Annuals and Perennials

A GARDENER'S ENCYCLOPEDIA

Annuals and Perennials

A GARDENER'S ENCYCLOPEDIA

SENIOR CONSULTANTS

Geoff Bryant and Tony Rodd

FIREFLY BOOKS

A FIREFLY BOOK

Published by Firefly Books Ltd. 2011

Photographs from the Global Book Publishing Photo Library © Global Book Publishing Pty Ltd 2011
Text © Global Book Publishing Pty Ltd 2011
Maps © Global Book Publishing Pty Ltd 2011

First printing

Publisher Cataloging-in-Publication Data (U.S.)
A CIP record of this book is available from the Library of Congress.

Library and Archives Canada Cataloguing in Publication
Bryant, Geoff
    Annuals and perennials : a gardener's encyclopedia / Geoff Bryant and Tony Rodd.
Includes index.
ISBN-13: 978-1-55407-837-0
ISBN-10: 1-55407-837-7
    1. Annuals (Plants)–Encyclopedias.
2. Perennials–Encyclopedias.
I. Rodd, Tony II. Title.
SB422.B79 2010   635.9'31203
C2010-906708-

Published in the United States by Firefly Books (U.S.) Inc.
P.O. Box 1338, Ellicott Station
Buffalo, New York 14205

Published in Canada by
Firefly Books Ltd.
66 Leek Crescent
Richmond Hill, Ontario L4B 1H1

Printed in China by 1010 Printing International Ltd
Color separation Pica Digital Pte Ltd, Singapore

Developed by Global Book Publishing
Level 8, 15 Orion Road, Lane Cove,
NSW 2066, Australia
Ph: (612) 9425 5800
Fax: (612) 9425 5804
E: rightsmanager@globalpub.com.au

MANAGING DIRECTOR
Chryl Campbell

EDITORIAL DIRECTOR
Sarah Anderson

ART DIRECTOR
Kylie Mulquin

PROJECT MANAGER
Dannielle Viera

SENIOR CONSULTANTS
Tony Rodd, Geoff Bryant

CONTRIBUTORS
Don Blaxell, David Bond, Peter Brownless, Geoff Bryant, Kate Bryant, Ian Connor, Penny Dunn, Richard Francis, William Grant, Ken Grapes, Sarah Guest, Sean Hogan, Melanie Kinsey, Folko Kullmann, Marilyn S. Light, Tony Lord, David Mabberley, Valda Paddison, Ron Parsons, Tony Rodd, Stephen Ryan, Julie Silk, Geoff Stebbings, Wendy Thomas, R. G. Turner, Jr., Ben-Erik van Wyk, Rachel Vogan, Scott Williams

EDITORS
Loretta Barnard, Kate Etherington, Janet Parker, Marie-Louise Taylor, Dannielle Viera

DESIGNERS
Stan Lamond, Kylie Mulquin, Jacqueline Richards

PROOFREADER
Puddingburn Publishing Services

INDEXER
Dannielle Viera

PUBLISHING COORDINATOR
Jessica Luca

PUBLISHING ASSISTANT
Kristen Donath

CAPTIONS
Front cover: *Geranium*, Hybrid Cultivar, 'Patricia'. Spine: *Erodium chrysanthum*. Back cover (left to right): *Osteospermum*, Hybrid Cultivar, 'Sunny Dark Gustaf'; *Helianthus* X *multiflora* 'Loddon Gold'; *Solenostemon scutellarioides*, Dragon Series, 'Black Dragon'; *Iris ensata* 'Flying Tiger'; *Maranta leuconeura* 'Tricolor'.

Page 1 (top to bottom): *Tagetes* 'Little Hero Fire'; *Hosta sieboldiana* 'Blue Angel'; *Lupinus*, Hybrid Cultivar, 'Candy Floss'. Page 2: *Cosmos bipinatus* 'Picotee Double'. Page 3 (top to bottom): *Pelargonium* 'Orsett'; *Petunia* X *hybrida*, Surfinia Series, Surfinia Blue Vein/'Sonsolos'. Pages 4–5: *Iris sibirica* 'Marcus Perry'. Pages 6–7: *Coreopsis lanceolata* 'Sterntaler'.

Contents

How This Book Works

Beautifully illustrated with hundreds of full-color photographs, this book provides an array of up-to-date information on over 1,300 annuals and perennials suitable for gardens of all sizes from all parts of the world. Because the large majority of garden enthusiasts live in the temperate zones, there is a more complete coverage of temperate plants than of tropical or alpine species.

The book begins with a comprehensive table of all the species in the book, containing at-a-glance information on height, spread, plant type, climate, frost tolerance, aspect, and more. Directly after the table are extensive individual plant entries, arranged alphabetically by genus name.

The symbol × before a genus or species name usually indicates a hybrid genus or species. The genus entries give the family to which the plant belongs, as well as geographical range, number of species, distinguishing features, commercial uses, and propagation and cultivation requirements of the genus as a whole.

Under every genus entry are a number of species entries (which include synonyms and common names, if applicable), each containing information such as the growth habit, flowering season, flower color, forms, and hardiness zones, with symbols denoting aspect, frost hardiness, spread, and height. The spread and height given apply to a mature plant in cultivation. The hardiness zones show the climatic areas in which plants can be grown. However, for annuals the minimum zone is that in which the plant can be raised and planted out over the spring to autumn period, disregarding winter hardiness.

Page heading
The heading on the left-hand page names the first genus or species entry on that page; the right-hand page heading names the last entry on that page.

Species entry
Contains detailed information on particular species and forms, and includes hardiness rating by zones.

Place of origin
The particular countries or regions of the world where the plant is naturally found.

Hardiness zones
The regions in which the plant can be successfully cultivated. See page 9 for more information.

Genus entry
Contains information about the genus as a whole, including geographical range, and cultivation and propagation requirements.

Synonyms
Incorrect botanical names by which the plant may have been known in the past.

Family name
The name of the group to which the genus belongs; related plant genera are placed in the same family.

Symbols
At-a-glance information about the plant—see the list of symbols on page 9 for their meaning.

Forms
Includes well-known or award-winning subspecies, varieties, forms, and cultivars of the species.

Common names
The non-botanical names by which the plant is generally known, usually in its native region.

Cultivation
General information on growing and propagating the members of the genus as a whole.

---

122   *Eryngium × oliverianum*

Eryngium × oliverianum
○/◑ ❄ ↔ 20–24 in (50–60 cm) ↕ 24–40 in (60–100 cm)
Perennial with long-stemmed, spiny, toothed leaves, rounded to heart-shaped, with 3 lobes on basal leaves. Bright metallic blue flowerheads, to 1¾ in (40 mm) across, with up to 15 narrow, spiny, purple bracts. Zones 5–9.

Eryngium variifolium
○/◑ ❄ ↔ 16–20 in (40–50 cm)
↕ 20–30 in (50–75 cm)
Native to North Africa. An evergreen perennial forming a thistle-like basal rosette of white-marbled, dark green, toothed leaves. Flowerheads purple-blue, to 1 in (25 mm) across, with up to 7 narrow, spiny, white-centered bracts. Zones 7–9.

ERYSIMUM
syn. *Cheiranthus*
WALLFLOWER
This genus in the cabbage (Brassicaceae) family, containing some 80 species of sometimes shrubby annuals and perennials, now includes many species formerly classified under *Cheiranthus*. The narrow green to blue-green leaves with shallow lobes are unremarkable, but the 4-petalled flowers are brightly colored, often fragrant, and frequently appear over a long season. In mild climates the bushy forms flower all year round. The hybrids come in a wide variety of colors.
CULTIVATION: Although most species of *Erysimum* are very hardy, they prefer a temperate climate with distinct seasons. Plant in

moist humus-rich soil and water well during the flowering period. They are often quite drought tolerant, but these plants will flower more abundantly with regular watering, feeding, trimming, and deadheading. Propagation of annual species is by seed; perennials can be propagated from seed, from small cuttings of non-flowering stems, or sometimes by division.

Erysimum, Hybrid Cultivar, 'Bowles' Mauve'

Erysimum bicolor
syn. *Cheiranthus bicolor*
○/◑ ❄ ↔ 24 in (60 cm) ↕ 36 in (90 cm)
Found in the Canary Islands and Madeira. Shrubby perennial with pointed, toothed, lance-shaped leaves. Scented flowers appear from spring onward, opening cream to orange-brown and ageing to mauve. Zones 9–10.

Erysimum cheiri
syn. *Cheiranthus cheiri*
WALLFLOWER
○/◑ ❄ ↔ 16 in (40 cm) ↕ 24 in (60 cm)
A native of southern Europe. Shrubby perennial, usually cultivated as biennial. Narrow deep green foliage; the lower leaves to 8 in (20 cm) long, becoming smaller higher up. Large heads of yellow and/or orange flowers. The cultivated forms, which are most likely hybrids, include 'Cloth of Gold', deep golden yellow flowers; Fair Lady (quite often called My Fair Lady) Strain, to 18 in (45 cm) tall, blooms in range of pastel shades; 'Fire King Improved', 16 in (40 cm) tall, brilliant orange-red flowers; 'Harpur Crewe', yellow double flowers; and Prince Series, stocky, to 18 in (45 cm) tall, in wide color range. Zones 7–9.

Erysimum Hybrid Cultivars
○/◑ ❄ ↔ 24 in (60 cm) ↕ 24–36 in (60–90 cm)
These bushy hybrids are of uncertain parentage. Though not long-lasting, they are easily propagated and flower virtually continuously. 'Bowles' Mauve' ★ (syn. 'E. A. Bowles'), best known, masses of small mauve-purple flowers; 'Gold Shot', 18 in (45 cm) tall, golden yellow flowers; 'Sunlight', yellow-flowered low spreader, about 4 in (10 cm) tall ; 'Wenlock Beauty', magenta flowers ageing to mauve; 'Winter Cheer', two-tone orange and light purple flowers. Zones 7–10.

ESCHSCHOLZIA
CALIFORNIA POPPY
Native to western North America and now widely naturalized, this genus in the poppy (Papaveraceae) family is made up of about 8 annuals and short-lived perennials. They have fine feathery foliage, often a rather grayish green, and in summer produce masses of bright golden yellow 4- to 8-petalled poppies that only open on sunny days. Modern seed strains come in many flower colors; the flowers are followed by long seed capsules.
CULTIVATION: These are easily grown in any sunny position with light, gritty, very well-drained soil, and often self-sow and naturalize. Most are very frost hardy and tolerate poor soil. Propagate from seed, which is best sown where it is required to grow.

Erysimum cheiri, Fair Lady Strain

Symbols

Each species entry in this book features symbols that provide at-a-glance information about the species.

★ Flora Award—the plant is recommended by
our consultants as outstanding in its group

↔ Spread—the width of the mature plant in cultivation

↑ Height—the height of the mature plant in cultivation

☼ Full Sun—the plant thrives in sunny conditions

☽ Half Sun—the plant thrives in dappled sunlight
or part-shade

☀ Shade—the plant thrives in shady conditions

❄ Frost Tolerance—the plant is fully hardy

❊ Frost Tolerance—the plant is frost hardy

❅ Frost Tolerance—the plant is half-hardy

✈ Frost Tolerance—the plant is frost tender

World Hardiness Zones

This world map is divided into Plant Hardiness Zones, which indicate how well cultivated plants survive the minimum winter temperature expected for each zone. The system was developed by the U.S. Department of Agriculture, originally for North America, but it now includes other geographical areas. Zone 1 applies to the cold subarctic climates of Alaska and Siberia, for example, whereas Zone 12 covers the warmest areas around the equator.

Both a minimum and maximum zone is given for every plant species listed in this book. A European native, *Rosa canina* will withstand the winter frosts occurring in parts of Zone 3, in which temperatures fall below –30°F (–34°C); it will also thrive up to Zone 10, where the minimum winter temperatures are above 30°F (–1°C). It is important to note that maximum temperatures also have an effect, and plants that can survive the cold of Zone 3 are unlikely to succeed in the heat of Zones 10 or 11.

Other climatic factors also affect plant growth. Humidity, day length, season length, wind, soil temperature, and rainfall all need to be considered.

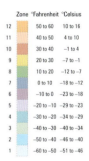

Zone	°Fahrenheit	°Celsius
12	50 to 60	10 to 16
11	40 to 50	4 to 10
10	30 to 40	–1 to 4
9	20 to 30	–7 to –1
8	10 to 20	–12 to –7
7	0 to 10	–18 to –12
6	–10 to 0	–23 to –18
5	–20 to –10	–29 to –23
4	–30 to –20	–34 to –29
3	–40 to –30	–40 to –34
2	–50 to –40	–46 to –40
1	–60 to –50	–51 to –46

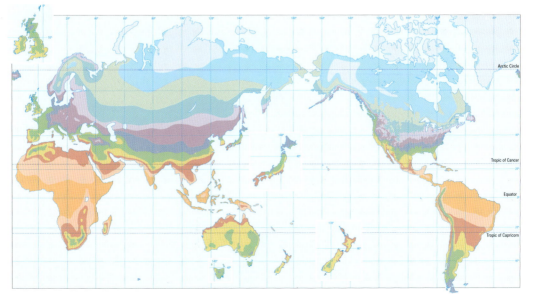

Annuals and Perennials

At the heart of many garden displays are annuals and perennials, which collectively offer an almost unrivaled choice of brilliantly colored blooms, across a wide range of garden situations. Annual plants have a frenetic life with only a short time to grow, flower, and set seed; they have no means of living through hard times, except as seed, so they must complete their life in a single season.

Perennials (more accurately known as herbaceous perennials to differentiate them from woody perennials such as trees) typically take more than a year to reach flowering size, but once they have, they bloom every year. Exceptions to this are monocarpic perennials such as the South American *Puya mirabilis*—they gradually build up the strength to flower, only then to die, having set thousands of seeds.

In the past, the traditional herbaceous border was a joy to behold, but its short season led many gardeners to abandon this type of garden. However, it is making a comeback, as today's range of herbaceous plants means that pretty perennials can enhance our gardens throughout much of the year, from hellebores flowering in late winter, and bergenias during spring, through to the last flowers of Japanese anemones in autumn.

As well as offering stunning deep red blooms that are excellent as cut flowers, *Gaillardia* ≥ *grandiflora* 'Burgunder' is both drought and heat tolerant.

Annuals and Perennials Finder

The following cultivation table features at-a-glance information for every species or hybrid with an individual entry in this book. Simply find the plant you wish to know more about, and run your eye along the row to discover its height and spread, whether it is frost tolerant or not, the aspect it prefers, and more.

The type of plant is abbreviated to **A**, **B**, or **P**:
A – the plant is an annual.
B – the plant is a biennial.
P – the plant is a perennial.

The climate(s) that each plant needs to thrive in the outdoors are given (some plants will grow in more than one climate), abbreviated to **C**, **W**, or **T**:
C – the plant prefers a cool climate.
W– the plant prefers a warm-temperate or subtropical climate.
T – the plant prefers a tropical climate.

The group that the plant belongs to is abbreviated to **B**, **C**, **G**, or **NA**:
B – the plant is a bromeliad.
C – the plant is carnivorous.
G – the plant is a gesneriad.
NA – the plant does not fit into one of the three groups given above.

The flowering and planting seasons are abbreviated to **A**, **W**, **Sp**, or **Su**:
A – the plant bears flowers or should be planted in autumn.
W– the plant bears flowers or should be planted in winter.
Sp – the plant bears flowers or should be planted in spring.
Su – the plant bears flowers or should be planted in summer.

Plant name	Height	Spread	Type	Climate	Group	Showy flowers	Showy foliage	Scented flowers	Planting season	Flowering season	Grow in pot/tub	Frost tolerant	Full Sun	Half Sun	Heavy shade
Abelmoschus manihot	3–6 ft (0.9–1.8 m)	3 ft (0.9 m)	P	W/T	NA	◆				W/Sp	Su	◆		◆	
Abelmoschus moschatus	4–6 ft (1.2–1.8 m)	30 in (75 cm)	A	W/T	NA	◆		◆	Sp	Su	◆		◆	
Acaena caesiiglauca	2 in (5 cm)	32 in (80 cm)	P	C/W	NA		◆			W/Sp	Su	◆	◆	◆	
Acaena microphylla	2 in (5 cm)	20 in (50 cm)	P	C/W	NA	◆				W/Sp	Su	◆	◆	◆	
Acanthus mollis	7 ft (2 m)	40–60 in (100–150 cm)	P	C/W	NA	◆	◆			W/Sp	Su		◆	◆	◆
Acanthus spinosus	36 in (90 cm)	40–60 in (100–150 cm)	P	C/W	NA	◆	◆			W/Sp	Su		◆	◆	◆
Achillea filipendulina	24–48 in (60–120 cm)	24–48 in (60–120 cm)	P	C/W	NA	◆				W/Sp	Su		◆	◆	
Achillea millefolium	12–30 in (30–75 cm)	18–30 in (45–75 cm)	P	C/W	NA	◆				W/Sp	Su/A		◆	◆	
Achillea ptarmica	30 in (75 cm)	30 in (75 cm)	P	C/W	NA	◆				W/Sp	Su		◆	◆	
Achillea Hybrid Cultivars	12–40 in (30–100 cm)	18–30 in (45–75 cm)	P	C/W	NA	◆				W/Sp	Su		◆	◆	
Achimenes longiflora	20–24 in (50–60 cm)	12–20 in (30–50 cm)	P	W/T	G	◆	◆			W/Sp	Su/A	◆			◆
Achimenes Hybrid Cultivars	3–6 in (8–15 cm)	10–15 in (25–38 cm)	P	W/T	G	◆	◆			W/Sp	Su/A	◆			◆
Aconitum carmichaelii	7 ft (2 m)	24–36 in (60–90 cm)	P	C	NA	◆				W/Sp	Su/A		◆	◆	◆
Aconitum napellus	5–6 ft (1.5–1.8 m)	24–32 in (60–80 cm)	P	C	NA	◆				W/Sp	Su/A		◆	◆	◆
Aconitum Hybrid Cultivars	4 ft (1.2 m)	24 in (60 cm)	P	C	NA	◆				W/Sp	Su/A		◆	◆	◆
Acorus calamus	4 ft (1.2 m)	3–7 ft (0.9–2 m)	P	C	NA	◆	◆			W/Sp	Su		◆	◆	◆
Acorus gramineus	16 in (40 cm)	18–36 in (45–90 cm)	P	C/W	NA		◆			W/Sp	Su		◆	◆	◆
Aechmea caudata	36 in (90 cm)	24 in (60 cm)	P	W	B	◆	◆			Sp	Su	◆			◆

Plant name	Height	Spread	Type	Climate	Group	Showy flowers	Showy foliage	Scented flowers	Planting season	Flowering season	Grow in pot/tub	Frost tolerant	Full Sun	Half Sun	Heavy shade
Aechmea chantinii	40 in (100 cm)	20 in (50 cm)	P	W/T	B	◆	◆		Sp	Su	◆				◆
Aechmea fasciata	27 in (70 cm)	16 in (40 cm)	P	W/T	B	◆	◆		Sp	Su	◆				
Aechmea fulgens	20 in (50 cm)	20 in (50 cm)	P	W/T	B	◆			Sp	Su	◆				
Aechmea gamosepala	30 in (75 cm)	10 in (25 cm)	P	W	B	◆			Sp	Su	◆	◆			
Aechmea nudicaulis	27–36 in (70–90 cm)	8 in (20 cm)	P	W/T	B	◆			Sp	Su	◆			◆	
Aechmea ornata	36 in (90 cm)	7 ft (2 m)	P	W	B	◆	◆		Sp	Su	◆				
Aechmea recurvata	8–16 in (20–40 cm)	8 in (20 cm)	P	W	B	◆	◆		Sp	Su	◆			◆	
Aechmea Hybrid Cultivars	12–36 in (30–90 cm)	12–24 in (30–60 cm)	P	W/T	B	◆	◆		Sp	Su	◆				
Aethionema grandiflorum	8–18 in (20–45 cm)	12–24 in (30–60 cm)	P	C	NA	◆			W	Sp/Su	◆	◆	◆		
Aethionema 'Warley Rose'	6 in (15 cm)	12 in (30 cm)	P	C	NA	◆			W	Sp/Su	◆	◆	◆		
Agapanthus inapertus	40–60 in (100–150 cm)	40–50 in (100–130 cm)	P	C/W	NA	◆			W/Sp	Su		◆	◆		
Agapanthus praecox	40 in (100 cm)	40–50 in (100–130 cm)	P	W	NA	◆			W/Sp	Su		◆	◆		
Agapanthus Hybrid Cultivars	15–60 in (38–150 cm)	12–30 in (30–75 cm)	P	C/W	NA	◆			W/Sp	Su	◆	◆	◆		
Agastache cana	20–24 in (50–60 cm)	12–18 in (30–45 cm)	P	W	NA	◆			W/Sp	Su		◆	◆		
Agastache foeniculum	20–32 in (50–80 cm)	18–24 in (45–60 cm)	P	W	NA	◆			W/Sp	Su		◆	◆		
Agastache rugosa	24–48 in (60–120 cm)	24 in (60 cm)	P	W	NA	◆			W/Sp	Su		◆	◆		
Agastache rupestris	18–36 in (45–90 cm)	18 in (45 cm)	P	W	NA	◆			W/Sp	Su		◆	◆		
Agastache Hybrid Cultivars	2–6 ft (0.6–1.8 m)	1–3 ft (0.3–0.9 m)	P	W	NA	◆			W/Sp	Su		◆	◆		
Ageratum houstonianum	6–30 in (15–75 cm)	6–20 in (15–50 cm)	A	W/T	NA	◆			Sp	Su	◆		◆		
Aglaonema commutatum	24–36 in (60–90 cm)	24 in (60 cm)	P	W/T	NA		◆		any	Su	◆		◆	◆	
Aglaonema costatum	12 in (30 cm)	24 in (60 cm)	P	W/T	NA		◆		any	Su	◆				
Aglaonema crispum	24–48 in (60–120 cm)	18–30 in (45–75 cm)	P	W/T	NA		◆		any	Su	◆			◆	◆
Ajuga pyramidalis	6–8 in (15–20 cm)	12–24 in (30–60 cm)	P	C/W	NA	◆	◆		W/Sp	Sp/Su		◆	◆	◆	
Ajuga reptans	4–8 in (10–20 cm)	12–48 in (30–120 cm)	P	C/W	NA	◆	◆		W/Sp	Sp/Su		◆	◆	◆	◆
Alcea rosea	2–8 ft (0.6–2.4 m)	2–3 ft (0.6–0.9 m)	B	C/W	NA	◆	◆		Sp	Su		◆	◆		
Alchemilla mollis	12–20 in (30–50 cm)	12–32 in (30–80 cm)	P	C	NA		◆		W/Sp	Su		◆	◆	◆	
Alchemilla xanthochlora	12–20 in (30–50 cm)	16–24 in (40–60 cm)	P	C	NA		◆		W/Sp	Su			◆	◆	
Alkanna orientalis	8–12 in (20–30 cm)	8–12 in (20–30 cm)	A	C/W	NA	◆		◆	W/Sp	Sp/Su			◆	◆	
Alkanna tinctoria	12–36 in (30–90 cm)	12–36 in (30–90 cm)	P	C	NA				W/Sp	Sp/Su			◆	◆	
Alocasia × amazonica	40–60 in (100–150 cm)	20–40 in (50–100 cm)	P	W/T	NA		◆		W/Sp	Su	◆				
Alocasia cuprea	40 in (100 cm)	30 in (75 cm)	P	W/T	NA		◆		W/Sp	Su	◆			◆	

Plant name	Height	Spread	Type	Climate	Group	Showy flowers	Showy foliage	Scented flowers	Planting season	Flowering season	Grow in pot/tub	Frost tolerant	Full Sun	Half Sun	Heavy shade
Alocasia sanderiana	40–60 in (100–150 cm)	20–36 in (50–90 cm)	P	W/T	NA		◆		W/Sp	Su	◆			◆	◆
Alpinia purpurata	8–12 ft (2.4–3.5 m)	2–4 ft (0.6–1.2 m)	P	W/T	NA	◆			W/Sp	Any	◆		◆	◆	
Alpinia zerumbet	6–10 ft (1.8–3 m)	2–3 ft (0.6–0.9 m)	P	W/T	NA	◆			Sp	Sp/Su	◆		◆	◆	
Alstroemeria psittacina	28–36 in (70–90 cm)	16–20 in (40–50 cm)	P	W	NA	◆			W/Sp	Su	◆	◆	◆	◆	
Alstroemeria Hybrid Cultivars	18–48 in (45–120 cm)	12–24 in (30–60 cm)	P	W	NA	◆			W/Sp	Su/A	◆	◆	◆	◆	
Alternanthera bettzichiana	2–3 ft (0.6–0.9 m)	2–3 ft (0.6–0.9 m)	A	W/T	NA		◆		Sp	Su			◆		
Amaranthus caudatus	36–48 in (90–120 cm)	24 in (60 cm)	A	W	NA	◆	◆		Sp	Su			◆		
Amaranthus tricolor	24–36 in (60–90 cm)	30 in (75 cm)	A	W	NA		◆		Sp	Su			◆		
Amsonia tabernaemontana	36 in (90 cm)	36–48 in (90–120 cm)	P	C/W	NA	◆			W/Sp	Sp/Su		◆	◆	◆	
Anagallis monelli	12–20 in (30–50 cm)	12–20 in (30–50 cm)	P	C/W	NA	◆			W/Sp	Sp/Su		◆	◆	◆	
Anaphalis margaritacea	32–40 in (80–100 cm)	16–24 in (40–60 cm)	P	C	NA	◆			W/Sp	Su			◆	◆	
Anaphalis triplinervis	32–36 in (80–90 cm)	16–20 in (40–50 cm)	P	C	NA	◆			W/Sp	Su			◆	◆	
Anchusa azurea	48 in (120 cm)	32 in (80 cm)	P	C/W	NA	◆			W/Sp	Sp/Su			◆		
Anchusa capensis	20 in (50 cm)	16 in (40 cm)	B	W	NA	◆			Sp	Su			◆		
Androsace lanuginosa	3 in (8 cm)	12–18 in (30–45 cm)	P	C	NA	◆			W/Sp	Su/A		◆	◆	◆	
Androsace rotundifolia	4–6 in (10–15 cm)	8 in (20 cm)	P	C	NA	◆			W/Sp	Sp/Su		◆	◆	◆	
Anemone blanda	4–8 in (10–20 cm)	6–12 in (15–30 cm)	P	C	NA	◆			A/W	W/Sp		◆		◆	◆
Anemone coronaria	16–24 in (40–60 cm)	8–16 in (20–40 cm)	P	C/W	NA	◆			A/W	Sp	◆	◆	◆	◆	◆
Anemone hupehensis	20–36 in (50–90 cm)	16–40 in (40–100 cm)	P	C	NA	◆			W/Sp	Su/A		◆		◆	◆
Anemone × hybrida	32–60 in (80–150 cm)	20–48 in (50–120 cm)	P	C	NA	◆			W/Sp	Su/A		◆		◆	◆
Anemone nemorosa	4–12 in (10–30 cm)	6–16 in (15–40 cm)	P	C	NA	◆			A/W	Sp		◆		◆	◆
Anemone pavonina	12 in (30 cm)	12–16 in (30–40 cm)	P	W	NA	◆			A/W	Sp		◆	◆	◆	
Anemone sylvestris	6–12 in (15–30 cm)	6–20 in (15–50 cm)	P	C	NA			◆	W	Sp/Su		◆		◆	
Angelonia angustifolia	18 in (45 cm)	12 in (30 cm)	A/P	W	NA	◆			Sp	Su	◆		◆		
Anigozanthos flavidus	10 ft (3 m)	3 ft (0.9 m)	P	W	NA	◆			W/Sp	Su			◆		
Anigozanthos manglesii	12–20 in (30–50 cm)	36 in (90 cm)	P	W	NA	◆			A/Sp	W/Sp			◆		
Anigozanthos Hybrid Cultivars	1–6 ft (0.3–1.8 m)	8–30 in (20–75 cm)	P	W	NA	◆			W/Sp	Sp/Su			◆	◆	
Antennaria dioica	8 in (20 cm)	24–36 in (60–90 cm)	P	C	NA	◆	◆		W/Sp	Su		◆	◆		
Anthemis punctata	16–24 in (40–60 cm)	12–20 in (30–50 cm)	P	C/W	NA	◆			W/Sp	Su			◆		
Anthemis tinctoria	24–36 in (60–90 cm)	20–40 in (50–100 cm)	P	C/W	NA	◆	◆		W/Sp	Sp–A		◆	◆		
Anthericum liliago	24–36 in (60–90 cm)	12 in (30 cm)	P	C/W	NA	◆			A/W	Sp		◆	◆		

Plant name	Height	Spread	Type	Climate	Group	Showy flowers	Showy foliage	Scented flowers	Planting season	Flowering season	Grow in pot/tub	Frost tolerant	Full Sun	Half Sun	Heavy shade
Anthurium andraeanum	20–48 in (50–120 cm)	12–24 in (30–60 cm)	P	W/T	NA	◆	◆		Any	Sp–A	◆			◆	◆
Anthurium scherzerianum	24–30 in (60–75 cm)	12–20 in (30–50 cm)	P	W/T	NA	◆	◆		Any	Sp–A	◆			◆	◆
Anthurium warocqueanum	24–60 in (60–150 cm)	3–10 ft (0.9–3 m)	P	T	NA		◆		Any	Sp–A	◆			◆	◆
Antirrhinum majus	12–60 in (30–150 cm)	6–20 in (15–50 cm)	A	C/W	NA	◆			Sp/Su	Sp–A		◆	◆	◆	
Antirrhinum molle	8–16 in (20–40 cm)	6–8 in (15–20 cm)	P	C/W	NA	◆			Sp/Su	Sp–A		◆	◆	◆	
Aponogeton distachyos	24–32 in (60–80 cm)	32–40 in (80–100 cm)	P	W	NA	◆		◆	W/Sp	Su			◆	◆	
Aquilegia caerulea	8–24 in (20–60 cm)	8–16 in (20–40 cm)	P	C	NA	◆			W/Sp	Sp/Su		◆	◆	◆	
Aquilegia canadensis	12–30 in (30–75 cm)	12–20 in (30–50 cm)	P	C/W	NA	◆			W/Sp	Sp/Su			◆		
Aquilegia chrysantha	32–36 in (80–90 cm)	12–32 in (30–80 cm)	P	C/W	NA	◆			W/Sp	Sp/Su			◆	◆	
Aquilegia formosa	20–36 in (50–90 cm)	12–20 in (30–50 cm)	P	C	NA	◆			W/Sp	Sp/Su			◆		
Aquilegia, McKana Group	32–48 in (80–120 cm)	12–20 in (30–50 cm)	P	C/W	NA	◆			W/Sp	Sp/Su		◆	◆	◆	
Aquilegia vulgaris	12–36 in (30–90 cm)	8–18 in (20–45 cm)	P	C/W	NA	◆			W/Sp	Sp/Su			◆	◆	
Aquilegia Hybrid Cultivars	18–36 in (45–90 cm)	12–24 in (30–60 cm)	P	C/W	NA	◆			W/Sp	Sp/Su			◆	◆	
Arabis × *arendsii*	4–8 in (10–20 cm)	12–24 in (30–60 cm)	P	C	NA	◆			W/Sp	Sp/Su	◆	◆	◆		
Arabis blepharophylla	4–6 in (10–15 cm)	6–8 in (15–20 cm)	P	C	NA	◆			W/Sp	Sp/Su	◆	◆	◆		
Arabis caucasica	6–12 in (15–30 cm)	8–20 in (20–50 cm)	P	C	NA	◆			W/Sp	Sp/Su	◆	◆	◆		
Arctotis acaulis	6–12 in (15–30 cm)	12–40 in (30–100 cm)	P	W	NA	◆			A–Sp	Any	◆	◆	◆		
Arctotis × *hybrida*	8–16 in (20–40 cm)	8–20 in (20–50 cm)	A/P	W	NA	◆			A–Sp	Any	◆		◆		
Arctotis venusta	16–24 in (40–60 cm)	8–16 in (20–40 cm)	A	W	NA	◆			Sp	Sp–A	◆		◆		
Arenaria montana	4–6 in (10–15 cm)	9–24 in (23–60 cm)	P	C	NA	◆			W/Sp	Sp/Su	◆	◆	◆	◆	
Arenaria purpurascens	4–6 in (10–15 cm)	9–24 in (23–60 cm)	P	C	NA	◆			W/Sp	Sp/Su	◆	◆	◆	◆	
Argemone mexicana	36 in (90 cm)	12–16 in (30–40 cm)	A	W	NA	◆	◆		Sp	Su/A			◆	◆	
Aristea major	3–5 ft (0.9–1.5 m)	24–36 in (60–90 cm)	P	W	NA	◆			W/Sp	Su			◆	◆	
Aristolochia clematitis	12–30 in (30–75 cm)	24 in (60 cm)	P	C/W	NA			◆	W/Sp	Su		◆	◆	◆	
Armeria juniperifolia	6 in (15 cm)	6–8 in (15–20 cm)	P	C/W	NA	◆			W/Sp	Su	◆	◆	◆	◆	
Armeria maritima	8–12 in (20–30 cm)	8–16 in (20–40 cm)	P	C/W	NA	◆			W/Sp	Su	◆	◆	◆	◆	
Armeria pseudarmeria	8–16 in (20–40 cm)	16–40 in (45–100 cm)	P	C/W	NA	◆			W/Sp	Su	◆	◆	◆	◆	
Artemisia lactiflora	5 ft (1.5 m)	24 in (60 cm)	P	C/W	NA	◆			W/Sp	Su			◆	◆	
Artemisia ludoviciana	36 in (90 cm)	36 in (90 cm)	P	C/W	NA		◆		W/Sp	Su			◆	◆	
Artemisia 'Powis Castle'	2 ft (0.6 m)	4 ft (1.2 m)	P	C/W	NA		◆		W/Sp	Su			◆	◆	
Artemisia stelleriana	18–24 in (45–60 cm)	18 in (45 cm)	P	C	NA		◆		W/Sp	Su			◆	◆	

Plant name	Height	Spread	Type	Climate	Group	Showy flowers	Showy foliage	Scented flowers	Planting season	Flowering season	Grow in pot/tub	Frost tolerant	Full Sun	Half Sun	Heavy shade
Arthropodium cirratum	20–30 in (50–75 cm)	24 in (60 cm)	P	W	NA	◆	◆		A–Sp	Su	◆		◆	◆	
Aruncus dioicus	2–6 ft (0.6–1.2 m)	4 ft (1.2 m)	P	C	NA	◆	◆		W/Sp	Su		◆		◆	
Asclepias linaria	24–36 in (60–90 cm)	24–36 in (60–90 cm)	P	W	NA	◆			W	Sp–A			◆		
Asclepias tuberosa	24–36 in (60–90 cm)	12 in (30 cm)	P	C/W	NA	◆			W/Sp	Sp–A		◆	◆		
Asparagus densiflorus	30–36 in (75–90 cm)	36 in (90 cm)	P	W	NA		◆		A/W	Sp/Su	◆	◆	◆		
Asparagus macowanii	6 ft (1.8 m)	8 ft (2.4 m)	P	W	NA	◆	◆		A/W	Su			◆		
Asperula gussonei	4 in (10 cm)	6–12 in (15–30 cm)	P	C/W	NA	◆	◆		A/W	Sp/Su	◆	◆	◆		
Asperula orientalis	8–12 in (20–30 cm)	16–24 in (40–60 cm)	A	C/W	NA	◆			Sp	Su		◆	◆	◆	
Asphodeline lutea	36–48 in (90–120 cm)	12 in (30 cm)	P	C/W	NA	◆		◆	A/W	Sp/Su		◆	◆		
Asphodelus aestivus	40 in (100 cm)	24 in (60 cm)	P	C/W	NA	◆			A/W	Sp		◆	◆		
Asphodelus albus	36 in (90 cm)	24 in (60 cm)	P	C/W	NA	◆			A/W	Sp		◆	◆		
Aspidistra elatior	16–24 in (40–60 cm)	16–36 in (40–90 cm)	P	C/W	NA			◆	Any	Sp/Su	◆	◆			◆
Astelia chathamica	3–6 ft (0.9–1.8 m)	5 ft (1.5 m)	P	W	NA		◆		Any	Su	◆	◆	◆	◆	
Astelia nervosa	3–7 ft (0.9–2 m)	5 ft (1.5 m)	P	W	NA		◆		Any	Su	◆		◆	◆	
Aster alpinus	4–10 in (10–25 cm)	8–32 in (20–80 cm)	P	C	NA	◆			A/W	Sp/Su	◆	◆	◆		
Aster amellus	24–27 in (60–70 cm)	12–20 in (30–50 cm)	P	C	NA	◆			W			◆	◆		
Aster ericoides	32–40 in (80–100 cm)	20–32 in (50–80 cm)	P	C	NA	◆			W	Su/A		◆	◆	◆	
Aster × frikartii	20–30 in (50–75 cm)	16–24 in (40–60 cm)	P	C	NA	◆			W/Sp	A		◆	◆	◆	
Aster lateriflorus	3–4 ft (0.9–1.2 m)	2–4 ft (0.6–1.2 m)	P	C	NA	◆			W	A		◆	◆	◆	
Aster novae-angliae	4–5 ft (1.2–1.5 m)	2–4 ft (0.6–1.2 m)	P	C	NA	◆			W/Sp	A		◆	◆	◆	
Aster novi-belgii	36–48 in (90–120 cm)	24–32 in (60–80 cm)	P	C	NA	◆			W/Sp	A		◆	◆	◆	
Aster turbinellus	4 ft (1.2 m)	3 ft (0.9 m)	P	C	NA	◆			W/Sp	A		◆	◆	◆	
Astilbe × arendsii	2–6 ft (0.6–1.8 m)	12–32 in (30–80 cm)	P	C	NA	◆	◆		W/Sp	Sp/Su		◆		◆	
Astilbe chinensis	to 7 ft (2 m)	12–20 in (30–50 cm)	P	C	NA	◆			W/Sp	Sp/Su		◆		◆	
Astilbe japonica	2–3 ft (0.6–0.9 m)	3 ft (0.9 m)	P	C	NA	◆			W/Sp	Sp/Su		◆		◆	
Astilbe simplicifolia	12–16 in (30–40 cm)	8–16 in (20–40 cm)	P	C	NA	◆			W/Sp	Sp/Su		◆		◆	
Astilbe Hybrid Cultivars	2–3 ft (0.6–0.9 m)	3 ft (0.9 m)	P	C	NA	◆			W/Sp	Sp/Su		◆		◆	
Astilboides tabularis	40–60 in (100–150 cm)	40–60 in (100–150 cm)	P	C/W	NA	◆			W	Su		◆			◆
Astrantia major	24–32 in (60–80 cm)	16–24 in (40–60 cm)	P	C	NA	◆			W/Sp	Su		◆		◆	
Astrantia maxima	27–36 in (70–90 cm)	20–24 in (50–60 cm)	P	C	NA	◆	◆		W/Sp	Su		◆		◆	
Atriplex hortensis	7–8 ft (2–2.4 m)	16–20 in (40–50 cm)	A	C/W	NA		◆		Sp	Su		◆	◆		

Plant name	Height	Spread	Type	Climate	Group	Showy flowers	Showy foliage	Scented flowers	Planting season	Flowering season	Grow in pot/tub	Frost tolerant	Full Sun	Half Sun	Heavy shade
Aubrieta Hybrid Cultivars	3–6 in (8–15 cm)	8–24 in (20–60 cm)	P	C/W	NA	◆			W/Sp	SpSu	◆	◆	◆		
Aurinia saxatilis	8–12 in (20–30 cm)	16–24 in (40–60 cm)	P	C/W	NA	◆			W/Sp	Sp/Su	◆	◆	◆		
Baileya multiradiata	8–20 in (20–50 cm)	4–12 in (10–30 cm)	P	C/W	NA	◆			W/Sp	Sp–A		◆	◆		
Ballota acetabulosa	40 in (100 cm)	24–32 in (60–80 cm)	P	C/W	NA	◆	◆		W/Sp	Su		◆	◆	◆	
Ballota pseudodictamnus	12–20 in (30–50 cm)	24–48 in (60–120 cm)	P	C/W	NA	◆	◆		W/Sp	Su		◆	◆		
Baptisia australis	2–4 ft (0.6–1.2 m)	4 ft (1.2 m)	P	C	NA	◆			W/Sp	Su		◆	◆		
Bassia scoparia	8–60 in (20–150 cm)	8–60 in (20–150 cm)	A	W	NA		◆		Sp	Su/A		◆	◆		
Begonia coccinea	48 in (120 cm)	24 in (60 cm)	P	W/T	NA	◆	◆		W/Sp	Sp	◆			◆	◆
Begonia × erythrophylla	8–16 in (20–40 cm)	16–24 in (40–60 cm)	P	W/T	NA		◆		Sp/Su	W/Sp	◆			◆	◆
Begonia fuchsioides	36 in (90 cm)	20 in (50 cm)	P	W/T	NA	◆	◆		Sp/Su	W	◆			◆	◆
Begonia grandis	24 in (60 cm)	12–18 in (30–45 cm)	P	W/T	NA	◆			Sp	Su/A	◆	◆		◆	◆
Begonia masoniana	12 in (30 cm)	12–16 in (30–40 cm)	P	W/T	NA		◆		W/Sp	Sp/Su	◆			◆	◆
Begonia metallica	48 in (120 cm)	20–32 in (50–80 cm)	P	W/T	NA	◆	◆		Sp/Su	Su/A	◆			◆	◆
Begonia, Cane-like Group	2–6 ft (0.6–1.8 m)	20–32 in (50–80 cm)	P	W/T	NA	◆	◆		Sp/Su	Any	◆			◆	
Begonia, Rex Cultorum Group	12–24 in (30–60 cm)	16–24 in (40–60 cm)	P	W/T	NA		◆		Sp/Su	Sp/Su	◆			◆	◆
Begonia, Rhizomatous Group	6–8 in (15–20 cm)	12–30 in (30–75 cm)	P	W	NA		◆		Sp/Su	Any	◆			◆	◆
Begonia, Semperflorens Group	12 in (30 cm)	12 in (30 cm)	A/P	W	NA	◆	◆		Sp	Su/A	◆		◆	◆	
Begonia, Shrub-like Group	12–36 in (30–90 cm)	18–48 in (45–120 cm)	P	W/T	NA	◆	◆		Sp/Su	Any	◆			◆	◆
Begonia, Thick-stemmed Group	12–18 in (30–45 cm)	12–18 in (30–45 cm)	P	W/T	NA	◆	◆		Sp/Su	Any	◆			◆	
Begonia, Trailing or Scandent Group	6–12 in (15–30 cm)	18–36 in (45–90 cm)	P	W/T	NA	◆		◆	Sp	Su/A	◆			◆	◆
Begonia, Tuberous Group	12–32 in (30–80 cm)	12–20 in (30–50 cm)	P	W	NA	◆			Sp	Su/A	◆	◆		◆	◆
Bellis perennis	2–4 in (5–10 cm)	4–8 in (10–20 cm)	P	C	NA			◆	W/Sp	Sp/Su	◆	◆	◆		
Bergenia cordifolia	16 in (40 cm)	48 in (120 cm)	P	C	NA	◆	◆		A/W	W/Sp		◆	◆		
Bergenia crassifolia	12 in (30 cm)	16–32 in (40–80 cm)	P	C	NA	◆	◆		A/W	Sp		◆	◆		
Bergenia × schmidtii	12 in (30 cm)	24–48 in (60–120 cm)	P	C	NA	◆	◆		A/W	W/Sp		◆	◆		
Bergenia Hybrid Cultivars	8–16 in (20–40 cm)	16–32 in (40–80 cm)	P	C	NA	◆	◆		A/W	Sp		◆	◆	◆	
Bidens ferulifolia	24–36 in (60–90 cm)	12–18 in (30–45 cm)	A/P	W	NA	◆			Sp	Su/A		◆	◆		
Billbergia amoena	24 in (60 cm)	12 in (30 cm)	P	W	B	◆	◆		W/Sp	Sp/Su	◆				◆
Billbergia elegans	12 in (30 cm)	4 in (10 cm)	P	W	B	◆	◆		W/Sp	Sp/Su	◆				◆
Billbergia euphemiae	24 in (60 cm)	8 in (20 cm)	P	W	B	◆			W/Sp	Sp/Su	◆				◆

Plant name	Height	Spread	Type	Climate	Group	Showy flowers	Showy foliage	Scented flowers	Planting season	Flowering season	Grow in pot/tub	Frost tolerant	Full Sun	Half Sun	Heavy shade
Billbergia nutans	10 in (25 cm)	6 in (15 cm)	P	W	B	◆			W/Sp	Sp/Su	◆	◆			◆
Billbergia pyramidalis	20 in (50 cm)	6 in (15 cm)	P	W	B	◆			W/Sp	Sp/Su	◆				◆
Billbergia zebrina	40 in (100 cm)	6 in (15 cm)	P	W	B	◆	◆		W/Sp	Sp/Su	◆				◆
Billbergia Hybrid Cultivars	24 in (60 cm)	8 in (20 cm)	P	W	B	◆	◆		W/Sp	Sp/Su	◆				◆
Boltonia asteroides	3–5 ft (0.9–1.5 m)	5 ft (1.5 m)	P	C/W	NA	◆			W/Sp	Su/A	◆	◆	◆		
Boykinia jamesii	2–6 in (5–15 cm)	6–8 in (15–20 cm)	P	C	NA	◆			W/Sp	Su	◆	◆		◆	
Brachyscome iberidifolia	2–16 in (5–40 cm)	8–12 in (20–30 cm)	A	W	NA	◆			W/Sp	Sp/Su			◆		
Brachyscome multifida	8–16 in (20–40 cm)	12–40 in (30–100 cm)	P	W	NA	◆			W/Sp	Sp–A	◆		◆		
Brachyscome Hybrid Cultivars	18 in (45 cm)	18 in (45 cm)	P	W	NA	◆			W/Sp	Sp/Su			◆	◆	
Bromelia pinguin	4 ft (1.2 m)	7 ft (2 m)	P	W/T	B	◆	◆		W/Sp	Sp/Su	◆				
Bromelia serra	24 in (60 cm)	7 ft (2 m)	P	W/T	B	◆			W/Sp	Sp/Su			◆		
Brunnera macrophylla	20 in (50 cm)	16–32 in (40–80 cm)	P	C	NA	◆	◆		A/W	Sp		◆		◆	
Calamintha grandiflora	2 ft (0.6 m)	3–4 ft (0.9–1.2 m)	P	C/W	NA	◆		◆	W/Sp	Su		◆	◆	◆	
Calamintha nepeta	32 in (80 cm)	3–5 ft (0.9–1.5 m)	P	C/W	NA	◆			W/Sp	Su		◆	◆		
Calathea burle-marxii	5 ft (1.5 m)	3–5 ft (0.9–1.5 m)	P	W/T	NA	◆	◆		W/Sp	Sp/Su	◆				◆
Calathea makoyana	24–32 in (60–80 cm)	16–32 in (40–80 cm)	P	W/T	NA		◆		W/Sp	Sp/Su	◆				
Calathea picturata	16–24 in (40–60 cm)	20–27 in (50–70 cm)	P	W/T	NA		◆		W/Sp	Sp/Su	◆				
Calathea zebrina	40 in (100 cm)	32–48 in (80–120 cm)	P	W/T	NA	◆	◆		W/Sp	Sp/Su	◆				
Calceolaria, Herbeohybrida Group	8–20 in (20–50 cm)	12–16 in (30–40 cm)	A/P	W	NA	◆			Su/A	W/Sp				◆	
Calceolaria integrifolia	4 ft (1.2 m)	8–12 in (20–30 cm)	P	W	NA	◆			W/Sp	Sp–A			◆	◆	
Calendula officinalis	12–24 in (30–60 cm)	12–18 in (30–45 cm)	A	C/W	NA	◆			A/W	Sp–A	◆	◆	◆		
Calibrachoa Hybrid Cultivars	3–8 in (8–20 cm)	12–24 in (30–60 cm)	P	W	NA	◆			Sp	Sp–A	◆	◆	◆	◆	
Callistephus chinensis	12–36 in (30–90 cm)	8–12 in (20–30 cm)	A	W	NA	◆			Sp	Su/A	◆	◆	◆		
Caltha palustris	12–24 in (30–60 cm)	16–24 in (40–60 cm)	P	C	NA	◆	◆		A/W	Sp/Su			◆	◆	◆
Campanula carpatica	6–12 in (15–30 cm)	12–16 in (30–40 cm)	P	C	NA	◆			W/Sp	Su		◆	◆	◆	
Campanula cochlearifolia	3 in (8 cm)	10 in (25 cm)	P	C	NA	◆			W/Sp	Su		◆	◆	◆	
Campanula garganica	6 in (15 cm)	6–12 in (15–30 cm)	P	C	NA	◆			W/Sp	Su		◆	◆		
Campanula glomerata	12–36 in (30–90 cm)	12–24 in (30–60 cm)	P	C	NA	◆			W/Sp	Su			◆	◆	
Campanula isophylla	6 in (15 cm)	12–18 in (30–45 cm)	P	C	NA	◆			W/Sp	Su	◆		◆	◆	
Campanula lactiflora	3–5 ft (0.9–1.5 m)	2 ft (0.6 m)	P	C	NA	◆			W/Sp	Su			◆	◆	
Campanula medium	24–36 in (60–90 cm)	12 in (30 cm)	B	W	NA	◆			Sp	Su	◆	◆	◆		

Plant name	Height	Spread	Type	Climate	Group	Showy flowers	Showy foliage	Scented flowers	Planting season	Flowering season	Grow in pot/tub	Frost tolerant	Full Sun	Half Sun	Heavy shade
Campanula persicifolia	24–36 in (60–90 cm)	18 in (45 cm)	P	C	NA	◆			W/Sp	Su		◆	◆		
Campanula portenschlagiana	6 in (15 cm)	18–24 in (45–60 cm)	P	C	NA	◆			W/Sp	Su	◆	◆	◆	◆	
Campanula poscharskyana	6–8 in (15–20 cm)	18–24 in (45–60 cm)	P	C	NA	◆			W/Sp	Su/A	◆	◆	◆		
Campanula punctata	12 in (30 cm)	18 in (45 cm)	P	C	NA	◆			W/Sp	Su	◆	◆	◆		
Campanula pyramidalis	4–7 ft (1.2–2 m)	2 ft (0.6 m)	B	W	NA	◆			Sp	Su	◆	◆	◆		
Campanula rapunculoides	36 in (90 cm)	24 in (60 cm)	P	C	NA	◆			W/Sp	Su		◆	◆		
Campanula rotundifolia	6–12 in (15–30 cm)	10–18 in (25–45 cm)	P	C	NA	◆			W/Sp	Su		◆	◆	◆	
Campanula takesimana	24 in (60 cm)	18 in (45 cm)	P	C/W	NA	◆			W/Sp	Su		◆		◆	
Canistrum fosterianum	24 in (60 cm)	8 in (20 cm)	P	W	B	◆	◆		Sp	Su	◆				◆
Canna glauca	4–6 ft (1.2–1.8 m)	1–3 ft (0.3–0.9 m)	P	W/T	NA	◆			W/Sp	Su			◆		
Canna indica	4–7 ft (1.2–2 m)	20–32 in (50–80 cm)	P	W/T	NA	◆	◆		W/Sp	Su/A		◆	◆	◆	
Canna iridiflora	10 ft (3 m)	20–32 in (50–80 cm)	P	W/T	NA	◆	◆		W/Sp	Su/A			◆		
Canna Hybrid Cultivars	2–7 ft (0.6–2 m)	3 ft (0.9 m)	P	W/T	NA	◆	◆		W/Sp	Su/A	◆	◆	◆	◆	
Carthamus tinctorius	24–40 in (60–100 cm)	16–20 in (40–50 cm)	A	C/W	NA	◆			Sp	Su			◆	◆	
Catananche caerulea	24–30 in (60–75 cm)	12–18 in (30–45 cm)	P	C/W	NA	◆			Sp	Su			◆	◆	
Catharanthus roseus	24 in (60 cm)	16 in (40 cm)	P	W/T	NA	◆			Sp	Su/A	◆		◆	◆	
Celmisia sessiliflora	2–6 in (5–15 cm)	6–40 in (15–100 cm)	P	C	NA	◆	◆		W/Sp	Su			◆	◆	
Celmisia spectabilis	8–12 in (20–30 cm)	20–48 in (50–120 cm)	P	C	NA	◆	◆		W/Sp	Su			◆	◆	
Celosia argentea	3–7 ft (0.9–2 m)	16–24 in (40–60 cm)	A	W	NA	◆	◆		Sp/Su	Su/A	◆		◆		
Centaurea cineraria	20–36 in (50–90 cm)	12–24 in (30–60 cm)	P	C/W	NA		◆		Sp	Su			◆	◆	
Centaurea cyanus	12–36 in (30–90 cm)	8–16 in (20–40 cm)	A/B/P	C/W	NA	◆			W/Sp	Sp/Su			◆	◆	
Centaurea dealbata	32–40 in (80–100 cm)	16–24 in (40–60 cm)	P	C	NA	◆	◆		Sp	Su			◆	◆	
Centaurea macrocephala	32–40 in (80–100 cm)	20–24 in (50–60 cm)	P	C	NA	◆	◆		Sp	Su			◆	◆	
Centaurea montana	24–32 in (60–80 cm)	12–40 in (30–100 cm)	P	C	NA	◆			W/Sp	Sp/Su			◆	◆	
Centranthus ruber	32–40 in (80–100 cm)	16–27 in (40–70 cm)	P	C/W	NA	◆		◆	W/Sp	Sp/Su			◆	◆	
Cephalotus follicularis	15 in (38 cm)	8 in (20 cm)	P	W	C	◆			A/W	Sp	◆			◆	
Cerastium boissieri	6–10 in (15–25 cm)	8–16 in (20–40 cm)	P	C/W	NA	◆			W/Sp	Sp/Su			◆	◆	
Cerastium tomentosum	4–6 in (10–15 cm)	40 in (100 cm)	P	C/W	NA	◆	◆		W/Sp	Sp/Su	◆		◆	◆	
Chelidonium majus	12–36 in (30–90 cm)	12–36 in (30–90 cm)	B/P	C	NA	◆			W/Sp	Su			◆	◆	◆
Chelone glabra	20–32 in (50–80 cm)	16–20 in (40–50 cm)	P	C	NA	◆			W/Sp	Su/A		◆	◆	◆	
Chelone lyonii	40–48 in (100–120 cm)	24–36 in (60–90 cm)	P	C	NA	◆			W/Sp	Su/A		◆	◆	◆	

Plant name	Height	Spread	Type	Climate	Group	Showy flowers	Showy foliage	Scented flowers	Planting season	Flowering season	Grow in pot/tub	Frost tolerant	Full Sun	Half Sun	Heavy shade
Chlorophytum comosum	12–24 in (30–60 cm)	12–24 in (30–60 cm)	P	W	NA		◆		Sp	Su	◆			◆	
Chlorophytum laxum	8–12 in (20–30 cm)	8–12 in (20–30 cm)	P	W/T	NA		◆		Sp	Su	◆			◆	
Chrysanthemum × grandiflorum	1–5 ft (0.3–1.5 m)	18–36 in (45–90 cm)	P	C/W	NA	◆			W/Sp	A	◆	◆	◆	◆	
Chrysanthemum weyrichii	4 in (10 cm)	16–24 in (40–60 cm)	P	C/W	NA	◆			W/Sp	Su/A	◆	◆	◆	◆	
Chrysogonum virginianum	6–10 in (15–25 cm)	24 in (60 cm)	P	C	NA	◆			A/W	Sp/Su	◆			◆	◆
Clarkia amoena	24 in (60 cm)	12 in (30 cm)	A	C/W	NA	◆			Sp	Sp/Su	◆	◆	◆		
Clarkia pulchella	12–18 in (30–45 cm)	12 in (30 cm)	A	C/W	NA	◆			Sp	Sp/Su	◆	◆	◆		
Clarkia unguiculata	24–30 in (60–75 cm)	12 in (30 cm)	A	C/W	NA	◆			Sp	Sp/Su	◆	◆	◆		
Clematis integrifolia	3 ft (0.9 m)	3–5 ft (0.9–1.5 m)	P	C	NA	◆			W/Sp	Sp–A		◆	◆	◆	
Cleome sesquiorygalis	5 ft (1.5 m)	20 in (50 cm)	A	W/T	NA	◆			Sp	Su/A			◆	◆	
Clivia miniata	16–24 in (40–60 cm)	24–40 in (60–100 cm)	P	W	NA	◆			W	Sp	◆			◆	
Clivia nobilis	16–24 in (40–60 cm)	20–36 in (50–90 cm)	P	W	NA	◆			W	Sp	◆			◆	
Codonopsis clematidea	32 in (80 cm)	20–60 in (50–150 cm)	P	C	NA	◆			W/Sp	Su/A		◆		◆	
Collinsia bicolor	12–24 in (30–60 cm)	6–12 in (15–30 cm)	A	C/W	NA	◆			Sp	Sp/Su	◆			◆	
Columnea 'Early Bird'	48 in (120 cm)	18 in (45 cm)	P	W/T	G	◆	◆		Any	Sp–A				◆	
Columnea gloriosa	12 in (30 cm)	18 in (45 cm)	P	W/T	G	◆			Any	Sp/Su				◆	◆
Columnea microphylla	6 ft (1.8 m)	2 ft (0.6 m)	P	W/T	G	◆			Any	Sp/Su				◆	
Columnea scandens	12 in (30 cm)	24 in (60 cm)	P	W/T	G	◆			Any	Sp/Su				◆	◆
Commelina tuberosa	12–36 in (30–90 cm)	18–30 in (45–75 cm)	P	W/T	NA	◆			W	Sp–A			◆	◆	
Consolida ajacis	32–40 in (80–100 cm)	6–12 in (15–30 cm)	A	W	NA	◆			Sp	Su			◆	◆	
Convolvulus sabatius	8–12 in (20–30 cm)	24–60 in (60–150 cm)	P	W	NA	◆			W/Sp	Sp/Su	◆	◆	◆	◆	
Convolvulus tricolor	20–40 in (50–100 cm)	12–32 in (30–80 cm)	A/P	W	NA	◆	◆		Sp	Sp/Su			◆	◆	
Coreopsis grandiflora	24 in (60 cm)	12–20 in (30–50 cm)	P	C/W	NA	◆			Sp	Sp/Su	◆	◆	◆	◆	
Coreopsis lanceolata	24 in (60 cm)	12–16 in (30–40 cm)	P	C	NA	◆			W/Sp	Su		◆	◆	◆	
Coreopsis 'Sunray'	20 in (50cm)	12–16 in (30–40 cm)	P	C/W	NA	◆			Sp	Sp/Su	◆	◆	◆	◆	
Coreopsis verticillata	36 in (90 cm)	16 in (40 cm)	P	C/W	NA	◆			Su	Su		◆	◆	◆	
Cornus canadensis	4–6 in (10–15 cm)	36 in (90 cm)	P	C	NA	◆			W	Su				◆	
Corydalis cashmeriana	10 in (25 cm)	12–32 in (30–80 cm)	P	C/W	NA	◆			W/Sp	Sp/Su				◆	
Corydalis flexuosa	12 in (30 cm)	12–32 in (30–80 cm)	P	C/W	NA			◆	W/Sp	Sp/Su				◆	
Corydalis ochroleuca	8–16 in (20–40 cm)	12–32 in (30–80 cm)	P	C/W	NA	◆			W/Sp	Sp/Su				◆	
Corydalis wilsonii	12–16 in (30–40 cm)	12–32 in (30–80 cm)	P	C/W	NA	◆			A/W	Sp		◆		◆	

Plant name	Height	Spread	Type	Climate	Group	Showy flowers	Showy foliage	Scented flowers	Planting season	Flowering season	Grow in pot/tub	Frost tolerant	Full Sun	Half Sun	Heavy shade
Cosmos bipinnatus	4–7 ft (1.2–2 m)	2–4 ft (0.6–1.2 m)	A	C/W	NA	◆			Sp	Su		◆	◆	◆	
Cosmos sulphureus	5–7 ft (1.5–2 m)	32–48 in (80–120cm)	A	C/W	NA	◆			Sp	Su		◆	◆	◆	
Costus igneus	20 in (50 cm)	20–40 in (50–100 cm)	P	W/T	NA	◆			A	W	◆			◆	
Costus pulverulentus	5–10 ft (1.5–3 m)	2–5 ft (0.6–1.5 m)	P	W/T	NA	◆			W	Sp–A	◆				◆
Cryptanthus acaulis	2 in (5 cm)	6 in (15 cm)	P	W	B		◆		Any	Sp/Su	◆				◆
Cryptanthus bivittatus	2 in (5 cm)	10 in (25 cm)	P	W/T	B		◆		Any	Sp/Su	◆				◆
Cryptanthus fosterianus	2 in (5 cm)	16 in (40 cm)	P	W/T	B		◆		Any	Sp/Su	◆				◆
Cryptanthus 'Rainbow Star'	16 in (40 cm)	16 in (40 cm)	P	W/T	B		◆		Any	Sp/Su	◆				◆
Cryptanthus zonatus	2 in (5 cm)	12 in (30 cm)	P	W/T	B		◆		Any	Sp/Su	◆				◆
Ctenanthe burle-marxii	18 in (45 cm)	12–18 in (30–45 cm)	P	W/T	NA		◆		Any	Sp/Su	◆				◆
Ctenanthe lubbersiana	18–24 in (45–60 cm)	18–24 in (45–60 cm)	P	W/T	NA		◆		Any	Sp/Su	◆				◆
Ctenanthe oppenheimiana	36 in (90 cm)	24–36 in (60–90 cm)	P	W/T	NA		◆		Any	Sp/Su	◆				◆
Cynoglossum amabile	20–24 in (50–60 cm)	12 in (30 cm)	B	C/W	NA	◆			W/Sp	Sp/Su		◆	◆	◆	
Cynoglossum nervosum	24–30 in (60–75 cm)	24 in (60 cm)	P	C	NA	◆			W/Sp	Sp/Su		◆	◆	◆	
Dampiera diversifolia	4–20 in (10–50 cm)	40–60 in (100–150 cm)	P	W	NA	◆			W	Sp/Su		◆	◆		
Darlingtonia californica	24–40 in (60–100 cm)	8–10 in (20–25 cm)	P	C	C		◆	◆	A/W	Sp/Su	◆	◆	◆	◆	
Darmera peltata	5–7 ft (1.5–2 m)	3–10 ft (0.9–3 m)	P	C/W	NA	◆			W	Sp					◆
Delphinium × *belladonna*	12–40 in (30–100 cm)	6–20 in (15–50 cm)	P	C	NA	◆			W	Sp/Su		◆	◆	◆	
Delphinium cardinale	3–7 ft (0.9–2 m)	8–20 in (20–50 cm)	P	C/W	NA	◆			W	Su			◆		
Delphinium elatum	2–6 ft (0.6–1.8 m)	8–20 in (20–50 cm)	P	C	NA	◆			W	Su			◆		
Delphinium grandiflorum	12–40 in (30–100 cm)	12–24 in (30–60 cm)	P	C	NA	◆			W	Su			◆		
Delphinium nudicaule	12–24 in (30–60 cm)	8–16 in (20–40 cm)	P	C/W	NA	◆			W	Sp/Su			◆		
Delphinium Hybrid Cultivars	4–7 ft (1.2–2 m)	1½–3 ft (0.5–0.9 m)	P	C/W	NA	◆			W	Sp/Su			◆		
Derwentia perfoliata	12–26 in (30–65 cm)	20–60 in (50–150 cm)	P	C	NA	◆			W/Sp	Sp/Su			◆		
Deuterocohnia brevifolia	2–4 in (5–10 cm)	4–12 in (10–30 cm)	P	C/W	B	◆	◆		W	Sp	◆	◆	◆	◆	
Deuterocohnia lorentziana	4 in (10 cm)	4 in (10 cm)	P	C/W	B	◆	◆		W	Sp	◆				◆
Dianella tasmanica	40 in (100 cm)	12 in (30 cm)	P	W/T	NA	◆	◆		A/W	Sp/Su	◆		◆	◆	
Dianthus alpinus	4–6 in (10–15 cm)	6–12 in (15–30 cm)	P	C	NA	◆			W	Sp/Su		◆	◆	◆	
Dianthus barbatus	12–24 in (30–60 cm)	6–12 in (15–30 cm)	A/P	C	NA	◆			W/Sp	Sp/Su		◆	◆	◆	
Dianthus caryophyllus	20–32 in (50–80 cm)	8–16 in (20–40 cm)	P	C	NA	◆			W			◆	◆	◆	
Dianthus deltoides	8–16 in (20–40 cm)	6–12 in (15–30 cm)	P	C	NA	◆			W	Sp/Su		◆	◆	◆	

Plant name	Height	Spread	Type	Climate	Group	Showy flowers	Showy foliage	Scented flowers	Planting season	Flowering season	Grow in pot/tub	Frost tolerant	Full Sun	Half Sun	Heavy shade
Dianthus gratianopolitanus	6–8 in (15–20 cm)	8–16 in (20–40 cm)	P	C	NA	♦		♦	W	Sp/Su	♦	♦	♦	♦	
Dianthus plumarius	6–14 in (15–35 cm)	8–16 in (20–40 cm)	P	C	NA	♦		♦	W	Sp/Su	♦	♦	♦	♦	
Dianthus superbus	20–30 in (50–75 cm)	12–20 in (30–50 cm)	P	C	NA	♦		♦	W	Sp/Su	♦	♦	♦	♦	
Dianthus Hybrid Cultivars	8–15 in (20–38 cm)	6–12 in (15–30 cm)	A/P	C	NA	♦		♦	W	Sp/Su	♦	♦	♦	♦	
Diascia barberae	12 in (30 cm)	12–16 in (30–40 cm)	P	W	NA	♦			W/Sp	Su	♦		♦	♦	
Diascia rigescens	16–20 in (40–50 cm)	24 in (60 cm)	P	W	NA	♦			W/Sp	Su	♦		♦	♦	
Diascia vigilis	20 in (50 cm)	48 in (120 cm)	P	W	NA	♦			W/Sp	Su/A	♦		♦	♦	
Diascia Hybrid Cultivars	8–18 in (20–45 cm)	12–24 in (30–60 cm)	P	W	NA	♦			W/Sp	Su			♦	♦	
Dicentra cucullaria	12–16 in (30–40 cm)	20–40 in (50–100 cm)	P	C	NA	♦	♦		A/W	Sp		♦	♦	♦	
Dicentra eximia	12–26 in (30–65 cm)	20–40 in (50–100 cm)	P	C	NA	♦	♦		A/W	Sp		♦	♦	♦	
Dicentra formosa	12–26 in (30–65 cm)	20–40 in (50–100 cm)	P	C	NA	♦	♦		A/W	Sp		♦	♦	♦	
Dicentra spectabilis	40–56 in (100–140 cm)	20–40 in (50–100 cm)	P	C	NA	♦	♦		A/W	Sp		♦	♦	♦	
Dichorisandra thyrsiflora	3–10 ft (0.9–3 m)	3 ft (0.9 m)	P	W/T	NA	♦	♦		A/W	Su/A	♦			♦	
Dicliptera suberecta	18–24 in (45–60 cm)	18–24 in (45–60 cm)	P	C/W	NA		♦		W	Su/A	♦	♦	♦		
Dieffenbachia seguine	3–6 ft (0.9–1.8)	18–24 in (45–60 cm)	P	W/T	NA		♦		Any	Sp/Su	♦		♦	♦	
Dietes bicolor	32–36 in (80–90 cm)	24–36 in (60–90 cm)	P	W	NA	♦			W	Sp/Su			♦	♦	♦
Dietes grandiflora	20–27 in (50–70 cm)	20–27 in (50–70 cm)	P	W	NA	♦			W	Su					♦
Digitalis grandiflora	40 in (100 cm)	20–24 in (50–60 cm)	B/P	C	NA	♦			A/W	Sp/Su		♦	♦	♦	
Digitalis lutea	24–40 in (60–100 cm)	16–24 in (40–60 cm)	P	C	NA	♦			A/W	Sp/Su		♦	♦	♦	
Digitalis mertonensis	20–30 in (50–75 cm)	16–20 in (40–50 cm)	P	C	NA	♦			A/W	Sp/Su		♦	♦	♦	
Digitalis purpurea	5–6 ft (1.5–1.8 m)	12–32 in (30–80 cm)	B	C	NA	♦			A/W	Su		♦	♦	♦	
Dimorphotheca sinuata	12–18 in (30–45 cm)	12 in (30 cm)	A	W	NA	♦			Sp	Sp/Su	♦		♦		
Dionaea muscipula	4 in (10 cm)	8 in (20 cm)	P	C/W	C		♦		W	Sp	♦	♦	♦	♦	
Dodecatheon dentatum	4–16 in (10–40 cm)	6–12 in (15–30 cm)	P	C	NA	♦			A/W	Sp/Su		♦	♦	♦	
Dodecatheon hendersonii	8–15 in (20–38 cm)	6–12 in (15–30 cm)	P	C	NA	♦			A/W	Sp/Su		♦	♦	♦	
Dodecatheon meadia	8–18 in (20–45 cm)	12 in (30 cm)	P	C	NA	♦			A/W	Sp		♦	♦	♦	
Dorotheanthus bellidiformis	2–6 in (5–15 cm)	8–16 in (20–40 cm)	A	W	NA	♦			Sp	Su	♦		♦		
Doryanthes excelsa	8–20 ft (2.4–6 m)	10 ft (3 m)	P	W	NA	♦	♦		W	Sp/Su			♦		
Doryanthes palmeri	3–10 ft (0.9–3 m)	3–10 ft (0.9–3 m)	P	W/T	NA	♦	♦		W	Sp			♦		
Drosera binata	12 in (30 cm)	8 in (20 cm)	P	W	C		♦		W	Sp	♦	♦	♦		
Drosera capensis	6 in (15 cm)	6 in (15 cm)	P	W	C	♦	♦		W	Sp	♦	♦	♦		

Plant name	Height	Spread	Type	Climate	Group	Showy flowers	Showy foliage	Scented flowers	Planting season	Flowering season	Grow in pot/tub	Frost tolerant	Full Sun	Half Sun	Heavy shade
Drosera pulchella	½ in (12 mm)	1¼ in (30 mm)	P	W	C	◆	◆		W	Sp	◆		◆		
Drosera rotundifolia	2 in (5 cm)	4 in (10 cm)	P	W	C		◆		W	Sp	◆	◆	◆		
Drosera zonaria	1 in (2.5 cm)	3 in (8 cm)	P	W	C		◆		W	Sp		◆	◆		
Drosophyllum lusitanicum	12 in (30 cm)	16 in (40 cm)	P	W	C	◆	◆		A/W	Sp	◆	◆	◆		
Dryas octopetala	3–4 in (8–10 cm)	40 in (100 cm)	P	C	NA	◆			A/W	Su		◆	◆		
Dyckia remotiflora	40 in (100 cm)	16 in (40 cm)	P	W	B	◆	◆	◆	A/W	Sp/Su	◆				◆
Echinops bannaticus	4 ft (1.2 m)	2 ft (0.6 m)	P	C	NA	◆	◆		W	Su/A		◆	◆	◆	
Echinops ritro	12–24 in (30–60 cm)	16–24 in (40–60 cm)	P	C	NA	◆	◆		W	Su/A		◆	◆	◆	
Echinops sphaerocephalus	3–7 ft (0.9–2 m)	16–32 in (40–80 cm)	P	C	NA	◆	◆		W	Su/A		◆	◆	◆	
Echium candicans	6 ft (1.8 m)	6 ft (1.8 m)	P	W	NA	◆			Any	Sp/Su			◆		
Echium vulgare	18–24 in (45–60 cm)	18–24 in (45–60 cm)	A/B	C/W	NA	◆			Sp	Su		◆	◆		
Edmondia pinifolia	12 in (30 cm)	12 in (30 cm)	P	W	NA	◆			W/Sp	Sp			◆		
Eichhornia crassipes	12 in (30 cm)	18 in (45 cm)	P	W/T	NA	◆			W/Sp	Su			◆		
Elodea canadensis	36 in (90 cm)	indefinite	P	C/W	NA			◆	Any	Su			◆	◆	
Emilia sonchifolia	6–20 in (15–50 cm)	6–10 in (15–25 cm)	A	W	NA	◆			Sp	Su	◆		◆		
Ensete ventricosum	30 ft (9 m)	15 ft (4.5 m)	P	W/T	NA	◆	◆		W/Sp	Su			◆		
Epilobium angustifolium	3–8 ft (0.9–2.4 m)	3–8 ft (0.9–2.4 m)	P	C	NA	◆			Sp	Su/A		◆	◆		
Epilobium canum	1–3 ft (0.3–0.9 m)	3–7 ft (0.9–2 m)	P	W	NA	◆	◆		W/Sp	Su/A		◆	◆		
Epilobium septentrionale	6–12 in (15–30 cm)	24–36 in (60–90 cm)	P	W	NA	◆	◆		W/Sp	Su/A		◆	◆		
Epimedium × cantabrigiense	12–24 in (30–60 cm)	12–18 in (30–45 cm)	P	C	NA	◆	◆		W	Sp			◆	◆	
Epimedium grandiflorum	8–12 in (20–30 cm)	8–12 in (20–30 cm)	P	C	NA	◆	◆		W	Sp			◆		◆
Epimedium × perralchicum	14–16 in (35–40 cm)	20–24 in (50–60 cm)	P	C	NA	◆	◆		W	Sp			◆		◆
Epimedium perralderianum	14–16 in (35–40 cm)	20–24 in (50–60 cm)	P	C	NA	◆	◆		W	Sp			◆		◆
Epimedium × versicolor	10–12 in (25–30 cm)	10–12 in (25–30 cm)	P	C	NA	◆	◆		W	Sp			◆		
Episcia cupreata	8–12 in (20–30 cm)	12–24 in (30–60 cm)	P	W/T	G	◆	◆		W/Sp	Su	◆			◆	◆
Episcia dianthiflora	8 in (20 cm)	18–36 in (45–90 cm)	P	W/T	G	◆	◆		W/Sp	Su	◆			◆	◆
Episcia Hybrid Cultivars	8–20 in (20–50 cm)	32–40 in (80–100 cm)	P	W/T	G	◆	◆		W/Sp	Sp–A	◆			◆	◆
Eranthis hyemalis	3–4 in (8–10 cm)	3–4 in (8–10 cm)	P	C	NA	◆			Su/A	W/Sp		◆		◆	
Erigeron glaucus	6–12 in (15–30 cm)	12–24 in (30–60 cm)	P	C/W	NA	◆			W/Sp	Sp/Su		◆	◆		
Erigeron karvinskianus	1–2 ft (0.3–0.6 m)	2–5 ft (0.6–1.5 m)	P	W	NA	◆			W/Sp	Sp–A	◆	◆	◆		
Erigeron pulchellus	6–16 in (15–40 cm)	8–16 in (20–40 cm)	B/P	C	NA	◆			W/Sp	Su		◆	◆		

Plant name	Height	Spread	Type	Climate	Group	Showy flowers	Showy foliage	Scented flowers	Planting season	Flowering season	Grow in pot/tub	Frost tolerant	Full Sun	Half Sun	Heavy shade
Erigeron 'Rosa Jewel'	18–30 in (45–75 cm)	16–24 in (40–60 cm)	P	C	NA	◆			W/Sp	Su		◆	◆		
Erigeron speciosus	18–30 in (45–75 cm)	16–24 in (40–60 cm)	P	C	NA	◆			W/Sp	Su		◆	◆		
Eriogonum arborescens	5 ft (1.5 m)	5 ft (1.5 m)	P	W	NA	◆			W/Sp	Su/A			◆	◆	
Eriogonum giganteum	8 ft (2.4 m)	10 ft (3 m)	P	W	NA	◆		◆	W/Sp	Su/A			◆		
Eriogonum umbellatum	6–18 in (15–45 cm)	3–4 ft (0.9–1.2 m)	P	C/W	NA	◆			W/Sp	Su			◆		
Erodium chrysanthum	4–6 in (10–15 cm)	12–16 in (30–40 cm)	P	C/W	NA	◆			W/Sp	Su		◆	◆	◆	
Erodium corsicum	8 in (20 cm)	12 in (30 cm)	P	C/W	NA	◆			W/Sp	Sp/Su		◆	◆		
Erodium reichardii	1–2 in (2.5–5 cm)	10 in (25 cm)	P	C/W	NA	◆			W/Sp	Su		◆	◆	◆	
Erodium × variabile	6–12 in (15–30 cm)	10 in (25 cm)	P	C/W	NA	◆			W/Sp	Su		◆	◆	◆	
Eryngium alpinum	24 in (60 cm)	24 in (60 cm)	P	C	NA	◆			W/Sp	Su		◆	◆	◆	
Eryngium amethystinum	28 in (70 cm)	20 in (50 cm)	P	C/W	NA	◆			W/Sp	Su			◆	◆	
Eryngium bourgatii	16 in (40 cm)	16 in (40 cm)	P	C/W	NA	◆			W/Sp	Su			◆	◆	
Eryngium giganteum	5 ft (1.5 m)	32 in (80 cm)	P	C	NA	◆			W/Sp	Su			◆	◆	
Eryngium × oliverianum	24–40 in (60–100 cm)	20–24 in (50–60 cm)	P	C	NA	◆			W/Sp	Su		◆	◆	◆	
Eryngium variifolium	20–30 in (50–75 cm)	16–20 in (40–50 cm)	P	C/W	NA	◆			W/Sp	Su			◆	◆	
Erysimum bicolor	36 in (90 cm)	24 in (60 cm)	P	W	NA			◆	W	Sp–A			◆	◆	
Erysimum cheiri	24 in (60 cm)	16 in (40 cm)	B/P	C/W	NA			◆	W/Sp	Sp–A			◆	◆	
Erysimum Hybrid Cultivars	24–36 in (60–90 cm)	24 in (60 cm)	P	C/W	NA			◆	W	Sp–A			◆	◆	
Eschscholzia caespitosa	10 in (25 cm)	10 in (25 cm)	A	W	NA	◆			Sp	Sp–A	◆	◆	◆		
Eschscholzia californica	8–24 in (20–60 cm)	8–16 in (20–40 cm)	A/P	C/W	NA	◆			W/Sp	Sp–A	◆	◆	◆		
Etlingera elatior	10–20 ft (3–6 m)	5–8 ft (1.5–2.4 m)	P	W/T	NA	◆			Sp	Su/A			◆	◆	
Eupatorium perfoliatum	3–5 ft (0.9–1.5 m)	3–5 ft (0.9–1.5 m)	P	C	NA	◆	◆		W/Sp	Su/A			◆	◆	
Eupatorium purpureum	6–10 ft (1.8–3 m)	6–10 ft (1.8–3 m)	P	C	NA	◆	◆	◆	W/Sp	Su/A			◆	◆	◆
Eupatorium rugosum	3–6 ft (0.9–1.8 m)	3–6 ft (0.9–1.8 m)	P	C	NA	◆			W/Sp	Su/A			◆	◆	
Euphorbia amygdaloides	20–32 in (50–80 cm)	24–40 in (60–100 cm)	P	C/W	NA	◆	◆		W/Sp	Sp/Su			◆	◆	◆
Euphorbia characias	6 ft (1.8 m)	5 ft (1.5 m)	P	W	NA	◆	◆		A/W	W–Su			◆	◆	
Euphorbia cyparissias	16 in (40 cm)	24 in (60 cm)	P	C/W	NA	◆			W/Sp	Sp/Su			◆	◆	
Euphorbia griffithii	36 in (90 cm)	36 in (90 cm)	P	C/W	NA	◆	◆		W/Sp	Su			◆	◆	
Euphorbia marginata	40 in (100 cm)	20 in (50 cm)	A	C/W	NA			◆	Sp	Su			◆	◆	
Euphorbia myrsinites	10 in (25 cm)	20 in (50 cm)	P	C/W	NA	◆	◆		A/W	Sp			◆		◆
Euphorbia nicaeensis	24 in (60 cm)	24 in (60 cm)	P	C/W	NA	◆			W/Sp	Sp/Su			◆	◆	

Plant name	Height	Spread	Type	Climate	Group	Showy flowers	Showy foliage	Scented flowers	Planting season	Flowering season	Grow in pot/tub	Frost tolerant	Full Sun	Half Sun	Heavy shade
Euphorbia polychroma	24 in (60 cm)	24 in (60 cm)	P	C/W	NA	◆	◆		W/Sp	Sp/Su		◆		◆	
Euphorbia schillingii	4 ft (1.2 m)	5 ft (1.5 m)	P	C/W	NA	◆			W/Sp	Su		◆	◆	◆	
Euphorbia seguieriana	20 in (50 cm)	32 in (80 cm)	P	C	NA	◆			W/Sp	Su			◆	◆	
Euphorbia sikkimensis	36 in (90 cm)	36 in (90 cm)	P	C/W	NA	◆	◆		W/Sp	Su			◆	◆	
Euryale ferox	3 ft (0.9 m)	5 ft (1.5 m)	A/P	W	NA	◆	◆		Sp	Su			◆	◆	
Eustoma grandiflorum	24–32 in (60–80 cm)	20 in (50 cm)	A/P	W	NA	◆			Sp	Su	◆	◆	◆	◆	
Evolvulus glomeratus	10–18 in (25–45 cm)	24–36 in (60–90 cm)	P	W/T	NA	◆			Sp	Sp–A	◆		◆		
Exacum affine	12–18 in (30–45 cm)	12 in (30 cm)	A/P	W/T	NA	◆		◆	Sp	Sp–A	◆		◆		
Farfugium japonicum	24–40 in (60–100 cm)	24–40 in (60–100 cm)	P	W	NA	◆	◆		W/Sp	W	◆			◆	
Felicia amelloides	16–24 in (40–60 cm)	24 in (60 cm)	P	W	NA	◆			W/Sp	Su	◆		◆		
Felicia fruticosa	36 in (90 cm)	36 in (90 cm)	P	W	NA	◆			W/Sp	Sp/Su			◆		
Filipendula purpurea	36–48 in (90–120 cm)	18 in (45 cm)	P	C	NA	◆	◆		A/W	Su		◆		◆	
Filipendula rubra	3–7 ft (0.9–2 m)	2 ft (0.6 m)	P	C	NA	◆	◆		A/W	Su		◆		◆	
Filipendula ulmaria	24–48 in (60–120 cm)	12–18 in (30–45 cm)	P	C	NA	◆	◆	◆	A/W	Su		◆		◆	
Filipendula vulgaris	24–36 in (60–90 cm)	18 in (45 cm)	P	C	NA	◆	◆		A/W	Su		◆		◆	
Fittonia albivenis	6 in (15 cm)	12–24 in (30–60 cm)	P	W/T	NA			◆	Any	Any	◆				◆
Gaillardia aristata	20 in (50 cm)	32 in (80 cm)	P	C/W	NA	◆			W/Sp	Su/A		◆	◆		
Gaillardia × grandiflora	24 in (60 cm)	40 in (100 cm)	P	C/W	NA	◆			W/Sp	Su/A		◆	◆		
Gaillardia pulchella	24 in (60 cm)	16 in (40 cm)	A	W	NA	◆			Sp	Su/A		◆	◆		
Galium odoratum	18 in (45 cm)	36 in (90 cm)	P	C	NA	◆		◆	W/Sp	Sp/Su		◆		◆	
Galium verum	3–4 ft (0.9–1.2 m)	3 ft (0.9 m)	P	C	NA	◆			W/Sp	Su/A		◆		◆	
Gaura lindheimeri	48–60 in (120–150 cm)	40 in (100 cm)	P	C/W	NA	◆			A/Sp	Sp/Su		◆	◆	◆	
Gazania rigens	8 in (20 cm)	40 in (100 cm)	P	W	NA	◆			W/Sp	Sp–A	◆		◆		
Gazania Hybrid Cultivars	4–6 in (10–15 cm)	20 in (50 cm)	P	W	NA	◆			W/Sp	Sp–A	◆		◆		
Genlisea violacea	1 in (2.5 cm)	2 in (5 cm)	P	W/T	C			◆	W/Sp	Sp/Su	◆			◆	
Gentiana acaulis	4 in (10 cm)	12 in (30 cm)	P	C	NA	◆			W/Sp	Sp/Su	◆	◆		◆	
Gentiana asclepiadea	16 in (40 cm)	24–40 in (60–100 cm)	P	C	NA	◆			W/Sp	Su/A		◆		◆	
Gentiana saxosa	8 in (20 cm)	12 in (30 cm)	P	C/W	NA	◆			W/Sp	Su	◆	◆		◆	
Gentiana septemfida	12 in (30 cm)	16 in (40 cm)	P	C	NA	◆			W/Sp	Su/A	◆	◆		◆	
Gentiana sino-ornata	6 in (15 cm)	12 in (30 cm)	P	C	NA	◆			W/Sp	A		◆		◆	
Gentiana verna	2 in (5 cm)	8–12 in (20–30 cm)	P	C	NA	◆			W/Sp	Sp/Su	◆	◆		◆	

Plant name	Height	Spread	Type	Climate	Group	Showy flowers	Showy foliage	Scented flowers	Planting season	Flowering season	Grow in pot/tub	Frost tolerant	Full Sun	Half Sun	Heavy shade
Geranium × cantabrigiense	8 in (20 cm)	24 in (60 cm)	P	C/W	NA	◆			W/Sp	Su	◆	◆	◆	◆	
Geranium cinereum	6 in (15 cm)	20 in (50 cm)	P	C/W	NA	◆			W/Sp	Su	◆	◆	◆	◆	
Geranium dalmaticum	6 in (15 cm)	20 in (50 cm)	P	C/W	NA	◆			W/Sp	Su	◆	◆	◆	◆	
Geranium endressii	18 in (45 cm)	24 in (60 cm)	P	C/W	NA	◆			W/Sp	Sp/Su		◆	◆	◆	
Geranium himalayense	18 in (45 cm)	40 in (100 cm)	P	C/W	NA	◆			W/Sp	Su			◆	◆	
Geranium incanum	40 in (100 cm)	40 in (100 cm)	P	C/W	NA	◆			W/Sp	Su			◆	◆	
Geranium macrorrhizum	20 in (50 cm)	40 in (100 cm)	P	C/W	NA	◆			W/Sp	Su			◆	◆	
Geranium maculatum	27 in (70 cm)	40 in (100 cm)	P	C/W	NA	◆			W/Sp	Sp/Su		◆	◆	◆	
Geranium maderense	60 in (150 cm)	60 in (150 cm)	P	C/W	NA	◆	◆		W/Sp	Sp/Su			◆	◆	
Geranium × magnificum	20 in (50 cm)	40 in (100 cm)	P	C/W	NA	◆			W/Sp	Su			◆	◆	
Geranium × oxonianum	24 in (60 cm)	48 in (120 cm)	P	C/W	NA	◆			W/Sp	Su			◆	◆	
Geranium phaeum	32 in (80 cm)	16 in (40 cm)	P	C/W	NA	◆			W/Sp	Su			◆	◆	
Geranium pratense	48 in (120 cm)	40 in (100 cm)	P	C/W	NA	◆			W/Sp	Su			◆	◆	
Geranium psilostemon	24–40 in (60–100 cm)	16–24 in (40–60 cm)	P	C/W	NA	◆			W/Sp	Su			◆	◆	
Geranium × riversleaianum	4 in (10 cm)	24 in (60 cm)	P	C/W	NA	◆			W/Sp	Su	◆	◆	◆	◆	
Geranium sanguineum	8 in (20 cm)	16 in (40 cm)	P	C/W	NA	◆			W/Sp	Su	◆	◆	◆	◆	
Geranium sylvaticum	27 in (70 cm)	40 in (100 cm)	P	C/W	NA	◆			W/Sp	Su			◆	◆	
Geranium wallichianum	6 in (15 cm)	24 in (60 cm)	P	C/W	NA	◆			W/Sp	Su	◆	◆	◆	◆	
Geranium Hybrid Cultivars	8–36 in (20–90 cm)	24–48 in (60–120 cm)	P	C/W	NA	◆			W/Sp	Su			◆	◆	
Gerbera jamesonii	27 in (70 cm)	30 in (75 cm)	P	W	NA	◆			Sp	A–Sp	◆	◆	◆		
Gerbera Hybrid Cultivars	8–18 in (20–45 cm)	12 in (30 cm)	P	W	NA	◆			Sp	A–Sp	◆			◆	
Geum chiloense	30 in (75 cm)	20 in (50 cm)	P	C/W	NA	◆			W/Sp	Su		◆	◆	◆	
Geum montanum	12 in (30 cm)	20 in (50 cm)	P	C	NA	◆			W/Sp	Sp/Su	◆	◆	◆	◆	
Geum rivale	12 in (30 cm)	30 in (75 cm)	P	C/W	NA	◆			W/Sp	Sp/Su			◆	◆	
Geum triflorum	16 in (40 cm)	16 in (40 cm)	P	C/W	NA	◆			W/Sp	Sp/Su			◆	◆	
Geum Hybrid Cultivars	36 in (90 cm)	36 in (90 cm)	P	C/W	NA	◆			W/Sp	Sp/Su		◆	◆	◆	
Gillenia trifoliata	48 in (120 cm)	48 in (120 cm)	P	C	NA	◆			W	Sp/Su			◆	◆	
Glaucium flavum	40 in (100 cm)	16 in (40 cm)	B/P	C/W	NA	◆	◆		Sp	Su			◆	◆	
Globba winitii	36 in (90 cm)	24 in (60 cm)	P	W	NA	◆			Sp	Su				◆	
Gloxinia perennis	24 in (60 cm)	15 in (38 cm)	P	W/T	G	◆			Sp	Su/A	◆			◆	
Gloxinia sylvatica	24 in (60 cm)	24 in (60 cm)	P	W/T	G	◆			Sp	Su/A	◆			◆	

Plant name	Height	Spread	Type	Climate	Group	Showy flowers	Showy foliage	Scented flowers	Planting season	Flowering season	Grow in pot/tub	Frost tolerant	Full Sun	Half Sun	Heavy shade
Gomphrena globosa	24 in (60 cm)	18 in (45 cm)	A	W	NA	◆			Sp	Su	◆	◆	◆		
Gunnera manicata	6–10 ft (1.8–3 m)	10–15 ft (3–4.5 m)	P	C/W	NA		◆		W	Sp/Su		◆	◆		
Gunnera prorepens	2–4 in (5–10 cm)	12–18 in (30–45 cm)	P	C/W	NA				W	Sp/Su		◆	◆		
Guzmania lingulata	12 in (30 cm)	8 in (20 cm)	P	W/T	B	◆	◆		W/Sp	Sp/Su	◆				◆
Guzmania musaica	20 in (50 cm)	16 in (40 cm)	P	W/T	B	◆	◆		W/Sp	Sp/Su	◆				◆
Guzmania wittmackii	30 in (75 cm)	36 in (90 cm)	P	W/T	B	◆			W/Sp	Sp/Su	◆				◆
Guzmania Hybrid Cultivars	18–36 in (45–90 cm)	10–24 in (25–60 cm)	P	W/T	B	◆			W/Sp	Sp/Su	◆				◆
Gynura aurantiaca	7–8 in (2–2.4 m)	4 ft (1.2 m)	P	W/T	NA		◆		Sp	W	◆				◆
Gypsophila cerastioides	3 in (8 cm)	8 in (20 cm)	P	C	NA	◆			W/Sp	Sp		◆	◆	◆	
Gypsophila paniculata	48 in (120 cm)	48 in (120 cm)	P	C	NA	◆		◆	W/Sp	Su		◆	◆	◆	
Gypsophila repens	4 in (10 cm)	24 in (60 cm)	P	C	NA	◆			W/Sp	Sp/Su		◆	◆	◆	
Gypsophila 'Rosenschleier'	12 in (30 cm)	36 in (90 cm)	P	C	NA	◆			W/Sp	Sp/Su	◆	◆	◆	◆	
Hedychium coccineum	7–10 ft (2–3 m)	2–5 ft (0.6–1.5 m)	P	W/T	NA	◆	◆		W	A		◆	◆	◆	
Hedychium coronarium	10 ft (3 m)	2–5 ft (0.6–1.5 m)	P	W/T	NA	◆	◆	◆	Sp			◆	◆	◆	
Hedychium gardnerianum	8 ft (2.4 m)	3–5 ft (0.9–1.5 m)	P	W	NA	◆			W	Su/A		◆	◆	◆	
Hedychium greenei	7 ft (2 m)	32–48 in (80–120 cm)	P	W/T	NA	◆			W	Su		◆	◆	◆	
Helenium autumnale	5 ft (1.5 m)	3 ft (0.9 m)	P	C	NA	◆			W/Sp	Su/A		◆	◆		
Helenium Hybrid Cultivars	40 in (100 cm)	40 in (100 cm)	P	C	NA	◆			W/Sp	Su/A		◆	◆		
Heliamphora heterodoxa	18 in (45 cm)	12 in (30 cm)	P	W/T	C		◆		W/Sp	W	◆		◆	◆	
Heliamphora minor	3 in (8 cm)	6 in (15 cm)	P	W	C		◆		W/Sp	Sp	◆		◆	◆	
Helianthus annuus	10–17 ft (3–5 m)	2–4 ft (0.6–1.2 m)	A	C/W	NA	◆			Sp	Su		◆	◆		
Helianthus maximilianii	7–10 ft (2–3 m)	2–3 ft (0.6–0.9 m)	P	C/W	NA	◆			Sp	A			◆		
Helianthus × multiflorus	7 ft (2 m)	2 ft (0.6 m)	P	C/W	NA	◆				Su/A			◆		
Helianthus salicifolius	10 ft (3 m)	2–4 ft (0.6–1.2 m)	P	C/W	NA	◆			Sp	A			◆		
Helianthus Hybrid Cultivars	4–7 ft (1.2–2 m)	3–4 ft (0.9–1.2 m)	P	C/W	NA	◆			Sp	Su		◆	◆		
Helichrysum ecklonis	4–16 in (10–40 cm)	16–24 in (40–60 cm)	P	W	NA	◆			W/Sp	Su	◆		◆		
Helichrysum frigidum	4 in (10 cm)	12 in (30 cm)	P	W	NA	◆			W/Sp	Sp/Su		◆	◆		
Helichrysum milfordiae	6 in (15 cm)	12 in (30 cm)	P	W	NA	◆			A/W	Sp		◆	◆		
Helichrysum petiolare	12–18 in (30–45 cm)	5 ft (1.5 m)	P	W	NA		◆		W/Sp	W			◆	◆	
Helichrysum splendidum	5 ft (1.5 m)	3 ft (0.9 m)	P	W	NA		◆		W/Sp	A/W		◆	◆		
Heliconia bihai	7–17 ft (2–5 m)	2–7 ft (0.6–2 m)	P	W/T	NA	◆			W/Sp	Sp–A				◆	

Plant name	Height	Spread	Type	Climate	Group	Showy flowers	Showy foliage	Scented flowers	Planting season	Flowering season	Grow in pot/tub	Frost tolerant	Full Sun	Half Sun	Heavy shade
Heliconia caribaea	7–17 ft (2–5 m)	2–7 ft (0.6–2 m)	P	W/T	NA	◆			W/Sp	Sp–A				◆	
Heliconia latispatha	10 ft (3 m)	3–4 ft (0.9–1.2 m)	P	W/T	NA	◆			W/Sp	Sp–A				◆	
Heliconia psittacorum	2–7 ft (0.6–2 m)	20–32 in (50–80 cm)	P	W/T	NA	◆			W/Sp	Sp–A				◆	
Heliconia wagneriana	12 ft (3.5 m)	4–7 ft (1.2–2 m)	P	W/T	NA	◆			W/Sp	Sp–A				◆	
Heliopsis helianthoides	2–5 ft (0.6–1.5 m)	1–2 ft (0.3–0.6 m)	P	C	NA	◆			W/Sp	Su/A		◆	◆		
Heliopsis Hybrid Cultivars	4 ft (1.2 m)	1–2 ft (0.3–0.6 m)	P	C	NA	◆			W/Sp	Su/A		◆	◆		
Heliotropium arborescens	3 ft (0.9 m)	20 in (50 cm)	P	W/T	NA	◆	◆	◆	Sp	Sp/Su			◆		
Helleborus argutifolius	40 in (100 cm)	24–40 in (60–100 cm)	P	C/W	NA	◆	◆		A/W	W/Sp		◆		◆	◆
Helleborus foetidus	24–32 in (60–80 cm)	24–40 in (60–100 cm)	P	C/W	NA	◆	◆		A/W	W/Sp		◆		◆	◆
Helleborus × hybridus	16 in (40 cm)	16–24 in (40–60 cm)	P	C	NA	◆			A/W	W/Sp		◆		◆	◆
Helleborus lividus	16 in (40 cm)	24 in (60 cm)	P	C/W	NA	◆			A/W	W/Sp		◆		◆	◆
Helleborus niger	12 in (30 cm)	12–20 in (30–50 cm)	P	C	NA	◆			A/W	W/Sp		◆		◆	◆
Helleborus × nigercors	24 in (60 cm)	24 in (60 cm)	P	C	NA	◆			A/W	W/Sp		◆		◆	◆
Helleborus orientalis	16 in (40 cm)	16–24 in (40–60 cm)	P	C	NA	◆			A/W	W		◆		◆	◆
Hemerocallis dumortieri	16 in (40 cm)	16–24 in (40–60 cm)	P	C/W	NA	◆		◆	W	Sp/Su		◆	◆	◆	
Hemerocallis fulva	3 ft (0.9 m)	4–5 ft (1.2–1.5 m)	P	C/W	NA	◆			W	Sp/Su		◆	◆	◆	
Hemerocallis lilio-asphodelus	24–40 in (60–100 cm)	40–48 in (100–120 cm)	P	C/W	NA	◆			W	Sp/Su		◆	◆	◆	
Hemerocallis middendorffii	18 in (45 cm)	20–24 in (50–60 cm)	P	C/W	NA	◆			W	Sp/Su		◆	◆	◆	
Hemerocallis minor	20 in (50 cm)	20–24 in (50–60 cm)	P	C/W	NA	◆			W	Sp/Su		◆	◆	◆	
Hemigraphis alternata	4 in (10 cm)	12–18 in (30–45 cm)	P	W/T	NA		◆		Sp	Any	◆			◆	
Hemigraphis repanda	4 in (10 cm)	12–18 in (30–45 cm)	P	W/T	NA		◆		Sp	Any	◆			◆	
Hepatica nobilis	3–4 in (8–10 cm)	4–6 in (10–15 cm)	P	C	NA	◆			W	Sp		◆			◆
Hesperis matronalis	32–36 in (80–90 cm)	16–20 in (40–50 cm)	B/P	C/W	NA	◆		◆	Sp	Sp/Su		◆	◆	◆	
Heuchera americana	18 in (45 cm)	16 in (40 cm)	P	C/W	NA	◆	◆		A–Sp	Sp–A		◆	◆	◆	
Heuchera × brizoides	12–30 in (30–75 cm)	12–18 in (30–45 cm)	P	C/W	NA	◆	◆	◆	A–Sp	Sp–A		◆	◆	◆	
Heuchera maxima	24 in (60 cm)	16–20 in (40–50 cm)	P	C/W	NA	◆	◆		A–Sp	Sp–A		◆	◆	◆	
Heuchera sanguinea	24 in (60 cm)	12–16 in (30–40 cm)	P	C/W	NA	◆			A–Sp	Sp–A		◆	◆	◆	
Heuchera Hybrid Cultivars	12–36 in (30–90 cm)	12–18 in (30–45 cm)	P	C/W	NA	◆	◆		A–Sp	Sp–A		◆	◆	◆	
× Heucherella tiarelloides	18 in (45 cm)	18 in (45 cm)	P	C/W	NA	◆	◆		W/Sp	Sp/Su		◆		◆	
× Heucherella Hybrid Cultivars	16–20 in (40–50 cm)	12–16 in (30–40 cm)	P	C/W	NA	◆	◆		W/Sp	Sp/Su		◆		◆	
Hibiscus cannabinus	12 ft (3.5 m)	6 ft (1.8 m)	A/P	W/T	NA	◆			Sp	Sp–A			◆		

Plant name	Height	Spread	Type	Climate	Group	Showy flowers	Showy foliage	Scented flowers	Planting season	Flowering season	Grow in pot/tub	Frost tolerant	Full Sun	Half Sun	Heavy shade
Hibiscus Herbaceous Hybrids	18 in–5 ft (45 cm–1.5 m)	2–4 ft (0.6–1.2 m)	P	C/W	NA	◆			W/Sp	Sp–A		◆	◆		
Hosta fortunei	36 in (90 cm)	32–48 in (80–120 cm)	P	C/W	NA		◆		W/Sp	Su		◆		◆	◆
Hosta lancifolia	18 in (45 cm)	16–20 in (40–50 cm)	P	C/W	NA		◆		W/Sp	Su		◆		◆	◆
Hosta minor	24 in (60 cm)	16 in (40 cm)	P	C/W	NA	◆	◆		W/Sp	Su		◆		◆	◆
Hosta plantaginea	26 in (65 cm)	32 in (80 cm)	P	C/W	NA	◆	◆	◆	W/Sp	Su		◆		◆	◆
Hosta sieboldii	20 in (50 cm)	32 in (80 cm)	P	C/W	NA	◆	◆		W/Sp	Su		◆		◆	◆
Hosta × *tardiana*	16 in (40 cm)	16–20 in (40–50 cm)	P	C/W	NA		◆		W/Sp	Su		◆		◆	◆
Hosta tardiflora	12 in (30 cm)	20 in (50 cm)	P	C/W	NA		◆		W/Sp	Su		◆		◆	◆
Hosta tokudama	18 in (45 cm)	32–48 in (80–120 cm)	P	C/W	NA		◆		W/Sp	Su		◆		◆	◆
Hosta undulata	12 in (30 cm)	16–20 in (40–50 cm)	P	C/W	NA		◆		W/Sp	Su		◆		◆	◆
Hosta ventricosa	40 in (100 cm)	24–32 in (60–80 cm)	P	C/W	NA	◆	◆		W/Sp	Su		◆		◆	◆
Hosta Hybrid Cultivars	6–36 in (15–90 cm)	12–60 in (30–150 cm)	P	C/W	NA	◆	◆		W/Sp	Su		◆		◆	◆
Houttuynia cordata	6–12 in (15–30 cm)	over 40 in (100 cm)	P	C/W	NA		◆		W/Sp	Su		◆	◆	◆	◆
Hunnemannia fumariifolia	18–36 in (45–90 cm)	10 in (25 cm)	A/P	W	NA	◆	◆		Sp	Su		◆	◆		
Hydrastis canadensis	12 in (30 cm)	8 in (20 cm)	P	C	NA		◆		W/Sp	Sp		◆			◆
Iberis amara	12 in (30 cm)	12–20 in (30–50 cm)	A	C/W	NA	◆			Sp	Su	◆		◆	◆	
Iberis gibraltarica	12 in (30 cm)	20–24 in (50–60 cm)	P	C/W	NA	◆			Sp	Su	◆	◆	◆	◆	
Iberis sempervirens	12 in (30 cm)	20–24 in (50–60 cm)	P	C/W	NA	◆			Sp	Sp/Su	◆	◆	◆	◆	
Iberis umbellata	12 in (30 cm)	16 in (40 cm)	A	C/W	NA	◆			Sp	Sp/Su	◆	◆	◆	◆	
Impatiens balsamina	27 in (70 cm)	12 in (30 cm)	A	W/T	NA	◆			Sp	Sp–A	◆			◆	◆
Impatiens hawkeri	3–7 ft (0.9–2 m)	16–40 in (40–100 cm)	P	W/T	NA	◆			Sp	All	◆			◆	◆
Impatiens New Guinea Hybrids	10–48 in (25–120 cm)	16–40 in (40–100 cm)	P	W/T	NA	◆			Sp	All	◆			◆	◆
Impatiens niamniamensis	36 in (90 cm)	16 in (40 cm)	P	W/T	NA	◆			Sp	All	◆			◆	◆
Impatiens sodenii	3–7 ft (0.9–2 m)	3–7 ft (0.9–2 m)	P	W/T	NA	◆			Sp	Su				◆	◆
Impatiens walleriana	8–24 in (20–60 cm)	8–20 in (20–50 cm)	A/P	W/T	NA	◆			Sp	Sp–A	◆			◆	◆
Incarvillea delavayi	20–24 in (50–60 cm)	12–16 in (30–40 cm)	P	C	NA	◆			W/Sp	Su		◆	◆		
Incarvillea emodi	16–20 cm (40–50 cm)	12–16 in (30–40 cm)	P	C	NA	◆			W/Sp	Sp		◆		◆	
Inula grandiflora	20–24 in (50–60 cm)	36–40 in (90–100 cm)	P	C/W	NA	◆			W/Sp	Su/A		◆	◆		
Inula helenium	8–10 ft (2.4–3 m)	3–4 ft (0.9–1.2 m)	P	C/W	NA	◆			W/Sp	Su/A		◆	◆	◆	
Inula magnifica	5–6 ft (1.5–1.8 m)	3–5 ft (0.9–1.5 m)	P	C/W	NA	◆			W/Sp	Su/A		◆	◆		
Ipomopsis rubra	3–6 ft (0.9–1.8 m)	18 in (45 cm)	B/P	C/W	NA	◆			W/Sp	Su/A		◆	◆		

Plant name	Height	Spread	Type	Climate	Group	Showy flowers	Showy foliage	Scented flowers	Planting season	Flowering season	Grow in pot/tub	Frost tolerant	Full Sun	Half Sun	Heavy shade
Iresine herbstii	18–24 in (45–60 cm)	12–18 in (30–45 cm)	A/P	W/T	NA		♦		Sp	Su	♦		♦		
Iris chrysographes	12–20 in (30–50 cm)	12 in (30 cm)	P	C/W	NA	♦			A/W	Sp/Su			♦	♦	
Iris cristata	4–5 in (10–12 cm)	12–20 in (30–50 cm)	P	C/W	NA	♦		♦	A/W	Sp			♦		♦
Iris douglasiana	20–32 in (50–80 cm)	18 in (45 cm)	P	C	NA	♦			A/W	Su			♦	♦	
Iris ensata	36 in (90 cm)	40 in (100 cm)	P	C	NA	♦			A/W	Su			♦	♦	
Iris foetidissima	18–30 in (45–75 cm)	18–30 in (45–75 cm)	P	C/W	NA	♦			A/W	Sp		♦		♦	♦
Iris × fulvala	18–30 in (45–75 cm)	10 in (25 cm)	P	C	NA	♦			A/W	Su			♦	♦	
Iris germanica	24–48 in (60–120 cm)	18–24 in (45–60 cm)	P	C	NA	♦			A/W	Su			♦	♦	
Iris innominata	8–10 in (20–25 cm)	10 in (25 cm)	P	C/W	NA	♦			A/W	Su			♦	♦	♦
Iris japonica	24–32 in (60–80 cm)	18–24 in (45–60 cm)	P	C/W	NA	♦			A/W	Sp			♦	♦	
Iris laevigata	2–5 ft (0.6–1.5 m)	5 ft (1.5 m)	P	C	NA	♦			A/W	Su			♦	♦	♦
Iris missouriensis	12–20 in (30–50 cm)	12 in (30 cm)	P	C	NA	♦			A/W	Sp/Su			♦	♦	
Iris pallida	36–48 in (90–120 cm)	12 in (30 cm)	P	C	NA	♦		♦	A/W	Su			♦	♦	
Iris pseudacorus	4–5 ft (1.2–1.5 m)	5–7 ft (1.5–2 m)	P	C	NA	♦			A/W	Sp/Su			♦	♦	
Iris pumila	4–6 in (10–15 cm)	4–6 in (10–15 cm)	P	C	NA	♦		♦	A/W	Sp			♦	♦	
Iris sibirica	18–48 in (45–120 cm)	8–24 in (20–60 cm)	P	C	NA	♦			A/W	Sp/Su			♦	♦	
Iris spuria	4–7 ft (1.2–2 m)	3–7 ft (0.9–2 m)	P	C	NA	♦			A/W	Sp			♦	♦	
Iris tectorum	12–16 in (30–40 cm)	12 in (30 cm)	P	C	NA	♦			A/W	Su			♦		♦
Iris unguicularis	12–15 in (30–38 cm)	16–20 in (40–50 cm)	P	C/W	NA	♦			A/W	W/Sp		♦	♦	♦	
Iris versicolor	8–32 in (20–80 cm)	10 in (25 cm)	P	C	NA	♦			A/W	Su			♦	♦	
Iris, Arilbred Hybrids	10–27 in (25–70 cm)	12 in (30 cm)	P	C/W	NA	♦			Su/A	Sp			♦	♦	
Iris, Bearded Hybrids	8–40 in (20–100 cm)	12–36 in (30–90 cm)	P	C/W	NA	♦			A/W	Sp/Su			♦	♦	
Iris, Californian Hybrids	12 in (30 cm)	10–20 in (25–50 cm)	P	C/W	NA	♦			A/W	Sp			♦	♦	♦
Iris, Louisiana Hybrids	18–60 in (45–150 cm)	3–7 ft (0.9–2 m)	P	C/W	NA	♦			A/W	Sp/Su			♦	♦	♦
Iris, Oncocyclus Hybrids	4–24 in (10–60 cm)	40 in (100 cm)	P	C/W	NA	♦			A/W	Sp			♦	♦	
Iris, Siberian Hybrids	18–48 in (45–120 cm)	8–24 in (20–60 cm)	P	C/W	NA	♦			W	Sp/Su			♦	♦	
Iris, Spuria Hybrids	30–48 in (75–120 cm)	18–24 in (45–60 cm)	P	C/W	NA	♦			A/W	Sp/Su			♦	♦	
Ismelia carinata	32–40 in (80–100 cm)	12–16 in (30–40 cm)	A	W/T	NA	♦			Sp	S/A			♦	♦	
Jasione laevis	8–20 in (20–50 cm)	8–10 in (20–25 cm)	P	C	NA	♦			W/Sp	Su			♦	♦	
Kirengeshoma palmata	48 in (120 cm)	30 in (75 cm)	P	C	NA	♦	♦		W/Sp	Su/A			♦		♦
Knautia arvensis	5 ft (1.5 m)	12 in (30 cm)	P	C/W	NA	♦			W/Sp	Su/A			♦	♦	

Plant name	Height	Spread	Type	Climate	Group	Showy flowers	Showy foliage	Scented flowers	Planting season	Flowering season	Grow in pot/tub	Frost tolerant	Full Sun	Half Sun	Heavy shade
Kniphofia caulescens	4 ft (1.2 m)	20 in (50 cm)	P	C/W	NA	◆			W/Sp	Su/A		◆	◆	◆	
Kniphofia northiae	5 ft (1.5 m)	40 in (100 cm)	P	W	NA	◆			W/Sp	Sp–A		◆	◆	◆	
Kniphofia × praecox	4–5 ft (1.2–1.5 m)	20–40 in (50–100 cm)	P	C/W	NA	◆			W/Sp	Su–W		◆	◆	◆	
Kniphofia rooperi	4 ft (1.2 m)	20–24 in (50–60 cm)	P	W	NA	◆			W/Sp	Su/A		◆	◆	◆	
Kniphofia thomsonii	4 ft (1.2 m)	16–24 in (40–60 cm)	P	W	NA	◆			W/Sp	Su/A			◆	◆	
Kniphofia uvaria	4 ft (1.2 m)	24 in (60 cm)	P	C/W	NA	◆			W/Sp	Su–W		◆	◆	◆	
Kniphofia Hybrid Cultivars	2–5 ft (0.6–1.5 m)	12–20 in (30–50 cm)	P	W	NA	◆			W/Sp	Su–W		◆	◆	◆	
Kohleria digitaliflora	12–24 in (30–60 cm)	12–24 in (30–60 cm)	P	W/T	G	◆			Sp	Su/A		◆		◆	
Kohleria eriantha	3–4 ft (0.9–1.2 m)	3–4 ft (0.9–1.2 m)	P	W/T	G	◆	◆		Sp	Sp/Su		◆		◆	
Lamium galeobdolon	8–16 in (20–40 cm)	48 in (120 cm)	P	C/W	NA		◆		W/Sp	Su		◆		◆	◆
Lamium garganicum	8–16 in (20–40 cm)	48 in (120 cm)	P	C/W	NA	◆			W/Sp	Su		◆		◆	◆
Lamium maculatum	6–20 in (15–50 cm)	24–60 in (60–150 cm)	P	C/W	NA		◆		W/Sp	Su		◆		◆	◆
Lathyrus laxiflorus	12 in (30 cm)	16–24 in (40–60 cm)	P	C	NA	◆			W/Sp	Su		◆	◆	◆	
Lathyrus odoratus	8 ft (2.4 m)	40 in (100 cm)	A	C/W	NA	◆		◆	Sp	Su		◆	◆		
Lathyrus splendens	7–10 (2–3 m)	3–7 ft (0.9–2 m)	P	W	NA	◆			Sp	Sp/Su		◆	◆		
Lathyrus vernus	12–24 in (30–60 cm)	24–40 in (60–100 cm)	P	C	NA	◆			W/Sp	Sp	◆	◆	◆		
Lavatera × clementii	6 ft (1.8 m)	6 ft (1.8 m)	P	C/W	NA	◆			W/Sp	Su/A		◆	◆		
Lavatera thuringiaca	6 ft (1.8 m)	3–4 ft (0.9–1.2 m)	P	C/W	NA	◆			W/Sp	Su/A		◆	◆		
Lavatera trimestris	24–48 in (60–120 cm)	18–36 in (45–90 cm)	A	C/W	NA	◆			Sp	Su		◆	◆		
Leonotis nepetifolia	3–4 ft (0.9–1.2 m)	8–12 in (20–30 cm)	A	W	NA	◆			Sp	W		◆	◆		
Leonotis ocymifolia	8 ft (2.4 m)	3 ft (0.9 m)	P	W	NA	◆			Sp	Su–W			◆		
Leontopodium alpinum	6 in (15 cm)	4–9 in (10–22 cm)	P	C	NA	◆	◆		W/Sp	Su	◆	◆	◆		
Lespedeza thunbergii	3–8 ft (0.9–2.4 ft)	5–10 ft (1.5–3 m)	P	C	NA	◆			W/Sp	Su/A		◆	◆		
Leucanthemum × superbum	48 in (120 cm)	40 in (100 cm)	P	C/W	NA	◆			W/Sp	Sp–A	◆	◆	◆	◆	
Leucanthemum vulgare	40 in (100 cm)	24 in (60 cm)	P	C	NA	◆			W/Sp	Su		◆	◆	◆	
Lewisia columbiana	12 in (30 cm)	8 in (20 cm)	P	C	NA	◆			W/Sp	Sp/Su	◆	◆	◆	◆	
Lewisia cotyledon	6–12 in (15–30 cm)	8 in (20 cm)	P	C	NA	◆			W/Sp	Sp/Su	◆	◆	◆	◆	
Lewisia 'Pinkie'	6–8 in (15–20 cm)	8 in (20 cm)	P	C	NA	◆			W/Sp	Sp/Su	◆	◆	◆	◆	
Lewisia rediviva	4 in (10 cm)	8 in (20 cm)	P	C	NA	◆			W/Sp	Sp/Su	◆	◆	◆	◆	
Lewisia tweedyi	8 in (20 cm)	8 in (20 cm)	P	C	NA	◆			W/Sp	Sp/Su	◆	◆	◆	◆	
Liatris aspera	40 in (100 cm)	12–20 in (30–50 cm)	P	C/W	NA	◆			W/Sp	Su/A	◆	◆	◆	◆	

Plant name	Height	Spread	Type	Climate	Group	Showy flowers	Showy foliage	Scented flowers	Planting season	Flowering season	Grow in pot/tub	Frost tolerant	Full Sun	Half Sun	Heavy shade
Liatris pycnostachya	60 in (150 cm)	10–18 in (25–45 cm)	P	C/W	NA	◆			W/Sp	Su/A		◆	◆	◆	
Liatris spicata	60 in (150 cm)	10–18 in (25–45 cm)	P	C/W	NA	◆			W/Sp	Su/A		◆	◆	◆	
Libertia formosa	18–36 in (45–90 cm)	24 in (60 cm)	P	W	NA	◆	◆		W/Sp	Sp			◆		
Libertia grandiflora	30 in (75 cm)	24 in (60 cm)	P	W	NA	◆	◆		W/Sp	Sp		◆	◆		
Libertia ixioides	8–12 in (20–30 cm)	24 in (60 cm)	P	W	NA			◆	W/Sp	Sp		◆	◆		
Libertia peregrinans	15–27 in (38–70 cm)	20 in (50 cm)	P	W	NA	◆			W/Sp	Sp		◆	◆	◆	
Ligularia dentata	30–60 in (75–150 cm)	40–60 in (100–150 cm)	P	C/W	NA	◆	◆		W/Sp	Su/A		◆		◆	◆
Ligularia przewalskii	7 ft (2 m)	40–48 in (100–120 cm)	P	C	NA	◆			W/Sp	Su/A		◆		◆	◆
Ligularia stenocephala	60 in (150 cm)	32–40 in (80–100 cm)	P	C/W	NA	◆	◆		W/Sp	Su/A		◆		◆	◆
Ligularia Hybrid Cultivars	3–7 ft (0.9–2 m)	32–60 in (80–150 cm)	P	C	NA	◆			W/Sp	Su/A		◆		◆	◆
Limonium brassicifolium	16 in (40 cm)	12 in (30 cm)	P	W	NA	◆			Sp	Su			◆	◆	
Limonium perezii	27 in (70 cm)	20 in (50 cm)	P	W	NA	◆			Sp	Sp/Su			◆		
Limonium sinuatum	16 in (40 cm)	16 in (40 cm)	A/P	W	NA	◆			Sp	Su			◆	◆	
Linaria maroccana	8–10 in (20–25 cm)	6–12 in (15–30 cm)	A	W	NA	◆			Sp	Su			◆		
Linaria purpurea	20–36 in (50–90 cm)	6–12 in (15–30 cm)	P	C/W	NA	◆			Sp	Su/A		◆	◆		
Linum 'Gemmell's Hybrid'	6 in (15 cm)	8 in (20 cm)	P	C/W	NA	◆			A/Sp	Su		◆	◆		
Linum grandiflorum	15–18 in (38–45 cm)	12 in (30 cm)	A	W	NA	◆			Sp	Su			◆		
Linum narbonense	12–24 in (30–60 cm)	12–18 in (30–45 cm)	P	C/W	NA	◆			Sp	Sp–A		◆	◆		
Linum perenne	12–18 in (30–45 cm)	12 in (30 cm)	P	C/W	NA	◆			Sp	Su		◆	◆		
Liriope muscari	12 in (30 cm)	18 in (45 cm)	P	C/W	NA	◆	◆		W/Sp	A	◆	◆	◆	◆	
Liriope spicata	10 in (25 cm)	18 in (45 cm)	P	C/W	NA	◆			W/Sp	Su	◆	◆	◆	◆	
Lobelia cardinalis	36 in (90 cm)	12–16 in (30–40 cm)	P	C/W	NA	◆	◆		W/Sp	Su/A		◆	◆	◆	
Lobelia erinus	8 in (20 cm)	12–16 in (30–40 cm)	A/P	C/W	NA	◆			Sp	Su/A	◆	◆	◆	◆	
Lobelia × gerardii	60 in (150 cm)	20–24 in (50–60 cm)	P	C/W	NA	◆			W/Sp	Su		◆	◆	◆	
Lobelia laxiflora	3 ft (0.9 m)	4 ft (1.2 m)	P	W	NA	◆			Sp	Su			◆	◆	
Lobelia siphilitica	24 in (60 cm)	16 in (40 cm)	P	C/W	NA	◆			W/Sp	Su/A		◆	◆	◆	
Lobelia tupa	6 ft (1.8 m)	3 ft (0.9 m)	P	W	NA	◆	◆		Sp	Su/A		◆	◆		
Lobularia maritima	10 in (25 cm)	8–16 in (20–40 cm)	A/P	C/W	NA	◆			Sp	Sp–A		◆	◆		
Lotus berthelotii	8 in (20 cm)	3–6 ft (0.9–1.8 m)	P	W	NA	◆	◆		A/Sp	Sp/Su	◆		◆		
Lotus maculatus	8 in (20 cm)	3–6 ft (0.9–1.8 m)	P	W	NA	◆			A/Sp	Sp/Su	◆		◆		
Ludwigia peruviana	20 in–8 ft (50 cm–2.4 m)	20 in–8 ft (50 cm–2.4 m)	P	C/W	NA	◆			Sp	Sp–A		◆	◆		

Plant name	Height	Spread	Type	Climate	Group	Showy flowers	Showy foliage	Scented flowers	Planting season	Flowering season	Grow in pot/tub	Frost tolerant	Full Sun	Half Sun	Heavy shade
Lunaria annua	30 in (75 cm)	12 in (30 cm)	B	C/W	NA	◆			A/Sp	Sp/Su		◆	◆	◆	
Lunaria rediviva	36–42 in (90–105 cm)	24 in (60 cm)	P	C/W	NA	◆		◆	A/Sp	Sp/Su		◆	◆	◆	
Lupinus chamissonis	2–7 ft (0.6–2 m)	4–10 ft (1.2–3 m)	P	W	NA	◆			Sp	Sp/Su			◆		
Lupinus polyphyllus	24–60 in (60–150 cm)	20–40 in (50–100 cm)	P	C	NA	◆			W/Sp	Su		◆		◆	
Lupinus texensis	12–24 in (30–60 cm)	12 in (30 cm)	A	C/W	NA	◆			A/W	Sp	◆	◆	◆		
Lupinus Hybrid Cultivars	2–4 ft (0.6–1.2 m)	2–5 ft (0.6–1.5 m)	P	C	NA	◆			W/Sp	Sp/Su	◆	◆	◆		
Lychnis × *arkwrightii*	12–30 in (30–75 cm)	16–24 in (40–60 cm)	P	C/W	NA	◆			W/Sp	Su		◆	◆	◆	
Lychnis chalcedonica	20 in (50 cm)	12–16 in (30–40 cm)	P	C/W	NA	◆			W/Sp	Su		◆	◆	◆	
Lychnis coronaria	16–32 in (40–80 cm)	20–40 in (50–100 cm)	B/P	C/W	NA	◆	◆		W/Sp	Su		◆	◆	◆	
Lychnis flos-cuculi	30 in (75 cm)	16 in (40 cm)	P	C	NA	◆			W/Sp	Su		◆	◆	◆	
Lychnis flos-jovis	32 in (80 cm)	16 in (40 cm)	P	C	NA	◆			W/Sp	Su		◆	◆	◆	
Lychnis viscaria	24 in (60 cm)	16 in (40 cm)	P	C/W	NA	◆			W/Sp	Su		◆	◆	◆	
Lysichiton americanus	3–4 ft (0.9–1.2 m)	4–5 ft (1.2–1.5 m)	P	C/W	NA	◆	◆		A/W	Sp		◆	◆	◆	
Lysimachia ciliata	40 in (100 cm)	20 in (50 cm)	P	C/W	NA	◆			W/Sp	Su		◆		◆	
Lysimachia clethroides	40 in (100 cm)	24 in (60 cm)	P	C/W	NA				W/Sp	Su		◆		◆	
Lysimachia congestiflora	6 in (15 cm)	8–16 in (20–40 cm)	P	C/W	NA				W/Sp	Su		◆		◆	
Lysimachia ephemerum	40 in (100 cm)	16–24 in (40–60 cm)	P	C/W	NA	◆			W/Sp	Su		◆		◆	
Lysimachia nummularia	2–4 in (5–10 cm)	24–40 in (60–100 cm)	P	C/W	NA	◆	◆		W/Sp	Su		◆		◆	◆
Lysimachia punctata	40 in (100 cm)	16–24 in (40–60 cm)	P	C/W	NA	◆			A/Sp	Su		◆		◆	
Lythrum salicaria	24–60 in (60–150 cm)	24 in (60 cm)	P	C/W	NA	◆			A/Sp	Su/A		◆	◆	◆	
Macleaya cordata	8 ft (2.4 m)	3 ft (0.9 m)	P	C/W	NA	◆	◆		A/Sp	Su		◆	◆		
Macleaya microcarpa	8 ft (2.4 m)	3 ft (0.9 m)	P	C/W	NA	◆	◆		A/Sp	A		◆	◆		
Maianthemum bifolium	5–6 in (12–15 cm)	40–48 in (100–120 cm)	P	C/W	NA	◆	◆		W/Sp	Sp		◆		◆	
Maianthemum canadense	7–8 in (18–20 cm)	36–40 in (90–100 cm)	P	C	NA	◆	◆	◆	W/Sp	Sp		◆		◆	
Maianthemum racemosum	2–3 ft (0.6–0.9 m)	2–4 ft (0.6–1.2 m)	P	C/W	NA	◆	◆		W/Sp	Su		◆		◆	◆
Malcolmia maritima	14 in (35 cm)	12 in (30 cm)	A	C/W	NA	◆		◆	Sp	Sp/Su	◆	◆	◆		
Malva alcea	40 in (100 cm)	24 in (60 cm)	P	C/W	NA	◆			Sp	Su/A		◆	◆		
Malva moschata	40 in (100 cm)	18 in (45 cm)	P	C/W	NA	◆			Sp	Su		◆	◆		
Malva sylvestris	3 ft (0.9 m)	7–25 ft (2–8 m)	B/P	C/W	NA	◆			Sp	Su/A		◆	◆		
Maranta leuconeura	10–12 in (25–30 cm)	10–12 in (25–30 cm)	P	W/T	NA		◆		Sp	Sp/Su	◆				◆
Marrubium incanum	20 in (50 cm)	24 in (60 cm)	P	C/W	NA	◆			Sp	Su		◆	◆		

Plant name	Height	Spread	Type	Climate	Group	Showy flowers	Showy foliage	Scented flowers	Planting season	Flowering season	Grow in pot/tub	Frost tolerant	Full Sun	Half Sun	Heavy shade
Matthiola incana	32 in (80 cm)	12 in (30 cm)	B	C/W	NA	◆		◆	W/Sp	Su	◆	◆	◆	◆	
Matthiola longipetala	20 in (50 cm)	10 in (25 cm)	A	C/W	NA	◆		◆	Sp	Su	◆	◆	◆	◆	
Mazus radicans	2 in (5 cm)	12 in (30 cm)	P	C	NA	◆	◆		Su/A	Sp/Su	◆	◆	◆		
Mazus reptans	2 in (5 cm)	20 in (50 cm)	P	C	NA	◆			Su/A	Sp/Su	◆	◆	◆		
Meconopsis betonicifolia	3–6 ft (0.9–1.8 m)	8–20 in (20–50 cm)	P	C	NA	◆			W/Sp	Sp/Su		◆		◆	◆
Meconopsis cambrica	12–24 in (30–60 cm)	8–16 in (20–40 cm)	P	C/W	NA	◆			W/Sp	Sp/Su		◆	◆	◆	
Meconopsis grandis	4 ft (1.2 m)	16–24 in (40–60 cm)	P	C	NA	◆			W/Sp	Sp/Su		◆		◆	
Meconopsis horridula	32 in (80 cm)	16 in (40 cm)	P	C	NA	◆			W/Sp	Su		◆		◆	
Meconopsis napaulensis	6–8 ft (1.8–2.4 m)	20–32 in (50–80 cm)	P	C/W	NA	◆			W/Sp	Sp/Su		◆		◆	◆
Meconopsis × sheldonii	4 ft (1.2 m)	16–24 in (40–60 cm)	P	C	NA	◆			W/Sp	Sp/Su		◆		◆	
Melampodium paludosum	24 in (60 cm)	36 in (90 cm)	A	W/T	NA	◆		◆	W/Sp	Sp–A	◆		◆		
Mentha × gracilis	12 in (30 cm)	36 in (90 cm)	P	C	NA		◆		W/Sp	Su/A			◆		
Mentha pulegium	8–12 in (20–30 cm)	20 in (50 cm)	P	C/W	NA	◆			W/Sp	Su/A	◆	◆	◆		
Mentha requienii	¾ in (1.8 cm)	27 in (70 cm)	P	C/W	NA			◆	W/Sp	Su	◆		◆		
Mentha × villosa	3 ft (0.9 m)	5 ft (1.5 m)	P	C	NA	◆			W/Sp	Su		◆	◆		
Menyanthes trifoliata	10–16 in (25–40 cm)	8–12 in (20–30 cm)	P	C	NA	◆	◆	◆	W/Sp	Su		◆	◆		
Mertensia sibirica	12–18 in (30–45 cm)	12 in (30 cm)	P	C	NA	◆			W/Sp	Sp/Su		◆	◆		
Mertensia simplicissima	6 in (15 cm)	18 in (45 cm)	P	C	NA	◆			W/Sp	Sp–A		◆	◆		
Mertensia virginica	12–24 in (30–60 cm)	12–24 in (30–60 cm)	P	C	NA	◆			W/Sp	Sp		◆		◆	
Meum athamanticum	18–24 in (45–60 cm)	12–18 in (30–45 cm)	P	C	NA			◆	Sp	Su		◆	◆		
Mimulus aurantiacus	4 ft (1.2 m)	3 ft (0.9 m)	P	C/W	NA	◆			W/Sp	Sp/Su			◆	◆	
Mimulus cardinalis	32–36 in (80–90 cm)	24–27 in (60–70 cm)	P	C/W	NA	◆			W/Sp	Su		◆	◆	◆	
Mimulus luteus	12–16 in (30–40 cm)	24–32 in (60–80 cm)	P	C/W	NA	◆			W/Sp	Sp–A		◆	◆	◆	
Mimulus ringens	3–4 ft (0.9–1.2 m)	4–5 ft (1.2–1.5 m)	P	C	NA	◆			W/Sp	Su		◆	◆		
Mimulus Hybrid Cultivars	8–36 in (20–90 cm)	12–32 in (30–80 cm)	P	C/W	NA	◆			W/Sp	Sp–A		◆	◆	◆	
Minuartia stellata	2 in (5 cm)	18 in (45 cm)	P	C/W	NA	◆			Sp/Su	Su	◆	◆	◆		
Mitchella repens	3 in (8 cm)	24 in (60 cm)	P	C	NA			◆	W/Sp	Su	◆	◆			◆
Moltkia × intermedia	8–10 in (20–25 cm)	16–20 in (40–50 cm)	P	C	NA	◆			W/Sp	Su		◆	◆		
Monarda didyma	3–4 ft (0.9–1.2 m)	24–40 in (60–100 cm)	P	C	NA	◆	◆		W/Sp	Su		◆	◆	◆	
Monarda fistulosa	3–4 ft (0.9–1.2 m)	24–40 in (60–100 cm)	P	C	NA	◆	◆		W/Sp	Su		◆	◆	◆	

Plant name	Height	Spread	Type	Climate	Group	Showy flowers	Showy foliage	Scented flowers	Planting season	Flowering season	Grow in pot/tub	Frost tolerant	Full Sun	Half Sun	Heavy shade
Monarda Hybrid Cultivars	20–60 in (50–150 cm)	20–32 in (50–80 cm)	P	C	NA	◆	◆		W/Sp	Su/A		◆	◆	◆	
Musa ornata	6–10 ft (1.8–3 m)	6 ft (1.8 m)	P	W/T	NA	◆	◆		W/Sp	Su			◆		
Musa velutina	5 ft (1.5 m)	3 ft (0.9 m)	P	W/T	NA	◆	◆		W/Sp	Sp			◆		
Myosotidium hortensia	12–16 in (30–40 cm)	24–40 in (60–100 cm)	P	C	NA	◆	◆		W/Sp	Su	◆	◆		◆	◆
Myosotis alpestris	12 in (30 cm)	16 in (40 cm)	P	C	NA	◆			A–Sp	Sp	◆	◆		◆	
Myosotis sylvatica	6–16 in (15–40 cm)	8–16 in (20–40 cm)	B/P	C	NA	◆			A–Sp	Su	◆	◆		◆	
Nelumbo lutea	7 ft (2 m)	7 ft (2 m)	P	C/W	NA	◆	◆	◆	W/Sp	Su		◆	◆		
Nelumbo nucifera	7 ft (2 m)	7 ft (2 m)	P	W/T	NA	◆	◆	◆	W/Sp	Su			◆		
Nemesia caerulea	16–24 in (40–60 cm)	16–24 in (40–60 cm)	P	W	NA	◆			A/Sp	Su	◆	◆	◆	◆	
Nemesia strumosa	6–20 in (15–50 cm)	8–16 in (20–40 cm)	A	W	NA	◆			Sp–A	Su		◆	◆	◆	
Nemesia Hybrid Cultivars	6–16 in (15–40 cm)	8–16 in (20–40 cm)	A	W	NA	◆			Sp–A	Su	◆		◆	◆	
Nemophila maculata	8–12 in (20–30 cm)	12–20 in (30–50 cm)	A	C/W	NA	◆			Sp/Su	Su			◆	◆	
Nemophila menziesii	4–6 in (10–15 cm)	12–20 in (30–50 cm)	A	C/W	NA	◆			Sp/Su	Su			◆	◆	
Neomarica caerulea	24–36 (60–90 cm)	12 in (30 cm)	P	W/T	NA	◆			A/W	Su			◆		
Neoregelia carolinae	12 in (30 cm)	24 in (60 cm)	P	W/T	B	◆	◆		W/Sp	Sp/Su	◆				◆
Neoregelia concentrica	12 in (30 cm)	32 in (80 cm)	P	W/T	B	◆	◆		W/Sp	Su	◆				◆
Neoregelia marmorata	20 in (50 cm)	40 in (100 cm)	P	W/T	B	◆	◆		W/Sp	Su	◆				◆
Neoregelia Hybrid Cultivars	6–20 in (15–50 cm)	4–40 in (10–100 cm)	P	W/T	B				W/Sp	Sp/Su	◆				◆
Nepenthes alata	15 ft (4.5 m)	20 in (50 cm)	P	W/T	C	◆			W/Sp	Su	◆	◆		◆	
Nepenthes ampullaria	20 ft (6 m)	20 in (50 cm)	P	W/T	C	◆			W/Sp	Su	◆		◆	◆	
Nepenthes burbidgeae	40 ft (12 m)	16 in (40 cm)	P	W/T	C	◆			W/Sp	Su	◆			◆	
Nepenthes fusca	35 ft (10 m)	14 in (35 cm)	P	W/T	C	◆			W/Sp	Su	◆			◆	
Nepenthes lowii	25 ft (8 m)	26 in (65 cm)	P	W/T	C	◆			W/Sp	Su	◆			◆	
Nepenthes maxima	10 ft (3 m)	30 in (75 cm)	P	W/T	C	◆			W/Sp	Su	◆			◆	
Nepenthes rajah	7 ft (2 m)	40 in (100 cm)	P	W/T	C	◆			W/Sp	Su	◆			◆	
Nepenthes spathulata	7 ft (2 m)	20 in (50 cm)	P	W/T	C	◆			W/Sp	Su	◆			◆	
Nepenthes tentaculata	7 ft (2 m)	20 in (50 cm)	P	W/T	C	◆			W/Sp	Su	◆			◆	
Nepenthes × *ventrata*	7 ft (2 m)	16 in (40 cm)	P	W/T	C	◆			W/Sp	Su	◆	◆		◆	
Nepenthes ventricosa	7 ft (2 m)	16 in (40 cm)	P	W/T	C	◆			W/Sp	Su	◆	◆		◆	
Nepeta camphorata	18 in (45 cm)	24 in (60 cm)	P	C/W	NA	◆	◆		W/Sp	Su		◆	◆	◆	
Nepeta clarkei	24–36 in (60–90 cm)	24 in (60 cm)	P	C/W	NA	◆	◆		W/Sp	Su		◆	◆	◆	

Plant name	Height	Spread	Type	Climate	Group	Showy flowers	Showy foliage	Scented flowers	Planting season	Flowering season	Grow in pot/tub	Frost tolerant	Full Sun	Half Sun	Heavy shade
Nepeta × faassenii	24 in (60 cm)	40 in (100 cm)	P	C/W	NA	◆	◆		W/Sp	Su		◆	◆	◆	
Nepeta grandiflora	24 in (60 cm)	24 in (60 cm)	P	C/W	NA	◆	◆		W/Sp	Su		◆	◆	◆	
Nepeta sibirica	40 in (100 cm)	40 in (100 cm)	P	C/W	NA	◆	◆		W/Sp	Sp/Su			◆	◆	
Nicotiana alata	24–36 in (60–90 cm)	12 in (30 cm)	A/P	C/W	NA	◆		◆	Sp	Su	◆		◆	◆	◆
Nicotiana langsdorffii	5 ft (1.5 m)	15 in (38 cm)	A	C/W	NA	◆			Sp	Su			◆	◆	
Nicotiana × sanderae	15–24 in (38–60 cm)	10 in (25 cm)	A	C/W	NA	◆		◆	Sp	Sp/Su	◆		◆	◆	
Nicotiana sylvestris	3–5 ft (0.9–1.5 m)	18–24 in (45–60 cm)	A	C/W	NA	◆			Sp	Su			◆	◆	
Nidularium fulgens	12 in (30 cm)	32 in (80 cm)	P	W/T	B	◆	◆		W/Sp	Sp/Su	◆				◆
Nidularium innocentii	14 in (35 cm)	36 in (90 cm)	P	W/T	B	◆	◆		W/Sp	Sp/Su	◆				◆
Nidularium Hybrid Cultivars	12–20 in (30–50 cm)	20–40 in (50–100 cm)	P	W/T	B	◆	◆		W/Sp	Sp/Su	◆				◆
Nierembergia caerulea	8–15 in (20–38 cm)	8 in (20 cm)	A/P	W	NA	◆			Sp	Su	◆		◆		
Nierembergia repens	2 in (5 cm)	18 in (45 cm)	P	W	NA	◆			Sp	Su	◆		◆		
Nigella damascena	20 in (50 cm)	10 in (25 cm)	A	C/W	NA	◆			Sp/Su	Su		◆	◆		
Nolana humifusa	4–6 in (10–15 cm)	12 in (30 cm)	A/P	W/T	NA	◆			Sp	Su			◆		
Nolana paradoxa	4–6 in (10–15 cm)	12 in (30 cm)	A/P	W/T	NA	◆			Sp	Su			◆		
Nuphar lutea	3–15 in (8–38 cm)	3–8 ft (0.9–2.4 m)	P	C/W	NA	◆	◆	◆	W/Sp	Su		◆	◆	◆	
Nymphaea alba	3–15 in (8–38 cm)	3–10 ft (0.9–3 m)	P	C/W	NA	◆	◆		W/Sp	Su			◆	◆	
Nymphaea caerulea	3–15 in (8–38 cm)	3–12 ft (0.9–3.5 m)	P	W/T	NA	◆	◆		W/Sp	Sp/Su			◆		
Nymphaea × daubenyana	3–15 in (8–38 cm)	3–6 ft (0.9–1.8 m)	P	W/T	NA	◆	◆		W/Sp	Sp/Su			◆		
Nymphaea lotus	3–15 in (8–38 cm)	3–12 ft (0.9–3.5 m)	P	W/T	NA	◆	◆		W/Sp	Sp/Su			◆		
Nymphaea mexicana	3–15 in (8–38 cm)	3–12 ft (0.9–3.5 m)	P	W/T	NA	◆	◆		W/Sp	Sp/Su			◆		
Nymphaea odorata	3–15 in (8–38 cm)	3–8 ft (0.9–2.4 m)	P	C/W	NA	◆	◆	◆	W/Sp	Su		◆	◆		
Nymphaea tetragona	3–15 in (8–38 cm)	12–48 in (30–120 cm)	P	C/W	NA	◆	◆	◆	W/Sp	Su			◆		
Nymphaea, Hardy Hybrids	3–15 in (8–38 cm)	3–8 ft (0.9–2.4 m)	P	C/W	NA	◆	◆		W/Sp	Sp/Su			◆		
Nymphaea, Tropical Day-Blooming Hybrids	3–15 in (8–38 cm)	3–12 ft (0.9–3.5 m)	P	W/T	NA	◆	◆	◆	W/Sp	Sp/Su			◆		
Nymphaea, Tropical Night-Blooming Hybrids	3–15 in (8–38 cm)	3–12 ft (0.9–3.5 m)	P	W/T	NA	◆	◆		W/Sp	Sp/Su			◆		
Nymphoides crenata	2–5 ft (0.6–1.5 m)	6 ft (1.8 m)	P	W	NA	◆	◆		W/Sp	Sp–A			◆		
Nymphoides peltata	12 in (30 cm)	3–8 ft (0.9–2.4 m)	P	C/W	NA	◆	◆		W/Sp	Su		◆	◆		
Ochagavia carnea	20 in (50 cm)	32 in (80 cm)	P	W	B	◆	◆		Sp	W			◆		

Plant name	Height	Spread	Type	Climate	Group	Showy flowers	Showy foliage	Scented flowers	Planting season	Flowering season	Grow in pot/tub	Frost tolerant	Full Sun	Half Sun	Heavy shade
Oenothera acaulis	6 in (15 cm)	16–24 in (40–60 cm)	B/P	C/W	NA	◆			W/Sp	Su		◆	◆		
Oenothera caespitosa	4–10 in (10–25 cm)	24 in (60 cm)	P	C	NA	◆		◆	W/Sp	Su		◆	◆		
Oenothera 'Crown Imperial'	16–20 in (40–50 cm)	12 in (30 cm)	P	C/W	NA	◆			W/Sp	Su		◆	◆		
Oenothera fruticosa	20–32 in (50–80 cm)	12–16 in (30–40 cm)	B/P	C/W	NA	◆			W/Sp	Su		◆	◆		
Oenothera 'Lemon Sunset'	40 in (100 cm)	16–32 in (40–80 cm)	P	C/W	NA	◆		◆	W/Sp	Su		◆	◆		
Oenothera macrocarpa	8–16 in (20–40 cm)	16–32 in (40–80 cm)	P	C/W	NA	◆			W/Sp	Su		◆	◆		
Oenothera speciosa	12–24 in (30–60 cm)	12–24 in (30–60 cm)	P	C/W	NA	◆			W/Sp	Su/A	◆	◆	◆		
Oenothera versicolor	24 in (60 cm)	16 in (40 cm)	P	C/W	NA	◆			W/Sp	Su		◆	◆		
Omphalodes cappadocica	8 in (20 cm)	12–18 in (30–45 cm)	P	C	NA	◆			A/Sp	Sp/Su		◆			◆
Omphalodes linifolia	12–18 in (30–45 cm)	6–10 in (15–25 cm)	A	C	NA	◆		◆	A/Sp	Su		◆	◆		
Omphalodes verna	6 in (15 cm)	24 in (60 cm)	P	C	NA	◆			A/Sp	Sp		◆			◆
Onopordum acanthium	8–10 ft (2.4–3 m)	6–7 ft (1.8–2 m)	B	C/W	NA	◆	◆		W/Sp	Su		◆	◆		
Onopordum acaulon	6 in (15 cm)	12–18 in (30–45 cm)	A/B	C/W	NA		◆		W/Sp	Su		◆	◆		
Ophiopogon japonicus	12 in (30 cm)	18 in (45 cm)	P	C/W	NA		◆		A/Sp	Su		◆	◆	◆	
Ophiopogon planiscapus	12–18 in (30–45 cm)	18 in (45 cm)	P	C/W	NA		◆		A/Sp	Su		◆	◆	◆	
Origanum × hybridum	8 in (20 cm)	12 in (30 cm)	P	W	NA	◆	◆		W/Sp	Su/A	◆		◆		
Origanum Hybrid Cultivars	4–12 in (10–30 cm)	12–24 in (30–60 cm)	P	C/W	NA	◆			W/Sp	Su/A	◆	◆	◆		
Orontium aquaticum	12–18 in (30–45 cm)	18–24 in (45–60 cm)	P	C/W	NA	◆	◆		W/Sp	Su		◆	◆		
Orthophytum navioides	4 in (10 cm)	40 in (100 cm)	P	W	B		◆		W/Sp	Su	◆		◆		
Orthophytum Hybrid Cultivars	10 in (25 cm)	4 in (10 cm)	P	W	B		◆		W/Sp	Su			◆		
Orthosiphon aristatus	36 in (90 cm)	36 in (90 cm)	P	W/T	NA			◆	W/Sp	Sp/Su			◆		
Osteospermum jucundum	12–20 in (30–50 cm)	20–32 in (50–80 cm)	P	W	NA	◆			W/Sp	Sp–A		◆	◆		
Osteospermum Hybrid Cultivars	8–12 in (20–30 cm)	16–24 in (40–60 cm)	P	W	NA	◆			W/Sp	Sp–A			◆		
Otacanthus caeruleus	36 in (90 cm)	20 in (50 cm)	P	W/T	NA	◆			Sp	Any	◆		◆	◆	
Oxalis acetosella	2–4 in (5–10 cm)	18–36 in (45–90 cm)	P	C/W	NA	◆			W/Sp	Su	◆	◆		◆	◆
Oxalis oregana	7–8 in (18–20 cm)	40 in (100 cm)	P	C/W	NA	◆	◆		W/Sp	Sp–A		◆			◆
Pachysandra terminalis	8–12 in (20–30 cm)	18 in (45 cm)	P	C/W	NA		◆	◆	W/Sp	Sp		◆		◆	◆
Paeonia cambessedesii	24 in (60 cm)	24 in (60 cm)	P	W	NA	◆			W	Sp		◆	◆		
Paeonia × chamaeleon	20 in (50 cm)	20 in (50 cm)	P	C	NA	◆			W	Sp		◆	◆		
Paeonia lactiflora	24 in (60 cm)	24 in (60 cm)	P	C	NA	◆		◆	W	Su		◆	◆		
Paeonia mascula	24–36 in (60–90 cm)	24 in (60 cm)	P	C	NA	◆			W	Sp		◆	◆		

Plant name	Height	Spread	Type	Climate	Group	Showy flowers	Showy foliage	Scented flowers	Planting season	Flowering season	Grow in pot/tub	Frost tolerant	Full Sun	Half Sun	Heavy shade
Paeonia mlokosewitschii	40 in (100 cm)	40 in (100 cm)	P	C	NA	◆			W	Sp		◆	◆		
Paeonia officinalis	15–24 in (38–60 cm)	24 in (60 cm)	P	C	NA	◆			W	Sp		◆	◆		
Paeonia peregrina	20 in (50 cm)	20 in (50 cm)	P	C	NA	◆			W	Sp		◆	◆	◆	
Paeonia tenuifolia	20–27 in (50–70 cm)	20–27 in (50–70 cm)	P	C/W	NA	◆			W	Sp		◆	◆		
Paeonia veitchii	24 in (60 cm)	20 in (50 cm)	P	C/W	NA	◆			W	Su		◆	◆		
Paeonia Hybrid Cultivars	30–36 in (75–90 cm)	30–36 in (75–90 cm)	P	C	NA	◆		◆	W	Sp		◆	◆		
Papaver alpinum	10 in (25 cm)	8–16 in (20–40 cm)	P	C	NA	◆			W/Sp	Su	◆	◆	◆	◆	
Papaver atlanticum	18 in (45 cm)	8–12 in (20–30 cm)	P	C/W	NA	◆			W/Sp			◆	◆	◆	
Papaver commutatum	16 in (40 cm)	16 in (40 cm)	A	W	NA	◆			W/Sp			◆	◆	◆	
Papaver × hybridum	8–20 in (20–50 cm)	6–10 in (15–25 cm)	P	C/W	NA	◆			W/Sp	Sp/Su		◆	◆	◆	
Papaver nudicaule	12–16 in (30–40 cm)	8–12 in (20–30 cm)	P	C/W	NA	◆			A–Sp	Sp/Su		◆	◆	◆	
Papaver orientale	24–40 in (60–100 cm)	12–20 in (30–50 cm)	P	C/W	NA	◆	◆		W/Sp	Su		◆	◆		
Papaver rhoeas	36–48 in (90–120 cm)	12–16 in (30–40 cm)	A	C/W	NA	◆			W/Sp	Su			◆	◆	
Papaver somniferum	36–48 in (90–120 cm)	12–24 in (30–60 cm)	A	C/W	NA	◆		◆	W/Sp	Su			◆	◆	
Paradisea liliastrum	16–24 in (40–60 cm)	10–12 in (25–30 cm)	P	C/W	NA			◆	W/Sp	Su			◆	◆	
Parahebe × bidwillii	4 in (10 cm)	6 in (15 cm)	P	C/W	NA	◆			W/Sp	Su	◆	◆	◆		
Parahebe cataractae	12 in (30 cm)	24 in (60 cm)	P	C/W	NA	◆			W/Sp	Su			◆		
Parahebe lyallii	8 in (20 cm)	18 in (45 cm)	P	C/W	NA	◆			W/Sp	Su	◆	◆	◆		
Paris polyphylla	36–40 in (90–100 cm)	8–12 in (20–30 cm)	P	C/W	NA	◆	◆		W/Sp	Su		◆		◆	◆
Paris quadrifolia	8–16 in (20–40 cm)	10–12 in (25–30 cm)	P	C	NA	◆	◆		W/Sp	Su		◆		◆	◆
Pelargonium australe	12 in (30 cm)	20 in (50 cm)	P	W	NA	◆			W/Sp	Sp/Su			◆		
Pelargonium crispum	30 (75 cm)	36 in (90 cm)	P	W	NA	◆	◆		W/Sp	Su	◆		◆		
Pelargonium graveolens	48 in (120 cm)	26 in (65 cm)	P	W	NA		◆		W/Sp	Su			◆		
Pelargonium odoratissimum	12 in (30 cm)	24 in (60 cm)	P	W	NA	◆	◆		W/Sp	Sp/Su	◆		◆		
Pelargonium quercifolium	3–5 ft (0.9–1.5 m)	24–32 in (60–80 cm)	P	W	NA		◆		W/Sp	Sp/Su			◆		
Pelargonium rodneyanum	8–12 in (20–30 cm)	12–20 in (30–50 cm)	P	W	NA	◆			Su/A	Sp			◆		
Pelargonium tomentosum	20 in (50 cm)	40 in (100 cm)	P	W	NA		◆		W/Sp	Sp/Su	◆		◆		
Pelargonium Hybrid Cultivars	6–60 in (15–150 cm)	8–40 in (20–100 cm)	P	W	NA	◆			W/Sp	Sp–A	◆		◆		
Peltandra virginica	12–36 in (30–90 cm)	12–36 in (30–90 cm)	P	C	NA	◆	◆		W/Sp	Sp		◆	◆		
Penstemon barbatus	40 in (100 cm)	12–20 in (30–50 cm)	P	C/W	NA	◆			W/Sp	Su		◆	◆	◆	
Penstemon campanulatus	12–24 in (30–60 cm)	8–12 in (20–30 cm)	P	W	NA	◆			W/Sp	Sp/Su			◆	◆	

Plant name	Height	Spread	Type	Climate	Group	Showy flowers	Showy foliage	Scented flowers	Planting season	Flowering season	Grow in pot/tub	Frost tolerant	Full Sun	Half Sun	Heavy shade
Penstemon davidsonii	4 in (10 cm)	20–24 in (50–60 cm)	P	C/W	NA	♦			W/Sp	Su		♦	♦	♦	
Penstemon digitalis	5 ft (1.5 m)	12–24 in (30–60 cm)	P	C/W	NA	♦			W/Sp	Su		♦	♦	♦	
Penstemon fruticosus	16 in (40 cm)	20 in (50 cm)	P	C/W	NA	♦			W/Sp	Sp/Su		♦	♦	♦	
Penstemon grandiflorus	40 in (100 cm)	12–20 in (30–50 cm)	P	C/W	NA	♦			W/Sp	Su		♦	♦	♦	
Penstemon heterophyllus	12–20 in (30–50 cm)	8–12 in (20–30 cm)	P	W	NA	♦			W/Sp	Su		♦	♦	♦	
Penstemon hirsutus	16–32 in (40–80 cm)	8–12 in (20–30 cm)	P	C/W	NA	♦			W/Sp	Su		♦	♦	♦	
Penstemon isophyllus	27 in (70 cm)	40 in (100 cm)	P	W	NA	♦			W/Sp	Sp			♦	♦	
Penstemon pinifolius	16 in (40 cm)	16–24 in (40–60 cm)	P	W	NA	♦			W/Sp	Su		♦	♦	♦	
Penstemon procerus	6–16 in (15–40 cm)	12–16 in (30–40 cm)	P	C/W	NA	♦			W/Sp	Su		♦	♦	♦	
Penstemon strictus	32 in (80 cm)	12–16 in (30–40 cm)	P	C/W	NA	♦			W/Sp	Su		♦	♦	♦	
Penstemon superbus	5–6 ft (1.5–1.8 m)	20–32 in (50–80 cm)	P	W	NA	♦			W/Sp	Su			♦	♦	
Penstemon Hybrid Cultivars	24–48 in (60–120 cm)	8–16 in (20–40 cm)	P	C/W	NA	♦			W/Sp	Su		♦	♦	♦	
Pentas lanceolata	6 ft (1.8 m)	3 ft (0.9 m)	A/P	W/T	NA	♦			Sp	Su			♦		
Peperomia argyreia	6–12 in (15–30 cm)	6–9 in (15–22 cm)	P	W/T	NA		♦		Any	Any	♦			♦	♦
Peperomia caperata	6–10 in (15–25 cm)	6–10 in (15–25 cm)	P	W/T	NA		♦		Any	Any	♦			♦	♦
Peperomia clusiifolia	6–10 in (15–25 cm)	6–10 in (15–25 cm)	P	W/T	NA		♦		Any	Any	♦			♦	♦
Peperomia griseoargentea	6–8 in (15–20 cm)	6–8 in (15–20 cm)	P	W/T	NA		♦		Any	Any	♦				♦
Peperomia obtusifolia	6–8 in (15–20 cm)	6–8 in (15–20 cm)	P	W/T	NA		♦		Any	Any	♦				♦
Peperomia orba	4–6 in (10–15 cm)	4–6 in (10–15 cm)	P	W/T	NA		♦		Any	Any	♦				♦
Pericallis × hybrida	16–32 in (40–80 cm)	16–40 in (40–100 cm)	P	W	NA	♦			Any	Sp/Su	♦			♦	♦
Perilla frutescens	24–40 in (60–100 cm)	18–24 in (45–60 cm)	A	W	NA	♦	♦		Sp	Su/A		♦	♦	♦	
Perovskia atriplicifolia	30–60 in (75–150 cm)	18–36 in (45–90 cm)	P	C	NA	♦			W/Sp	Su/A		♦	♦		
Persicaria affinis	8–10 in (20–25 cm)	20–24 in (50–60 cm)	P	C/W	NA	♦			W/Sp	Su		♦	♦		
Persicaria amplexicaulis	3–4 ft (0.9–1.2 m)	3–4 ft (0.9–1.2 m)	P	C	NA	♦	♦		W/Sp	Su/A		♦	♦		
Persicaria bistorta	6–30 in (15–75 cm)	6–30 in (15–75 cm)	P	C	NA	♦	♦		W/Sp	Su		♦		♦	
Persicaria capitata	3–6 in (8–15 cm)	6–12 in (15–30 cm)	P	C/W	NA	♦	♦		W/Sp	Su/A		♦	♦		
Persicaria orientalis	36–60 in (90–150 cm)	15–18 in (38–45 cm)	A	C/W	NA	♦			W/Sp	Su/A		♦	♦		
Persicaria virginiana	24–48 in (60–120 cm)	32–60 in (80–150 cm)	P	C/W	NA		♦		W/Sp	Su		♦	♦	♦	
Petunia axillaris	12–20 in (30–50 cm)	16–24 in (40–60 cm)	A	W	NA	♦		♦	Sp	Su			♦	♦	
Petunia × hybrida	4–16 in (10–40 cm)	8–40 in (20–100 cm)	A	C/W	NA	♦			Sp	Sp–A			♦	♦	
Petunia integrifolia	12–20 in (30–50 cm)	16–24 in (40–60 cm)	A/P	W	NA	♦			Sp	Su		♦	♦	♦	

Plant name	Height	Spread	Type	Climate	Group	Showy flowers	Showy foliage	Scented flowers	Planting season	Flowering season	Grow in pot/tub	Frost tolerant	Full Sun	Half Sun	Heavy shade
Phacelia campanularia	6–24 in (15–60 cm)	6–24 in (15–60 cm)	A	C/W	NA	◆			Sp	Sp		◆	◆		
Phacelia tanacetifolia	6–60 in (15–150 cm)	4–24 in (10–60 cm)	A	C/W	NA	◆			Sp	Sp		◆	◆		
Phlomis cashmeriana	36 in (90 cm)	36 in (90 cm)	P	W	NA	◆	◆		W/Sp	Su		◆	◆		
Phlomis 'Edward Bowles'	36 in (90 cm)	36 in (90 cm)	P	W	NA	◆	◆		W/Sp	Su		◆	◆		
Phlomis purpurea	24 in (60 cm)	24 in (60 cm)	P	W	NA	◆	◆		W/Sp	Su		◆	◆		
Phlomis russeliana	36 in (90 cm)	24 in (60 cm)	P	W	NA	◆	◆		W/Sp	Su		◆	◆		
Phlomis tuberosa	36 in (90 cm)	36 in (90 cm)	P	W	NA	◆	◆		W/Sp	Su		◆	◆		
Phlox adsurgens	4–6 in (10–15 cm)	12–20 in (30–50 cm)	P	C/W	NA	◆			W/Sp	Sp/Su	◆	◆	◆	◆	
Phlox bifida	4–8 in (10–20 cm)	12–16 in (30–40 cm)	P	C/W	NA	◆		◆	W/Sp	Sp/Su		◆	◆	◆	
Phlox divaricata	12–18 in (30–45 cm)	24–40 in (60–100 cm)	P	C	NA	◆			W/Sp	Sp		◆	◆	◆	
Phlox douglasii	2–6 in (5–15 cm)	12–20 in (30–50 cm)	P	C/W	NA	◆			W/Sp	Sp/Su		◆	◆	◆	
Phlox drummondii	6–16 in (15–40 cm)	8–16 in (20–40 cm)	A	C/W	NA	◆			Sp	Su		◆	◆	◆	
Phlox maculata	27 in (70 cm)	16 in (40 cm)	P	C/W	NA	◆			W/Sp	Su			◆	◆	
Phlox paniculata	24–48 in (60–120 cm)	16–40 in (40–100 cm)	P	C/W	NA	◆			W/Sp	Su			◆	◆	
Phlox subulata	2–4 in (5–10 cm)	12–20 in (30–50 cm)	P	C/W	NA	◆			W/Sp	Sp/Su	◆	◆	◆	◆	
Phormium cookianum	4–8 ft (1.2–2.4 m)	7–8 ft (2–2.4 m)	P	C/W	NA		◆		Any	Su		◆	◆		
Phormium Hybrid Cultivars	1–6 ft (0.3–1.8 m)	1–6 ft (0.3–1.8 m)	P	C/W	NA		◆		Any	Su		◆	◆		
Physalis alkekengi	12–24 in (30–60 cm)	12–24 in (30–60 cm)	P	C	NA				W/Sp	Su		◆	◆		
Physostegia virginiana	32–48 in (80–120 cm)	12–20 in (30–50 cm)	P	C/W	NA	◆			W/Sp	Su/A		◆	◆	◆	
Phytolacca americana	12 ft (3.5 m)	3 ft (0.9 m)	P	C/W	NA	◆	◆		W/Sp	Su/A		◆	◆		
Pilea involucrata	4–18 in (10–45 cm)	6–12 in (15–30 cm)	P	W/T	NA		◆		Any	Su	◆			◆	
Pilea peperomioides	6–20 in (15–50 cm)	6–20 in (15–50 cm)	P	W/T	NA		◆		Any	Su	◆				
Pinguicula emarginata	1½ in (35 mm)	4 in (10 cm)	P	W	C	◆			Sp	Su	◆	◆	◆	◆	
Pinguicula moranensis	2 in (5 cm)	10 in (25 cm)	P	W	C	◆			Sp	Su	◆	◆		◆	
Pinguicula vulgaris	6 in (15 cm)	5 in (12 cm)	P	C	C	◆			Sp	Su	◆	◆	◆	◆	
Pistia stratiotes	4–6 in (10–15 cm)	4–6 in (10–15 cm)	P	W/T	NA		◆		Su	Su			◆		
Pitcairnia atrorubens	32 in (80 cm)	8 in (20 cm)	P	W/T	B	◆			Any	Su					◆
Pitcairnia heterophylla	20 in (50 cm)	20 in (50 cm)	P	W/T	B	◆			Any	Su					◆
Platycodon grandiflorus	27 in (70 cm)	24 in (60 cm)	P	C	NA	◆			W/Sp	Su		◆	◆	◆	
Plectranthus ciliatus	2–4 in (5–10 cm)	4 in (10 cm)	P	W	NA	◆	◆		W/Sp	A/W	◆			◆	
Plectranthus ecklonii	5 ft (1.5 m)	3 ft (0.9 m)	P	W	NA	◆			W/Sp	A			◆		

Plant name	Height	Spread	Type	Climate	Group	Showy flowers	Showy foliage	Scented flowers	Planting season	Flowering season	Grow in pot/tub	Frost tolerant	Full Sun	Half Sun	Heavy shade
Plectranthus forsteri	3–8 ft (0.9–2.4 m)	10 ft (3 m)	P	W	NA	◆			W/Sp	Su/A				◆	
Plectranthus neochilus	18 in (45 cm)	24 in (60 cm)	P	W	NA	◆	◆		W/Sp	Su			◆	◆	
Plectranthus oertendahlii	8–12 in (20–30 cm)	36 in (90 cm)	P	W	NA	◆	◆		W/Sp	Any	◆			◆	
Plectranthus verticillatus	12 in (30 cm)	40 in (100 cm)	P	W	NA	◆			W/Sp	Su				◆	
Podophyllum peltatum	24 in (60 cm)	24 in (60 cm)	P	C	NA	◆	◆	◆	W/Sp	Sp			◆	◆	
Polemonium caeruleum	12–36 in (30–90 cm)	12–20 in (30–50 cm)	P	C	NA	◆			A–Sp	Sp/Su			◆	◆	
Polemonium pulcherrimum	20–24 in (50–60 cm)	20–24 in (50–60 cm)	P	C	NA	◆			A–Sp	Sp/Su		◆	◆	◆	
Polemonium reptans	8–27 in (20–70 cm)	12–27 in (30–70 cm)	P	C	NA	◆			A–Sp	Sp/Su			◆	◆	
Polygala chamaebuxus	2–6 in (5–15 cm)	15 in (38 cm)	P	C	NA	◆			W/Sp	Sp			◆	◆	
Polygonatum odoratum	36 in (90 cm)	24 in (60 cm)	P	C	NA	◆	◆	◆	W/Sp	Sp/Su			◆		◆
Pontederia cordata	48 in (120 cm)	27 in (70 cm)	P	C	NA	◆			W/Sp	Su			◆	◆	
Portea petropolitana	7 ft (2 m)	3 ft (0.9 m)	P	W/T	B	◆	◆		W/Sp	Su	◆				◆
Portulaca grandiflora	6–12 in (15–30 cm)	6–12 in (15–30 cm)	A	W	NA	◆			Sp	Su	◆		◆	◆	
Potamogeton perfoliatus	2 in (5 cm)	15 ft (4.5 m)	P	C/W	NA			◆	W/Sp				◆	◆	
Potentilla alba	10 in (25 cm)	10 in (25 cm)	P	C	NA	◆	◆		W/Sp	Sp/Su	◆		◆	◆	
Potentilla atrosanguinea	36 in (90 cm)	36 in (90 cm)	P	C	NA	◆			W/Sp	Su/A			◆	◆	
Potentilla aurea	12 in (30 cm)	12 in (30 cm)	P	C	NA	◆			W/Sp	Sp/Su	◆		◆	◆	
Potentilla megalantha	8–12 in (20–30 cm)	8–12 in (20–30 cm)	P	C	NA	◆			W/Sp	Su/A	◆		◆	◆	
Potentilla nepalensis	12–24 in (30–60 cm)	12–24 in (30–60 cm)	P	C	NA	◆			W/Sp	Su			◆	◆	
Potentilla neumanniana	3–4 in (8–10 cm)	6–12 in (15–30 cm)	P	C	NA	◆			W/Sp	Sp			◆	◆	
Potentilla nitida	2–4 in (5–10 cm)	5–16 in (12–40 cm)	P	C	NA	◆	◆		W/Sp	Su			◆	◆	
Potentilla × tonguei	6–10 in (15–25 cm)	12–20 in (30–50 cm)	P	C	NA	◆			W/Sp	Su			◆	◆	
Primula alpicola	16–36 in (40–90 cm)	10–16 in (25–40 cm)	P	C	NA	◆			A–Sp	Sp/Su		◆		◆	◆
Primula auricula	4–8 in (10–20 cm)	6–16 in (15–40 cm)	P	C	NA	◆			A–Sp	Sp		◆		◆	
Primula beesiana	32 in (80 cm)	20 in (50 cm)	P	C	NA	◆			A–Sp	Su		◆			◆
Primula bulleyana	24 in (60 cm)	12–27 in (30–70 cm)	P	C	NA	◆			A–Sp	Sp/Su				◆	◆
Primula capitata	10–15 in (25–38 cm)	12–18 in (30–45 cm)	P	C	NA	◆		◆	W/Sp	Sp/Su	◆	◆		◆	
Primula denticulata	8–12 in (20–30 cm)	10–18 in (25–45 cm)	P	C	NA	◆			A–Sp	Sp				◆	◆
Primula elatior	6–12 in (15–30 cm)	6–16 in (15–40 cm)	P	C	NA	◆			A–Sp	Sp/Su				◆	◆
Primula farinosa	8 in (20 cm)	12 in (30 cm)	P	C	NA	◆			A–Sp	Sp	◆	◆		◆	
Primula florindae	36 in (90 cm)	8–16 in (20–40 cm)	P	C	NA	◆		◆	A–Sp	Sp/Su		◆		◆	◆

Plant name	Height	Spread	Type	Climate	Group	Showy flowers	Showy foliage	Scented flowers	Planting season	Flowering season	Grow in pot/tub	Frost tolerant	Full Sun	Half Sun	Heavy shade
Primula japonica	18 in (45 cm)	12–24 in (30–60 cm)	P	C	NA	◆			A–Sp	Sp/Su		◆		◆	◆
Primula juliae	2 in (5 cm)	6–10 in (15–25 cm)	P	C	NA	◆			A–Sp	Sp		◆		◆	◆
Primula × kewensis	12 in (30 cm)	12–18 in (30–45 cm)	P	C/W	NA	◆		◆	A/W	Sp	◆			◆	◆
Primula malacoides	12 in (30 cm)	16 in (40 cm)	A	C/W	NA	◆			A/W	W/Sp	◆		◆	◆	
Primula obconica	8 in (20 cm)	8–16 in (20–40 cm)	A	C/W	NA	◆			A/W	W/Sp	◆			◆	◆
Primula, Pruhonicensis Hybrids	4–12 in (10–30 cm)	6–16 in (15–40 cm)	P	C	NA	◆			A–Sp	W/Sp	◆	◆		◆	◆
Primula × pubescens	6 in (15 cm)	10 in (25 cm)	P	C	NA	◆			A–Sp	Sp	◆	◆		◆	◆
Primula pulverulenta	36 in (90 cm)	20 in (50 cm)	P	C	NA	◆			A–Sp	Sp/Su		◆		◆	◆
Primula rosea	4–6 in (10–15 cm)	6–15 in (15–38 cm)	P	C	NA	◆			A–Sp	Sp		◆		◆	◆
Primula sieboldii	12 in (30 cm)	12–24 in (30–60 cm)	P	C	NA	◆			A–Sp	Sp/Su		◆		◆	◆
Primula sikkimensis	12–36 in (30–90 cm)	10–24 in (25–60 cm)	P	C	NA	◆			A–Sp	Sp/Su		◆		◆	◆
Primula veris	12 in (30 cm)	16 in (40 cm)	P	C	NA	◆		◆	A–Sp	Sp/Su		◆		◆	◆
Primula vulgaris	4–6 in (10–15 cm)	6–16 in (15–40 cm)	P	C	NA	◆		◆	A–Sp	Sp	◆	◆		◆	◆
Prunella grandiflora	12–24 in (30–60 cm)	12–24 in (30–60 cm)	P	C	NA	◆			Sp	Su		◆	◆		
Prunella laciniata	9–12 in (22–30 cm)	9–12 in (22–30 cm)	P	C	NA	◆			Sp	Sp/Su		◆	◆		
Psylliostachys suworowii	12–36 in (30–90 cm)	12–16 in (30–40 cm)	A	C/W	NA	◆			Sp	Su/A	◆	◆	◆		
Pulmonaria angustifolia	8–16 in (20–40 cm)	16–40 in (40–100 cm)	P	C	NA	◆	◆		A–Sp	Sp				◆	◆
Pulmonaria mollis	16 in (40 cm)	40 in (100 cm)	P	C	NA	◆	◆		A–Sp	Sp/Su				◆	◆
Pulmonaria rubra	12–18 in (30–45 cm)	20–40 in (50–100 cm)	P	C	NA	◆	◆		A–Sp	Sp/Su				◆	◆
Pulmonaria saccharata	12–16 in (30–40 cm)	16–32 in (40–80 cm)	P	C	NA	◆	◆		A–Sp	Sp				◆	◆
Pulmonaria vallarsae	12–18 in (30–45 cm)	20–40 in (50–100 cm)	P	C	NA	◆	◆		A–Sp	Sp/Su				◆	◆
Pulmonaria Hybrid Cultivars	8–16 in (20–40 cm)	16–40 in (40–100 cm)	P	C	NA	◆	◆		A–Sp	Sp/Su				◆	◆
Pulsatilla albana	8 in (20 cm)	8 in (20 cm)	P	C	NA	◆	◆		A/W	Sp/Su		◆	◆	◆	
Pulsatilla halleri	10 in (25 cm)	12 in (30 cm)	P	C	NA	◆	◆		A/W	Sp		◆	◆	◆	
Pulsatilla patens	6–10 in (15–25 cm)	8–12 in (20–30 cm)	P	C	NA	◆	◆		A/W	Sp		◆	◆	◆	
Pulsatilla pratensis	12 in (30 cm)	16 in (40 cm)	P	C	NA	◆	◆		A/W	Sp		◆	◆	◆	
Pulsatilla vulgaris	8–15 in (20–38 cm)	8–16 in (20–40 cm)	P	C	NA	◆	◆		A/W	Sp		◆	◆	◆	
Puya berteroniana	15 ft (4.5 m)	7 ft (2 m)	P	C/W	B	◆	◆		A/W	Sp/Su		◆	◆		
Puya chilensis	15 ft (4.5 m)	7 ft (2 m)	P	C/W	B	◆	◆		A/W	Sp/Su		◆	◆		
Puya venusta	40 in (100 cm)	20 in (50 cm)	P	W	B	◆	◆		A/W	Sp/Su		◆	◆		
Quesnelia liboniana	32 in (80 cm)	4 in (10 cm)	P	W/T	B	◆			W	Sp					◆

Plant name	Height	Spread	Type	Climate	Group	Showy flowers	Showy foliage	Scented flowers	Planting season	Flowering season	Grow in pot/tub	Frost tolerant	Full Sun	Half Sun	Heavy shade
Quesnelia marmorata	24 in (60 cm)	4 in (10 cm)	P	W/T	B	◆			W	Sp					◆
Ramonda myconi	4–5 in (10–12 cm)	7–8 in (18–20 cm)	P	C	G	◆			W/Sp	Sp/Su	◆	◆		◆	
Raoulia australis	½ in (12 mm)	12 in (30 cm)	P	C	NA		◆		W/Sp	Su	◆	◆	◆		
Raoulia eximia	12 in (30 cm)	20 in (50 cm)	P	C	NA		◆		W/Sp	Su	◆	◆	◆		
Ratibida columnifera	24 in (60 cm)	18 in (45 cm)	P	C	NA	◆			W/Sp	Su/A			◆	◆	
Ratibida pinnata	48 in (120 cm)	12–18 in (30–45 cm)	P	C	NA	◆			W/Sp	Su/A			◆	◆	
Rehmannia elata	40–60 in (100–150 cm)	20–32 in (50–80 cm)	P	W	NA	◆			W/Sp	Sp/Su				◆	
Reineckea carnea	8 in (20 cm)	6–12 in (15–30 cm)	P	C/W	NA	◆		◆	W/Sp	Sp		◆		◆	
Reseda lutea	20–27 in (50–70 cm)	20–27 in (50–70 cm)	A	C/W	NA	◆			Sp	Su			◆	◆	
Reseda luteola	36–48 in (90–120 cm)	8–12 in (20–30 cm)	A/P	C/W	NA	◆			W/Sp	Su			◆	◆	
Reseda odorata	12–24 in (30–60 cm)	7–8 in (18–20 cm)	A	C/W	NA	◆		◆	Sp	Su			◆	◆	
Rheum australe	5 ft (1.5 m)	5 ft (1.5 m)	P	C	NA		◆		W/Sp	Su		◆	◆	◆	
Rheum palmatum	5–8 ft (1.5–2.4 m)	5 ft (1.5 m)	P	C	NA		◆		W/Sp	Su			◆	◆	
Rhodanthe chlorocephala	12–24 in (30–60 cm)	8–12 in (20–30 cm)	A	W	NA	◆			A–Sp	W–Su			◆		
Rhodanthe manglesii	12–18 in (30–45 cm)	6–12 in (15–30 cm)	A	W	NA	◆			W/Sp	Sp			◆	◆	
Rhodanthemum gayanum	8–12 in (20–30 cm)	24–40 in (60–100 cm)	P	W	NA	◆			W/Sp	W/Sp	◆	◆	◆		
Rhodanthemum hosmariense	4–8 in (10–20 cm)	12–16 in (30–40 cm)	P	W	NA	◆	◆		W/Sp	Sp–A	◆		◆		
Rodgersia aesculifolia	5–7 ft (1.5–2 m)	3–7 ft (0.9–2 m)	P	C	NA	◆	◆		W/Sp	Su			◆		◆
Rodgersia pinnata	32–48 in (80–120 cm)	3–7 ft (0.9–2 m)	P	C	NA	◆	◆		W/Sp	Su			◆		◆
Rodgersia podophylla	32–48 in (80–120 cm)	3–7 ft (0.9–2 m)	P	C	NA	◆	◆		W/Sp	Su			◆		◆
Rodgersia sambucifolia	24–36 in (60–90 cm)	24–48 in (60–120 cm)	P	C	NA	◆	◆		W/Sp	Su			◆		◆
Romneya coulteri	8 ft (2.4 m)	7 ft (2 m)	P	C/W	NA	◆	◆		W/Sp	Su/A			◆	◆	
Rudbeckia fulgida	40 in (100 cm)	24–48 in (60–120 cm)	P	C/W	NA	◆			W/Sp	Su/A			◆	◆	◆
Rudbeckia 'Herbstsonne'	6 ft (1.8 m)	3 ft (0.9 m)	P	C/W	NA	◆			W/Sp	Su/A			◆	◆	
Rudbeckia hirta	5–7 ft (1.5–2 m)	32–48 in (80–120 cm)	B/P	C/W	NA	◆			W/Sp	Su/A			◆	◆	
Rudbeckia laciniata	7–10 ft (2–3 m)	3–7 ft (0.9–2 m)	P	C/W	NA	◆			W/Sp	Su/A			◆	◆	
Rudbeckia nitida	5–7 ft (1.5–2 m)	32–48 in (80–120 cm)	P	C/W	NA	◆			W/Sp	Su/A			◆	◆	
Rudbeckia occidentalis	5–7 ft (1.5–2 m)	32–48 in (80–120 cm)	P	C/W	NA	◆			W/Sp	Su			◆	◆	
Ruellia brittoniana	24–36 in (60–90 cm)	18–24 in (45–60 cm)	P	W	NA	◆			W/Sp	Sp–A			◆	◆	
Ruellia makoyana	6–12 in (15–30 cm)	15–18 in (38–45 cm)	P	W/T	NA	◆	◆		W/Sp	All	◆		◆		
Rumex sanguineus	20–40 in (50–100 cm)	12–36 in (30–90 cm)	P	C/W	NA		◆		W/Sp	Su			◆	◆	

Plant name	Height	Spread	Type	Climate	Group	Showy flowers	Showy foliage	Scented flowers	Planting season	Flowering season	Grow in pot/tub	Frost tolerant	Full Sun	Half Sun	Heavy shade
Rumex vesicarius	8–10 in (20–25 cm)	6–8 in (15–20 cm)	A	C/W	NA	◆	◆		W/Sp	Sp		◆	◆		
Ruscus aculeatus	30–40 in (75–100 cm)	40 in (100 cm)	P	C/W	NA			◆	W/Sp	Sp		◆	◆	◆	
Ruscus hypoglossum	18–26 in (45–65 cm)	40 in (100 cm)	P	C/W	NA			◆	W/Sp	Sp		◆	◆	◆	
Sagina subulata	1 in (25 mm)	12 in (30 cm)	P	C	NA			◆	W/Sp	Su		◆	◆	◆	
Sagittaria graminea	20 in (50 cm)	12 in (30 cm)	P	All	NA	◆	◆		W/Sp	Su		◆	◆		
Saintpaulia ionantha	4–10 in (10–25 cm)	8–16 in (20–40 cm)	P	W/T	G	◆	◆		Sp	All	◆				◆
Saintpaulia shumensis	2–6 in (5–15 cm)	6–10 in (15–25 cm)	P	W/T	G	◆	◆		Sp	All	◆				◆
Saintpaulia Hybrid Cultivars	2–8 in (5–20 cm)	4–12 in (10–30 cm)	P	W/T	G	◆			Sp	All	◆				◆
Salpiglossis sinuata	16–24 in (40–60 cm)	8–12 in (20–30 cm)	A	W	NA	◆			Sp	Su/A	◆	◆	◆	◆	
Salvia argentea	24–36 in (60–90 cm)	24–36 in (60–90 cm)	P	W	NA	◆	◆		W/Sp	Su		◆	◆		
Salvia blepharophylla	8–12 in (20–30 cm)	20–27 in (50–70 cm)	P	W	NA	◆			W/Sp	Su/A				◆	
Salvia chiapensis	16–24 in (40–60 cm)	16–24 in (40–60 cm)	P	W	NA	◆			W/Sp	Sp–A			◆	◆	
Salvia coccinea	40 in (100 cm)	20–32 in (50–80 cm)	A	W	NA	◆			Sp	Su/A			◆	◆	
Salvia discolor	32–40 in (80–100 cm)	32–40 in (80–100 cm)	P	W	NA	◆	◆		W/Sp	Su/A			◆	◆	
Salvia dorisiana	36–48 in (90–120 cm)	36 in (90 cm)	P	W	NA	◆		◆	Sp	W			◆		
Salvia elegans	6 ft (1.8 m)	3 ft (0.9 m)	P	C/W	NA	◆			W/Sp	Sp–A		◆	◆		
Salvia farinacea	36–48 in (90–120 cm)	24 in (60 cm)	A/P	W	NA	◆	◆		Sp	Su/A			◆		
Salvia fulgens	48 in (120 cm)	30 in (75 cm)	P	W	NA	◆			W/Sp	Su			◆		
Salvia gesneriiflora	26 in (65 cm)	10 in (25 cm)	P	W	NA	◆			W/Sp	Su/A			◆		
Salvia greggii	12–36 in (30–90 cm)	12–36 in (30–90 cm)	P	W	NA	◆			W/Sp	Su/A			◆		
Salvia guaranitica	4–5 ft (1.2–1.5 m)	16–27 in (40–70 cm)	P	C/W	NA	◆			W/Sp	Su/A		◆	◆		
Salvia indica	24–36 in (60–90 cm)	24 in (60 cm)	P	W	NA	◆			A/W	Sp			◆		
Salvia involucrata	5 ft (1.5 m)	5 ft (1.5 m)	P	W	NA	◆	◆		W/Sp	Su/A			◆	◆	
Salvia leucantha	36 in (90 cm)	36 in (90 cm)	P	W	NA	◆	◆		W/Sp	Su			◆		
Salvia microphylla	4 ft (1.2 m)	3 ft (0.9 m)	P	W	NA	◆			W/Sp	Su/A		◆	◆		
Salvia nemorosa	24–36 in (60–90 cm)	12–24 in (30–60 cm)	P	C/W	NA	◆			W/Sp	Sp		◆	◆		
Salvia patens	12–24 in (30–60 cm)	12–24 in (30–60 cm)	P	W	NA	◆			W/Sp	Su/A				◆	
Salvia pratensis	36 in (90 cm)	12 in (30 cm)	P	C/W	NA	◆			W/Sp	Sp/Su		◆	◆		
Salvia przewalskii	12–24 in (30–60 cm)	12–24 in (30–60 cm)	P	W	NA	◆			W/Sp	Su		◆	◆		
Salvia roemeriana	12 in (30 cm)	12 in (30 cm)	P	C/W	NA	◆			W/Sp	Su		◆	◆	◆	
Salvia spathacea	12–36 in (30–90 cm)	12–36 in (30–90 cm)	P	C/W	NA	◆	◆		W/Sp	Sp/Su		◆	◆	◆	

Plant name	Height	Spread	Type	Climate	Group	Showy flowers	Showy foliage	Scented flowers	Planting season	Flowering season	Grow in pot/tub	Frost tolerant	Full Sun	Half Sun	Heavy shade
Salvia splendens	8–48 in (20–120 cm)	8–32 in (10–80 cm)	A/P	W	NA	◆			Sp	Su/A				◆	
Salvia × sylvestris	20–40 in (50–100 cm)	20–40 in (50–100 cm)	P	C/W	NA	◆			W/Sp	Su		◆	◆		
Salvia uliginosa	3–6 ft (0.9–1.8 m)	3 ft (0.9 m)	P	W	NA	◆			W/Sp	Su/A			◆		
Salvia verticillata	40 in (100 cm)	32 in (80 cm)	P	C/W	NA	◆			W/Sp	Su		◆	◆		
Salvia Hybrid Cultivars	20–60 in (50–150 cm)	16–48 in (40–120 cm)	A	C/W	NA	◆			Sp	Su/A		◆	◆	◆	
Sanguinaria canadensis	8 in (20 cm)	4 in (10 cm)	P	C	NA	◆			A/W	Sp		◆		◆	◆
Sanguisorba canadensis	48–60 in (120–150 cm)	24–36 in (60–90 cm)	P	C	NA	◆			W/Sp	Su		◆	◆		
Sanvitalia procumbens	6–8 in (15–20 cm)	12 in (30 cm)	A	C/W	NA	◆			Sp	Su			◆	◆	
Saponaria ocymoides	6–12 in (15–30 cm)	12–20 in (30–50 cm)	P	C/W	NA	◆			W/Sp	Su	◆	◆	◆		
Saponaria officinalis	12–24 in (30–60 cm)	20–40 in (50–100 cm)	P	C/W	NA	◆			W/Sp	Su/A	◆	◆	◆		
Saponaria × olivana	2 in (5 cm)	8 in (20 cm)	P	C/W	NA	◆			W/Sp	Sp	◆	◆	◆		
Sarracenia alata	27 in (70 cm)	12 in (30 cm)	P	C/W	C		◆	◆	W/Sp	Sp	◆	◆	◆		
Sarracenia × catesbaei	18 in (45 cm)	12 in (30 cm)	P	C/W	C		◆	◆	W/Sp	Sp	◆	◆	◆		
Sarracenia × exornata	14 in (35 cm)	12 in (30 cm)	P	C/W	C		◆	◆	W/Sp	Sp	◆	◆	◆		
Sarracenia flava	30 in (75 cm)	12 in (30 cm)	P	C/W	C		◆	◆	W/Sp	Sp	◆	◆	◆		
Sarracenia 'Juthatip Soper'	18 in (45 cm)	12 in (30 cm)	P	C/W	C		◆	◆	W/Sp	Sp	◆	◆	◆		
Sarracenia leucophylla	24 in (60 cm)	12 in (30 cm)	P	C/W	C		◆	◆	W/Sp	Sp	◆	◆	◆		
Sarracenia minor	24 in (60 cm)	12 in (30 cm)	P	C/W	C		◆	◆	W/Sp	Sp	◆	◆	◆		
Sarracenia × mitchelliana	18 in (45 cm)	12 in (30 cm)	P	C/W	C		◆	◆	W/Sp	Sp	◆	◆	◆		
Sarracenia × moorei	40 in (100 cm)	12 in (30 cm)	P	C/W	C		◆	◆	W/Sp	Sp	◆	◆	◆		
Sarracenia oreophila	24 in (60 cm)	12 in (30 cm)	P	C/W	C		◆	◆	W/Sp	Sp	◆	◆	◆		
Sarracenia psittacina	10 in (25 cm)	20 in (50 cm)	P	C/W	C		◆	◆	W/Sp	Sp	◆	◆	◆		
Sarracenia purpurea	12 in (30 cm)	24 in (60 cm)	P	C/W	C		◆	◆	W/Sp	Sp	◆	◆	◆		
Sarracenia × readii	24 in (60 cm)	12 in (30 cm)	P	C/W	C		◆	◆	W/Sp	Sp	◆	◆	◆		
Sarracenia × stevensii	24 in (60 cm)	12 in (30 cm)	P	C/W	C		◆	◆	W/Sp	Sp	◆	◆	◆		
Saxifraga andersonii	4 in (10 cm)	12 in (30 cm)	P	C	NA	◆			W/Sp	Sp	◆	◆	◆		
Saxifraga callosa	10 in (25 cm)	8 in (20 cm)	P	C	NA	◆			W/Sp	Su		◆	◆		
Saxifraga cochlearis	8 in (20 cm)	6 in (15 cm)	P	C	NA	◆			W/Sp	Su	◆	◆	◆		
Saxifraga oppositifolia	1 in (2.5 cm)	8 in (20 cm)	P	C	NA	◆			W/Sp	Sp	◆	◆	◆	◆	
Saxifraga paniculata	6 in (15 cm)	10 in (25 cm)	P	C	NA	◆			W/Sp	Su	◆	◆	◆		
Saxifraga spathularis	8–12 in (20–30 cm)	6–8 in (15–20 cm)	P	C/W	NA	◆			W/Sp	Su		◆	◆	◆	

Plant name	Height	Spread	Type	Climate	Group	Showy flowers	Showy foliage	Scented flowers	Planting season	Flowering season	Grow in pot/tub	Frost tolerant	Full Sun	Half Sun	Heavy shade
Saxifraga stolonifera	16 in (40 cm)	12 in (30 cm)	P	C/W	NA	◆	◆		W/Sp	Su		◆	◆	◆	◆
Saxifraga umbrosa	12 in (30 cm)	12 in (30 cm)	P	C	NA	◆			W/Sp	Sp/Su		◆	◆		
Saxifraga × urbium	12 in (30 cm)	18–36 in (45–90 cm)	P	C	NA	◆			W/Sp	Su		◆	◆		
Saxifraga Hybrid Cultivars	3–12 in (8–30 cm)	6–18 in (15–45 cm)	P	C	NA	◆			W/Sp	Sp/Su		◆	◆	◆	
Scabiosa atropurpurea	16–36 in (40–90 cm)	16–30 in (40–75 cm)	A/B/P	C/W	NA	◆		◆	Sp	Su/A			◆	◆	
Scabiosa caucasica	20–36 in (50–90 cm)	16–18 in (40–45 cm)	P	C/W	NA	◆			W/Sp	Su/A		◆	◆	◆	
Scabiosa columbaria	24 in (60 cm)	16 in (40 cm)	B/P	C/W	NA	◆			W/Sp	Su		◆	◆	◆	
Scabiosa lucida	12 in (30 cm)	12–20 in (30–50 cm)	P	C/W	NA	◆			W/Sp	Su/A		◆	◆		
Scaevola aemula	6 in (15 cm)	20 in (50 cm)	P	W	NA	◆			W/Sp	Sp/Su	◆		◆		
Schaueria flavicoma	36 in (90 cm)	24 in (60 cm)	P	W/T	NA	◆	◆		W/Sp	Sp/Su	◆		◆		
Schizanthus pinnatus	8–20 in (20–50 cm)	8–16 in (20–40 cm)	A	W	NA	◆			Sp	Su/A	◆		◆	◆	
Schizanthus × wisetonensis	12–20 in (30–50 cm)	12 in (30 cm)	A	W	NA	◆			Sp	Su/A	◆		◆		
Scleranthus biflorus	2–4 in (5–10 cm)	12 in (30 cm)	P	C	NA			◆	Sp	Su		◆	◆		
Scrophularia auriculata	36–48 in (90–120 cm)	36–48 in (90–120 cm)	P	C/W	NA			◆	W/Sp	Su		◆			
Scutellaria alpina	6–10 in (15–25 cm)	18 in (45 cm)	P	C	NA	◆			W/Sp	Sp/Su	◆	◆	◆		
Scutellaria incana	24–48 in (60–120 cm)	24 in (60 cm)	P	C/W	NA	◆			W/Sp	Su/A	◆	◆	◆	◆	
Scutellaria indica	6 in (15 cm)	12 in (30 cm)	P	C/W	NA	◆			W/Sp	Su		◆	◆	◆	
Scutellaria orientalis	12–18 in (30–45 cm)	6–10 in (15–25 cm)	P	C/W	NA	◆			W/Sp	Su		◆	◆		
Sedum spectabile	27 in (70 cm)	16–32 in (40–80 cm)	P	C/W	NA	◆	◆		W/Sp	Su/A		◆	◆		
Sedum telephium	24 in (60 cm)	24–32 in (60–80 cm)	P	C/W	NA	◆	◆		W/Sp	Su		◆	◆		
Sedum Hybrid Cultivars	12–24 in (30–60 cm)	12–24 in (30–60 cm)	P	C/W	NA	◆			W/Sp	Su/A		◆	◆		
Semiaquilegia ecalcarata	12 in (30 cm)	8–10 in (20–25 cm)	P	C	NA	◆	◆		W/Sp	Su	◆	◆	◆	◆	◆
Senecio cineraria	20 in (50 cm)	16 in (40 cm)	P	C/W	NA		◆		A–Sp	Su		◆	◆		
Senecio vira-vira	16–24 in (40–60 cm)	12–24 in (30–60 cm)	P	W	NA		◆		A–Sp	Su			◆	◆	
Serissa japonica	18 in (45 cm)	18 in (45 cm)	P	W	NA	◆	◆		W/Sp	Sp–A	◆		◆		
Shortia galacifolia	6 in (15 cm)	10 in (25 cm)	P	C	NA	◆	◆		Su/A	Sp	◆	◆			◆
Shortia soldanelloides	6 in (15 cm)	10 in (25 cm)	P	C	NA	◆	◆		Su/A	Sp	◆	◆			◆
Sidalcea candida	24–36 in (60–90 cm)	20 in (50 cm)	P	C/W	NA	◆			W/Sp	Su		◆	◆		
Sidalcea malviflora	24–40 in (60–100 cm)	16–30 in (40–75 cm)	P	C/W	NA	◆			W/Sp	Sp–A		◆	◆	◆	
Sidalcea Hybrid Cultivars	24–32 in (60–80 cm)	16–24 in (40–60 cm)	P	C/W	NA	◆			W/Sp	Sp–A		◆	◆	◆	
Silene acaulis	2 in (5 cm)	4 in (10 cm)	P	C	NA	◆			W/Sp	Sp/Su		◆	◆		

Plant name	Height	Spread	Type	Climate	Group	Showy flowers	Showy foliage	Scented flowers	Planting season	Flowering season	Grow in pot/tub	Frost tolerant	Full Sun	Half Sun	Heavy shade
Silene alpestris	6–12 in (15–30 cm)	12 in (30 cm)	P	C	NA	◆			W/Sp	Su		◆	◆	◆	
Silene dioica	24 in (60 cm)	12 in (30 cm)	P	C	NA	◆			W/Sp	Su		◆	◆	◆	
Silene fimbriata	40 in (100 cm)	24 in (60 cm)	P	C	NA	◆			W/Sp	Su		◆	◆	◆	
Silene laciniata	36 in (90 cm)	8 in (20 cm)	P	C/W	NA	◆			W/Sp	Su			◆	◆	
Silene schafta	4 in (10 cm)	8 in (20 cm)	P	C	NA	◆			W/Sp	Su/A	◆	◆	◆	◆	
Silene uniflora	4–8 in (10–20 cm)	4 in (10 cm)	P	C	NA	◆			W/Sp	Su			◆	◆	
Silphium laciniatum	5–10 ft (1.5–3 m)	3–4 ft (0.9–1.2 m)	P	C	NA	◆			W/Sp	Su		◆	◆	◆	
Silphium perfoliatum	5 ft (1.5 m)	3 ft (0.9 m)	P	C/W	NA	◆			W/Sp	Su		◆	◆	◆	
Silphium terebinthinaceum	7–10 ft (2–3 m)	3–6 ft (0.9–1.8 m)	P	C	NA	◆			W/Sp	Su		◆	◆	◆	
Silybum marianum	4 ft (1.2 m)	2 ft (0.6 m)	B	C/W	NA	◆	◆		W/Sp	Sp/Su			◆	◆	
Sinningia canescens	10 in (25 cm)	10 in (25 cm)	P	W/T	G	◆	◆		Sp	Su	◆			◆	◆
Sinningia cardinalis	8–12 in (20–30 cm)	12 in (30 cm)	P	W/T	G	◆	◆		Sp	Su	◆			◆	◆
Sinningia × pumila	4–6 in (10–15 cm)	6–12 in (15–30 cm)	P	W/T	G	◆			Sp	Su	◆			◆	◆
Sinningia speciosa	8–12 in (20–30 cm)	12–20 in (30–50 cm)	P	W/T	G	◆	◆		Sp	Su	◆			◆	◆
Sisyrinchium 'Biscutella'	12 in (30 cm)	6 in (15 cm)	P	C/W	NA	◆			W/Sp	Su		◆	◆		
Sisyrinchium 'Californian Skies'	12 in (30 cm)	8 in (20 cm)	P	C/W	NA	◆			W/Sp	Su/A		◆	◆		
Sisyrinchium californicum	24 in (60 cm)	6 in (15 cm)	P	C/W	NA	◆			W/Sp	Su		◆	◆		
Sisyrinchium graminoides	20 in (50 cm)	8 in (20 cm)	P	C/W	NA	◆			W/Sp	Su/A		◆	◆		
Sisyrinchium striatum	32 in (80 cm)	14 in (35 cm)	P	W	NA	◆			W/Sp	Su		◆	◆		
Smithiantha zebrina	18–24 in (45–60 cm)	10–18 in (25–45 cm)	P	W/T	G	◆	◆		W/Sp	Su	◆				◆
Solanum quitoense	7 ft (2 m)	7 ft (2 m)	P	W/T	NA			◆	Sp	Su			◆		
Soldanella alpina	3–6 in (8–15 cm)	8 in (20 cm)	P	C	NA	◆			W/Sp	Sp/Su	◆	◆	◆		
Soldanella carpatica	3–6 in (8–15 cm)	8 in (20 cm)	P	C	NA	◆			W/Sp	Sp		◆	◆	◆	
Soldanella villosa	6–12 in (15–30 cm)	8–12 in (20–30 cm)	P	C	NA	◆			W/Sp	Sp		◆	◆	◆	
Soleirolia soleirolii	2–4 in (5–10 cm)	2–4 ft (0.6–1.2 m)	P	W/T	NA		◆		Any	Su	◆			◆	◆
Solenostemon scutellarioides	12–24 in (30–60 cm)	12–24 in (30–60 cm)	P	W/T	NA		◆		Sp/Su	Su	◆			◆	◆
Solidago bicolor	40 in (100 cm)	24 in (60 cm)	P	C	NA	◆			W/Sp	Su/A		◆	◆	◆	
Solidago californica	40–48 in (100–120 cm)	24–32 in (60–80 cm)	P	C/W	NA	◆			W/Sp	A		◆	◆	◆	
Solidago canadensis	60 in (150 cm)	40 in (100 cm)	P	C	NA	◆			W/Sp	Su/A		◆	◆	◆	
Solidago rugosa	60 in (150 cm)	40 in (100 cm)	P	C	NA	◆			W/Sp	Su		◆	◆	◆	
Solidago virgaurea	40 in (100 cm)	24 in (60 cm)	P	C	NA	◆			W/Sp	Su/A		◆	◆	◆	

Plant name	Height	Spread	Type	Climate	Group	Showy flowers	Showy foliage	Scented flowers	Planting season	Flowering season	Grow in pot/tub	Frost tolerant	Full Sun	Half Sun	Heavy shade
Solidago Hybrid Cultivars	24–60 in (60–150 cm)	12–48 in (30–120 cm)	P	C	NA	◆			W/Sp	Su/A		◆	◆	◆	
× *Solidaster luteus*	32–36 in (80–90 cm)	12–15 in (30–38 cm)	P	C/W	NA	◆			W/Sp	Su/A		◆	◆		
Spathiphyllum cannifolium	40 in (100 cm)	40 in (100 cm)	P	W/T	NA	◆	◆		W/Sp	Sp/Su	◆				◆
Spathiphyllum wallisii	24–48 in (60–120 cm)	20–40 in (50–100 cm)	P	W/T	NA	◆	◆	◆	W/Sp	Sp/Su	◆				◆
Spathiphyllum Hybrid Cultivars	12–72 in (30–180 cm)	12–60 in (30–150 cm)	P	W/T	NA	◆	◆		W/Sp	Sp/Su	◆				◆
Sphaeralcea coccinea	6–18 in (15–45 cm)	6–12 in (15–30 cm)	P	C/W	NA	◆			W/Sp	Su		◆	◆		
Sphaeralcea munroana	8–36 in (20–90 cm)	12–27 in (30–70 cm)	P	C/W	NA	◆			W/Sp	Su		◆	◆		
Stachys byzantina	18 in (45 cm)	24 in (60 cm)	P	C	NA		◆		A/Sp	Sp/Su		◆	◆		
Stachys citrina	8 in (20 cm)	12 in (30 cm)	P	C	NA	◆	◆		A/Sp	Su		◆	◆		
Stachys coccinea	24 in (60 cm)	18 in (45 cm)	P	C/W	NA	◆			A/Sp	Sp–A		◆	◆		
Stachys macrantha	18–24 in (45–60 cm)	12–18 in (30–45 cm)	P	C	NA	◆	◆		A/Sp	Su		◆	◆		
Stachys officinalis	12–36 in (30–90 cm)	18–36 in (45–90 cm)	P	C	NA	◆	◆		A/Sp	Su/A		◆	◆		
Stellaria holostea	20–24 in (50–60 cm)	3–7 in (0.9–2 m)	P	C/W	NA	◆			W/Sp	Sp/Su		◆		◆	
Stokesia laevis	10–30 in (25–75 cm)	8–16 in (20–40 cm)	P	C/W	NA	◆			Sp	Su/A	◆	◆	◆	◆	
Strelitzia juncea	5 ft (1.5 m)	3–5 ft (0.9–1.5 m)	P	W/T	NA	◆	◆		W/Sp	Sp/Su			◆		
Strelitzia reginae	6 ft (1.8 m)	3 ft (0.9 m)	P	W/T	NA	◆	◆		W/Sp	W/Sp	◆		◆		
Streptocarpus candidus	12 in (30 cm)	10–16 in (25–40 cm)	P	W/T	G	◆		◆	W/Sp	Su	◆			◆	◆
Streptocarpus caulescens	12–20 in (30–50 cm)	12–20 in (30–50 cm)	P	W/T	G	◆			W/Sp	Su–W	◆			◆	◆
Streptocarpus cyaneus	6–8 in (15–20 cm)	12–20 in (30–50 cm)	P	W/T	G	◆			W/Sp	Sp/Su	◆			◆	◆
Streptocarpus glandulosissimus	12–20 in (30–50 cm)	12–20 in (30–50 cm)	P	W/T	G	◆			W/Sp	All	◆			◆	◆
Streptocarpus kirkii	12–16 in (30–40 cm)	8–12 in (20–30 cm)	P	W/T	G	◆			W/Sp	W	◆			◆	◆
Streptocarpus saxorum	4–6 in (10–15 cm)	8–16 in (20–40 cm)	P	W/T	G	◆	◆		W/Sp	All	◆			◆	◆
Streptocarpus wendlandii	12 in (30 cm)	30 in (75 cm)	P	W/T	G	◆			W/Sp	Su	◆			◆	◆
Streptocarpus Hybrid Cultivars	12–20 in (30–50 cm)	12–20 in (30–50 cm)	P	W/T	G	◆			W/Sp	Sp/Su	◆			◆	◆
Strobilanthes anisophyllus	5 ft (1.5 m)	5 ft (1.5 m)	P	W/T	NA		◆		W/Sp	Su/A			◆		
Strobilanthes dyerianus	36 in (90 cm)	36 in (90 cm)	P	W/T	NA		◆		W/Sp	Sp/Su			◆		
Strobilanthes gossypinus	3–5 ft (0.9–1.5 m)	20–30 in (50–75 cm)	P	W/T	NA	◆			W/Sp	Su				◆	
Stromanthe sanguinea	3–5 ft (0.9–1.5 m)	2–3 ft (0.6–0.9 m)	P	W/T	NA	◆	◆		W/Sp	Su				◆	◆
Stylidium graminifolium	10–20 in (25–50 cm)	10 in (25 cm)	P	W	NA	◆			W/Sp	Su	◆		◆		
Stylidium lineare	6–12 in (15–30 cm)	4 in (10 cm)	P	W	NA	◆			W/Sp	Su/A	◆		◆		
Stylophorum diphyllum	18 in (45 cm)	12 in (30 cm)	P	C	NA	◆	◆		A–Sp	Sp		◆			◆

Plant name	Height	Spread	Type	Climate	Group	Showy flowers	Showy foliage	Scented flowers	Planting season	Flowering season	Grow in pot/tub	Frost tolerant	Full Sun	Half Sun	Heavy shade
Stylophorum lasiocarpum	12 in (30 cm)	12 in (30 cm)	P	C	NA	◆	◆		A–Sp	Sp		◆			◆
Sutera cordata	3 in (8 cm)	20 in (50 cm)	P	W	NA	◆			Sp	All	◆		◆		
Sutera grandiflora	40 in (100 cm)	24 in (60 cm)	P	W	NA	◆			Sp	Su/A	◆		◆		
Swainsona formosa	3–4 ft (0.9–1.2 m)	3–7 ft (0.9–2 m)	P	W	NA	◆			W/Sp	W–Su			◆		
Swainsona galegifolia	2 ft (0.6 m)	6 ft (1.8 m)	P	W	NA	◆			W/Sp	Sp/Su			◆		
Symphyandra hofmannii	12–24 in (30–60 cm)	6–12 in (15–30 cm)	P	C	NA				W/Sp	Su		◆	◆	◆	
Symphytum asperum	4–5 ft (1.2–1.5 m)	5–7 ft (1.5–2 m)	P	C/W	NA	◆	◆		W/Sp	Su		◆	◆		
Symphytum caucasicum	24–32 in (60–80 cm)	24–32 in (60–80 cm)	P	C/W	NA	◆	◆		W/Sp	Su		◆	◆		
Symphytum 'Goldsmith'	10–12 in (25–30 cm)	12–20 in (30–50 cm)	P	C/W	NA	◆	◆		W/Sp	Sp/Su		◆	◆	◆	
Symphytum grandiflorum	15–16 in (38–40 cm)	20–24 in (50–60 cm)	P	C/W	NA	◆	◆		W/Sp	Sp/Su		◆	◆		
Symphytum 'Hidcote Blue'	18–20 in (45–50 cm)	18–20 in (45–50 cm)	P	C/W	NA	◆	◆		W/Sp	Sp/Su		◆	◆		
Symphytum ibericum	16 in (40 cm)	12 in (30 cm)	P	C/W	NA	◆			W/Sp	Sp/Su		◆	◆	◆	
Synthyris missurica	16–24 in (40–60 cm)	12 in (30 cm)	P	C	NA			◆	W/Sp	Sp/Su		◆		◆	◆
Synthyris reniformis	2–6 in (5–15 cm)	4 in (10 cm)	P	C	NA			◆	W/Sp	Sp/Su		◆		◆	◆
Tacca integrifolia	24–48 in (60–120 cm)	24 in (60 cm)	P	W/T	NA	◆	◆		A/W	Sp/Su	◆		◆		
Tagetes lucida	16–40 in (40–100 cm)	16–32 in (40–80 cm)	P	W/T	NA	◆			Sp	Su	◆		◆	◆	
Tagetes patula	8–20 in (20–50 cm)	6–12 in (15–30 cm)	A	W	NA	◆			Sp	Su/A	◆		◆		
Tagetes tenuifolia	12–32 in (30–80 cm)	12–24 in (30–60 cm)	A	W	NA	◆			Sp	Su/A	◆		◆		
Tagetes Hybrid Cultivars	8–12 in (20–30 cm)	6–12 in (15–30 cm)	A	W	NA	◆			Sp	Sp–A	◆		◆		
Talinum paniculatum	40 in (100 cm)	16–20 in (40–50 cm)	P	W	NA	◆			W/Sp	Sp/Su			◆	◆	
Tanacetum balsamita	36 in (90 cm)	18 in (45 cm)	P	C/W	NA	◆	◆		Sp	Su/A		◆	◆		
Tanacetum camphoratum	27 in (70 cm)	20 in (50 cm)	P	W	NA	◆	◆		Sp	Su/A		◆	◆		
Tanacetum coccineum	18–30 in (45–75 cm)	18 in (45 cm)	P	C/W	NA	◆			Sp	Su/A		◆	◆		
Tanacetum corymbosum	36 in (90 cm)	18 in (45 cm)	P	C/W	NA	◆			Sp	Su/A		◆	◆		
Tanacetum niveum	36 in (90 cm)	24 in (60 cm)	P	C/W	NA	◆	◆		Sp	Sp/Su		◆	◆		
Tapeinochilos ananassae	5–7 ft (1.5–2 m)	2–3 ft (0.6–0.9 m)	P	W/T	NA	◆			W/Sp	Su					◆
Telekia speciosa	4–6 ft (1.2–1.8 m)	4–6 ft (1.2–1.8 m)	P	C	NA	◆		◆	W/Sp	Su		◆		◆	
Tellima grandiflora	24 in (60 cm)	24 in (60 cm)	P	C/W	NA	◆	◆		A–Sp	Su		◆			◆
Teucrium chamaedrys	12–24 in (30–60 cm)	24–36 in (60–90 cm)	P	C/W	NA	◆			W/Sp	Su		◆	◆		
Teucrium cossonii	8 in (20 cm)	24 in (60 cm)	P	W	NA	◆			W/Sp	Sp–A		◆	◆		
Teucrium hircanicum	24 in (60 cm)	24 in (60 cm)	P	C/W	NA	◆			W/Sp	Su/A		◆	◆		

Plant name	Height	Spread	Type	Climate	Group	Showy flowers	Showy foliage	Scented flowers	Planting season	Flowering season	Grow in pot/tub	Frost tolerant	Full Sun	Half Sun	Heavy shade
Teucrium polium	4–16 in (10–40 cm)	6–12 in (15–30 cm)	P	C/W	NA	◆			W/Sp	Su		◆	◆		
Teucrium scorodonia	24 in (60 cm)	18 in (45 cm)	P	C/W	NA	◆	◆		W/Sp	Su/A		◆	◆	◆	
Thalia dealbata	3–6 ft (0.9–1.8 m)	20–30 in (50–75 cm)	P	W	NA	◆	◆		W/Sp	Su/A			◆		
Thalictrum aquilegiifolium	60 in (150 cm)	20–40 in (50–100 cm)	P	C/W	NA	◆	◆		W/Sp	Su		◆	◆	◆	
Thalictrum delavayi	4–5 ft (1.2–1.5 m)	16–24 in (40–60 cm)	P	C/W	NA	◆	◆		W/Sp	Su		◆	◆	◆	
Thalictrum dioicum	12–30 in (30–75 cm)	12–16 in (30–40 cm)	P	C/W	NA	◆	◆		W/Sp	Su		◆		◆	◆
Thalictrum flavum	40 in (100 cm)	16–20 in (40–50 cm)	P	C/W	NA	◆	◆		W/Sp	Su		◆	◆	◆	
Thalictrum kiusianum	6–12 in (15–30 cm)	12–20 in (30–50 cm)	P	C/W	NA	◆	◆		W/Sp	Su		◆		◆	
Thalictrum minus	3–5 ft (0.9–1.5 m)	20–32 in (50–80 cm)	P	C/W	NA	◆	◆		W/Sp	Su		◆	◆	◆	
Thalictrum rochebruneanum	40 in (100 cm)	16–20 in (40–50 cm)	P	C/W	NA	◆	◆		W/Sp	Su		◆	◆	◆	
Thermopsis rhombifolia	36 in (90cm)	24 in (60 cm)	P	C/W	NA	◆			W/Sp	Sp/Su		◆	◆		
Thermopsis villosa	3–5 ft (0.9–1.5 m)	2 ft (0.6 m)	P	C/W	NA	◆			W/Sp	Sp/Su		◆	◆	◆	
Thymus caespititius	2 in (5 cm)	15 in (38 cm)	P	C/W	NA	◆			W/Sp	Sp		◆	◆		
Thymus × citriodorus	6–12 in (15–30 cm)	24 in (60 cm)	P	C/W	NA	◆	◆		W/Sp	Su		◆	◆		
Thymus Coccineus Group	3–4 in (8–10 cm)	14 in (35 cm)	P	C/W	NA	◆			W/Sp	Su		◆	◆		
Thymus herba-barona	4 in (10 cm)	24 in (60 cm)	P	C/W	NA	◆			W/Sp	Su		◆	◆		
Thymus mastichina	6–12 in (15–30 cm)	16 in (40 cm)	P	C/W	NA	◆			W/Sp	Su		◆	◆		
Thymus polytrichus	2 in (5 cm)	24 in (60 cm)	P	C/W	NA	◆			W/Sp	Su		◆	◆		
Thymus pseudolanuginosus	1–3 in (2.5–8 cm)	24 in (60 cm)	P	C/W	NA	◆	◆		W/Sp	Su		◆	◆		
Tiarella cordifolia	12 in (30 cm)	16–20 in (40–50 cm)	P	C	NA	◆			W/Sp	Su		◆		◆	◆
Tiarella polyphylla	12–18 in (30–45 cm)	16–20 in (40–50 cm)	P	C	NA	◆			W/Sp	Sp/Su		◆		◆	◆
Tiarella wherryi	8–12 in (20–30 cm)	16–20 in (40–50 cm)	P	C	NA	◆	◆		W/Sp	Su		◆		◆	◆
Tiarella Hybrid Cultivars	12–18 in (30–45 cm)	16–20 in (40–50 cm)	P	C	NA	◆	◆		W/Sp	Su		◆		◆	◆
Tillandsia aeranthos	6 in (15 cm)	6 in (15 cm)	P	W/T	B	◆			W/Sp	Su					◆
Tillandsia bergeri	6 in (15 cm)	6 in (15 cm)	P	W/T	B	◆			W/Sp	Su					◆
Tillandsia butzii	12 in (30 cm)	4 in (10 cm)	P	W/T	B	◆	◆		W/Sp	Su					◆
Tillandsia crocata	8 in (20 cm)	6 in (15 cm)	P	W/T	B	◆	◆	◆	W/Sp	Su					◆
Tillandsia cyanea	10 in (25 cm)	10 in (25 cm)	P	W/T	B	◆		◆	W/Sp	Su					◆
Tillandsia dyeriana	6 in (15 cm)	6 in (15 cm)	P	W/T	B	◆			W/Sp	Su					◆
Tillandsia fasciculata	40 in (100 cm)	20 in (50 cm)	P	W/T	B	◆			W/Sp	Su					◆
Tillandsia fuchsii	8 in (20 cm)	4 in (10 cm)	P	W/T	B	◆			W/Sp	Su					◆

Plant name	Height	Spread	Type	Climate	Group	Showy flowers	Showy foliage	Scented flowers	Planting season	Flowering season	Grow in pot/tub	Frost tolerant	Full Sun	Half Sun	Heavy shade
Tillandsia imperialis	20 in (50 cm)	16 in (40 cm)	P	W/T	B	♦	♦		W/Sp	Su					♦
Tillandsia ionantha	2 in (5 cm)	3 in (8 cm)	P	W/T	B		♦		W/Sp	Su					♦
Tillandsia leiboldiana	24 in (60 cm)	10 in (25 cm)	P	W/T	B	♦	♦		W/Sp	Su					♦
Tillandsia lindenii	27 in (70 cm)	16 in (40 cm)	P	W/T	B	♦	♦	♦	W/Sp	Su					♦
Tillandsia magnusiana	6 in (15 cm)	6 in (15 cm)	P	W/T	B	♦			W/Sp	Su					♦
Tillandsia recurvata	4 in (10 cm)	2½–8 in (6–20 cm)	P	W/T	B	♦			W/Sp	Su				♦	
Tillandsia streptophylla	18 in (45 cm)	8 in (20 cm)	P	W/T	B	♦			W/Sp	Su					♦
Tillandsia stricta	8 in (20 cm)	6 in (15 cm)	P	W/T	B	♦			W/Sp	Su					♦
Tillandsia tectorum	20 in (50 cm)	12 in (30 cm)	P	W/T	B	♦	♦		W/Sp	Su					♦
Tillandsia tenuifolia	6 in (15 cm)	6 in (15 cm)	P	W/T	B	♦			W/Sp	Su					♦
Tillandsia usneoides	24 in (60 cm)	4 in (10 cm)	P	W/T	B		♦	♦	W/Sp	Su					♦
Tillandsia Hybrid Cultivars	4–36 in (10–90 cm)	4–24 in (10–60 cm)	P	W/T	B	♦	♦	♦	W/Sp	Su					♦
Tithonia rotundifolia	3–6 ft (0.9–1.8 m)	2 ft (0.6 m)	A	W	NA	♦			Sp	Su/A			♦		
Tolmiea menziesii	18–24 in (45–60 cm)	3–6 ft (0.9–1.8 m)	P	C/W	NA		♦		Any	Sp/Su	♦	♦			♦
Torenia fournieri	12 in (30 cm)	10 in (25 cm)	A	W/T	NA	♦			Sp	Sp/Su	♦			♦	♦
Torenia Hybrid Cultivars	12–15 in (30–38 cm)	10 in (25 cm)	A	W/T	NA	♦			Sp	Sp–A	♦			♦	♦
Townsendia formosa	12–16 in (30–40 cm)	10–12 in (25–30 cm)	P	C/W	NA	♦			W/Sp	Su		♦	♦		
Townsendia parryi	10–15 in (25–38 cm)	10–15 in (25–38 cm)	B/P	C	NA	♦			W/Sp	Su		♦	♦		
Trachelium caeruleum	24–36 in (60–90 cm)	18 in (45 cm)	P	W	NA	♦			Sp	Su			♦		
Trachystemon orientalis	2–3 ft (0.6–0.9 m)	3–7 ft (0.9–2 m)	P	C/W	NA	♦	♦		W/Sp	W/Sp		♦			♦
Tradescantia Andersoniana Group	8–20 in (20–50 cm)	12–48 in (30–120 cm)	P	C/W	NA	♦	♦		W/Sp	Sp–A		♦		♦	
Tradescantia fluminensis	12–20 in (30–50 cm)	24–60 in (60–150 cm)	P	W	NA	♦	♦		W/Sp	Su				♦	♦
Tradescantia spathacea	15 in (38 cm)	12–16 in (30–40 cm)	P	W/T	NA		♦		W/Sp	Any	♦			♦	♦
Tradescantia virginiana	12–20 in (30–50 cm)	20–48 in (50–120 cm)	P	C/W	NA	♦			W/Sp	Su		♦		♦	
Tradescantia zanonia	24–40 in (60–100 cm)	5 ft (1.5 m)	P	W/T	NA	♦	♦		W/Sp	Su–W				♦	♦
Trichostema lanatum	2–5 ft (0.6–1.5 m)	2 ft (0.6 m)	P	W	NA	♦			A/Sp	Sp/Su		♦	♦		
Tricyrtis formosana	36 in (90 cm)	18 in (45 cm)	P	C	NA	♦			Sp	Su/A		♦			♦
Tricyrtis hirta	36 in (90 cm)	24 in (60 cm)	P	C	NA	♦			W/Sp	A		♦			♦
Tricyrtis macrantha	30 in (75 cm)	24 in (60 cm)	P	C	NA	♦			Sp	A		♦			♦
Tricyrtis macropoda	30 in (75 cm)	24 in (60 cm)	P	C	NA	♦			Sp	Su		♦			♦
Trifolium pannonicum	8 in (20 cm)	8 in (20 cm)	P	C	NA	♦	♦		W/Sp	Su		♦	♦	♦	

Plant name	Height	Spread	Type	Climate	Group	Showy flowers	Showy foliage	Scented flowers	Planting season	Flowering season	Grow in pot/tub	Frost tolerant	Full Sun	Half Sun	Heavy shade
Trifolium repens	2 in (5 cm)	8–16 in (20–40 cm)	P	C/W	NA	◆	◆	◆	W/Sp	Su		◆	◆	◆	
Trifolium rubens	12–24 in (30–60 cm)	18–24 in (45–60 cm)	P	C/W	NA	◆	◆		W/Sp	Su		◆	◆	◆	
Trifolium uniflorum	2–4 in (5–10 cm)	8–16 in (20–40 cm)	P	C/W	NA	◆			W/Sp	Sp/Su		◆	◆	◆	
Trillium chloropetalum	20 in (50 cm)	20 in (50 cm)	P	C	NA	◆	◆	◆	A/W	Sp		◆		◆	◆
Trillium cuneatum	24 in (60 cm)	16 in (40 cm)	P	C	NA	◆	◆	◆	A/W	Sp		◆		◆	◆
Trillium erectum	20 in (50 cm)	20 in (50 cm)	P	C	NA	◆	◆		A/W	Sp		◆		◆	◆
Trillium grandiflorum	18 in (45 cm)	20 in (50 cm)	P	C	NA	◆	◆		A/W	Su		◆		◆	◆
Trillium luteum	18 in (45 cm)	18 in (45 cm)	P	C	NA	◆	◆	◆	A/W	Sp		◆		◆	◆
Trillium ovatum	20 in (50 cm)	20 in (50 cm)	P	C	NA			◆	A/W	Sp		◆		◆	◆
Trillium sessile	12 in (30 cm)	12–16 in (30–40 cm)	P	C	NA	◆	◆	◆	A/W	Sp		◆		◆	◆
Trollius chinensis	36 in (90 cm)	18 in (45 cm)	P	C	NA	◆			W/Sp	Su		◆	◆	◆	
Trollius × cultorum	24–36 in (60–90 cm)	18 in (45 cm)	P	C	NA	◆			W/Sp	Su		◆	◆	◆	
Tropaeolum ciliatum	20 ft (6 m)	20 ft (6 m)	P	W	NA	◆	◆		W/Sp	Su		◆		◆	
Tropaeolum peregrinum	8 ft (2.4 m)	8 ft (2.4 m)	P	W	NA	◆	◆		W/Sp	Su/A			◆	◆	
Utricularia alpina	12 in (30 cm)	6 in (15 cm)	P	W	C	◆			W/Sp	Sp/Su	◆			◆	
Utricularia bisquamata	2 in (5 cm)	3 in (8 cm)	P	W	C	◆			W/Sp	Sp/Su	◆			◆	
Utricularia calycifida	6 in (15 cm)	4 in (10 cm)	P	W	C	◆			W/Sp	Sp/Su	◆			◆	
Utricularia dichotoma	6–18 in (15–45 cm)	8 in (20 cm)	P	W	C	◆			W/Sp	Sp/Su	◆			◆	
Utricularia inflata	12 in (30 cm)	12 in (30 cm)	P	W/T	C	◆			W/Sp	Sp/Su				◆	
Utricularia menziesii	3 in (8 cm)	2 in (5 cm)	P	W	C	◆			W/Sp	Sp/Su	◆			◆	
Utricularia praelonga	18 in (45 cm)	12 in (30 cm)	P	W/T	C	◆			W/Sp	Sp/Su	◆			◆	
Utricularia reniformis	18 in (45 cm)	18 in (45 cm)	P	W/T	C	◆	◆		W/Sp	Sp/Su	◆			◆	
Utricularia uniflora	8 in (20 cm)	3 in (8 cm)	P	W	C	◆			W/Sp	Sp/Su	◆			◆	
Uvularia grandiflora	12–24 in (30–60 cm)	12–24 in (30–60 cm)	P	C/W	NA	◆	◆		Sp–A	Sp/Su		◆			◆
Uvularia perfoliata	16 in (40 cm)	12–18 in (30–45 cm)	P	C/W	NA	◆	◆		Sp–A	Sp/Su		◆			◆
Valeriana montana	10 in (25 cm)	10 in (25 cm)	P	C	NA	◆			A/Sp	Su		◆		◆	
Valeriana phu	36 in (90 cm)	18 in (45 cm)	P	C	NA		◆		A/Sp	Su		◆	◆		
Vancouveria chrysantha	12 in (30 cm)	12 in (30 cm)	P	C	NA	◆	◆		A–Sp	Su		◆	◆	◆	
Vancouveria hexandra	12 in (30 cm)	12 in (30 cm)	P	C	NA	◆	◆		A–Sp	Sp/Su		◆	◆	◆	
Veratrum album	24 in (60 cm)	24 in (60 cm)	P	C/W	NA	◆	◆		A/Sp	Su		◆		◆	
Veratrum nigrum	24–48 in (60–120 cm)	24 in (60 cm)	P	C/W	NA	◆	◆		A/Sp	Su		◆		◆	

Plant name	Height	Spread	Type	Climate	Group	Showy flowers	Showy foliage	Scented flowers	Planting season	Flowering season	Grow in pot/tub	Frost tolerant	Full Sun	Half Sun	Heavy shade
Verbascum acaule	4 in (10 cm)	4 in (10 cm)	P	C/W	NA	◆			W/Sp	Sp–A	◆	◆	◆	◆	
Verbascum blattaria	5–6 ft (1.5–1.8 m)	12–20 in (30–50 cm)	B	C/W	NA	◆			W/Sp	Su/A		◆	◆	◆	
Verbascum bombyciferum	6–8 ft (1.8–2.4 m)	24–40 in (60–100 cm)	B	C/W	NA	◆	◆		W/Sp	Su		◆	◆	◆	
Verbascum chaixii	36–48 in (90–120 cm)	12–24 in (30–60 cm)	P	C/W	NA	◆			W/Sp	Su		◆	◆	◆	
Verbascum dumulosum	8 in (20 cm)	12–16 in (30–40 cm)	P	W	NA	◆	◆		W/Sp			◆	◆	◆	
Verbascum olympicum	5–6 ft (1.5–1.8 m)	20–40 in (50–100 cm)	B/P	C/W	NA	◆	◆		W/Sp	Su		◆	◆	◆	
Verbascum phoeniceum	8–16 in (20–40 cm)	12–16 in (30–40 cm)	B/P	C/W	NA	◆			W/Sp	Su		◆	◆	◆	
Verbascum thapsus	6–7 ft (1.8–2 m)	20–32 in (50–80 cm)	B	C/W	NA	◆			W/Sp	Su		◆	◆	◆	
Verbascum Hybrid Cultivars	12–60 in (30–150 cm)	12–20 in (30–50 cm)	P	C/W	NA	◆		◆	W/Sp	Sp–A		◆	◆	◆	
Verbena bonariensis	3–5 ft (0.9–1.5 m)	24 in (60 cm)	A/P	C/W	NA	◆			Sp	Sp–A			◆	◆	
Verbena canadensis	8 in (20 cm)	16 in (40 cm)	P	C	NA	◆			W/Sp	Sp–A			◆	◆	
Verbena rigida	24–36 in (60–90 cm)	12 in (30 cm)	P	W	NA	◆			W/Sp	Su			◆	◆	
Verbena tenera	12–20 in (30–50 cm)	12–20 in (30–50 cm)	P	W	NA	◆			W/Sp	Su			◆		
Verbena tenuisecta	12–20 in (30–50 cm)	12–20 in (30–50 cm)	A/P	W	NA	◆			W/Sp	Su			◆		
Verbena Hybrid Cultivars	12–24 in (30–60 cm)	24–40 in (60–100 cm)	P	C	NA	◆			W/Sp	Su/A	◆	◆	◆		
Veronica alpina	2–6 in (5–15 cm)	8–16 in (20–40 cm)	P	C	NA	◆			W/Sp	Sp/Su		◆	◆	◆	
Veronica austriaca	6–16 in (15–40 cm)	10–24 in (25–60 cm)	P	C/W	NA	◆			W/Sp	Sp/Su	◆	◆	◆	◆	
Veronica beccabunga	4–6 in (10–15 cm)	8–20 in (20–50 cm)	P	C	NA	◆			W/Sp	Su			◆	◆	
Veronica chamaedrys	6–10 in (15–25 cm)	12–20 in (30–50 cm)	P	C	NA	◆			W/Sp	Sp/Su		◆	◆	◆	
Veronica cinerea	2–4 in (5–10 cm)	6–10 in (15–25 cm)	P	C/W	NA	◆			W/Sp	Su		◆	◆	◆	
Veronica gentianoides	12–24 in (30–60 cm)	12–24 in (30–60 cm)	P	C	NA	◆			W/Sp	Sp/Su		◆	◆	◆	
Veronica longifolia	20–48 in (50–120 cm)	16–30 in (40–75 cm)	P	C	NA	◆			W/Sp	Su/A		◆	◆	◆	
Veronica pectinata	2–8 in (5–20 cm)	12–16 in (30–40 cm)	P	C	NA	◆			W/Sp	Sp/Su		◆	◆	◆	
Veronica petraea	4–6 in (10–15 cm)	8–12 in (20–30 cm)	P	C	NA	◆			W/Sp	Su/A		◆	◆	◆	
Veronica prostrata	2–4 in (5–10 cm)	8–16 in (20–40 cm)	P	C	NA	◆			W/Sp	Sp/Su		◆	◆	◆	
Veronica spicata	12–24 in (30–60 cm)	12–32 in (30–80 cm)	P	C	NA	◆			W/Sp	Su	◆	◆	◆	◆	
Veronica wormskjoldii	4–12 in (10–30 cm)	8–20 in (20–50 cm)	P	C	NA	◆			W/Sp	Su		◆	◆	◆	
Veronicastrum virginicum	2–6 ft (0.6–1.8 m)	1–3 ft (0.3–0.9 m)	P	C	NA	◆			W/Sp	Su			◆	◆	
Victoria amazonica	10–12 in (25–30 cm)	15–20 ft (4.5–6 m)	P	W/T	NA	◆	◆	◆	W/Sp	Su/A			◆		
Victoria 'Longwood Hybrid'	10–12 in (25–30 cm)	12–40 ft (3.5–12 m)	P	W/T	NA	◆	◆	◆	W/Sp	Su/A			◆		
Viguiera multiflora	30–40 in (75–100 cm)	30–40 in (75–100 cm)	P	W/T	NA	◆			W/Sp	Su			◆		

Plant name	Height	Spread	Type	Climate	Group	Showy flowers	Showy foliage	Scented flowers	Planting season	Flowering season	Grow in pot/tub	Frost tolerant	Full Sun	Half Sun	Heavy shade
Vinca difformis	12 in (30 cm)	5–10 ft (1.5–3 m)	P	C/W	NA	◆			W/Sp	Sp		◆	◆	◆	◆
Vinca major	18 in (45 cm)	5–10 ft (1.5–3 m)	P	C/W	NA	◆	◆		W/Sp	Sp–A		◆	◆	◆	◆
Vinca minor	8 in (20 cm)	5–10 ft (1.5–3 m)	P	C/W	NA	◆	◆		W/Sp	Sp–A	◆	◆	◆	◆	◆
Viola adunca	2–4 in (5–10 cm)	12–16 in (30–40 cm)	P	C	NA	◆			W/Sp	Sp		◆		◆	◆
Viola blanda	3–6 in (8–15 cm)	12–20 in (30–50 cm)	P	C	NA	◆	◆		W/Sp	Sp		◆		◆	◆
Viola canina	4–12 in (10–30 cm)	12–20 in (30–50 cm)	P	C	NA	◆	◆		W/Sp	Su		◆		◆	
Viola cornuta	6–12 in (15–30 cm)	8–14 in (20–35 cm)	A/P	C/W	NA	◆			W/Sp	Sp/Su		◆	◆	◆	
Viola cucullata	4–6 in (10–15 cm)	8–16 in (20–40 cm)	P	C	NA	◆	◆		W/Sp	Sp/Su		◆	◆	◆	
Viola hederacea	2–3 in (5–8 cm)	6–12 in (15–30 cm)	P	W	NA	◆			W/Sp	Sp–A			◆	◆	◆
Viola jooi	2–4 in (5–10 cm)	8–14 in (20–35 cm)	P	C/W	NA	◆	◆		W/Sp	Sp/Su		◆	◆	◆	
Viola odorata	4–6 in (10–15 cm)	12–24 in (30–60 cm)	P	C/W	NA	◆	◆	◆	W/Sp	Sp/Su	◆	◆		◆	◆
Viola pedata	4–6 in (10–15 cm)	8–16 in (20–40 cm)	P	C	NA	◆	◆		W/Sp	Sp		◆		◆	
Viola riviniana	4–6 in (10–15 cm)	8–24 in (20–60 cm)	P	C	NA	◆	◆		W/Sp	Sp/Su		◆		◆	◆
Viola septentrionalis	4–6 in (10–15 cm)	6–16 in (15–40 cm)	P	C	NA	◆	◆		W/Sp	Sp/Su		◆		◆	◆
Viola sororia	2–6 in (5–15 cm)	6–16 in (15–40 cm)	P	C	NA	◆	◆		W/Sp	Sp/Su	◆	◆		◆	◆
Viola tricolor	4–14 in (10–35 cm)	6–16 in (15–40 cm)	A/B/P	C/W	NA	◆			W/Sp	Sp/Su	◆	◆	◆	◆	◆
Viola Hybrid Cultivars	6–12 in (15–30 cm)	8–16 in (20–40 cm)	A/P	C/W	NA	◆			W/Sp	W–Su	◆	◆	◆	◆	
Vriesea carinata	14 in (35 cm)	12 in (30 cm)	P	W/T	B	◆	◆		W/Sp	Sp/Su					◆
Vriesea erythrodactylon	16 in (40 cm)	16 in (40 cm)	P	W/T	B	◆	◆		W/Sp	Sp/Su					◆
Vriesea fenestralis	40 in (100 cm)	27 in (70 cm)	P	W/T	B	◆	◆		W/Sp	Sp/Su	◆				◆
Vriesea fosteriana	60 in (150 cm)	40 in (100 cm)	P	W/T	B	◆	◆		W/Sp	Sp/Su					◆
Vriesea malzinei	32 in (80 cm)	16 in (40 cm)	P	W/T	B	◆	◆		W/Sp	Sp/Su					◆
Vriesea saundersii	24 in (60 cm)	16 in (40 cm)	P	W/T	B	◆	◆		W/Sp	Sp/Su	◆				
Vriesea splendens	40 in (100 cm)	20 in (50 cm)	P	W/T	B	◆	◆		W/Sp	Sp/Su					◆
Vriesea Hybrid Cultivars	16–36 in (40–90 cm)	8–20 in (20–50 cm)	P	W/T	B	◆	◆		W/Sp	Sp/Su	◆				◆
Wachendorfia thyrsiflora	4–7 ft (1.2–2 m)	2–4 ft (0.6–1.2 m)	P	W	NA		◆		W/Sp	Su			◆		
Waldsteinia fragarioides	2 in (5 cm)	12–20 in (30–50 cm)	P	C	NA	◆	◆		W/Sp	Sp		◆	◆	◆	
Waldsteinia ternata	6 in (15 cm)	24 in (60 cm)	P	C	NA	◆	◆		W/Sp	Sp/Su				◆	
Wittrockia superba	16 in (40 cm)	55 in (140 cm)	P	W/T	B	◆	◆		W/Sp	Sp/Su	◆				◆
Xanthorrhoea australis	3 ft (0.9 m)	3 ft (0.9 m)	P	W	NA	◆	◆	◆	A/Sp	Sp			◆		
Xanthorrhoea glauca	20 ft (6 m)	3 ft (0.9 m)	P	W	NA	◆	◆	◆	A/Sp	Sp			◆		

Plant name	Height	Spread	Type	Climate	Group	Showy flowers	Showy foliage	Scented flowers	Planting season	Flowering season	Grow in pot/tub	Frost tolerant	Full Sun	Half Sun	Heavy shade
Xanthorrhoea johnsonii	7 ft (2 m)	3 ft (0.9 m)	P	W	NA	◆	◆	◆	A/Sp	Sp			◆		
Xanthorrhoea quadrangulata	7–10 ft (2–3 m)	4–7 ft (1.2–2 m)	P	W	NA	◆	◆	◆	A/Sp	A			◆		
Xanthosoma undipes	7–10 ft (2–3 m)	7–10 ft (2–3 m)	P	W/T	NA	◆	◆		W/Sp	Sp/Su			◆		
Xeranthemum annuum	10–36 in (25–90 cm)	10–36 in (25–90 cm)	A	C/W	NA	◆			Sp	Su/A		◆	◆		
Xerochrysum bracteatum	36 in (90 cm)	16 in (40 cm)	A/P	W	NA	◆			Sp	Su	◆	◆	◆		
Zaluzianskya ovata	8–10 in (20–25 cm)	20–24 in (50–60 cm)	P	W	NA	◆			W/Sp	Su/A	◆		◆		
Zingiber spectabile	5–7 ft (1.5–2 m)	3 ft (0.9 m)	P	W/T	NA	◆	◆		W/Sp	Su			◆		
Zingiber zerumbet	6–8 ft (1.8–2.4 m)	3 ft (0.9 m)	P	W/T	NA	◆	◆		W/Sp	Su		◆	◆		
Zinnia angustifolia	8–16 in (20–40 cm)	12–20 in (30–50 cm)	A	W	NA	◆			Sp	Su	◆		◆		
Zinnia elegans	8–40 in (20–100 cm)	8–18 in (20–45 cm)	A	W	NA	◆			Sp	Su	◆		◆		
Zinnia haageana	24 in (60 cm)	12–24 in (30–60 cm)	A	W	NA	◆			Sp	Su	◆		◆	◆	

ABELMOSCHUS

This genus belonging to the mallow (Malvaceae) family consists of about 15 species of annuals, perennials, and soft-wooded shrubs native to warmer parts of Asia and Africa. Allied to *Hibiscus*, its flowers have a single bract wrapping around the base of the sepals, splitting down one side as the flower expands. Leaves are usually maple-like or divided into finger-like lobes. Flowers are often showy, in shades of pink, red, or yellow, and are followed by elongated pods. *Abelmoschus esculentus* is grown as a vegetable (okra). The leafy young shoots of most species can be used as pot greens.

CULTIVATION: These plants do best in a sunny sheltered position and well-drained soil, fertilized in summer. Propagate from basal cuttings or seed sown in late spring.

Abelmoschus manihot
syn. *Hibiscus manihot*
AIBIKA
☼ ❄ ↔ 3 ft (0.9 m) ↕ 3–6 ft (0.9–1.8 m)
Shrubby Southeast Asian perennial. Large, deeply lobed leaves. Pale yellow flowers with a dark purplish eye appear at the branch tips, in summer. Zones 8–12.

Abelmoschus moschatus
syn. *Hibiscus abelmoschus*
MUSKMALLOW
☼ ☇ ↔ 30 in (75 cm) ↕ 4–6 ft (1.2–1.8 m)
Variable species from tropical Asia to northern Australia. Stems and leaves bear bristly hairs; leaf lobes triangular. Flowers white, pink, or yellow, with a dark eye, in summer. Ornamental strains grown as annuals. **'Mischief'** and **'Oriental Pink'**, colorful cultivars. The **Pacific Series**, scarlet and pink flowers. Zones 10–12.

ACAENA
BIDDY BIDDY, NEW ZEALAND BURR, SHEEP'S BURRS
This genus of creeping perennials and evergreen subshrubs is a member of the rose (Rosaceae) family. It contains about 100 species native to California and Hawaii, USA, Central and South America, Australia, and New Zealand, often found growing in mountainous areas. The leaves are small and often fern-like, bright green to grayish blue and bronze-purple. Tiny spherical to spike-like flowerheads are held above the foliage, and the spiny burrs that follow are very ornamental in some species. They are ideal as ground cover plants and for growing over walls.

CULTIVATION: These grow readily in poor soil but must be well drained. They prefer full sun but tolerate light shade. Most are hardy but they may be deciduous in areas with prolonged frosts. Propagate from rooted stem pieces or seed in autumn and spring.

Acaena caesiiglauca
☼ ❄ ↔ 32 in (80 cm) ↕ 2 in (5 cm)
A New Zealand species with small pinnately divided leaves of bluish gray, silky beneath. Small white flowerheads are held well above the foliage, followed by brown spiny burrs. Zones 6–10.

Acaena microphylla
☼ ❄ ↔ 20 in (50 cm) ↕ 2 in (5 cm)
From New Zealand's North Island, this ground-hugging species has fine ferny foliage of green or bronze. The tiny cream flowers are followed by eye-catching, spiny, red burrs in late summer. **'Kupferteppich'** (syn. *A. m.* 'Copper Carpet') has green to bronze leaves. Zones 6–10.

Abelmoschus moschatus 'Oriental Pink'

ACANTHUS
BEAR'S BREECHES
From the acanthus (Acanthaceae) family, this genus includes 30 species of perennials and shrubs from the temperate and tropical Old World regions. Cultivated species are valued for their bold, often near-evergreen foliage and upright flower spikes. The leaves, which form a basal clump, are usually large, glossy, and pinnately lobed, lobes toothed or spiny. The flowers are tubular, tend to be mauve and white, and partially enclosed within conspicuous bracts. Large seed pods follow.

CULTIVATION: Species are mostly cold tolerant but prefer mild winters. Plant in moist, well-drained, humus-rich soil. Many have heavy roots and divide easily, otherwise raise from spring-sown seed. May self-sow freely and can sucker.

Acanthus mollis
BEAR'S BREECHES
☼/◐ ❄ ↔ 40–60 in (100–150 cm) ↕ 7 ft (2 m)
From southern Europe and northwest Africa. Deep green, deeply toothed, soft-spined, pinnate or doubly pinnate leaves up to 36 in (90 cm) long. White flowers flushed pale purple in toothed mauve bracts on stems up to 2 m (7 ft) tall. **'Candelabrum'**, large-lobed flowers on sometimes branching stems. Zones 6–10.

Acanthus spinosus
☼/◐ ❄ ↔ 40–60 in (100–150 cm) ↕ 36 in (90 cm)
Found around the Mediterranean. Similar to *Acanthus mollis* but with leaves more deeply divided, broader and spinier. White,

Acanthus spinosus 'Lady Moore'

sometimes mauve-tinted flowers in spiny bracts. 'Lady Moore', variegated leaves and purple and white flowers. Zones 6–10.

ACHILLEA

MILFOIL, YARROW

This genus of about 100 species of clumping or mat-forming perennial plants is a member of the large daisy (Asteraceae) family. They are found throughout Europe and northern and western Asia in a range of habitats, including alpine. Some can be invasive. The foliage is usually finely divided with a fern-like appearance and is often aromatic. Usually grouped in flat corymbs, the small flowerheads are white and pale cream, lemon, and pink, with many cultivars in brighter colors.
CULTIVATION: Most yarrows can easily be grown in well-drained soil in full sun. They can tolerate quite poor conditions and are frost hardy to 5°F (−15°C). Alpine species require perfect drainage and protection from winter rain if downy-leafed. Propagation is by division or from seed.

Achillea filipendulina

☼ ❋ ↔ 24–48 in (60–120 cm) ↕ 24–48 in (60–120 cm)
Robust species from central and western Asia. Divided, hairy, aromatic leaves to 8 in (20 cm) long. Tiny gold flowers crowded in flattened flowerheads, to 4 in (10 cm) across, in summer. 'Cloth of Gold', 'Gold Plate', and 'Parker's Variety' are improved cultivars 4–6 ft (1.2–1.8 m) high with bright golden flowerheads up to 6 in (15 cm) across. 'Schwellenburg', about 18 in (45 cm) high with lemon yellow flowers. Zones 5–10.

Achillea millefolium

MILFOIL, YARROW

☼ ❋ ↔ 18–30 in (45–75 cm) ↕ 12–30 in (30–75 cm)
Weedy species from western Asia and Europe. Naturalized in temperate regions, too invasive for most gardens. Fern-like leaves. Flat sprays of small dull white flowerheads in summer–autumn. 'Cerise Queen', cherry red, vigorous. Zones 3–10.

Achillea ptarmica

SNEEZEWORT

☼ ❋ ↔ 30 in (75 cm) ↕ 30 in (75 cm)
From Europe. Vigorous spreading mats of dark green, narrow, serrated leaves. Loose heads of small white flowers in summer. Tolerant of damp sites. 'The Pearl', profuse double white flowers. Zones 6–10.

Achillea Hybrid Cultivars

☼ ❋ ↔ 18–30 in (45–75 cm) ↕ 12–40 in (30–100 cm)
Numerous cultivars in bright shades make excellent border plants. Anthea/'Anblo', pale yellow flowers, silvery foliage; 'Apfelblüte' (syn. Apple Blossom), rose pink flowers; 'Coronation Gold', bright yellow; 'Fanal' (syn. 'The Beacon'), crimson-red, yellow centers; 'Heidi', bright salmon, yellow centers; 'Lachsschönheit', salmon fading to pale pink; 'Moonshine', bright yellow flowers over silvery foliage; and 'Paprika', bright red, yellow centers. Quick to flower from seed are 'Taygetea', gray foliage, lemon yellow

Achillea, Hybrid Cultivar, 'Paprika'

flowers; 'Terracotta', rusty orange; 'Walther Funcke', red, yellow centers; 'Wesersandstein', salmon fading to cream. Zones 3–10.

ACHIMENES

Found in tropical Americas, including the West Indies, this genus is a member of the African violet (Gesneriaceae) family and has some 25 species of winter-dormant fleshy-stemmed perennials ranging from ground covers, usually cultivated in hanging baskets, to shrubby species. Deep green, somewhat fleshy, simple elliptical to lance-shaped, tooth-edged leaves are covered with fine downy hair. The flowers are long-tubed with 5 lobes on 2 lips—2 lobes above, 3 below. Flowers appear in the leaf axils, either singly or in small groups.
CULTIVATION: Some are grown as house or greenhouse plants, others as annuals. All thrive outdoors in tropical and subtropical gardens. Plant rhizomes in spring in moist, humus-rich, well-drained soil in a bright but not too hot position. Feed and water well while in growth; dry off in autumn. Propagate by division.

Achimenes, Hybrid Cultivar, 'Lachs Charm'

Achimenes longiflora

◑ ✦ ↔ 12–20 in (30–50 cm)
↕ 20–24 in (50–60 cm)
Shrubby species found from Mexico to Panama. Deep green, lance-shaped leaves. White, mauve, purple to maroon flowers to 2½ in (6 cm) wide, borne singly. Zones 10–12.

Achimenes Hybrid Cultivars

◑ ✦ ↔ 10–15 in (25–38 cm) ↕ 3–6 in (8–15 cm)
Achimenes hybrids vary in size, growth habit, and flower color. 'Endeavor', deep orchid pink flowers, leaves bronzy; 'Glacier', 24 in (60 cm) tall, upright, white flowers tinted blue; 'Lachs Charm', bright reddish pink flowers, small purple blotch; 'Peach Blossom', trailer with salmon pink flowers; 'Pendant Purple', vigorous trailer with bright purple-blue flowers; 'Ruby', 12 in (30 cm) tall, bushy with masses of deep purple-red flowers; and 'Show-off', to 16 in (40 cm), bushy, heavy crop of lavender-pink flowers. Zones 10–12.

Aconitum napellus

Aconitum carmichaelii

ACONITUM

BADGER'S BANE, MONKSHOOD, WOLFSBANE

This genus in the buttercup (Ranunculaceae) family has around 100 species of often tuberous biennials and perennials found in northern temperate zones. Completely dormant over winter, they quickly develop a clump of deeply lobed fan-shaped leaves from which emerge erect stems bearing racemes of hooded or helmet-shaped flowers, usually white, creamy yellow, or mauve-blue to purple in color. Flowers mainly from summer to autumn. Monkshood sap contains several toxic alkaloids, principally aconitine.

CULTIVATION: *Aconitum* species are mostly very hardy and easily grown in full sun or half-sun in moist, humus-rich, well-drained soil. Propagation is by division when dormant or from seed.

Aconitum carmichaelii

☼/☀ ❄ ↔ 24–36 in (60–90 cm) ↑ 7 ft (2 m)

From China. Upright growth with dark green, 3- to 5-lobed, toothed, leathery leaves with pale undersides. Dense spikes of white to mauve helmet-shaped flowers, deep purple inside. Cultivars include 'Arendsii' and 'Kelmscott' (Wilsonii Group) ★. Zones 3–9.

Aconitum napellus

FRIAR'S CAP, HELMET FLOWER, MONKSHOOD

☼/☀ ❄ ↔ 24–32 in (60–80 cm)
↑ 5–6 ft (1.5–1.8 m)

Found in Europe and temperate Asia. Upright perennial with dark green slightly hairy leaves with 5 to 7 toothed lobes. Bright purple-blue helmet-shaped flowers in dense heads atop tall stems, late summer–autumn. Zones 5–9.

Aconitum Hybrid Cultivars

☼/☀ ❄ ↔ 24 in (60 cm) ↑ 4 ft (1.2 m)

Several hybrid monkshoods, varying in size, color, and flowering season, are sometimes listed under the name *A. × cammarum* (*A. variegatum × A. napellus*), but as they are not all of this parentage this grouping seems inappropriate. Popular hybrids include 'Bressingham Spire', strongly upright, with long spikes

of purple-blue flowers; *A. × cammarum* 'Grandiflorum Album', large heads of white flowers; 'Ivorine', with creamy white flowers; 'Spark's Variety', tall, non-twining, open plant, bright purple-blue flowers; and 'Stainless Steel', gray-green foliage and white-centered metallic blue flowers. Zones 4–9.

ACORUS

SWEET FLAG

Making up the family Acoraceae, this rather sedge-like genus of 2 evergreen perennial species occurs around pond margins in temperate East Asia and southeast USA. The narrow iris-like leaves in fans are often variegated in the cultivated forms. In summer they produce flowers in which the typically showy arum spathe is leaf-like and inconspicuous. The flowerhead (spadix) is pronounced but not a feature.

CULTIVATION: *Acorus* species are tough and easily grown. Plant in damp or boggy soil, preferably by a pond, and cut back or divide occasionally to encourage fresh young leaves. Propagation is by division or from seed if available.

Acorus calamus

CALAMUS, FLAGROOT, MYRTLE FLAG, SWEET CALAMUS, SWEET FLAG

☼/☀ ❄ ↔ 3–7 ft (0.9–2 m) ↑ 4 ft (1.2 m)

Originally from temperate Eurasia and eastern North America but now widely naturalized in the Northern Hemisphere. Has iris-like leaves to 5 ft (1.5 m) long and a narrow yellow-green spadix to 4 in (10 cm) long. 'Variegatus' ★ has cream and yellow variegated leaves. Zones 3–10.

Acorus gramineus

☼/☀ ❄ ↔ 18–36 in (45–90 cm) ↑ 16 in (40 cm)

From Japan and possibly nearby mainland Asia, very similar to *A. calamus* but smaller grassy leaves, to 18 in (45 cm) long. Spadix broad and up to 3 in (8 cm) long. Several foliage cultivars, including 'Hakuro-nishiki', 'Ōgon' (syn. 'Wogon'), 'Pusillus', and 'Variegatus' (syn. 'Aureovariegatus'). Zones 5–10.

Acorus gramineus 'Hakuro-nishiki'

AECHMEA

This genus is a member of the pineapple (Bromeliaceae) family and has around 80 species, ranging in size from 4 in (10 cm) to 7 ft (2 m) in diameter, and more than 500 cultivars. They come from the humid regions of Central America, ranging from the upper reaches of the Amazon and the hot dry areas of Bahia in Brazil to cooler areas in the southern parts of Brazil and Argentina. Most grow on trees in their natural environment, though some grow on rocks. The edges of the leaves are toothed, with the teeth ranging from very fine to most vicious. The flowerheads vary from short to elongated cones. Many have bright red banner-like primary bracts under the flower branches, which attract hummingbirds. The small-petalled flowers come in various colors. The fruit can be brightly colored, from yellow to red to blue to purple.

CULTIVATION: Recommended for indoor culture if in flower; for greenhouse or conservatory in cool-temperate areas; or outdoors, with protection from direct continuous sunlight and extremes of rain, in warm-temperate, subtropical, and tropical areas. Water when potting mix is dry. No extra fertilizer needed if potting mix is of good quality. Propagate from seed or by offset.

Aechmea caudata

☀ ❄ ↔ 24 in (60 cm) ↑ 36 in (90 cm)

Originates in the southern part of Brazil and is hardier than most other species. Leaves, to 40 in (100 cm) long, form an open funnel-shaped rosette. Flower stem to 36 in (90 cm) high; flowerhead erect, to 10 in (25 cm) long, with side spikes at the base, yellow petals. *A. c.* var. *variegata*, a more robust variegated form. Zones 9–11.

Aechmea chantinii

☀ ❄ ↔ 20 in (50 cm) ↑ 40 in (100 cm)

Originates in the upper reaches of the Amazon and likes hot humid conditions. Leaves to 40 in (100 cm) long, with strong white cross-banding, forming a loose funnel-shaped rosette. Flower stem to 40 in (100 cm) high; flowerhead open, with mainly yellow side spikes on long stems; orange flowers. Lower side spikes have large bright red primary bracts that hang down. This species has numerous cultivars, usually describing the leaf color, for example, 'Ash Blond', 'Black Goddess', and 'Green Ice'. Variegated cultivars include 'Samurai' and 'Shogun'. Zones 9–12.

Aechmea fasciata

Aechmea fasciata

☀ ❄ ↔ 16 in (40 cm) ↑ 27 in (70 cm)

From southern parts of Brazil. Leaves to 3 ft (0.9m) long, forming a slender funnel-shaped rosette. Leaves strongly cross-banded in white and in some forms almost totally covered with white scales. Flower stem to 27 in (70 cm) high. Flowerhead conical, bracts pink with a light covering of white scales. Flowers blue, ageing to red. There are variegated forms, and non-spined forms such as 'Morgana' and 'Kiwi'. Zones 9–12.

Aechmea fulgens

☀ ❄ ↔ 20 in (50 cm) ↑ 20 in (50 cm)

From eastern Brazil. Leaves 16 in (40 cm) long, forming a dense funnel-shaped rosette. Flower stem to 20 in (50 cm) high. Flowerhead to 8 in (20 cm) high, narrowly pyramidal with a few red side branches at the base. Dark red flowers scattered along branches, blue petals soon changing to red. Zones 9–12.

Aechmea gamosepala

MATCHSTICK PLANT

☀ ❄ ↔ 10 in (25 cm) ↑ 30 in (75 cm)

From southern parts of Brazil. Leaves to 22 in (55 cm) long, forming a dense funnel-form rosette. Flower stem to 30 in (75 cm) high. Flowerhead a narrow cylinder to 10 in (25 cm) long, with flowers standing at right angles from the center stem like matches, red with blue petals. Zones 8–11.

Aechmea nudicaulis

☀ ❄ ↔ 8 in (20 cm) ↑ 27–36 in (70–90 cm)

Found from southern Mexico to southern Brazil. Variable in size. Leaves 36 in (90 cm) long, green through to reddish, commonly with white bands, forming a tight tube. Flowerhead cylindrical with many flowers sticking out from the center stem. Bright red bracts under flowerhead. Flowers mainly yellow. Zones 9–12.

Aechmea ornata

☀ ❄ ↔ 7 ft (2 m) ↑ 36 in (90 cm)

From southern Brazil. Leaves green, 36 in (90 cm) long, with small teeth, forming open rosette. Flowerhead a short cylinder with bristles and many flowers on all sides. Petals red or blue. Large red erect bracts under flowerhead. *A. o.* var. *hoehneana*, blue-petalled form. *A. o.* var. *nationalis*, variegated form. Zones 9–11.

Aechmea recurvata

☀ ❄ ↔ 8 in (20 cm) ↑ 8–16 in (20–40 cm)

From southern Brazil. Leaves green, to 16 in (40 cm) long, moderately spined, forming an open rosette from a bulbose base. Flowerhead almost globular, red bracts on the outside, reddish purple petals. 'Aztec Gold' is variegated. Zones 8–11.

Aechmea Hybrid Cultivars

☀ ❄ ↔ 12–24 in (30–60 cm) ↑ 12–36 in (30–90 cm)

Nearly all the more popular *Aechmea* species have been used in the breeding of hybrids. 'Bastantha', leaves light yellowish green, red below; 'Burning Bush', bright red flower stem and branches, cream flowers; 'Fascini', large green rosette with branched long-lasting carmine flowers; 'Fia', gray-green leaves, red bracts, flowers with yellow ovaries and red sepals; 'Foster's Favorite', red-black leaves, pendent flowerhead, coral petals tipped blue; 'Friederike', spineless; 'J C Superstar', open funnel-shaped rosette, red bracts, pale petals; 'Royal Wine', light green leaves, maroon undersides, orange and blue flowers; 'Shelldancer', leaves apple green with red tips, side spikes, flowers white at base, petals blue. Zones 9–12.

Aechmea recurvata 'Aztec Gold'

AETHIONEMA

STONE CRESS

The 40-odd species in this genus of the cabbage (Brassicaceae) family are annuals and perennials distributed from Europe and the Mediterranean to southwest Asia. Most are low, spreading, or mounding plants that thrive in rockery conditions. They have simple, small, fleshy leaves on wiry stems that can become a tangled mass of branches and foliage tufts. In spring and summer flower-heads form at stem tips, bearing dense clusters of tiny 4-petalled flowers. Well-grown plants are smothered in blooms.
CULTIVATION: These plants are hardy to repeated frosts but per-haps a little tender for harsh continental winters. Plant in full sun in gritty well-drained soil with extra humus for moisture retention. Many appreciate a light dressing of dolomite. Water if necessary when flowering but otherwise keep dry. Propagate from seed or cuttings or by layering. May self-sow.

Aethionema grandiflorum

☀ ❄ ↔ 12–24 in (30–60 cm)
↕ 8–18 in (20–45 cm)
Found in the Caucasus and nearby parts of Iran and Iraq. Can mound up to form a moderately sized shrub. Blue-green foli-age and bright pink flowers, each slightly more than ½ in (12 mm) wide. Zones 7–9.

Aethionema 'Warley Rose'

☀ ❄ ↔ 12 in (30 cm) ↕ 6 in (15 cm)
Most widely grown *Aethionema*. Blue-green foliage. Flowers bright rosy red, borne profusely from late spring to sum-mer's end. May be short lived. Zones 6–9.

AGAPANTHUS

AFRICAN LILY, LILY-OF-THE-NILE

This southern African genus consists of 10 species of fleshy-rooted perennials of the onion (Alliaceae) family. Long, strappy, fleshy leaves form dense clumps of evergreen or deciduous foliage. Tall flower stems with heads of tubular to bell-shaped flowers, usually blue, are held above the foliage. Flowers of evergreens appear over a long season in frost-free climates, and in summer elsewhere. Their narrow, rather upright habit makes them ideal border plants. Dwarf forms are superb in large rockeries or containers.
CULTIVATION: Easily grown in any well-drained soil in sun or half-sun, they will withstand drought and poor soil but produce more flowers with good conditions. Slugs and snails often damage the young foliage. Propagate by division in winter or raise from seed.

Agapanthus inapertus

DRAKENSBERG AGAPANTHUS, DROOPING AGAPANTHUS

☀ ❄ ↔ 40–50 in (100–130 cm) ↕ 40–60 in (100–150 cm)
Deciduous, from southeastern South Africa. Dense clumps of blue-tinted leaves to 27 in (70 cm) long. Pendulous, purple-blue, sometimes white, tubular flowers on stems to 5 ft (1.5 m) tall. *A. i.* subsp. *hollandii*, taller stems and flared flowers. Zones 7–10.

Agapanthus praecox

☀ ❄ ↔ 40–50 in (100–130 cm) ↕ 40 in (100 cm)
Evergreen, fleshy, bright green leaves to 27 in (70 cm) long. Wide-opening pale to mid-blue flowers on stems to 36 in (90 cm) tall. Most widely cultivated species in warm-temperate gardens. *A. p.* subsp. *orientalis*, smaller, forms dense foliage clumps with tightly packed heads of small bright blue flowers. Zones 8–11.

Agapanthus Hybrid Cultivars

☀ ❄ ↔ 12–30 in (30–75 cm) ↕ 15–60 in (38–150 cm)
Variable group, ranging from plants for large gardens to those for rockeries or tubs. Mainly easily grown in areas with not too severe winters. Cultivars include 'Baby Blue', dwarf, with bright blue flowers on 12–16 in (30–40 cm) stems; 'Elaine', upright, vigorous, deep purple-blue flowers on 4 ft (1.2 m) high stems; 'Ellamae', bright violet-blue flowers on stems to 5 ft (1.5 m); 'Henryi', dwarf, narrow leaves, white flowers on 18 in (45 cm) stems; 'Lilliput', dwarf, dark blue flowers on 18 in (45 cm) tall stems; 'Loch Hope', large heads of dark blue flowers, 4 ft (1.2 m) stems, late-flowering; 'Midnight Blue'/'Monmid', compact, deep purple-blue flowers on 16 in (40 cm) stems; 'Peter Pan', dwarf, mid-blue flowers on 12 in (30 cm) stems; 'Queen Anne', bright blue flowers on 24 in (60 cm) stems; 'Rancho White', white flowers on stems to 18 in (45 cm); 'Storm Cloud', intense purple-blue flowers on 4 ft (1.2 m) stems; and 'Tinkerbell', leaves edged cream, pale blue flowers on 16 in (40 cm) stems. Zones 7–11.

AGASTACHE

GIANT HYSSOP, MEXICAN HYSSOP

There are 20 species of very aromatic perennials in this genus, a member of the mint (Lamiaceae) family. They are native to North America, China, and Japan where they grow in dry scrub and fields. Leaf shape varies from pointed oval to almost triangular or lance shaped, the margins being shallowly to finely toothed. Flowers may be red, orange, rose, violet, blue, or white, typically tubular with two lips. They are borne in densely packed whorls on spikes or narrow panicles in summer and are very popular with bees.
CULTIVATION: Grow in well-drained soil in a sunny position. Most species tolerate some frost; give the more tender ones a warm shel-tered site in cooler climates or grow as annuals. They can be prone to fungal diseases in summer. Propagate from seed or cuttings.

Agastache cana

HUMMINGBIRD PLANT, MOSQUITO PLANT

☀ ❄ ↔ 12–18 in (30–45 cm) ↕ 20–24 in (50–60 cm)
Woody-based perennial from southern USA. Slightly downy triangular or pointed oval leaves. Flower spikes to 12 in (30 cm) long, whorls of rose-colored tubular flowers. 'Heather Queen' ★ has bright pink flowers. Zones 7–11.

Agapanthus inapertus

Agastache foeniculum

syns *Agastache anethiodora*, *A. anisata*

ANISE HYSSOP

☼ ❄ ↔ 18–24 in (45–60 cm)

↑ 20–32 in (50–80 cm)

Very aromatic plant from North America. Leaves triangular to pointed oval with toothed margins, downy beneath. Short, densely packed flower spikes bear small violet-blue flowers. Zones 8–10.

Agastache rugosa

HUO XIANG, KOREAN MINT, WRINKLED GIANT HYSSOP

☼ ❄ ↔ 24 in (60 cm) ↑ 24–48 in (60–120 cm)

Erect perennial from China and Japan. Coarsely toothed ovate leaves, hairy undersides. In summer, short compact spikes bear small tubular flowers of violet to rose. 'Honeybee White' and 'Honeybee Blue' ('Licorice Blue' may be the prior name for this) are compact plants. Zones 7–11.

Ageratum houstonianum 'Azure Pearl'

Agastache rupestris

LICORICE MINT, SUNSET HYSSOP, THREADLEAF GIANT HYSSOP

☼ ❄ ↔ 18 in (45 cm) ↑ 18–36 in (45–90 cm)

A very aromatic species found from southwestern USA to northern Mexico. Grayish green thread-like leaves. Orange flowers with lavender calyces in summer. 'Sunset', slightly shorter. Zones 5–9.

Agastache Hybrid Cultivars

☼ ❄ ↔ 1–3 ft (0.3–0.9 m) ↑ 2–6 ft (0.6–1.8 m)

The crossing of several species has resulted in cultivars of varying heights and colors. Cultivars include 'Apricot Sunrise', grayish green foliage, orange flowers; 'Blue Fortune', bluish purple flowers; 'Firebird', coppery orange tones; 'Tangerine Dreams', similar to 'Apricot Sunrise' but taller; 'Tutti Frutti', grayish green leaves, raspberry red flowers. Zones 7–10.

AGERATUM

FLOSS FLOWER

Found in the tropical Americas, including the West Indies, this genus containing 43 species of annuals, perennials, and shrubs is a member of the daisy (Asteraceae) family. Best known for the annual bedding species, *Ageratum houstonianum*, the genus is characterized by flowerheads in which the ray florets are tubular filaments rather than petal-like, creating a fine feathery effect. The size of the plants varies considerably with the species, but most of the garden forms are compact and

Agastache foeniculum

have hairy or felted leaves, generally with toothed edges.

CULTIVATION: Plant in full sun in gritty well-drained soil that remains moist during the flowering season. Most perennial and shrubby species can tolerate only light frosts and may be grown outdoors only in mild areas. Raise annuals from seed, usually sown in spring; propagate perennials from half-hardened cuttings.

Ageratum houstonianum

☼ ❄ ↔ 6–20 in (15–50 cm) ↑ 6–30 in (15–75 cm)

Annuals from Central America and West Indies. Pointed oval to poplar-shaped, downy, tooth-edged, dull green leaves to nearly 4 in (10 cm) long. Large dense or open heads of blue or lavender flowers. Garden forms include pink and white flowers. Popular cultivars include 'Azure Pearl', 12 in (30 cm) tall, mid-blue flowers; 'Blue Danube', up to 6 in (15 cm) tall, mound forming, blue flowers; 'Blue Horizon', 24–30 in (60–75 cm) tall, purple-blue flowers; 'Blue Lagoon', 8 in (20 cm) tall, neat rounded blue flowers; 'Blue Mink' ★, 12 in (30 cm) tall, light dusky blue flowers; 'Pacific', 8 in (20 cm) tall, purple-blue flowers; and 'Red Top', 24–28 in (60–70 cm) tall, bushy purple-red flowers. Among several seedling strains of uniform size one of the best is the Hawaii Series—neat rounded plants around 8 in (20 cm) tall—including: 'Hawaii Blue', 'Hawaii Pink Shell', 'Hawaii Royal', and 'Hawaii White'. Zones 10–12.

AGLAONEMA

This genus in the arum (Araceae) family has some 25 species of herbaceous evergreens, found from eastern India to southern China and south to Indonesia and the Philippines. Clustered fleshy stems are short, or may grow slowly to over 3 ft (0.9 m) long. Leaves crowded at stem tips are mostly ovate or elliptical, somewhat leathery, and often patterned in gray or cream. Flower spikes project from among the leaf bases. Red or yellow fruits are berry-like. Used indoors, or outdoors under trees in tropical gardens.

CULTIVATION: Require a humid, virtually frost-free environment and grow best in filtered light; some tolerate deep shade. Pot in a free-draining medium and feed regularly through summer; remove longer stems. Propagate from stem cuttings or by division.

Aglaonema costatum

Aglaonema commutatum

☼/◐ ▨ ↔ 24 in (60 cm) ↑ 24–36 in (60–90 cm)
Most widely cultivated species, from the Philippines and eastern
Indonesia. Stems sprawl as they elongate. Leaves narrowly ovate,
dull dark green with feathery gray markings. *A. c.* var. *maculatum*,
leaves with light green markings. *A. c.* '**Pseudobracteatum**', larger
areas of white and pale green along veins; '**Treubii**', narrower
deep green leaves, pale gray pattern; '**White Rajah**', erect thin
leaves, much more white and cream than green. Zones 10–12.

Aglaonema costatum

☼/◐ ▨ ↔ 24 in (60 cm) ↑ 12 in (30 cm)
From the Malay Peninsula, low-growing plant with short trailing
stems and short dark green leaves with paler midrib; flower spikes
few, with white spathe, to 1½ in (35 mm) long, in summer.
'**Foxii**', scattered, small, white spots, white midrib. Zones 10–12.

Aglaonema crispum

syn. *Aglaonema robelinii*
PAINTED DROP-TONGUE
☼/◐ ▨ ↔ 18–30 in (45–75 cm)
↑ 24–48 in (60–120 cm)
Robust clumping plant with erect stems, from
Philippines. Elliptical leaves to 12 in (30 cm)
long, gray with dark green zone along midrib.
Flower spikes clustered, spathe yellowish, to
3 in (8 cm) long. Zones 10–12.

AJUGA

BUGLE
Members of the mint (Lamiaceae) family, the
40-odd, low, spreading annuals and perennials in this genus
occur throughout temperate Eurasia, Africa, and Australia, and
are widely naturalized elsewhere. Many spread by fleshy stems,
others self-layer as they grow. Leaves are in whorls on narrow
angular stems. Conical, short-stemmed, upright flowerheads with
small, often purple-blue flowers appearing from the axils of leaf
bracts, bloom mainly from late spring into summer. Use as a
quick ground cover around small shrubs or in containers, but
take care to control their spread.

CULTIVATION: Most grow very freely in any well-drained soil.
Some need to be cut back routinely. Propagation of perennials
is by division or from self-rooted layers; annuals from seed.

Ajuga pyramidalis

PYRAMID BUGLE
☼/◐ ✳ ↔ 12–24 in (30–60 cm) ↑ 6–8 in (15–20 cm)
Mat-forming European perennial. Rosettes of dark green, finely
toothed leaves to 4 in (10 cm) long. Leafy pyramidal flowerheads with mauve-blue flowers backed by purple-bronze bracts.
'**Metallica Crispa**', wavy-edged purple-bronze foliage. Zones 6–10.

Ajuga reptans

☼/◐ ✳ ↔ 12–48 in (30–120 cm) or more ↑ 4–8 in (10–20 cm)
A temperate Eurasian native. Sometimes invasive. Foliage often
purple tinted. Flowers in blue to purple shades, sometimes pink.
Cultivars include '**Atropurpurea**', deep purple-bronze foliage,
dark flowers; '**Braunherz**', very dark, glossy, purple-bronze leaves;
'**Burgundy Glow**', gray-green leaves, reddish markings; '**Burgundy
Lace**', purple-bronze, cream, and green variegation; '**Catlin's
Giant**', bronze-green leaves, tall flower spikes; '**Jungle Beauty**',
large deep green leaves, bright purple-blue flowers; '**Jungle Bronze**',
vigorous and upright, large wavy-edged bronze leaves; '**Multi-
color**' (syns '**Rainbow**', '**Tricolor**'), cream, pink, and green foliage;
'**Pink Elf**', compact, deep pink flowers; '**Pink Surprise**', bronze,
gray, and green variegated foliage, bronze in winter, pink flowers;
and '**Purple Torch**', bronze foliage, pink flowers. Zones 5–10.

ALCEA

HOLLYHOCK
A member of the mallow (Malvaceae) family, this genus contains
about 60 species of biennials and short-lived perennial herbs
native to central and southwestern Asia.
Some are naturalized around the Mediterranean. Flowers, to 4 in (10 cm) across and
borne on stems to 7 ft (2 m) tall in summer,
have 5 petals and may be pink, purple, yellow, or white. Stamens form a prominent
central column, usually yellow. A quint-
essential English cottage garden style plant.
CULTIVATION: Grow in a sunny position in
rich soil, moist but well drained. Stake plants
on exposed sites and water in dry spells. Rust
is a problem, and it is best to renew plants
each year. Propagate from seed sown in late
summer or early spring.

Alcea rosea

Alcea rosea

syn. *Althaea rosea*
HOLLYHOCK
☼ ✳ ↔ 2–3 ft (0.6–0.9 m) ↑ 2–8 ft (0.6–2.4 m)
Cultivated and naturalized in many places but thought to orig-
inate from Turkey or Asia. Rounded leaves have 3 to 7 lobes.
Flowers single or double, to 4 in (10 cm) across, shades of pink,
purple, yellow, and white. Wide range of cultivars and seed lines.
'**Nigra**', dark maroon single flowers. Zones 3–10.

ALCHEMILLA
BEAR'S FOOT, LADY'S MANTLE, LION'S FOOT

This widespread genus of around 300 species of clump-forming soft-stemmed perennials from Eurasia, Africa, and Central and South America belongs to the rose (Rosaceae) family. Foliage, on fine stems that often self-layer, is hand-shaped with rounded lobes, covered in fine hairs. Sprays of tiny yellow-green flowers are borne from late spring.
CULTIVATION: Cultivated species are temperate-zone plants that prefer cool, moist, well-drained conditions with shade from the hottest sun. Propagation is usually by division when dormant, but can be raised from seed.

Alchemilla mollis ★
LADY'S MANTLE

☼/◐ ❄ ↔ 12–32 in (30–80 cm) ↕ 12–20 in (30–50 cm)
Mounding spreading species found from Romania to Greece and Iran. Toothed leaves, finely hairy above, densely hairy below. Sprays of yellow-green flowers in summer. Zones 4–9.

Alchemilla xanthochlora
◐ ❄ ↔ 16–24 in (40–60 cm) ↕ 12–20 in (30–50 cm)
Mounding and spreading European species. Yellow-green, kidney-shaped, toothed, 9- to 11-lobed leaves, hairless above, hairy below. Yellow-green flowers in summer. Zones 5–9.

ALKANNA
This is a genus of about 30 frost-hardy annual and perennial species found from southern Europe to Iran, and it is a member of the borage (Boraginaceae) family. The plants have branching terminal inflorescences with a long tubular corolla and a downy ring in the center. The leaves are smooth-edged and hairy. Fruits are elongated calyces.
CULTIVATION: These plants prefer rich warm soil in an open sunny position. Propagate from seed.

Alkanna orientalis
☼ ❄ ↔ 8–12 in (20–30 cm) ↕ 8–12 in (20–30 cm)
Annual found from southwest Europe to southwest Asia. White or yellow scented flowers to ½ in (12 mm) wide. Hairy green to whitish green leaves to 3 in (8 cm) long, lance-shaped or narrowly egg-shaped. Zones 6–9.

Alkanna tinctoria
ALKANET, DYER'S BUGLOSS

☼ ❄ ↔ 12–36 in (30–90 cm) ↕ 12–36 in (30–90 cm)
Perennial from central and southern Europe. Bright purplish blue flowers to ½ in (12 mm) wide with funnel-shaped corolla. Bristly, smooth-edged, linear to egg-shaped leaves to 3 in (8 cm) long. Extensive root system and a hairy angular stem. Zones 5–8.

ALOCASIA
Comprising 70 species, this genus of the arum (Araceae) family occurs in a variety of habitats, from lowland rainforests to road-sides, swamps, and mountain regions from tropical southern Asia, Indonesia, Malaysia, New Guinea, and Australia, to islands of the Pacific. The species are perennial, evergreen, very small to massive herbs, even tree-like, with corms, runners, or above-ground stems. Leaves are several with sheathing leaf stalk, simple, broadly or narrowly arrowhead-shaped, with entire or deeply lobed margins, but usually heart-shaped at the base. The major veins are often strikingly prominent in some species. Inflorescences are borne at or near the apex of the leafy plant, 2 or more together, the spathes constricted, the spadix in 4 parts, lowermost female, then sterile, then male, then a sterile appendage. The female flower has no petals or sepals, consisting only of the single-celled ovary and stigma. Male flowers consist of 3 to 8, stalkless, narrow anthers united into a pyramid shape. Fruit is a globular berry containing several seeds.
CULTIVATION: Propagate from seed and stem cuttings or by division of fleshy stem. All species require warm moist conditions in shady sheltered locations, and are grown in greenhouses and conservatories in all regions but the tropics.

Alocasia × amazonica
☀ ⚘ ↔ 20–40 in (50–100 cm) ↕ 40–60 in (100–150 cm)
A hybrid of *A. lowii* and *A. sanderiana*, its origins are unknown. Leaves to 24 in (60 cm) long and 12 in (30 cm) wide, arrowhead-shaped, upperside dark green, midrib yellow-greenish white, other veins silvery white. Underside dull purple, major veins green-white. Leaf stalk green, 18 in (45 cm) long. '**Magnifica**', more intensely silver coloration on upperside, all purple below; '**Randall**', larger in all parts. Zones 11–12.

Alocasia × amazonica

Alocasia cuprea

◐ ✂ ↔ 30 in (75 cm) ↑ to 40 in (100 cm)

Occurs in forests of Malaysia and Borneo. Perennial herb, fleshy-stemmed, leaf stalks 24 in (60 cm) long, leaf blades oblong to oval, somewhat arrowhead-shaped, surface raised between the lateral veins giving a quilted appearance, upperside with dark green and copper-colored areas, underside reddish purple. Spathes purple, to 6 in (15 cm) long. Flowers in summer. Zones 11–12.

Alocasia sanderiana

syns *Alocasia sanderana*, *A. sanderi*, *Schizocasia sanderiana*

◑/◐ ✂ ↔ 20–36 in (50–90 cm)
↑ 40–60 in (100–150 cm)

Perennial herb. Common in cultivation but endangered in the wild; its only known habitat is the moist forests of Mindanao in the Philippines. Leaves broadly arrowhead-shaped, shiny, blackish green on the upperside, main veins and edges silvery white, underside green, 20 in (50 cm) long, leaf stalks 24 in (60 cm) long. Spathe is greenish, shorter than leaves, flowering intermittent. Attractive cultivars include '**Nobilis**' and '**Van Houtte**'. Zones 11–12.

ALPINIA

GINGER LILY

The 200 species of fleshy-stemmed perennials in this genus, which belongs to the ginger (Zingiberaceae) family, are native to tropical regions of Asia, Australia, and some Pacific islands. Lance-shaped leaves are arranged in 2 ranks along reed-like stems from 3–12 ft (0.9–3.5 m) tall depending on the species. The inflorescences are usually showy and long-lasting. The true flowers are often enclosed at first within colorful bracts.
CULTIVATION: In warm climates grow in sun or half-sun in fertile moist soil. Most species will withstand a little frost but need 4 to 5 months of growth to flower, so in cool climates start earlier indoors or grow under glass in bright filtered light, water plentifully and maintain high humidity. Propagate from seed or by division.

Alpinia zerumbet

Alpinia purpurata

RED GINGER

◑/◐ ⬡ ↔ 2–4 ft (0.6–1.2 m) ↑ 8–12 ft (2.4–3.5 m)

From Melanesia. Large leaves, up to 32 in (80 cm) long, prominent midribs. The long-lasting rich red flowerheads are borne on upright inflorescences for much of the year. Zones 10–11.

Alpinia purpurata

Alpinia zerumbet

syns *Alpinia nutans*, *A. speciosa*
PINK PORCELAIN LILY, SHELL GINGER

◑/◐ ⬡ ↔ 2–3 ft (0.6–0.9 m) ↑ 6–10 ft (1.8–3 m)

From eastern Asia and New Guinea. Most widely grown species. Glossy leathery leaves. Pendulous inflorescence to 16 in (40 cm) long. Pale pink or white bracts at first enclose yellow and red flowers, borne in spring and summer. '**Variegata**', pale yellow striped leaves. Zones 9–11.

ALSTROEMERIA

LILY OF THE INCAS, PERUVIAN LILY

This genus in the Alstroemeriaceae family has around 50 species of fleshy-rooted perennials. Found in South America, often at altitude, they are known for their long-lasting beautifully marked flowers but notorious for their vigorous roots and self-sowing. *A. psittacina* is considered a weed in some areas. Foliage is mid-green, usually lance-shaped, and slightly twisted. It is carried on tall stems that terminate in many flowered heads of 6-petalled lily-like blooms of many shades.
CULTIVATION: Though rather frost tender—the roots should be insulated with mulch—these species are easily grown in any sunny position with moderately fertile well-drained soil that can be kept moist during the flowering season. Propagate by division when dormant, or from seed.

Alstroemeria psittacina

syn. *Alstroemeria pulchella*

◑/◐ ❄ ↔ 16–20 in (40–50 cm) ↑ 28–36 in (70–90 cm)

This Brazilian species has leaves up to 3 in (8 cm) long, and heads of red-flushed green flowers with maroon flecks, borne in summer. '**Royal Star**' (syn. 'Variegata') is variegated. Zones 8–10.

Alstroemeria Hybrid Cultivars

◐ ❄ ↔ 12–24 in (30–60 cm) ↑ 18–48 in (45–120 cm)

Alstroemerias hybridize freely, and in recent years the range has increased enormously. Popular hybrids include '**Aimi**', 2 ft (0.6 m) tall, pink-blushed pale creamy yellow flowers with deep brown flecks; '**Amanda**', white-flushed pink flowers with green petal tips and dark flecks; '**Apollo**', 3 ft (0.9 m) tall, white flowers with deep yellow center and brown flecks; '**Belinda**', soft yellow flowers with darker center and brown flecks; '**Blue Heaven**', 3–4 ft (0.9–1.2 m) tall, lavender blue flowers with pale center and red-brown flecks; '**Blushing Bride**', 3 ft (0.9 m) tall, white flowers with faint pink blush; '**Evening Song**', 3 ft (0.9 m) tall, deep magenta flowers with yellow throat and dark flecks; '**Friendship**', 3 ft (0.9 m) tall, soft yellow flowers with deep brown markings and a darker center, and hint of purple at the petal tips; '**Fuego**' ★, 5–6 ft (1.5–1.8 m) tall, fiery red flowers with small yellow throat; Ilona/ '**Stalona**', soft orange-red flowers with creamy yellow throat and dark flecks; Irena/'**Statiren**', white-flushed pink flowers with near-red mid-stripe and dark flecks; '**Marina**', 20–30 in (50–75 cm) tall, magenta-pink flowers with small yellow throat and dark flecks; '**Marissa**', 3 ft (0.9 m) tall, rose pink flowers lightening to cream mid-petal with yellow throat and dark flecks; '**Napoli**', magenta-purple flowers with faint yellow throat and dark flecks; '**Odessa**', 3–4 ft (1–1.2 m) tall, white flowers flushed and tipped deep red-pink, with yellow throat and red flecks; Olga/ '**Stalog**', white flowers with yellow center and red flecks; '**Orange Gem**', 3 ft (0.9 m) tall, orange flowers with golden yellow throat and dark flecks; '**Orange Glory**', 3 ft (0.9 m) tall, deep orange flowers with dark markings and golden throat; Queen Elizabeth The Queen Mother/'**Stamoli**', brown-marked cream flowers flushed with pink; Rebecca/'**Stabec**', 3 ft (0.9 m) tall, cream flowers with deep pink blotches, yellow center and dark flecks; '**Red Beauty**', 3 ft (0.9 m) tall, with black-flecked, red-orange flowers with yellow-throats, '**Romy**', 4–5 ft (1.2–1.5 m) tall, white flowers with yellow center and red flecks; '**Tessa**', 30 in (75 cm) tall, brown-flecked red flowers with small yellow center; and '**Yellow Friendship**', black-flecked bright yellow flowers.

The **Little Miss Series** are dwarf plants, 6–12 in (15–30 cm) tall, with large flowers, strong stems and a long flowering period. They include '**Little Miss Olivia**', '**Little Miss Roselind**', '**Little Miss Sophie**', and '**Little Miss Tara**'.

The Dutch-raised **Princess Series** is a range of compact hybrids that grow 12–18 in (30–45 cm) tall and are long flowering because they are sterile. They are ideal as potted plants. This series includes Princess Daniela/'**Stapridani**', Princess Ivana/'**Staprivane**', Princess Monica/ '**Staprimon**', Princess Morana/'**Staprirana**', Princess Oxana/'**Staprioxa**', Princess Pamela/ '**Stapripame**', Princess Sissi/'**Staprisis**', and Princess Zavina/'**Staprivina**'. Zones 7–10.

ALTERNANTHERA

CHAFF FLOWER, COPPERLEAF, JOYWEED

A genus of about 200 low, compact, trailing or erect, aquatic, annual or perennial herbs from tropical to subtropical Americas belonging to the amaranth (Amaranthaceae) family. The spikes of small flowers have bracts but no petals. They are often grown for their brightly colored foliage, which is smooth-edged or densely toothed. CULTIVATION: Adaptable to most soils, they do best in a protected, warm, sunny position in rich soil with frequent watering. Regularly clip plants for border displays. In cooler climates plants should be lifted after first frosts. Propagate by division or from cuttings taken in late summer or spring.

Alstroemeria, Hybrid Cultivar, 'Apollo'

Alternanthera bettzichiana

CALICO PLANT

☼ ✻ ↔ 2–3 ft (0.6–0.9 m) ↕ 2–3 ft (0.6–0.9 m)

Annual or short-lived perennial native to Brazil. Erect habit; insignificant flowers; narrow spoon-shaped leaves of khaki to yellow, with red to purple markings. Usually grown for its foliage. '**Brilliantissima**' has vivid red leaves. Zones 10–12.

AMARANTHUS

There are about 60 species of weedy annuals and short-lived perennials in this genus, which is a member of the amaranth (Amaranthaceae) family. They have a worldwide distribution, often being found in wasteland areas. Species range from tall to prostrate, with long, often drooping, tassels of small red or green flowers. Individual flowers are either male or female and may be borne on separate plants. Some species are cultivated as leaf or grain crops in tropical areas, while those with dramatic flowers or colorful foliage are popular in the ornamental garden and for floristry. CULTIVATION: These are easily grown in well-drained fertile soil in full sun. Protect tall varieties from strong wind. In cooler climates sow seed under glass in early spring and plant out after danger of frosts has passed. In warmer areas seed can be sown outdoors later in the season.

Amaranthus caudatus 'Green Tails'

Amaranthus caudatus

LOVE-LIES-BLEEDING, TASSEL FLOWER, VELVET FLOWER

☼ ✻ ↔ 24 in (60 cm) ↕ 36–48 in (90–120 cm)

Native to Peru, Africa, and India, this annual or short-lived perennial has dull green leaves, as well as drooping crimson-purple tassels, up to 12 in (30 cm) long, in summer. Cultivars include '**Green Tails**' and '**Viridis**' (syn. '**Green Thumb**'). Zones 8–11.

Amaranthus tricolor
CHINESE SPINACH, JOSEPH'S COAT, TAMPALA

☼ ❄ ↔ 30 in (75 cm) ↑ 24–36 in (60–90 cm)

Bushy annual from Africa and Asia. Grown as a leaf vegetable or, in varieties which have colorful foliage, for its ornamental value. Appearing in summer, the flower spikes are green or red. '**Joseph's Coat**' has red and gold upper leaves. Zones 8–11.

AMSONIA
BLUE STAR

Found from southern Europe, through temperate Asia including Japan, and in North America, this genus of the dogbane (Apocynaceae) family has some 20 species of perennials and subshrubs characterized by milky sap and simple narrow leaves. Flowers, though small, are an unusual shade of blue and mass in heads above the foliage. While not spectacular, most species are distinctive, adding something different to the perennial border.

CULTIVATION: These plants prefer a climate with distinct seasons. Most are easily cultivated in a quite sunny position with well-drained soil kept moist in the growing season. Propagate perennials by division during dormancy or as growth starts. Those with firmer stems will also grow from summer cuttings.

Amsonia tabernaemontana
BLUE DOGBANE, BLUE STAR

☼/❂ ❄ ↔ 36–48 in (90–120 cm) ↑ 36 in (90 cm)

Clump-forming perennial of eastern USA. Upright green stems, simple lance-shaped leaves to 3 in (8 cm) long. Heads of pale blue flowers in mid-spring–late summer. Zones 4–9.

ANAGALLIS
PIMPERNEL

This primrose (Primulaceae) family genus includes 20 species, found over much of the globe, especially temperate zones. The soft-stemmed, low, spreading plants, mostly biennials or perennials, behave as annuals in cold climates. The leaves are small and simple. The small flowers are brightly colored, pink, red, or blue. Some may be weeds, but are not invasive.

Anaphalis triplinervis 'Sommerschnee'

CULTIVATION: Grow in a sunny spot with moist well-drained soil. Cultivated species are easily maintained by pinching to shape; not invasive. Propagate from seed, base cuttings, or layers.

Anagallis monelli
BLUE PIMPERNEL

☼/❂ ❄ ↔ 12–20 in (30–50 cm) ↑ 12–20 in (30–50 cm)

Mediterranean native, small perennial. Dark green leaves. Flowers single but abundant, bright blue, red-tinted undersides. Cultivars include '**Pacific Blue**' ★ and '**Phillipii**'. Zones 7–10.

ANAPHALIS
PEARLY EVERLASTING

This genus in the daisy (Asteraceae) family consists of around 100 species of perennials that may be upright, low and bushy, or trailing. Though found across northern temperate zones and on tropical mountains, a feature common to all is that the foliage and stems are covered with a fine white to gray hair. Leaves are simple, linear to lance-shaped, attached to stems without stalks. Flowerheads form dense downy heads, and while they lack ray florets, papery white bracts create a similar effect. Cut flowers last well but the plants are grown as much for their foliage.

CULTIVATION: Mostly very hardy. Plant in full sun with gritty well-drained soil kept moist in summer. Dry winter conditions are preferable. Cut back hard in spring to encourage strong new growth. Propagate from seed, base cuttings, or by division.

Anaphalis margaritacea
PEARLY EVERLASTING

☼ ❄ ↔ 16–24 in (40–60 cm) ↑ 32–40 in (80–100 cm)

Widespread in northern temperate areas. Leaves gray-green above with white hair below. In summer, flowerheads are clustered in corymbs to 6 in (15 cm) wide with opalescent bracts. Zones 3–9.

Anaphalis triplinervis
PEARLY EVERLASTING

☼ ❄ ↔ 16–20 in (40–50 cm) ↑ 32–36 in (80–90 cm)

Central Asian species, found from Afghanistan to southwest China. Clump-forming. Spatula-shaped gray-green leaves to 4 in (10 cm) long. Dome-shaped heads of white flowerheads in summer. '**Sommerschnee**', larger, with silvery white flowers. Zones 5–9.

ANCHUSA
ALKANET, BUGLOSS

Classified in the borage (Boraginaceae) family, this genus includes some 35 species of biennials and perennials from Europe, western Asia, and Africa. They are strong growers, usually clump-forming, with upright stems and simple, pointed, elliptical leaves that can be quite large at the base of the clump. Heads of small 5-petalled flowers in shades from pale blue to purple open through late spring and summer.

CULTIVATION: Species thrive in most conditions except very poor soil, deep shade, or drought. Ample feeding and mulching in winter and water in the growing season promotes flowering. Perennials may be divided in winter or very early spring; annuals or biennials must be raised from seed, preferably sown in autumn so young plants can start growth early in spring.

Anchusa azurea
syn. *Anchusa italica*

☼/◐ ❄ ↔ 32 in (80 cm) ↕ 48 in (120 cm)

Perennial, native to the Mediterranean region and western Asia. Bristly red-tinted stems with lower leaves to 12 in (30 cm) long. Flowers blue to purple, ½ in (12 mm) wide, 5-petalled, in late spring–summer. Cultivars include '**Dropmore**', compact and bushy, large deep blue flowers; and '**Opal**', compact, grayish foliage, light blue flowers. Zones 3–9.

Anchusa capensis
☼ ⁑ ↔ 16 in (40 cm) ↕ 20 in (50 cm)

Hairy biennial from South Africa with narrow lance-shaped leaves to 5 in (12 cm) long. White-centered bright blue flowers through summer. Treated as a spring-sown annual where summers are long. Zones 9–11.

ANDROSACE
ROCK JASMINE

This genus of 100 species of annual, biennial, and perennial herbs belongs to the primrose (Primulaceae) family. They are alpine plants from northern temperate regions, growing in scree at high altitudes and in turf at lower altitudes. The dainty flowers, usually less than ½ in (12 mm) across, have short tubular bases flaring to flat openfaced petals. They are white, pink, or red with a central eye that is often yellow or orange.
CULTIVATION: These plants need perfect drainage, good air circulation, and careful watering. Grow in a cool greenhouse or outdoors in troughs in a low-fertility gritty mix. Prevent collar rot with a gritty mulch on the soil surface and water from beneath. Cover outdoor troughs with glass in winter to protect from rain. Propagate from seed (germination may take 2 years), or cuttings or runners of some species.

Androsace lanuginosa ★
☼ ❄ ↔ 12–18 in (30–45 cm) ↕ 3 in (8 cm)

From the Himalayas. Prostrate perennial forming a mat of foliage covered in silvery hairs. Small dense heads of pale pink, darker-eyed flowers in summer–early autumn. '**Leichtlinii**' has deeper pink flowers. Zones 6–9.

Androsace rotundifolia
☼ ❄ ↔ 8 in (20 cm) ↕ 4–6 in (10–15 cm)

Hairy perennial from northern India. Rosettes of small, round, lobed leaves; densely packed, pale pink flowers, in spring–early summer. Zones 4–9.

ANEMONE
WINDFLOWER

Widespread in temperate regions of both hemispheres, this genus is a member of the buttercup (Ranunculaceae) family, and has some 120 species of perennials. Their roots may be tuberous, fleshy-

Anchusa azurea

stemmed or fibrous, and develop into clumps of finely divided foliage. Bowl-shaped flowers, single or in small clusters, sit on wiry stems well above the foliage. Most species flower in spring shortly after the foliage appears, but some continue into early summer and a few species bloom in autumn.
CULTIVATION: The wood anemones prefer woodland conditions with dappled shade, but most species thrive in a sunny border with moist well-drained soil. Propagation is by division in winter when dormant, or from seed in the case of strains grown as annuals.

Anemone blanda
◐/◑ ❄ ↔ 6–12 in (15–30 cm) ↕ 4–8 in (10–20 cm)

Found from southeastern Europe to the Caucasus region. Strong fleshy stems and ferny base leaves. Flowers 1–1¾ in (25–40 mm) wide, white, blue, mauve, or pink, from late winter. '**Atrocaerulea**' (syn. 'Ingramii'), deep blue flowers; '**Radar**', white-centered deep magenta-pink flowers; '**White Splendour**', tall grower, large white flowers, pink-tinted inside. Zones 5–9.

Anemone coronaria
FLORIST'S ANEMONE, WIND POPPY, WINDFLOWER

☼/◐ ❄ ↔ 8–16 in (20–40 cm) ↕ 16–24 in (40–60 cm)

Tuberous-rooted native of southeastern Europe and northern Mediterranean. Finely divided ferny base foliage and simple leaves on flower stems. Large spring flowers in most shades except yellow. Parent of many cultivars and a large range of garden hybrids, such as the **Mona Lisa Series**, which grow to 24 in (60 cm) tall with flowers to 4 in (10 cm) wide in all colors. Zones 8–10.

Anemone blanda

Anemone hupehensis var. japonica

Anemone pavonina

Anemone sylvestris

Anemone hupehensis

☼/☀ ❄ ↔ 16–40 in (40–100 cm) ↑ 20–36 in (50–90 cm)
Fibrous-rooted, late summer- to autumn-flowering species from China and Japan. Coarsely toothed, lightly downy, 3-part foliage. Upright branching flower stems with large flowers, usually white but often in pink shades. Fluffy seedheads follow. *A. h.* var. *japonica*, *A. h.* var. *japonica* 'Prinz Heinrich', and *A. h.* 'Hadspen Abundance' are attractive forms. Zones 6–9.

Anemone × hybrida

☼/☀ ❄ ↔ 20–48 in (50–120 cm) ↑ 32–60 in (80–150 cm)
Garden hybrids of uncertain origin. 'Géantes des Blanches', 4 ft (1.2 m) tall, large, white, semi-double flowers; 'Honorine Jobert' ★, 4 ft (1.2 m) tall, large, white, single flowers with pale pink reverse; 'Margarete', 3 ft (0.9 m) tall, pink double flowers; 'September Charm' (syn. *A. hupehensis* 'September Charm'), 30 in (75 cm) high, tall, pink flowers, often drooping. Zones 6–9.

Anemone nemorosa

WINDFLOWER, WOOD ANEMONE

☼/☀ ❄ ↔ 6–16 in (15–40 cm) ↑ 4–12 in (10–30 cm)
Fleshy-stemmed, spring-flowering, European native usually found in woodlands. Leaflets are in 3s, coarsely toothed, and/or finely divided. Flowers are around 1 in (25 mm) wide, usually white in the wild but garden forms come in a range of mauve and pink shades. Cultivars include 'Allenii', 'Pallida', 'Robinsoniana', and 'Vestal'. Zones 5–9.

Anemone pavonina

ANEMONE OF GREECE

☼/☀ ❄ ↔ 12–16 in (30–40 cm) ↑ 12 in (30 cm)
Clump-forming tuberous species native to the Mediterranean region. Three-part base foliage deeply divided and ferny, bright green. In spring, 2–4 in (5–10 cm) wide flowers in a range of colors. Allow to dry off after flowering. Zones 8–10.

Anemone sylvestris

SNOWDROP ANEMONE, SNOWDROP WINDFLOWER

☀ ❄ ↔ 6–20 in (15–50 cm) ↑ 6–12 in (15–30 cm)
A spreading fleshy-stemmed European species that is found to occur in a range of conditions from lowland woods to subalpine

regions. The species has deeply divided, deep green, hand-shaped leaves and, appearing from late spring, scented white flowers that are up to 3 in (8 cm) wide, often slightly drooping. These are followed by fluffy seedheads. Cultivars include 'Elise Fellman' (syn. 'Flore Pleno') and 'Grandiflora'. Zones 4–9.

ANGELONIA

There are some 30 species of subshrubs or perennials in this genus in the foxglove (Scrophulariaceae) family. Native to central and southern America, they grow in damp open spaces. Leaves are usually small and simple. The short, 5-lobed, tubular flowers are mauve, blue, or white and are produced for much of the year. In cool and temperate climates these are usually treated as annuals.
CULTIVATION: Grow in a sunny position in a moist but well-drained light soil. Indoors they require bright filtered light in a potting mix with added organic matter and should be kept moist. Propagate from seed or softwood cuttings, or by division.

Angelonia angustifolia

☼ ❄ ↔ 12 in (30 cm) ↑ 18 in (45 cm)
From Mexico and West Indies. Small pointed leaves with serrated edges, and racemes of mauve to violet flowers in summer. Colored strains are available in white (alba), purple, purple and white, and rose pink. Zones 9–11.

ANIGOZANTHOS

KANGAROO PAW

This genus contains 11 species of evergreen sword-leafed perennials of the bloodroot (Haemodoraceae) family, all of which are confined naturally to southwestern Australia. The foliage is dark green and varies from grassy to iris-like. Spikes or panicles of intriguingly furry tubular blooms are borne on stems 1–6 ft (0.3–1.8 m) tall, usually in warmer months. Flowers are around 1¼ in (30 mm) long and occur in green and warm shades of gold, pink, red, and russet brown, depending on the species. The flower stems last well when cut.
CULTIVATION: Plant in a sunny position with perfect drainage. Better if watered well in the growing season but will tolerate drought. Blackened foliage signals ink disease, which can be very damaging, as can slugs and snails. Propagation in gardens is mostly by careful division. Species may be raised from seed.

Anigozanthos flavidus

GREEN KANGAROO PAW, TALL KANGAROO PAW

↔ 3 ft (0.9 m) ↕ 10 ft (3 m)

Found in moist positions in forested regions of southern and southwestern Australia on sandy and gravelly soils. Summer-flowering perennial with green leaves to 3 ft (0.9 m) long. Flowering stems smooth, green, to 10 ft (3 m) tall. Hairy, tubular flowers are green or yellow-green, sometimes red, orange, or pink. Zones 9–11.

Anigozanthos manglesii

MANGLES' KANGAROO PAW, RED AND GREEN KANGAROO PAW

↔ 36 in (90 cm) ↕ 12–20 in (30–50 cm)

Usually a short-lived perennial, this species occurs on well-drained sandy soils along the western coast of Western Australia. Leaves flat, smooth, gray-green. Flower stems red, woolly, hairy, rarely branched. Tubular flowers green, red at base, in late winter–early summer. Zones 9–10.

Anigozanthos manglesii

Anigozanthos Hybrid Cultivars

↔ 8–30 in (20–75 cm) ↕ 1–6 ft (0.3–1.8 m)

There are now many attractive cultivars being offered to the gardening public. Cultivars include '**Autumn Sunrise**' ★, orange flowers in late spring–summer; '**Big Red**', many red flowers; '**Copper Charm**', tall scapes of orange flowers in spring; '**Dwarf Delight**', red hairs on yellow-green flowers; '**Hickman's Delight**', dark green leaves, dark red flowers; '**Little Jewel**', glossy green evergreen leaves, red flowers in spring; '**Mini Red**', compact plant, dense clusters of red flowers; '**Patricia**', red-brown flowers in spring; '**Pink Joey**', pale, purplish pink flowers; '**Red Cross**', large deep burgundy-colored flowers with a yellow spot at the base; '**Regal Claw**', red to orange flowers over most of the year; '**Ruby Jools**', leaves semi-deciduous, flowers red-green; '**Space Age**', red flowers; '**Spence's Spectacular**', red-brown flowers, deciduous leaves; '**Sue Dixon**', flowers red near base merging to yellow-green near lobes; and '**Velvet Harmony**', very dark, woolly, purplish flowers. The **Bush Gems Series** comes in a wide variety of colors. Zones 9–11.

ANTENNARIA

CAT'S EARS, EVERLASTING, LADIES' TOBACCO, PUSSY-TOES

Found in the northern temperate zone, especially in Asia and North America, this genus in the daisy (Asteraceae) family includes some 45 species of near-evergreen perennials characterized by a low, spreading habit and densely felted foliage. Flowerheads, on felted stems well above the foliage, are small, lack ray florets (petals), and are held within dry bracts. They are usually white, cream or pink, the foliage and growth habit perhaps being more important than the flowers.

CULTIVATION: These plants are used mainly as small-scale ground covers for rockeries and alpine troughs and to provide a foliage color contrast for showier plants. Grow in a sunny position with well-drained, somewhat gritty soil that can be kept moist in summer. Established plants can be divided or will self-layer, or fresh stocks can be raised from seed.

Antennaria dioica

CATSFOOT

↔ 24–36 in (60–90 cm) ↕ 8 in (20 cm)

Widespread in northern temperate zone. Mat-forming with felted, silver-gray, spatula-shaped leaves. White, cream, pink, or red flowerheads, on sturdy stems, in summer. Zones 5–9.

ANTHEMIS

DOG FENNEL

This genus in the daisy (Asteraceae) family contains around 100 species. These aromatic perennials and small shrubs are found mainly in the Mediterranean region and western Asia. Their leaves are usually very finely divided, sometimes gray-green or silvery, and form a base foliage clump with the yellow or white, rarely mauve, daisy flowers held above it.

CULTIVATION: Hardy, easily grown in moist, fertile, well-drained soil in full sun. Cut back after flowering for bushiness. May be short-lived. but easily propagated from cuttings and seed; some perennials may be divided.

Anthemis punctata

↔ 12–20 in (30–50 cm) ↕ 16–24 in (40–60 cm)

Found in Europe, the Mediterranean islands, and North Africa. Woody-based perennial with silky, white, pinnate leaves to around 4 in (10 cm) long. Abundant white flowerheads in summer. *A. p.* subsp. *cupaniana* ★ from Sicily has silver-gray foliage and is a vigorous grower. Zones 7–9.

Anthemis tinctoria

DYER'S CHAMOMILE, YELLOW CHAMOMILE

↔ 20–40 in (50–100 cm) ↕ 24–36 in (60–90 cm)

A shrubby perennial found from Europe to western Asia. Masses of golden flowerheads during the warmer months. Popular cultivars include '**E. C. Buxton**' (syn. '**Mrs E. C. Buxton**'), '**Golden Rays**', '**Sauce Hollandaise**', and '**Wargrave Variety**' (syn. '**Wargrave**'). Zones 6–9.

Anthemis tinctoria 'Wargrave Variety'

Anthurium andraeanum

ANTHERICUM

There are over 50 species of perennial herbs in this genus which belongs to the agave (Agavaceae) family. They are found in southern Europe, Turkey, and Africa, growing in dry meadows and open scrub. They have short fleshy stems and fleshy roots and form clumps of narrow grass-like leaves. The flowering stems are tall and slender and bear airy sprays of white starry flowers in late spring and early summer.
CULTIVATION: Grow in full sun in fertile well-drained soil. Most species prefer alkaline conditions. Do not allow to dry out during the growth period. Propagate from seed or by division.

Anthericum liliago
ST BERNARD'S LILY
☼ ❄ ↔ 12 in (30 cm) ↕ 24–36 in (60–90 cm)
Native to alpine meadows of southern Europe. Grass-like leaves to 16 in (40 cm) long. Starry white flowers, 1 in (2.5 cm) wide, borne on slender stems, in late spring. *A. l.* var. *major* has taller flowering stems and somewhat bigger flowers. Zones 7–9.

ANTHURIUM

This genus from the tropical Americas belongs to the arum (Araceae) family and encompasses around 900 species of evergreen perennials and climbers. They are widely grown as houseplants but also grown outdoors in the tropics. The large, elliptical, lance- or arrow-shaped leaves are usually held upright on stiff stems that emerge from a stout rootstock that may also produce aerial roots. The flowerheads consist of a shield-shaped spathe surrounding a protruding spadix. The spathe and spadix tend to be the same colour, often bright red. Anthuriums last well as cut flowers and are an important industry in Hawaii.
CULTIVATION: Mainly epiphytes in the wild, they adapt well to container and garden cultivation, thriving in bright humid conditions with moist humus-rich soil. Completely intolerant of frost, they cope with cool conditions quite well, though prolonged warmth is required for flowering.

Anthurium andraeanum
FLAMINGO FLOWER
☼/◐ ⚘ ↔ 12–24 in (30–60 cm) ↕ 20–48 in (50–120 cm)
From Colombia and Ecuador. Dark green arrowhead-shaped leaves up to 20 in (50 cm) long on equally long stalks. Bright, deep red, glossy, heavily veined, heart-shaped spathe with white to cream spadix and red fruit. Cultivars include 'Lady Ruth', probably of hybrid origin, 'Rhodochlorum', 'Rubrum', and 'Small Talk Pink'. Zones 11–12.

Anthurium scherzerianum ★
☼/◐ ⚘ ↔ 12–20 in (30–50 cm) ↕ 24–30 in (60–75 cm)
Compact terrestrial species from Costa Rica. Popular house plant. Narrow elliptical to lance-shaped leaves to 10 in (25 cm) long on slightly shorter stems. Stems extend beyond foliage, often red. Spathes bright red, broad. Spadix orange to red, twisted. Fruit red. Zones 11–12.

Anthurium warocqueanum
QUEEN ANTHURIUM
☼/◐ ⚘ ↔ 3–10 ft (0.9–3 m) ↕ 24–60 in (60–150 cm)
From Colombia. Spreading ground cover sometimes climbing to over 5 ft (1.5 m). Stunning pendent, elongated, heart-shaped leaves to 3 ft (0.9 m) long, dark green with velvety texture and large pale-green veins. Flowers on short stems among foliage. Spathe green and spadix yellow green. Zone 12.

ANTIRRHINUM
SNAPDRAGON
Found in temperate Northern Hemisphere areas, this genus of around 40 species of annuals, perennials, and subshrubs belongs to the figwort or foxglove (Scrophulariaceae) family. Most species are compact, forming a low mound of simple rounded to lance-shaped leaves, sometimes with a gray-green tint. Flowering stems develop from late spring and carry heads of the familiar lobed blooms.
CULTIVATION: These species grow best in a fertile, moist, humus-rich soil in full sun. The Mediterranean species are reasonably drought tolerant but need moisture to flower well. Rust diseases can cause problems in humid conditions. Propagation is from seed, though the perennial species will grow from cuttings of non-flowering stems.

Antirrhinum majus, Chimes Series, 'Chimes Red'

Antirrhinum majus
☼/◐ ❄ ↔ 6–20 in (15–50 cm)
↕ 12–60 in (30–150 cm)
Southwest European perennial, usually treated as an annual. Upright bushy habit, dark green, elliptical leaves. Flowers in upright racemes, usually pink in wild, but cultivated in most colors except blue. Popular seedling series include the dwarf **Candelabra Series** and **Chimes Series,** particularly 'Chimes Red' ★, the mid-height **Sonnet Series**, and the slightly taller, often double-flowered **Liberty Series**. Zones 7–10.

Antirrhinum molle

☼/◐ ❊ ↔ 6–8 in (15–20 cm) ↑ 8–16 in (20–40 cm)

Native to Portugal and northeastern Spain. Downy elliptical leaves, flowers pale pink or white with yellow throat and downy exterior. '**Avalanche**', white flowers with a small yellow patch on lower lip, blooms for most of the year. Zones 7–10.

APONOGETON

A member of the family Aponogetonaceae, this genus consists of some 44 species of aquatic herbaceous perennials from many tropical and subtropical areas, some of which have become weedy in areas where they are not native. The foliage can be submerged or floating, rather like that of a waterlily. The flowers are produced in a compound panicle that sits above the water. These can make attractive pond plants, and the more tropical species are often used in indoor heated aquariums. CULTIVATION: Plant *Aponogeton* species in mud in the bottom of a pond, either in full sun or half-shade. Propagation is from fresh seed, or by division.

Aquilegia canadensis

Aponogeton distachyos

CAPE POND WEED, WATER HAWTHORN

☼/◐ ✢ ↔ 32–40 in (80–100 cm) ↑ 24–32 in (60–80 cm)

From South Africa, this species is naturalized in parts of Australia. It has oblong floating leaves. Its white and purple scented flowers are seen in a forked spike just above water level, during summer. The flowers are edible. Zones 9–11.

AQUILEGIA

COLUMBINE, GRANNY'S BONNET

This genus in the buttercup (Ranunculaceae) family has about 70 species, found over much of the temperate and subarctic Northern Hemisphere. Fine-stemmed, often blue-green foliage emerges from a woody rootstock. Flowering stems usually reach above the foliage and carry spurred, bell-shaped, often pendulous flowers. Some are short-flowering, others bloom through much of late spring and summer. CULTIVATION: An adaptable genus, with species suitable for woodland, rockeries, and perennial borders. Generally they prefer a cool-winter climate and a place in half-sun with cool, moist, humus-rich, well-drained soil. Often attracts aphids. Some species can be divided when dormant but propagation is usually from seed. May self-sow, can be invasive.

Aquilegia caerulea

BLUE COLUMBINE, ROCKY MOUNTAIN COLUMBINE

☼/◐ ❊ ↔ 8–16 in (20–40 cm)

↑ 8–24 in (20–60 cm)

From high woodlands and mountains of western USA. Large flowers. White to cream petals, blue or pink sepals, long spurs. Zones 3–9.

Aquilegia canadensis

CANADA COLUMBINE, MEETING HOUSES, ROCK BELLS, WILD COLUMBINE

◐ ❊ ↔ 12–20 in (30–50 cm) ↑ 12–30 in (30–75 cm)

Found over much of eastern North America. Soft yellow, red-spurred flowers are borne on many-branched, wiry stems. Prefers rockery or woodland conditions. Flowers popular with hummingbirds. Zones 2–10.

Aquilegia chrysantha

GOLDEN COLUMBINE

◐ ❊ ↔ 12–32 in (30–80 cm)

↑ 32–36 in (80–90 cm)

Found in southern USA. Vigorous tall stems and large bright yellow flowers with long curved spurs, slightly paler in color. Several cultivars available, including double-flowered, white, and very tall types. '**Denver Gold**', huge flowers to 3 in (8 cm) wide; '**Yellow Queen**', larger, brighter yellow flowers than species. Zones 3–10.

Aquilegia formosa

WESTERN COLUMBINE

◐ ❊ ↔ 12–20 in (30–50 cm) ↑ 20–36 in (50–90 cm)

From western USA, this species has a graceful open habit with many small, orange-red, short-spurred flowers on each of its stems. An excellent source of nectar for hummingbirds, butterflies and bees. A number of cultivars are available, including dwarf types, and it is widely hybridized. Zones 3–9.

Aquilegia, McKana Group

☼/◐ ❊ ↔ 12–20 in (30–50 cm) ↑ 32–48 in (80–120 cm)

These hybrids between several North American species cover a wide color range. Most of the hybrids in the group are tall upright plants with long-spurred flowers and contrasting colors of corolla and sepals. Zones 3–10.

Aquilegia chrysantha

Aquilegia, Hybrid Cultivar, Songbird Series, 'Cardinal'

Aquilegia vulgaris

☼/◐ ❄ ↔ 8–18 in (20–45 cm) ↑ 12–36 in (30–90 cm)

Found over most of Europe. Ferny foliage; flowers with hooked spurs in white and shades of blue, mauve, and red, including double-flowered forms. The wild species is seldom seen in gardens but there are many cultivars. Single-flowered cultivars include '**Heidi**', purple-red-stemmed, nodding, soft pink flowers; '**Hensol Harebell**', short-spurred, mauve-blue flowers; and '**Nivea**' (syn. 'Munstead White'), gray-green foliage; pure white flowers. Double-flowered cultivars can be divided into the following groups. **Flore Pleno Group**, elongated flowers, rounded petals, includes '**Graeme Iddon**', tall, white flowers, has spawned a range of double-flowered forms; and '**Rougham Star**', flowers with white inner petals, mauve-blue outer petals and sepals. **Stellata Group**, star-shaped double flowers, radiating pointed petals, includes '**Black Barlow**', deep purple to near black flowers; '**Blue Barlow**', double blue flowers; '**Nora Barlow**' ★, green, white, and pink pompon-like flowers; and '**Rose Barlow**', mid-pink and cream flowers. **Vervaeneana Group**, marbled green and gold foliage and variable flower color. Zones 3–10.

Aquilegia Hybrid Cultivars

☼/◐ ❄ ↔ 12–24 in (30–60 cm)
↑ 18–36 in (45–90 cm)

Aquilegias have been so widely hybridized, particularly among the American species, that there are now hybrids in almost any conceivable size and flower color. *A.* 'Crimson Star', 24 in (60 cm) tall, large, red-spurred cream flowers. The **Butterfly Series** includes '**Brimstone**', cream and soft yellow; and '**Holly Blue**', white to pale mauve petals, powder blue sepals. The **Songbird Series**, compact foliage clump, 24 in (60 cm) flower stems, large flowers in many shades, includes '**Bluebird**', very large flowers, white petals, soft blue sepals; '**Cardinal**', white petals with pink markings, dark red sepals; '**Dove**', pure white; '**Goldfinch**', bright yellow; '**Redwing**', white to cream petals, deep red sepals; and '**Robin**', white to pale pink petals, dusky deep pink sepals. The **State Series** includes '**Alaska**', pure white flowers; '**Colorado**', semi-double flowers, mauve and white petals with purple sepals; '**Florida**', yellow petals, creamy white sepals; '**Kansas**', bright yellow petals, vivid red sepals; and '**Louisiana**', creamy white petals, deep red sepals. Zones 4–10.

ARABIS

ROCK CRESS

This genus belongs to the cabbage (Brassicaceae) family and has around 120 species of annuals and perennials, mainly evergreen and sometimes woody-stemmed. Widespread in the northern temperate zones, especially Eurasia and western North America, they tend to be small plants that are often most at home in rock crevices. Their leaves are simple, sometimes downy or gray-green, and are often borne in tufted rosettes. In spring and early summer they carry upright sprays of small 4-petalled flowers, usually white or purple.

CULTIVATION: Most are hardy and easily grown in any temperate climate. Plant in a sunny position with well-drained soil that remains moist in summer. Ideal in rockeries or spilling over banks. Many species appreciate a light dressing of lime. Remove spent flowerheads to keep tidy and encourage continued blooming. Propagation is mainly from seed, though perennials will grow from base cuttings and a few species can be divided with care.

Arabis × *arendsii*

☼/◐ ❄ ↔ 12–24 in (30–60 cm) ↑ 4–8 in (10–20 cm)

Garden hybrid between *A. aubrietoides* and *A. caucasica*. Usually low and spreading, with tufted foliage clumps. Flower stems up to 6 in (15 cm) high, with deep pink flowers. '**Compinkie**' (syn. *A. caucasica* 'Compinkie'), bright pink flowers; '**Monte Rosa**', maroon flowers; '**Rubin**', wine red flowers. Zones 5–9.

Arabis blepharophylla

☼/◐ ❄ ↔ 6–8 in (15–20 cm)
↑ 4–6 in (10–15 cm)

Californian perennial with small rosettes of deep to bright green leaves. Flowers deep pink to purple-red. '**Frühlingszauber**' (syn. 'Spring Charm') is a compact cultivar with bright magenta flowers. Zones 7–9.

Arabis caucasica

☼/◐ ❄ ↔ 8–20 in (20–50 cm)
↑ 6–12 in (15–30 cm)

Arabis caucasica 'Schneehaube'

Perennial from southern European mountains. Gray-green leaves. White flowers, rarely pink, from spring to early summer. Sometimes confused with *A. alpina* in cultivation. '**Pinkie**', bright pink flowers; '**Flore Pleno**', more upright growth habit, white double flowers; '**Schneehaube**' (syn. 'Snowcap'), low and spreading with white flowers; '**Variegata**', white-edged leaves, masses of white flowers. Zones 4–9.

ARCTOTIS

AFRICAN DAISY

Found from the southern tip of Africa northward to Angola, this genus in the daisy (Asteraceae) family consists of around 50 species of low spreading annuals and perennials that often produce masses of large and brightly colored flowerheads. The leaves are simple, usually lance-shaped and frequently have felted undersides. For much of the year in mild climates the foliage is topped by 1–4 in (2.5–10 cm) wide flowers in a range of colors.
CULTIVATION: They thrive in light well-drained soil and full sun. They are drought tolerant but will flower more heavily if watered well in the growing season. Propagate from seed, though perennials grow readily from cuttings of non-flowering stems.

Arctotis acaulis

☼ ❄ ↔ 12–40 in (30–100 cm) ↕ 6–12 in (15–30 cm)
Clumping rosette-forming perennial. Wavy, lobed, or toothed leaves. Flowerheads to 4 in (10 cm) wide, ray florets mainly in yellow, orange, or red shades, disc florets deep purple. 'Magenta', long-stemmed purple-red flowers. Zones 8–10.

Arctotis × hybrida

☼ ⚘ ↔ 8–20 in (20–50 cm) ↕ 8–16 in (20–40 cm)
Compact plants, usually with silvery foliage. Often treated as annuals in cool climates. Many popular named cultivars and seedling strains. 'Flame' ★, bright orange flowers; 'Mahogany', deep red-brown flowers; 'Red Devil', bright red. Zones 9–11.

Arctotis venusta

BLUE-EYED AFRICAN DAISY

☼ ⚘ ↔ 8–16 in (20–40 cm) ↕ 16–24 in (40–60 cm)
Annual with deeply lobed to almost pinnate, downy, gray-white leaves and heavily ribbed flower stems. Flowers in cultivation are variably colored but wild plants usually have deep magenta ray florets and purple-blue disc florets. Zones 9–11.

ARENARIA

SANDWORT

This genus of about 160 low-growing, largely perennial, woody herbs and some annuals from the pink (Caryophyllaceae) family is found across the temperate Northern Hemisphere. They are ideal rock-garden plants and compact ground covers. The branching stems bear masses of dense, often hairy foliage. Abundant, small, star-like flowers, normally white and 5-petalled, grow in cymes or solitary. The shallow root system can make them drought sensitive. Fruit is a cylindrical or ovoid capsule with 6 lobes.
CULTIVATION: Most species need partial shade and protection from hot afternoon sun, especially in hot climates. They will tolerate poor soils, but the soil should be moist, sandy, and well drained. Shallow roots will require mulching or frequent watering around, but not over, the plant. Propagate by division, from seed in autumn or spring, or from softwood cuttings in early summer.

Arctotis × *hybrida* 'Red Devil'

Arenaria montana

☼/◐ ❄ ↔ 9–24 in (23–60 cm) ↕ 4–6 in (10–15 cm)
Vigorous perennial from southwestern Europe. Loose mats of narrow, gray-green, hairy leaves. Small white flowers, in spring–early summer. 'Avalanche', more profuse, larger white flowers. Zones 4–8.

Arenaria purpurascens

☼/◐ ❄ ↔ 9–24 in (23–60 cm) ↕ 4–6 in (10–15 cm)
Evergreen, tufted, mat-forming perennial with small, sharply pointed, glossy leaves, from northern Spain. Many small clusters of 1 to 4 tiny, pale to deep purplish pink flowers, in early spring–summer. 'Elliot's Variety', abundant pink flowers. Zones 4–8.

ARGEMONE

A genus of 23 species of annual or perennial herbs and a shrub, in the poppy (Papaveraceae) family. Occurs in North and South America, West Indies, and Hawaii, in drier plant communities, commonly colonizing. Erect stems are produced from fleshy roots, leaves entire or deeply lobed, prickly or smooth, bluish green. Flowers broad and shallow, white, yellow, or mauve, in clusters or singly, in summer–autumn. Fruits are prickly pods, containing many blackish seeds. Stems contain a yellowish latex.
CULTIVATION: Propagate from seed. Grow in full sun in well-draining gravelly soils. Self-seeding occurs with some species.

Argemone mexicana

MEXICAN POPPY, PRICKLY POPPY

☼ ❄ ↔ 12–16 in (30–40 cm) ↕ to 36 in (90 cm)
Erect, spreading annual. Leaves deeply lobed, with silvery spines. Yellow flowers, to 3 in (8 cm) across, in summer–autumn. A weed from southern USA to Central America. 'White Lustre', white flowers; 'Yellow Lustre', orange-yellow flowers. Zones 8–10.

ARISTEA

This genus belonging to the iris (Iridaceae) family has about 50 mainly evergreen species of fleshy-stemmed perennials found in Africa from the tropics to South Africa and Madagascar. They have upright sword-shaped leaves, in fans. The 6-petalled flowers, borne on branching stems with somewhat flattened segments, occur in shades of blue, lavender, and purple, and are short-lived. The flowering season ranges from late winter to summer.

CULTIVATION: Tolerant of only light frosts, most prefer to grow in sun or half-sun with a light but humus-rich, moist, well-drained soil. Plants can be divided but resent disturbance, so they are usually propagated from seed, which may be sown in autumn in frost-free areas, otherwise in spring.

Aristea major

◐/◑ ❄ ↔ 24–36 in (60–90 cm) ↕ 3–5 ft (0.9–1.5 m)
From the Cape region of South Africa. Blue-green leaves, 3–4 ft (0.9–1.2 m) long. Rootstock can form a trunk. Dense clusters of soft blue flowers, to 1½ in (35 mm) wide, in summer. Zones 9–10.

Aristea major

ARISTOLOCHIA

BIRTHWORT, DUTCHMAN'S PIPE

This genus of about 300 species ranging from vigorous climbers to perennials, both deciduous and evergreen, found throughout tropical and temperate regions, is a member of the birthwort (Aristolochiaceae) family. Stems are usually thick and fissured; leaves vary from entire to lobed, often being heart-shaped. The flowers, which trap pollinating insects, have bladder-like bases and contorted, tubular shapes. They range from less than 3 in (8 cm) to giants of 20 in (50 cm) and many have an offensive smell. Flowers are mottled in shades of brown, pink, purple, and ivory. The common name, birthwort, comes from the herbal use of some species as an aid to childbirth.

CULTIVATION: Many of the vigorous climbers are hardy only to 23°F (–5°C) and better suit the greenhouse in cooler areas. Where suitable, grow outdoors in sun or half-sun in rich well-drained soil. Climbers require support and can be pruned in late winter. Propagate from softwood cuttings or seed, or by division.

Aristolochia clematitis

◐/◑ ❄ ↔ 24 in (60 cm) ↕ 12–30 in (30–75 cm)
Native to Europe and naturalized in the UK and North America. Herbaceous species with heart-shaped leaves. Small dull greenish yellow flowers appear among the foliage in summer. Zones 6–10.

ARMERIA

SEA PINK, THRIFT

Armeria belongs to the leadwort (Plumbaginaceae) family. The genus comprises around 80 species of herbaceous and shrubby perennials found in Eurasia, North Africa, and the American Pacific coast. They form clumps of simple linear leaves, with rounded heads of tiny flowers with colorful bracts held in spring and summer.

CULTIVATION: They occur in a wide range of environments and are easily cultivated, being especially at home in rockeries. Most are hardy and prefer moist well-drained soil and a position in full or half-sun. Propagate from seed or cuttings, or by the careful division of well-established clumps.

Armeria juniperifolia

◐/◑ ❄ ↔ 6–8 in (15–20 cm) ↕ 6 in (15 cm)
Small shrubby perennial native to Spain. Very short, finely hairy, aromatic, grassy leaves. Flower stems less than 2 in (5 cm) long. Pink to magenta flowerheads, ½ in (12 mm) wide. 'Bevan's Variety' is a compact cultivar with dark foliage and short-stemmed pink flowerheads. Zones 8–10.

Armeria maritima

◐/◑ ❄ ↔ 8–16 in (20–40 cm) ↕ 8–12 in (20–30 cm)
This mounding perennial or subshrub is found across the northern temperate zone. It has grassy deep green leaves to 4 in (10 cm) long. Flower stems grow to 12 in (30 cm) tall with 1 in (25 mm) wide heads of white, pink, or red flowers. A. m. subsp. californica, from California, USA, mounds to 6 in (15 cm) high and has lavender-pink flowerheads on short stems. A. m. 'Bee's Ruby', 'Bloodstone' ★, 'Corsica', 'Isobel Burdett', 'Rubrifolia', and 'Vindictive' are attractive cultivars. Zones 4–10.

Armeria maritima

Artemisia 'Powis Castle'

Armeria pseudarmeria

☀ ❄ ↔16–40 in (40–100 cm)
↕8–16 in (20–40 cm)

This dwarf subshrub or woody-based perennial is a native of coastal Portugal. Has fine grassy leaves around 1 in (25 mm) long. Flower stems are tall compared to the plant, with white to deep pink flowerheads to 2 in (5 cm) wide. '**Rubra**', is a red-flowered cultivar; '**Westacre Beauty**' has soft pink flowers. Zones 8–10.

ARTEMISIA

This genus of about 300 species of evergreen herbs and shrubs is spread throughout northern temperate regions with some also found in southern Africa and South America. It is a member of the daisy (Asteraceae) family but they bear small dull white or yellow flowerheads without ray florets. The attractive foliage is well dissected and of palest gray to silver. The plants are frequently aromatic. Tarragon, the popular culinary herb, is a member of this genus (*Artemisia dracunculus*).
CULTIVATION: These shrubs are ideal for hot dry areas as most can withstand considerable periods of drought. They should be grown in a full-sun position in well-drained soil. Their silvery leaves provide an attractive foliage contrast in borders, and when clipped some species can be used as a low hedge. Prune quite hard in spring and lightly clip at flowering time if the flowers are not wanted. Propagation is usually from softwood or half-hardened cuttings in summer.

Artemisia lactiflora

WHITE MUGWORT

☀ ❄ ↔24 in (60 cm) ↕5 ft (1.5 m)

From China. A perennial species forming clumps of green divided leaves. Tall showy plumes of tiny cream flowers in mid-summer. Requires more moisture than most species. Mahogany stems and purplish green foliage are a feature of the **Guizhou Group**. Zones 4–10.

Artemisia ludoviciana

syns *Artemisia gnaphalodes*, *A. purshiana*
CUDWEED, SILVER WORMWOOD, WESTERN MUGWORT, WHITE SAGE

☀ ❄ ↔36 in (90 cm) ↕36 in (90 cm)

Native to USA. Perennial herb with white downy stems and narrow, silvery gray, aromatic foliage. Sprays of tiny grayish white flowers in summer. *A. l.* subsp. *mexicana* var. *albula* has lance-shaped leaves, white and hairy. *A. l.* '**Silver Queen**' and '**Valerie Finnis**' are attractive cultivars. Zones 5–10.

Artemisia 'Powis Castle' ★

☀ ❄ ↔4 ft (1.2 m) ↕2 ft (0.6 m)

Similar to *A. arborescens* but its habit is more sprawling, with woody stems usually lying on the ground. This is possibly a hybrid between *A. arborescens* and *A. pontica*. Zones 7–10.

Artemisia stelleriana

BEACH WORMWOOD, DUSTY MILLER, OLD WOMAN

☀ ❄ ↔18 in (45 cm) ↕18–24 in (45–60 cm)

Evergreen fleshy-stemmed perennial from northeastern Asia and eastern USA. Heavily felted gray-white leaves, deeply lobed. Sprays of tiny yellow flowers in summer. '**Boughton Silver**' and '**Mori**' are white-leafed prostrate forms. Zones 3–9.

ARTHROPODIUM

This genus in the family Laxmanniaceae has about 12 species of evergreen or deciduous fleshy-stemmed perennials found mostly in Australia and New Zealand. Plants form clumps of linear leaves. The white to pale mauve and violet flowers have 6 petals with yellow and purple stamens. They are borne in panicles.
CULTIVATION: In warm areas, grow in well-drained soil in sun or half-sun. Where frosts are worse, choose a warm sheltered site or grow in a greenhouse. Propagate from seed or by division.

Arthropodium cirratum

Arthropodium cirratum

RENGARENGA, ROCK LILY

☀/❄ ❄ ↔24 in (60 cm) ↕20–30 in (50–75 cm)

Variable evergreen species, native to New Zealand. Fleshy strap-shaped leaves, to 24 in (60 cm) long, may have bluish green overtones. Flowering stems bear airy panicles of starry white flowers, early to mid-summer. Zones 9–11.

ARUNCUS

GOAT'S BEARD

This genus is a member of the rose (Rosaceae) family and contains 2 or 3 species of deciduous perennials native to northern temperate and subarctic regions. They are grown for their large fern-like leaves and tiny flowers.
CULTIVATION: Grow in moist soil in half-sun. Propagate by division in autumn or early spring, or from seed sown in autumn.

Aruncus dioicus

syns *Aruncus sylvester*, *A. vulgaris*, *Spiraea aruncus*
GOAT'S BEARD

☀ ❄ ↔4 ft (1.2 m) ↕2–6 ft (0.6–1.8 m)

From Europe and northern Asia. Imposing plant forming large clumps. Panicles of cream flowers, up to 20 in (50 cm) long, in summer. Weed in much of Australia. Zones 3–9.

ASCLEPIAS

MILKWEED

This American and African genus is a member of the dogbane (Apocynaceae) family and comprises over 100 species, including annuals, perennials, subshrubs, and shrubs. These plants have simple, narrow, elliptical to lance-shaped leaves. They produce heads of small 5-petalled flowers followed by seed pods, sometimes oddly shaped, tightly packed with small seeds, each with a small parachute of silky down. All parts of the plants exude a milky sap if they are cut, hence the common name. The sap is poisonous in some species.
CULTIVATION: Easily grown in light, well-drained soil in full sun, milkweeds will, however, have more luxuriant foliage and will flower more heavily if well-fed and watered. They grow readily and quickly from seed, and can be treated as annuals or short-lived perennials. Some species can be propagated from cuttings. Trim to shape, not into bare wood, as plants can be slow to recover from harsh pruning.

Asclepias linaria

PINE-NEEDLE MILKWEED, PINELEAF MILKWEED, THREADLEAF MILKWEED
☼ ❄ ↔ 24–36 in (60–90 cm) ↕ 24–36 in (60–90 cm)
From arid areas of California and Arizona, USA, and Mexico. Shrubby perennial with fine needle-like foliage. Flowers for long periods with small, white, 5-petalled flowers in clusters to 2 in (5 cm) wide. Zones 9–11.

Asclepias tuberosa ★

BUTTERFLY WEED, PLEURISY ROOT
☼ ❄ ↔ 12 in (30 cm) ↕ 24–36 in (60–90 cm)
Native to eastern and southern USA. Woody-based perennial herb. Narrow lance-shaped leaves on crowded stems. Heads of yellow, orange, or vermilion flowers. Pointed seed head to 6 in (15 cm) long. Zones 3–9.

Asclepias tuberosa

ASPARAGUS

syns *Myrsiphyllum*, *Protasparagus*
ASPARAGUS

A genus of about 300 perennial herbs, shrubs, or climbers that grow from a tuberous rhizome. Mostly from Africa and Asia, they belong to the asparagus (Asparagaceae) family. Leaves are small, scaly, and often spiny. Cladophylls (flattened stems that function as a leaf) are green and often needle-like. The green, yellow, or white flowers are small. Fruit is a round berry.
CULTIVATION: These plants prefer rich moist soils in a protected position with filtered sunlight. Propagate by division of crowded roots or from seed. Edible asparagus *(A. officinalis)* is grown from 1-year-old crowns planted in mid- to late winter, spaced 12 in (30 cm) apart, in heavily mulched rows 4–6 ft (1.2–1.8 m) apart. Harvest when spears are 6–10 in (15–25 cm) tall by breaking off at ground level. Full production in 2 to 3 years after planting; plants can produce for up to 25 years.

Asparagus densiflorus

syn. *Protasparagus densiflorus*
ASPARAGUS FERN, EMERALD FERN, FOXTAIL SHRUB, SPRENGER ASPARAGUS
☼ ❄ ↔ 36 in (90 cm) ↕ 30–36 in (75–90 cm)
Evergreen trailing plant, native to subtropical South Africa. Thick tuberous roots, No leaves but needle-like branchlets or cladophylls on green or brown, wiry, spiny stems. Small white flowers on axillary racemes in spring and summer. Small bright red berries in winter. Popular cultivars include '**Compactus**' (syn. 'Nanus'), '**Deflexus**', '**Myersii**', and '**Sprengeri**' *(syn. A. sprengeri).* Zones 7–11.

Asparagus macowanii

syns *Asparagus zuluensis*, *Protasparagus macowanii*
☼/❄ ❄ ↔ 8 ft (2.4 m) ↕ 6 ft (1.8 m)
From the South African provinces of Eastern Cape, KwaZulu-Natal, and Mpumalanga. Robust plant with many stems about 1 in (25 mm) thick, springing like giant asparagus spears from a raised root-mass, each whitish stem living for many years, branched above into dense, fine, pale-green foliage. Profuse pure white flowers in mid-summer. Small blackish berries in winter. Zones 9–11.

ASPERULA

WOODRUFF

A genus of around 100 species of annuals, perennials, and small shrubs in the madder (Rubiaceae) family found from Europe through Asia to Australia. Most are mat-forming, with spreading sometimes bristly stems clothed with whorls of simple, narrow, sometimes faintly downy leaves. Some are more upright, often spreading by runners. Tiny, bell- or funnel-shaped, 4-petalled flowers appear in the leaf axils, or in clusters at the stem tips, from spring through summer. The heavy-flowering species smother themselves in bloom.

CULTIVATION: Plant in a bright position with moist, fertile, well-drained soil and trim after flowering. The smaller species are marvellous rockery plants. Propagate from seed, base cuttings, by division or layers, as appropriate.

Asperula gussonei

☀ ❄ ↔ 6–12 in (15–30 cm) ↕ 4 in (10 cm)

Sicilian perennial that forms a mat or tufts of silvery blue-gray whorled leaves around ½ in (12 mm) long. Densely packed heads of up to 15, minute, pale pink to red flowers. Zones 7–10.

Asperula orientalis

syn. *Asperula azurea*

BLUE WOODRUFF

☀/◐ ❄ ↔ 16–24 in (40–60 cm) ↕ 8–12 in (20–30 cm)

Annual from southern Europe, western Asia, and the Middle East. Rangy upright habit with widely spaced whorls of green leaves to 2 in (5 cm) long. Terminal heads of lavender-blue funnel-shaped flowers. Often self-sows. Zones 8–10.

ASPHODELINE

This genus is a member of the asphodel (Asphodelaceae) family. It has 18 to 20 species of fleshy-stemmed perennial or biennial herbs native to southern Europe where they grow on rocky slopes and in scrubby areas. They are clump-forming plants with gray-ish green linear leaves, sometimes with slightly serrated margins. The flowers are about 1¼ in (30 mm) across and are borne in spring and summer. They have 6 flaring petals, yellow or white tinged pink, and are scented in some species.

CULTIVATION: Useful plants for the border, rockery, or for natural-izing. Grow in moderately fertile soil in full sun. Propagate from seed or by division of clumps.

Asphodeline lutea ★

JACOB'S ROD, KING'S SPEAR, YELLOW ASPHODEL

☀ ❄ ↔ 12 in (30 cm) ↕ 36–48 in (90–120 cm)

From the Mediterranean. Narrow silvery leaves to 12 in (30 cm) long. Fragrant yellow flowers, borne on stiff spikes, in late spring–summer. Decorative seed pods. Zones 7–10.

ASPHODELUS

There are 12 species of clump-forming, swollen-rooted perennials in this genus in the asphodel (Asphodelaceae) family. They are found from the Mediterranean to the Himalayas, growing in scrub and on rocky slopes. The leaves are linear, up to 24 in (60 cm) long, and may be flat or cylindrical. The flowers have 6 whorled tepals and are white or pink with green or brown veining. Flowering stems vary in length, from 7 ft (2 m) tall in one species to non-existent in another, which flowers within the basal rosette.

CULTIVATION: *Asphodelus* is best grown in moderately fertile soil in a position that receives full sun. Some of the species, such as the low-growing *A. acaulis,* are better suited to the rockery as they require sharp drainage. Propagate from seed or by division.

Asperula orientalis

Asphodelus aestivus

☀ ❄ ↔ 24 in (60 cm) ↕ 40 in (100 cm)

Native to the Canary Islands and Mediterranean regions. Long, flat, basal leaves, flowering stems with short side branches. Its flowers are starry white, with a central brown stripe on each petal. Spring-flowering species. Zones 7–10.

Asphodelus albus

☀ ❄ ↔ 24 in (60 cm) ↕ 36 in (90 cm)

Native to southern and western Europe and northern Africa, this species has linear leaves that are up to 24 in (60 cm) long. Flowering stems, 12–36 in (30–90 cm) tall, bear white to pale pink flowers, with a pinkish brown stripe on each petal, in spring. Zones 6–10.

Asphodeline lutea

ASPIDISTRA

Found from the Himalayas to Japan, the 8 ever-green perennial species in this genus belong to the family Ruscaceae. Spreading from thick rhi-zomes, they form clumps of tough, deep green, elliptical to lance-shaped leaves that emerge directly from the ground on a strong leaf stalk, either singly or in small clusters. Small, stemless, purple-red to brown, bell- to urn-shaped flowers open from spring.

CULTIVATION: Easily grown outdoors in a mild temperate climate, preferring a shady spot with warm, moist, well-drained soil. They spread well, making an excellent large-scale ground cover.

Aspidistra elatior

BAR ROOM PLANT, CAST-IRON PLANT

☀ ❄ ↔ 16–36 in (40–90 cm) ↕ 16–24 in (40–60 cm)

A Chinese native. Veined, overarching, leathery leaves to 24 in (60 cm) long emerge singly. Flowers unobtrusive, bell-shaped, cream with purple spots to overall purple. Popular house plant, coping well with lack of light. Zones 7–10.

Aster × frikartii 'Mönch'

CULTIVATION: Mostly frost tolerant, they prefer well-drained soil that stays moist in the growing season. A sunny, airy, open position ensures maximum flowering and minimum mildew, a problem in humid conditions. Cut back hard after flowering. Propagate by winter division or from spring softwood cuttings.

ASTELIA

This genus is a member of the family Asteliaceae and contains 25 species of clump-forming evergreen perennials with attractive sword-like leaves. Most species are native to New Zealand with others scattered around Southern Hemisphere islands and Australia. Their natural habitat ranges from alpine areas to lowland forests, and many species are epiphytes. They are primarily grown for their foliage, which has a silvery sheen. The leaves can range in length from 3 in (8 cm) to 7 ft (2 m). The flowers are unisexual and insignificant but are followed by red berries.
CULTIVATION: Most are frost hardy and can be grown outdoors in a fertile moisture-retentive soil in full sun or half-sun. In very cold areas they need a warm sheltered position, or a greenhouse. Propagate by division in spring.

Astelia chathamica
☼/◐ ❄ ↔ 5 ft (1.5 m) ↕ 3–6 ft (0.9–1.8 m)
From New Zealand's Chatham Islands. Ornamental species forming clumps of broad, arching, sword-like leaves with a deep silvery sheen. Zones 8–10.

Astelia nervosa
☼ ❄ ↔ 5 ft (1.5 m) ↕ 3–7 ft (0.9–2 m)
A variable species from New Zealand. Foliage ranges from reddish tones through green to silver, leaves 2–7 ft (0.6–2 m) long. Named color forms are often available. Zones 8–10.

ASTER
MICHAELMAS DAISY
Found across the temperate Northern Hemisphere and into South America, this group of 250 species of mainly herbaceous perennials is the type genus for the daisy (Asteraceae) family. Upright plants that often sprawl under the weight of their foliage and flowers, they usually have simple linear to lance-shaped leaves, sometimes hairy and/or serrated. A few species flower in spring but most bloom in late summer and autumn, producing large heads of small to medium-sized daisies in a range of colors, all with a central eye of purple or yellow.

Aster alpinus
ALPINE ASTER
☼ ❄ ↔ 8–32 in (20–80 cm)
↕ 4–10 in (10–25 cm)
Spreading, sometimes mounding perennial from mountains of southern Europe. Simple spatula-to lance-shaped base foliage. In spring and summer, masses of short-stemmed daisies, to slightly under 2 in (5 cm) wide, in white and all shades of pink, mauve, and purple. Zones 3–9.

Aster amellus
☼ ❄ ↔ 12–20 in (30–50 cm) ↕ 24–27 in (60–70 cm)
Upright Eurasian perennial. Faintly downy stems, green lance-shaped leaves around 2 in (5 cm) long. In autumn, terminal clusters of 2 in (5 cm) wide daisies, violet pink in the wild. Popular cultivars include 'Framfieldii', 'Jacqueline Genebrier', 'King George', 'Sonia', and 'Veilchenkönigin'. Zones 5–9.

Aster ericoides
HEATH ASTER
☼/◐ ❄ ↔ 20–32 in (50–80 cm) ↕ 32–40 in (80–100 cm)
Branching, bushy, North American perennial with narrow leaves to 2½ in (6 cm) long. Blooms in summer and autumn with masses of small daisies on leafy flower stems. Many cultivars, of which 'Pink Cloud' ★, to 3 ft (0.9 m) tall, with bronze new growth and billows of small pink flowers, is typical. Zones 3–9.

Aster × frikartii
☼/◐ ❄ ↔ 16–24 in (40–60 cm) ↕ 20–30 in (50–75 cm)
Garden hybrid between A. amellus and A. thomsonii. Upright perennial with dark green, elongated, lance-shaped base leaves. In autumn, branching sprays of 2 in (5 cm) wide daisies in shades of lavender and purple-blue. 'Mönch' and 'Wunder von Stäfa' are two cultivars with lavender-blue flowers. Zones 4–9.

Aster lateriflorus
☼/◐ ❄ ↔ 2–4 ft (0.6–1.2 m) ↕ 3–4 ft (0.9–1.2 m)
This upright to spreading North American perennial has base leaves to 6 in (15 cm) long, and is autumn-flowering, with sprays of pink-centered white to lavender-pink flowers on downy wiry stems. A. l. var. horizontalis is a spreading variety with brown-centered cream flowers. A. l. 'Prince' ★ is a typical cultivar and grows to 24 in (60 cm) tall, with bronze leaves and pink-centered white flowerheads. Zones 3–9.

Aster novae-angliae

NEW ENGLAND ASTER

☀/◑ ❄ ↔ 2–4 ft (0.6–1.2 m) ↕ 4–5 ft (1.2–1.5 m)

A bushy autumn-flowering perennial that comes from eastern North America. It has lance-shaped base leaves up to 5 in (12 cm) long, and dense sprays of yellow-centered soft purple flowerheads up to 1¾ in (40 mm) wide. Cultivars include '**Andenken an Alma Pötschke**', cerise pink flowers; '**Barr's Pink**', small, deep pink, double flowers; '**Harrington's Pink**', small, soft pink, semi-double flowers; '**Hella Lacy**', violet-blue flowers; and '**Purple Dome**', dwarf, covered in purple flowers. Zones 2–9.

Aster novi-belgii

MICHAELMAS DAISY, NEW YORK ASTER

☀/◑ ❄ ↔ 24–32 in (60–80 cm) ↕ 36–48 in (90–120 cm)

This North American perennial is similar to *A. novae-angliae* except that it is slightly shorter and its leaves are more noticeably toothed. Over 400 cultivars have been raised and include '**Coombe Violet**', tall, deep purple flowers; '**Ernest Ballard**', 30 in (75 cm) tall, bright pink, named after the famous hybridizer; '**Little Red Boy**', masses of bright cerise-red flowers; '**Marie Ballard**', lavender blue, very fully double flowers; and '**Professor Anton Kippenberg**', lavender blue flowers. Zones 2–9.

Aster novae-angliae
'Andenken an Alma Pötschke'

Aster turbinellus

☀/◑ ❄ ↔ 3 ft (0.9 m) ↕ 4 ft (1.2 m)

Branching, multi-stemmed, autumn-flowering perennial from eastern USA. Lance-shaped 3 in (8 cm) long base leaves, fringed with fine hairs. Flowerheads 1 in (25 mm) wide, pink, borne singly on the stems but in large numbers. Zones 5–9.

ASTILBE

FALSE SPIRAEA

Found mainly in temperate East Asia, this perennial genus of the saxifrage (Saxifragaceae) family includes just 12 species that have been extensively selected and hybridized. Their toothed pinnate or bipinnate leaves sprout directly from rhizomes and soon form a large foliage clump. Long-stemmed plumes of tiny flowers appear in spring and summer, in white and all shades of pink, mauve, and red.

CULTIVATION: Astilbes are not drought tolerant nor do they thrive in the hot summer sun. Instead they prefer moist, humus-rich, woodland soil and dappled sunlight. They often thrive around pond margins but also tolerate being in well-drained soils.

Astilbe × arendsii

◑ ❄ ↔ 12–32 in (30–80 cm) ↕ 2–6 ft (0.6–1.8 m)

This group of garden hybrids involves several parent species. Both flowers and foliage are highly variable. Popular named forms include '**Anita Pfeifer**', 24 in (60 cm) tall, finely divided foliage and feathery sprays of pink flowers; '**Brautschleier**' (syn. 'Bridal Veil'), 30 in (75 cm) tall, white flowers, early-flowering;

'**Bumalda**', 24 in (60 cm) high, white flowers with a faint pink blush, bronze foliage; '**Fanal**' ★, 24 in (60 cm) tall, dark, red-tinted foliage, deep red flowers; '**Federsee**', 24 in (60 cm) tall, sprays of deep pink flowers; '**Gertrud Brix**', 24 in (60 cm) tall, deep red flowers, bronze foliage; '**Gloria**', 27 in (70 cm) tall, deep pink flowers; '**Hyazinth**', 36 in (90 cm) tall, bright green foliage, lilac-pink flower sprays; '**Irrlicht**', 24 in (60 cm) tall, purple-tinted foliage and white flower sprays; '**Mainz**', 24 in (60 cm) tall, deep rose-pink flowers; '**Rosa Perle**' (syn. 'Pink Pearl'), 30 in (75 cm) tall, silvery to pink flowers; **Showstar Group**, dwarf seedling strain in a mixed color range; '**Spinell**', 36 in (90 cm) tall, orange-red flowers; '**Venus**', 36 in (90 cm) tall, bright green foliage, sprays of pink flowers; '**Weisse Gloria**', 36 in (90 cm) tall, sprays of white flowers; and '**William Reeves**', 24 in (60 cm) tall, deep pinkish red flowers. Zones 6–9.

Astilbe chinensis

◑ ❄ ↔ 12–20 in (30–50 cm) ↕ to 7 ft (2 m)

Native to China and Japan. Foliage with large and coarsely toothed leaflets. Flowerheads short-stemmed with strongly up-right plumes. Several natural varieties, including: *A. c.* var. *davidii*, bronze young leaves and purple-pink flower plumes to 7 ft (2 m) tall; *A. c.* var. *pumila*, just 10 in (25 cm) tall, with green foliage and dense plumes of deep pink flowers; and *A. c.* var. *taquetii* '**Superba**', with magenta flowers on brown stems to 4 ft (1.2 m) tall. *A. c.* '**Visions**', 18 in (45 cm) tall, honey-scented, deep pink to red flower sprays and bronze foliage. Zones 5–9.

Astilbe japonica

◑ ❄ ↔ 3 ft (0.9 m) ↕ 2–3 ft (0.6–0.9 m)

Endemic to Japan, known chiefly by its cultivars and hybrids. Leaves bi- or tripinnate, flowers white, in pyramidal panicles to 8 in (20 cm) long in late spring–early summer. Zones 5–9.

Astilbe × *arendsii* 'Gloria'

Astilbe chinensis 'Visions'

Astilbe simplicifolia

☀ ❊ ↔ 8–16 in (20–40 cm) ↕ 12–16 in (30–40 cm)

Compact Japanese species. Foliage often simple, glossy, ovate, and lobed but sometimes more deeply divided. Starry white flowers in narrow upright plumes. Several cultivars, including 'Bronze Elegance' and 'Hennie Graefland'. Zones 7–9.

Astilbe Hybrid Cultivars

☀ ❊ ↔ 3 ft (0.9 m) ↕ 2–3 ft (0.6–0.9 m)

These cultivars have *A. japonica* as a major part of their heritage. 'Betsy Cuperus', 36 in (90 cm) tall, arching panicles of soft pink flowers; 'Deutschland', 20 in (50 cm) tall, pure white flowers; 'Europa', 24 in (60 cm) high, pale pink flowers; 'Montgomery', 30 in (75 cm) tall, red flowers, red-tinted foliage; 'Red Sentinel', 24–36 in (60–90 cm) high, bronze leaves, open sprays of red flowers on red stems; 'Straussenfeder' (syn. 'Ostrich Feather'), 36 in (90 cm) high, salmon pink to soft red flowers in arching sprays. Zones 6–9.

Astilbe, Hybrid Cultivar, 'Red Sentinel'

ASTILBOIDES

A genus of the saxifrage (Saxifragaceae) family containing only one species, a herbaceous perennial once included in the genus *Rodgersia*. It comes from China and differs from its former relatives mainly in its leaf shape. It is grown for its huge leaves and racemes of tiny white flowers in summer. CULTIVATION: It grows best in moist soils in a cool sheltered spot and is usually seen at its best near water. Propagation is from seed or by division when dormant.

Astilboides tabularis

syn. *Rodgersia tabularis*

☀ ❊ ↔ 40–60 in (100–150 cm) ↕ 40–60 in (100–150 cm)

This impressive perennial has huge, bright green, circular leaves to 36 in (90 cm) across, with the stem attached to the center. Above the foliage are its large fluffy heads of tiny white flowers, produced in summer. Zones 7–10.

Astrantia major

ASTRANTIA

MASTERWORT, PINCUSHION FLOWER

Primarily European, this genus of 10 species of perennials also occurs westward to Asia, often in alpine meadows or woodlands. Belonging to the carrot (Apiaceae) family, they bear small pastel-toned flowers in dome-shaped heads (umbels). The true flowers are often less showy than the surrounding papery bracts. The foliage, which forms a basal clump and spreads by runners, is hand-shaped, with 3 to 7 toothed lobes. CULTIVATION: Apart from an intolerance of prolonged dry conditions, these grow freely in any cool-temperate garden with moderately fertile free-draining soil. Foliage may be lusher in shade, a consideration with variegated cultivars, but they usually flower best in at least half-sun. Propagate by division when dormant or from seed, which needs stratification.

Astrantia major

GREATER MASTERWORT

☀ ❊ ↔ 16–24 in (40–60 cm) ↕ 24–32 in (60–80 cm)

From central and eastern Europe. Leaves with 3 to 7, broad, toothed lobes. Floral bracts white through red, often green tinted or veined. *A. m.* subsp. *involucrata*, long narrow bracts creating a lacy flowerhead; 'Moira Reid', pink-tinted early blooms; 'Shaggy', green-tipped white flowers. *A. m.* var. *rosea*, green-tinted pale pink inflorescences. *A. m.* 'Rubra' ★, deep purple-red inflorescence; 'Sunningdale Variegated', pink-flushed white flowerheads. Zones 6–9.

Astrantia maxima

☀ ❊ ↔ 20–24 in (50–60 cm) ↕ 27–36 in (70–90 cm)

Large leaves with 3 to 5 finely toothed lobes. Pink flowerheads, lighter center, bracts fused to create a ruff, in summer. Zones 6–9.

ATRIPLEX

SALTBUSH

From all continents except Antarctica, there are around 300 species included in this genus in the goosefoot or saltbush (Chenopodiaceae) family. *Atriplex* includes many shrubs, as well as annuals and perennials, that are multi-branched with wiry crooked twigs. The leaves are fleshy, and may be covered in fine whitish scales giving the foliage a silvery or pale bluish cast. Flowers are small, of different sexes often on different plants. CULTIVATION: These plants are suited to hot, dry, or saline environments, including exposed seashores. All require full sun and do best in a well-drained soil of moderate fertility. They can be cut back hard, responding with thicker foliage, and trained into hedges. Propagate from softwood cuttings or seed. Soak seed to simulate the effect of rain needed for these plants to germinate.

Atriplex hortensis

FAT HEN, FRENCH SPINACH, MOUNTAIN SPINACH, ORACH, SALTBUSH, SEA PURSLANE

☀ ❊ ↔ 16–20 in (40–50 cm) ↕ 7–8 ft (2–2.4 m)

An erect annual from Asia, with grayish leaves, that has naturalized in most temperate parts of the world. Leaves heart-shaped to triangular, slightly serrated, 4–6 in (10–15 cm) long, green or purplish brown, and used in cooking. Terminal clusters of insignificant green or red flowers, without petals, in summer, followed by tiny brown plate-like seeds. *A. h.* var. *rubra*, purple leaves. *A. h.* 'Cuptorosea' and 'Rosea' are popular. Zones 6–11.

AUBRIETA

AUBRETIA

Found from Europe to central Asia, the 12 evergreen cushion or mat-forming perennials of this genus are members of the cabbage (Brassicaceae) family. They are smothered in tiny, 4-petalled, purple, mauve, or white blooms in spring and early summer. The foliage is small and simple, usually dull gray-green and finely downy, often with small lobes or teeth. They are excellent choices for rockeries, flower borders, or spilling over banks. CULTIVATION: Hardy in most temperate zones, aubrietas prefer gritty well-drained soil in full or half-sun. Water during the flowering season and give an occasional light dressing of lime. Although perennial, at nurseries aubretias are often sold with the bedding annuals and may be treated as such. However, if left to grow on they become far more impressive plants. Propagate from seed, layers, or small basal cuttings or by division.

Aubrieta Hybrid Cultivars

☀ ❄ ↔ 8–24 in (20–60 cm) ↕ 3–6 in (8–15 cm)
Garden hybrids are derived from several species. All are matforming, but otherwise highly variable. 'Argenteovariegata', silver-edged leaves and purple flowers; 'Blue Cascade', strongly trailing habit, may mound, purple-blue flowers; 'Blue King', mauve-blue flowers in abundance; 'Bressingham Pink', clusters of large, pink, double flowers; 'Campbellii', mauve-blue double flowers; 'Doctor Mules', neat, compact habit with attractive violet-blue flowers; 'Hendersonii', low spreader with purple flowers, well suited to rock walls and banks; 'Novalis Blue', bright mauve-blue flowers; 'Rokey's Purple', deep purple flowers; 'Whitewell Gem', purple-violet flowers. Zones 7–10.

AURINIA

A genus of 7 species of perennials and biennials of the cabbage (Brassicaceae) family, found in central and southern Europe and eastward to Turkey and the Black Sea region. They are small carpeting plants that form loose basal rosettes of leaves that emerge from a sometimes thickened rootstock. Leaves are often covered with fine hairs, giving them a silver-gray appearance. Heads of small bright yellow or white flowers open from spring, often almost hiding the foliage. CULTIVATION: Best suited to a cool-temperate climate where frosts are not severe, these are superb plants for rockeries or alpine troughs. They prefer a position in full sun and need perfectly drained gritty soil that is kept moist in spring and early summer. All species may be propagated from seed, and the perennials can also be grown from self-layered pieces or by taking small tip cuttings.

Aubrieta, Hybrid Cultivar, 'Whitewell Gem'

Aurinia saxatilis

syn. *Alyssum saxatile*
BASKET OF GOLD, YELLOW ALYSSUM
☀ ❄ ↔ 16–24 in (40–60 cm) ↕ 8–12 in (20–30 cm)
From central and southeastern Europe. Low, carpeting perennial with small silver-gray leaves. Sprays of pale to bright yellow flowers, from spring. Hardiest species by far. 'Citrina' is heavy-blooming, bright yellow flowers; 'Compacta' has golden flowers on 8 in (20 cm) high stems. Zones 3–9.

BAILEYA

This small genus from western North America is part of the daisy (Asteraceae) family. It comprises just 3 species of annuals and perennials; one, *B. multiradiata*, is sometimes grown for a bright splash of color in summer and autumn, especially in arid areas. *Baileya* species have opposite pairs of hairy, gray-green, pinnate leaves and have an open habit, rarely growing to more than 12–16 in (30–40 cm) tall. Their cosmos-like yellow flowerheads are held clear of the foliage on long stems, appearing from early summer and continuing until the first frosts. CULTIVATION: *Baileya* plants thrive in semi-desert conditions and, although sometimes considered weeds, they are one of the most reliable and colorful summer annuals for arid gardens. Plant in full sun and water only to get plants established or if dry conditions persist. Remove spent flowerheads to prolong blooming. Propagation is from seed, which may be sown in situ or started under cover and then transplanted.

Aurinia saxatilis 'Compacta'

Baileya multiradiata

DESERT BAILEYA, DESERT MARIGOLD, PAPER DAISY, WILD MARIGOLD
☀ ❄ ↔ 4–12 in (10–30 cm) ↕ 8–20 in (20–50 cm)
Native to southern USA and Mexico. Short-lived perennial with grayish green foliage. Bright yellow flowers, 2 in (5 cm) across and resembling marigolds, are borne from spring to autumn. Needs perfect drainage to prevent rotting. Zones 7–10.

Baptisia australis

CULTIVATION: Grow in full sun in deep, well-drained, neutral or slightly acidic soil. Most species grow happily in poorly nourished soils. Stake tall plants in exposed positions. Propagate by division or from seed.

Baptisia australis

syn. *Baptisia caerulea*

BLUE FALSE INDIGO

⚬ ❋ ↔ 4 ft (1.2 m) ↑ 2–4 ft (0.6–1.2 m)

Native to central and eastern USA, but threatened in some states. Upright or spreading bushy perennial with bluish green foliage. Spikes of purplish blue flowers in summer. Erect, inflated, dark gray seed pods can be dried for floral arrangements. Zones 5–9.

BALLOTA

Found from Europe through the Mediterranean region to western Asia, this mint (Lamiaceae) family genus is composed of 35 species of perennials and subshrubs. Bushy and spreading, they are grown primarily for their hairy gray-green stems and foliage, which in the best forms are heavily felted. The leaves may be evergreen or deciduous and are aromatic, oval to heart-shaped, with conspicuously toothed edges. In summer, small upright spikes of white, cream, or lilac-pink flowers appear.
CULTIVATION: Plants tolerate hardy to moderate frosts and are very easily grown in full or half-sun in a moist well-drained soil. Cut the evergreen types back hard in spring. Will naturalize and can become quite invasive. Propagate by division, or from basal cuttings or seed.

Ballota acetabulosa

⚬/◐ ❋ ↔ 24–32 in (60–80 cm) ↑ 40 in (100 cm)
Shrubby semi-evergreen perennial. Native to Greece, Turkey, and eastern Mediterranean islands. Woolly stems and foliage. Leaves heart-shaped, pale green, to 2 in (5 cm) long, with toothed edges. Up to 12 purple-marked white flowers per head, ½ in (12 mm) wide, in summer. Zones 8–10.

Ballota pseudodictamnus

⚬ ❋ ↔ 24–48 in (60–120 cm) ↑ 12–20 in (30–50 cm)
Evergreen subshrub found from Turkey through Crete to North Africa. Rounded, toothed, felted, gray-green leaves to 2 in (5 cm) long. White or mauve flowers with darker spotting, in large green calyces, in summer. Zones 8–10.

BAPTISIA

FALSE INDIGO, WILD INDIGO

Belonging to the pea-flower subfamily of the legume (Fabaceae) family, this genus contains about 17 species of perennial herbs native to the USA. They grow in sand, gravel, and other poor soils in dry woodlands and open areas. Plants have a shrubby habit, spreading or erect, to 7 ft (2 m) tall, with trifoliate leaves. Spikes of lupin-like flowers are white, yellow, or purplish blue. Once used in dye-making as a substitute for true indigo.

BASSIA

A genus of 26 densely branching, shrubby annuals or perennials belonging to the goosefoot (Chenopodaceae) family, *Bassia* plants are found in warm-temperate parts of the Northern Hemisphere. One species is grown for its foliage. Leaves are usually narrow and smooth-edged, and the flowers are normally inconspicuous spikes. Fruits are achenes (small, dry, single-seeded fruits).
CULTIVATION: Sow seed in spring where plants are to grow, in most soils, including saline. Propagate from seed or cuttings.

Bassia scoparia

syns *Kochia scoparia, K. trichophylla*

BELVEDERE, BURNING BUSH, FIREBUSH, FIREWEED, KOCHIA, SUMMER CYPRESS

⚬ ❋ ↔ 8–60 in (20–150 cm) ↑ 8–60 in (20–150 cm)
Annual originally from temperate Asia, now naturalized through Europe and North America. Narrow flat leaves, normally mid-green, turning purple-red in late summer. Small inconspicuous flower clusters same color as leaves. With maturity, plant breaks off at base and rolls away, dispersing seed. Zones 8–11.

BEGONIA

Found through the tropics and subtropics but most diverse in the Americas, this group of around 900 species of perennials, shrubs, and climbers belongs to the family Begoniaceae. They may be fibrous- or rhizome-rooted or tuberous, with foliage emerging from the rootstock or held on cane-like stems. Leaves variable but are often lobed and finely hairy. Flowers are also variable.
CULTIVATION: Mostly frost tender, they are treated as annuals outdoors or grown indoors in cool climates. Plants prefer a bright but not sunny position with fertile, cool, moist, soil rich in humus. Water and feed well. Watch for fungal diseases. Propagate by division or from offsets, leaf cuttings, or seed, depending on type.

Begonia coccinea

ANGEL-WING BEGONIA

◐/⚬ ⁂ ↔ 24 in (60 cm) ↑ 48 in (120 cm)
Fibrous-rooted, from Brazil. Stems upright, succulent. Lush green, pointed, wing-shaped leaves, to 6 in (15 cm) long, red undersides. Large racemes of bright red flowers in spring. Zones 10–12.

Begonia × *erythrophylla*

BEEFSTEAK BEGONIA

☼/◐ ⚘ ↔16–24 in (40–60 cm) ↑8–16 in (20–40 cm)

Rhizome-rooted. Rounded wavy leaves, deep green, red below, with hairs. Small pink flowers in winter–spring. Zones 10–12.

Begonia fuchsioides

FUCHSIA BEGONIA

☼/◐ ⚘ ↔20 in (50 cm) ↑36 in (90 cm)

From Venezuela. Fibrous-rooted species. Succulent upright stems. Toothed, pointed, wing-shaped leaves, to 2 in (5 cm) long, bright green above, red-tinted below. Pendulous sprays of pink to red 1¼ in (30 mm) wide flowers in winter. Zones 10–12.

Begonia grandis

EVANS' BEGONIA, HARDY BEGONIA

☼/◐ ✳ ↔12–18 in (30–45 cm) ↑24 in (60 cm)

From China and Japan. Perennial with loose sprays of flower clusters over large clump of leaves. Green heart-shaped leaves, thick, succulent, ruby red veins on lower surfaces. Flowers pink, in drooping cymes, appear in late summer–autumn. 'Heron's Pirouette' blooms from early summer until autumn. Zones 6–9.

Begonia masoniana

IRON CROSS BEGONIA

☼/◐ ⚘ ↔12–16 in (30–40 cm) ↑12 in (30 cm)

Rhizome-rooted, from New Guinea. Leaves asymmetrical, pointed, wing- to heart-shaped, to 8 in (20 cm) long, toothed, hairy, with puckered surface, light green with dark central markings. Upright sprays of small pale green flowers in spring–summer. Zones 10–12.

Begonia metallica

METALLIC-LEAF BEGONIA

☼/◐ ⚘ ↔20–32 in (50–80 cm) ↑48 in (120 cm)

Fibrous-rooted, from Brazil. Leaves asymmetrical, pointed oval, to 6 in (15 cm) long, serrated edges, steely purple-blue upper surface veining. Many-flowered sprays of single 1¼ in (30 mm) wide, light to deep pink flowers in summer–autumn. Zones 10–12.

Begonia Hybrid Cultivars

Begonia is such a large genus and many of the species interbreed so freely that countless hybrids have been introduced over the years. These largely fall into eight quite clear-cut groups. While there are several subgroups, these are the main divisions.

CANE-LIKE GROUP

☼ ⚘ ↔20–32 in (50–80 cm) ↑2–6 ft (0.6–1.8 m)

Tall upright stems. Leaves, usually wing-shaped, vary in size, texture, and color; may be deeply lobed, feathery; often silvery or red-tinted. Small red, pink, or salmon flowers in sprays. 'Flamingo Queen', pink flowers, spotted leaves; 'Honeysuckle', fragrant pink flowers; 'Irene Nuss' ★, coral pink flowers, bronze leaves; 'Looking Glass', pink flowers, leaves silvery; 'Orange Rubra', orange flowers, mid-green leaves. Zones 9–11.

REX CULTORUM GROUP

☼/◐ ⚘ ↔16–24 in (40–60 cm) ↑12–24 in (30–60 cm)

Leaves large, exquisitely colored and marked, heavily veined and textured, velvety, often hairy at edges. Upper surfaces have combinations of bronze-green, bright green, silver, pink, and white; undersides usually purple-red. Clusters of small pink flowers. 'Merry Christmas', pink flowers, red leaves; 'Silver Queen', pink flowers, silvery leaves; 'Tinsel', purple-tinged leaves. Zones 10–12.

RHIZOMATOUS GROUP

☼/◐ ⚘ ↔12–30 in (30–75 cm) ↑6–8 in (15–20 cm)

Grow from spreading or upright rhizomes. Often fleshy leaves, to 12 in (30 cm) wide. Leaf shape, texture, and color variable, often red-tinted undersides and wavy edges. Flowers few to many, mostly pink. Cultivars include 'Munchkin' and 'Tiger Paws'. Zones 9–11.

SEMPERFLORENS GROUP

☼/◐ ⚘ ↔12 in (30 cm) ↑12 in (30 cm)

Small bushy perennials, usually treated as bedding annuals. Bright green or red, glossy, waxy leaves. Small, white, pink, or red flowers, usually single. Suit cool, fairly moist summers. **All Round Series**, bronze or green foliage; **Alfa Series**, vigorous plants, bronze foliage, including 'Alfa Pink'; **Ambassador Series**, compact with mid-green foliage; **Cocktail Series**, single flowers, bronze foliage; **Expresso Series**, bronze foliage, including 'Expresso Scarlet'; **Inferno Series**, vigorous and resilient, including 'Inferno Apple Blossom'; **Olympia Series**, green foliage, including 'Olympia White'; **Prelude Series**, early blooming, rich green foliage; **Senator Series**, early blooming, bronze foliage. Zones 9–11.

Begonia coccinea

Begonia, Cane-like Group, 'Flamingo Queen'

Begonia, Rex Cultorum Group, 'Tinsel'

SHRUB-LIKE GROUP

◐/◉ ❄ ↔ 18–48 in (45–120 cm) ↑ 12–36 in (30–90 cm)
Bushy plants with dense growth habit; leaves variably sized, colored, and textured, hairy or smooth, often red-veined. Flowers usually pink or cream, sometimes red or white, usually small and clustered. Popular cultivars include 'Cockatoo', 'Ginny', 'Red Amigo', 'Richmondensis' ★, and 'Thurstonii'. Zones 9–12.

THICK-STEMMED GROUP

◐/◉ ❄ ↔ 12–18 in (30–45 cm)
↑ 12–18 in (30–45 cm)
Strong fleshy stems. Variably colored leaves, more than 6 in (15 cm) long, deeply toothed, lobed, or smooth-edged. Small flowers, usually white or pink, sometimes scented. 'Boomer', bronze leaves, white flowers. Zones 9–12.

TRAILING OR SCANDENT GROUP

◐/◉ ❄ ↔ 18–36 in (45–90 cm)
↑ 6–12 in (15–30 cm)
Low spreading plants with lax stems. Usually grown in hanging baskets but sometimes climbing. Leaves usually small to medium-sized, smooth or hairy, often dark green. Sprays of small white, pink, or red flowers, often scented. Zones 9–12.

TUBEROUS GROUP

◐/◉ ❄ ↔ 12–20 in (30–50 cm) ↑ 12–32 in (30–80 cm)
These grow from large flat tubers, producing short, heavy, succulent stems carrying large, often hairy leaves. Huge range of flower types and colors, including many that resemble roses. They are suitable for indoor or outdoor cultivation, flowering mainly from mid-summer to frost. Popular cultivars include 'Coppelia', 'Fairylight', and 'Roy Hartley'. The Non-Stop Series and Pin-up Series ★ include a variety of attractive plants. Zones 8–10.

BELLIS

BELLIS DAISY, BRUISEWORT, LAWN DAISY
This European and Mediterranean genus of 7 species of annual and perennial daisies (family Asteraceae) includes the common

Begonia, Tuberous Group, 'Coppelia'

daisy *(B. perennis)*. Cultivated forms have much larger flowerheads with many more ray florets and a wider color range than wild plants. *Bellis* plants form flat rosettes of spoon- to kidney-shaped leaves and carry their flowerheads on individual stems.
CULTIVATION: Best in cool-temperate climates in a sunny or part-shaded open position with good air movement and soil that remains moist during the growing season. White rust and mildew can occur in humid conditions. The fancy cultivars are propagated by division, the others from seed.

Bellis perennis

Bellis perennis

BELLIS DAISY, ENGLISH DAISY
◉ ❄ ↔ 4–8 in (10–20 cm) ↑ 2–4 in (5–10 cm)
Originally from temperate Eurasia but now naturalized in most temperate zones. Leaves 1–2 in (25–50 mm) long, broad, spatula-shaped. White flowers, sometimes tinted pink, with yellow centers, from late winter. Popular cultivars include 'Dresden China', the Pomponette Series, and 'Rob Roy'. Zones 4–10.

BERGENIA

PIGSQUEAK
Found in Asia, from Afghanistan to Mongolia, this genus of the saxifrage (Saxifragaceae) family is made up of 8 species of perennials. Large leathery leaves sprout from tough, woody, fleshy stems. Leaves are broad, often light green, and usually at least 8 in (20 cm) long. They are complemented by long-stemmed heads of 5-petalled flowers in spring. Species most often have pink flowers but garden forms occur in white and shades of pink, red, and mauve.
CULTIVATION: For lush foliage, plant in cool moist conditions in part-shade in soil rich in humus. Plants in full sun often flower well but at the expense of their leaves, which burn. Excellent in large rockeries. Propagate by division after flowering.

Bergenia cordifolia

HEARTLEAF SAXIFRAGE, PIGSQUEAK
◐ ❄ ↔ 48 in (120 cm) ↑ 16 in (40 cm)
Found in the mountains of Siberia and Mongolia. Rounded toothed-edged leaves, to 8 in (20 cm) long, on strong stalks. Bright pink flowers on red stems from late winter.Popular cultivars include 'Perfecta', 'Purpurea', and 'Redstart'. Zones 3–10.

Bergenia crassifolia

◐ ❄ ↔ 16–32 in (40–80 cm) ↑ 12 in (30 cm)
From Siberia and Mongolia. Shallowly toothed, rounded leaves up to 8 in (20 cm) long, but can be considerably smaller. Magenta to cerise flowers on strong red stems. Zones 3–9.

Bergenia × schmidtii

◐ ❄ ↔ 24–48 in (60–120 cm) ↑ 12 in (30 cm)
Variable hybrid with large rounded leaves and deep pink to magenta flowers. Blooms very early, in winter and early spring; protect the flowers from frost. Zones 5–10.

Bergenia Hybrid Cultivars

☼/◗ ❄ ↔ 16–32 in (40–80 cm) ↕ 8–16 in (20–40 cm)

These plants need some sunlight for the best leaf color. Cultivars include '**Abendglut**' (syn. 'Evening Glow'), compact, wavy-edged red-tinted foliage, purple-red semi-double flowers; '**Ballawley**' (syn. 'Delbees'), glossy leaves, purple-tinted in winter, red flowers; '**Bressingham White**', pure white flowers; '**Eroica**', bronze- to purple-tinted foliage, purple-red flowers; '**Morgenröte**' (syn. 'Morning Blush'), large bronze green leaves and deep purple-red flowers; '**Rosi Klose**', dark green leaves, pink flowers; '**Silberlicht**' (syn. 'Silver Light'), large leaves, white flowers ageing to pink; and '**Sunningdale**', bronze-to red-tinted winter foliage, deep lavender-pink flowers. Zones 3–9.

BIDENS

BEGGAR'S TICK, BURR MARIGOLD, SPANISH NEEDLES, STICK TIGHT, TICKSEED

This genus of about 200 annual and perennial species belongs to the daisy (Asteraceae) family. It has a worldwide distribution, with its largest numbers in temperate and tropical Africa and America. The few ornamental forms are used as annual bedding plants. The sticking hooks on the seeds help them to become dispersed over wide areas.

CULTIVATION: These plants require little more than a sunny well-drained site with reasonable moisture-retentive soil. Plant after frosts in very cold climates. Propagate from seed or by division of the perennial forms.

Bidens ferulifolia

APACHE BEGGARTICKS

☼ ❄ ↔ 12–18 in (30–45 cm) ↕ 24–36 in (60–90 cm)

From Arizona (USA), Mexico, and Guatemala. Annual or perennial with ferny foliage. Golden wide-rayed daisies, about 1¼ in (30 mm) across, from late summer to autumn. '**Golden Goddess**' and '**Goldmarie**' are improved selections. '**Golden Eye**', Goldie/ '**Innbid**', and '**Peters Goldteppich**' ★, trailing cultivars. Zones 8–11.

BILLBERGIA

This bromeliad (Bromeliaceae) family genus has 65 species and some 500 cultivars. It can be divided into 2 main groups: one from the warmer parts of South America and Mexico, the other from Brazil. Leaves form a tubular rosette, and come in all colors and markings; colors are more evident when plants are grown in good light. Flowerheads usually vary from spherical to cylindrical and can have a long stem, so the flowerhead hangs outside the leaf tube. Beneath the flowerhead are large, banner-like, red bracts. Flowers are long, thin, and tubular, topped with petals of many different colors in odd combinations.

Billbergia nutans

CULTIVATION: Indoor culture recommended if in flower; in greenhouse in cool-temperate areas; outdoors with protection from direct sunlight and rain in warm-temperate, subtropical, and tropical areas. Water when potting mix is dry. Adding fertilizer to good quality potting mix is not necessary. Propagate from seed or offsets.

Bergenia, Hybrid Cultivar, 'Sunningdale'

Billbergia amoena

☀ ❄ ↔ 12 in (30 cm) ↕ 24 in (60 cm)

Native to southern Brazil. Leaves green to red, sometimes with white spots. Flowerhead erect, mainly green, with up to 20 flowers; petals green, sometimes with blue tips. Beneath flowerhead are 7 or 8 red bracts, erect or drooping. Zones 9–10.

Billbergia elegans

☀ ❄ ↔ 4 in (10 cm) ↕ 12 in (30 cm)

Native to southern Brazil. Leaves green with white bands, becoming reddish in good light. Flowerhead erect but sometimes slightly bent, salmon pink, up to 8 flowers with blue-tipped green petals. Several salmon pink bracts below flowerhead. Zones 9–10.

Billbergia euphemiae

☀ ❄ ↔ 8 in (20 cm) ↕ 24 in (60 cm)

Native to eastern Brazil. Leaves green, sometimes purple. Flower stem erect to slightly bent. Flowerhead mainly yellow, to 6 in (15 cm) long, with up to 30 flowers, petals purple. This species is not as hardy as some of the other *Billbergia* species. Zones 9–10.

Billbergia nutans

FRIENDSHIP PLANT, QUEEN'S TEARS, TARTAN FLOWER

☀ ❄ ↔ 6 in (15 cm) ↕ 10 in (25 cm)

From southern Brazil to Uruguay. Leaves green, thin, to 24 in (60 cm) long. Flowerheads nodding, few green and pink flowers, blue-edged petals. Commonly grown bromeliad, but plants may really be the hybrid cultivar 'Albertii'. Zones 8–10.

Billbergia pyramidalis

☀ ⚘ ↔ 6 in (15 cm) ↑ 20 in (50 cm)

From eastern Brazil. Leaves light to dark green, sometimes with narrow white bands, teeth small. Flowerhead erect, mainly red with frosting, pyramidal shape, up to 40 flowers. Many large red bracts beneath flowerhead. Petals red with bluish tips. *B. p.* var. *concolor* (syn. *B. p.* var. *thyrsoidea*), large, wide, pale green leaves and faint blue hue to petal ends. Zones 9–10.

Billbergia zebrina

☀ ⚘ ↔ 6 in (15 cm) ↑ 40 in (100 cm)

From southern Brazil and adjacent countries. Leaves to 3 in (8 cm) wide, pale green with white cross-bands. Flowerhead hanging, to 16 in (40 cm) long, felty, yellowish green. Up to 8 large pale pink to rose bracts above flowerhead. Zones 9–10.

Billbergia Hybrid Cultivars

☀ ⚘ ↔ to 8 in (20 cm) ↑ to 24 in (60 cm)

A range of hybrids with beautiful flowers. 'Afterglow', green-petalled flowers, large red bracts; 'Albertii', green-petalled flowers, blue petal edges; 'Breauteana', drooping flowerhead, mainly light pink with dark blue petals; 'Catherine Wilson', erect flowerhead, mainly green, with rose-colored bracts below; 'Domingos Martins', flowerhead to 6 in (15 cm) long, almost totally red, petals blue; 'Euphemie Waterman', compact flowerhead, leaves maroon with silvery bands; 'Fascinator', drooping flowerhead comprising about 15 blooms, petals green with blue edges, large red bracts; 'Hallelujah', flowerhead mainly light green, erect, up to 10 flowers with blue tips; 'Manda's Othello', flowerhead erect, mainly pale pink with blue-tipped petals, red bracts beneath; 'Muriel Waterman', flowerhead slightly bent, mainly green to pale pink with blue petals, flowers rarely; 'Platinum', flowerhead felty, erect, then curved, up to 14 flowers, pale green and pale red with dark blue-tipped petals; 'Poquito Blanco', flowerhead erect with few flowers, mainly pale pink, petals pale green with purple edges; 'Windii', large rose red bracts cover hanging flowerhead, mainly green and white, petals green with blue edges. Zones 9–10.

BOLTONIA

FALSE CHAMOMILE

A genus of about 8 species in the daisy (Asteraceae) family, these tall perennials are found in central and eastern USA and northeastern Asia, where they grow in moist soils. Their upright leafy stems bear masses of daisy-like flowers in late summer and autumn. The flowers have a yellow eye and are white, pink, mauve, or purple in color.
CULTIVATION: Showy and easily grown in borders or "wild" gardens, these plants can be cultivated in any moderately fertile soil in full sun or part-shade. Stake in exposed positions. Regular division will maintain vigor. Propagate by division or from seed.

Billbergia zebrina

Boltonia asteroides

☼ ❀ ↔ 5 ft (1.5 m) ↑ 3–5 ft (0.9–1.5 m)

Clump-forming perennial from eastern USA. Leaves narrow, to 4 in (10 cm) long. Erect leafy stems bear masses of starry white daisies in late summer–autumn. *B. a.* var. *latisquama*, taller plant bearing large mauve daisies. *B. a.* 'Snowbank', strong grower to 7 ft (2 m) tall, white daisies. Zones 4–10.

BOYKINIA

There are about 9 species of perennial herbs in this genus in the saxifrage (Saxifragaceae) family. They are native to moist woodlands of North America and Japan. They have creeping rhizomes and form clumps of rounded or kidney-shaped leaves. The tiny flowers are borne on crowded panicles. They are white, yellowish green, or purple.
CULTIVATION: Best suited to "wild" or woodland gardens, or rockeries. Grow in moist well-drained soil in light shade. Propagate by division.

Boykinia jamesii

syn. *Telesonix jamesii*

☼ ❀ ↔ 6–8 in (15–20 cm) ↑ 2–6 in (5–15 cm)

Compact low-growing species from northwestern USA. Leaves small, toothed, kidney-shaped. Flowers small, purple-red, in early summer. Grow in cool greenhouse or trough. Zones 5–9.

BRACHYSCOME

syn. *Brachycome*

DAISY

A popular genus of annuals, perennials, and subshrubs in the daisy (Asteraceae) family. There are 90 to 100 species in the genus, with many cultivars. They occur throughout Australia from coastal to alpine habitats. Leaves are small, bright green, and generally multi-lobed, divided, and/or toothed. Plants can form mats or be suckering or rounded compact bushes. Flowers are a typical daisy type in shades of pink, mauve, blue, purple, lemon, and white, generally with yellow centers. These daisies are popular in rock gardens, pots, hanging baskets, on banks, and at the front of garden borders. Some cultivars have arisen by chance but others are the result of deliberate breeding programs to improve color selections and the size of the flowers.
CULTIVATION: Any well-drained soil in either full or half-sun will do; some plants are more drought/frost tolerant than others. Propagation is from seed, with named cultivars propagated from cuttings or by division.

Brachyscome iberidifolia

SWAN RIVER DAISY

☼ ⚘ ↔ 8–12 in (20–30 cm) ↑ 2–16 in (5–40 cm)

Erect annual daisy with pinnate leaves. Flowers 1 in (25 mm) in diameter in blue, purple, or white throughout spring–summer.

Can be frost tender. Cultivars include '**Blue Mist**', attractive blue flowers; '**Blue Star**' ★, purple-tinted flowers with quilled petals, lightly scented. Zones 9–11.

Brachyscome multifida
CUT-LEAF DAISY, HAWKESBURY RIVER DAISY

☼ ⚘ ↔ 12–40 in (30–100 cm) ↕ 8–16 in (20–40 cm)

Soft, much-divided foliage on a mounding form. Flowers generally purple but can be pink or white. Likes well-drained soil and will tolerate frost. May layer but does not sucker. *B. m.* var. *dilatata*, rounded form, leaves more wedge-shaped than species; '**Break O' Day**', hardier and more compact than species, bears deep mauve flowers from spring to autumn. *B. m.* '**Evan**', cushion-like, deep mauve flowers from spring to autumn; '**White Surprise**', similar to species, except flowers are white. Zones 9–11.

Brachyscome Hybrid Cultivars
☼/◐ ⚘ ↔ 18 in (45 cm) ↕ 18 in (45 cm)

These hybrids, mostly of *B. angustifolia* and *B. iberidifolia*, are compact heavy-flowering plants. '**Blue Haze**', compact, low growing, mauve-blue flowers; '**City Lights**', mounding form with large light lavender blue flowers; '**Just Jayne**', compact plant that does sucker, bearing white to pale pink flowers in autumn; '**New Amethyst**', fine foliage, small dark purple flowers in spring–autumn; '**Strawberry Mousse**', reddish mid-green foliage, spoon-shaped lobed leaves, bright pink flowers; '**Toucan Tango**' (syn. 'Ultra'), lacy foliage, violet-blue flowers year round; '**Valencia**', mauve-pink flowers 1½ in (35 mm) in diameter, flowers year round in tropics. Zones 9–11.

BROMELIA
In 1753 Linnaeus named *Bromelia pinguin*, and this genus gave the bromeliad (Bromeliaceae) family its name. Found in Mexico, the Caribbean islands, and Central America south to Argentina. Leaves are long, narrow, and leathery with large curved spines along edges. When flowering the center turns bright red and a dense head or panicle of flowers emerges. There are about 50 species, but only 6 are popularly grown. Perhaps the most hardy is *B. serra,* with *B. pinguin* and its variegated form the most common. CULTIVATION: Recommended for a greenhouse in cool-temperate areas, or outdoors in warm-temperate, subtropical, and tropical areas. Bromelias send out underground fleshy stems, so are best grown in large tubs. Water when potting mix is dry. No extra fertilizer. Propagate from seeds or offsets.

Bromelia pinguin
PINGUIN, PINUELA

◐ ⚘ ↔ 7 ft (2 m) ↕ 4 ft (1.2 m)

Clumping species from tropical America. Many rosettes, each with up to 40 spiny leaves to 6 ft (1.8 m) long and 2 in (5 cm) wide, light gray-green flushed with red. Large panicles of white to pink flowers; small, fleshy, yellow fruits. Zones 10–12.

Brachyscome iberidifolia 'Blue Star'

Bromelia serra
☼ ⚘ ↔ 7 ft (2 m) ↕ 24 in (60 cm)

From Bolivia to northern Argentina. Leaves green, short spines on edges. Flower stem short. Flowerhead globular, 2½ in (6 cm) wide. Petals blue-purple. Bright red, stiff, spiny bracts up to 8 in (20 cm) long beneath the flowerhead. Zones 9–11.

BRUNNERA
This genus of 3 species of fleshy-stemmed herbaceous perennials of the borage (Boraginaceae) family comes from temperate Eurasia. The species are closely related to the forget-me-nots and resemble them in flower. Sprays of tiny blue or white flowers appear in spring. However, the rounded to heart-shaped leaves of *Brunnera* are far larger than those of the common forget-me-nots and, as the garden forms are often variegated, the foliage is as much a feature as the flowers. CULTIVATION: These plants are most at home in a temperate climate with cool summers. Extremely hardy and easily grown in woodland conditions with dappled sunlight and moist, humus-rich, well-drained soil. Propagate from seed or division of established clumps near the end of the dormant period, *Brunnera* species often naturalize.

Brunnera macrophylla

Brunnera macrophylla
◐ ❄ ↔ 16–32 in (40–80 cm) ↕ 20 in (50 cm)

A Eastern European perennial with finely hairy, broad, heart-shaped leaves to 6 in (15 cm) long on 8 in (20 cm) stalks. Soft blue flowers are held above the foliage on 20 in (50 cm) stems. '**Hadspen Cream**', one of several variegated cultivars, cream-spotted light green leaves, blue flowers. Zones 3–9.

Calamintha nepeta

CALAMINTHA
CALAMINT

This mint (Lamiaceae) family genus is made up of 7 species of sometimes shrubby perennials found in the northern temperate zones excluding East Asia. The foliage is evergreen in mild climates but in cool winters plants may die back to a basal clump. Their aromatic pointed oval leaves are often slightly glossy and have toothed edges. Flower stems develop in summer and carry tubular pink to mauve flowers in the leaf axils near their tips.
CULTIVATION: Hardiness varies with the species, although the majority will tolerate quite severe frosts. Plant in a bright but not baking position with moist, humus-rich, well-drained soil. Some species have vigorous rhizomes and these can be slightly invasive. Propagation is by division, or from basal cuttings or seed.

Calamintha grandiflora
LARGE-FLOWERED CALAMINT

☼/◑ ❊ ↔ 3–4 ft (0.9–1.2 m) ↑ 2 ft (0.6 m)
Native to southern Europe and North Africa. Bushy plant with spreading rootstock. Dark green, downy, toothed leaves to 3 in (8 cm) long. Flowers 1½ in (35 mm) long, pink to mauve, borne singly or up to 5 in a cluster. 'Variegata' (syn. 'Fornsett Form'), compact. Zones 5–10.

Calamintha nepeta
LESSER CALAMINT

◑ ❊ ↔ 3–5 ft (0.9–1.5 m) ↑ 32 in (80 cm)
Spreading rhizome-rooted perennial found from Britain to southern Europe. Downy gray-green stems and leaves, to 1¼ in (30 mm) long. Aromatic. Flowers mauve-pink, ½ in (12 mm) long, up to 15 in a cluster. Zones 6–10.

CALATHEA

Found from Mexico to northern Argentina, this large genus of 300 evergreen, tuberous, or rhizome-rooted perennials belongs in the arrowroot (Marantaceae) family. They are upright in habit, with bold and often strikingly marked elliptical foliage, and they are commonly grown as house plants. There are 3 basic forms of calatheas: dense clumps of short-stemmed leaves; more open

clumps of leaves with long leaf stalks; and those with their foliage on cane-like stems. Leaves can be as much as 5 ft (1.5 m) long, though 6–10 in (15–25 cm) is more common. The flowers, backed by colored bracts, are usually held in a cone-like structure.
CULTIVATION: Calatheas require warm, humid, frost-free conditions. A draft-free shaded position with moist, humus-rich, well-drained soil is best. Propagate by division.

Calathea burle-marxii
☀ ⚥ ↔ 3–5 ft (0.9–1.5 m) ↑ 5 ft (1.5 m)
Upright cane-stemmed Brazilian species with leaves often over 24 in (60 cm) long, and bright green with a yellow-green midrib and gray-green undersides. Large heads of cream to yellow flowers, which are sometimes tinted blue or purple. Zones 11–12.

Calathea makoyana
CATHEDRAL WINDOWS, PEACOCK PLANT
☀ ⚥ ↔ 16–32 in (40–80 cm) ↑ 24–32 in (60–80 cm)
From Brazil. Short-stemmed, 12 in (30 cm) long, translucent leaves, midrib and main vein darker green bordered with cream, green and maroon below. White flowers, green bracts. Zones 11–12.

Calathea picturata
☀ ⚥ ↔ 20–27 in (50–70 cm) ↑ 16–24 in (40–60 cm)
From Brazil. Short-stemmed leaves to 10 in (25 cm) long, dark green with white along midrib and inside margin, maroon undersides. The white patches often join to form white-centered leaves. White flowers. Zones 11–12.

Calathea makoyana

Calathea zebrina
ZEBRA PLANT
☀ ⚥ ↔ 32–48 in (80–120 cm) ↑ 40 in (100 cm)
From Brazil. Short canes with velvety, light and dark green banded leaves to 27 in (70 cm) long, pale midrib, maroon undersides. White to mauve flowers with purple-brown bracts. Zones 11–12.

CALCEOLARIA

Found from Mexico to southern South America, this genus of 300 species or so in the foxglove (Scrophulariaceae) family includes perennials and shrubs. Leaves tend to be light green and are covered with fine hairs and small glands that make them sticky. Flowers are very distinctive. They are 2-lipped with a small hooded upper lip and a large lower lip that is inflated and pouch-like. Yellow, orange, and red shades dominate the flower colors.
CULTIVATION: While calceolarias vary in their frost hardiness and sun tolerance, they prefer cool moist soil conditions. Work high-humus compost into soil before planting. Shrubby species become untidy after a few years; pruning rejuvenates them, but replacement with new plants is usually more successful. Seed germinates well, but tip cuttings strike quickly and are the preferred method.

Calceolaria, Herbeohybrida Group

LADIES' PURSES, POCKETBOOK PLANT, SLIPPER FLOWER

◑ ↔ 12–16 in (30–40 cm) ↕ 8–20 in (20–50 cm)

These perennials are treated as annuals. Large winter flowers in shades of reds, oranges, and yellows (some speckled or blotched), characteristic pouch-like lip and hairy leaves. **Sunset Series** produces bushy plants and short-stemmed flowers for a long period; flowers scarlet, yellow, rich red, and copper-orange. **'Sunset Red'**, brilliant red to orange flowers. Zones 9–11.

Calceolaria, Herbeohybrida Group, Sunset Series, 'Sunset Red'

Calceolaria integrifolia

☼/◑ ❄ ↔ 2–6 ft (0.6–1.8 m) ↕ 4 ft (1.2 m)

Native to Chile. Most commonly cultivated species. Woody shrubby perennials. Leaves toothed, light green, sticky, slightly puckered, fine brown hairs beneath. Flowers yellow or rusty orange, sometimes with contrasting spots, borne all year, particularly abundant in warmer months. Trim in early spring. Popular cultivars include **'Goldbouquet'**, **'Golden Nugget'**, **'Kentish Hero'** ★, and **'Russet'**. Zones 8–10.

CALENDULA

A genus of about 20 species of annual and perennial herbs in the daisy (Asteraceae) family. They are found around the Mediterranean area and Atlantic Islands where they are often found growing on disturbed ground, particularly *C. officinalis*, which is a widespread garden escapee. All have alternate simple leaves; some of these are aromatic. The cheerful yellow or orange daisies appear for long periods throughout the year. The common name marigold is today also associated with some *Tagetes* species. CULTIVATION: Very easily grown in any well-drained soil in full sun. Sow seed in situ or under glass in spring in cooler areas, or earlier in warmer areas. Successive sowings and deadheading will result in a display over many months, from spring to autumn in cooler areas and throughout the year in warm ones.

Calendula officinalis ★

COMMON MARIGOLD, POT MARIGOLD, SCOTCH MARIGOLD

☼ ❄ ↔ 12–18 in (30–45 cm) ↕ 12–24 in (30–60 cm)

Originally from southern Europe but now widely naturalized. Bushy annual with slightly downy leaves. Orange or yellow daisies, to 3 in (8 cm) wide, in spring–autumn. **Bon Bon Series**, a mix of apricot, yellow, and orange flowers; **'Dwarf Gem'**, double, large, apricot, yellow, and orange daisies; **Fiesta Gitana Group** ★, a mix of cream, yellow, orange, and bi-colored flowers; **'Greenheart Orange'**, orange petals and a green center to flowers; **'Orange Salad'**, petals are a saffron substitute; **Kablouna Series**, short ray florets and prominent quilled centers, mixed yellow, orange, and apricot flowers; **Pacific Beauty Series**, tall-stemmed, yellow, orange, and apricot flowers; **'Radio'**, orange flowers, quilled petals resembling cactus-type dahlia. Zones 6–10.

CALIBRACHOA

syn. *Petunia* (in part)

A genus in the nightshade (Solanaceae) family, *Calibrachoa* is closely related to *Petunia* and its 25 species are found across much the same region of South America, from southern Brazil across to Peru and Chile; one species, *C. parviflora*, extends north to southern USA. They are weak evergreen perennials and subshrubs, mostly sprawling or prostrate with leaves under 1 in (25 mm) long. Flowers are smaller than in most petunias, under 1 in (25 mm) across and short-tubed, arising from leaf axils in continuous succession. After the release of the patented **Million Bells Series** in the 1990s, many strains followed with a wider range of colors and more compact or trailing habits. They flower almost continuously with adequate light and warmth. CULTIVATION: They will tolerate light frosts and thrive in sun or semi-shade. Mostly grown in pots or baskets; can be treated as annuals or short-lived perennials. Plant in a free-draining medium and apply weak fertilizer at intervals throughout the growing season, pinch back the longer shoots to increase the number of flowers. Water only when the soil is almost dry. Propagate from tip cuttings but be aware that propagation for sale may infringe plant patents.

Calibrachoa Hybrid Cultivars

☼/◑ ❄ ↔ 12–24 in (30–60 cm) ↕ 3–8 in (8–20 cm)

Valued for their low mounding or trailing habit and profusion of small flowers, mid-spring–late autumn or virtually year-round in warm climates. **Million Bells Series** are yellow-throated flowers in shades from white to lemon, pink, red, and purple, mounding to 6 in (15 cm). Flowers in the **Trailing Million Bells Series** are only 3 in (7 cm) or so high, spilling over edges of baskets or planter boxes. Flowers in the **Colorburst Series** come in cherry, red, rose and violet. Flowers of the German-bred **Minifamous Series** (syn. Selecta Series) include some rich colors, especially oranges, reds, and yellows, and also bicolors. The **Liricashower Series** include strong reds and yellows as well as pastels, with flat open blooms. Zones 8–11.

Calibrachoa, Hybrid Cultivar, 'Colorburst Violet'

CALLISTEPHUS

CHINA ASTER

The sole species in this genus is an annual daisy in the family
Asteraceae, from China. However, despite being just one species,
it has been developed into an array of garden varieties, which
have flowers in white and all shades of pink, mauve-blue, red,
and purple in single- and double-flowered
styles, all of which last well when cut. It is
naturally a sturdy upright plant, though
dwarf forms are available.
CULTIVATION: Plant in the full sun with moist
well-drained soil and feed occasionally with
liquid fertilizer. Err on the cautious side with
feeding or you may produce foliage at the
expense of flowers. Raise from seed. Spring-
sown seed begins flowering by early summer;
stagger sowing for a succession of blooms.

Callistephus chinensis

☀ ❄ ↔ 8–12 in (20–30 cm)
↑ 12–36 in (30–90 cm)
Dark green, pointed oval leaves to over 3 in (8 cm) long, with
coarsely toothed edges. Flowerheads are 2–4 in (5–10 cm) across,
borne singly on long stems. **Milady Series Mixed**, strong-growing
and bushy yet compact series growing to around 10 in (25 cm)
tall, available in a wide color range. Zones 8–11.

CALTHA

This buttercup (Ranunculaceae) family genus contains 10 species
of herbaceous perennials, widespread in temperate regions of
both hemispheres. Often very much like buttercups in general
appearance, they have fleshy, bright to deep green, kidney- to
heart-shaped leaves on sturdy leaf stalks and develop into
mounding clumps of foliage. Flowers white to pale yellow or
gold; although petalless, their
5 or more petal-like sepals give them a buttercup-like appearance.
Double-flowered forms are common. Flowering season varies.
CULTIVATION: These plants are mostly very frost tolerant with a
preference for damp soil and partly shaded conditions, though
ordinary well-drained humus-rich garden soil in a woodland
environment is perfectly acceptable. Their roots spread readily.
Most are easily propagated by division.

Caltha palustris

syn. *Caltha polypetala*

KING CUP, MARSH MARIGOLD

☀/☀ ❄ ↔ 16–24 in (40–60 cm)
↑ 12–24 in (30–60 cm)
Widespread throughout the northern temperate zone. Upright or spreading habit, with
kidney-shaped leaves, 4–8 in (10–20 cm)
wide. Bright golden yellow flowerheads on
upright stems, in late spring–early summer.
Several double-flowered cultivars with rounded heads available, including **'Flore Pleno'**
and the dark-leafed **'Monstrosa'**. Zones 3–9.

Callistephus chinensis

CAMPANULA

This large genus of about 300 species of hardy annual, biennial,
and perennial plants belongs to the bellflower (Campanulaceae)
family. It contains a number of popular and beautiful garden
plants. Many are native to Mediterranean areas, the Balkans, and
Caucasus region. Some are from North America and temperate
Asia. Their growth habit is ground-hugging
and clump-forming, or erect and branching.
A few species are invasive. Leaves are usually
alternately arranged. Flowers are in shades of
blue, mauve, pale pink, and white. They
range from large drooping bells to delicate
open stars, and are borne on panicles, spikes,
or singly. The variety of species allows for
choices for a range of garden types.
CULTIVATION: Most species grow easily in any
reasonably fertile well-drained soil in sun or
half-sun. Some alpine species require grittier
soil and dislike winter wet. Propagate from
seed, basal cuttings or by division.

Campanula carpatica

syn. *Campanula turbinata*

CARPATHIAN BELLFLOWER, TUSSOCK BELLFLOWER

☀/☀ ❄ ↔ 12–16 in (30–40 cm) ↑ 6–12 in (15–30 cm)
From the Carpathian Mountains. Low-growing spreading perennial forming a thick clump of small, bright green, egg-shaped
leaves. In summer the plant is covered with pale blue or white,
upward facing, open cup-shaped flowers, 1–2 in (2.5–5 cm)
in diameter. Eccellent ground cover. *C. c. f. alba* has white
flowers. *C. c.* cultivars include **'Blaue Clips'**, blue flowers; **'Blue
Moonlight'**, very open flowers, light grayish-blue; **'Chewton Joy'**,
light blue petals edged with deeper blue. Zones 3–9.

Campanula cochlearifolia

syn. *Campanula pusilla*

FAIRIES' THIMBLES

☀ ❄ ↔ 10 in (25 cm) ↑ 3 in (8 cm)
Creeping fleshy-stemmed perennial from the European Alps.
Forms tight clumps of small rounded leaves. Bell-shaped pale
lavender-blue flowers hang from wiry stems for long periods
over summer. *C. c.* var. *alba* has white flowers. The *C. c.* **Baby
Series** includes **'Blue Baby'**, prolific, pale blue
flowers; **'Bavaria Blue'**, a very compact plant
with dark blue flowers; **'Elizabeth Oliver'**,
double pale blue flowers. Zones 6–9.

Campanula garganica

syn. *Campanula elatines* var. *garganica*

☀ ❄ ↔ 6–12 in (15–30 cm) ↑ 6 in (15 cm)
Native to Italy. Low-growing perennial
forms tight clumps of small light green
leaves. Masses of small, starry, light blue
flowers on lax panicles, for long periods in
summer. **'Dickson's Gold'** (syn. 'Aurea'),
golden foliage. Zones 5–9.

Caltha palustris 'Flore Pleno'

Campanula glomerata
CLUSTERED BELLFLOWER

☼ ❄ ↔ 12–24 in (30–60 cm)
↑ 12–36 in (30–90 cm)

Perennial, native to Europe and Asia. Forms clumps by suckering. Bristly stems, purplish blue flowers. Long flowering period over summer. *C. g.* var. *acaulis*, very dwarf plants. *C. g.* 'Nana', 'Purple Pixie', and 'Superba' all have deep purple flowers. Zones 4–9.

Campanula isophylla
FALLING STARS, ITALIAN BELLFLOWER, STAR OF BETHLEHEM

☼ ❄ ↔ 12–18 in (30–45 cm) ↑ 6 in (15 cm)

From northern Italy, trailing perennial with small heart-shaped leaves. Smothered in 1 in (25 mm) wide, starry, mid-blue flowers in summer. Suitable for hanging baskets. Protect from winter wet. Cultivars include 'Alba', 'Stella Blue', and 'Stella White'. Zones 7–9.

Campanula portenschlagiana

Campanula lactiflora
MILKY BELLFLOWER

☼ ❄ ↔ 2 ft (0.6 m) ↑ 3–5 ft (0.9–1.5 m)

From the Caucasus region. Upright perennial. Well-branched, leafy, arching stems. Milky blue bell-shaped flowers in wide showy panicles in summer. 'Alba', white flowers; 'Loddon Anna', soft pinkish white flowers; 'Macrantha', large violet-purple flowers; 'Prichard's Variety', violet-blue flowers. Zones 5–9.

Campanula medium
CANTERBURY BELLS, CUP AND SAUCER

☼ ❄ ↔ 12 in (30 cm) ↑ 24–36 in (60–90 cm)

Native to southern Europe. Biennial. Soft, hairy, lance-shaped leaves. Showy bell-shaped white, pink, or blue flowers, in summer. Popular as cut flowers. 'Calycanthema' has petal-like calyx. Zones 8–10.

Campanula persicifolia
PEACH-LEAFED BELLFLOWER, WILLOW BELLFLOWER

☼ ❄ ↔ 18 in (45 cm)
↑ 24–36 in (60–90 cm)

Native to Europe, eastern Asia, and northern Africa. Perennial. Narrow wavy-edged leaves. Open, blue, bell-shaped flowers, on showy stems in summer. Long-flowering. Many single and double cultivars, including 'Bennett's Blue' (syn. 'Wortham Belle'), 'Boule de Neige', 'Chettle Charm', 'Fleur de Neige', and 'Planiflora' (syn. 'Nitida'). Zones 4–9.

Campanula punctata

Campanula portenschlagiana
syn. *Campanula muralis*

☼/❋ ❄ ↔ 18–24 in (45–60 cm) ↑ 6 in (15 cm)

From southern Europe. A vigorous alpine perennial with small heart-shaped leaves. It is smothered through the summer months

with erect starry flowers of lavender-blue. 'Resholdt's Variety' produces deep vivid blue flowers. Zones 4–9.

Campanula poscharskyana
SERBIAN BELLFLOWER

☼ ❄ ↔ 18–24 in (45–60 cm) ↑ 6–8 in (15–20 cm)

Native to Croatia. Vigorous alpine perennial. Bears starry flowers, lavender to violet, in summer–autumn. Spreads rapidly in rock gardens. 'Blue Gown', large mid-blue flowers; 'Blue Waterfall', vigorous and free-flowering, dark blue flowers with lighter centers; 'E. H. Frost' bears milky white starry flowers; 'Erich G. Arends' has blue flowers; 'Lisduggan Variety', lavender-pink flowers; 'Multiplicity' ★, double lavender-blue flowers; 'Stella', bright blue flowers. Zones 6–9.

Campanula punctata
syn. *Campanula nobilis*

☼ ❄ ↔ 18 in (45 cm) ↑ 12 in (30 cm)

From Siberia and Japan. A somewhat invasive perennial forming clumps of pointed heart-shaped leaves. Tubular, pendulous, bell-shaped flowers, cream, flushed with pink and spotted inside with red. *C. p.* f. *rubriflora*, narrow cream flowers tinged pink to purple, heavily spotted with red inside. *C. p.* 'Cherry Bells', cherry red with paler edging. Zones 6–9.

Campanula pyramidalis
CHIMNEY BELLFLOWER

☼ ❄ ↔ 2 ft (0.6 m) ↑ 4–7 ft (1.2–2 m)

From Europe. Short-lived clumping perennial usually grown as biennial. Broad, pointed, serrated-edged leaves. Tall branching stems of densely packed open bell-shaped flowers in pale blue or white. Summer-flowering. Best grown in the conservatory in cooler areas. Zones 8–10.

Campanula rapunculoides

☼/◐ ❄ ↔ 24 in (60 cm) ↑ 36 in (90 cm)

Native to Europe. Robust, invasive perennial forming large patches of serrated nettle-like leaves. Tall stems of nodding bell-shaped flowers in shades of blue to violet in summer. Zones 4–9.

Campanula rotundifolia

BLUEBELL, HAREBELL

◐ ❄ ↔ 10–18 in (25–45 cm) ↑ 6–12 in (15–30 cm)

Found throughout much of the Northern Hemisphere. Fleshy-stemmed perennial. Heart-shaped leaves forming rosettes. Dainty bell-shaped flowers, white to deep blue, on slender stems during summer. Buds upright but flowers hang when opened. Zones 3–9.

Campanula takesimana

◐ ❄ ↔ 18 in (45 cm) ↑ 24 in (60 cm)

From Korea, a rather invasive fleshy-stemmed perennial. Forms basal rosettes of large leaves. Bears tall stems of long, drooping, tubular bellflowers in summer. Flowers creamy white to lilac-pink on the outside, and spotted maroon inside. **'Beautiful Trust'** (syn. 'Beautiful Truth') has drooping spidery petals, pure white; 'Elizabeth' ★, prolific and long flowering. Zones 4–9.

CANISTRUM

These bromeliads from eastern to southeastern Brazil belong to the pineapple (Bromeliaceae) family. There are only 7 species. They form erect spreading rosettes to 24 in (60 cm) high and 16 in (40 cm) wide. The leaves sometimes have black teeth, are generally narrow and green, and some have dark markings. The flower stem is long and the globular flowerhead is enclosed by mainly red (sometimes orange) bracts, which may spread outward. The petals are white to rose to yellow in color.

CULTIVATION: These plants are recommended for indoor culture if in flower, for greenhouse or similar in cool-temperate areas, or outdoors with protection from direct continuous sunlight and extremes of rain in warm-temperate, subtropical, and tropical areas.

Canna iridiflora

Canistrum fosterianum

☼ ◑ ↔ 8 in (20 cm) ↑ 24 in (60 cm)

A tubular rosette a little flared at the top, leaves green with variable black markings on the outside. The flowerhead, to 4 in (10 cm) in diameter, appears just above the leaf tube and has spreading red bracts. Petals are white. Zones 9–12.

CANNA

CANNA LILY, INDIAN SHOT

Found throughout the New World in tropical and subtropical areas and widely naturalized elsewhere, this Cannaceae family genus has 9 species. They are vigorous plants with strong, upright, reed-like pseudostems that sprout from rhizomes and which bear long lance-shaped leaves. Heads of striking lily-like flowers, usually in shades of yellow, tangerine, and red, are borne.

CULTIVATION: Although they are often tropical in origin most can withstand light frosts as dormant roots if well insulated with mulch. Plant in full sun in moist, humus-rich, well-drained soil and feed well. Propagate selected forms by division in early spring. Seeds will often self-sow but rarely result in superior plants.

Canna glauca

☼ ❄ ↔ 1–3 ft (0.3–0.9 m) ↑ 4–6 ft (1.2–1.8 m)

Native to wetlands of tropical America. Bluish green pointed leaves to 20 in (50 cm) long. Large pale yellow flowers in summer. Zones 8–12.

Canna indica

syn. *Canna edulis*

INDIAN SHOT, QUEENSLAND ARROWROOT

☼/◐ ❄ ↔ 20–32 in (50–80 cm) ↑ 4–7 ft (1.2–2 m)

Widespread in the tropics. Leaves to 20 in (50 cm) long, often purple-tinted. Flowerheads upright, usually simple but sometimes branched. Red to orange flowers, rarely pink, often with contrasting spots, to slightly over 2 in (5 cm) wide. Zones 8–12.

Canna iridiflora

☼/◐ ❄ ↔ 20–32 in (50–80 cm) ↑ 10 ft (3 m)

Found from Costa Rica to Peru. Banana-like blue-green leaves to 4 ft (1.2 m) long. They bear simple or few-branched heads of semi-pendent, long-tubed, deep pink to orange flowers from late summer to mid-autumn. Many plants cultivated under this name are now thought to be the hybrid *C.* × *ehemanii*. Zones 8–12.

Canna Hybrid Cultivars

☼/◐ ❄ ↔ 3 ft (0.9 m) ↑ 2–7 ft (0.6–2 m)

Large range of garden hybrids with complex and often uncertain parentage. The names *C.* × *generalis* and *C.* × *orchioides* have been used for these plants in the past. Ranging in size from 24 in (60 cm) dwarfs to over 7 ft (2 m) tall. Wide range of flower colors and forms. 'Durban', 4 ft (1.2 m) tall, with yellow-striped purple-red leaves, bright red flowers; 'Erebus', 6 ft (1.8 m) tall, silvery blue-green leaves, salmon pink flowers; 'Lucifer' ★, 30 in (75 cm) high, dark foliage and yellow-edged red flowers; 'Minerva', 5 ft (1.5 m) tall, white and green striped foliage, yellow flowers opening from red buds over a long season; 'Pink Sunburst', 3 ft (0.9 m) high, pink-tinted yellow and green striped leave and salmon pink flowers; 'Red King Humbert', 7 ft (2 m) tall, bronze foliage and blood red flowers; 'Roi Humbert', 7–8 ft (2–2.4 m) tall, deep bronze foliage, orange-red flowers, sometimes yellow-marked; 'Striata' (syn. 'Pretoria'), 6 ft (1.8 m) tall, leaves banded in light and dark shades of green, orange-pink flowers; Tropicanna/'Phasion', 7 ft (2 m) tall, vivid purple-red and yellow-orange striped foliage, bright orange flowers. Zones 8–12.

CARTHAMUS

A genus of 14 species of thistle-like annuals and perennials of the daisy (Asteraceae) family. Found mainly around the Mediterranean and in western Asia, one species, the common *C. tinctorius*, now has a much wider distribution. Other species are seldom grown as they tend to become invasive. They are upright plants with stems that branch near the top to make a bushy clump of foliage. The leaves tend to be simple or pinnate with spine-tipped teeth. The whole plant is covered in fine downy hairs. Thistle-like heads with yellow, gold, pink, or violet ray florets appear in summer. Spiny bracts surround the base of the flowerheads. CULTIVATION: They are easily grown in any sunny position with light, gritty, well-drained soil. Sometimes used as a quick filler in annual or perennial borders, they are more likely to be seen as a field-grown commercial crop or as a weed on waste ground.

Carthamus tinctorius

FALSE SAFFRON, SAFFLOWER

☼ ❈ ↔ 16–20 in (40–50 cm) ↕ 24–40 in (60–100 cm)
Native to the Mediterranean region. Lower leaves may be simple or pinnate, sometimes spiny; those on flower stem usually simple and spine-tipped. Flowerheads yellow, gold to orange or red, rarely white. Summer-flowering. '**Orange Gold**' has intensely golden yellow flowerheads. Zones 4–10.

CATANANCHE

CUPID'S DART

This small genus, belonging to the daisy (Asteraceae) family, contains 5 species of annual or perennial herbs found in countries bordering the Mediterranean, inhabiting dry grassy areas. Leaves are usually long and narrow and arise at base of clump. Flowering stems are long and wiry, bearing cornflower-like flowers of blue, white, or yellow. Bracts below the flowers are transparent and papery, often with a silver tinge.
CULTIVATION: *C. caerulea* is usually the only species seen in cultivation. Grow in full sun in any well-drained soil. It tends to be short-lived as a perennial, especially when grown in heavy clay, and can be treated as an annual. Plants propagated from seed will flower in the first year. Propagate by division in winter.

Canna, Hybrid Cultivar, '**Tropicanna**'/'Phasion'

Catananche caerulea

BLUE CUPIDONE, BLUE SUCCORY, CUPID'S DART

☼ ❈ ↔ 12–18 in (30–45 cm)
↕ 24–30 in (60–75 cm)
Native to southwestern Europe and northern Africa. Low clumps of narrow, lance-shaped, grayish green leaves, sometimes with a few long teeth. Delicate stems of blue to mauve flowers, like cornflowers in color and appearance, in summer. '**Major**' has flowers of deep blue. Zones 7–10.

CATHARANTHUS

Although related to the common periwinkle *(Vinca)*, the 8 annuals and perennials of this genus, in the dogbane (Apocynaceae) family, are less hardy and tolerate little or no frost. All Madagascan natives, they are bushy plants with simple elliptical leaves on semi-succulent stems. Flat, 5-petalled flowers, mainly in pink and mauve shades, appear at the stem tip and leaf axils. Considered a weed in the tropics and subtropics, the commonly cultivated species *C. roseus* is a perennial often grown as a greenhouse plant or summer bedder in temperate gardens.
CULTIVATION: Very easily grown in sun or part-shade, periwinkles are drought tolerant but flower more heavily with summer moisture. Pinch back to encourage bushiness. In cool areas where winter frost would be fatal, bring plants indoors or discard and replace in spring. Propagate from seed or half-hardened summer cuttings.

Catharanthus roseus

Catharanthus roseus

syn. *Vinca rosea*

MADAGASCAR PERIWINKLE, ROSE PERIWINKLE

☼/◐ ✦ ↔ 16 in (40 cm) ↕ 24 in (60 cm)
Upright perennial from Madagascar. Glossy deep green leaves with pale midrib, to 2 in (5 cm) long. Mauve-throated, soft pink to red, 5-petalled flowers, with red "eye." '**Albus**', white flowers; '**Blue Pearl**', 18 in (45 cm) tall, white-centered lavender blue to mauve flowers; '**Blush Cooler**', very pale pink flowers, light red center, one of the compact, 12 in (30 cm) tall, heavy-flowering **Cooler Series**; '**Pacifica Punch**', deep pink flowers with slightly darker center, one of the 18 in (45 cm) tall **Pacifica Series**; '**Parasol**', white flowers to 2 in (5 cm) wide, with red eye; the **Pretty Series**, very heat-tolerant; '**Stardust Orchid**', cream-centered deep pink flowers, up to 16 in (40 cm) tall. Zones 11–12.

CELMISIA
MOUNTAIN DAISY, SNOW DAISY

Mainly from New Zealand, with a few species in southeastern Australia, this genus in the daisy (Asteraceae) family has some 60 species of perennials and subshrubs that frequently occur in subalpine and alpine regions where they often dominate the vegetation and may carpet large areas. They form basal rosettes or tufts of simple narrow leaves, sometimes ribbed, often with a covering of downy hair on the undersides. This hair can also cover the upper surfaces of young leaves. Woody stems can develop at the base, especially among the larger spreading species. The flowerheads are simple daisies with white ray florets around a central swelling of golden yellow disc florets. They are borne one head to a stem and appear mainly around mid-summer.
CULTIVATION: Only a few species adapt well to cultivation; many are difficult to grow outside their natural environment. They prefer a cool-summer temperate climate and should be planted in gritty, humus-rich, moist, well-drained soil in full or half-sun. Propagate from seed or by division.

Celmisia sessiliflora
WHITE CUSHION DAISY

☀/◑ ❀ ↔ 6–40 in (15–100 cm)
↑ 2–6 in (5–15 cm)
From South and Stewart Islands, New Zealand, common at altitude. Densely branched subshrub forming cushions of stiff, thick, silvery leaves less than 1 in (25 mm) long. Flowerheads abundant, usually at foliage level. Zones 7–9.

Celmisia spectabilis
COTTON DAISY, COTTON PLANT

☀/◑ ❀ ↔ 20–48 in (50–120 cm)
↑ 8–12 in (20–30 cm)
New Zealand species, found from the central North Island southward. The leaves are bright green, 4–6 in (10–15 cm) long with silver to buff-colored hairs, and grow in dense tufts. Plants can spread with age as a dense ground cover. Flowerheads to 2 in (5 cm) wide, on sturdy downy stems, in summer. Zones 7–9.

CELOSIA
COCKSCOMB, WOOLFLOWER

Found in the tropics of Asia, Africa, and the Americas, this genus of around 50 species of annuals and perennials belongs to the amaranth (Amaranthaceae) family. *C. argentea* var. *cristata*, an annual, is the only widely cultivated species and it has been developed into many variably flowered and colored seedling strains. Upright plants, some are up to 6 ft (1.8 m) tall, though most are far smaller. They have simple lance-shaped leaves up to 6 in (15 cm) long and tiny vivid yellow, orange, or red flowers massed in upright plumes or combs (cristate).
CULTIVATION: Although it can be grown far outside its natural range, *Celosia* needs ample warmth to perform well. Plant in fertile well-drained soil in full sun and water well. Raise from seed.

Celosia argentea
☀/◑ ✈ ↔ 16–24 in (40–60 cm) ↑ 3–7 ft (0.9–2 m)
Quick-growing annual, widespread in the tropics. Leaves lance-shaped to 6 in (15 cm) long. Tiny white flowers in upright spikes to 3 in (8 cm) long. Usually seen as *C. a.* var. *cristata*; cultivated forms have green, purple, or red foliage and many flower colors and styles: **Childsii Group**, rounded to globose flowerheads; **Cristata** or **Cockscomb Group**, flowerheads terminal, flattened and broad, resembling a rooster's comb; **Plumosa Group**, upright plumes of flowers, not always terminal, cultivars include 'Apricot Brandy', 'Forest Fire', 'Castle Mix', 'New Look', and 'Venezuela'; **Pyramidalis Group**, flowerheads broad-based, tapering evenly to a point, often included with Plumosa Group. Zones 11–12.

CENTAUREA
CORNFLOWER, KNAPWEED, STAR THISTLE

Widespread in temperate zones, this genus is a member of the daisy (Asteraceae) family and encompasses around 450 species of annuals, perennials, and subshrubs. A variable lot, most species are readily identifiable by their thistle-like flowerheads, which emerge from an egg-shaped receptacle known as an involucre. The flowerheads often have distinctly different inner and outer florets, with the outer having 5 longer petals. The range of flower colors includes white, yellow, pink, blue, and mauve. Plant size varies with the species; common features are pinnately lobed foliage, often silver-gray, and an upright habit.

Celosia argentea var. *cristata*, Plumosa Group, 'Venezuela'

CULTIVATION: Plant in full sun, in light well-drained soil. Good ventilation will lessen any mildew problems. Annuals can be raised from seed; perennials also propagated by division or from softwood cuttings of non-flowering stems.

Centaurea cineraria ★
syn. *Centaurea gymnocarpa*
DUSTY MILLER

☀ ❀ ↔ 12–24 in (30–60 cm) ↑ 20–36 in (50–90 cm)
From western and southern Italy. Perennial sometimes treated as an annual. Very decorative silver-gray pinnate leaves, Flowerheads purple-pink. Zones 7–10.

Centaurea cyanus
BACHELOR'S BUTTON, BLUEBOTTLE, CORNFLOWER

☀ ❀ ↔ 8–16 in (20–40 cm) ↑ 12–36 in (30–90 cm)
Annual or biennial from temperate Eurasia. Narrow green to blue-green leaves, sometimes silvery when young. Flowerheads are usually blue in the species but garden forms include white and a wide range of pink and blue shades. The flowering season is from late spring to summer; deadheading will prolong flowering. 'Blue Diadem', large, ruffled, double, deep blue heads; the Florence Series, a dwarf strain, to around 14 in (35 cm) high, wide color range. Zones 2–10.

Centaurea dealbata

Centaurea dealbata
PERSIAN CORNFLOWER

☼ ❋ ↔ 16–24 in (40–60 cm) ↕ 32–40 in (80–100 cm)

Caucasian and northern Iranian perennial. The pinnate leaves, to 8 in (20 cm) long, are green above with gray furry undersides. Pink to purple flowerheads are borne in summer. '**Steenbergii**', large, vigorous, with attractive deep pink flowerheads. Zones 3–9.

Centaurea macrocephala
GLOBE CORNFLOWER

☼ ❋ ↔ 20–24 in (50–60 cm) ↕ 32–40 in (80–100 cm)

Erect perennial native to the Caucasus region. Green lance-shaped leaves covered with minute silvery hairs. Large yellow flowerheads. Zones 3–9.

Centaurea montana
MOUNTAIN BLUET, PERENNIAL CORNFLOWER

☼ ❋ ↔ 12–40 in (30–100 cm) ↕ 24–32 in (60–80 cm)

Perennial from mountains of Europe. Spreads by rhizomes and may form large clump of broad, green, lance-shaped leaves, sometimes pinnate at base. Flowerheads violet to purple-blue. '**Alba**', low-growing, white-flowered cultivar. Zones 3–9.

CENTRANTHUS

This genus belongs to the valerian (Valerianaceae) family, and consists of 12 species of annual and perennial subshrubs from Europe and the Mediterranean, of which only one, *Centranthus ruber*, is widely cultivated. Forming clumps of upright stems with simple, lance-shaped, blue-green leaves and topped with inflorescences of tiny honey-scented flowers, the species can be 2–5 ft (0.6–1.5 m) tall. The flowers are most often a dusky crimson shade but may be white or pink.

CULTIVATION: These drought-tolerant and adaptable plants are very easily grown in any sunny well-drained position. Alkaline soil is preferred but not essential. To prevent seeding, cut back flower stems as soon as they fade. *C. ruber* is inclined to self-sow and is considered a weed in parts of New Zealand.

Centranthus ruber
JUPITER'S BEARD, RED VALERIAN

☼/☽ ❋ ↔ 16–27 in (40–70 cm) ↕ 32–40 in (80–100 cm)

Found in Europe, North Africa, and western Asia. Blue-green oval to lance-shaped leaves, are sometimes finely toothed, to 3 in (8 cm) long. Tiny, fragrant, deep rose pink to red flowers massed in upright heads. '**Albus**' has white flowers. Zones 6–10.

CEPHALOTUS

A carnivorous pitcher plant and the only genus in the family Cephalotaceae, this is only found on the southwestern coast of Western Australia. Its small but very strong pitchers resemble little moccasins. Although a perennial, its growth slows and sometimes stops in the cool winters. In spring the plant produces non-carnivorous waxy leaves; as the weather warms, the carnivorous pitchers develop. Formed in a rosette, the outward-facing pitchers are covered in fine white hairs. The pitchers have a ribbed rim, a central rib, and 2 side ribs that slope toward the opening. In half-sun the pitchers are bright green but turn dark burgundy in full sun. Insects are attracted to the plant by the bright colors and the nectar just inside the pitcher's rim.

CULTIVATION: Grow in pots in a mixture of 3 parts peat, 1 part vermiculite and 2 parts sand or in a sunny bog garden. They do best in full sun (the pots can stand in water trays in summer); keep the soil just damp in the cooler months as plants are prone to root rot. Use a soil fungicide every few months. In its natural habitat, temperatures can reach up to 104°F (40°C) in summer but the winter nights are cool to cold. Propagate by division or from stem cuttings in late spring to early summer.

Cephalotus follicularis
ALBANY PITCHER PLANT, WESTERN AUSTRALIAN PITCHER PLANT

☽ ⚘ ↔ 8 in (20 cm) ↕ 15 in (38 cm)

Robust rootstock that produces many short stems bearing 2 types of leaves: simple, spoon-shaped, green, fleshy, oval; and leaves modified to a pitcher-shaped container with a hinged lid, green, brown or red. Flowering stem can be 2 ft (0.6 m) high. Zone 9.

Cephalotus follicularis

CERASTIUM

A genus of about 100 species in the pink (Caryophyllaceae) family. Mostly annuals or perennials, the majority are vigorous carpeting ground covers or tufting plants; many are classed as weeds. Mainly found in Europe and North America, from temperate to arctic zones. Generally the leaves are small and are often hairy, giving a silvery appearance. The flowers are usually small and white. They are popular in rock gardens or massed in borders. CULTIVATION: A well-drained soil in a position in full sun is a must for these plants. Some species can cope with poor or rocky soils. Propagation is from seed, cuttings, or by division.

Cerastium boissieri

syn. *Cerastium boissierianum*
☼ ❄ ↔ 8–16 in (20–40 cm)
↑ 6–10 in (15–25 cm)
European species, found particularly in Spain. Hairy white leaves. White flowers. Does well in sunny dry rock crevices. Zones 6–11.

Cerastium tomentosum

SNOW-IN-SUMMER
☼ ❄ ↔ 40 in (100 cm) ↑ 4–6 in (10–15 cm)
This species ranges widely through mountains of Europe and western Asia. A vigorous mat-former, this plant has whitish-woolly foliage. Profuse heads of starry white flowers, to 1 in (25 mm) wide, in spring–summer. Zones 6–11.

CHELIDONIUM

There is just one species of biennial or perennial herb in this genus of the poppy (Papaveraceae) family. It is native to Europe and western Asia and naturalized in the eastern USA. Variable species, branching from the base and with pinnate leaves, often with a 3-lobed terminal leaflet. Golden yellow flowers, to 1 in (25 mm) wide with 4 petals, are borne in loose terminal clusters. CULTIVATION: This plant is suitable for the wild garden and shady corners in a range of soil types. It self-sows readily. Propagate from seed sown in situ.

Chelidonium majus

GREATER CELANDINE
☼/◑ ❄ ↔ 12–36 in (30–90 cm) ↑ 12–36 in (30–90 cm)
From Europe, western Asia, naturalized elsewhere. Brittle leafy stems. Summer-flowering. *C. m.* var. *laciniatum*, deeply cut leaves. *C. m.* 'Flore Pleno', more common double form. Zones 6–9.

CHELONE

SHELL FLOWER, TURTLE'S HEAD
This North American genus in the foxglove (Scrophulariaceae) family contains 6 species of herbaceous perennials. They have opposite leaves and bear tubular flowers with 2 lips. White to purple blooms are produced from mid-summer till cold weather arrives. They are long lasting if cut; seed heads can be dried. CULTIVATION: These are happy in moisture-retentive soil in a half-sun to sunny position. Propagate by division, or from seed.

Chelone glabra

SNAKE HEAD, TURTLE'S HEAD
☼/◑ ❄ ↔ 16–20 in (40–50 cm) ↑ 20–32 in (50–80 cm)
From eastern and southern North America. White flowers, often stained pink or purple, to 1 in (25 mm) long, throughout summer and autumn. Zones 3–9.

Chelone lyonii ★

☼/◑ ❄ ↔ 24–36 in (60–90 cm) ↑ 40–48 in (100–120 cm)
Tall upright species, mainly found in Tennessee and North Carolina, USA. Deep pink flowers with a yellow beard on the inside lower lip, to 1 in (25 mm) long, throughout summer and into autumn. Zones 4–9.

Chlorophytum comosum 'Variegatum'

CHLOROPHYTUM

This genus in the sisal (Agavaceae) family contains about 215 species of fleshy-stemmed perennials native to tropical and subtropical regions of Africa, Asia, and 1 species extending to northern Australia. They range in height from 4–24 in (10–60 cm), with linear to lance-shaped leaves arising from the root-stock. Small white flowers are borne in loose sparse panicles, and the flowering stems form new plantlets in some species. CULTIVATION: A few species are cultivated for their foliage. The most commonly seen is the popular house plant *C. comosum*. In warmer areas where outdoor cultivation is possible, grow in light shade in well-drained soil. Can be grown as a ground cover. Indoor plants need bright indirect light and watering well when in full growth.

Chlorophytum comosum

SPIDER PLANT
◑ ✄ ↔ 12–24 in (30–60 cm) ↑ 12–24 in (30–60 cm)
From South Africa. Leaves to 16 in (40 cm) long, green or striped white. Loose panicles of small starry flowers. Can be invasive in mild moist climates. 'Variegatum', white or cream margins; 'Vittatum', recurved leaves with central white stripe. Zones 9–11.

Chlorophytum laxum

◑ ✄ ↔ 8–12 in (20–30 cm) ↑ 8–12 in (20–30 cm)
From tropical Africa to Southeast Asia and northern Australia. Fleshy-rooted perennial with linear leaves striped creamy white. Small white flowers are borne in loose panicles. Zones 10–12.

CHRYSANTHEMUM

syn. *Dendranthema*
Although once referred to as *Dendranthema*, the florists' chrysanthemum is now correctly known under its old name. There are about 40 species, mainly from East Asia. CULTIVATION: Florists' chrysanthemums prefer a heavier richer soil and will tolerate some shade. Pinch back when young and disbud to ensure the best flower show. Annual species are raised from seed; the florists' forms by division when dormant or from half-hardened summer cuttings.

Chrysanthemum × *grandiflorum*

syn. *Dendranthema* × *grandiflorum*

FLORISTS' CHRYSANTHEMUM

☼/◐ ❀ ↔ 18–36 in (45–90 cm) ↕ 1–5 ft (0.3–1.5 m)

Encompassing a large group of hybrids, chrysanthemums are available from florists throughout the year; under garden conditions they are autumn-flowering. Although they tend to have similar lobed aromatic leaves, chrysanthemums occur in a wide range of plant sizes and flower types and are classified in groups based on flower characteristics. The United States National Chrysanthemum Society Standards recognizes these 13 classes.

1. **Irregular incurved:** Very large ball-shaped heads, with incurving florets, the lower ones often loose and irregular, creating a skirt. '**Gold Creamest**', '**Palisade**', and '**Shamrock**' are examples.

2. **Reflexed:** Medium-sized to large heads, regular, downward curving florets, overlap neatly like scales or feathers. Included in this class are '**Euro**', '**Fiji**', and Robin/'**Yorobi**'.

3. **Regular incurved:** Heads 4–6 in (10–15 cm) wide, near-spherical flowers, upward-curving florets. Includes '**Heather James**'.

4. **Decorative:** Compact, rather flattened heads, distinct but short ray florets, no visible disc florets. Includes most of those known as spray chrysanthemums. Usually over 18 in (45 cm) tall. Popular examples include Barbara/'**Yobarbara**', '**Fortune**', '**Margaret**', '**Red Headliner**', '**Salmon Margaret**', '**Storm King**', Sundoro/'**Yosun**', '**Wendy**', and '**Wildfire**'.

5. **Intermediate incurved:** Similar to irregular incurved but with smaller flowerheads, still around 6 in (15 cm) wide. Includes '**Primrose Allouise**' and '**Royal Touch**'.

6. **Pompon:** Small, densely petalled, spherical heads ranging from 1–4 in (2.5–10 cm) wide. Usually under 18 in (45 cm) tall. Popular hybrids include '**Carillon**', '**Cheers**', and '**Ping Pong**'.

7. **Single and semi-double:** Simple heads, often very large, visible and clearly defined disc florets surrounded by one or more rows of ray florets. Singles sometimes known as 'daisies.' This group includes '**Amber Enbee Wedding**', '**Buckeye**', '**Golden Megatime**', '**Megatime**', '**Poser**', '**Splendor**', '**Tiger**', and '**Tracy**'.

8. **Anemone:** Basically semi-double in structure with a clearly defined halo of outer ray florets but smaller ray florets clustered and mounding at the center, and concealing the disc. Includes '**Day's End**', '**Pennine Marie**', '**Pennine Oriel**', '**Powder Puff**', '**Score**', '**Sunny Le Mans**', and '**Yellow Pennine Oriel**'.

9. **Spoon:** Semi-double heads, clearly defined disc florets. Ray florets long, narrow, broaden to spoon shape at tips. Cultivars include '**Citrine**', and '**Seminole**'.

10. **Quill:** Large, regularly shaped heads, long, straight tubular florets open at tips. Includes '**Pennine Flute**'.

11. **Spider:** Long, drooping, tubular florets, either narrow or broad, and often coiled or recurved at the tips. Popular hybrids include '**Dusky Queen**', '**Mixed Spider**', and '**Yellow Knight**' ★.

12. **Brush or Thistle:** Very narrow, often twisted florets, lower of which stand out at right angles from stem.

13. **Unclassified:** Catch-all grouping covering blooms yet to be formally classified or not falling into any other categories. Includes '**Angora**', '**Beacon**', '**Bronze Cassandra**', '**Cherry Nathalie**', '**Eastleigh**', '**George Griffiths**', '**Harlekijn**', '**Lemon Fiji**', '**Mancetta Bride**', '**Mavis**', '**Myss Madi**', '**Pennine Lace**', '**Pink Gin**', '**Roy Coopland**', '**Rynoon**', '**Southway Swan**', and '**Weldon**'. Zones 5–10.

Chrysanthemum weyrichii

syn. *Dendranthema weyrichii*

MIYABE DAISY

☼/◐ ❀ ↔ 16–24 in (40–60 cm) ↕ 4 in (10 cm)

Spreading perennial native to Japan. Leaves fleshy, glossy bright green, on purple-tinted stems. Short-stemmed flowerheads 1½ in (40 mm) wide with white or pink ray florets, in summer–autumn. '**Pink Bomb**' and '**White Bomb**', heavy-flowering. Zones 4–9.

CHRYSOGONUM

Part of the daisy (Asteraceae) family, this genus contains only one species—a low perennial herb native to eastern USA. It is a good ground cover for partly shaded borders and edges of woodlands. CULTIVATION: Plants prefer moist well-drained soil and part- to full shade. Propagate by division in early spring or early autumn; it also self-sows. Self-sown seedlings may be transplanted.

Chrysogonum virginianum

GOLDEN STAR, GREEN AND GOLD

◐/☼ ❀ ↔ 24 in (60 cm) ↕ 6–10 in (15–25 cm)

Coarse hairy leaves, serrated margin. Flowers yellow with 5 slightly notched petals, 1–1½ in (25–35 mm) wide, flowers from spring to early summer, and sporadically during summer. Will grow in colder areas provided it gets good snow cover. Zones 5–9.

Chrysanthemum × *grandiflorum*, 7. Single, '*Tiger*'

Chrysanthemum × *grandiflorum*, 11. Spider, '*Mixed Spider*'

Chrysanthemum weyrichii

CLARKIA

FAREWELL TO SPRING, GODETIA

This genus of 33 species of annual herbs belongs to the evening-primrose (Onagraceae) family. The majority are native to western North America. They are cultivated for their showy funnel-shaped flowers, which occur in shades of pink, red, purple, and sometimes yellow and white, from late spring to summer. The petals are often splashed with red or white. The flowers are long-lasting.
CULTIVATION: Grow in full sun in low to moderately fertile well-drained soil. They dislike hot humid conditions, so in warmer areas seed should be sown in autumn so that the plants will flower before the summer heat becomes intense. In cooler areas sow in early spring.

Clarkia amoena
syns *Clarkia grandiflora, Godetia amoena*
SATIN FLOWER
☀ ❋ ↔ 12 in (30 cm) ↑ 24 in (60 cm)
Showy species from northern California, USA. Densely packed spikes of cup-shaped flowers of pink to lavender, sometimes darkening at the base or shading to white, centers usually splashed with dark red. 'Grandiflora' (syn. 'Whitneyi'), flowers in shades of rose, pink, lavender, red, and white. Zones 7–10.

Clarkia pulchella
☀ ❋ ↔ 12 in (30 cm) ↑ 12–18 in (30–45 cm)
Found from the Rocky Mountains to the Pacific Coast, USA. Compact species. Frilly flowers of bright pink to lavender, sometimes with white or purple veining. Double forms of mixed colors are most commonly grown. Zones 7–10.

Clarkia unguiculata
syn. *Clarkia elegans*
☀ ❋ ↔ 12 in (30 cm) ↑ 24–30 in (60–75 cm)
From California. Commonly grown species with many cultivars. Flowers, 1 in (25 mm) across, ranging through pink, purple, and red shades, also yellow and white. Zones 7–10.

CLEMATIS

LEATHER VINE, TRAVELLER'S JOY, VIRGIN'S BOWER

This genus of over 200 species, in the buttercup (Ranunculaceae) family, encompasses a huge range of forms. *Clematis* species are mainly climbing or scrambling but sometimes shrubby or perennial, deciduous or evergreen, flowering at any time in any color, occurring in both northern and southern temperate zones and at higher altitudes in the tropics. Leaves may be simple or pinnate. Flowers are nearly always showy, with 4 to 8 petal-like sepals. Fluffy seed heads follow.
CULTIVATION: Foliage should be in the sun while the roots are kept cool and moist. Incorporate plenty of humus-rich compost before

Clarkia pulchella, double mixed

planting, and water well. Clematis wilt disease is a problem in many areas. Propagate from cuttings or layers. Species may be raised from seed, but sex will be undetermined before flowering.

Clematis integrifolia
☀/☀ ❋ ↔ 3–5 ft (0.9–1.5 m) ↑ 3 ft (0.9 m)
Deciduous perennial or subshrub found from Europe to central Asia. Simple, lance-shaped leaves with downy undersides. Pendulous, flattened, bell-shaped flowers, to 4 in (10 cm) wide, deep violet-blue. Zones 3–9.

CLEOME

SPIDER FLOWER

This largely tropical and subtropical genus of around 150 species of annuals and perennials belongs to the small caper (Capparidaceae) family. The commonly grown species are upright summer annuals. Their large palmate leaves have fine-toothed edges and stems that are sometimes spiny. Their 4-petalled flowers have long, protruding, filament-like stamens and are carried in apical heads with the filaments facing outward.
CULTIVATION: In areas with a warm summer the annuals are easily grown in any sheltered sunny position with moist, fertile, free-draining soil. Deadheading the flowers encourages longer blooming. With the exception of a few species, the perennials will not tolerate frost and need at least subtropical conditions. Propagate from spring-sown seed.

Cleome sesquiorygalis
syn. *Cleome spinosa*
SPIDER FLOWER
☀/☀ ❊ ↔ 20 in (50 cm) ↑ 5 ft (1.5 m)
Upright annual from southern Brazil, Paraguay, and northern Argentina. Palmate leaves with 5 to 7 finely toothed hairy leaflets to over 4 in (10 cm) long. Flowers clustered in terminal heads, petals to 1¼ in (30 mm) long with long filaments. In white and many shades of pink to purple. Several seedling strains and named forms, such as the **Queen Series**: 'Cherry Queen', 'Helen Campbell' (syn. 'White Queen'), 'Mauve Queen', 'Pink Queen', 'Purple Queen', 'Rose Queen', 'Ruby Queen'. Zones 10–12.

CLIVIA

FIRE LILY

This genus in the amaryllis (Amaryllidaceae) family consists of 4 species of perennials from southern Africa. Clump-forming with stocky rhizomes, they have long, bright green, strappy leaves and at various times, depending on the species, produce strong flower stems topped with heads of large funnel-shaped flowers in shades of yellow, orange, and red. Red berries follow flowering.

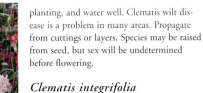
Cleome sesquiorygalis

CULTIVATION: Tolerating only light frosts but otherwise quite easily grown, clivias are superb as greenhouse container plants. Outdoors they will be happiest when grown in dappled shade. Water well during the warmer months and allow to dry off for winter. Propagation is usually by division.

Clivia miniata
FIRE LILY

☀ ❄ ↔ 24–40 in (60–100 cm)
↕ 16–24 in (40–60 cm)

Leaves to 24 in (60 cm) long, sometimes quite broad. Wide open, funnel-shaped, yellow-throated, orange to nearly red flowers. Spring-flowering. *C. m.* f. *citrina*, primrose yellow flowers; cultivars include '**Vico Yellow**'. *C. m.* '**Aurea**', '**Flame ★**', '**Megen**', and '**Striata**' are attractive cultivars. Zones 9–11.

Clivia miniata 'Vico Yellow'

Clivia nobilis
GREENTIP FIRE LILY

☀ ❄ ↔ 20–36 in (50–90 cm) ↕ 16–24 in (40–60 cm)

Hardiest and most easily grown *Clivia*. Leaves to 18 in (45 cm) long, very finely toothed, producing a rough texture. Heads of green-tipped, yellow to red flowers. Spring-flowering. Zones 9–11.

CODONOPSIS
BONNET BELLFLOWER

This genus in the bellflower (Campanulaceae) family has around 30 species of herbaceous perennials that will climb on structures but prefer to scramble through surrounding vegetation. They have wiry, often twining stems and simple light-textured leaves of variable shape. The flowers are nodding, bell-shaped, with conspicuous calyces, and although fairly large they are often a pale blue-green color that merges well with the foliage. CULTIVATION: They are mostly very hardy and easily grown in any temperate climate with reasonable summer rainfall. They prefer woodland conditions with dappled light and cool, moist, humus-rich, well-drained soil. Try to remove the tangle of dry foliage and stems after it has died off, otherwise it may become very untidy. Propagate by division when dormant, or raise from seed.

Codonopsis clematidea

☀ ❄ ↔ 20–60 in (50–150 cm) ↕ 32 in (80 cm)

From central Asia. Slightly downy, 1 in (25 mm) long leaves tinted blue-green. In summer, very pale blue bell-shaped flowers, orange and black markings within. Zones 4–9.

COLLINSIA

This genus of 25 species of hardy annuals belongs to the foxglove (Scrophulariaceae) family. They are native to western North America and Mexico. They are grown for their attractive, tubular, 2-lipped flowers that are borne in whorls on slender stems. The flowers are in shades of white, lilac, rose, violet, and blue, and are often bicolored. Flowering is in spring and summer.

CULTIVATION: Grow these plants in a rich, moist, but well-drained soil in sun or half-sun. They can also be grown as pot plants in a conservatory, with shade from the hottest sun and a fortnightly dressing of weak liquid fertilizer. Propagate from seed.

Collinsia bicolor
syn. *Collinsia heterophylla*
CHINESE HOUSES, INNOCENCE

☀ ❄ ↔ 6–12 in (15–30 cm) ↕ 12–24 in (30–60 cm)

From California. Slender plants with lance-shaped leaves. Tubular 2-lipped flowers, borne on spikes in whorls of 2 to 7 blooms. Upper lip and tube are white, lower lip is rosy purple. Zones 7–10.

COLUMNEA

This mainly epiphytic genus of the African violet family (Gesneriaceae) contains around 160 species native to the New World tropics. They have arching to trailing or pendulous stems that form a crown of foliage. The small leaves are oval to lance-shaped and flowers are tubular.

CULTIVATION: Intolerant of frost, these are house or greenhouse plants outside the subtropics. They need a steady temperature, not necessarily hot, dappled light and shelter from cold drafts. Allow to dry in winter. Propagate from half-hardened tip cuttings.

Columnea 'Early Bird' ★

☀ ✦ ↔ 18 in (45 cm) ↕ 48 in (120 cm)

Bright yellow flowers, red-orange edges, 2–3 in (5–8 cm) wide. Small, shiny, mid-green leaves, darker tips. Zones 11–12.

Columnea gloriosa ★
GOLDFISH PLANT

☀/◐ ✦ ↔ 18 in (45 cm) ↕ 12 in (30 cm)

Central American species. Stems arch up before trailing. Hairy, pointed, oval leaves. Yellow-throated orange-red flowers borne singly, with hooded upper lip. Zones 11–12.

Columnea microphylla

☀/◐ ✢ ↔ 2 ft (0.6 m) ↑ 6 ft (1.8 m)

Costa Rican species. Long, trailing stems. Red-haired rounded leaves less than ½ in (12 mm) long, with red undersides. Flowers borne singly, up to 3 in (8 cm) long, yellow markings, large hooded upper lip. Calyces often red-tinted, finely toothed. Zones 11–12.

Columnea scandens

☀/◐ ✢ ↔ 24 in (60 cm) ↑ 12 in (30 cm)

From the West Indies and Central America. Cascading, sometimes arching stems. Deep green leaves, fine red hairs. Narrow flowers, singly or in pairs, fine-haired, nearly 3½ in (9 cm) long, red or yellow. Zones 11–12.

COMMELINA

DAY FLOWER, WIDOW'S TEARS

There are around 100 species of mainly perennial herbs in this genus, which gives its name to the spiderwort (Commelinaceae) family. They are native to mainly tropical and subtropical regions. The roots are often tuberous and the stems are usually slender and sprawling, rooting at the nodes. The flowers are held within spathe-like folded bracts. Commonly grown species have blue flowers, but white, yellow, rose, and lilac flowers occur.
CULTIVATION: Grow in full sun in any well-drained soil. In cooler climates the tuberous species should be lifted in autumn. Propagate from seed or cuttings.

Commelina tuberosa

☀/◐ ❁ ↔ 18–30 in (45–75 cm) ↑ 12–36 in (30–90 cm)

Variable perennial with tuberous roots, occurring from southern Mexico to Peru, in mountains. "Typical" form is low, spreading, and mounding. Brilliant blue flowers open continuously in spring–autumn. **Coelestis Group** (syn. *Commelina coelestis*) includes taller, more erect forms, larger flowers. Zones 9–12.

Convolvulus tricolor

Columnea microphylla

CONSOLIDA

LARKSPUR

This Eurasian genus in the buttercup (Ranunculaceae) family has around 40 species. Larkspurs have fine feathery foliage, and about half their height is taken up with upright, sometimes branching heads of 5-petalled flowers that make excellent cut flowers. Some parts of the plant, especially the seeds, are poisonous.
CULTIVATION: Plant these in fertile well-drained soil in full sun. They thrive in most conditions and will often self-sow, although the flowers of wild seedlings rarely amount to much. They may need staking. Raise from seed.

Consolida ajacis

syns *Consolida ambigua*, *Delphinium ajacis*
LARKSPUR

☀/◐ ❁ ↔ 6–12 in (15–30 cm)
↑ 32–40 in (80–100 cm)

Mediterranean native with lacy finely cut foliage in basal clumps and wiry upright stems bearing heads of many spurred flowers in shades of blue, pink, or white. Garden forms occur in wide color range and include double flowers. **Giant Imperial Series**, including 'Giant Imperial Blue Spire', 'Giant Imperial Pink Perfection', and 'Giant Imperial White King', double flowers covering the entire color range with long spikes that last well and keep their color when dried. The **Dwarf Hyacinth Series** has short tightly packed spikes. Zones 9–11.

CONVOLVULUS

This genus of the family Convolvulaceae contains around 100 species of twining climbers, soft-stemmed shrubs, and herbaceous perennials from many temperate regions. The leaves are mostly narrow and thin textured. The widely flared funnel-shaped flowers bloom in succession over a long period.
CULTIVATION: Most *Convolvulus* species are hardy plants adaptable to a range of soils and situations, but all prefer a sunny position. Trim shrubby species regularly to encourage density of growth. They are easily propagated from cuttings.

Convolvulus sabatius ★

syn. *Convolvulus mauritanicus*

☀/◐ ❈ ↔ 24–60 in (60–150 cm) ↑ 8–12 in (20–30 cm)

Low spreading perennial species. Native to Italy and North Africa. Trailing stems. Fine-haired, gray-green, oval leaves to 1½ in (35 mm) long. Groups of 1 to 3 flowers in the leaf axils, pale mauve to purple, sometimes pink, to 1 in (25 mm) in diameter. Zones 8–10.

Convolvulus tricolor

☀/◐ ❈ ↔ 12–32 in (30–80 cm) ↑ 20–40 in (50–100 cm)

Found through southern Europe and in North Africa. Annual or short-lived shrubby or small climbing perennial. Small, pointed, oval leaves. Flowers to 2 in (5 cm) wide, borne singly in the leaf axils, in blue shades, often with a yellow throat. **Ensign Series**, brightly colored flowers with contrasting markings: 'Blue Ensign', white-edged, yellow-throated, deep blue flowers. Zones 8–10.

COREOPSIS

TICKSEED

Found in the Americas, especially in south-western USA and Mexico, the 80-odd annuals and perennials (rarely shrubs) in this genus belong to the daisy (Asteraceae) family. They are compact plants that flower profusely, providing spectacular summer color. Most are 2–4 ft (0.6–1.2 m) tall, with narrow, sometimes lobed leaves. Flowers are usually golden yellow, though garden forms occur in a variety of shades. The tips of the ray florets are often toothed as if cut with pinking shears.
CULTIVATION: Plant in a sunny position in light well-drained soil. These flower better with summer moisture but are quite drought tolerant. All can be raised from seed; the perennials will also grow from divisions or small basal cuttings from non-flowering stems.

Coreopsis 'Sunray'

Coreopsis grandiflora

◐/◑ ❄ ↔ 12–20 in (30–50 cm) ↕ 24 in (60 cm)
Bushy perennial from central and southern USA. Leaves to 4 in (10 cm) long; lower leaves often entire, upper tending toward pinnate. Long-stemmed flowerheads to slightly over 2 in wide, with around 8 ray florets. In the wild, colors range from pale yellow to gold. Flowers from late spring. 'Calypso', 14 in (35 cm) tall, cream variegated foliage, small red spots on ray florets; 'Early Sunrise', 18 in (45 cm) tall, gold double flowers; 'Kelvin Harbutt', up to 36 in (90 cm) tall, golden yellow flowerheads with red-brown disc florets. Zones 7–10.

Coreopsis lanceolata

◐/◑ ❄ ↔ 12–16 in (30–40 cm) ↕ 24 in (60 cm)
Tough perennial from central and southeastern USA. Leaves to 6 in (15 cm) long, lance-shaped to linear. Yellow flowerheads to 2½ in (6 cm) wide, usually with around 8 ray florets, in summer. A weed in Australia. 'Baby Gold', 16 in (40 cm) tall, golden flowers; 'Baby Sun' (syn. 'Sonnenkind'), 12 in (30 cm) tall, gold flowers; 'Sterntaler', 16 in (40 cm) tall, gold flowers, ray florets with bronze-red basal blotch. Zones 3–9.

Coreopsis 'Sunray' ★

◐/◑ ❄ ↔ 12–16 in (30–40 cm) ↕ 20 in (50 cm)
Compact bushy plant with entire and pinnate foliage, bright green, leaflets often narrow. Glowing yellow double flowers from late spring. Often listed as a *C. grandiflora* cultivar. Zones 7–10.

Coreopsis verticillata

◐/◑ ❄ ↔ 16 in (40 cm) ↕ 36 in (90 cm)
Upright perennial from southeastern USA. Sticky doubly pinnate leaves, 3 leaflets per section, may be very narrow, to 2½ in (6 cm)

long. Bright yellow flowerheads to 2 in (5 cm) wide, in summer. Attractive cultivars include 'Golden Gain', 20 in (50 cm) tall, narrow leaf segments, bright yellow flowers; 'Grandiflora' (syn. 'Golden Shower'), 24 in (60 cm) tall, large bright yellow flowers; 'Moonbeam', 20 in (50 cm) tall, soft yellow flowers; and 'Zagreb', 12 in (30 cm) tall, pale gold flowers. Zones 6–10.

CORNUS

DOGWOOD

There are about 65 species of deciduous and evergreen trees, shrubs, and herbs in this genus of the family Cornaceae, nearly all from eastern Asia, North America, and Europe. A few are ornamental, garden-grown for their autumn leaf color, colored winter stems, or their branches covered in blankets of "flowers," composed of large petals or wide decorative bracts surrounding small insignificant flowers. Other species are bractless. The simple oval leaves are usually opposite. The fleshy fruits have stones.
CULTIVATION: They need sun or part-shade, good drainage, and a fertile neutral to acid soil. Those grown for their winter stem color are best grown in full sun and cut back in early spring. Propagate the multi-stemmed species by layering of sucker growths, from hardwood cuttings taken in summer or autumn, or from seed cleaned and cold-stratified for at least 3 months. The large-bracted species can be raised from seed (also stratified), from half-hardened cuttings in summer, or by grafting.

Cornus canadensis

Cornus canadensis

BUNCHBERRY, CREEPING DOGWOOD
◑ ❄ ↔ 36 in (90 cm) ↕ 4–6 in (10–15 cm)
Found from Greenland to Alaska. Hardy, low, deciduous perennial, spreading by rhizomes. Whorls of ovate to lance-shaped leaves, vivid red autumn color. Large white bracts around flowerheads. Summer-flowering. Red edible fruit. Likes cool moist conditions. Zones 2–8.

CORYDALIS

The 300-odd species of annuals and perennials in this genus belong to the poppy (Papaveraceae) family. Mainly confined to the northern temperate zones, the perennials spread by rhizomes or tubers to form clumps of ferny, often blue-green foliage. Their flowers are borne in racemes and are tubular, with 4 tiny petals and a long spur. The flowers are showy, combining well with the delicate foliage. The blue-flowered *C. flexuosa* and its cultivars are probably the most widely grown of the genus. CULTIVATION: These plants are mostly very hardy, preferring temperate climates that have distinct seasons. Woodland or rockery conditions are best, with moist, cool, humus-rich, well-drained soil. If soil remains moist, they will grow in full sun, though part-shade is preferable. Propagate by division or from seed.

Corydalis cashmeriana
☀ ❄ ↔ 12–32 in (30–80 cm) ↑ 10 in (25 cm)
Perennial from the Himalayas. Bright green ferny foliage with leaflets to 1 in (25 mm) long. Bright blue flowers, conspicuously spurred, ½–1 in (12–25 mm) long, in racemes of up to 8 blooms. Late spring- to summer-flowering. Zones 5–9.

Corydalis flexuosa
☼/☀ ❄ ↔ 12–32 in (30–80 cm) ↑ 12 in (30 cm)
Perennial from southwestern China. Blue-green leaves die after flowering. Bright blue flowers, mildly scented, spurred, to 1 in

Corydalis flexuosa 'Père David'

(25 mm) long, in spring–early summer. Attractive cultivars include 'Bronze Leaf', leaves purplish, especially at tips, light blue flowers; 'China Blue', deep blue flowers; 'Père David', bright blue flowers to 2 in (5 cm) long; and 'Purple Leaf', deep blue flowers, purplish foliage. Zones 5–9.

Corydalis ochroleuca
☀ ❄ ↔ 12–32 in (30–80 cm) ↑ 8–16 in (20–40 cm)
Southern European perennial. Leaves strongly blue-green. Flowers very pale yellow to cream, ½ in (12 mm) long. Zones 5–9.

Corydalis wilsonii
☀ ❄ ↔ 12–32 in (30–80 cm)
↑ 12–16 in (30–40 cm)
Chinese perennial. Bright green to bronze-green, finely divided, ferny leaves to 4 in (10 cm) long. Small racemes of bright yellow flowers with yellow-green tips, in spring. Zones 7–9.

COSMOS
MEXICAN ASTER

This genus of the daisy (Asteraceae) family is found in the Americas from the tropics to the warm temperate zones. It contains 26 species, including both annuals and perennials, of which 3 are commonly grown. The common annual cosmos (*C. bipinnatus*) has fine feathery foliage and showy, large, wide-open flowers with 8 ray florets. It is available in many colors and varieties, from dwarf to 7 ft (2 m) tall. The common perennial species have broader leaves and smaller flowers than the annual *C. bipinnatus*, but are interesting for their colors and scents. CULTIVATION: Annual species should be planted out only when all danger of frost has passed; perennials tolerate occasional moderate frosts. Plant in full sun with moist, well-drained soil. Do not overfeed or the plants may become top-heavy; they may need staking anyway. Propagate the annuals from seed and the perennials from basal cuttings.

Cosmos bipinnatus
☼/☀ ❄ ↔ 2–4 ft (0.6–1.2 m) ↑ 4–7 ft (1.2–2 m)
Annual native to Mexico and southern USA. Ferny pinnate leaves to over 4 in (10 cm) long, with very fine narrow leaflets. Flower-heads large and long-stemmed. Pink to lavender flowers in the wild, but many garden forms and seedling strains. 'Candystripe', 24 in (60 cm) tall, white flowers with red stripes; 'Dazzler', 4 ft (1.2 m) tall, bright crimson flowers; 'Picotee' 30 in (75 cm) tall, white to pale pink flowers flushed and edged deep pinkish red; Sensation Series, 3–4 ft (0.9–1.2 m) tall, wide color range; Sonata Series, 24–36 in (60–90 cm) tall, simple, daisy-like flowers in shades of pink and white; 'Sweet Dreams', 30–36 in (75–90 cm), soft pink flowers with darker center. Zones 7–11.

Cosmos sulphureus
☼/☀ ❄ ↔ 32 in–48 in (80 cm–120 cm) ↑ 5–7 ft (1.5–2 m)
Annual found from northern South America to Mexico. Pinnate, sometimes faintly hairy leaves to 14 in (35 cm) long.

Cosmos bipinnatus

Flowerheads deep yellow through orange to red. Several seedling strains. '**Bright Lights**', to 4 ft (1.2 m) tall, yellow, orange and red shades; '**Cosmic Yellow**', to 24 in (60 cm) tall, bright yellow single and semi-double flowers; **Ladybird Series**, 12–16 in (30–40 cm) tall, pale yellow to deep red flowers; '**Sunny Red**', 12–16 in (30–40 cm) tall, bright red flowers. Zones 7–11.

COSTUS

SPIRAL FLAG, SPIRAL GINGER

This genus in the ginger (Zingiberaceae) family has around 90 rhizome-rooted perennial species and is found throughout the tropics. They form clumps of strong cane-like stems with lance-shaped leaves, usually around 8–10 in (20–25 cm) long, spiralling around them. Their spikes of 3-petalled flowers, subtended by bracts and sometimes a ruff of leaves, are bright, flat, and crepe-textured. They usually bloom in the warmer months; then the spike develops into a cone-like fruit, best removed to encourage repeat flowering.

CULTIVATION: Many can survive in mild climates if the soil does not freeze and the summers are warm enough to encourage strong growth. Propagate from seed, from spring basal cuttings, or by dividing clumps in late winter or very early spring.

Costus igneus

FIERY COSTUS

☀ ⛊ ↔ 20–40 in (50–100 cm) ↑ 20 in (50 cm)

Brazilian species with purple-tinted stems and 4–8 in (10–20 cm) long, dark green leaves with reddish undersides. Bright orange flowers through winter. Little or no dormant period. Zones 10–12.

Costus pulverulentus

☀ ⛊ ↔ 2–5 ft (0.6–1.5 m) ↑ 5–10 ft (1.5–3 m)

Found from southern Mexico to Peru. Narrow, velvety, blue-green leaves to 12 in (30 cm) long, with red-tinted undersides and silvery veins. Upright inflorescences to 3 in (7.5 cm) long, with bright red flowers. Zones 10–12.

CRYPTANTHUS

EARTH STARS

The 50 species of this genus in the pineapple (Bromeliaceae) family are found from eastern to southern Brazil, growing in the ground or on rocks, under the protection of trees or bushes. They are generally small and flattened, with an irregular star shape. The triangular leaves are stiff and broad and of many colors, often with crossbands or longitudinal stripes. There are 2 main groups. One has no flower stem and the flowerhead nestles in the center of the plant; there is male dominance in the flowers in the center but female dominance in the outer flowers. The other group has similar flowers throughout the flowerhead, which is on a short stem. The petals are white for both groups.

CULTIVATION: These need more moisture than most bromeliads, and protection in the winter. They are best grown in shallow pots, and are recommended for indoor culture and greenhouse

Cryptanthus zonatus

Costus pulverulentus

conditions in cool-temperate areas, or outdoors with protection from direct continuous sunlight and extremes of rain in warm-temperate, subtropical, and tropical areas. Water when potting mix is dry. Fertilizer extra to that already incorporated in good quality potting mix is not necessary. Propagate from offsets.

Cryptanthus acaulis

☀ ⛊ ↔ 6 in (15 cm) ↑ 2 in (5 cm)

The most common and most hardy of the genus; can survive 32°F (0°C). Plant more circular in general shape than the more usual oval. Leaves triangular, to 4 in (10 cm), a scurfy green, sometimes reddish. Zones 9–10.

Cryptanthus bivittatus

☀ ⛊ ↔ 10 in (25 cm) ↑ 2 in (5 cm)

Plant resembles an open star. Leaves dark green with 2 broad, longitudinal, white or pinkish stripes. The center of '**Starlite**' (syn. '**Starlight**') is cream to light pink instead of dark green; '**Pink Starlite**', center stripe dark green, rest of leaf hot pink. Zones 10–12.

Cryptanthus fosterianus

☀ ⛊ ↔ 16 in (40 cm) ↑ 2 in (5 cm)

Narrow oval plant, irregular in shape. Leaves to 12 in (30 cm) long, thick and fleshy, wavy along the edges, coloring maroon with wavy gray crossbands. Zones 10–12.

Cryptanthus 'Rainbow Star'

☀ ⛊ ↔ 16 in (40 cm) ↑ 16 in (40 cm)

Variegated plant, leaves striped in green, white, and pink. Two forms, one stiffer leafed than other. Best allowed to offset freely; when settled into a large clump it will flower. Zones 10–12.

Cryptanthus zonatus

☀ ⛊ ↔ 12 in (30 cm) ↑ 2 in (5 cm)

Oval plant, irregular in shape. Leaves grow to 8 in (20 cm) long and are thick, fleshy, wavy along edges, mainly green, with wavy, shiny, gray crossbands. Zones 10–12.

Ctenanthe oppenheimiana 'Tricolor'

CTENANTHE

This genus in the arrowroot (Marantaceae) family contains about 15 species of evergreen perennials. They are native to Costa Rica and Brazil, where they grow on damp forest floors and in scrub. Arising from rhizomes, stems are single or branching, with leaves arising from sheaths at the nodes. The leaves are leathery, oblong, pointed, usually matt, often with colored markings. CULTIVATION: In suitably warm climates grow in a shady sheltered position. In temperate climates they are cultivated as indoor plants. Grow in bright filtered light. During active growth, water moderately and apply liquid fertilizer fortnightly. Propagate by division or from cuttings.

Ctenanthe burle-marxii

☀ ╫ ↔ 12–18 in (30–45 cm) ↑ 18 in (45 cm)
From Brazil. Leaves to 6 in (15 cm) long, pale green, with sickle-shaped darker markings on upperside and dark purple beneath. Leaf sheaths also tinged purple. Zones 10–12.

Ctenanthe lubbersiana ★

☀ ╫ ↔ 18–24 in (45–60 cm) ↑ 18–24 in (45–60 cm)
From Brazil. Widely branching stems with narrow oblong leaves, deep green with yellow variegation on upperside, pale green beneath. Zones 10–12.

Ctenanthe oppenheimiana

syn. *Maranta lubbersiana*
NEVER NEVER PLANT
☀ ╫ ↔ 24–36 in (60–90 cm) ↑ 36 in (90 cm)
From eastern Brazil. Bushy plant with leathery oblong leaves to 16 in (40 cm) long, green, with silvery marking on upperside and deep red beneath. 'Tricolor', dark green leaves with irregular creamy yellow markings. Zones 10–12.

CYNOGLOSSUM

HOUND'S TONGUE
This genus in the borage (Boraginaceae) family has around 55 species of annuals, biennials, and perennials, found mainly in the temperate zones. They have simple, elongated, elliptical to lance-shaped leaves, often densely covered with fine hairs, that form a basal foliage clump. Upright flower stems emerge from the clump, branching into racemes of small 5-petalled flowers, usually in vivid blue shades. The flowers appear mainly in summer. CULTIVATION: Most will tolerate quite severe short frosts, if not prolonged freezing. Perfect drainage is essential and summer moisture will improve flowering, so incorporate extra grit and humus. Deadhead the plants frequently to prolong flowering. Taller types may need to be staked or tied back. *Cynoglossum* are ideal for border planting. They can be raised from seed; the perennial species can also be propagated from basal cuttings.

Cynoglossum amabile

CHINESE FORGET-ME-NOT
☀/◐ ❄ ↔ 12 in (30 cm) ↑ 20–24 in (50–60 cm)
Biennial from temperate East Asia. Oval to lance-shaped basal leaves to 8 in (20 cm) long, often finely hairy. Sprays of white, pink, or blue flowers, ¼ in (6 mm) wide. 'Firmament', dwarf cultivar, gray-green leaves and slightly pendulous bright blue flowers. Zones 7–10.

Cynoglossum nervosum

HAIRY HOUND'S TOOTH
☀/◐ ❄ ↔ 24 in (60 cm) ↑ 24–30 in (60–75 cm)
Bushy upright perennial, native to the Himalayas. Oblong green leaves with short stiff hairs; intense blue flowers, in late spring, last for about 4 weeks. Soil must be well drained. Very suitable for a woodland setting, or for an informal garden. Zones 4–9.

DAMPIERA

Endemic to Australia, this large genus of 66 species is part of the Goodeniaceae family. Most of the species are perennial herbs with a few shrubby species occurring in a range of soil types from pure sand to clay, and in habitats from forests and woodlands to arid parts of the continent, and from sea level to montane. Most species occur in the southwest of Western Australia. Leaf shape ranges from simple and smooth-edged to lobed or toothed, basal or alternate on the stems, glabrous to densely woolly hairy. The flowers are an irregular shape, borne singly or in terminal or axillary clusters. Color is predominantly blue with some species' flowers being mauve to purple, only a couple of species being white, pink, or yellow. A few species produce suckers. CULTIVATION: Propagation is from stem or leaf cuttings, or by division of the suckering species. Seeds are not easily obtained, but even when available, germination is not assured. Smoke treatment has been successful with germinating some of the western species, but cultivation of most of these has been rather difficult in non-Mediterranean climates of eastern Australia and elsewhere. Several other species now commonly cultivated. Tissue culture is a propagation method.

Dampiera diversifolia ★

☀ ❄ ↔ 40–60 in (100–150 cm) ↑ 4–20 in (10–50 cm)
A perennial prostrate herb from habitats in southwestern Australia, suckering readily in cultivated forms. Lance-shaped,

glabrous, slightly toothed basal leaves. Prostrate stems with smaller leaves, narrow and not toothed. Purple-blue flowers, borne in leaf axils during spring to summer, in great profusion, almost obscuring rest of plant. Zones 8–10.

DARLINGTONIA

CALIFORNIA PITCHER PLANT, COBRA LILY

This is a single species genus, belonging to the pitcher-plant (Sarraceniaceae) family, which also includes *Heliamphora* and *Sarracenia*. The plant grows in and around springs and streams, in sphagnum bogs, and wherever it has access to cool running water. Found at both high and low altitudes in northern California and southern Oregon, USA, this carnivorous herbaceous perennial is characterized by the cobra-like head of the pitcher, which resembles a snake poised to strike, fangs and all! Insects are attracted by the bright green or dark red pitchers and smell of nectar from around the rim. The nectar lures an insect to where it is trapped by downward pointing hairs and dissolved in liquid at base of pitcher. Unlike that of *Sarracenia*, this liquid does not contain digestive enzymes and the insect's body is broken down by bacteria.

CULTIVATION: These plants should be grown in sphagnum moss, in concrete or terracotta pots standing in a saucer of water, in full or half-sun. The most important key to growing *Darlingtonia* plants successfully is to keep their roots cool. In warm to hot weather, use chilled water. Propagate by removing the new plantlets that grow on the end of the fleshy stem.

Delphinium × belladonna

Darlingtonia californica ★

☼/◐ ❄ ↔ 8–10 in (20–25 cm) ↕ 24–40 in (60–100 cm)
Perennial pitcher plant. Slender pitchers have bulbous hood with fishtail or fang-like tongues protruding from the hood's base. Red and green nodding flowers stand singly on a leafless stalk, in spring–late summer. Zones 6–9.

DARMERA

syn. *Peltiphyllum*

This genus of one species is native to western North America and is a member of the saxifrage (Saxifragaceae) family. It is a large herbaceous perennial, found along stream sides and in damp woods, grown for its dramatic foliage and early flowers. It is recommended for a bog garden or fernery.

CULTIVATION: Plant in moist to wet soils, rich in organic matter, in a cool sheltered site. Propagate by division of established clumps, although raising from seed is an option if sown fresh.

Darmera peltata

syn. *Peltiphyllum peltatum*

❄ ❄ ↔ 3–10 ft (0.9–3 m) ↕ 5–7 ft (1.5–2 m)
Herbaceous perennial with rounded heads of tiny pink flowers prior to foliage in very early spring. Huge leaves soon follow like bright green umbrellas. Dwarf form also grown. Zones 6–10.

DELPHINIUM

This genus is sometimes known as larkspur, although that name is best reserved for its relatives in the genus *Consolida*. A member of the buttercup (Ranunculaceae) family, *Delphinium* consists of around 250 species of annuals, biennials, and perennials. Most species form a basal clump of finely divided or lobed foliage, from which develops an upright spike bearing long-spurred, 4-petalled flowers backed by 5 sepals that sometimes become bract-like. Plant sizes vary markedly with the species: the smaller species may not exceed 12 in (30 cm) tall, while the fancy hybrids can grow to over 7 ft (2 m). Flower colors vary, but *Delphinium* is best known for the intense blue flowers it often produces.

CULTIVATION: They do best in an open airy position that lessens the risk of mildew. However, the more exposed the location, the more important it is that the plants are staked to prevent damage from wind. Plant in moist, humus-rich, fertile soil and water well while in flower. Propagate from seed or basal cuttings, or by division.

Delphinium × belladonna

☼/◐ ❄ ↔ 6–20 in (15–50 cm)
↕ 12–40 in (30–100 cm)
Perennial hybrid crosses between *D. elatum* and *D. grandiflorum*. Compact, sometimes dwarf, with finely divided dark green foliage. Flowers to 1¼ in (30 mm) wide. Many selected forms, including 'Bellamosum', intensely dark blue flowers; 'Blue Sensation', bright mid-blue flowers; and 'Cliveden Beauty', light sky blue flowers. Zones 3–9.

Delphinium cardinale

☼/◐ ❄ ↔ 8–20 in (20–50 cm) ↕ 3–7 ft (0.9–2 m)
A short-lived perennial, sometimes annual or biennial, from California, USA. Dark green, finely divided, basal foliage. Wiry upright flower stems; widely spaced red flowers, with yellow centers, in summer. Zones 8–10.

Darlingtonia californica

Delphinium grandiflorum 'Tom Pouce'

Delphinium elatum

☼/◑ ❄ ↔ 8–20 in (20–50 cm) ↑ 2–6 ft (0.6–1.8 m)
Summer-flowering Eurasian perennial. Downy or hairy leaves
with 5 to 7 lobes toothed or further divided. Strong upright
flower stems, dense racemes of blue flowers, in summer. Zones 3–9.

Delphinium grandiflorum

syn. *Delphinium chinense*
☼/◑ ❄ ↔ 12–24 in (30–60 cm) ↑ 12–40 in (30–100 cm)
Perennial from temperate East Asia. Low bushy foliage clump,
very finely divided bright green leaves. Racemes of vivid blue
flowers, sometimes quite tall and upright, usually short and lax.
'Blue Butterfly', masses of deep blue flowers on short stems;
'Tom Pouce', bright gentian blue flowers. Zones 3–9.

Delphinium nudicaule

☼/◑ ❄ ↔ 8–16 in (20–40 cm) ↑ 12–24 in (30–60 cm)
Perennial from California, USA. Short-lived, sometimes annual
or biennial. Leaves coarsely lobed, secondary divisions fine,
downy, dull green. Wiry flower stems with widely spaced,
orange-red flowers marked yellow on upper lips, from late
spring. Zones 8–10.

Delphinium Hybrid Cultivars

☼ ❄ ↔ 1½–3 ft (0.5–0.9 m) ↑ 4–7 ft (1.2–2 m)
Extensively selected and hybridized to produce the Elatum
Group, which includes 'Albert Shepherd', medium height, light
blue flowers with pink flush and buff center; 'Angela Harbutt',
medium to tall, pinkish mauve; 'Blue Dawn', medium to tall,
bright deep blue with white eye; 'Blue Lagoon', medium to tall,
pure dark blue with light eye; 'Blue Nile', low-growing, clear
mid-blue with contrasting white eye; 'Bruce', tall, deep violet-
purple with lavender to gray eye; 'Cassius', medium height,
mid-blue often suffused with mauve, black center; 'Claire', low-
growing, pale pink to nearly white at the center; 'Clifford Park',
medium height, shades of pink; 'Conspicuous', medium height,
mauve with large brown center; 'Constance Rivett', medium
height, pure white; 'Cupid', short, blue with white eye; 'Emily

Hawkins', tall and strong-growing, lavender suffused with blue,
buff center; 'Fanfare', tall, pale silvery mauve, early flowering;
'Faust', tall, intense almost metallic deep blue with hint of
purple; 'Fenella', medium height, bright pure blue with black
center; 'Gillian Dallas', medium height, gray-blue with white
center, late flowering; 'Giotto', medium height, purple-blue with
mustard center; 'Harlekijn', deep violet, semi-double with blackish center; 'Kathleen Cooke', medium height, mid-blue with
white eye; 'Langdon's Royal Flush', medium height, dusky pink
with white center; 'Loch Leven', low-growing, light blue with
white eye; 'Lord Butler', low-growing, soft mid-blue with white
eye, compact and heavy flowering; Magic Fountain Series ★,
seedling strain, in wide color range; 'Michael Ayres', medium
height, deep pinkish violet with dark center; 'Mighty Atom',
short semi-double, deep mauve, late flowering; 'Min', medium
height, lavender with dark veining; the New Century hybrids, to
over 4 ft (1.2 m) tall, come in a wide range of colors; 'Our Deb',
mid-sized, soft pink with dark eye; 'Rosemary Brock', medium
height, soft mid-pink with a buff center; 'Sandpiper' ★, tall,
white with black center; 'Spindrift', medium height, flower variable, usually turquoise shade but sometimes also with blue or pink
flowers; 'Sungleam', medium height, creamy yellow with yellow
eye; 'Thamesmead', short to medium, gentian blue with black
eye; 'Tiddles', medium height, semi-double, dusky mauve; and
'Walton Gemstone', medium height, pale lavender blue flowers
with white eye. Zones 3–9.

DERWENTIA

This small genus of 8 species is a member of the foxglove
(Scrophulariaceae) family, and occurs in subalpine to lower
mountain regions of southeastern Australia. They are evergreen
perennials or subshrubs, with the ability to re-sprout from the
rootstock. Leaves are opposite and variously shaped, some species
being highly glaucous. White, blue, or mauve flowers are borne
in dense spikes in spring and summer.
CULTIVATION: Propagation is usually from cuttings, with most
success being from fresh new growth taken from sprouting rootstocks. Seeds are not readily obtained, but if available they should
be sown when fresh.

Delphinium, Hybrid Cultivar,
'Albert Shepherd'

Delphinium, Hybrid Cultivar,
'Clifford Park'

Derwentia perfoliata
syns *Parahebe perfoliata, Veronica perfoliata*
DIGGER'S SPEEDWELL

☀ ❄ ↔ 20–60 in (50–150 cm) ↑ 12–26 in (30–65 cm)

Occurs in a range of habitats from central New South Wales, generally above 1,640 ft (500 m) altitude, south to eastern and central western Victoria, Australia. Small shrubby perennial with woody rootstock. Stems mostly held erect, glaucous, with finely toothed, oval-shaped, leathery leaves, in 2s or 3s at nodes. Bluish flowers in terminal and axillary spikes, in spring–summer. Propagate from seeds and cuttings. Zones 8–9.

DEUTEROCOHNIA
syn. *Abromeitiella*

Mainly found from northern Argentina, Peru, and Bolivia, this genus of 15 species is a member of the pineapple (Bromeliaceae) family. The rosette-forming plants are sun-loving and prickly, growing in the ground or on rocks, and they form large clumps. There are 2 groups of species: one consists of low-growing plants that look like cushions in the wild, generally with green tubular flowers; the other group is made up of larger plants that have mainly yellow flowers on long stems. The genus is unique among bromeliads because it has perennial flowering shoots that produce new branches each year.
CULTIVATION: Smaller species can be grown indoors, larger species are best in greenhouses or conservatories in cool-temperate areas, or outdoors in warm-temperate, subtropical, and tropical areas. Water when dry; do not over-fertilize. Propagate from seed or offsets.

Deuterocohnia brevifolia ★
syn. *Abromeitiella brevifolia*

☀/◑ ❄ ↔ 4–12 in (10 cm) ↑ 2–4 in (5–10 cm)

From northern Argentina. The plants eventually form broad mounds. Triangular green leaves, with a few spines along edge. Flowers green, tubular, solitary, and stalkless among leaves. *D. b.* subsp. *chlorantha*, more flexible spines on leaf. Zones 8–10.

Deuterocohnia lorentziana
syn. *Abromeitiella lorentziana*

☀ ❄ ↔ 4 in (10 cm) ↑ 4 in (10 cm)

From northern Argentina. Clump-forming plants. Triangular grayish leaves, few spines along edge. Petals tubular, green. Zones 8–10.

DIANELLA
A member of the daylily (Hemerocallidaceae) family, this genus of evergreen perennials has some 20 species from Australia, New Zealand, and Pacific Islands. One tropical species *(D. ensifolia)* extends to mainland Asia as far as China, Japan, and India, and

Deuterocohnia lorentziana

to East Africa and Madagascar. *Dianella* are herbaceous plants with fibrous roots, often with underground rhizomes. The stems are creeping or erect, bearing a terminal fan of leaves. The leaves are grass-like, in 2 ranks, sheathing at the base and often with the lower edges folded and fused together. Inflorescence is a loose panicle with flowers on nodding stalks. The flowers have perianth segments, in 2 whorls of 3, blue to white, sometimes tinged green or purple. Fruit is a pale blue to dark purple-blue berry. Seeds are black and shiny.
CULTIVATION: In warmer regions they are grown in borders or wild plantings; elsewhere best under glass. Some will tolerate temperatures down to 20°F (–7°C) or even lower, others are frost tender. Tolerate light shade. These plants are easily propagated by division or from seed.

Dianella tasmanica
syns *Dianella archeri, D. densa, D. hookeri*
BLUE FLAX-LILY, TASMANIAN FLAX-LILY

☀ ❄ ↔ 12 in (30 cm) ↑ 40 in (100 cm)

Occurs in forests of southeastern Australia. Tufted perennial, rarely forms clumps. Leaves to 40 in (100 cm) long, green, inflorescences may exceed the leaves in length. Blue flowers in spring–summer. Large globular berries, bluish purple, containing many shiny black seeds. Zones 8–10.

DIANTHUS
CARNATION, PINK

The 300 or so species in this genus in the pink (Caryophyllaceae) family are tufting or spreading perennials largely from the Eurasian region. Most have narrow, somewhat grassy, blue-green leaves emerging directly from a dense basal clump or on wiry spreading stems. The flowers are simple 5-petalled structures, often with a powerful spicy scent. Flower stem length varies greatly. The common flower color is pink, and the petal edges ragged, which appear as if cut with pinking shears. Most species flower from late spring.
CULTIVATION: Plant in a bright, open position in moist, well-drained, humus-rich soil. Most appreciate a little lime and need regular feeding to prevent center of clump from dying out. Propagate from seed or small basal cuttings known as "slips," or by division.

Dianella tasmanica

Dianthus alpinus
☀/◑ ❄ ↔ 6–12 in (15–30 cm) ↑ 4–6 in (10–15 cm)

Short-lived perennial from European Alps. Leaves dark green and grassy. Flowers deep pinkish red with darker spots, white eye. 'Joan's Blood', maroon-centered with deep red flowers. Zones 3–9.

Dianthus gratianopolitanus 'Baker's Variety'

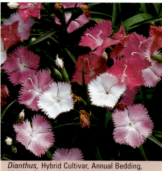

Dianthus, Hybrid Cultivar, Annual Bedding, Melody Series, 'Melody Pink Blush'

Dianthus, Hybrid Cultivar, Perennial, Perpetual-flowering, Self, 'Terra'

Dianthus barbatus ★

SWEET WILLIAM

☼/◑ ❉ ↔ 6–12 in (15–30 cm) ↕ 12–24 in (30–60 cm)

Short-lived, southern European perennial usually grown as annual. Clump of lance-shaped leaves. Pinked flowers clustered in heads. Seedling strains in many colors and patterned forms. **Auricula-eyed Group**, contrasting colored ring near center. Zones 4–9.

Dianthus caryophyllus

CARNATION

☼/◑ ❉ ↔ 8–16 in (20–40 cm) ↕ 20–32 in (50–80 cm)

Perennial from Mediterranean region. Leaves sheathed, gray-green to blue-green, on wiry spreading stems. Flowerheads on upright, sometimes spindly stems, strongly fragrant. Wild plants have pink flowers, garden forms many colors. **Knight Series** includes '**Crimson Knight**', '**White Knight**', and '**Yellow Knight**'. Zones 8–10.

Dianthus deltoides

MAIDEN PINK

☼/◑ ❉ ↔ 6–12 in (15–30 cm) ↕ 8–16 in (20–40 cm)

Eurasian perennial, forming carpet, sometimes mounding, of small green to blue-green leaves with spreading narrow-leafed stems around the edge. Flowers usually borne singly, in pink shades, often with dark central spotting, pinked. '**Albus**', white flowers; '**Brilliancy**', deep crimson flowers. Zones 3–9.

Dianthus gratianopolitanus

syn. *Dianthus caesius*

CHEDDAR PINK

☼/◑ ❉ ↔ 8–16 in (20–40 cm) ↕ 6–8 in (15–20 cm)

Mat-forming perennial native to central and western Europe. Older leaves can be small and very densely packed. Fragrant pink to crimson flowers, usually borne singly, pinked. '**Baker's Variety**' and '**Flore Pleno**', semi-double flowers. Zones 3–9.

Dianthus plumarius

PINK

☼/◑ ❉ ↔ 8–16 in (20–40 cm) ↕ 6–14 in (15–35 cm)

Perennial from eastern and central Europe. Loose tuft of blue-green foliage. Flowers pink or white, often with darker markings or center. Zones 3–9.

Dianthus superbus

☼/◑ ❉ ↔ 12–20 in (30–50 cm) ↕ 20–30 in (50–75 cm)

Strong-growing Eurasian perennial with spreading stems. Flowers usually borne singly, with pink to purple-pink, highly scented, deeply cut petals. *D. s.* var. *longicalycinus*, mauve to light purple flowers with elongated calyx. Zones 4–9.

Dianthus Hybrid Cultivars

☼/◑ ❉ ↔ 6–12 in (15–30 cm) ↕ 8–15 in (20–38 cm)

The many carnations and pinks and their cultivars are divided into groups based on growth habit, flower color and style. Zones 8–10.

ANNUAL BEDDING DIANTHUS

Although sometimes really perennial, these small plants are grown as annuals. In many ways they resemble sweet William (*D. barbatus*), but they are available in a wider range of sizes and growth forms, including some suitable for hanging baskets. Popular annual dianthus include **Floral Lace Series**, masses of small flowers with pinked edges; and **Melody Series**, mainly single-colored in pink shades and white.

PERENNIAL DIANTHUS

Countless hybrids have been raised, either as garden plants or for the cut-flower trade. There are three main groups of dianthus hybrids that are further divided, primarily by flower type.

Border carnations

Tall growers that are derived from *D. caryophyllus*. Flowers are usually strongly scented, often fully double, with or without pinked edges. They bloom mainly in spring and early summer, and are divided as follows:

Fancies: Flowers basically one color but with flecks, spots, or small sectors of another color. '**Brookham Fancy**', yellow flowers with pink flecks.

Selfs: Flowers all one color. '**Cathlene Hitchcock**', soft pink flowers; '**Fiery Cross**', vivid red; '**Golden Cross**' soft yellow; '**Grey Dove**', dusky mauve.

Clove-scented: Flowers strongly scented, color may be variable. '**Candy Clove**', red-striped white flowers.

Picotees: One base color edged with another color. The edging width is variable. '**Eva Humphries**', purple-edged white.

Perpetual-flowering Carnations

The tallest carnations, often with flower stems that need staking or tying. Not hardy to repeated severe frosts, and best grown in mild climates for their year-round flowering.

The rare Malmaison carnation has strong foliage and flower stems, and very intense clove perfume. **'Duchess of Westminster'**, with large cream flowers, is the most widely grown Malmaison.

Perpetuals are widely cultivated as greenhouse plants for florists. Popular forms, all doubles unless stated otherwise, follow: **Fancies:** **'Bright Rendez-vous'**, creamy white flowers, with soft pink lacing; **'Cheerio'**, pinkish white and red; **'Crimson Tempo'**, rich red; **'Havana'**, red and yellow; **'Impulse'**, creamy white, deep pinkish red; **'New Tempo'**, pinkish white and red; **'Rendez-vous'**, white laced with deep pink; **'Tempo'**, white with fine red lacing, a few red sectors; **'Tundra'**, yellow laced with light red; **'Yellow Rendez-vous'**, soft yellow laced with deep pink.

Selfs: **'Delphi'**, white flowers; **'Mambo'**, bright yellow; **'Moutarde'**, yellow; **'Pink Dona'**, shades of pink ; **'Prado'**, creamy pale green; **'Raggio di Sole'**, orange; **'Terra'**, salmon to pink.

Spray carnations: Flowers usually smaller, 5 to 6 per stem. **'Fiorella'**, yellow and red; **'Ibiza'**, yellow; **'Kortina'**, purple-red.

Pinks

Developed from *D. plumarius* but often crossed with other species and hybrids. The most common cross is with the perpetual-flowering carnations, which gave rise to the Allwoodii Pinks. Flowers may or may not be fragrant, nearly always pinked edges.

Fancies: **'Dad's Favourite'** (syn. 'Dad's Favorite'), white flowers, maroon lacing and center, double; **'Gran's Favourite'**, white, pinkish red lacing, double; **'Red Ensign'**, deep pink, white lacing.

Selfs: **'Becky Robinson'**, deep pink flowers; **'Bovey Belle'**, purple, double; **'Carmine Letitia Wyatt'**, deep pink, semi-double, scented; **'Devon Pride'**, bright pink; **'Dwarf Helen'**, pink, double; **'Inglestone'**, bright pink; **'Lemsii'**, small, pink; **'Letitia Wyatt'** ★, bright pink, double, scented; **'Lionheart'**, red, sometimes lighter edges, single, scented; **'Neon Star'**, bright purple-pink, single, scented; **'Valda Wyatt'**, pink, double, scented; **'Whatfield Cancan'**, soft pink, frilled double, scented; **'White Joy'**, white, sometimes flushed pale pink, double.

Allwoodii Pinks: Usually *D. plumarius* × *D. alpinus* hybrids. **'Whatfield Ruby'**, vivid crimson flowers, gray foliage.

Bicolors: **'Cranmere Pool'**, white to pale pink flowers, deep red center, double; **'Doris'** ★, light pink with purple-red center, double; **'Houndspool Ruby'** (syn. 'Ruby Doris'), deep pink with crimson center, double, sport of 'Doris'; **'Monica Wyatt'**, pink with red center, double; **'Peach Mambo'**, cream with soft orange-pink center, double; **'Rose Monica Wyatt'**, deep pink with red center, double.

Old-Fashioned Pinks: Usually forms of *D. plumarius* but are sometimes hybrids or just varieties of indeterminate origin. **'Earl of Essex'**, deep pink, double flowers; well-known, very fragrant; **'Mrs Sinkins'**, white double flowers; **'Pike's Pink'**, pink semi-double flowers.

DIASCIA

TWINSPUR

This South African genus of around 50 species of annuals and perennials belongs to the foxglove (Scrophulariaceae) family. They are generally low mounding or spreading plants with upright or semi-trailing stems and small oval to elliptical leaves with toothed edges. The flowers, in shades of mauve, pink, and soft orange, are tiny but showy, because they are massed in racemes at the stem tip, mainly in the summer.

CULTIVATION: Plant these in a bright open position with good air movement, and well-drained humus-rich soil that is kept moist throughout the flowering season. Pinch back to keep the plants bushy, and deadhead regularly to encourage continued blooming. Propagate from seed or from cuttings.

Diascia barberae

☼/◗ ❄ ↔ 12–16 in (30–40 cm) ↕ 12 in (30 cm)

From the Drakensberg region of southern Africa. Upright or sprawling perennial. Flowers bright pink, with conspicuous spurs and small yellow patch, maroon edge and spots. **'Blackthorn Apricot'**, low growing, apricot-pink to soft orange flowers; **'Fisher's Flora'**, heart-shaped leaves, dark-centered flowers with two yellow spots; **'Ruby Field'**, pinkish red flowers. Zones 8–10.

Diascia rigescens

☼/◗ ❄ ↔ 24 in (60 cm) ↕ 16–20 in (40–50 cm)

From Drakensberg region of southern Africa. Sprawling perennial. Pointed oval leaves, sometimes with fine red edge. Upright flower spikes, closely spaced flowers, less open heads than other species. Deep pink flowers, distinct keel on the lower lobe. Zones 8–10.

Diascia vigilis

☼/◗ ❄ ↔ 48 in (120 cm) ↕ 20 in (50 cm)

From Drakensberg region of southern Africa. Strong-growing perennial with slightly glossy fleshy leaves. Soft pink flowers, small dark spots in the throat. Continues flowering later than other species. **'Jack Elliott'**, larger mid-pink flowers. Zones 8–10.

Diascia vigilis

Dicentra spectabilis

Diascia Hybrid Cultivars

☀ ❄ ↔ 12–24 in (30–60 cm) ↕ 8–18 in (20–45 cm)

The species tend to interbreed freely when cultivated and produce many intermediate hybrids. Attractive examples include Coral Belle/'Hecbel', narrow, slightly glossy leaves, coral red flowers, semi-trailing habit, good in baskets; **'Joyce's Choice'**, heart-shaped leaves, apricot-pink flowers; **'Langthorn's Lavender**, pretty pink-mauve flowers; **'Lilac Belle'**, small leaves, light purple flowers with a conspicuous lower lip; Little Dancer/'Pendan', small heart-shaped leaves, vivid pink flowers, very good in baskets; Redstart/'Hecstart', coral pink to red flowers; **'Rupert Lambert'** ★, deep pink flowers, to around 10 in (25 cm) tall and twice as wide, blooms from summer through to autumn; **'Salmon Supreme'**, light salmon pink flowers with darker spots; Sydney Olympics/'Hecsyd', light salmon pink flowers, compact, heavy-flowering; and **'Twinkle'**, dark foliage, purple-pink flowers, trailing habit, good in baskets. Zones 8–10.

DICENTRA

BLEEDING HEART

This genus of around 20 species of annuals and perennials from North America and Asia belongs in the poppy (Papaveraceae) family, though the resemblance may not be obvious. Most species have roots adapted as storage organs, as tap roots, rhizomes, or tubers. The foliage, ferny and often finely cut, disappears for winter, but redevelops quickly with the arrival of spring, the larger species often making noticeable daily growth. The flowers have 4 petals, the outer pair creating a pouched structure that largely envelops the inner pair. The pendulous flowers appear in spring, and are borne in clusters on stems rising above the foliage, mostly in white, pink, or cream shades.
CULTIVATION: These species prefer a cool moist soil that is humus-rich, fertile, and well drained. They thrive in woodlands and perennial borders, and the smaller forms also do well in rockeries. Best lightly shaded from hottest sun. Propagate from seed or basal cuttings, or by division.

Dicentra cucullaria

DUTCHMAN'S BREECHES

☀/☼ ❄ ↔ 20–40 in (50–100 cm)
↕ 12–16 in (30–40 cm)

Perennial from eastern North America. Leaves green, lacy, fern-like, with blue-green undersides, finely divided. Small flowers, heart-shaped but inner petals protruding, white or pink, tipped yellow. Flowers look like upside-down bloomers. May cause dermatitis in some people. Zones 5–9.

Dicentra eximia

STAGGERWEED, TURKEY CORN

☀/☼ ❄ ↔ 20–40 in (50–100 cm)
↕ 12–26 in (30–65 cm)

Perennial found over much of the USA. Blue-green leaves are finely divided. Sprays of pink or white heart-shaped flowers. The plant is somewhat toxic to stock. Zones 5–9.

Dicentra formosa

syn. *Dicentra eximia* of gardens

WILD BLEEDING HEART

☀/☼ ❄ ↔ 20–40 in (50–100 cm) ↕ 12–26 in (30–65 cm)

Perennial, native to western North America. Ferny leaves with blue-green undersides. Panicles up to 30 flowers, most commonly deep pink, sometimes yellow, and rarely white. *D. formosa* and *D. eximia* have been confused in cultivation and it now appears that they may be one quite variable species. **'Aurora'**, gray-green leaves, white flowers; **'Bacchanal'**, gray-green foliage, pinkish red flowers; **'Bountiful'**, light blue-green leaves, deep pink flowers; **'Langtrees'**, very compact, blue-green leaves, pink-tinted cream flowers; **'Luxuriant'** ★, blue-green foliage, deep cherry pink to red flowers; **'Stuart Boothman'**, blue-green leaves with narrow leaflets, deep pink flowers on short stems; **'Zestful'**, light blue-green foliage and deep purple-pink flowers. Zones 4–9.

Dicentra spectabilis

BLEEDING HEART

☀/☼ ❄ ↔ 20–40 in (50–100 cm) ↕ 40–56 in (100–140 cm)

Vigorous perennial from Japan, northeastern China, and Russia's far east. Leaves coarsely divided. Upright often red-tinted flower stems with up to 15 large, pink, heart-shaped flowers with slightly protruding white inner petals. **'Alba'**, pure white flowers. Zones 6–9.

DICHORISANDRA

This genus of about 25 species from Central and South America belongs to the spiderwort (Commelinaceae) family. All are perennials, sometimes becoming shrubby, with soft stems and glossy green leaves, sometimes striped with cream or purple. The small flowers are borne in dense terminal spikes and are blue or purple.
CULTIVATION: *Dichorisandra* species are best grown in shady or only partly sunny, sheltered positions in moist soil. They are somewhat frost tender but in cold climates plants can be over-wintered in a greenhouse. Propagation is from division or from cuttings taken in summer.

Dichorisandra thyrsiflora

BLUE GINGER

◐ ◑ ↔ 3 ft (0.9 m) ↕ 3–10 ft (0.9–3 m)

From northern South America. Dark green glossy leaves. Terminal clusters of purple-blue flowers, on stems to 10 ft (3 m) high, depending upon growing conditions. Zones 9–12.

DICLIPTERA

This genus of about 150 annual and perennial herbs and shrubs belongs to the acanthus (Acanthaceae) family, and is native to tropical and warm-temperate regions. Stems are usually 6-angled. Flowers are borne in terminal clusters with 2-lipped tubular corollas, expanding toward the throat.
CULTIVATION: These plants are easily grown in average well-drained soils in full sun and will tolerate some shade and drought. Suited to containers or hanging baskets. Propagate from seed or cuttings.

Dichorisandra thyrsiflora

Dicliptera suberecta

syns *Jacobina suberecta, Justicia suberecta*

HUMMINGBIRD PLANT, KING'S CROWN

☀ ❄ ↔ 18–24 in (45–60 cm) ↕ 18–24 in (45–60 cm)

Perennial subshrub from Uruguay. Slender, velvety, gray foliage on erect or arching stems. Simple smooth-edged leaves. Two-lipped, rusty reddish orange, tubular flowers. Summer- to autumn-flowering. Zones 7–11.

DIEFFENBACHIA

DUMB CANE, MOTHER-IN-LAW'S TONGUE, TUFTROOT

This genus of about 25 evergreen, erect, perennial herbs from tropical America belongs to the arum (Araceae) family and is grown for the patterned foliage. Large oval-shaped leaves, spotted or streaked with cream, spread out from a stout central stem. Flowers are borne on long spikes with a green boat-shaped spathe blade. These are very poisonous plants; contact with the sap will cause the tongue to swell.
CULTIVATION: *Dieffenbachia* are ideal as houseplants in bright light and rich moist soil, preferring full sun or partial shade and high humidity. Protect from frost or plant in frost-free areas. Propagate from stem or root cuttings or by division of established clumps.

Dieffenbachia seguine

SPOTTED DUMBCANE

☀/◐ ✿ ↔ 18–24 in (45–60 cm)
↕ 3–6 ft (0.9–1.8 m)

Variable perennial from tropical America. Cane-like stems; large, leathery, oval-shaped leaves, with pointed tips. '**Amoena**', very robust, thick stems, large green leaves evenly marked in cream; '**Exotica**', compact form, pointed oval-shaped leaves sprinkled

with ivory cream; '**Maculata**', bright green leaves spotted with cream; '**Rudolph Roehrs**', leaves mostly yellow, spotted with ivory, ribbed, deep green margin; '**Superba**', fresh green leaves variegated with creamy white; '**Tropic Snow**' (syns 'Snow Queen', 'Tropic Topaz', 'Hi-color'), dense tall plant, known by its heavy cream leaf markings. Zones 10–12.

DIETES

This genus belongs to the iris (Iridaceae) family and has 6 species of evergreen clumping plants, 5 from southern Africa and 1 from Lord Howe Island, Australia. The flat flowers are held above the leaves. They make strong bold feature plants. The flowers individually only last a day or two, but the flowering season can last a long time.
CULTIVATION: Able to endure only very light frosts, they will tolerate sun or deep shade, poor soils, and dry conditions. Propagate from seed; they can be divided, but tend to resent disturbance.

Dietes bicolor

☀/◐ ✿ ↔ 24–36 in (60–90 cm) ↕ 32–36 in (80–90 cm)

Well-known rhizomatous species from the East Cape, South Africa. Long, arching, deep green, strap-like leaves overtopped by flat lemon flowers with contrasting, brown, basal blotches. Spring- to summer-flowering. Zones 9–11.

Dietes grandiflora

syn. *Dietes iridioides* 'Johnsonii'

WILD IRIS

☀ ✿ ↔ 20–27 in (50–70 cm) ↕ 20–27 in (50–70 cm)

Perennial from forests of South Africa. Sword-shaped dark green leaves, broader than *D. bicolor*. Large white flowers marked with yellow and brown blotches. Summer-flowering. Zones 9–11.

Dieffenbachia seguine

Digitalis purpurea, Excelsior Group

DIGITALIS

FOXGLOVE

This genus, once confined to Eurasia and North Africa, now occurs in most temperate regions of the world. A member of the foxglove (Scrophulariaceae) family, it has around 20 species of biennials and perennials. They form a basal clump of coarse, often elliptical, heavily veined leaves. The upright flower stems carry smaller leaves and many downward-facing, 4-lobed, bell-shaped flowers that open progressively upwards along the spike in a long flowering period. Most flower from late spring into summer, in pink, lavender, purple, yellow, cream, or white. All parts of the plants are toxic if swallowed; the leaves may irritate the skin.
CULTIVATION: These are easily cultivated in most temperate areas. Plant in moist, humus-rich soil, water well in spring, and while in flower. Biennials must be raised from seed, but perennials will also grow from basal offshoots.

Digitalis grandiflora

syn. *Digitalis ambigua*
LARGE YELLOW FOXGLOVE
☼/◐ ❄ ↔ 20–24 in (50–60 cm) ↑ 40 in (100 cm)
European biennial or short-lived perennial. Lush dark green leaves, toothed; leafy flower stems. Flowers pale yellow, darker veining. 'Carillon', to 24 in (60 cm) tall, primrose yellow flowers. Zones 4–9.

Digitalis lutea

STRAW FOXGLOVE
☼/◐ ❄ ↔ 16–24 in (40–60 cm) ↑ 24–40 in (60–100 cm)
Native to Europe and North Africa. Leaves dark green, hairless, finely to heavily serrated. Soft yellow or white flowers. Zones 4–9.

Digitalis mertonensis

STRAWBERRY FOXGLOVE
☼/◐ ❄ ↔ 16–20 in (40–50 cm) ↑ 20–30 in (50–75 cm)
Widely grown perennial garden hybrid. Large, downy, pinkish red to purple-pink flowers. Compact plant with lush foliage and tightly packed flowers. Zones 4–9.

Digitalis purpurea

COMMON FOXGLOVE
☼/◐ ❄ ↔ 12–32 in (30–80 cm)
↑ 5–6 ft (1.5–1.8 m)
Biennial from western Europe and now widely naturalized, often considered a weed. Strongly upright flower stems. Many pink, purple, or white flowers, heavily spotted within, from early summer. *D. p.* subsp. *heywoodii*, silvery foliage, white and cream flowers. *D. p.* f. *albiflora*, flowers often free of throat markings. *D. p.*, Excelsior Group, flowers surrounding the stem, in a mix of colors; 'Sutton's Apricot', creamy salmon pink flowers. Zones 4–9.

DIMORPHOTHECA

This genus of 7 species of annuals, perennials, and subshrubs is a member of the daisy (Asteraceae) family. They are native to southern and tropical Africa. Stems may be upright or sprawling and the leaves simple or divided, sometimes scented. They flower prolifically from spring to late summer. The typical daisy flowers have white or yellow rays that are purplish blue or coppery beneath, creating an attractive contrast.
CULTIVATION: Grow in full sun in a well-drained soil. In cooler areas the protection of a hot sunny wall will promote flowering. Propagate annuals from seed; others from seed or cuttings.

Dimorphotheca sinuata

NAMAQUALAND DAISY
syn. *Dimorphotheca aurantiaca* of gardens
☼ ❄ ↔ 12 in (30 cm) ↑ 12–18 in (30–45 cm)
Native to South Africa. Annual with narrow coarsely toothed leaves. Dark-centered daisies in range of colors from white to orange, including some pastel shades. Zones 9–11.

DIONAEA

This single-species genus belongs to the sundew (Droseraceae) family. The Venus flytrap is found in coastal areas of North and South Carolina, USA, in damp acidic soil. It captures its prey in traps that snap shut when the trap's trigger hairs have been touched more than once in quick succession. Digestive enzymes enter the trap and the soft tissue of the insect is dissolved.
CULTIVATION: Grow in pots containing either just peat moss or 1 part sand to 3 parts peat, in full sun to half-sun. Water by tray; when winter dormancy approaches, remove pots from trays and only water once a week. Remove any black leaves or traps. Repot every couple of years. Propagate by division at the end of winter.

Dionaea muscipula ★

VENUS FLYTRAP
☼/◐ ❄ ↔ 8 in (20 cm) ↑ 4 in (10 cm)
Leaves green, each leaf blade having 2 eyelid-shaped fringed lobes. Each lobe has 3 fine trigger hairs. Small white flowers on a leafless stalk, at the end of spring. 'Akai Ryu', bright

burgundy traps in full sun; '**Fang**' and '**Sawtooth**', edges of the traps have jagged "teeth" rather than a fringe. Zones 8–11.

DODECATHEON

AMERICAN COWSLIP, SHOOTING STARS

This charming genus of some 14 species of small rosette-forming herbaceous perennials is a member of the primrose (Primulaceae) family, and is native to North America. These plants produce several flowers per stem, in spring, with fully reflexed petals like those of a cyclamen.
CULTIVATION: These frost-hardy plants grow naturally in moist meadows and mountain pastures, and usually perform best in a cool rock garden or pot. Propagate from freshly sown seed in autumn; division in late winter, just before the plants break dormancy, is also possible.

Dodecatheon dentatum

☼/◐ ❄ ↔6–12 in (15–30 cm)
↕4–16 in (10–40 cm)
North American species, found from Oregon and Washington through Idaho to Arizona, USA. Rosette-forming herbaceous perennial. Leaves oblong to lance-shaped, bright green, sometimes with finely toothed margins. White flowers, turned-back petals, yellow anthers. Spring- to early summer-flowering. Zones 5–9.

Dodecatheon hendersonii

MOSQUITO-BILLS, SAILOR'S CAP

☼/◐ ❄ ↔6–12 in (15–30 cm) ↕8–15 in (20–38 cm)
From California, USA. Deep green, fleshy, oval leaves. Flowers in heads of 2 to 3. Pinkish purple turned-back petals, yellow anthers. Zones 6–9.

Dodecatheon meadia

syn. **Dodecatheon pauciflorum**
AMERICAN COWSLIP, EASTERN SHOOTING STAR, SHOOTING STAR

☼/◐ ❄ ↔12 in (30 cm) ↕8–18 in (20–45 cm)
From eastern USA. Oblong leaves. Flowers in heads of 10 to 20, turned-back petals usually purple, cream to white base, sometimes pink or white. **D. m. f. album**, white flowers. Zones 3–9.

DOROTHEANTHUS

LIVINGSTONE DAISY

This genus of 6 species of succulent annuals, belonging to the iceplant (Aizoaceae) family, is confined to South Africa. They are spreading or mounding plants with thickened leaves that have a crystalline surface, creating a sugar-coated look. The flowers are daisy-like, often very abundant, in a range of colors, mainly shades of pink or white but also yellow, orange, red, and purple. Mostly ephemeral, these subdesert plants can race into growth with the arrival of rain. In frost-free climates they may grow at any time but in temperate areas they are mainly summer-flowering.
CULTIVATION: Plant in spring in a bright sunny position to ensure maximum flowering time. Soil should be light, gritty, and well-drained, but the plants do need occasional watering when they are flowering. Deadhead frequently to encourage blooms over a longer period. In cooler climates, sow seed under glass in winter or spring. Propagation is from seed.

Dorotheanthus bellidiformis

☼ ◱ ↔8–16 in (20–40 cm) ↕2–6 in (5–15 cm)
From South Africa. Low spreading plant. Red-tinted stems, fleshy gray-green leaves, rough textured surface. Daisy-like flowers in mainly pink to purple shades but also white. Garden forms with yellow and multi-colored flowers may be hybrids. Zones 9–11.

Dionaea muscipula

DORYANTHES

This genus of 2 species of large perennial herbs has its own family, Doryanthaceae, and occurs in woodlands, open forests, and rocky hillsides on well-draining soils in eastern Australia. The leaves are lance-shaped and pointed. Flower stalks can exceed the leaves in length by 2 to 3 times. Flowers are in terminal heads, each large, red, and with 6 equal segments. Fruits are 3-celled capsules. Plants are long-lived in cultivation.
CULTIVATION: Propagation is usually from seeds, but flowering could be up to 10 years from germination. Division of clumps, or from suckers, will produce flowering plants more quickly.

Doryanthes excelsa

GIANT LILY, GYMEA LILY, ILLAWARRA LILY

☼ ◱ ↔10 ft (3 m) ↕20 ft (2.4–6 m)
Found in woodlands on sandy soils in the central coast region of New South Wales, Australia. Leaves bright or slightly yellowish green, generally stiff and erect. Flower stalk, to 20 ft (6 m) long, terminating in a dense head of many red flowers, in spring–summer. Each flower contains large quantities of nectar. Dark colored capsules. Zones 9–11.

Dodecatheon meadia

Doryanthes palmeri

SPEAR LILY

☼ ⚘ ↔ 3–10 ft (0.9–3 m) ↕ 3–10 ft (0.9–3 m)

From northern New South Wales and southern Queensland, Australia. Leaves long, bright green, lance-shaped, cylindrical appendage at apex. Flower stalks to 17 ft (5 m) long, tending to arch. Brownish flowers in spring. Capsules greenish. Zones 10–12.

DROSERA

SUNDEW

A diverse genus of more than 130 carnivorous plants found on every continent except Antarctica, *Drosera* belongs to the sundew (Droseraceae) family. Almost half the species are native to Australia but are also found in South America, New Zealand, and Borneo. Their size and shape is varied. The tentacle-covered leaves can be erect, climbing, fan-leafed, or arranged in a rosette. All species trap prey by luring an insect to sticky, dew-like liquid sparkling on the red tentacles on the sundew's leaves.

CULTIVATION: Growing conditions for *Drosera* vary but they can be divided into the groups below. Some species grow in both tropical and temperate zones. Many grow easily from leaf cuttings.

   Tropical species: Grow in sphagnum moss, in pots in tray of water in shade. Need high humidity. Best if temperature does not fall below 59°F (15°C).

   Subtropical species: Use a soil mix of 3 parts peat and 2 parts sand; keep soil damp. Full sun to part-shade. Some species tolerate light frosts, but are best treated as an annual in colder areas. Grow in a greenhouse or on a sunny windowsill.

   Temperate species: Use a soil mix of 3 parts peat to 2 parts sand. Stand containers in water. Full sun in temperate climates, part-shade in warmer areas. Plants usually dormant in winter.

   Tuberous species: Use a soil mix of 3 parts peat to 2 parts sand. Pots should be kept dry and out of direct sunlight during summer dormancy. Start to water by tray as winter approaches and new growth appears. Protect from frosts.

Drosera binata

FORKED SUNDEW

☼ ❄ ↔ 8 in (20 cm) ↕ 12 in (30 cm)

From east coast of Australia and New Zealand. Leaf blades fork in-to "Y" shape. Slender green to yellow leaves, densely covered with tentacles. Temperate to subtropical (*see* Cultivation). Zones 8–10.

Drosera capensis

CAPE SUNDEW

☼ ❄ ↔ 6 in (15 cm) ↕ 6 in (15 cm)

From the Cape region of South Africa, found growing in bogs, marshes, and wet grasslands. Slender green leaves, covered in fine red tentacles; ends of leaves are rounded and curl around trapped prey. Older plants produce a woody trunk with green foliage at top. Pretty pink flowers on leafless stalk in spring. Does not experience dormancy in winter. Easy sundew to grow. Temperate to subtropical (*see* Cultivation). Zones 8–11.

Drosera pulchella

PRETTY SUNDEW

☼ ⚘ ↔ 1¼ in (30 mm) ↕ ½ in (12 mm)

Found in swamps, wet peat, and damp sandy soil in Western Australia. Rosette sundew with round, tentacled, green leaves on broad stalks. Flowers in spring on 2 or 3 leafless stalks; can be white, pink, orange, or dark red with metallic sheen. Dormant in wild in hot dry summer, but not in cultivation if plant is kept moist. Subtropical (*see* Cultivation). Zones 9–11.

Drosera rotundifolia

ROUND-LEAFED SUNDEW

☼ ✳ ↔ 4 in (10 cm) ↕ 2 in (5 cm)

Most widely distributed of temperate sundews, found in Asia, Europe, and North America in sphagnum bogs. Cup-shaped leaves on fine stalk. Tiny flowers, white to pink, on leafless stalk, in spring–summer. Temperate (*see* Cultivation). Zones 3–9.

Drosera zonaria

PAINTED SUNDEW

☼ ❄ ↔ 3 in (8 cm) ↕ 1 in (2.5 cm)

Sundew from Western Australia. Rounded leaves with short stems in overlapping rosette. Green leaves, usually red around the edges. Flowers white, rare. Tuberous (*see* Cultivation). Zones 8–10.

DROSOPHYLLUM

DEWY PINE, PORTUGUESE SUNDEW

A carnivorous single species genus of the sundew (Droseraceae) family, the Portuguese sundew is found in Spain, Morocco, and Portugal. A small perennial shrub, it grows in dry sandy soil on coastal hills, often among short fir trees (*Pinus pinaster*). The

Drosera binata

Drosera capensis

Drosera zonaria

plant has a dewy appearance, caused by the droplets of sticky mucus on the leaves. Small insects get trapped on the leaves by the very sticky liquid; the leaves then secrete a digestive enzyme which dissolves the prey's soft tissue.
CULTIVATION: Grow in mix of 3 parts sand to 1 part peat, add a teaspoon of limestone or dolomite to a 6 in (15 cm) clay pot. Place the clay pot in a plastic pot containing live sphagnum moss (ensure the plastic pot has a large drainage hole), in full sun. Water by tray, never from above. Allow the pot to dry out for one day each month. Small plantlets frequently appear among the branches, and these can be removed and planted once they have 10 or 12 leaves; dip stem in rooting hormone and plant in mix of 1 part sand to 2 parts peat.

Drosophyllum lusitanicum
☼ ❄ ↔ 16 in (40 cm) ↕ 12 in (30 cm)
Woody base. Up to 100 slender green leaves covered in sticky red liquid; leaves uncurl outwardly. Bright yellow flowers appear in spring. Zones 8–10.

DRYAS
MOUNTAIN AVENS
This small genus of 3 species, all evergreen mat-forming plants from arctic and Northern Hemisphere alpine regions, belongs to the rose (Rosaceae) family. The foliage resembles that of the oak *(Quercus),* although on a miniature scale. The flowers have 8 petals, unlike most Rosaceae members. They are comparatively large, white or lemon in color, and are produced in summer, held well clear of the foliage, and followed by large fluffy seed heads.
CULTIVATION: These prefer a sunny moist aspect in non-tropical climates in a rock garden or between pavers. They are ideal ground covers over small bulbs. Propagate by division, or from cuttings or freshly sown seed.

Dryas octopetala ★
MOUNTAIN AVENS
☼ ❄ ↔ over 40 in (100 cm) ↕ 3–4 in (8–10 cm)
Northern European species. Glossy, dark green, oak-shaped leaves, white reverse turns coppery in winter. White flowers, in summer. Fluffy seed heads. Zones 3–9.

DYCKIA
This genus in the pineapple (Bromeliaceae) family consists of more than 120 species, mostly from Brazil, Argentina, and neighboring countries, with only a few in cultivation. They are clumpforming plants. The leaves are triangular, usually green and very succulent, with mostly weak teeth on the edges. The generally long flower stems do not emerge from the plant's center, which means the plant does not die after flowering as with most other members of the Bromeliaceae. The flowerhead is sometimes single, sometimes open-branched, each branch having many well-spaced yellow to orange flowers.
CULTIVATION: Grow in well-drained sandy soil mix, in greenhouses or conservatories, in cool-temperate areas, or outdoors in warm-

Dryas octopetala

temperate, subtropical, and tropical areas. Water when potting mix is dry. Do not over-fertilize. Propagate from seed or offsets.

Dyckia remotiflora
☼ ⚘ ↔ 16 in (40 cm) ↕ 40 in (100 cm)
Found from southern Brazil to Argentina. Terrestrial bromeliads. Slow clump-forming plants. Narrow, triangular, dark green leaves. Flowerhead a single stem with a few yellow flowers scattered on all sides. Mainly grown in open rockeries. Zones 9–11.

ECHINOPS
GLOBE THISTLE
This genus, containing about 120 species of thistle-like perennials found from Europe eastward to central Asia and southward to the mountains of Africa, is from the daisy (Asteraceae) family. The leaves are spine-tipped and usually deeply lobed, and may be simple or have up to 3 large leaflets. The flowers, appearing in summer–early autumn, are small, mostly white to mauve-blue, borne in spherical heads without ray florets, and backed by often spiny basal bracts, which are sometimes colored. The flowerheads are sometimes dried but tend to disintegrate rather quickly.
CULTIVATION: These are mostly very hardy plants and easily grown in any temperate climate garden with a moderately fertile, well-drained soil. They are best grown in a fairly open position to reduce the risk of mildew. Propagated mainly from seed but easily divided in late winter.

Echinops bannaticus
☼/◐ ❄ ↔ 2 ft (0.6 m) ↕ 4 ft (1.2 m)
Found from Greece to the Czech Republic. Upright stem; finely hairy leaves, angularly lobed almost to the midrib, a few narrow spines; downy stems. Gray-blue flowerheads, to 2 in (5 cm) across, lighter in bud. 'Blue Globe', dark blue flowerheads, 2½ in (6 cm) across; 'Taplow Blue', bright steel blue flowerheads. Zones 3–9.

Echinops bannaticus 'Taplow Blue'

Echinops ritro

☼/◐ ❄ ↔ 16–24 in (40–60 cm) ↑ 12–24 in (30–60 cm)
Eurasian species. Leaves finely hairy, narrow, triangular, deeply
lobed, with small spines. Flowerheads deep steel blue to purple,
rarely white, to nearly 2 in (5 cm) wide. *E. r.* subsp. *ruthenicus*
(syn. *E. ruthenicus*), leaves with small spines and white woolly
hair on undersides, steel blue flowerheads; *E. r.* 'Blue Glow',
large light blue flowerheads. Zones 3–9.

Echinops sphaerocephalus

☼/◐ ❄ ↔ 16–32 in (40–80 cm) ↑ 3–7 ft (0.9–2 m)
Native to southern and central Russia. Downy
deeply lobed leaves, short spines, white hair on
undersides. White to pale ash gray flowerheads,
to over 2 in (5 cm) across. Zones 3–9.

ECHIUM

This genus contains about 60 species in the
borage (Boraginaceae) family, a large proportion
of which are endemic to the Canary Islands and
Madeira. Some of these endemics are shrubs or
giant biennials. The remaining species are found
in parts of the Mediterranean region, through
western Asia, and in parts of Africa. These are
nearly all smaller annuals, biennials, or perennials,
generally beginning as a rosette of narrow leaves
clothed in stiff hairs. Bell-shaped flowers, usually
blue, pink, purple, or reddish in color, are carried
in branched, usually erect, spikes in spring and summer.
CULTIVATION: The shrubby species of *Echium* thrive best with only
moderate amounts of fertilizer and water. The herbaceous species
can be fertilized and watered more liberally. All do best in full
sun. The species that are from the Canary Islands are less frost
hardy than the European species. They are usually propagated
from seed, but cuttings may be taken in spring or summer.
These plants have a tendency to self-seed in mild climates,
so they must be positioned carefully.

Edmondia pinifolia

Echium candicans ★

syn. *Echium fastuosum*
PRIDE OF MADEIRA
☼ ◑ ↔ 6 ft (1.8 m) ↑ 6 ft (1.8 m)
Native to the Canary Islands and Madeira. Thick-stemmed, soft-
wooded, evergreen shrub, with large densely hairy leaves, to 10 in
(25 cm) long. Clusters of about 8 blue flowers with protruding
pink to lilac-purple stamens, borne in a spiky
panicle, in early spring–early summer. May naturalize in cool climates. Zones 9–10.

Echium vulgare

BLUE WEED, VIPER'S BUGLOSS
☼ ❄ ↔ 18–24 in (45–60 cm)
↑ 18–24 in (45–60 cm)
From Europe and western Asia. Biennial usually
grown as an annual. Often confused with *E.
plantagineum* but bristlier, with smaller flowers.
Branching spikes of intense violet-blue flowers,
to ¾ in (18 mm), in summer. Zones 7–10.

EDMONDIA

This small genus, containing 3 species of perennials and small shrubs in the daisy (Asteraceae)
family, is confined to the Cape region of South
Africa. The flowerheads are composed of disc
florets only, the daisy appearance is given by
the papery bracts surrounding the flowerheads.
CULTIVATION: Best grown in relatively frost-free regions in well-
drained soil in full sun. Propagate from seed in spring or from
cuttings during summer or autumn.

Edmondia pinifolia

☼ ❄ ↔ 12 in (30 cm) ↑ 12 in (30 cm)
Evergreen perennial. Small narrow leaves, white felting on undersurface. The flowerheads are surrounded by crimson bracts,
borne at branch tips, in spring. Zones 8–9.

EICHHORNIA

This genus contains 7 species from tropical America, and belongs
to the pickerelweed (Pontederiaceae) family. The plants are rhizomatous aquatics, usually perennial, with floating or submerged
leaves. The stems are short and floating, and may be detaching or
rooted in mud. The shiny hairless leaves form either floating or
emergent rosettes; when free-floating they have tufts of thread-
like roots below. Leaves have either narrow cylindrical stalks or,
in floating species, elliptical stalks inflated with air-filled tissue.
The inflorescence is a spike or panicle; flowers have 6 lobes,
arising from a tube at the base, and are usually violet to blue
with white or yellow markings. Fruit is a many-seeded capsule.
CULTIVATION: These plants do not tolerate frost and generally
require water at least 6 in (15 cm) deep. They respond to dissolved nutrients with faster growth; in hotter climates growth
is so rapid that planting is not recommended in any but small
ponds. Some species are prohibited in some areas as a weed.
Propagation is by division.

Echium candicans

Eichhornia crassipes
WATER HYACINTH

☼ ⚬ ↔ 18 in (45 cm) ↑ 12 in (30 cm)

Usually a free-floating plant. Swollen leaf stalks and leaf blades raised above the water act as sails. Violet-blue flowers in summer; some selections tinted pink or yellow. Introduced as an ornamental, but has spread to choke many tropical waterways and naturalize in many parts of the world. Regarded as a noxious weed in many countries, its use must be carefully planned. Zones 10–12.

ELODEA
syn. *Anacharis*

This genus in the frogbit (Hydrocharitaceae) family contains 12 species. These prolific freshwater plants, native to North and South America, are useful in aquariums, ponds, and water gardens. Because they are submersed, they protect spawning and young fish; they also counteract algae build-up. Some species are free floating, some rooted.

Emilia sonchifolia

Even in aquariums, rooted species can grow to 15 ft (4.5 m).
CULTIVATION: For best results, grow in full sun in slow-moving or still water. Under ideal conditions, *Elodea* can spread rapidly. Reproduce from cuttings.

Elodea canadensis
CANADIAN PONDWEED, WATERWEED

☼ ✽ ↔ indefinite ↑ 36 in (90 cm)

From North America. Excellent perennial oxygenator for water gardens, can become invasive. Densely branched stems, whorls of dark green pointed leaves, minute white flowers in summer. Dies back in winter. Zones 3–10.

EMILIA

There are about 24 species of rather sparse annual herbs in this genus in the daisy (Asteraceae) family. They are found throughout Polynesia, India, and tropical Africa. Their foliage is reminiscent of sow thistles, and the finely rayed flowers, which are borne singly or in small corymbs, are in bright shades of purple, scarlet, yellow, or orange.
CULTIVATION: These are easily grown in most soils in full sun; plant close together for the best effect. Propagate from seed.

Emilia sonchifolia
FLORA'S PAINTBRUSH, TASSEL FLOWER

☼ ⚬ ↔ 6–10 in (15–25 cm) ↑ 6–20 in (15–50 cm)

Annual from tropical Asia and Africa. Rosettes of lyre-shaped leaves, sometimes bluish green. Tassel-like flowers in shades of scarlet, brilliant orange, or yellow in summer. Zones 9–11.

ENSETE

Members of the banana (Musaceae) family, to which this genus belongs, are really giant, tree-like, perennial herbs. *Ensete* is a

Eichhornia crassipes

genus of 7 species of ornamental bananas found in tropical Asia and Africa. The large solitary trunk or pseudostem is composed of the sheathing bases of the huge leaves, the blades of which are easily frayed by strong winds. Flowers are carried in large pendulous inflorescences at the end of arching stems, and develop into small, dry, inedible bananas containing hard seeds.
CULTIVATION: These are easy to grow, and do not require as much warmth as their edible relatives. The plants will survive all year in a mild frost-free climate; otherwise, treat them as annuals. Plant in moist, rich, well-drained soil in full sun or part-shade. They are usually propagated from seed, though it is sometimes possible to remove and strike basal suckers with roots.

Ensete ventricosum
ABYSSINIAN BANANA, ETHIOPIAN BANANA

☼ ⚬ ↔ 15 ft (4.5 m) ↑ 30 ft (9 m)

African species. Huge crown of leaves, to 20 ft (6 m) long, tinted purple. '**Maurelii**', large, broad, red-tinged leaves. Zones 9–12.

EPILOBIUM
WILLOW HERB

This genus of about 200 species of annuals, perennials, and subshrubs in the evening primrose (Onagraceae) family is found in temperate climates around the world. Some are weedy. They are mostly rhizomatous plants. The leaves are opposite, and usually 4-ranked. Flowers are mostly pink or white, borne in succession in upper leaf axils, with long calyx tube and 4 petals, which are often notched. Fruit is a slender capsule. Some species from western North America have a more shrubby habit and scarlet flowers.
CULTIVATION: These plants are best suited to wild gardens or areas where they can spread freely. Grow in full sun in moisture-retentive soil. Alpine species need perfect drainage and protection from the hottest sun. Propagation is from seed or cuttings.

Epilobium angustifolium, in the wild, Wyoming, USA

their biggest asset, and the dainty spring flowers occur in a range of colors, often with long curved spurs.
CULTIVATION: Most prefer a cool shaded aspect under deciduous trees in humus-rich soil; many are quite drought tolerant once established. Propagate by division in late winter.

Epilobium angustifolium
syn. *Chamerion angustifolium*
FIREWEED, FRENCH WILLOW, GREAT WILLOW HERB, ROSEBAY WILLOW HERB
☼ ✲ ↔ 3–8 ft (0.9–2.4 m) ↕ 3–8 ft (0.9–2.4 m)
Found throughout Northern Hemisphere. Invasive vigorous perennial. Willowy stems; narrow alternately arranged leaves. Racemes of pink to purplish flowers in summer–early autumn. Zones 3–9.

Epilobium canum
syns *Zauschneria californica, Z. cana*
CALIFORNIA FUCHSIA, ZAUSCHNERIA
☼ ✲ ↔ 2–3 ft (0.6–0.9 m) ↕ 1–3 ft (0.3–0.9 m)
Ranging from Oregon and Wyoming to California and New Mexico, USA, and northwestern Mexico. Variable semi-deciduous plant; foliage gray-green; brilliant scarlet funnel-shaped flowers 1–2 in (2.5–5 cm) long, in summer–autumn. 'Solidarity Pink', reddish pink flowers. *E. c.* subsp. *latifolium* (syn. *Zauschneria californica* subsp. *latifolia*), leaves broader, less grayish. Zones 8–10.

Epilobium septentrionale
syns *Epilobium canum* subsp. *septentrionale*, *Zauschneria septentrionalis*
HUMBOLDT COUNTY FUCHSIA, WHITE LEAF FUCHSIA
☼ ✲ ↔ 24–36 in (60–90 cm)
↕ 6–12 in (15–30 cm)
A mat-forming, semi-evergreen perennial from California, USA. Short, oval to lance-shaped, gray to gray-green leaves. Succession of tubular scarlet flowers in late summer-autumn. 'Select Mattole', silvery gray leaves. Zones 7–10.

EPIMEDIUM
BARRENWORT, BISHOP'S HAT, BISHOP'S MITER, HORNY GOAT WEED
This genus has about 44 species. Both evergreen and deciduous, they are clumping to slightly running perennials in the barberry (Berberidaceae) family that are found mainly in Asia but extend to the Mediterranean. They have attractive foliage, which is often

Epimedium × *cantabrigiense*
☼ ✲ ↔ 12–18 in (30–45 cm)
↕ 12–24 in (30–60 cm)
Heart-shaped evergreen leaves, downy beneath, with a few marginal spines. Stems of dainty red and pale yellow flowers in spring. Zones 5–9.

Epimedium grandiflorum
☼ ✲ ↔ 8–12 in (20–30 cm)
↕ 8–12 in (20–30 cm)
From Japan, China, and Northern Korea. Widespread more or less deciduous species. clumping habit. Heart-shaped leaves. Small spurred flowers in shades of white, yellow, pink or purple. More selected clones than any other species. 'Lilacinum', lilac flowers; 'Lilafee', magenta flowers; 'Rose Queen' ★, deep pink flowers with white-tipped spurs. Zones 5–9.

Epimedium × *perralchicum*
☼ ✲ ↔ 20–24 in (50–60 cm) ↕ 14–16 in (35–40 cm)
Forms large solid clumps of evergreen foliage, bronze when young. Sprays of bright yellow spurless flowers. 'Frohnleiten', spikier foliage and larger flowers. Zones 7–9.

Epimedium perralderianum
☼ ✲ ↔ 20–24 in (50–60 cm) ↕ 14–16 in (35–40 cm)
From northern Africa. Evergreen with a slowly spreading habit. Leaves with 3 toothed leaflets, bronze ageing to green. Yellow flowers with short brown spurs. Zones 7–9.

Epimedium × *versicolor* 'Sulphureum'

Epimedium × *versicolor*
☼ ✲ ↔ 10–12 in (25–30 cm)
↕ 10–12 in (25–30 cm)
Range of evergreen clump-forming garden hybrids. Spiny-edged leaves often richly colored with bronze when young. Pink and yellow flowers have short spurs that do not exceed the length of the calyx. 'Neosulphureum', soft lemon flowers; 'Sulphureum', bright yellow flowers with slightly longer spurs. Zones 5–9.

EPISCIA
This genus of 9 species from tropical America belongs to the African violet (Gesneriaceae) family. They are epiphytic or terrestrial herbs and are exceptional in the family in having runners. The leaves are opposite, often colored, and in equal or unequal pairs; when unequal the smaller one is often deciduous. The

flowers are borne in stalked racemes in the leaf axils, and may be clustered or solitary. The calyx has 5 green or colored sepals, which are sometimes joined at the base. The corolla is funnel-shaped with 5 spreading lobes. The fruit is a 2-valved capsule containing many elliptical seeds.
CULTIVATION: In temperate areas *Episcia* need greenhouse culture and are often grown in hanging baskets, but in the tropics they can be grown outside. These plants are difficult to overwinter in the poor light of temperate regions, but can be readily propagated from cuttings, which root easily, or from seed.

Episcia cupreata
CARPET PLANT, FLAME VIOLET
◐/◑ ❋ ↔ 12–24 in (30–60 cm)
↕ 8–12 in (20–30 cm)
Native to Central and South America. Evergreen creeping perennial. Leaves oval, brown to dark green, wrinkled, downy, flecked with copper and purple underneath. Clusters of scarlet flowers with a yellow ring, throat sometimes spotted with purple, in summer. 'Acajou', lighter-colored leaves, silvery markings; 'Chocolate Soldier', large brown leaves

Episcia cupreata

with silvery gray center band; 'Country Cowgirl', silvery green pebble-textured leaves with copper-green margins; 'Metallica', copper leaves marked with silver, red flowers; 'Silver Sheen', bright copper-green margins on leaves, yellow, lilac, or red flowers; 'Tetra', large orange-red flowers with wavy lobes, orange-yellow inside; 'Tropical Topaz', bright yellow flowers. Zones 10–12.

Episcia dianthiflora
syn. *Alsobia dianthiflora*
LACE-FLOWER VINE
◐/◑ ❋ ↔ 18–36 in (60–90 cm) ↕ 8 in (20 cm)
Found from southern Mexico to Costa Rica. Low-growing evergreen perennial. Leaves dark green, toothed, elliptical to oval-shaped, to 1¾ in (40 mm) long, often veined with purple-red. Solitary, pearly white, tubular flowers, spotted with purple at base, conspicuously fringed rounded petals, in summer. Zones 10–12.

Episcia Hybrid Cultivars
◐/◑ ✿ ↔ 32–40 in (80–100 cm) ↕ 8–20 in (20–50 cm)
The best of the many hybrid cultivars tend to be compact plants that flower heavily, often with marked foliage. 'Chocolate 'n' Cherries', very dark bronze foliage, yellow-dotted bright red flowers; 'Star of Bethlehem', dark bronze leaves with red undersides, distinctive bright pink flowers with a broad white margin; 'Toy Silver', very dwarf, with leaves of dark green heavily veined with silver-gray, bright red flowers. Zones 10–12.

ERANTHIS
WINTER ACONITE
The 7 species in this genus of small tuberous plants from the buttercup (Ranunculaceae) family are found in the damp deciduous woodlands of Europe and Asia. In similar cool, damp, summer-shady situations they colonize and extend their territory. The

cupped golden flowers, each held on a single stem, are encircled with pronounced green "ruffs," and appear in late winter.
CULTIVATION: Transplant in early spring while the plants are in leaf. Grow in moisture-retentive soil, with plenty of winter sun. Propagate by dividing the tubers or from seed.

Eranthis hyemalis
◑ ❋ ↔ 3–4 in (8–10 cm) ↕ 3–4 in (8–10 cm)
Originally found from southern France to Bulgaria; now naturalized over a far wider range. Brilliant golden flowers, like buttercups, often appearing before snow-melt, held on short curved stems. Stems elongate and straighten as the flower develops. Bright green, lobed, and circular basal leaves emerge after the flowers fade. Plant beneath deciduous trees in alkaline soils. Zones 5–8.

ERIGERON
FLEABANE
The 200 or so species of annuals and perennials in this genus in the daisy (Asteraceae) family are found throughout temperate regions, particularly in North America, and grow in a variety of habitats. Their daisy flowers usually have numerous narrow rays in shades of white, pink, or lavender, occasionally yellow. Cultivars extend the color range. Plants vary from the low alpine species, suitable for a rock garden, to larger-flowered species growing to 30 in (75 cm) or more. They flower profusely, often over a long season.
CULTIVATION: Apart from the alpine species, which need protection in winter and very good drainage, most are easily grown in full sun in any reasonable soil. Propagate from seed or by division.

Erigeron glaucus
BEACH ASTER, SEASIDE DAISY
◑ ❋ ↔ 12–24 in (30–60 cm) ↕ 6–12 in (15–30 cm)
From western USA. Somewhat succulent straggly perennial, with broadly oval leaves. Large gold-centered daisies with lilac to violet rays in late spring–early summer. 'Arthur Menzies', compact form, pink daisies; 'Rose Purple', pink-purple daisies. Zones 3–10.

Erigeron glaucus

Erigeron speciosus 'Quakeress'

Erigeron karvinskianus
syn. *Erigeron mucronatus*
MEXICAN DAISY, SANTA BARBARA DAISY
☼ ❄ ↔ 2–5 ft (0.6–1.5 m) ↑ 1–2 ft (0.3–0.6 m)
Perennial from highlands of southern Mexico, Central America, and Venezuela. Mounds of small toothed leaves on slender stems. Airy masses of small, white to pink, yellow-centered daisies all year round in frost-free areas, from spring to autumn in colder regions. Popular ground cover, but sometimes a weed. Zones 8–11.

Erigeron pulchellus
ROBIN'S PLANTAIN
☼ ❄ ↔ 8–16 in (20–40 cm) ↑ 6–16 in (15–40 cm)
Native to North America. Biennial or short-lived perennial with creeping rhizomes. Leaves spoon-shaped. Dainty pale pink or pale purple daisies with yellow centers in summer. Zones 4–9.

Erigeron 'Rosa Jewel'
☼ ❄ ↔ 16–24 in (40–60 cm) ↑ 18–30 in (45–75 cm)
An attractive hybrid with bright pink daisy-like flowers, similar to *E. speciosus* in other respects. Zones 3–9.

Erigeron speciosus
☼ ❄ ↔ 16–24 in (40–60 cm)
↑ 18–30 in (45–75 cm)
From northwestern USA. Popular perennial. Prolific blue daisies with yellow centers in summer. *E. s.* var. *macranthus*, slightly larger flowers. Many cultivars in shades of pink and blue. 'Rosa Jewel' ★ (syn. 'Pink Jewel'), bright pink flowers; 'Quakeress', light mauve-pink flowers. Zones 3–9.

ERIOGONUM
WILD BUCKWHEAT
This genus from western North America belongs to the knotweed (Polygonaceae) family, and includes about 150 annuals, perennials, and small evergreen shrubs of varied habit, most of which grow from a basal rosette of leaves. Small flowers appear in dense clusters or umbels, and the fruit is a 3-angled achene. *Eriogonum* species are good rockery or background plants for drier gardens.
CULTIVATION: Adaptable to a wide range of climates, they will grow in sun or part-shade in a well-drained, preferably sandy, soil. They require plenty of water in warm conditions but need to be drier in winter. Remove spent flowerheads. Propagate from seed sown in spring or from cuttings. The root clumps of perennial species may be divided.

Eriogonum arborescens
SANTA CRUZ ISLAND BUCKWHEAT
☼/❂ ⚘ ↔ 5 ft (1.5 m) ↑ 5 ft (1.5 m)
From California, USA. Peeling bark. Narrow near-linear leaves with slightly rolled edges and felted undersides. White to pale pink flowers, in downy inflorescences 2–6 in (5–15 cm) wide, in early summer–autumn. Good cut flower. Zones 9–10.

Eriogonum giganteum
SAINT CATHERINE'S LACE
☼ ⚘ ↔ 10 ft (3 m) ↑ 8 ft (2.4 m)
From the Santa Barbara Islands off southern California, USA. Rounded evergreen shrub, with a central trunk, and leathery, oval, grayish white leaves. Flat clusters of woolly flowerheads, to 12 in (30 cm) across, white slowly fading to rusty red. Summer-flowering. Zones 9–11.

Eriogonum umbellatum
SULFUR FLOWER
☼ ❄ ↔ 3–4 ft (0.9–1.2 m) ↑ 6–18 in (15–45 cm)
From northwestern USA and southwestern Canada. Variable, low-spreading, perennial herb. Rosettes of spatula-shaped, purplish-tinged, stalked leaves, finely hairy underneath, in winter. Loose ball-like clusters of bright sulfur yellow or cream flowers in summer. Zones 6–10.

ERODIUM
HERONSBILL, STORKSBILL
This genus in the geranium (Geraniaceae) family includes 60 species of perennials and a few annuals and subshrubs. They are found in sunny rocky areas in mountainous regions of Europe, Asia, Australia, and South America. Some are mat-forming, others are erect, growing to 20 in (50 cm) tall. The leaves are lobed or pinnately divided, often finely and ornately, sometimes silvery gray. The charming 5-petalled flowers have 5 stamens. Some species carry male and female flowers on separate plants. The flowers are pink, red, purple, blue, yellow, or white, and often veined or stained with darker tones.
CULTIVATION: Grow the smaller species in rockeries, pots, or a greenhouse; the taller plants are ideal in borders. Heronsbills need full sun and well-drained slightly alkaline soil. Propagate annuals from seed; perennials from seed or cuttings, or by division.

Erodium chrysanthum

Erodium chrysanthum
☀ ❋ ↔ 12–16 in (30–40 cm) ↕ 4–6 in (10–15 cm)

From Greece. Low tufts of ferny silvery leaves. Saucer-shaped pale lemon flowers, to ¾ in (18 mm) across, in summer. Zones 7–10.

Erodium corsicum
☀ ❋ ↔ 12 in (30 cm) ↕ 8 in (20 cm)

From Corsica and Sardinia. Short-lived mat-forming perennial. Downy silvery gray foliage. Small, crumpled, oval leaves with wavy margins. Flowers rose pink, to ¾ in (18 mm) across, in late spring–summer. '**Rubrum**', deeper pink flowers. Zones 8–10.

Erodium reichardii
ALPINE GERANIUM

☀ ❋ ↔ 10 in (25 cm) ↕ 1–2 in (2.5–5 cm)

From Majorca and Corsica. Mat-forming species. Small, crinkled, scallop-edged leaves. Delicate white flowers with pink veins, to ½ in (12 mm) across, in summer. Good choice for rock garden. '**Charm**', white flowers. Zones 7–10.

Erodium reichardii 'Charm'

Erodium × variabile
☀ ❋ ↔ 10 in (25 cm) ↕ 6–12 in (15–30 cm)

These hybrids of *E. corsicum* and *E. reichardii* are intermediate between the parents. '**Bishop's Form**', deep pink flowers with reddish veins; '**Derek**' (syn. *E. reichardii* 'Derek'), very compact, with deep pink flowers; '**Flora Pleno**', small, pale or deep pink, double flowers; '**Roseum**', pink flowers veined with crimson. Zones 7–10.

ERYNGIUM

Belonging to the carrot (Apiaceae) family, this genus of more than 200 species of annuals, biennials, and perennials is found throughout most of the temperate world. Although the flower stems often carry rudimentary leaves, the foliage, which can be very spiny, is almost entirely basal, often forming a large clump. Unlike most umbellifers, with their open airy flowerheads, the flowerheads of *Eryngium* are thistle-like, with the flowers clustered in a central cone surrounded by spiny bracts, often in shades of metallic blue or silver gray. Flowerheads and foliage last well when cut and have a certain charm when dried. Summer is the main flowering season. CULTIVATION: Their hardiness varies with the species, though most will tolerate at least moderate frosts. Some are drought tolerant; most are comfortable in moist well-drained soil with regular watering during the growing season. Propagate by division or from seed.

Eryngium alpinum
☀/◑ ❋ ↔ 24 in (60 cm) ↕ 24 in (60 cm)

Perennial, found from western France to the Balkans. Long-stemmed leaves, deeply lobed, spiny, triangular to heart-shaped, to 6 in (15 cm) long. Purple-blue flowerheads surrounded by a large feathery ruff of spiny, 2½ in (6 cm) long, metallic purple-blue bracts. '**Blue Star**', to 30 in (75 cm) tall, bracts more blue than purple. Zones 6–9.

Eryngium amethystinum
AMETHYST SEA HOLLY

☀/◑ ❋ ↔ 20 in (50 cm) ↕ 28 in (70 cm)

Found around the Adriatic to Sicily. Perennial. Leaves to 6 in (15 cm) long, palmately lobed and further divided into narrow spine-tipped segments. Many near-spherical purple-blue flowerheads surrounded by narrow, spiny, purple-tinted bracts, to 2 in (5 cm) long. Zones 7–9.

Eryngium bourgatii
MEDITERRANEAN SEA HOLLY

☀/◑ ❋ ↔ 16 in (40 cm) ↕ 16 in (40 cm)

Native to Spain and the Pyrenees. Perennial, forms low clump of foliage. Leaves much-divided, spiny, rounded, to 3 in (8 cm) across. Branching inflorescence of many flowerheads, to over ½ in (12 mm) wide, with up to 12 narrow light mauve-blue bracts that are not always spiny. '**Oxford Blue**', attractive silver-blue bracts and darker flowerheads. Zones 5–10.

Eryngium giganteum
MISS WILLMOTT'S GHOST

☀/◑ ❋ ↔ 32 in (80 cm) ↕ 5 ft (1.5 m)

Perennial, native to Caucasus region. Long-stemmed triangular leaves, to 6 in (15 cm) long, deeply toothed, and spiny. Green to silvery mauve-blue flowerhead, surrounded by up to 10 large, spiny, silver-white bracts. Zones 6–9.

Eryngium bourgatii cultivar

Eryngium × oliverianum

☼/◐ ❄ ↔ 20–24 in (50–60 cm) ↑ 24–40 in (60–100 cm)

Perennial with long-stemmed, spiny, toothed leaves, rounded to heart-shaped, with 3 lobes on basal leaves. Bright metallic blue flowerheads, to 1¾ in (40 mm) across, with up to 15 narrow, spiny, purple bracts. Zones 5–9.

Eryngium variifolium

☼/◐ ❄ ↔ 16–20 in (40–50 cm)
↑ 20–30 in (50–75 cm)

Native to North Africa. An evergreen perennial forming a thistle-like basal rosette of white-marbled, dark green, toothed leaves. Flowerheads purple-blue, to 1 in (25 mm) across, with up to 7 narrow, spiny, white-centered bracts. Zones 7–9.

ERYSIMUM

syn. *Cheiranthus*

WALLFLOWER

This genus in the cabbage (Brassicaceae) family, containing some 80 species of sometimes shrubby annuals and perennials, now includes many species formerly classified under *Cheiranthus*. The narrow green to blue-green leaves with shallow lobes are unremarkable, but the 4-petalled flowers are brightly colored, often fragrant, and frequently appear over a long season. In mild climates the bushy forms flower all year round. The hybrids come in a wide variety of colors.

CULTIVATION: Although most species of *Erysimum* are very hardy, they prefer a temperate climate with distinct seasons. Plant in

Erysimum, Hybrid Cultivar, 'Bowles' Mauve'

moist humus-rich soil and water well during the flowering period. They are often quite drought tolerant, but these plants will flower more abundantly with regular watering, feeding, trimming, and deadheading. Propagation of annual species is by seed; perennials can be propagated from seed, from small cuttings of non-flowering stems, or sometimes by division.

Erysimum bicolor

syn. *Cheiranthus bicolor*

☼/◐ ❄ ↔ 24 in (60 cm) ↑ 36 in (90 cm)

Found in the Canary Islands and Madeira. Shrubby perennial with pointed, toothed, lance-shaped leaves. Scented flowers appear from spring onward, opening cream to orange-brown and ageing to mauve. Zones 9–10.

Erysimum cheiri

syn. *Cheiranthus cheiri*

WALLFLOWER

☼/◐ ❄ ↔ 16 in (40 cm) ↑ 24 in (60 cm)

A native of southern Europe. Shrubby perennial, usually cultivated as biennial. Narrow deep green foliage; the lower leaves to 8 in (20 cm) long, becoming smaller higher up. Large heads of yellow and/or orange flowers. The cultivated forms, which are most likely hybrids, include '**Cloth of Gold**', deep golden yellow flowers; **Fair Lady** (quite often called **My Fair Lady**) **Strain**, to 18 in (45 cm) tall, blooms in range of pastel shades; '**Fire King Improved**', 16 in (40 cm) tall, brilliant orange-red flowers; '**Harpur Crewe**', yellow double flowers; and **Prince Series**, stocky, to 18 in (45 cm) tall, in wide color range. Zones 7–9.

Erysimum Hybrid Cultivars

☼/◐ ❄ ↔ 24 in (60 cm) ↑ 24–36 in (60–90 cm)

These bushy hybrids are of uncertain parentage. Though not long-lasting, they are easily propagated and flower virtually continuously. '**Bowles' Mauve**' ★ (syn. *E. A. Bowles*), best known, masses of small mauve-purple flowers; '**Gold Shot**', 18 in (45 cm) tall, golden yellow flowers; '**Sunlight**', yellow-flowered low spreader, about 4 in (10 cm) tall, ; '**Wenlock Beauty**', magenta flowers ageing to mauve; '**Winter Cheer**', two-tone orange and light purple flowers. Zones 7–10.

ESCHSCHOLZIA

CALIFORNIA POPPY

Native to western North America and now widely naturalized, this genus in the poppy (Papaveraceae) family is made up of about 8 annuals and short-lived perennials. They have fine feathery foliage, often a rather grayish green, and in summer produce masses of bright golden yellow 4- to 8-petalled poppies that only open on sunny days. Modern seed strains come in many flower colors; the flowers are followed by long seed capsules.

CULTIVATION: These are easily grown in any sunny position with light, gritty, very well-drained soil, and often self-sow and naturalize. Most are very frost hardy and tolerate poor soil. Propagate from seed, which is best sown where it is required to grow.

Erysimum cheiri, Fair Lady Strain

Eschscholzia caespitosa

TUFTED CALIFORNIA POPPY

☼ ❄ ↔ 10 in (25 cm) ↑ 10 in (25 cm)

From northern California and Oregon, USA. Fast-growing annual. Leaves very finely divided, feathery, green to blue-green. Bright yellow flowers, 2 in (5 cm) across. '**Sundew**', to 6 in (15 cm) tall, lemon yellow flowers. Zones 7–10.

Eschscholzia californica

CALIFORNIA POPPY

☼ ❄ ↔ 8–16 in (20–40 cm)
↑ 8–24 in (20–60 cm)

From western USA and northern Baja California, Mexico. Now regarded as weed in parts of Australia. Annual or short-lived perennial. Leaves variable but usually finely divided, feathery, blue-green. Cup-shaped flowers to over 2 in (5 cm) across, usually bright orange but often yellow, rarely cream or pink. Seedling strains available in many colors and forms, including double flowers. '**Dali**', interesting soft apricot-colored flowers with 2 rows of petals; '**Red Chief**', striking red flowers. Zones 6–10.

Eschscholzia californica

ETLINGERA

About 60 species of rhizomatous perennials occur in this genus, which is a member of the ginger (Zingiberaceae) family, and is found from Sri Lanka to New Guinea. The stems are cane-like and the long leaves are borne in 2 ranks. Terminal flowerheads arise from the rhizomes on separate leafless stems; these are made up of small flowers and are surrounded by large, colorful, petal-like bracts.
CULTIVATION: In suitably warm climates grow these plants in sun or part-shade in moist humus-rich soil. In cool climates grow indoors in bright filtered light and maintain high humidity. Water well and feed regularly during growth periods. Propagation is from seed or by division.

Etlingera elatior

syns *Nicolaia elatior, Phaeomeria magnifica, P. speciosa*

PHILIPPINE WAX FLOWER, TORCH GINGER

☼/◐ ✦ ↔ 5–8 ft (1.5–2.4 m)
↑ 10–20 ft (3–6 m)

From western Indonesia and the Malay Peninsula. Spectacular plant with large linear leaves. Cone-like heads of pink to bright red, densely packed, small flowers and waxy bracts of the same color, the outer bracts large and flaring, in summer–autumn. Zones 11–12.

EUPATORIUM

In the broadest sense, this is a genus of more than 450 species, but some botanists have preferred to split off several other genera, leaving only about 40 species in a more narrowly defined *Eupatorium*. As the genus is traditionally understood, *Eupatorium* includes annuals, perennials, subshrubs, and shrubs within the daisy (Asteraceae) family, and is native to eastern North America, Central America and South America, with a very few species in Europe and Asia. All the species of *Eupatorium* have whorled or opposite leaves on simple or branched stems, the stems terminating in corymbs or panicles of small flowerheads, which are the plants' most decorative feature. The fruit is plumed, like thistledown. The flowers are attractive to butterflies.
CULTIVATION: These plants require a sunny position in well-drained but moist fertile soil. Growing tips can be pinched back to encourage compact growth. Propagate in spring from seed or cuttings of green wood, or by dividing root clumps when the plant is dormant; protect from frosts.

Eupatorium perfoliatum

BONESET, THOROUGHWORT

☼ ✦ ↔ 3–5 ft (0.9–1.5 m) ↑ 3–5 ft (0.9–1.5 m)

Native to southeastern USA. Aromatic herbaceous perennial. Erect, branching, hairy stems. Lance-shaped leaves, opposite, wrinkled, toothed, to 8 in (20 cm) long; downy underside. Pairs of leaves joined at base. Large, flat-topped, terminal, compound heads of 10 to 40 tubular white flowers, sometimes tinged with purple, from late summer to autumn. Flowering does not occur until the second year. Zones 3–4.

Eupatorium purpureum ★

JOE PYE WEED, TRUMPET WEED

☼/◐ ✦ ↔ 6–10 ft (1.8–3 m)
↑ 6–10 ft (1.8–3 m)

From eastern USA. Herbaceous perennial. Strong dark red stems. Large whorls of elliptical leaves that are finely toothed, with a purplish tinge. Inflorescence of a half-rounded panicle with 5 to 15 fragrant flowerheads, purple or pale pink to greenish yellow or rose-purple, in late summer–autumn. *E. p.* subsp. *maculatum* (syn. *E. maculatum*), smaller, with a flat-topped panicle of 15 pale or rose purple flowerheads. Zones 3–9.

Eupatorium rugosum

syn. *Ageratina altissima*

FALL POISON, SNOW THOROUGHWORT, WHITE SNAKEROOT

☼ ✦ ↔ 3–6 ft (0.9–1.8 m) ↑ 3–6 ft (0.9–1.8 m)

From northeastern North America. Perennial herb. Hairy stems. Leaves opposite, elliptical, grayish to purplish green, toothed. Flat-topped clusters of white flowers, at stem tips, in late summer. '**Braunlaub**', young foliage and flowers tinted brown. Zones 4–6.

Etlingera elatior

Euphorbia amygdaloides 'Purpurea'

Euphorbia characias subsp. wulfenii 'Bosahan'

Euphorbia griffithii 'Fireglow'

EUPHORBIA

This large genus of about 2,000 species of annuals, perennials, shrubs, and trees, both evergreen and deciduous, is distributed throughout the world. It gives its name to the large and diverse family Euphorbiaceae. *Euphorbia* alone takes in a very diverse range of forms and natural habitats, from spiny and succulent cactus-like species occurring mainly in hot dry areas to leafy perennials from cool-temperate climates. All species contain a poisonous milky sap which can cause severe irritation if it contacts the skin and, if rubbed into the eyes, may bring on temporary blindness. The true flowers are tiny, with separate male and female forms attached to a smooth cup-like structure, or cyathium. Cyathia are generally accompanied by bracts, which may be larger and are often colored, such as the scarlet bracts of poinsettia *(E. pulcherrima)*. These cyathia and bracts may be arranged in repeatedly branched inflorescences and sometimes form large flowerheads. The flowering times of many species are rainfall dependent; in temperate climates with even rainfall, the likely flowering time is from late spring to mid-summer.
CULTIVATION: Provide similar growing conditions to the plant's natural habitat. In cool-temperate climates most succulent and subtropical species will require greenhouse protection; some will grow in dry rock gardens. Avoid the toxic sap when pruning and disposing of branches. Some species can only be propagated from seed, others can be grown from stem-tip cuttings or by division.

Euphorbia amygdaloides
WOOD SPURGE

☼/◐ ❄ ↔ 24–40 in (60–100 cm) ↑ 20–32 in (50–80 cm)
From temperate Eurasia. Sspreading, mounding, leafy perennial. Soft stems densely foliaged with spatula-shaped leaves, to over 3 in (8 cm) long; often purple-tinted with a slight sheen. Sprays of showy yellow-green flowerheads throughout spring and summer. *E. a.* var. *robbiae*, more robust dark foliage, spreading rosettes. *E. a.* 'Purpurea', stems and foliage strongly tinted with purple-red, new growth is red-wine colored. Zones 7–10.

Euphorbia characias
☼ ❄ ↔ 5 ft (1.5 m) ↑ 6 ft (1.8 m)
Various forms from the Mediterranean region and southern Europe. Perennial subshrub or shrub with soft stems. Narrow,

elliptical, gray-green leaves. Heads of up to 20 small purple-green or yellow flowers, backed by conspicuous yellow-green whorled bracts, usually in late winter–early summer. The yellow-green-flowered *E. c.* subsp. *wulfenii* ★, with its various cultivars, is more widely cultivated than the species; 'Bosahan', variegated leaves, pale yellow flowers; 'John Tomlinson', 16 in (40 cm) long heads of bright yellow-green flowers. Zones 8–10.

Euphorbia cyparissias
CYPRESS SPURGE

☼/◐ ❄ ↔ 24 in (60 cm) ↑ 16 in (40 cm)
Widespread in Europe. Perennial, spreads by rhizomes, forms a clump of narrow stems with narrow green leaves, 1¾ in (40 mm) long, which may redden in sun or drought. Yellow-green inflorescence surrounded by mauve- to red-tinted feathery bracts in late spring to mid-summer. 'Fens Ruby', bright red bracts, near-yellow flowerheads, very compact. Zones 4–9.

Euphorbia griffithii
☼ ❄ ↔ 36 in (90 cm) ↑ 36 in (90 cm)
From the Himalayas. Widely grown and usually a perennial, can become shrubby in mild climates. Narrow leaves are, to 5 in (12 cm) long, dark green, tinted pink to orange. Flowerheads, with vivid orange-red bracts in summer, develop coppery tones with age. 'Fireglow', vivid red bracts. Zones 5–10.

Euphorbia marginata
GHOST WEED, SNOW ON THE MOUNTAIN

☼/◐ ❄ ↔ 20 in (50 cm) ↑ 40 in (100 cm)
Native to North America. Annual. Dense mound of light green, soft, downy leaves, to 3 in (8 cm) long, edged in white, sometimes entirely white at the top of the plant. White bracts in summer. Contact with sap can cause severe skin problems. Zones 4–10.

Euphorbia myrsinites ★
CREEPING SPURGE, DONKEY TAIL

◐ ❄ ↔ 20 in (50 cm) ↑ 10 in (25 cm)
From Eurasia. Clump-forming perennial with sprawling stems. Leaves spiralled, finely toothed, pointed, fleshy, blue-green, to 1¾ in (40 mm) long. Bright green cyathia with chrome yellow bracts in spring. Zones 6–10.

Euphorbia nicaeensis

☀ ❄ ↔ 24 in (60 cm) ↕ 24 in (60 cm)

From Europe. Attractive bushy perennial. Stems often tinged red and well covered with narrow bluish gray leaves. Floral bracts are a contrasting yellow-green. Zones 6–10.

Euphorbia polychroma

CUSHION SPURGE

◐ ❄ ↔ 24 in (60 cm) ↕ 24 in (60 cm)

From Eurasia. Clump-forming perennial. Bright green, elliptical, velvety leaves, to about 2 in (5 cm) long. Bright yellow-green, sometimes red-tinted, flowerheads in spring–summer. '**Major**', compact, chrome yellow flowerheads. Zones 6–9.

Euphorbia schillingii

☀/◐ ❄ ↔ 5 ft (1.5 m) ↕ 4 ft (1.2 m)

From Nepal. Shrubby perennial. Bright green leaves, narrow, elliptical, to 3 in (8 cm) long. Showy yellow-green flowerheads with rounded green bracts, in summer. Zones 7–9.

Euphorbia schillingii

Euphorbia seguieriana

☀/◐ ❄ ↔ 32 in (80 cm) ↕ 20 in (50 cm)

Found from central Europe to Pakistan and Siberia. Woody-based perennial. Forms clump of blue-green stems; similarly colored, pointed, linear leaves, to 1½ (35 mm) long. Large heads of yellow-green cyathia and yellow bracts, in summer. *E. s.* **subsp.** *niciciana,* less crowded flowerheads. Zones 5–9.

Euphorbia sikkimensis ★

☀/◐ ❄ ↔ 36 in (90 cm) ↕ 36 in (90 cm)

From the eastern Himalayas. Rhizome-rooted perennial with upright stems and narrow elliptical leaves, up to 4 in (10 cm) long, and often red-tinted. Attractive pink new growth. Showy orange-red flowerheads in summer. Zones 6–9.

EURYALE

This genus has just one species and belongs to the waterlily (Nymphaeaceae) family. It is found from northern India to China and Japan. It is a very large, perennial, aquatic plant with a massive rhizome. The leaves are round, ribbed, and very prickly. Flowers consist of 4 sepals and numerous petals, which are shorter than the sepals. The fruit is a prickly berry with many seeds. CULTIVATION: This is often grown as an annual in tropical greenhouses, where it is raised from seed sown immersed in water at 70–73°F (21–23°C).

Euryale ferox

☀ ❄ ↔ 5 ft (1.5 m) ↕ 3 ft (0.9 m)

Leaves 2–5 ft (0.6–1.5 m) across; upperside dull green, with sparse prickles; undersurface reddish, densely armed with prickles. Summer flowers often do not open, remaining more or less submerged. Sepals green; petals red to purple or lilac. Zones 8–11.

EUSTOMA

LISIANTHUS, PRAIRIE GENTIAN, TEXAS BLUEBELL

This genus of family Gentianaceae has 3 species of annuals or short-lived perennials found from southern USA to northern South America. They form clumps of fleshy oval to narrowly elliptical leaves, producing showy 5- to 6-petalled, funnel- to bell-shaped flowers, up to 2 in (5 cm) wide, in summer. Some species carry flowers singly, but the cultivated plants have many-flowered stems up to 24 in (60 cm) long, with blooms in a wide range of colors and in double-flowered forms.
CULTIVATION: These are usually grown as annuals. Slow-growing, they need prolonged warm conditions to flower well. Plant in full or half-sun with fertile, moist, well-drained soil. The heavy flower stems are best staked. May be propagated by cuttings but better if raised fresh from seed.

Eustoma grandiflorum ★

syns *Eustoma russellianum, Lisianthus grandiflorus*

☀/◐ ❄ ↔ 20 in (50 cm) ↕ 24–32 in (60–80 cm)

Annual or short-lived perennial from southern USA and Mexico. Upright blue-green stems; fleshy, blue-green, pointed oval leaves, to 3 in (8 cm) long. Heads of bell-shaped flowers, to 2½ in (6 cm) across. **Echo** mixed color strain, to 24 in (60 cm) tall, in lilac-, blue-, pink-, yellow-, and white-flowered forms as well as picotee-edged; '**Forever Blue**', to 12 in (30 cm) tall, large purple-blue flowers; **Heidi Series**, to 18 in (45 cm) tall, in many colors; **Mermaid Series**, including early-flowering dwarf '**Lilac Rose**', light purple-pink single flowers. Zones 9–11.

Eustoma grandiflorum 'Forever Blue'

EVOLVULUS

This genus of about 100 species comes mostly from tropical and warm-temperate parts of the Americas. It belongs to the bind-weed (Convolvulaceae) family. These plants are annuals, perennials, or subshrubs, often creeping but never climbing. The leaves are small, simple, and often narrow. The inflorescences are borne in the leaf axils or at the ends of the stems, each with one to several flowers with 5 small sepals. The corolla is funnel-shaped to flat, blue or pink to white, and has a lobed to smooth margin. The dry seed capsule is spherical to ovate in shape and contains 1 to 4 small seeds.

CULTIVATION: These plants thrive in well-drained soil in full sun. Propagate by root division or from cuttings; the shorter-lived species are readily raised from seed.

Evolvulus glomeratus

Evolvulus glomeratus
syn. *Evolvulus pilosus* of gardens

⬜ ⚘ ↔ 24–36 in (60–90 cm)
↕ 10–18 in (25–45 cm)

American species, found from South Dakota and Montana to Texas and Arizona, USA. Evergreen perennial. Dense mound of foliage emerging from mass of rhizomes; leaves gray-green with soft silky hairs. Long succession of brilliant blue flowers with a small white eye, 1 in (25 mm) across, in spring–autumn, wilting after noon in hot weather. Sold under the names 'Blue Daze', 'Hawaiian Blue Eyes', and 'Sapphire', but these are doubtfully distinct as cultivars. Often grown in hanging baskets. Zones 9–11.

EXACUM

There are about 25 species of tender annuals, biennials, and perennials in this genus, which is a member of the gentian (Gentianaceae) family and is native to the Old World tropics. The leaves are opposite, oval or elliptic, and often stalkless. Clusters of flowers, sometimes fragrant, are borne on leafy stems. The flowers consist of a narrow tube flaring to 5 flattened petal lobes with protruding yellow stamens.

CULTIVATION: These are popular in temperate regions as pot plants for the house or conservatory. Grow in well-drained but moist potting mix in a well-lit position. These plants can also be grown

Felicia fruticosa

outdoors as a bedding annual but they are suitable for permanent outdoor cultivation only in humid tropical and subtropical areas. Propagation is from seed.

Exacum affine
GERMAN VIOLET, PERSIAN VIOLET

⬜ ✿ ↔ 12 in (30 cm)   ↕ 12–18 in (30–45 cm)

A native of the island of Socotra at the mouth of the Red Sea. Annual or short-lived perennial with pointed oval leaves. Small fragrant flowers, ranging in color from sky blue to pale and deep violet, in spring–autumn. Zones 10–12.

FARFUGIUM

This genus of only 2 species belongs to the daisy (Asteraceae) family, and is native to East Asia. The handsome plants are evergreen perennials with large, deep green, kidney-shaped leaves and clusters of yellow daisies from autumn to winter.

CULTIVATION: Members of this genus are hardy, and easily grown in temperate zones in cool, moist, humus-rich soil. They will grow in damp areas but prefer woodland conditions with good drainage. Full sun is tolerated, but foliage will become lusher in partial shade. Good indoor pot plants in colder climates. Propagation is by division in late winter and spring.

Farfugium japonicum
syn. *Ligularia tussilaginea*

☀ ✿ ↔ 24–40 in (60–100 cm)   ↕ 24–40 in (60–100 cm)

Native to Japan, evergreen herbaceous perennial. The only species usually cultivated. Large, kidney-shaped, rich green leaves. Yellow flowers, widely spaced rays, in winter. 'Argenteum', leaves edged with white; 'Aureomaculatum' ★ (leopard plant), irregular yellow spots on leaf; 'Crispatum' (syn. 'Cristata'), green leaves, crumpled crested edges. Zones 8–11.

FELICIA

This is a genus of about 80 species of annuals, perennials, sub-shrubs, and shrubs belonging to the daisy (Asteraceae) family, mostly evergreen. Most species are from South Africa, with a few species from eastern Africa and Arabia. Preferring open, sunny, low-humidity areas, most species need frost-free conditions. These plants are grown for their mainly blue flowerheads with yellow disc florets. Mauve, pink, and white forms are also available, as are some new cultivars. The shrubby forms are popular as annual container and patio plants, and will overwinter in a greenhouse in colder areas.

CULTIVATION: Members of this genus grow outdoors in moderately fertile soil, but prolonged damp conditions can kill them. When grown in containers they need a loam-based compost with added grit for drainage. The flowering season can be prolonged by removing dead flowers. Propagation is from seed sown in spring, or by taking stem-tip cuttings in summer and overwintering them in frost-free conditions.

Felicia amelloides

syns *Agathaea coelestis*, *Felicia aethiopica*
BLUE DAISY, BLUE MARGUERITE

☼ ⁑ ↔ 24 in (60 cm) ↑ 16–24 in (40–60 cm)
South African perennial, trailing and/or up-right stems. Fine-haired leaves light green. Solitary flowers, vivid yellow disc florets, light to dark blue ray florets. Summer-flowering. '**Blue Eyes**', deep blue flowers; '**Santa Anita**', heavy flowering, hardier. Zones 9–10.

Felicia fruticosa

☼ ⁑ ↔ 36 in (90 cm) ↑ 36 in (90 cm)
Evergreen species, native to South Africa. Linear leaves densely packed. Ray florets pink, purple, or white, with yellow disc. Fruits are hairy. Lengthy flowering season through spring–summer; can be extended by dead-heading. Zones 9–11.

Fittonia albivenis 'Nana'

FILIPENDULA

DROPWORT, MEADOWSWEET

This genus in the rose (Rosaceae) family has about 10 species of tuberous clump-forming perennials. They are native to northern temperate regions, where they are usually found growing in damp habitats. These tall attractive plants have large divided leaves, and bear plumes of tiny white or pink flowers.
CULTIVATION: Grow in part-shade in moist humus-rich soil that does not dry out in summer. Propagate from seed or by division.

Filipendula purpurea

☼ ❋ ↔ 18 in (45 cm) ↑ 36–48 in (90–120 cm)
Native to Japan. Stems and leaf stalks often purple. Stiff, palmate, dark green leaves. Plumes of small deep pink to purplish red flowers, in summer. Zones 6–9.

Filipendula rubra

QUEEN OF THE PRAIRIE

☼ ❋ ↔ 2 ft (0.6 m) ↑ 3–7 ft (0.9–2 m)
From eastern USA. Vigorous perennial, forming large clumps of deeply divided foliage. Tall stems of peachy pink flowers are borne in plumes in summer. '**Venusta**' ★ (syn. 'Magnifica'), deep rose flowers. Zones 2–9.

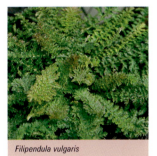

Filipendula vulgaris

Filipendula ulmaria

MEADOWSWEET, QUEEN OF THE MEADOWS

☼ ❋ ↔ 12–18 in (45–60 cm) ↑ 24–48 in (60–120 cm)
From Europe and Western Asia. Clump-forming perennial. Stems tinged red to purple. Large divided leaves, dark green uppersurface, paler-colored and hairy underside. Showy plumes of creamy white fragrant flowers in summer. '**Aurea**', golden yellow foliage; '**Flore Pleno**', double white flowers; '**Rosea**', soft pink flowers; '**Variegata**', dark green leaves with bright yellow central marking. Zones 3–9.

Filipendula vulgaris

syn. *Filipendula hexapetala*
DROPWORT

☼ ❋ ↔ 18 in (45 cm) ↑ 24–36 in (60–90 cm)
From Europe and northern and central Asia. Tuberous with deeply cut fern-like leaves. Small white flowers, often tinged reddish purple, borne in feathery heads in summer. Zones 3–9.

FITTONIA

Usually seen as house plants, the 2 species of low, spreading, evergreen perennial in this tropical South American genus belong to the acanthus (Acanthaceae) family. The plants form a mat of stems that root as they creep across the ground. The stems and undersides of the oval leaves are downy. The foliage is the main attraction, not the rather inconspicuous spikes of tiny creamy white flowers. The leaves are deep green to olive, sometimes red-tinted, with pink to red, or silvery white veins.
CULTIVATION: These do not tolerate prolonged cool conditions, let alone frost; they need a warm, humid, draft-free environment with moist, well-drained, humus-rich soil. They thrive in terrariums and are easily propagated by removing small rooted pieces.

Fittonia albivenis

MOSAIC PLANT

☼ ✦ ↔ 12–24 in (30–60 cm) ↑ 6 in (15 cm)
From Ecuador, Peru, and the western edge of Brazil. Mat-forming, with stems rooting at nodes. Leaves broadly rounded at tip, dark green with network of contrasting veins. Flowers small, cream, for much of the year. '**Nana**', smaller leaves. **Argyroneura Group** (syns *F. argyroneura*, *F. verschaffeltii* var. *argyroneura*), leaves deep green, veined white or faintly pink. **Verschaffeltii Group** (syn. *F. verschaffeltii*), leaves dark bronzy green, veins pink. Zones 11–12.

GAILLARDIA

BLANKET FLOWER, FIREWHEEL

This genus of around 30 species of annual, biennial, and perennial daisies (family Asteraceae) occurs mainly in southern Canada, USA, and Mexico. In summer and autumn the small plants are covered with 2–4 in (5–10 cm) wide flowerheads. The ray florets are typically red at the center with a yellow outer half. Garden forms occur in a range of warm tones.
CULTIVATION: Hardiness varies with the species. Plant in a sunny open position with gritty well-drained soil that remains moist during the growing season. Deadhead on a regular basis. Propagate from seed or basal cuttings, or by division.

Gaillardia aristata

☼ ❈ ↔ 32 in (80 cm) ↕ 20 in (50 cm)

Perennial, widespread in western North America. Very hairy stems and leaves, with basal leaves to 8 in (20 cm) long. Narrow lance-shaped leaves may have small basal lobes and/or toothed edges. Flowerheads to 4 in (10 cm) wide with ray florets no more than 1 in (25 mm) long, yellow or yellow with red base; disc florets usually same color as base of ray florets. **Zones 6–10.**

Gaillardia × grandiflora

☼ ❈ ↔ 40 in (100 cm) ↕ 24 in (60 cm)

Garden hybrid between *G. aristata* and *G. pulchella*. 'Burgunder' (syn. 'Burgundy'), deep red flowers; 'Dazzler', 12 in (30 cm) tall, red ray florets tipped golden yellow; 'Indian Yellow', bright golden yellow flowers; Goblin/'Kobold' ★, 16 in (40 cm) tall, red ray florets with yellow border; 'Gaiety' and 'Monarch', hybrids and double-flowered forms in mixed red and gold shades. **Zones 5–10.**

Gaillardia pulchella

☼ ❈ ↔ 16 in (40 cm) ↕ 24 in (60 cm)

Fast-growing hairy annual from northeastern Mexico and neighboring parts of eastern and central USA. Leaves to over 3 in (8 cm) long, sometimes lobed and/or toothed. Flowerheads around 2½ in (6 cm) wide, ray florets yellow, red, or red with yellow tips. 'Lollipop', to 18 in (45 cm) tall, yellow, red, and orange; 'Red Plume',

Gaillardia × grandiflora Goblin/'Kobold'

12–18 in (30–45 cm) tall, red double flowers; 'Yellow Plume', 12–18 in (30–45 cm) tall, yellow double flowers. **Zones 8–10.**

GALIUM

BEDSTRAW, CLEAVERS, WOODRUFF

A widespread genus in the madder (Rubiaceae) family with around 400 species of often sprawling annuals and perennials, this includes a few useful species and some rather persistent weeds. Plants are characterized by weak angular stems that spread through surrounding growth and may adhere to it by sticky coatings and/or fine hooked hairs. The small bright green leaves are sometimes in opposite pairs but more often in distinct whorls at intervals. Tiny white or yellow flowers, either solitary or in small clusters, appear in the leaf axils and at the stem tips.
CULTIVATION: Hardiness varies; most thrive in temperate climates. Easily grown in any well-drained soil in full sun or half-sun. Mostly propagated from seed; perennials also by division.

Galium odoratum

syn. *Asperula odorata*

SWEET WOODRUFF, WOODRUFF

☼ ❈ ↔ 36 in (90 cm) ↕ 18 in (45 cm)

The most attractive species. Aromatic carpet-forming perennial from Europe and North Africa. Stiff, narrow, prickly, elliptic leaves, to 2 in (5 cm) long, and with rough margins, in 6 to 8 neat whorls. Fragrant white flowers, 1½ in (35 mm) across, in terminal clusters, in spring–summer. **Zones 3–9.**

Galium verum

OUR LADY'S BEDSTRAW, YELLOW BEDSTRAW

☼ ❈ ↔ 3 ft (0.9 m) ↕ 3–4 ft (0.9–1.2 m)

Clump-forming perennial from North America, Europe, and Asia. Small narrow leaves, to 1¼ in (30 mm) long, in whorls of 6 or 8, rough margins rolled under and tipped with bristles. Dense spikes of small, star-shaped, bright yellow flowers in summer–autumn. Can be invasive and weedy. **Zones 2–10.**

GAURA

The 21 annual and perennial species in this North American genus are well worth growing. Members of the evening primrose (Onagraceae) family, they generally form a clump of irregularly shaped basal leaves from which emerge wiry stems bearing graceful, airy, 4-petalled, white to soft pink flowers. The stems may be more than 36 in (90 cm) tall and appear throughout the warmer months. Various pink-flowered and dwarf cultivars are available.
CULTIVATION: *Gaura* species prefer full sun with light, gritty, well-drained soil. While drought-tolerant, they flower better with summer moisture. Deadhead routinely and cut back hard after flowering. Propagate from seed in autumn and spring, or from basal cuttings in summer.

Gaura lindheimeri

☼/☀ ❈ ↔ 40 in (100 cm) ↕ 48–60 in (120–150 cm)

Vigorous heavy-flowering perennial from Texas and Louisiana, USA. Forms a clump of upright stems with narrow, elliptical, toothed leaves to 4 in (10 cm) long. Sprays of pink-tinted white

Gaura lindheimeri 'Whirling Butterflies'

flowers to over 1 in (25 mm) wide, upper petals large and wing-like, in spring–summer. **'Corrie's Gold'**, foliage edged in golden yellow; **'Karalee Petite'**, 24 in (60 cm) tall, deep pink flowers; **'Siskiyou Pink'**, bright pink flowers; **'Whirling Butterflies'**, 24 in (60 cm) tall, heavy-blooming, large flowers. Zones 5–9.

GAZANIA
TREASURE FLOWER

The 16 species of annuals and perennials belonging to this genus in the daisy (Asteraceae) family are found mainly in South Africa, with 1 species extending the range to the tropics. They are low, near-evergreen, clump-forming plants with simple, narrow, lance-shaped, sometimes downy leaves with paler undersides. Their flowers, which appear throughout the warmer months, are large, brightly colored, often interestingly marked, and always showy. While the species usually have yellow or orange flowers, garden forms are available in a large color range.
CULTIVATION: Apart from being somewhat frost tender and resenting wet winters, they are easily grown in any open sunny position with gritty very free-draining soil. They appreciate additional humus but will grow in poor dry soils. Propagation is by division, or from basal cuttings or seed.

Gazania, Hybrid Cultivar, 'Christopher Lloyd'

Gazania rigens
TREASURE FLOWER

☀ ❄ ↔ 40 in (100 cm) ↑ 8 in (20 cm)

Perennial with fleshy stems that strike root as they spread, forming large leafy clump. Leaves to over 4 in (10 cm) long, smooth-edged or near-pinnately lobed, deep green to bronze above, white hair below. Long-stemmed flowerheads to 3 in (8 cm) wide, ray florets orange with black base, disc florets yellow or reddish orange. *G. r.* var. *uniflora*, small flowerheads, yellow ray florets, and silvery foliage. *G. r.* **'Variegata'**, foliage variegated with gold or cream, orange flowers. Zones 9–11.

Gazania Hybrid Cultivars

☀ ❄ ↔ 20 in (50 cm) ↑ 4–6 in (10–15 cm)

There is a wide variety of garden forms, sizes, and flower colors. **'Aztec'**, soft silvery gray foliage, white ray florets shading to purple-brown at the center; **'Aztec Queen'**, yellow ray florets with red-brown base; **'Blackberry Ripple'**, buff ray florets with purple midstripe; **'Bronze Gnome'**, compact, bronze double flowers; **'Christopher Lloyd'**, ray florets light red, darkening near center, green base; **'Cookei'**, silvery gray foliage, burnt orange petals shading to taupe toward center; **'Copper King'**, large copper-red flowers; **'Cream Dream'**, silver-gray foliage, cream ray florets with green base; **'Fiesta Red'**, rusty red ray florets with orange base; **'Michael'**, dark foliage, yellow ray florets with black base; **'Moonglow'**, golden double flowers. Also available as mixed color seedling strains: **Chansonette Series**, early-flowering; **Daybreak** and **Mini-star Series**, compact; **Talent Series**, gray-leafed. Zones 9–11.

GENLISEA
CORKSCREW PLANT

This genus of carnivorous plants belonging to the bladderwort (Lentibulariaceae) family has about 15 species. They come from Africa, Madagascar, and South America, growing in very wet soils along watercourses and in swampy savannahs. These small perennial plants produce 2 types of leaves: green spoon-shaped or lance-shaped leaves above the ground and carnivorous corkscrew-like leaves below ground. These carnivorous leaves fork into 2 prongs, at the base of which is a mouth in which very small prey are captured. Once inside the mouth, the prey cannot escape because inward-pointing hairs block their way, forcing them up through the trap into the digestive chamber.

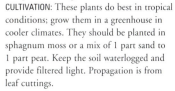

CULTIVATION: These plants do best in tropical conditions; grow them in a greenhouse in cooler climates. They should be planted in sphagnum moss or a mix of 1 part sand to 1 part peat. Keep the soil waterlogged and provide filtered light. Propagation is from leaf cuttings.

Genlisea violacea

☀ ❄ ↔ 2 in (5 cm) ↑ 1 in (2.5 cm)

Native of Brazil. Dense rosettes of green, 1 in (2.5 cm) long, spoon-shaped leaves. Violet-like flowers on 4 in (10 cm) leafless stalks. Zones 9–12.

GENTIANA
GENTIAN

This genus has around 400 widely distributed species of annuals, biennials, and perennials and is the type genus for its family, the Gentianaceae. Most form a compact clump of simple pointed leaves, sometimes in rosettes. The trumpet- or bell-shaped flowers may be blue, white, cream, yellow, or purple.
CULTIVATION: Gentians prefer a climate with distinct seasons and grow best in full sun/half-sun with moist, well-drained, humus-rich soil, perhaps with a little dolomite lime. The small species thrive in rockeries. Propagate by division or from seed.

Gentiana acaulis

☼ ✳ ↔ 12 in (30 cm) ↑ 4 in (10 cm)

Found from Spain to the Balkans. Perennial. Clump of short-stemmed, 1 in (25 mm) long, elliptical leaves in basal rosettes. Solitary, deep blue, green-spotted, flared bell-shaped flowers to 2 in (5 cm) long. Spring- to early summer-flowering. 'Rannoch', 2 in (5 cm) tall, dark-centered, deep blue flowers with fine green and/or white stripes. Zones 3–9.

Gentiana asclepiadea

WILLOW GENTIAN

☼ ✳ ↔ 24–40 in (60–100 cm) ↑ 16 in (40 cm)

Eurasian herbaceous perennial with arching stems to 24 in (60 cm) long. Finely tapering, 2–3 in (5–8 cm) long, oval to lance-shaped leaves. Narrow bell-shaped flowers to 1¼ in (30 mm) long, in clusters of 2 to 3 in leaf axils, mauve to purple-blue with darker spotting. Summer- to autumn-flowering. Zones 6–9.

Gentiana saxosa

☼ ❄ ↔ 12 in (30 cm) ↑ 8 in (20 cm)

Near-prostrate herbaceous perennial from New Zealand. Rosettes of purple-tinted, spatula-shaped, basal leaves, to more than 1¼ in (30 mm) long. Short upright flower stems with purple-veined, white, open bell-shaped flowers, solitary or in small heads. Summer-flowering. Zones 8–9.

Gentiana septemfida ★

☼ ✳ ↔ 16 in (40 cm) ↑ 12 in (30 cm)

Native to western and central Asia. Perennial with spreading, sometimes upright stems. Paired pointed oval leaves to nearly 1¾ in (40 mm) long and clusters of light-spotted, bright blue, bell-shaped flowers, to 1¾ in (40 mm) long. Summer- to autumn-flowering. *G. s.* var. *lagodechiana*, branching stems, solitary flowers. Zones 3–9.

Gentiana sino-ornata

☼ ✳ ↔ 12 in (30 cm) ↑ 6 in (15 cm)

Spreading perennial from western China and Tibet. Stems root as they spread. Loose rosettes of narrow lance-shaped leaves to more than 1¼ in (30 mm) long. Solitary, vivid blue, funnel-shaped flowers, to more than 2 in (5 cm) long, lighter inside, with purple and white bands. Autumn-flowering. Zones 6–9.

Gentiana verna

☼ ✳ ↔ 8–12 in (20–30 cm) ↑ 2 in (5 cm)

Prostrate European perennial. Leaves bright green, oval, to 1 in (25 mm) long. Starry vivid blue flowers, pale-centered, usually solitary, to 1 in (25 mm) wide, in spring–summer. Zones 5–9.

GERANIUM

CRANESBILL

The plants often called geraniums in fact belong in the genus *Pelargonium*. While both genera are members of the geranium (Geraniaceae) family, true geraniums are a very different group of some 300 species of perennials and subshrubs, sometimes evergreen, that are widespread in temperate zones. Their leaves, usually palmately lobed, with toothed lobes, are often finely hairy. They bloom in summer and have simple, flat, 5-petalled flowers in pink or purple-blue shades, less commonly white or purple-black. The flowers develop into long narrow fruits.
CULTIVATION: Most species are hardy and will grow in a range of conditions, preferring full sun or half-sun and moist humus-rich soil. The rhizomes can be invasive. Propagate from seed, cuttings, or by division. May self-sow.

Geranium × cantabrigiense

◐/☼ ✳ ↔ 24 in (60 cm) ↑ 8 in (20 cm)

A low spreading *G. macrorrhizum* × *G. dalmaticum* hybrid. Aromatic, bright green, rounded leaves, to 3 in (8 cm) wide, divided into 7 toothed lobes. Flowers to 1 in (25 mm) wide, pink or white with pink center. 'Biokovo', pink-flushed white flowers; 'Cambridge', deep pink to magenta flowers. Zones 5–9.

Geranium cinereum

◐/☼ ✳ ↔ 20 in (50 cm) ↑ 6 in (15 cm)

Found in southern Europe and Turkey. Spreading perennial, rosettes of 5- to 7-lobed gray-green leaves, to 2 in (5 cm) wide. Small heads of often dark-veined white to deep pink flowers, to 1 in (25 mm) wide. 'Purple Pillow', very compact habit, striking funnel-shaped purple-red flowers. Zones 5–9.

Geranium dalmaticum

◐/☼ ✳ ↔ 20 in (50 cm) ↑ 6 in (15 cm)

Small slow-spreading native of Albania and southwest Balkans. Glossy 5- to 7-lobed leaves, to 1¾ in (40 mm) wide. Airy sprays

Gentiana acaulis

Geranium × cantabrigiense

Geranium dalmaticum

of bright pink 5-petalled flowers to more than 1¼ in (30 mm) wide, in summer. Zones 5–9.

Geranium endressii

☼/☽ ❄ ↔ 24 in (60 cm) ↑ 18 in (45 cm)
Long-flowering evergreen perennial from the Pyrenees. Basal leaves 5-lobed, to 6 in (15 cm) wide, upper leaves 3- to 5-lobed and smaller. Foliage reddens in winter. Heads of dark-veined bright pink flowers to 1¾ in (40 mm) wide. '**Beholder's Eye**', good for use as ground cover, dark pink flowers; '**Castle Drogo**', pink flowers with large petals that overlap each other. Zones 5–9.

Geranium himalayense

☼/☽ ❄ ↔ 40 in (100 cm) ↑ 18 in (45 cm)
Found from northern Afghanistan to Nepal. Spreading habit with hairy stems and leaves. Basal leaves to 8 in (20 cm) wide, 7-lobed and toothed, upper leaves considerably smaller. Airy sprays of deep purple-blue flowers, to more than 2 in (5 cm) wide, often pink- or white-centered. '**Baby Blue**', compact habit, vivid bright blue flowers; '**Gravetye**' (syn. 'Alpinum'), intense blue flowers, red-tinted autumn foliage; '**Plenum**' (syn.'Birch Double'), compact habit, small leaves, purple-blue double flowers. Zones 4–9.

Geranium incanum

☼/☽ ❄ ↔ 40 in (100 cm) ↑ 40 in (100 cm)
Evergreen South African species, with branching main stems; long-stemmed, aromatic, bright green leaves, sometimes paired, finely cut into 5 narrow toothed lobes, downy white undersides. Airy sprays of long-stemmed, light-centered, magenta flowers to more than 1¼ in (30 mm) wide. Zones 8–11.

Geranium macrorrhizum

☼/☽ ❄ ↔ 40 in (100 cm) ↑ 20 in (50 cm)
Spreading clump-forming perennial native to southern Europe. The leaves are 4–8 in (10–20 cm) wide, with 5 to 7 lobes, toothed and further divided. Flower stems to 12 in (30 cm) tall. Densely clustered heads of pink to purple-red flowers in summer. '**Album**', white flowers with red-tinted sepals; '**Bevan's Variety**', small leaves, bright magenta flowers; '**Czakor**', low-growing, magenta flowers with dark sepals; '**Ingwersen's Variety**', light glossy green leaves, pale pink flowers. Zones 4–9.

Geranium phaeum

Geranium maculatum

☼/☽ ❄ ↔ 40 in (100 cm) ↑ 27 in (70 cm)
Bushy North American perennial found from Manitoba, Canada, to Kansas, USA. Basal leaves to 8 in (20 cm) wide, upper leaves to 4 in (10 cm) wide, 5- to 7-lobed, further divided and toothed. Heads of upward-facing deep pink flowers, to 1¾ in (40 mm) wide, in late spring–summer. Zones 4–9.

Geranium maderense

Geranium maderense

☼/☽ ❄ ↔ 60 in (150 cm) ↑ 60 in (150 cm)
This native of Madeira is regarded as the largest geranium. Shrubby habit with rosettes of deeply lobed and divided leathery leaves, to 12 in (30 cm) wide, long purple-tinted stalks. Large, hairy, purple-stemmed flowerheads with many dark-veined deep pink to magenta flowers, to 1¾ in (40 mm) wide. Zones 9–11.

Geranium × magnificum

☼/☽ ❄ ↔ 40 in (100 cm) ↑ 20 in (50 cm)
Garden hybrid. Leaves to 4 in (10 cm) wide, 9- to 11-lobed, toothed; hairy stems. Heads of dark-veined purple flowers to more than 1¾ in (40 mm) wide, in mid-summer. Zones 5–9.

Geranium × oxonianum

☼/☽ ❄ ↔ 48 in (120 cm) ↑ 24 in (60 cm)
Hybrid between *G. endressii* and *G. versicolor*. Spreads to cover large area. Leaves with 5 fairly shallow lobes, 2–4 in (5–10 cm) wide, sometimes larger. Masses of dark-veined light pink flowers to 1 in (25 mm) wide. *G. × o.* f. *thurstonianum,* deep purple-pink flowers, thin petals. *G. × o.* '**A. T. Johnson**', pale silvery pink flowers; '**Claridge Druce**', vigorous, hairy stems, dark leaves, deep pink flowers; '**Rose Clair**', small with purple to pink flowers; '**Sherwood**', starry flowers with very narrow pale pink petals; '**Wargrave Pink**', many soft orange-pink flowers. Zones 5–9.

Geranium phaeum

BLACK WIDOW
☼/☽ ❄ ↔ 16 in (40 cm) ↑ 32 in (80 cm)
Upright, bushy, European perennial with 9-lobed leaves, larger at the base. Heads of 1 in (25 mm) wide flowers, mauve, maroon, to dark purple-red, sometimes near-black. '**Album**' ★, large white flowers; '**Lily Lovell**', large purple flowers. Zones 5–9.

Geranium pratense 'Mrs Kendall Clark'

Geranium sylvaticum

Geranium, Hybrid Cultivar, 'Patricia'

Geranium pratense
MEADOW CRANESBILL

☼/◐ ❄ ↔ 40 in (100 cm) ↕ 48 in (120 cm)

Sturdy spreading perennial found from central Europe to western Himalayas. Upright stems, leaves 4–8 in (10–20 cm) wide, 7 to 9 deep pinnate lobes, toothed. Flowerheads crowded to rather open; blue flowers to 2 in (50 mm) wide. '**Mrs Kendall Clark**', pale flowers with translucent veins; '**Splish-splash**', pale flowers randomly sectored and flecked with light purple-blue. Zones 5–9.

Geranium psilostemon

☼/◐ ❄ ↔ 16–24 in (40–60 cm) ↕ 24–40 in (60–100 cm)

Upright slightly spreading perennial from northeastern Turkey. Leaves 2–8 in (5–20 cm) wide, deeply lobed, and further divided. Erect heads of black-centered magenta flowers, to over 1¼ in (30 mm) wide. Zones 6–9.

Geranium × riversleaianum

☼/◐ ❄ ↔ 24 in (60 cm) ↕ 4 in (10 cm)

Garden hybrid. Low spreading habit with small, 7-lobed, bronze green leaves. Open heads of dark-veined, funnel-shaped, pink flowers, to more than 1¼ in (30 mm) wide. '**Mavis Simpson**', light-centered flowers; '**Russell Prichard**', deep pink flowers, sharply toothed leaves. Zones 7–10.

Geranium sanguineum
BLOODY CRANESBILL

☼/◐ ❄ ↔ 16 in (40 cm) ↕ 8 in (20 cm)

Low, slowly spreading, bushy Eurasian perennial. Leaves 2–4 in (5–10 cm) wide, 5- to 7-lobed, further divided. Many flowers, borne singly, magenta to purple-red, to over 1¼ in (30 mm) wide. *G. s.* var. *striatum* is small plant with dark-veined soft pink flowers, of which '**Splendens**' is taller form. *G. s.* Alan Bloom/ 'Bloger', small leaves, compact habit, deep magenta flowers; '**Album**', white flowers; '**Max Frei**', similar to Alan Bloom/'Bloger' but darker foliage, longer flower stems. Zones 5–9.

Geranium sylvaticum

◐ ❄ ↔ 40 in (100 cm) ↕ 27 in (70 cm)

Native to Europe and northern Turkey, usually growing in moist places. Leaves finely hairy, 2–8 in (5–20 cm) wide, 7 to 9 deep lobes, further divided and toothed. Dense heads of usually mauve-blue but sometimes white to magenta flowers, to 1¼ in (30 mm) wide. '**Album**', pure white flowers; '**Mayflower**', purplish blue flowers with pale centers. Zones 4–9.

Geranium wallichianum

☼/◐ ❄ ↔ 24 in (60 cm) ↕ 6 in (15 cm)

Spreading mountain perennial found from northeastern Afghanistan to Kashmir. Paired, 3- to 5-lobed, deeply divided and toothed leaves, about 3 in (8 cm) wide, often long-stemmed. Bowl-shaped, light-centered, magenta or light purple flowers, to over 1¼ in (30 mm) wide. '**Buxton's Variety**' ★ (syn. 'Buxton's Blue'), prostrate habit and light-centered bright mauve-blue flowers. Zones 7–10.

Geranium Hybrid Cultivars

☼/◐ ❄ ↔ 24–48 in (60–120 cm) ↕ 8–36 in (20–90 cm)

Geraniums tend to sport readily and interbreed freely, so there are many garden forms in assorted sizes and flower colors. '**Ann Folkard**', trailing habit, yellow-green foliage, magenta flowers with dark-center; '**Ballerina**', red-veined purple-pink flowers, notched petal tips; '**Frances Grate**', silvery foliage, reddish purple flowers; '**Johnson's Blue**' ★, 18 in (45 cm) tall, bushy to semi-trailing habit, bright blue to purple-blue flowers; '**Nimbus**', 16 in (40 cm) tall, glossy foliage, starry purple flowers; '**Patricia**', spreading, rather open habit with black-centered magenta-pink flowers; '**Philippe Vapelle**', 16 in (40 cm) tall, large leaves, densely foliaged, dark-veined lavender blue flowers; '**Pink Spice**', trailing, dark bronze foliage, small pink flowers; '**Rambling Robin**', mounding, spreading habit, lavender-blue flowers; Rozanne/'Gerwat', to 20 in (50 cm) tall, variegated foliage, large violet-blue flowers; '**Sue Crûg**', bushy habit, mauve-pink flowers, with darker centers and veins. Zones 6–9.

GERBERA
BARBERTON DAISY, TRANSVAAL DAISY

Some 40 species of daisy (Asteraceae) family perennials make up this genus, best known for its winter-flowering South African representatives; other species occur in western and southern Asia. Resembling highly sophisticated dandelions, they have a basal rosette of deeply lobed and softly toothed spatula- to lance-shaped leaves, and from the center of the rosette emerge strong flower stems, each bearing one large daisy head. Available in a wide color range and double flowers.

CULTIVATION: Gerberas are tender but can tolerate light frosts if kept barely moist in winter. Plant in full sun with deep, light, humus-rich soil with added grit for drainage. Popular as a house plant and cut flower. Propagation is from seed or by careful division after flowering.

Gerbera jamesonii ★

BARBERTON DAISY

☼ ❄ ↔ 30 in (75 cm) ↑ 27 in (70 cm)

Native to South Africa and Swaziland. Long-stemmed, deep green, dandelion-like leaves with coarse lobes and finely hairy undersides. Leaves can be more than 24 in (60 cm) long but usually considerably smaller. Flowerheads long-stemmed, to 4 in (10 cm) wide, usually in yellow, orange, or red shades. Zones 8–11.

Gerbera Hybrid Cultivars

☼ ✂ ↔ 12 in (30 cm) ↑ 8–18 in (20–45 cm)

These plants produce a long succession of large flowerheads throughout much of the year, in both pastel and strong colors. **Dwarf Pandora Series**, large single blooms on short stems, in a mix of reds, oranges, yellows, pinks, and whites, usually 3 to 6 open at any one time. **Fantasia Double Series**, very large double blooms with quilled central florets, in a range of soft colors. **Happipot Series**, large blooms in vivid shades, deep green leaves. Zones 9–11.

GEUM

AVENS

This genus in the rose (Rosaceae) family, consisting of around 40 species and perennials, is widely distributed in the temperate regions. The plants are either rosette-forming or spread by rhizomes or runners, with their finely hairy pinnate or lobed leaves arising directly from the roots. From late winter to late summer, depending on the species, they produce flower stems bearing showy flowers that resemble tiny single roses, usually in bright shades of yellow, orange, pink, or red. Bristly dry fruits follow the flowers.

CULTIVATION: The small species are popular for rockeries, while larger forms suit perennial borders. Plant in a sunny position with moist well-drained soil that does not become compacted. Propagate by division when dormant, or raise from seed.

Geum chiloense

☼/◐ ❄ ↔ 20 in (50 cm) ↑ 30 in (75 cm)

Heavy-flowering Chilean perennial that has been extensively developed in cultivation. Basal rosette of long leaves divided into many toothed 1 in (25 mm) lobes. Erect flower stems with terminal panicles of bright red flowers. Summer-flowering. 'Farncombe', orange-yellow, semi-double, upward facing flowers; 'Werner Arends' (syn. 'Borisii'), many light orange-red semi-double flowers. Zones 5–9.

Geum chiloense
'Werner Arends'

Geum montanum

ALPINE AVENS

☼/◐ ❄ ↔ 20 in (50 cm) ↑ 12 in (30 cm)

Native to the mountains of central and southern Europe. Creeping rhizome-rooted perennial. Rosettes of bright green pinnate leaves, to 6 in (15 cm) long, large terminal leaflet making up half that length. Small heads of bright yellow flowers, to more than 1 in (25 mm) wide, in spring–early summer. Zones 6–9.

Geum rivale

INDIAN CHOCOLATE, WATER AVENS

☼/◐ ❄ ↔ 30 in (75 cm) ↑ 12 in (30 cm)

Eurasian and North American native forming a small clump and spreading by rhizomes. Slightly pendulous heads of creamy yellow flowers within downy purple-red calyces. Leaves to 12 in (30 cm) long, pinnate, with 7 to 13 toothed leaflets. 'Leonardii' (syn. 'Leonard's Variety'), soft orange-red flowers. Zones 3–9.

Geum triflorum

LION'S BEARD, OLD MAN'S WHISKERS, PRAIRIE SMOKE, PURPLE AVENS

☼/◐ ❄ ↔ 16 in (40 cm) ↑ 16 in (40 cm)

North American species. Ferny leaves, to 6 in (15 cm) long, gray-green, sometimes very downy. Flower stems to 16 in (40 cm) tall, with clusters of small, maroon-tinted, yellow flowers. Zones 6–9.

Geum Hybrid Cultivars

☼/◐ ❄ ↔ to 36 in (90 cm) ↑ 36 in (90 cm)

Geums hybridize freely. 'Beech House Apricot', flower stems to 8 in (20 cm), light yellow to apricot flowers; 'Coppertone', pale-apricot flowers; 'Fire Opal', 30 in (75 cm) tall, semi-double orange-red flowers; 'Lady Stratheden', 24 in (60 cm) tall, bright yellow double flowers; 'Mrs J. Bradshaw' ★, 24 in (60 cm) tall, bright red semi-double flowers; 'Starker's Magnificum', flower stems to 16 in (40 cm), flowers soft orange-pink; 'Tangerine', 5 in (12 cm) flower stems, bright orange flowers. Zones 6–9.

Gerbera Hybrid Cultivar

GILLENIA

This North American genus of 2 species of rhizome-rooted perennials belongs to the rose (Rosaceae) family. They form shrubby
clumps of upright, arching, branching stems bearing stemless
trifoliate leaves with toothed leaflets that turn orange in autumn.
Loose sprays of 5-petalled flowers appear from spring to summer,
with calyces that last long after the flowers have fallen, enlarging
and reddening as the small seed heads develop.
CULTIVATION: These are very hardy but do best when protected
from hot sun. They are easily grown in dappled light and moist,
humus-rich, well-drained soil. Propagate from stratified seed,
or by dividing established clumps as they
enter or leave dormancy in autumn or spring.

Gillenia trifoliata
BOWMAN'S ROOT, INDIAN PHYSIC

☀ ❄ ↔ 48 in (120 cm) ↑ 48 in (120 cm)
Found in eastern North America, from
Ontario to Georgia. Leaves with serrated
pointed oval leaflets to nearly 3 in (8 cm)
long. Flowers to 1 in (25 mm) wide, white,
sometimes pink- or purple-tinted. Zones 4–9.

GLAUCIUM
HORNED POPPY, SEA POPPY

This genus in the poppy (Papaveraceae) family has around
25 species of annuals, biennials, and perennials and is found from
Europe to North Africa, central and western Asia, often in coastal
areas. They are similar in general appearance to poppies but are
clearly differentiated by the long horn-shaped seed capsules that
follow the flowers. Most species have blue-green leaves, toothed
and often pinnately lobed, in a basal rosette. Upright, sometimes
branching flower stems with small leaves emerge from the rosette
in summer, and carry 4-petalled flowers, usually 2–4 in (5–10 cm)
wide, in warm shades of yellow, orange, or red.
CULTIVATION: These plants are hardy to moderate frosts and are
very easily grown in any temperate climate with reasonably warm
summers. Plant in full sun with light, rather gritty, free-draining

Gloxinia sylvatica

soil. Most species, even the perennial ones, are propagated
from seed and may self-sow, though rarely invasively.

Glaucium flavum
YELLOW-HORNED POPPY

☀ ❄ ↔ 16 in (40 cm) ↑ 40 in (100 cm)
Biennial or short-lived perennial from Europe, North Africa,
and the Middle East. Hairy, pinnately lobed, toothed, blue-green
leaves. Branching stems with bright yellow or orange flowers, to
2 in (5 cm) wide. Narrow curved seed pods, to 12 in (30 cm) long.
G. f. f. fulvum, grayish foliage, orange-yellow flowers. Zones 7–10.

Glaucium flavum

GLOBBA

There are about 70 species of tender, fleshy-
stemmed, rhizomatous perennials in this
genus, which is a member of the ginger
(Zingiberaceae) family. They are native to
forested areas of southeastern Asia and northeastern India. The lance-shaped to oblong
leaves are carried on reed-like pseudostems to
3 ft (0.9 m) tall. Pendulous terminal racemes
bear oddly shaped flowers, often spurred,
with protruding stamens and colorful bracts.
CULTIVATION: In warm areas grow these plants outdoors in a shady
well-drained situation. In cooler climates start plants indoors in
spring and place outside after danger of frost has passed, or grow
indoors in bright indirect light with high humidity. Propagate
from the bulbils produced on the flowering stems.

Globba winitii

☀ ◗ ↔ 24 in (60 cm) ↑ 36 in (90 cm)
From Thailand. The most commonly grown species. Long leaves,
heart-shaped bases, hairy beneath. Flowers have magenta bracts
with yellow floral parts. Zones 9–11.

GLOXINIA

Not to be confused with Sinningia, which includes the florist's
gloxinia, this genus of some 8 species of perennials and subshrubs
in the African violet (Gesneriaceae) family occurs in Central
America and tropical South America. They are mostly small plants
that form bushy clumps of stems bearing opposite pairs of simple
pointed oval leaves, often finely toothed. The stems and foliage
are usually covered with fine velvety hairs. Single or paired
funnel- or bell-shaped flowers appear in the leaf axils.
CULTIVATION: These adapt well to pot cultivation and are usually
grown as house or greenhouse plants outside the tropics. They
prefer even warm temperatures, absence of cool drafts, and ample
humidity. Plant in half-sun or full shade in moist, humus-rich,
free-draining soil. Propagate from seeds or stem or leaf cuttings.

Gloxinia perennis

☀ ◗ ↔ 15 in (38 cm) ↑ 24 in (60 cm)
Perennial from Colombia to Peru. Heart-shaped, hairy, toothed
leaves, to 8 in (20 cm) long, pale red underneath. Solitary lower
flowers, upper flowers in racemes with bell-shaped pale purple
corollas, purple-blotched throat, late summer–autumn. Zones 10–12.

Gloxinia sylvatica

◐ ✚ ↔ 24 in (60 cm) ↑ 24 in (60 cm)

Native to Bolivia and Peru. Mounds, then spreads by runners, to become slightly trailing. Lustrous, narrow, lance-shaped leaves. Orange-red to red bell-shaped flowers, to 1 in (25 mm) long, held clear of the foliage in terminal clusters, in cooler months. 'Bolivian Sunset', red flowers with orange interior. Zones 10–12.

GOMPHRENA

Native to tropical parts of the Americas and Australia, the 90-odd annuals and perennials in this genus are members of the amaranth (Amaranthaceae) family. The flowers are borne in small, usually upright, heads. The cultivated species form bushy mounds with leaves that are simple narrow oblongs in opposite pairs. The stems are finely hairy, the leaves less so. The flower-heads are borne on wiry stems and held just above the foliage. Each head is a short plume of many tiny flowers, usually creamy yellow, mauve, or pink in the species. CULTIVATION: Out of the tropics these plants are treated as annuals; they need long warm summers to flower. Plant in moist humus-rich soil and water well; do not overfeed. Propagate from seed.

Gomphrena globosa

BACHELOR'S BUTTON, GLOBE AMARANTH

☀ ✳ ↔ 18 in (45 cm) ↑ 24 in (60 cm)

From Panama and Guatemala. Bushy annual with slightly hairy pointed leaves. Flowers papery and round, white through to red, purple, and yellow, in summer. 'Lavender Lady', lavender-colored flowers; 'Strawberry Fields', flowers scarlet to crimson. Zones 7–11.

GUNNERA

There are 40 to 50 species of fleshy stemmed perennials in this genus in the family Gunneraceae. They are native to Australasia, South Africa, South America, and the Pacific. Species range from tiny ground huggers to spectacular giants of 7 ft (2 m) or more. Grown for their foliage, which may be round to oval, heart-shaped or deeply lobed, with or without toothed margins. Tiny greenish yellow or red flowers are borne on spikes in summer, and followed by red, orange, yellow, or white berries. CULTIVATION: These are excellent plants for waterside planting. Grow in moisture-retentive soils in full sun. Cover the crowns of large species with a protective mulch in winter. Propagate from seed or by division.

Gunnera manicata

syn. *Gunnera brasiliensis*

GIANT RHUBARB

☀ ✳ ↔ 10–15 ft (3–4.5 m) ↑ 6–10 ft (1.8–3 m)

Spectacular species from South America. Rhubarb-like leaves, 7 ft (2 m) or more across, sharply toothed, spiny beneath. Tiny greenish red flowers on erect spikes 3–6 ft (0.9–1.8 m) tall. Zones 7–9.

Gunnera prorepens

☀ ✳ ↔ 12–18 in (30–45 cm) ↑ 2–4 in (5–10 cm)

Mat-forming stoloniferous perennial from New Zealand. Small, round-toothed, ovate leaves, bronze to purplish green. Male and

Gunnera manicata

female flowers on separate plants; the female plants bear short spikes of dense red berries after flowering. Zones 8–10.

GUZMANIA

This genus of about 200 usually epiphytic species and more than 200 hybrids belongs to the bromeliad (Bromeliaceae) family. The plants are found mainly in Ecuador and Colombia and also in Central America and the West Indies. They grow up to 40 in (100 cm) high and wide but are mostly smaller, with green, spineless, strap-like leaves, sometimes finely lined or cross-banded on the undersides, forming an open rosette. The flower stem is usually conspicuous and the flowerhead is globular to cylindrical, with side branches and flowers on all sides. Beneath each branch or flower there are generally brilliantly colored bracts in yellow to orange to red shades. Petals are white or yellow. CULTIVATION: Recommended for indoor culture if in flower, for greenhouse in cool-temperate areas, or outdoors with protection from continuous sunlight and excessive heat in warm-temperate, subtropical, and tropical areas. Prefers a damp atmosphere and a constant warm temperature. Water when potting mix is dry. Do not over-fertilize. Propagate from seed or offsets.

Guzmania lingulata

◐ ✚ ↔ 8 in (20 cm) ↑ 12 in (30 cm)

Widespread from the West Indies and Central America to Bolivia and Brazil. Leaves 18 in (45 cm) long, forming a dense spreading rosette. Flower stem usually shorter than leaves. Flowerhead globular with up to 50 flowers, petals white, nestling in a bed of large red to pink bracts. *G. l.* var. *cardinalis* has bright red hooded bracts, foliage often striped. *G. l.* 'Estrella', orange-red flowerhead; 'Empire', smaller form with orange-red star-shaped flowerhead; 'Fortuna', white-tipped brilliant red bracts; 'Rondo', similar to 'Empire' but with red-striped leaves. Zones 10–12.

Guzmania musaica

↔16 in (40 cm) ↑20 in (50 cm)

From Panama and Colombia. Strap-like leaves, to 27 in (70 cm) long, can be totally green on both sides, or green on top and purple beneath, or with fine, dark, irregular, transverse lines, forming an open rosette. Flower stem shorter than leaves. Spherical flowerhead, with up to 25 white flowers mainly pointing upward. Below each flower is a small red bract. Zones 10–12.

Guzmania wittmackii

↔36 in (90 cm) ↑30 in (75 cm)

From Colombia and Ecuador. Green strap-like leaves, 32 in (80 cm) long, forming an open funnel-shaped rosette. Flower stem equal in length to leaves. Flowerhead long and slender with very small branches. Below each branch is a long thin bract, to 3 in (8 cm) long, which can be red, orange, white, or even green. Flowers have long white petal tube, about 3 in (8 cm) long. Zones 10–12.

Guzmania, Hybrid Cultivar, 'Grand Prix'

Guzmania Hybrid Cultivars

↔10–24 in (25–60 cm) ↑18–36 in (45–90 cm)

Most of these have brilliantly colored and large inflorescence bracts. **'Amaranth'**, green leaves with brownish lines on undersides, intense raspberry-purple flower bracts, petals white; **'Attila'**, dark green rosette, red bracts, yellow flowers; **'Caroline'**, bright green rosette, pinkish red bracts; **'Cherry'**, leaves reddish green with faint striping at the base, vibrant cherry red bracts, yellow flowers. **'Cherry Smash'**, **'Grand Prix'** ★, **'Grapeade'**, **'Orangeade'**, and **'Samba'**, similar but have different-colored bracts. Some forms also have variegated leaves. Zones 9–12.

GYNURA

VELVET PLANT

This genus of some 50 species of perennials and subshrubs belongs in the daisy (Asteraceae) family and comes from the tropics, ranging from Java through Thailand to China all the way to East Africa. Often brightly colored, the flowers are small. These plants are grown for their handsome velvet-covered foliage.

CULTIVATION: Except in the tropics, where they can be grown outside in part-shade, these plants are usually grown indoors. Propagate from cuttings; fresh young stock grown each year is best.

Gynura aurantiaca

PURPLE VELVET PLANT, ROYAL VELVET PLANT, VELVET PLANT

↔4 ft (1.2 m) ↑7–8 ft (2–2.4 m)

Trailing, soft-wooded, evergreen plant from Java. Rich purple bristles cover the 8 in (20 cm) long, spearhead-shaped, scalloped leaves and stems. Small orange flowers, to 1 in (25 mm) wide, in open clusters, in winter. **'Purple Passion'** (syn. *G. sarmentosa* of gardens), more trailing, stems and leaves covered with purple bristles. Zones 10–12.

GYPSOPHILA

BABY'S BREATH

Related to the pink (Caryophyllaceae) family, the 100-odd annuals and perennials in this genus occur naturally in temperate Eurasia. They can be spreading mat-forming plants studded with pink or white blooms, or upright shrubby species with billowing heads of tiny flowers. Leaves are simple linear to lance-shaped, sometimes rather fleshy, and often blue-green. *G. paniculata* and its cultivars are very popular cut flowers.

CULTIVATION: *Gypsophila* means lime-loving, but most species are happy in any neutral to slightly alkaline soil that is fertile, moist, and well-drained. Mat-forming species are superb rockery plants. Plant in full sun. Larger types will often rebloom if cut back after their first flush. Propagate from basal cuttings or seed.

Gypsophila cerastioides

↔8 in (20 cm) ↑3 in (8 cm)

Mat-forming perennial from the Himalayas. Small, downy, gray-green leaves with small sprays of pink-veined white or mauve flowers to over ½ in (12 mm) wide. Zones 5–9.

Gypsophila repens

Gypsophila paniculata

BABY'S BREATH

☼/◐ ❄ ↔ 48 in (120 cm) ↕ 48 in (120 cm)

Rhizome-rooted perennial found from central Europe to central Asia. Forms a bushy clump of narrow blue-gray leaves to 3 in (8 cm) long, often hidden below billowing panicles massed with tiny white or pink flowers. 'Bristol Fairy' ★, the most widely grown form, has relatively large white double flowers. Zones 4–9.

Gypsophila repens

☼/◐ ❄ ↔ 24 in (60 cm) ↕ 4 in (10 cm)

Mat-forming perennial from the mountains of central and southern Europe. Narrow, pointed oval, blue-green leaves to more than ½ in (12 mm) long. Sprays of up to 25 tiny, white, pink, or mauve flowers. 'Rosa Schönheit' (syn. 'Rose Beauty'), rose pink flowers. Zones 4–9.

Gypsophila 'Rosenschleier'

syn. *Gypsophila* 'Rosy Veil'

☼ ❄ ↔ 36 in (90 cm) ↕ 12 in (30 cm)

Pale pink-flowered hybrid. Blue-green leaves. Zones 4–9.

HEDYCHIUM

GARLAND LILY, GINGER LILY

This genus is a member of the ginger (Zingiberaceae) family and includes some 40 species of perennials with heavy rhizomes from which emerge strong cane-like pseudostems with large leaves like those of canna lilies. Native to tropical Asia, the Himalayan region, and Madagascar, they have naturalized elsewhere and have become troublesome at times, one species being a serious pest in northern New Zealand. Ginger lilies are grown mainly for their colorful and fragrant flowerheads, in which are clustered many slender-tubed flowers with protruding anthers. The flowers appear in summer and are mainly in yellow or pink shades. CULTIVATION: They are mostly tolerant of very light frosts and capable of reshooting from the rootstock. Plant in sun or shade with fertile, moist, humus-rich, well-drained soil. Cut back the spent flower stems and any old, unproductive canes to encourage fresh growth. Propagate by division or from seed.

Hedychium coccineum

RED GINGER LILY, SCARLET GINGER LILY

☼/◐ ❄ ↔ 2–5 ft (0.6–1.5 m) ↕ 7–10 ft (2–3 m)

Himalayan native with very narrow leaves to 20 in (50 cm) long. Heads of pink, orange, or red flowers with similarly colored lower lip and filaments. Autumn-flowering. 'Tara', large spikes of orange flowers. Zones 7–12.

Hedychium coronarium

BUTTERFLY LILY, GARLAND FLOWER, WHITE GINGER

☼/◐ ❄ ↔ 2–5 ft (0.6–1.5 m) ↕ 10 ft (3 m)

Indian species with lance-shaped leaves to 24 in (60 cm) long and a little more than 4 in (10 cm) wide. Heads of very fragrant white butterfly-like flowers with yellow-green markings. Spring-flowering. 'F. W. Moore', soft yellow-brown flowers with orange markings. Zones 8–12.

Hedychium greenei

Hedychium gardnerianum

GINGER LILY, KAHILI GINGER

☼/◐ ❄ ↔ 3–5 ft (0.9–1.5 m) ↕ 8 ft (2.4 m)

Northern Indian and Himalayan native. Leaves to 16 in (40 cm) long. Dense spikes of many cream and yellow flowers with conspicuous red filaments. Summer- to autumn-flowering. Very vigorous species. Zones 8–11.

Hedychium greenei

☼/◐ ❄ ↔ 32–48 in (80–120 cm) ↕ 7 ft (2 m)

Summer-flowering native of Bhutan. Very narrow leaves to 10 in (25 cm) long and bright red flowers in 5 in (12 cm) long spikes. May form bulbils in the leaf axil near flowerheads. Zones 8–12.

HELENIUM

SNEEZEWEED

This mainly North American genus in the daisy (Asteraceae) family contains about 40 species of annuals, biennials, and perennials. Most form an upright foliage clump and have simple lance-shaped leaves, usually covered with fine hairs. From mid-summer into autumn they produce large flowerheads with a central cone of disc florets and large often slightly drooping ray florets. Yellow and orange to red shades are common. CULTIVATION: Hardiness of these plants varies but most species are very frost tolerant. Plant in a sunny, open position in moist, well-drained soil. Regular removal of dead flowers prolongs flowering; alternatively pick the flowers for use as a cut flower to encourage repeat flowering. Propagation is by division, or from basal cuttings or seed.

Helenium autumnale

SNEEZEWEED

☼ ❄ ↔ 3 ft (0.9 m) ↕ 5 ft (1.5 m)

North American perennial making a dense clump of stems with narrow, usually serrated, leaves to 6 in (15 cm) long topped with many 2 in (5 cm) wide, bright yellow to golden flowerheads each with up to 20 reflexed ray florets. 'Sunshine Hybrid' is a seedling strain with yellow, orange, red-brown, and red flowers in a range of color patterns. Zones 3–9.

Helenium, Hybrid Cultivar, 'Waldtraut'

Helenium Hybrid Cultivars

☀ ❀ ↔ 40 in (100 cm) ↕ 40 in (100 cm)

These are heavy-flowering plants usually more compact than the species. '**Moerheim Beauty**', red-brown to red flowers, strongly downward-angled ray florets; Pipsqueak/'**Blopip**', 18 in (45 cm) tall, yellow ray florets and red-brown disc florets; '**Waldtraut**' ★, burnt orange and gold flowers; '**Wyndley**', gold to tawny brown ray florets, brown disc florets. Zones 5–9.

HELIAMPHORA

MARSH PITCHER, SUN PITCHER

A carnivorous genus of 9 known species in the pitcher plant (Sarraceniaceae) family, native to Brazil, Guyana, and Venezuela. They have tubular green to red pitchers that range from 1¾ in (40 mm) to 20 in (50 cm) in height, and most have a small overhanging cap. The pitchers are arranged in a rosette attached to a stem at the base. Insects are attracted to the plant by the bright colors and nectar under the lid of the pitcher. The upper interior of the pitcher is covered in down-ward-pointing hairs, and then it becomes smooth and slippery. Insects slide into the well of water and are digested by the plant.
CULTIVATION: Grow in full sun in sphagnum or a mix of 4 parts peat to 1 part perlite. In very hot weather pots should be placed in shade or in trays of water. Keep soil moist, water over-head, mist regularly. Use a weak liquid fertilizer every couple of weeks. Ideal temperatures are 65–80°F (18–26°C) during the day and 35–50°F (2–10°C) overnight. These plants do well in a cool or warm greenhouse. Propagate by division in spring.

Heliamphora heterodoxa

☀/❁ ❦ ↔ 12 in (30 cm) ↕ 18 in (45 cm)

From Venezuela. Lime green pitchers, usually red toward the top. Pitcher lid green on young plants, red on older ones. Pink and white flowers in early to mid-winter. Easy to grow. Zones 10–12.

Heliamphora minor

☀/❁ ❀ ↔ 6 in (15 cm) ↕ 3 in (8 cm)

From Auyan Tepuis and Chimanta Tepuis in Venezuela. The smallest species. Cone-shaped, green to red, 3 in (8 cm) high pitchers. Emerging pitchers are covered in fine white hairs; older pitchers have hairs along central seam and near rim. Pink flowers in spring. *H. m.* × *heterodoxa*, pale pink flowers. Zones 8–10.

HELIANTHUS

SUNFLOWER

This genus of 70 annuals and perennials in the daisy (Asteraceae) family is from the Americas and is best known for the common or giant sunflower *(H. annuus)*, which is both popular as an orna-mental and widely grown commercially for its seeds and the oil extracted from them. Other species are smaller and tend to have lance-shaped rather than heart-shaped leaves. Most have bristly stems. The flowers are held above the foliage and are nearly always yellow. Double-flowered forms are common. Flowerheads turn to follow the sun.
CULTIVATION: Plant in a sunny, open position with fertile, moist, well-drained soil. Mildew can be a problem but usually only when the plants are past their best. Propagate annuals from seed and perennials also by division and from basal cuttings.

Helianthus annuus

COMMON SUNFLOWER

☀ ❀ ↔ 2–4 ft (0.6–1.2 m) ↕ 10–17 ft (3–5 m)

Quick-growing annual native to USA. Broad, bristly, toothed, pointed heart-shaped leaves to 16 in (40 cm) long. Flowerheads to 12 in (30 cm) wide from mid-summer, ray florets golden yellow around a purple-brown disc. '**Music Box**', mixed color seedling strain with 2-tone ray florets, 30 in (75 cm) tall; '**Ring of Fire**', 5 ft (1.5 m) tall, flower 5 in (12 cm) wide, yellow and red ray florets; '**Ruby Eclipse**', 6 ft (1.8 m) tall, red-tinted primrose ray florets, red at base, no pollen; '**Sunrich Orange**', 5 ft (1.5 m) tall, bright orange ray florets, no pollen; '**Teddy Bear**', 3 ft (0.9 m) tall, fully double, golden yellow flowers 5 in (12 cm) wide. Zones 4–11.

Helianthus annuus 'Ruby Eclipse'

Helianthus maximilianii

☀ ❀ ↔ 2–3 ft (0.6–0.9 m) ↕ 7–10 ft (2–3 m)

Erect perennial found from Texas, USA, to southern Canada. Forms a bushy base of 8 in (20 cm) long, often shallowly toothed, blue-green, lance-shaped, rough-textured leaves. Deep golden yellow flowerheads to 4 in (10 cm) wide in autumn. Zones 4–9.

Helianthus × *multiflorus*

☀ ❀ ↔ 2 ft (0.6 m) ↕ 7 ft (2 m)

Garden hybrid. Perennial. Coarsely hairy, lance-shaped lower leaves to 8 in (20 cm) long. Flowerheads to nearly 5 in (12 cm) wide, often double, from late summer until first frost. '**Capenoch Star**', 5 ft (1.5 m) tall, soft yellow flowerheads; '**Loddon Gold**', 5 ft (1.5 m) tall, golden yellow, double flowerheads. Zones 5–9.

Helianthus salicifolius

☀ ✳ ↔ 2–4 ft (0.6–1.2 m) ↑ 10 ft (3 m)

Perennial, native to south-central USA. Drooping, slightly hairy, narrowly lance-shaped leaves to 8 in (20 cm) long. Flowerheads to 3 in (8 cm) wide, yellow ray florets around a dark disc, in autumn. 'Golden Pyramid', 5 ft (1.5 m) tall, has a double row of yellow ray florets. Zones 4–9.

Helianthus Hybrid Cultivars

☀ ✳ ↔ 3–4 ft (0.9–1.2 m)
↑ 4–7 ft (1.2–2 m)

These hybrid cultivars are robust hardy plants popular with gardeners. 'Italian White', 5 ft (1.5 m) tall, very pale yellow flowers; 'Monarch', 6 in (15 cm) wide flowerheads, double row of golden ray florets; 'Moonshadow', 4 ft (1.2 m) tall, near-white ray florets; 'Newcutt Gold', rich yellow flowers; 'Sunbeam', 5 ft (1.5 m) tall, golden ray florets, outer disc florets yellow around a green center; 'Sunny', double row of bright yellow blooms; 'Vanilla Ice', 5 ft (1.5 m) tall, starry, flowerheads, creamy yellow ray florets around a dark disc. Zones 5–10.

Helichrysum milfordiae

HELICHRYSUM

A member of the daisy (Asteraceae) family, this genus was formerly estimated to have over 600 mainly perennial species, but many of these are now considered better placed in other genera; some are yet to be formally renamed. The plants have simple, often heavily felted leaves, usually in pale green to gray-green shades. Tiny flowers, usually quite heavily clustered and conspicuous, lack ray florets or petals but have white to yellow, pink, or purple papery bracts around each flowerhead.
CULTIVATION: Most species tolerate drought once established. Plant in full sun with light, gritty, very well-drained soil. Their frost hardiness varies, but few will tolerate prolonged cold; if wet at the same time, they tend to rot before they are killed by frost. Any trimming or shaping should be done in spring. Propagation is from seed (some species self-sow freely), or layers can be pegged down at any time, or half-hardened tip cuttings, which strike well in both summer and autumn.

Helichrysum ecklonis

☀ ✴ ↔ 16–24 in (40–60 cm) ↑ 4–16 in (10–40 cm)

Carpeting South African perennial, sometimes upright habit. Rosettes of oblong leaves to 8 in (20 cm) long with patchy covering of down, sometimes cobweb-like. Flowerheads solitary, to 1¼ in (30 mm) wide, white to purple. Summer-flowering. Zones 9–11.

Helichrysum frigidum

☀ ✳ ↔ 12 in (30 cm) ↑ 4 in (10 cm)

Mat-forming plant from Sardinia and Corsica. Forms a dense carpet with many narrow, ¼ in (6 mm) long, white to gray downy leaves. Numerous white flowerheads to ½ in (12 mm) wide, solitary. Excellent for rock gardens. Spring- to summer-flowering. Zones 8–10.

Helichrysum milfordiae

☀ ✳ ↔ 12 in (30 cm) ↑ 6 in (15 cm)

Cushion-forming plant from South Africa. Densely downy, spatula-shaped, leaves to ½ in (12 mm) long. Deep pink to red buds open to white flowerheads, to 1½ in (35 mm) wide. Spring-flowering. Zones 8–10.

Helichrysum petiolare

LICORICE PLANT, LIQUORICE PLANT

☀ ✴ ↔ 5 ft (1.5 m) ↑ 12–18 in (30–45 cm)

South African native. Forms a mounding ground cover. Long soft stem; rounded leaves to over 1¼ in (30 mm) long. Leaves and stems covered in pale gray down. Small, dull white flowerheads loosely clustered. Winter-flowering. 'Limelight', distinctive pale yellow-green foliage; 'Variegatum', gray and cream variegated leaves. Zones 9–11.

Helichrysum splendidum

☀ ✳ ↔ 3 ft (0.9 m) ↑ 5 ft (1.5 m)

From eastern and southern Africa. Narrowly lance-shaped leaves to over 2 in (5 cm) long with a thin covering of down. Tiny yellow to orange flowerheads clustered together. Autumn- to winter-flowering. Zones 8–11.

HELICONIA

FALSE BIRD OF PARADISE, LOBSTER CLAW, WILD PLANTAIN

Widespread in the American tropics, southern Asia, and the Pacific Islands, this group of around 100 species of evergreen perennials is from the banana (Musaceae) family. Ranging from small clumps to tree-like species and with large leaves resembling those of canna lilies or bananas, they are impressive foliage plants but their main feature is the floral inflorescence in which small flowers are each backed by a colorful bract that overlaps with the next flower to form a long spiral. Most members of this genus bloom continuously.
CULTIVATION: All but a very few species will not do well in prolonged cool conditions. Plant in a part-shaded, warm, sheltered place with moist, humus-rich, well-drained soil. Water and feed well. Remove spent inflorescences to encourage flowering. Propagate by division, or from offsets or seed if available.

Helichrysum frigidum

Heliconia bihai
MACAW FLOWER, WILD PLANTAIN

☼ ❄ ↔ 2–7 ft (0.6–2 m) ↑ 7–17 ft (2–5 m)

From Central America and tropical South America. Forms clump of banana-like stems with leaves often red-veined, to 6 ft (1.8 m) long, though usually much shorter. Long upright inflorescence with up to 20 green-edged red bracts around green-tipped white flowers. '**Aurea**', bracts with a broad gold edge; '**Chocolate Dancer**', deep red-brown bracts edged gold; '**Emerald Forest**', narrow bright green bracts; '**Schaefer**', brilliant red bracts edged orange; '**Yellow Dancer**', yellow bracts tipped green. Zones 10–12.

Heliconia caribaea
BALISIER, WILD PLANTAIN

☼ ❄ ↔ 2–7 ft (0.6–2 m) ↑ 7–17 ft (2–5 m)

From West Indies. Banana-like stems; pointed elliptical leaves to 4 ft (1.2 m) long. Short upright inflorescence, up to 15 golden yellow to red bracts, often green-tipped. Flowers white, green-tipped. '**Barbados Flat**', flat inflorescence, red-brown bracts edged yellow; '**Gold**', golden yellow bracts; '**Flash**', bracts with yellow base, red center, green edges. Zones 10–12.

Heliconia latispatha

☼ ❄ ↔ 3–4 ft (0.9–1.2 m) ↑ 10 ft (3 m)

Found from southern Mexico to Colombia and Venezuela. Broad, sometimes red-edged leaves to over 5 ft (1.5 m) long. Upright inflorescence, long narrow bracts, yellow with a broad red edge. Zones 10–12.

Heliconia psittacorum
PARAKEET FLOWER, PARROT FLOWER

☼ ❄ ↔ 20–32 in (50–80 cm) ↑ 2–7 ft (0.6–2 m)

From eastern Brazil and the southern West Indies. Banana-like growth habit; slender stems; narrow leaves to 20 in (50 cm) long, edges and stalks often red. Tall, upright inflorescence. Few large bracts, pink, orange, or red. Cultivars in range of colors. '**Strawberries and Cream**', creamy yellow bracts tinged pink. Zones 10–12.

Heliconia wagneriana

☼ ❄ ↔ 4–7 ft (1.2–2 m) ↑ 12 ft (3.5 m)

Banana-like species found from Central America to northern Colombia. Wavy-edged leaves to over 6 ft (1.8 m) long. Inflorescence upright, to 18 in (45 cm) long. Bracts deep pink, orange, or red with creamy yellow keel and green edges. Zones 10–12.

HELIOPSIS
FALSE SUNFLOWER, OX-EYE

From North America, this genus of 13 species of loosely branched, erect, perennial herbs is a member of the daisy (Asteraceae) family. Flowerheads of bright yellow daisy-like flowers are produced from mid-summer to autumn, over a long period.

Heliconia caribaea

CULTIVATION: Fully frost hardy, these plants prefer full sun and average soil kept moist during summer. Staking may be needed. Propagate from seed or divide clumps in spring or autumn.

Heliopsis helianthoides
EVERLASTING SUNFLOWER, FALSE SUNFLOWER, SMOOTH OX-EYE

☼ ❄ ↔ 1–2 ft (0.3–0.6 m) ↑ 2–5 ft (0.6–1.5 m)

Perennial found from Ontario, Canada, to Florida and Mississippi, USA. Smooth, oval- to sword-shaped, coarse-toothed, leaves, to 6 in (15 cm) long. Many terminal flowerheads of yellow daisy-like flowers, to 3 in (8 cm) across. *H. h.* var. *scabra*, double orange-yellow flowers, very rough stems and leaves; '**Incomparabilis**', single orange-yellow flowers; '**Light of Loddon**', double bright golden orange flowers. Zones 3–9.

Heliopsis Hybrid Cultivars

☼ ❄ ↔ 1–2 ft (0.3–0.6 cm) ↑ 4 ft (1.2 m)

Perennials with mid-green leaves. '**Goldgefieder**' (ox-eye), late-flowering, 4–5 ft (1.2–1.5 m) tall, double golden flowers; Loraine Sunshine/'**Helhan**', dwarf, white leaves with green veins, large golden yellow flowers. Zones 3–9.

HELIOTROPIUM

This is a genus in the borage family (Boraginaceae) with about 250 species of annuals, perennials, subshrubs, and evergreen shrubs from tropical and warmer temperate climates around the world. The fragrant flowers can be white, yellow, blue, or purple.

CULTIVATION: Most of the species prefer fertile free-draining soils, summer moisture and shelter from cold. Full sun to filtered light is their favored habitat. Shelter from frosts. Prune moderately after flowering to encourage new shoots. Propagate from soft-tip cuttings or half-hardened cuttings in a warm and moist situation.

Heliotropium arborescens
CHERRY PIE, COMMON HELIOTROPE

☼ ❄ ↔ 20 in (50 cm) ↑ 3 ft (0.9 m)

From Peru, Ecuador, and Bolivia. Spreading, evergreen plant. Narrow oval leaves dark and shiny above, paler reverse. Abundant fragrant mauve to purple flowers, from early spring to late summer. '**Black Beauty**' ★, very dark purple-black flowers; '**Chatsworth**', purple flowers; '**Fragrant Delight**', dark purple flowers; '**Iowa**', purple-tinted foliage, dark purple flowers; '**Lord Roberts**', compact growth, violet flowers; '**Marine**', compact growth, purple-blue flowers; '**Princess Marina**', dark violet-blue flowers. Zones 9–12.

HELLEBORUS
LENTEN ROSE, WINTER ROSE

This genus of 15 species of buttercup (Ranunculaceae) family perennials is found in the temperate zone from Europe to western China. They are mainly low-growing plants with short-stemmed, often toothed, palmate foliage emerging direct from a rhizome. The simple, 5-petalled, bowl-shaped flowers appear from mid-winter into spring and occur in unusual shades of green, dusky pink, and maroon as well as white. At the center of the flower are prominent greenish nectaries and yellow stamens.

CULTIVATION: Most prefer woodland conditions with deep, fertile, humus-rich, well-drained soil and dappled shade. Some of the smaller types are well suited to rock gardens. Many are near-evergreen but benefit from having old foliage removed when dormant. Propagate by division or from seed, which may require 2 periods of stratification. Naturalizes in suitable climates.

Heliotropium arborescens

Helleborus argutifolius
syns *Helleborus corsicus*,
H. lividus subsp. *corsicus*
☼/◐ ❀ ↔ 24–40 in (60–100 cm) ↕ 40 in (100 cm)
Native to islands of Corsica, France, and Sardinia, Italy. Evergreen, leathery leaves with soft-spined toothed leaflets to 8 in (20 cm) long, sometimes gray-green. Large heads of green flowers to 2 in (5 cm) wide. Winter- to spring-flowering. 'Janet Starnes', mottled cream foliage; 'Pacific Frost', mottled cream and pink foliage, narrow leaflets, pale flowers, sometimes maroon-tinted. Zones 7–10.

Helleborus foetidus
BEAR'S FOOT, STINKING HELLEBORE, STINKWORT
☼/◐ ❀ ↔ 24–40 in (60–100 cm) ↕ 24–32 in (60–80 cm)
Evergreen found from Britain to Hungary. Foliage is pungent if crushed. Dark green leaves with 5 to 13 narrow leaflets, longest to 8 in (20 cm) long, toothed. Green flowers, often red-tinted, bell-shaped, 1 in (25 mm) wide, on upright stems. 'Green Giant', bright green flowers, finely divided foliage; 'Miss Jekyll', fragrant flowers; Sierra Nevada Group, 12 in (30 cm) high; Wester Flisk Group, red-tinted stems and leaves, gray-green flowers. Zones 6–9.

Helleborus × hybridus
☼/◐ ❀ ↔ 16–24 in (40–60 cm)
↕ 16 in (40 cm)
Hybrids of *H. orientalis* and other species. 'Alberich', purple-black flowers; 'Banana Split', large creamy yellow flowers; 'Blue Spray', bell-shaped smoky purple flowers; 'Fred Whitsey', white flowers with purple spots and streaks; 'Hades', dark-speckled gray-blue flowers; 'Mardi Gras', red-blotched white flowers; 'Pleiades', dwarf, red-flecked white flowers; 'Southern Belle', lavender flowers on tall stems; 'Trotter's Spotted', large purple-spotted white flowers. Zones 5–9.

Helleborus lividus
☼/◐ ❀ ↔ 24 in (60 cm) ↕ 16 in (40 cm)
Evergreen from Mallorca, Spain. Simple 3-part, deep green, purple-tinted leaves. Flowers bright green flushed purple to all purple, from mid-winter. May rot in cold wet winters. Zones 8–10.

Helleborus niger
CHRISTMAS ROSE
☼/◐ ❀ ↔ 12–20 in (30–50 cm) ↕ 12 in (30 cm)
Evergreen from Alps of northern Italy to southern Germany. Deep green, leathery, serrated leaves, with 5 to 9 broad leaflets, to 8 in (20 cm) long. White flowers on strong stems, sometimes flushed pink. Winter- to spring-flowering. *H. n.* subsp. *macranthus*, large flowers, blue-green leaves. *H. n.* 'Potter's Wheel', white

Helleborus niger

flowers to 4 in (10 cm) wide; 'White Magic', dark-stemmed white flowers, pink-tinted with age. Zones 3–9.

Helleborus × nigercors
☼/◐ ❀ ↔ 24 in (60 cm) ↕ 24 in (60 cm)
Leaves evergreen, large, gray-green, 3 to 7 leaflets coarsely toothed and often soft-spined. Heads of large blue-green-tinted white flowers from mid-winter. Zones 7–10.

Helleborus orientalis ★
LENTEN ROSE
☼/◐ ❀ ↔ 16–24 in (40–60 cm)
↕ 16 in (40 cm)
Semi-evergreen from northern Turkey and Greece. Leaves with 7 to 9 leaflets. Flowers pure white to red-black, often dark-spotted. Winter-flowering. *H. o.* subsp. *abchasicus*, red to purplish flowers; *H. o.* subsp. *a.*, Early Purple Group (syn. *Helleborus atrorubens*), flowers greenish purple. *H. o.* subsp. *guttatus*, white flowers, dark-spotted. *H. o.* subsp. *orientalis*, white flowers. Zones 5–9.

Hemerocallis minor

HEMEROCALLIS

DAYLILY

Daylilies are so named because each of their funnel- to bell-shaped flowers lasts only one day, though they carry a succession of blooms from late spring until autumn. Once classified with the true lilies, this group of 15 species of rhizome-rooted perennials from temperate East Asia is now the type genus for its own family, the Hemerocallidaceae. They form clumps of grassy or iris-like leaves with sometimes branching racemes of 6-petalled flowers in a range of warm yellow, apricot, and red shades. All parts of the plant, especially the buds and flowers, are edible.

CULTIVATION: They are hardy and easily grown in a sunny or part-shaded position with fertile, moist, well-drained soil. Slugs and snails often badly disfigure the foliage. Take care when siting as the flowers turn to face the sun. Rust disease is a problem in some areas. Propagation is usually by division.

Hemerocallis dumortieri

LEMON LILY

☼/◐ ✹ ↔16–24 in (40–60 cm)
↑16 in (40 cm)
Compact, early-flowering species from Korea and eastern Russia. Very narrow leaves to 14 in (35 cm) long. Flower stems, red-tinted, unbranched and only slightly exceeding foliage height, bearing just 2 to 4 fragrant golden flowers to a little over 2 in (5 cm) wide, backed by broad bracts. Zones 4–9.

Hemerocallis fulva

☼/◐ ✹ ↔4–5 ft (1.2–1.5 m) ↑3 ft (0.9 m)
Wild origin uncertain, may be a hybrid. Leaves to over 24 in (60 cm) long, strappy. Flower stems usually 2-branched with up to 20, dark-striped, light orange-brown, 3–4 in (8–10 cm) wide flowers. 'Kwanzo' (syn. 'Kwanzo Flore Pleno'), dark-centered

double flowers; 'Kwanzo Variegata', same flowers, creamy white-edged foliage. Zones 4–9.

Hemerocallis lilio-asphodelus

CUSTARD LILY

☼/◐ ✹ ↔40–48 in (100–120 cm)
↑24–40 in (60–100 cm)
An early-flowering Chinese species. Very narrow sickle-shaped leaves to over 24 in (60 cm) long. Wiry, branching flower stems carry up to 12 night-scented pale yellow flowers to 3 in (8 cm) wide. Zones 4–9.

Hemerocallis middendorffii

☼/◐ ✹ ↔20–24 in (50–60 cm)
↑18 in (45 cm)
Native to Japan and nearby mainland north-eastern Asia. Leaves strappy, to 12 in (30 cm) long. Flower stems unbranched, with scented yellow flowers clustered together. Zones 5–9.

Hemerocallis minor

☼/◐ ✹ ↔20–24 in (50–60 cm) ↑20 in (50 cm)
From Japan and nearby parts of China. Very narrow leaves to 18 in (45 cm) long. Flower stems with 2 or sometimes more branches bearing up to 5 soft yellow flowers to over 2 in (5 cm) wide. Zones 4–9.

HEMIGRAPHIS

This genus, which is a member of the acanthus (Acanthaceae) family, contains about 90 species of annuals, perennials, and subshrubs that are native to tropical Asia. They have low-growing slender stems with opposite leaves that usually have toothed or scalloped margins. The foliage is the most attractive feature of most species. The small flowers are tubular with 5 petal lobes and have conspicuous bracts. They are carried on terminal spikes, which appear intermittently through the year.

CULTIVATION: In tropical and subtropical regions these plants can be grown as ground cover outdoors in positions in partial shade. In other areas they are suitable for indoor plants and as ground cover in the tropical greenhouse. In these situations they require filtered light and plentiful watering during the growing period. Propagation is from cuttings.

Hemigraphis alternata

Hemigraphis alternata

syn. Hemigraphis colorata
METAL LEAF, RED IVY

☀ ✦ ↔12–18 in (30–45 cm) ↑4 in (10 cm)
From India and Java. Prostrate perennial rooting at the nodes. It is grown for its attractive, scallop-edged, oval leaves, which are purple beneath and dark bluish green above with a metallic sheen. Flowers are small and white. 'Exotica' has puckered leaves with rolled margins. Zones 11–12.

Hemigraphis repanda

☼ ✦ ↔ 12–18 in (30–45 cm) ↑ 4 in (10 cm)

Native to Malaysia. Prostrate perennial rooting at the nodes. Slender stems flushed with maroon. Lance-shaped leaves with scalloped edges are satiny gray flushed with maroon or purple. Zones 11–12.

HEPATICA

This is a small genus of 10 species belonging to the buttercup (Ranunculaceae) family, closely related to *Anemone*. They are native to northern temperate zones in woodland settings. The leaves are basal, usually 3- to 5-lobed, leathery in texture, and often persist throughout winter. The flowers, produced in very early spring, are bowl-shaped and borne one per stem and are white, pink, and blue to purple.

CULTIVATION: As they are woodlanders by nature, a cool aspect in humus-rich soil is best, and as the plants are small in stature, the intimacy of a small pocket in a shaded rock garden makes a good setting. Propagate from freshly sown seed or by division of selected clones, which will take time to re-establish.

Heuchera americana

Hepatica nobilis

☼ ❋ ↔ 4–6 in (10–15 cm) ↑ 3–4 in (8–10 cm)

European native. Mid-green leaves with 3 rounded lobes, underside sometimes purplish. Open bowl-shaped flowers, to 1 in (25 mm) across, in shades of white through pink to blue and almost purple. Many selections in a range of colors and with double flowers. Zones 5–9.

HESPERIS

This genus belongs to the cabbage (Brassicaceae) family and consists of 60 biennials and short-lived perennials of upright habit from central and southwest Asia and the Mediterranean region. Erect stems are clothed with oblong leaves and topped with open clusters of 4-petalled flowers in shades of yellow, white, or purple, often sweetly scented, particularly in the evenings.

CULTIVATION: These plants are suitable for the border or wild garden. They will do best in full sun or light shade and prefer a neutral to alkaline soil. Although they tolerate poor soils, they will perform better if the ground is enriched. Inspect periodically for mildew. Propagation is from seed, which will usually self-sow, or from cuttings of the sterile double forms.

Hesperis matronalis

DAMASK VIOLET, DAME'S VIOLET, SWEET ROCKET

☼/☀ ❋ ↔ 16–20 in (40–50 cm) ↑ 32–36 in (80–90 cm)

Well-known biennial or short-lived perennial from southern Europe through to central Asia. Dark green leaves to 8 in (20 cm) long. Clusters of scented flowers, 1¾ in (40 mm) across, in late spring–summer. Forms with both white and lilac, single and double flowers are grown. Zones 3–10.

HEUCHERA

ALUM ROOT, CORAL BELLS

This genus, a member of the saxifrage (Saxifragaceae) family, consists of around 55 near-evergreen perennials native to North America. The species form a dense clump of basal foliage with rounded to kidney-shaped, toothed leaves on thin wiry leaf stalks. The branching flower stems are also very fine and from late spring to autumn carry sprays of tiny flowers, usually 5-petalled but sometimes petal-less.

CULTIVATION: They are mostly very hardy and adaptable and are suitable for perennial borders or rock gardens, depending on size. Plant in full or half-sun with fertile, moist, humus-rich, well-drained soil. Remove flower stems as they fade. Propagate by division or from seed sown fresh in early autumn.

Heuchera americana

ROCK GERANIUM

☼/☀ ❋ ↔ 16 in (40 cm) ↑ 18 in (45 cm)

Evergreen North American native with downy, broad, lobed, heart-shaped leaves about 3 in (8 cm) long, sometimes white mottled. Upright flower stems with narrow heads of faintly pink-tinted cream flowers. 'Garnet', leaves which are red when young, developing a red center in winter; 'Lace Ruffles', ruffled, silver-mottled leaves, white flowers; 'Ring of Fire', red-veined green foliage turning pink in winter with pale edges; 'Velvet Night', darkest purple-black leaves overlaid with metallic purple. Zones 4–10.

Heuchera × brizoides

☼/☀ ❋ ↔ 12–18 in (30–45 cm) ↑ 12–30 in (30–75 cm)

These are a mixed group, sharing simple green, lobed, heart-shaped leaves and differing mainly in flower color. **Bressingham hybrids**, with graceful, airy flowerheads, many shades of pink, red, and white; Firefly/'**Leuchtkäfer**', coral pink, faintly scented; '**Freedom**', dwarf form, flowers bright pink; '**June Bride**', white flowers. Zones 4–10.

Heuchera × brizoides

Heuchera maxima

Heuchera, Hybrid Cultivar, 'Strawberry Candy'

Heuchera maxima

☼/◗ ❋ ↔ 16–20 in (40–50 cm) ↑ 24 in (60 cm)
Evergreen species from western USA. Rounded, toothed leaves to more than 6 in (15 cm) wide, underside veins downy. Pinkish white flowers in warmer months. Zones 6–10.

Heuchera sanguinea

☼/◗ ❋ ↔ 12–16 in (30–40 cm) ↑ 24 in (60 cm)
Evergreen, from New Mexico and Arizona, USA. Roughly kidney-shaped leaves to 2 in (5 cm) wide, with irregular lobes and downy undersides. Bright red flowers. 'Brandon Pink', bright coral-pink flowers, green and white leaves; 'Monet', white-variegated green foliage, red flowers; 'Northern Fire', pinkish red flowers, green leaves, vigorous; 'Singham', bright green leaves, hot pink flowers; 'Snow Storm', white-mottled foliage, red flowers; 'Splendens', deep red flowers; 'Virginalis', white flowers. Zones 3–9.

Heuchera Hybrid Cultivars

☼/◗ ❋ ↔ 12–18 in (30–45 cm)
↑ 12–36 in (30–90 cm)
In recent years many Heuchera hybrids have been introduced, with interesting foliage. 'Amber Waves', light golden bronze foliage and deep pink flowers; 'Autumn Haze', purple leaves overlaid silver, pink flowers; 'Chocolate Ruffles' ★, deep bronze-green foliage with purple-brown overtones, white flowers; 'Fireglow', red blooms; 'Mint Frost', green leaves overlaid silver, cream lowers; 'Persian Carpet', silver-marked red to purple-red leaves, buff flowers; 'Petite Marble Burgundy', compact, silver-marked, purple-red leaves, pinkish flowers; 'Pewter Moon', silver-veined deep purple-red foliage; 'Pewter Veil', purple-red foliage overlaid silver-gray; 'Plum Pudding', purple-brown leaves with red undersides, cream flowers; 'Red Spangles', plain green leaves, bright red flowers; 'Ruby Veil', deep maroon and silver-gray upper leaves, purple-red undersides; 'Santa Ana Cardinal' (H. maxima × H. sanguinea), tall, rounded bright green leaves, deep pink to red flowers; 'Snow

Angel', red flowers, white-flecked green foliage; 'Strawberry Candy', green leaves overlaid silver, pink flowers; 'Wendy' ★ (H. maxima × H. sanguinea), large light green leaves, soft pink flowers. Canyon Series, compact evergreen hybrids with small, lobed, rounded to heart-shaped leaves, usually deep green, sometimes with hint of purple; many tiny flowers in upright, airy sprays. Original varieties include 'Canyon Delight', tall, deep pink to red; 'Canyon Pink', bright pink. Canyon Quartet Series includes 'Canyon Bell', short stems, bright red flowers; 'Canyon Chimes', tall stems, red flowers; 'Canyon Duet', bicolor red and white flowers; and 'Canyon Melody', smaller plant, pink and white flowers. Zones 5–10.

× HEUCHERELLA

This group of garden hybrids in the saxifrage (Saxifragaceae) family are crosses between the genera Heuchera and Tiarella. They are sterile hybrids with evergreen maple-shaped leaves that often color well in winter and sprays of tiny dainty pale pink to white flowers on upright stems in late spring.
CULTIVATION: These hybrids are best grown in humus-rich moist soils in cool woodland-type aspects where they make attractive slow-moving ground covers. Propagation is by division.

× Heucherella tiarelloides

☼/◗ ❋ ↔ 18 in (45 cm) ↑ 18 in (45 cm)
Smooth, light green, divided leaves heart-shaped at the base. Stems of pink flowers above foliage in spring–summer. Zones 5–9.

× Heucherella Hybrid Cultivars

☼/◗ ❋ ↔ 12–16 in (30–40 cm) ↑ 16–20 in (40–50 cm)

× Heucherella, Hybrid Cultivar, 'Viking Ship'

Evergreen perennials with striking foliage. 'Bridget Bloom', heart-shaped mid-green leaves, heavy brown markings, white flower spikes in spring–autumn; 'Dayglo Pink', mid-green leaves, chocolate-colored inlay, purple foliage tones in winter, brilliant pink flowers; 'Kimono', tawny flowers, in summer–autumn; 'Viking Ship', silver leaves in spring, coral-pink flowers. Zones 5–9.

HIBISCUS

GIANT MALLOW, MALLOW, ROSE MALLOW
This genus of over 200 annual or perennial herbs, shrubs, or trees in the mallow (Malvaceae) family is widely distributed throughout warm-temperate, subtropical, and tropical regions of the world. They are grown mostly for their large dramatic flowers, borne singly or in terminal clusters, usually lasting for just a day. The open bell-shaped flowers appear in a wide variety of colors, and are characterized by a prominent staminal column and a darker coloring in the center. The alternate simple leaves are usually palmate. The fruit is a capsule.
CULTIVATION: Most species of Hibiscus are drought tender and rather frost tender, and prefer a position in full sun in a rich and moist soil. Many will tolerate hard pruning after flowering to maintain shape. Perennials are propagated from seed or by

division, while annuals are best grown from seed in the growing position. Shrub types can be propagated from cuttings, by grafting, or from seed sown in containers for later transplanting.

Hibiscus cannabinus
BIMLI, DECCAN HEMP, INDIAN HEMP, KENAF
☼ ❄ ↔ 6 ft (1.8 m) ↕ 12 ft (3.5 m)
Fast-growing annual or short-lived, shrubby perennial, thought to be from East Indies. Long stems used for fiber. Pale yellow, sometimes pale purple flowers in racemes, reddish purple column and center. Leaves prickly, deeply lobed, serrated. Zones 10–12.

Hibiscus Herbaceous Hybrids
☼ ❄ ↔ 2–4 ft (0.6–1.2 m)
↕ 18 in–5 ft (45 cm–1.5 m)
Perennials derived mainly from *H. moscheutos*. Leaves vary from toothed to deeply lobed. Succession of large, flat to funnel-shaped flowers from upper leaf axils in shades from white or pale pink to dark red, sometimes with dark eye. '**Davis Creek**', deep pink to red flowers; '**Lady Baltimore**', pink flowers; '**Miss Kitty**', yellow flowers. Zones 5–10.

HOSTA
syn. *Funkia*
PLANTAIN LILY
This genus from the agave (Agavaceae) family contains about 40 perennial species. Hostas are clump-forming, and grown primarily for their large, bold, heart-shaped leaves. In addition to green, blue, and grayish tones, some cultivars have variegated or yellow-green foliage. The flowers are funnel-shaped and borne in racemes atop erect stems. They are usually white, mauve, or purple, appear from mid-summer, and are sometimes scented. CULTIVATION: Although sun-tolerant cultivars have been raised, hostas prefer shaded conditions with moist, cool, humus-rich, well-drained soil. Water and feed well during the growing season. Propagate by dividing as the first buds show. The young shoots are very vulnerable to slug and snail damage.

Hosta fortunei
◖/☼ ❄ ↔ 32–48 in (80–120 cm) ↕ 36 in (90 cm)
Wild status uncertain—it is perhaps Japanese but may be a garden hybrid from Europe. Wavy, deep green, heart- to lance-shaped leaves tapering to a fine point, often variegated. Mauve flowers on leafy stems. '**Albomarginata**', large white-edged leaves; '**Albopicta**', large, thin leaves, maturing to green with hint of cream; '**Antioch**', dark green leaves, yellow edge turning cream; '**Aurea**', leaves yellow, turning light green; '**Aureomarginata**', clearly defined gold-edged leaves; '**Elizabeth Campbell**', leaves with broad green edge and light green central zone; '**Francee**', white-edged deep green leaves, slightly puckered; '**Gold Haze**', like 'Aurea' but slower to turn green; '**Gold Standard**', green-gold leaves, clearly defined dark green edge; '**Goldbrook Gold**', yellow-gold leaves; '**Joker**', gray-green to blue-green leaves; '**Mary Marie Ann**', bright green edges around a broad yellow-green center;

Hibiscus, Herbaceous Hybrid, 'Davis Creek'

'**Minuteman**', bright green leaves, with irregular broad white edge; '**North Hills**', mid-green leaves with irregular narrow white edge; '**Striptease**', heart-shaped blue-green leaves with narrow cream and green central zone; '**Whirlwind**', mid-green, broad yellow-gold center. Zones 6–10.

Hosta lancifolia
◖/☼ ❄ ↔ 16–20 in (40–50 cm)
↕ 18 in (45 cm)
Not known in the wild. Narrow, deep green, lance-shaped leaves to around 6 in (15 cm) long, tapering to a fine point. Flower stems leafy, flowers purple. Zones 6–10.

Hosta minor
KIRIN GIBOSHI
◖/☼ ❄ ↔ 16 in (40 cm) ↕ 24 in (60 cm)
Korean species cultivated in Japan. Clump of small, dark green, pointed oval to heart-shaped leaves to 3 in (8 cm) long. Tall flower stem with deep mauve flowers. Zones 6–10.

Hosta plantaginea
AUGUST LILY, MARUBA
◖/☼ ❄ ↔ 32 in (80 cm) ↕ 26 in (65 cm)
Native to China and Japan. Grown as much for flowers as foliage. Leaves bright green, wavy, deeply veined, lance-shaped tapering to fine point, to 10 in (25 cm) long. Flowers white, may be mauve-tinted, large, scented. *H. p.* var. *japonica* (syn. *H. p.* var. *grandiflora*), taller flower stems, larger flowers. *H. p.* '**Honey Bells**', mauve-tinted flowers; '**Venus**', double flowers. Zones 8–10.

Hosta sieboldii
KOBA GIBOSHI
◖/☼ ❄ ↔ 32 in (80 cm) ↕ 20 in (50 cm)
Native to Japan and Sakhalin Island. Finely pointed, often undulating and puckered, lance-shaped leaves to 6 in (15 cm) long, deep green with white edges. Mauve flowers. *H. s. f. kabitan*, small, green-edged golden leaves. *H. s.* '**Krossa Cream Edge**', narrow, cream-edged leaves; '**Wogon**', lime green leaves. Zones 5–10.

Hosta fortunei 'Whirlwind'

Hosta × *tardiana*

◑/◐ ❄ ↔ 16–20 in (40–50 cm) ↑ 16 in (40 cm)

Hybrids between *H. sieboldiana* var. *elegans* and *H. tardiflora*. Mainly forming mounding clumps of heavily veined blue-green leaves, sometimes variegated. Flower stems fairly short, flowers cream to pale mauve. '**Brother Ronald**', dark blue-green leaves to over 6 in (15 cm) long; '**Camelot**', wide spreading, broad, heart-shaped, intensely blue-green leaves to 8 in (20 cm) long, lavender flowers; '**Devon Blue**', pointed, gray-marked, blue-green leaves to over 6 in (15 cm) long; '**Halcyon**', heart-shaped blue-green leaves to 8 in (20 cm) long, many lavender-gray flowers; '**Moody Blues**', broad, intensely blue-green leaves, pale lavender flowers. Zones 6–10.

Hosta tardiflora

◑/◐ ❄ ↔ 20 in (50 cm) ↑ 12 in (30 cm)

Unknown in the wild. Prominently veined, glossy, olive green, sometimes undulating, lance-shaped leaves to 6 in (15 cm) long. Flower stem to 14 in (35 cm) long but held at around a 45° angle, flowers mauve in cream to purple bracts. Zones 6–10.

Hosta tokudama

TOKUDAMA GIBOSHI

◑/◐ ❄ ↔ 32–48 in (80–120 cm) ↑ 18 in (45 cm)

Unknown in the wild, long cultivated in Japan. Broad oval to heart-shaped leaves, puckered surface, bright blue-green, to 10 in (25 cm) long and wide. Flowers lavender-gray to white. *H. t.* f. *aureonebulosa*, leaves irregular, large central yellow-green area. *H. t.* '**Love Pat**', possibly of hybrid origin, heavily textured, deep blue-green leaves, mauvish white flowers. Zones 6–10.

Hosta undulata

SUJI GIBOSHI

◑/◐ ❄ ↔ 16–20 in (40–50 cm) ↑ 12 in (30 cm)

Unknown in the wild, long cultivated in Japan. Dark green leaves, narrow central band of creamy white, pointed elliptical, wavy edged, to nearly 6 in (15 cm) long. Flowers pale purple within greenish white bracts. '**Albomarginata**', leaves with white edges, wavy but not twisted; '**Variegata**' *(syn. H. u.* var. *undulata)*, leaves with central area cream and 2-tone green; '**Univittata**', large leaves with narrow central creamy white zone; '**White Christmas**', white leaves with narrow irregular green edge. Zones 6–10.

Hosta ventricosa

MURASAKI GIBOSHI

◑/◐ ❄ ↔ 24–32 in (60–80 cm) ↑ 40 in (100 cm)

Chinese species long cultivated in Japan. Deep green, broad, often wavy, heart-shaped leaves to 10 in (25 cm) long. Tall flower stems, light purple flowers. *H. v.* var. *aureomaculata*, young leaves with bright yellow center. *H. v.* '**Peedee Elfin Bells**', pendulous flowers. Zones 6–10.

Hosta Hybrid Cultivars

◑/◐ ❄ ↔ 12–60 in (30–150 cm) ↑ 6–36 in (15–90 cm)

In recent decades hostas have been among plant breeders' favorites, and extensive hybridizing has produced a myriad of foliage forms. '**Allan P. McConnell**', medium height, dark green with white edge, purple flowers; '**August Moon**', tall, wavy yellow-gold leaves, lavender flowers; '**Blue Moon**', low-growing, small blue-green leaves, white flowers; '**Brim Cup**', tall, puckered, light yellow-green leaves with irregular green center, mauve flowers; '**Candy Hearts**', tall blue-green leaves, pale mauve flowers; '**County Park**', tall, broad, flat, mid-green leaves, white flowers; '**Devon Gold**', medium height, small yellow-green leaves, purple flowers; '**Floradora**', medium height, neat heart-shaped mid-green leaves, pale mauve flowers; '**Gold Edger**', low-growing, golden green leaves, white flowers; '**Green Piecrust**', tall, large mid-green wavy-edged leaves, lavender flowers; '**Ground Sulphur**', medium height, low spreader, bright yellow-green leaves; '**Island Charm**', medium height, small pink-stemmed bright green leaves with yellow center, lavender flowers; '**Julie Morss**', medium height, yellow-gold leaves with green edges, lavender-pink flowers; '**June**', medium height, small yellow-centered blue-green leaves, violet flowers; '**King Michael**', tall, large lustrous mid-green leaves, white flowers; '**Krossa Regal**', tall, long-stemmed blue-green leaves, white to pale mauve flowers; '**Lady Isobel Barnett**', tall, very large mid-green leaves with creamy yellow margin, white to pale lavender flowers; '**Medusa**', medium height, narrow green-edged cream leaves, purple flowers; '**Midwest Magic**', tall, yellow-green leaves with darker edges, lavender flowers; '**Patriot**', tall, dark green leaves with broad white edge, violet flowers; '**Paul's Glory**', medium height, heavily puckered yellow-centered blue-green leaves, lavender flowers; '**Pearl Lake**', tall, small mid-green leaves, many lavender flowers; '**Pizzazz**', medium height, broad

Hosta tardiflora

Hosta undulata 'White Christmas'

Hosta, Hybrid Cultivar, 'August Moon'

blue-green leaves with thin irregular yellow edges, pale mauve flowers; '**Radiant Edger**', tall, small mid-green leaves with yellow-green edges, mauve flowers; '**Royal Standard**', tall, glossy mid-green leaves, fragrant white flowers; '**Ryan's Big One**', tall, very large puckered blue-green leaves, pale lavender flowers; '**September Sun**', tall, leaves initially yellow-green becoming green-edged, white flowers; '**Shade Fanfare**', medium height, puckered white-edged blue-green leaves, pale mauve flowers; '**Summer Music**', medium height, slightly twisted dark green leaves with white to cream center, pale mauve flowers; '**Tall Boy**', tall, long-stemmed mid-green leaves, purple flowers on tall stems; '**Torchlight**', medium height, dark green leaves with broad white edge, lavender flowers; '**Veronica Lake**', medium height, blue-green leaves with white to light green edges, pale mauve flowers; '**Wide Brim**', tall, blue-green leaves with creamy yellow edge, mauve flowers; '**Yellow Waves**', low-growing, small yellow-gold leaves, mauve flowers. Zones 6–10.

HOUTTUYNIA

This genus of a only single species from East Asia belongs to the lizard's-tail (Saururaceae) family. It is a widely spreading herbaceous perennial with heart-shaped leaves and cones of tiny yellow flowers surrounded by 4 white petal-like bracts. The leaves can be eaten raw or cooked and have a peppery taste.
CULTIVATION: This grows well in moist to wet soil, even slightly submerged in water, and is happy in full sun or half-shade. It can become invasive and hard to remove; grow in pots kept off the ground to restrict spread. Propagate by division.

Houttuynia cordata

☼◐/◐ ❊ ↔ over 40 in (100 cm)
↕ 6–12 in (15–30 cm)
Herbaceous plant China and Japan. Aromatic heart-shaped leaves to 3½ in (9 cm) long, deep green often stained burgundy. White-bracted flower clusters atop red stems from mid-summer onward. '**Chameleon**' (syns *H. c.* 'Court Jester', *H. c.* 'Tricolor', *H. c.* 'Variegata'), slightly less vigorous, leaves broadly edged in yellow and stained red; '**Flore Pleno**', masses of white bracts arranged like little cones. Zones 5–10.

HUNNEMANNIA
GOLDEN CUP, MEXICAN TULIP POPPY

This genus belongs to the poppy (Papaveraceae) family and contains one fast-growing species of perennial that is often grown as an annual. It is native to highland areas of Mexico. Although rather woody at the base, it is of delicate appearance with finely divided bluish gray foliage. The clear yellow flowers may be single or semi-double, and are up to 3 in (8 cm) in diameter, appearing in summer.
CULTIVATION: Grow in full sun in a well-drained soil. It will not tolerate wet conditions in the cooler months. Deadhead regularly to encourage a longer flowering season. Care should be taken not to disturb the roots on transplanting. Propagate from seed.

Houttuynia cordata 'Chameleon'

Hunnemannia fumariifolia

☼ ❊ ↔ 10 in (25 cm) ↕ 18–36 in (45–90 cm)
Perennial or annual. Attractive bluish gray filigree leaves. Satiny flowers clearest yellow, held above foliage in summer. Zones 8–10.

HYDRASTIS

This genus, a member of the buttercup (Ranunculaceae) family, contains only 2 species of low-growing perennial herbs, one native to Japan and the other to eastern North America.
CULTIVATION: These grow best in conditions similar to its natural habitat—the forest floor. Plant in a shady position with rich moist soil that has been enriched with leafmold. Add more leafmold or similar organic matter every year. Propagate from seed or by division.

Hydrastis canadensis
EYE ROOT, GOLDENSEAL, GROUND RASPBERRY, INDIAN DYE, JAUNDICE ROOT, ORANGEROOT, TURMERIC, YELLOW PUCCOON

☼ ❊ ↔ 8 in (20 cm) ↕ 12 in (30 cm)
Perennial woodland herb from eastern North America. Each stem has 2 large, serrated, 5-lobed, wrinkled leaves; small white flowers in spring. Raspberry-like fruit, in cluster of red berries, follows in summer. Endangered species. All parts poisonous. Zones 6–8.

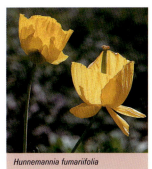
Hunnemannia fumariifolia

IBERIS
CANDYTUFT

Popular for the bold effect of their massed heads of white, pink, mauve, or purple flowers, the 30-odd annuals, perennials, and subshrubs in this genus in the cabbage (Brassicaceae) family are found from western and southern Europe to western Asia. They usually have simple, small, narrow leaves; when not flowering they form a rounded bush. Their flowerheads open in summer, on short stems holding them clear of the foliage.
CULTIVATION: Plant in a sunny position with light yet moist, well-drained soil. A light dressing of dolomite lime is appreciated. Deadhead regularly. Propagate the annuals from seed and the perennials and subshrubs from seed or small cuttings.

Iberis gibraltarica

Iberis amara
ANNUAL CANDYTUFT

☀/◐ ❄ ↔ 12–20 in (30–50 cm) ↑ 12 in (30 cm)

Western European annual. Small, lance-shaped, sometimes toothed leaves often hidden under massed heads of white, pink, or purple flowers in summer. Zones 7–11.

Iberis gibraltarica
GIBRALTAR CANDYTUFT

☀/◐ ❄ ↔ 20–24 in (50–60 cm) ↑ 12 in (30 cm)

Evergreen species from Gibraltar. Forms neat mound of narrow stems with rosettes of small leaves at tips. Heads of white, lavender, or pink-tinted flowers in summer. Zones 7–10.

Iberis sempervirens

☀/◐ ❄ ↔ 20–24 in (50–60 cm) ↑ 12 in (30 cm)

Spreading evergreen plant from southern Europe with small oblong leaves, mainly clustered at stem tips. Flowerheads to 2 in (5 cm) wide, usually white, in spring–summer. 'Flore-Plena', compact habit, double flowers; 'Purity', to 8 in (20 cm) high; Snowflake/'Schneeflocke' ★, low-growing, silvery white flowers; 'Weisser Zwerg' (syn. 'Little Gem'), 6 in (15 cm) high, early flowers. Zones 7–10.

Iberis umbellata

☀/◐ ❄ ↔ 16 in (40 cm) ↑ 12 in (30 cm)

Annual from southern Europe. Very narrow lance-shaped leaves may be toothed. Purple flowers in spring–summer. Flash Series, white, shades of pink, mauve, purple, and red flowers. Grow from autumn-sown seed in mild areas; summer annual elsewhere. Zones 7–10.

IMPATIENS
BALSAM, BUSY LIZZIE, WATER FUCHSIA

The type genus giving its name to the balsam (Balsaminaceae) family is home to around 850 species of annuals, perennials, and subshrubs found worldwide except in Australasia, South America, and the polar regions. These are generally soft-stemmed plants with simple, pointed, lance-shaped leaves, often with toothed edges. Flowers in many colors appear throughout the year in mild areas and have 5 petals, an upper standard and the lower 4 fused into 2 pairs, the sepals also partly fused to form a spur. Ripe seed pods explosively eject their contents at a touch.
CULTIVATION: Grow the annuals as summer plants in cooler climates outside the recommended zones; perennials need mild winter conditions. Provide shade from the hottest sun and plant in deep, cool, moist, humus-rich soil. Feed well. Propagate annuals from seed, the perennials also by cuttings. Some species self-sow and are slightly invasive.

Impatiens balsamina
BALSAM

◐/☀ ✦ ↔ 12 in (30 cm) ↑ 27 in (70 cm)

Vigorous upright annual from East Asia. Toothed lance-shaped leaves. Flowers to nearly 2 in (5 cm) wide, clustered, in many colors, mainly pink, mauve to red shades. Conspicuous seed pods burst when ripe. Garden seedling strains include Camellia-flowered Series, large double flowers; and Tom Thumb Series, low-growing double-flowered. Zones 10–12.

Impatiens hawkeri
syn. *Impatiens schlechteri*

◐/☀ ✦ ↔ 16–40 in (40–100 cm) ↑ 3–7 ft (0.9–2 m)

Shrubby, continuous-flowering, evergreen perennial from New Guinea and Solomon Islands. Heavy fleshy stems; pointed oval to lance-shaped leaves, toothed, usually red or red-tinted. Long-spurred flowers to over 3 in (8 cm) wide, white, or pink, red, and purple shades. Zones 10–12.

Impatiens New Guinea Hybrids

◐/☀ ✦ ↔ 16–40 in (40–100 cm) ↑ 10–48 in (25–120 cm)

These are usually cultivars of *I. hawkeri* or hybrids with *I. linearifolia*. They are available in many striking combinations of flower and foliage. Bonita Series includes Improved Quepos/'Kimpque', bright reddish flowers, dark red-tinted green leaves, and Sarchi/'Kisar', deep magenta flowers, dark green leaves; Celebration Series, 'Light Lavender II', mauve flowers, mid-green leaves; Celebrette Hot Pink/'Balcebhopi', vivid magenta flowers and mid-green leaves; Paradise Series, includes Pascua/'Kipas', deep pink flowers, mid-green leaves, Tagula/'Kigula', pale pink flowers with red upper petal, dark green leaves, and Timor/'Kitim', deep orange-red flowers, red-tinted bright green leaves; 'Tango' ★, bright orange flowers, bronze-green leaves. Zones 10–12.

Impatiens niamniamensis

Impatiens niamniamensis

◐/☀ ✦ ↔ 16 in (40 cm) ↑ 36 in (90 cm)

Continuous-flowering evergreen perennial from tropical east Africa. Deeply toothed leaves. Large, heavy-textured, long-spurred, deep red flowers with yellow upper petal. Zones 10–12.

Impatiens sodenii

☀/◑ ✦ ↔ 3–7 ft (0.9–2 m) ↑ 3–7 ft (0.9–2 m)

Shrubby evergreen perennial from tropical east Africa. Whorls of toothed lance-shaped leaves. Long-stemmed flowers to over 2 in (5 cm) wide, in lavender and pink shades or white, in summer. Zones 10–12.

Impatiens walleriana

syns *Impatiens holstii, I. sultani*

☀/◑ ✦ ↔ 8–20 in (20–50 cm)
↑ 8–24 in (20–60 cm)

Continuous-flowering, shrubby, evergreen, tropical east African perennial; often treated as annual. Fleshy, succulent stems; toothed lance-shaped leaves, often red-tinted. Spurred flat-faced flowers, evenly sized petals; most colors except yellow and blue. '**Blackberry Ice**', double purple-red flowers; **Carousel Mix**, rosebud doubles in wide range of colors; **Dazzler Series**, many single flowers in warm pastel shades; **Deco Series**, spreading, single flowers in all shades; **Fiesta Series**, rosebud double flowers in many shades including bicolors; **Garden Leader Series** comes in a wide range of colors; **Ice Series**, white-marked foliage, rosebud double flowers in all shades; **Merlot Series**, bright green foliage, single flowers in all colors; **Super Elfin Series**, very compact, single flowers in all shades; **Tempo Series**, compact plants, large flowers; '**Victorian Rose**', spreading habit, semi-double deep pink flowers. Double and variegated cultivars are propagated from cuttings, the rest from seed. Zones 10–12.

INCARVILLEA

This group of 14 species from central and eastern Asia includes annuals and perennials, some of which are slightly woody, and belongs in the trumpet-vine (Bignoniaceae) family. Depending on which species you plant, they can make exotic-looking rock-garden or border plants. The flowers are trumpet-shaped with flared and often undulated edges, and are usually a bright pink to magenta, although yellow forms have been discovered. Most species have a long flowering period; besides the decorative value of the flowers, the foliage is usually also attractive.
CULTIVATION: Grow in moisture-retentive but not wet soil, sheltered from the hottest afternoon sun. Propagate from fresh seed or by division, although established plants resent disturbance.

Incarvillea delavayi

☀ ❄ ↔ 12–16 in (30–40 cm) ↑ 20–24 in (50–60 cm)

Rosette-forming species from western China. Long compound leaves. Up to 10 large rich pink trumpets per stem, to 3 in (8 cm) across, with yellow throat, held above the foliage, in early to mid-summer. '**Snowtop**', white with yellow throat. Zones 6–9.

Incarvillea emodi

☀ ❄ ↔ 12–16 in (30–40 cm) ↑ 16–20 in (40–50 cm)

Rosette-forming perennial from Afghanistan, Pakistan, and northern India. Large leaves; stems of deep pink trumpets with yellow throat, each bloom 2½ in (6 cm) long, in spring. Zones 7–9.

INULA

Members of this large genus in the daisy (Asteraceae) family are found in a wide range of habitats, from Europe through to subtropical Africa and Asia. Most are herbaceous perennials, with some biennials and annuals, the perennial species being those most commonly grown. Some can be invasive. The basal leaves tend to be largest, the leaves reducing in size toward the top of the stems. All have yellow daisy flowers produced mainly in summer. CULTIVATION: Despite the range of habitats from which they originate, most species like a sunny aspect and rich moist soil. The dwarf species are suited to the larger rock garden, while the taller species can be planted in the wilder parts of the garden or among other perennials in the border. Propagation is from seed or by division.

Impatiens sodenii

Inula grandiflora

syns *Inula glandulosa, I. orientalis*

☀ ❄ ↔ 36–40 in (90–100 cm) ↑ 20–24 in (50–60 cm)

From the Caucasus region. Smooth-edged hairy leaves, to 5 in (12 cm) long. Yellow flowers, to 3 in (8 cm) across. Zones 6–10.

Inula helenium

ELECAMPANE

☀/◑ ❄ ↔ 3–4 ft (0.9–1.2 m) ↑ 8–10 ft (2.4–3 m)

Tall, robust, somewhat invasive species from temperate Eurasia. Large hairy lower leaves, to 27 in (70 cm) long, serrated and undulating edges. Spikes of yellow daisy flowers. Zones 5–10.

Inula magnifica

syn. *Inula afghanica*

☀ ❄ ↔ 3–5 ft (0.9–1.5 m) ↑ 5–6 ft (1.5–1.8 m)

Robust, impressive, herbaceous perennial from Caucasus region. Large, deep green, basal leaves, to 10 in (25 cm) long, hairy beneath. Large open clusters of yellow daisies. Zones 6–10.

Inula helenium

IPOMOPSIS

This genus in the phlox (Polemoniaceae) family has 24 species of annuals and perennials that are native to western North America, with outlying species found in Florida, USA, and temperate South America. Leaves often form a basal rosette and may be either smooth or pinnately divided. The tubular flowers, in shades of red, yellow, pink, white, or violet, are borne in loose racemes in spring and summer.

CULTIVATION: In cooler climates they can be grown as temporary summer bedding or in the conservatory or greenhouse. Elsewhere, grow in full sun in fertile well-drained soil. Propagate from seed.

Ipomopsis rubra

syn. *Gilia rubra*

STANDING CYPRESS

☼ ❁ ↔ 18 in (45 cm) ↕ 3–6 ft (0.9–1.8 m)

From South Carolina, Florida, and Texas, USA. Erect unbranched perennial or biennial. Basal rosettes of thread-like leaves. Stems of tubular flowers, scarlet with speckled yellow throats, from summer to autumn. Zones 7–10.

IRESINE

BLOODLEAF

There are about 80 species of annuals, perennials, and subshrubs in this genus, which belongs to the amaranth (Amaranthaceae) family. They are native to the Americas and Australia. The simple leaves are often brilliantly colored with contrasting veins, and it is for this feature that these plants are cultivated. The spikes of small white or green flowers are of little ornamental significance.

Iresine herbstii 'Brilliantissima'

CULTIVATION: Grow outdoors all year round in tropical and subtropical areas. In cooler regions, grow outside in summer. Plant in well-drained moisture-retentive soil in full sun for best leaf coloring. Can be used in summer bedding schemes and in pots, both indoors and outdoors. Pinch growing tips to maintain bushiness. Propagate from cuttings, seed, or by division.

Iresine herbstii

BEEF PLANT, BEEF STEAK PLANT, BLOOD-LEAF

☼ ⚵ ↔ 12–18 in (30–45 cm) ↕ 18–24 in (45–60 cm)

Native to Brazil. Perennial, often renewed annually in cultivation. Green, purple, or red stems. Pointed oval leaves, deep purple with pink veins to green with yellow veins. 'Aureo-reticulata', green, gold, and red leaves; 'Brilliantissima', crimson leaves. Zones 9–12.

IRIS

Iris is the type genus for the family Iridaceae. The 300-odd species, which are divided into various sections, and scattered over the northern temperate zones, occur in bulbous, rhizomatous, and fibrous-rooted forms. The sword-shaped foliage, often arranged in fans, is sometimes variegated. The flowers have 6 petals, usually in the fleur-de-lis pattern of 3 upright standards and 3 downward-curving falls, which may be bearded, beardless, or crested, and occurring in all colors.

CULTIVATION: Bog irises need a sunny position in damp soil. Woodland irises thrive in dappled sunlight with moist well-drained soil. Bearded irises need sun, and dry soil after flowering. Rockery irises need a sunny spot in moist, well-drained, gritty soil. Propagate by division when dormant, less commonly by seed.

Iris chrysographes

GOLD NET IRIS, GOLD PATTERN IRIS

☼ ❁ ↔ 12 in (30 cm) ↕ 12–20 in (30–50 cm)

Fleshy-stemmed beardless iris from China, Myanmar, and Tibet. Strappy grayish green leaves. Flowers purple-black, gold streaks on falls. 'Black Knight', purple-black flowers. Zones 7–10.

Iris cristata

CRESTED IRIS

◐ ❁ ↔ 12–20 in (30–50 cm) ↕ 4–5 in (10–12 cm)

Dainty herbaceous woodlander from eastern USA, with exposed, creeping, fleshy stems, and fans of bright green strappy leaves. Produces lightly scented light blue to purple flowers, on stems to height of leaves, with white markings on falls and yellow crests. Spring-flowering. A white-flowered form also grown. Zones 6–10.

Iris douglasiana

☼ ❁ ↔ 18 in (45 cm) ↕ 20–32 in (50–80 cm)

Fleshy-stemmed beardless iris from California and Oregon, USA. Loose clumps of dark green ribbed leaves. Branching flower stems. Blooms, in summer, vary in color from cream to deep reddish purple, veining usually in darker tones. Zones 7–9.

Iris ensata ★

syn. *Iris kaempferi*

JAPANESE WATER IRIS, WOODLAND IRIS

☼ ❁ ↔ 40 in (100 cm) ↕ 36 in (90 cm)

Native to Europe, Asia, and North America. Tall, dark green, strappy, grass-like foliage. Single, occasionally branched stems of

Iris chrysographes 'Black Knight'

flowers vary in color from red, purple, or blue, held well above foliage, in early summer. Will grow in shallow water. Not tolerant of dry hot conditions. '**Flying Tiger**', white flowers, heavily veined in violet; '**Hekito**', deep blue flowers, blue-tipped; '**Hue and Cry**', red-veined plum-red flowers; '**Rose Queen**', soft pink flowers, darker veined falls; '**Variegata**', purple-red flowers, variegated foliage; '**Yaemo-miji**', cerise-purple flowers streaked with white. Zones 5–8.

Iris foetidissima
GLADDON, GLADWYN, ROAST BEEF PLANT, STINKING GLADWYN
☀/☀ ❋ ↔ 18–30 in (45–75 cm)
↕ 18–30 in (45–75 cm)
Vigorous, fleshy-stemmed, beardless iris, native to Europe and north Africa. Glossy, deep green, sword-shaped leaves, odorous when crushed. Spring flowers unspectacular, buff-yellow and dusty dull purple. '**Variegata**', boldly white-striped leaves. Zones 6–10.

Iris ensata 'Flying Tiger'

Iris × fulvala
☀ ❋ ↔ 10 in (25 cm) ↕ 18–30 in (45–75 cm)
Hybrid beardless irises. Purplish red flowers, in summer. Needs very moist soil. Zones 7–10.

Iris germanica
☀ ❋ ↔ 18–24 in (45–60 cm)
↕ 24–48 in (60–120 cm)
Rhizomatous bearded iris. Origin uncertain, widely naturalized. Blue, white, and yellow flowers, to 4 in (10 cm) wide, yellow beards. Zones 5–9.

Iris pseudacorus 'Variegata'

Iris innominata
☀/☀ ❋ ↔ 10 in (25 cm) ↕ 8–10 in (20–25 cm)
Fleshy-stemmed beardless iris, native to Oregon and California, USA, with narrow dark green leaves. Slender-petalled flowers, cream to purple, with darker veining, in summer. Zones 8–10.

Iris japonica
syns *Iris chinensis, I. fimbriata*
☀ ❋ ↔ 18–24 in (45–60 cm) ↕ 24–32 in (60–80 cm)
Fleshy-stemmed crested iris from central China and Japan. Shiny dark green leaves in fans. Pale lavender flowers with orange markings, ruffled and fringed at margins, borne on branching airy stems, in spring. Zones 8–10.

Iris laevigata
JAPANESE WATER IRIS, RABBIT EAR IRIS
☀/☀ ❋ ↔ 5 ft (1.5 m) ↕ 2–5 ft (0.6–1.5 m)
From Japan. Robust upright irises, grow in water and boggy areas. Will naturalize on edges of swamps and ponds. Tall spikes

of purple, mauve, and white flowers, above foliage, in summer. Large floppy petals hang gracefully toward the ground. '**Variegata**', to 16 in (40 cm) tall, green leaves striped with large white veins, purple-blue flowers, on short stems, Zones 3–9.

Iris missouriensis
☀ ❋ ↔ 12 in (30 cm) ↕ 12–20 in (30–50 cm)
Fleshy-stemmed beardless iris from western North America. Narrow grayish green leaves. White, blue, or purple flowers, long narrow falls, in late spring–summer. Zones 3–8.

Iris pallida
syns *Iris glauca, I. odoratissima*
DALMATIAN IRIS
☀ ❋ ↔ 12 in (30 cm) ↕ 36–48 in (90–120 cm)
Fleshy-stemmed bearded iris from the European Alps. Stiff, sword-like, bluish green foliage. Large fragrant flowers, blue with yellow beards, in early summer. *I. p.* **subsp.** *cengialti* ★ (syn. *I. cengialti*), greener leaves than species, dark purple flowers. *I. p.* '**Argentea Variegata**', white stripes on leaf edges; '**Variegata**', creamy yellow leaf markings. Zones 5–9.

Iris pseudacorus
YELLOW FLAG
☀ ❋ ↔ 5–7 ft (1.5–2 m) ↕ 4–5 ft (1.2–1.5 m)
Robust, potentially weedy water iris from Europe, Middle East, and northern Africa. Long, upright, rich green leaves die down in winter. Bright yellow flowers with brown markings on falls, 4 in (10 cm) across, just below the tallest leaves. '**Variegata**', boldly cream-variegated leaves fade to green after flowering. Zones 6–10.

Iris tectorum

Iris unguicularis

Iris versicolor

Iris pumila
DWARF BEARDED IRIS

☼ ❄ ↔ 4–6 in (10–15 cm) ↕ 4–6 in (10–15 cm)

Dainty rock-garden iris, found from eastern Europe to the Ural Mountains of Russia. Solitary flowers, perfumed, blue, purple, or yellow, in mid-spring. Zones 5–10.

Iris sibirica

☼ ❄ ↔ 8–24 in (20–60 cm) ↕ 18–48 in (45–120 cm)

From Europe and northern Asia. Rhizomatous beardless iris. Thin, grassy, bright green leaves. Purple-blue flowers, dark veins on falls, to 3 in (8 cm) wide, in late spring–summer. Zones 4–9.

Iris spuria

☼ ❄ ↔ 3–7 ft (0.9–2 m) ↕ 4–7 ft (1.2–2 m)

From northern and northwestern Iran. Colonizing iris. Flowers from pale and dark blues through to whites, creams, and mauves. Plants need rich warm soils. *I. s.* subsp. *halophila*, pale to deep yellow flowers, dark green strappy foliage. Zones 6–9.

Iris tectorum
ROOF IRIS

☼ ❄ ↔ 12 in (30 cm) ↕ 12–16 in (30–40 cm)

Native to China. Fleshy-stemmed crested iris. Light green leaves. Bluish purple flowers, darker veining, in early summer. Zones 6–9.

Iris unguicularis
syn. *Iris stylosa*
ALGERIAN IRIS, WINTER IRIS

☼/❄ ❄ ↔ 16–20 in (40–50 cm) ↕ 12–15 in (30–38 cm)

Evergreen species from Mediterranean region. Grows well in hot dry aspects. Tough grassy leaves and pale lavender to blue flowers, hidden among leaves, in winter–early spring. 'Mary Barnard', deep violet-blue flowers. Zones 7–10.

Iris versicolor

☼ ❄ ↔ 10 in (25 cm) ↕ 8–32 in (20–80 cm)

From eastern USA. Vigorous, water-loving, fleshy-stemmed, beardless iris. Broad, ribbed, green foliage. Many small flowers in bluish purple shades, with darker veining, carried on branching flower spikes. Summer-flowering species. Zones 4–9.

Iris Hybrid Cultivars
ARILBRED HYBRIDS

☼ ❄ ↔ 12 in (30 cm) ↕ 10–27 in (25–70 cm)

Large flowers in a range of purple shades and yellow, with colored markings, in early spring. Require a dry dormant summer season. 'Oyez', 24 in (60 cm) high, white flowers, dark purple veins on standards and falls. Zones 3–9.

BEARDED HYBRIDS

☼ ❄ ↔ 12–36 in (30–90 cm) ↕ 8–40 in (20–100 cm)

Hardy perennials. Grown from rhizomes. Will produce more flowers in cooler climates. Upright pale blue-green foliage. Large heads of flowers, in blues, purples, and browns through to oranges, whites, and yellows, in late spring. Flowers have standards and falls, with a distinctive beard on each fall. Do not cover rhizomes with soil, as they will rot and die. Need well-drained and fertile soil in full sun. Divide every 5 to 7 years.

Miniature Dwarf Bearded Hybrids: Less than 8 in (20 cm) high. Small flowers, 1½–3 in (35–80 mm) wide, in spring.

Standard Dwarf Bearded Hybrids: Flower well in cool maritime climates. Height of 8–15 in (20–38 cm). Form good clumps. Flowers in late spring. Need good cold period through winter to perform well. 'Bromyard', early season, blue-gray standards, blue-purple and ocher falls, blue-gray beards; 'Eyebright', yellow flowers with deep brown lines, creamy yellow beards; 'Flower Shower', ruffled flowers in violet and white; 'Honington', cream-yellow flowers; 'Rain Dance', early season, violet-blue flowers, matching violet-blue beards; 'Tirra Lirra', mauve flowers.

Intermediate Bearded Hybrids: These hybrids reach 16–27 in (40–70 cm) high. Medium-sized plants bear blooms that are also medium-sized. Will flower well in most areas, flowers well able to support themselves on their stems. Do well in wind-prone areas, but need full sun. 'Arctic Fancy', pure white flowers with purple markings; 'Eye Magic', yellow flowers, with red thumbprint on falls; 'Happy Mood' ★, creamy flowers edged in lavender; 'Maui Moonlight', mid-season, rich lemon flowers. Other popular Intermediate Bearded Hybrids include 'Katie-Koo', 'Miss Carla', 'Sherbet Lemon', and 'Templecloud'.

Miniature Tall Bearded Hybrids: Sharing a similar flowering season to the Tall Bearded Hybrids, and reaching similar height to Border Bearded Hybrids, these hybrids produce smaller flowers on wiry stems. '**Bumblebee Deelite**', yellow standards, maroon falls edged with yellow; '**Frosted Velvet**', two-tone flowers with white centers, rich velvet purple falls edged in white.

Border Bearded Hybrids: Flowering at same time as Tall Bearded Hybrids, but with somewhat smaller flowers held on stalks 16–27 in (40–70 cm) high. '**Apricot Frosty**', white flowers, deep apricot falls, apricot beards; '**Brown Lasso**', deep butterscotch and yellow flowers, petals edged in pale lavender.

Tall Bearded Hybrids: Well-branched spikes of robust large flowers, may be ruffled or smooth-edged. Can reach height of 27–40 in (70–100 cm). Good for cutting. '**Apricorange**', orange flowers; '**Berry Sherbet**', early flowering, pink and violet flowers; '**Blue-Eyed Brunette**', ruffled bronze flowers, blue beards; '**Breakers**', mid-blue ruffled flowers; '**Celebration Song**', late season, pinkish standards, lavender-blue falls; '**Champagne Elegance**' ★, apricot flowers, yellow standards, white falls edged in apricot, yellow-red beards, large number of blooms; '**Cinderella's Coach**', pumpkin orange flowers, bright red to tangerine beards, ruffled flowers; '**Cupid's Arrow**', pink to maroon flowers; '**Dazzling Gold**', mid-season, yellow and red flowers; '**Designing Woman**', rosy lilac standards and falls, coral beards, very wavy and ruffled blooms; '**Dusky Challenger**', large, ruffled, black-purple flowers; '**Early Light**', creamy yellow ruffled flowers; '**Good Morning America**', mid-season, pale blue flowers; '**Hello Darkness**', mid-season, rich velvet black flowers; '**Honky Tonk Blues**', mid-season, blue-violet, heavily washed over a white base, giving a soft blue effect, wide ruffled blooms; '**Incantation**', mid-season, bluish standards, pure white falls; '**In Town**', mid-season, lilac blue standards, with slightly ruffled purple falls; '**Jesse's Song**', white center bleeding into violet, lemon beard, violet edging; '**Stepping Out**', similar to 'Jesse's Song'; '**Thornbird**', yellowish standards, greenish brown falls; '**Vanity**', pink flowers, salmon pink beards. Other attractive Tall Bearded Hybrids include '**Bewick Swan**', '**Meg's Mantle**', '**Paradise**', '**Paradise Bird**', '**Phil Keen**', '**Precious Heather**', and '**Sun Miracle**'. Zones 3–9.

CALIFORNIAN HYBRIDS

☼/◐ ❋ ↔ 12 in (30 cm)
↑ 10–20 in (25–50 cm)

Hybrids of about 6 iris species from California and Oregon, sometimes known as Pacific Coast Hybrids, wide color range, from yellow to pink and purple. Long bloom period from spring. '**Broadleigh Carolyn**', compact white flowers, mauve-purple veining and yellow blotches in eye; '**Broadleigh Rose**', rich rose pink flowers, yellow and cream blotches in eye; '**Broadleigh Sybil**', creamy apricot standards, deep rose pink falls. Zones 5–9.

LOUISIANA HYBRIDS

☼/◐ ❋ ↔ 3–7 ft (0.9–2 m) ↑ 18–60 in (45–150 cm)

Adaptable to growing in water and also on edges of ponds and rivers. Will grow in ordinary garden soil if given plenty of water. Need well-prepared soil, with good amount of humus. Will grow in full sun or part-shade. Flowers from pinks, yellows, and blues to oranges, purples, and browns. '**Marie Caillet**', ruffled violet-blue flowers, yellow signals. Zones 6–9.

ONCOCYCLUS HYBRIDS

☼ ❋ ↔ 40 in (100 cm) ↑ 4–24 in (10–60 cm)

Similar to bearded iris, but smaller. One flower on each stem. Characteristic large blotch and dark veining on flowers. Adaptable to hot dry climates. Large seed heads in autumn. Zones 7–9.

SIBERIAN HYBRIDS

☼ ❋ ↔ 8–24 in (20–60 cm) ↑ 18–48 in (45–120 cm)

Adaptable irises, happy in heavy clay soils. Flower spikes taller than foliage, up to 5 flowers on each stem; flowers blue-violet or white. Flowers of '**Annemarie Troeger**' in 2 shades of blue, white signals; '**Harpswell Happiness**', ruffled white flowers; '**Pink Haze**', lavender-pink flowers, red-violet veins on falls; '**White Swirl**', pure white flowers, yellow blotches, flared outer petals. Zones 4–9.

SPURIA HYBRIDS

☼ ❋ ↔ 18–24 in (45–60 cm)
↑ 30–48 in (75–120 cm)

Tall plants with large flowers in white and yellow to red and purple shades, in spring–summer. '**Shelford Giant**', mid-season, large lemon and white flowers. Zones 4–9.

Iris, Hybrid Cultivar, Bearded, Tall, 'Cinderella's Coach'

Iris, Hybrid Cultivar, Louisiana, 'Marie Caillet'

Ismelia carinata

ISMELIA

This genus of around 5 species of annuals and short-lived perennials in the daisy (Asteraceae) family, which was established with the break-up of the genus *Chrysanthemum*, may prove to be indistinguishable from *Xanthopthalmum*. Found around the Mediterranean region and on Madeira and the Canary Islands, they are bushy plants with upright stems that sometimes become woody at the base. The foliage is pinnately lobed, sometimes with very narrow lobes, and may be toothed. The daisy-like flowerheads are often brightly colored and appear in abundance. CULTIVATION: These plants are intolerant of repeated frosts but are otherwise very adaptable in mild climates. Plant in a bright position with light well-drained soil. Water well when in bud and flower, but otherwise keep rather dry. Usually raised from seed, although perennial species may also be propagated from half-hardened stem cuttings.

Ismelia carinata

syns *Chrysanthemum carinatum, Ismelia versicolor*
☼/◐ ✷ ↔ 12–16 in (30–40 cm) ↕ 32–40 in (80–100 cm)
Annual of obscure origin, probably from Morocco. Upright stems; bright green, fleshy, pinnately lobed leaves. Flowerheads to 4 in (10 cm) diameter, disc florets dark, ray florets multicolored in yellow, orange, and red tones with light base, in summer–early autumn. 'Court Jesters', popular mixed color strain. Summer annual in cool areas. Zones 10–12.

JASIONE

SHEEP'S BIT
There are about 20 species of annuals, perennials, and biennials in this genus, which belongs to the bellflower (Campanulaceae) family. These plants are native to Europe and regions of the Mediterranean, where they grow in grassland. Plants form tufts of narrow grassy foliage. Their small blue flowers are borne in compact terminal heads reminiscent of scabious, and are surrounded by 1 or more rows of bracts. Flowers occur in summer. CULTIVATION: The small *Jasione* species are best grown in the rock garden while the taller ones are suitable for the front of the border. Grow in full sun in a well-drained sandy soil. Propagation is by division or from seed.

Jasione laevis

syn. *Jasione perennis*
SHEEP'S BIT, SHEPHERD'S SCABIOUS
☼ ✷ ↔ 8–10 in (20–25 cm) ↕ 8–20 in (20–50 cm)
From southern and western Europe. Perennial forming dense tufts of narrow leaves. The blue flowerheads are a little over 1 in (25 mm) wide and have numerous bracts. 'Blaulicht' (syn. 'Blue Light') has globose flowerheads of vivid blue. Zones 5–9.

KIRENGESHOMA

This genus of a single species, a woodland perennial from Japan and Korea, is a member of the hydrangea (Hydrangeaceae) family. These plants have large, maple-like, soft green leaves, and drooping thick-petalled flowers, shaped like a shuttlecock, are produced in late summer. CULTIVATION: Give *Kirengeshoma* a cool shaded aspect, sheltered from the wind, in moist humus-rich soil. Propagation is from seed freshly sown or by careful division of established clumps.

Kirengeshoma palmata

☀ ✷ ↔ 30 in (75 cm) ↕ 48 in (120 cm)
Elegant, arching, herbaceous perennial from Japan and Korea. Leaves to 8 in (20 cm) long on black stems. Pale lemon flowers to 1½ in (35 mm) long, in late summer. Zones 5–9.

KNAUTIA

This genus of some 60 species of annuals and herbaceous perennials is a member of the teasel (Dipsacaceae) family. They can be found in Europe, the Caucasus region, Siberia, and the Mediterranean region in a wide range of habitats, from woods to meadows and rocky hillsides. They have flowers very like those of *Scabiosa* species, consisting of a cluster of small flowers that look like a single bloom. Their open airy habit makes them useful in the border or the wild garden. CULTIVATION: Grow these plants in any well-drained fertile soil in full sun. Propagation is usually from seed and they will usually self-seed, sometimes to the extent of weediness.

Knautia arvensis

syn. *Scabiosa arvensis*
BLUE BUTTONS, FIELD SCABIOUS
☼ ✷ ↔ 12 in (30 cm) ↕ 5 ft (1.5 m)
Upright clumping perennial from Europe through to Siberia via the Caucasus, Iran, and central Asia. Hairy dull green leaves, smooth-edged through to indented, and up to 10 in (25 cm) long. Erect branched flower stems. Soft lilac-blue flowerheads, 1½ in (35 mm) across, from mid-summer through to cooler months. Zones 6–10.

KNIPHOFIA

RED-HOT POKER, TORCH LILY

Most of the nearly 70 species in this genus in the asphodel (Asphodelaceae) family are South African clump-forming perennials with grassy to sword-shaped, often evergreen, foliage that emerges from vigorous rhizomes. They are grown for their spikes of intensely colored, usually orange and/or yellow flowers, borne mainly from autumn to spring in bottlebrush heads at the top of strong, tall, upright stems. Many hybrids and cultivars are available in a variety of sizes and flower colors.

CULTIVATION: Hardiness varies, though none will tolerate repeated heavy frosts. Plant in an open sunny position in moist, humus-rich, well-drained soil. Water and feed well during active growth. Most will tolerate salt winds and thrive near the coast. Propagation is usually by division after flowering or from seed.

Kniphofia caulescens

☼/◐ ❄ ↔ 20 in (50 cm) ↕ 4 ft (1.2 m)

Tough evergreen alpine species. Narrow but thick blue-green leaves on "trunk" to 12 in (30 cm) high. Coppery flower stems and densely packed heads of pink-tinted cream flowers opening from red buds, in late summer–autumn. Zones 7–10.

Kniphofia northiae

☼/◐ ❄ ↔ 40 in (100 cm) ↕ 5 ft (1.5 m)

Evergreen perennial. Thick, broader, slightly blue-green leaves with deep central keel. Dense cylindrical heads of yellow flowers opening from red buds, in late spring–autumn. Zones 8–10.

Kniphofia × praecox

RED-HOT POKER

☼/◐ ❄ ↔ 20–40 in (50–100 cm) ↕ 4–5 ft (1.2–1.5 m)

Wild hybrids from South Africa, also garden hybrids. Evergreen perennial. Dense basal clumps of narrow deeply channeled leaves. Strong upright flower stems. Cylindrical to rounded heads of bright orange, yellow, or cream flowers, mainly in late summer–winter. Zones 7–10.

Kniphofia rooperi

☼/◐ ❄ ↔ 20–24 in (50–60 cm) ↕ 4 ft (1.2 m)

Evergreen perennial. Thick leaves with conspicuous keels. From late summer, large spherical heads of bright red flowers appear; lower flowers often yellow-green. Zones 8–10.

Kniphofia thomsonii

☼/◐ ❄ ↔ 16–24 in (40–60 cm) ↕ 4 ft (1.2 m)

From Kenya. Usually evergreen. Narrow leaves. Strong flower stems, large cylindrical heads of deep dusky red flowers, yellow-gold at base of head, in mid-summer to autumn. *K. t.* var. *snowdenii* is deciduous. Zones 9–11.

Kniphofia uvaria

☼/◐ ❄ ↔ 24 in (60 cm) ↕ 4 ft (1.2 m)

Evergreen perennial. Thick, deeply channeled leaves. Strong flower stems with ovoid heads of yellow-tipped, bright orange-red, tubular flowers, in late summer–autumn. Parent of many garden hybrids. Zones 5–10.

Kniphofia Hybrid Cultivars

☼/◐ ❄ ↔ 12–20 in (30–50 cm) ↕ 2–5 ft (0.6–1.5 m)

Many hybrids. 'Bees' Sunset', deciduous, leaves with serrated edges, yellow-orange flowers on dark stems to 3 ft (0.9 m) tall; 'Green Jade', evergreen, flowers initially pale cream ageing through cream to white, 5 ft (1.5 m) stems; 'Ice Queen', deciduous, green buds open pale yellow and age to off-white, 5 ft (1.5 m) stems; 'Little Maid', deciduous, fine grassy leaves, green buds open soft yellow and age to cream, 24 in (60 cm) stems; 'Painted Lady', dusky red flowers age to orange-pink, 3 ft (0.9 m) stems; 'Primrose Beauty', fine grassy foliage, bright yellow flowers, 24 in (60 cm) stems; 'Royal Standard', deciduous, bright yellow flowers open from red buds, stocky 3 ft (0.9 m) stems; 'Sunset', orange to red flowers; 'Tetbury Torch', broad, slightly blue-green leaves, golden yellow flowers open from orange buds, 3 ft (0.9 m) stems; 'Yellowhammer', spring-flowering, bright yellow flowers, 4 ft (1.2 m) stems. Zones 8–10.

Kniphofia caulescens

Kniphofia northiae

Kniphofia, Hybrid Cultivar, 'Little Maid'

Kniphofia, Hybrid Cultivar, 'Primrose Beauty'

Lamium maculatum 'Pink Pewter'

KOHLERIA

These 50 hairy herbs and shrubs, native to tropical Central and South America, are part of the African violet (Gesneriaceae) family, and are often cultivated as house plants. Large rhizomes grow across the soil surface and the thick, serrated, hairy or velvety leaves are often mottled with red. Trumpet-shaped flowers with erect, thick, hairy sepals and tubular corollas, usually in colors ranging from yellow through red to purple, are covered with red hairs and spotted on the inside with a contrasting color. CULTIVATION: These plants prefer moist well-drained soil, kept drier in winter, in full sun or part-shade. Propagate in spring by division of rhizomes or from seed sown in spring.

Kohleria digitaliflora

syn. *Kohleria warscewiczii*

☀ ❄ ↔ 12–24 in (30–60 cm)
↕ 12–24 in (30–60 cm)
Erect perennial from Colombia. Hairy white stems and dark green narrowly oval to sword-shaped leaves to 8 in (20 cm) long. Stalked clusters of very hairy flowers with white corolla tubes to 1¼ in (3 cm) long, flushed with deep rose, and green lobes spotted with purple, in summer–autumn. Zones 8–10.

Kohleria eriantha

☀ ❄ ↔ 3–4 ft (0.9–1.2 m) ↕ 3–4 ft (0.9–1.2 m)
Shrubby perennial from tropical Colombia. Reddish, densely hairy stems and oval to spear-shaped, deep green, velvety leaves, to 5 in (12 cm) long, with hairy red margins. Clusters of up to 4 drooping flowers, fuzzy, with corolla tubes to 2 in (5 cm) long, of scarlet-orange, with lobes ¼ in (6 mm) across, spotted with yellow, in late spring–summer. Zones 8–10.

Kohleria eriantha

LAMIUM

DEAD-NETTLE

This is the type genus for the mint (Lamiaceae) family. This group of about 50 species of low-growing annuals and perennials, which often spreads by rhizomes or runners, occurs naturally in Europe, North Africa, and temperate Asia, but some are also widely naturalized elsewhere and have become weeds. The opposite pairs of toothed, pointed, heart-shaped leaves resemble those of stinging nettles but lack the sting. They can be eaten as a salad vegetable. The small flowers, usually yellow, pink, or white, emerge in spring near the stem tips in leafy heads (verticillasters). CULTIVATION: These are very hardy and easily grown in any partly shaded or shaded position in moist, humus-rich, well-drained soil. Variegated forms often need more light to maintain their color. Propagate at any time from cuttings or by division.

Lamium galeobdolon

syns *Galeobdolon luteum, Lamiastrum galeobdolon*
YELLOW ARCHANGEL

◑/☀ ❄ ↔ 48 in (120 cm) ↕ 8–16 in (20–40 cm)
Vigorous, creeping or scrambling, near-evergreen perennial from temperate Eurasia. Leaves narrow, dark green, to over 2 in (5 cm) long, deeply toothed edges. Heads of up to 10 yellow flowers, to ¾ in (18 mm) long, in summer. **'Hermann's Pride'** ★, narrow leaves, silver streaks and spots; **'Silver Angel'**, low spreader, stems initially upright, silver-marked leaves. Zones 6–10.

Lamium garganicum

◑/☀ ❄ ↔ 48 in (120 cm) ↕ 8–16 in (20–40 cm)
From Europe, western Asia, and North Africa. Mat-forming, spreading, scrambling, near-evergreen perennial. Leaves broad, dull mid-green, toothed, triangular, to 3 in (8 cm) long. Heads of up to 8 widely spaced purple-pink to red flowers, to over 1 in (25 mm) long, in summer. Zones 6–10.

Lamium maculatum

◑/☀ ❄ ↔ 24–60 in (60–150 cm)
↕ 6–20 in (15–50 cm)
From Europe, western Asia, and North Africa. Spreading, sometimes mounding or scrambling, near-evergreen perennial. Stems long, rooting as they spread, with downy, toothed, pointed oval to triangular, often white-marked leaves, to over 3 in (8 cm) long. Heads of up to 8 widely spaced pinkish red to purple, rarely white, flowers, to ¾ in (18 mm) long, in summer. **'Album'**, silver blotched leaves, white flowers; **'Anne Greenaway'**, tricolor foliage, silver center outlined in dark green on yellow-green base, light purple flowers; **'Aureum'**, yellow-green leaves with white centers, pink flowers; **'Beacon Silver'**, silver leaves with thin green margin, pink to purplish flowers; **'Pink Nancy'**, silver leaves with thin green margin, pale pink flowers; **'Pink Pewter'**, green leaves overlaid with silver-gray, deep pink flowers; **'White Nancy'**, silver leaves with thin green margin, white flowers. Zones 4–10.

LATHYRUS

SWEET PEA, VETCHLING, WILD PEA

This genus in the pea-flower subfamily of the legume (Fabaceae) family has 110 species of annuals and perennials from Eurasia, North America, temperate South America, and the mountains

of east Africa. Many are climbers, others are low-spreading plants, and some are shrubby. The climbers support themselves with tendrils growing at the tips of the pinnate leaves, where the terminal leaflets would normally be. The typical pea-flowers occur in many colors, and may be borne singly or in racemes.
CULTIVATION: The non-climbing perennials will tolerate partial shade, but otherwise grow these species in sunny well-ventilated conditions. Plant in moist well-drained soil; provide stakes or wires for climbers. Propagate the annuals from seed sown in early spring, or in autumn–winter in mild climates, and the perennials by division when dormant.

Lathyrus laxiflorus

☼/◐ ❄ ↔ 16–24 in (40–60 cm) ↑ 12 in (30 cm)
From southeastern Europe. Low, somewhat spreading perennial. Paired lance-shaped leaflets, to 1¾ in (40 mm) long. Sprays of up to 6 white-centered violet flowers, ¾ in (18 mm) across, in summer. Zones 7–9.

Lathyrus odoratus

SWEET PEA
☼ ❄ ↔ 40 in (100 cm) ↑ 8 ft (2.4 m)
From Italy and the Mediterranean islands. Highly scented annual climber. Paired blue-green leaflets. Racemes of up to 3 violet and purple-red flowers in summer. Garden forms are heavier flowering, very wide range of colors. '**Alan Williams**', buff-pink and white flowers; '**Annie Good**', pink tonings; '**Anniversary**' ★, white with pink edge; '**Bijou Mix**', only 12 in (30 cm) tall, many colors; '**Brian Clough**', orange and white; '**Charlie's Angel**', blue and lavender; '**Eclipse**', deep lavender; '**Evening Glow**', mid-pink and orange; '**Firebird**', orange-red; '**Jill Walton**', cream and pale pink, darker edge; '**Lilac Ripple**', white and mauve; '**Midnight**', deep purple-red; '**Noel Sutton**', deep blue; '**Spencer Mixed**', large-flowered mixed color strains; '**Teresa Maureen**', lavender and cerise, purplish edge; '**Wiltshire Ripple**', brown-red and white; '**Winner**', red flowers suffused with orange. Cultivars with small, fragrant, single flowers, often known as **Heirloom** style, include '**Blanche Ferry**', pink and white bicolor; '**Cupani**', compact, very fragrant, purple and red flowers; '**Old Spice Mix**', very fragrant flowers in wide color range, including bicolor and striped; and '**Painted Lady**', pale pink and deep cherry red flowers. Zones 8–11.

Lathyrus splendens

PRIDE OF CALIFORNIA
☼ ❄ ↔ 3–7 ft (0.9–2 m) ↑ 7–10 ft (2–3 m)
From northern Baja California, Mexico. Shrubby, sometimes scrambling, evergreen perennial. Leaves tendril-tipped, with up to 10 leaflets to nearly 3 in (8 cm) long. Racemes of up to 12 violet to purple-red flowers, 1¾ in (40 mm) across. Zones 8–10.

Lathyrus odoratus 'Brian Clough'

Lathyrus vernus

SPRING VETCH
☼ ❄ ↔ 24–40 in (60–100 cm) ↑ 12–24 in (30–60 cm)
From Europe. Semi-evergreen perennial. Leaves with 1 to 2 pairs of leaflets. Racemes of up to 15 flowers, ¾ in (18 mm) across, purple-red ageing to blue-green, in early spring. '**Alboroseus**', pink and white flowers; '**Rosenelfe**', pale pink flowers. Zones 4–9.

LAVATERA

TREE MALLOW
There are 25 species of evergreen or deciduous annuals, biennials, perennials, and softwooded shrubs in this genus within the mallow (Malvaceae) family found from the Mediterranean to the northwestern Himalayas, and in parts of Asia, Australia, California (USA), and Baja California (Mexico). The leaves are usually palmately lobed and slightly downy, and most species have attractive hibiscus-like flowers with prominent staminal columns, in colors ranging from white to a rosy purple. *Lavatera* is closely related to *Malva*, and following recent botanical studies several of its species have been reclassified as *Malva* species.
CULTIVATION: Shrubby mallows are suitable for planting in mixed borders, where they will bloom abundantly throughout summer. They should be grown in full sun in light well-drained soil. Too rich a soil will result in an excess of foliage at the expense of flowers. Prune after flowering to prevent legginess. Mallows tend to be short lived; softwood cuttings taken in spring or early summer strike readily and are the usual method of propagation for shrubby species.

Lavatera × *clementii*

☼ ❄ ↔ 6 ft (1.8 m) ↑ 6 ft (1.8 m)
Vigorous upright plants. Sometimes short lived. '**Barnsley**' ★, masses of pale pink flowers; '**Bredon Springs**' ★, deep pink flowers; '**Rosea**', tall, gray-tinted foliage, dusky pink flowers. Zones 8–10.

Lavatera × *clementii* 'Barnsley'

Lavatera thuringiaca

TREE MALLOW

※ ❄ ↔ 3–4 ft (0.9–1.2 m) ↑ 6 ft (1.8 m)

Shrubby evergreen perennial from central Europe. Rose pink flowers for several months in summer–autumn. Zones 8–11.

Lavatera trimestris

ANNUAL MALLOW, REGAL MALLOW, ROSE MALLOW,
ROYAL MALLOW

※ ❄ ↔ 18–36 in (45–90 cm)
↑ 24–48 in (60–120 cm)

Bushy easy-to-grow annual native to Mediterranean region. No need to stake. Silky cup-shaped flowers. 'Ruby Regis', to 24 in (60 cm) tall, cerise pink flowers; 'Silver Cup', 24 in (60 cm) tall, pink flowers. Zones 8–10.

LEONOTIS

Comprising 15 species, this genus of soft-wooded annuals, perennials, and evergreen to semi-deciduous subshrubs in the mint (Lamiaceae) family, with the exception of one widely distributed tropical species, occurs wild in tropical and southern Africa. Opposite pairs of mid-green leaves are borne on upright squarish stems, and in late summer to winter whorls of narrow 2-lipped flowers are arranged densely around the stems.

CULTIVATION: These are warm-climate plants that can be grown under cover in frost-prone areas. They need moderately fertile soil in full sun and ample water in the growing season. The somewhat brittle stems can be cut back in spring. Propagate from seed or from softwood cuttings in summer.

Leonotis nepetifolia

※ ❄ ↔ 8–12 in (20–30 cm) ↑ 3–4 ft (0.9–1.2 m)

From India and Africa; now naturalized in parts of North America. Upright annual. Serrated leaves, to 5 in (12 cm) long. Curved orange trumpet-flowers in winter. Zones 8–11.

Leonotis ocymifolia

syn. *Leonotis leonurus*

LION'S TAIL, WILD DAGGA

※ ◗ ↔ 3 ft (0.9 m) ↑ 8 ft (2.4 m)

Clump-forming plant, semi-deciduous or evergreen depending on climate. Upright stems. Bright orange woolly flowers in late summer–winter. 'Alba' and 'Harrismith White', white-flowered plants. Zones 9–11.

LEONTOPODIUM

A rock garden favorite, *Leontopodium* is a member of the daisy (Asteraceae) family. The approximately 60 species are hardy, herbaceous, alpine perennials. Most are native to the mountain regions of east and central Asia, with only one species occurring in Europe. The gray-green leaves are basal or alternate, and coated with white hairs. The flowerheads are small and white.

Leontopodium alpinum

In the wild, these tufted herbs grow in alpine meadows, on scree slopes, and among rocks, in cool to cold climates.

CULTIVATION: These plants require a well-drained gritty or sandy soil and a sunny position. They will not tolerate damp conditions, and generally prefer cooler temperatures. Propagate from seed.

Leontopodium alpinum

EDELWEISS

※ ❄ ↔ 4–9 in (10–22 cm) ↑ 6 in (15 cm)

The only European species, from the Alps, Carpathians, and Pyrenees. Creeping short-lived perennial. Leaves silvery gray, 2–3 in (5–8 cm) long. Star-shaped white flowers with central yellow floret surrounded by long floral bracts in early summer. Zones 4–8.

LESPEDEZA

This genus is a member of the large pea-flower subfamily of the legume (Fabaceae) family. It contains about 40 species of usually prostrate annuals and perennials and deciduous shrubs, which are found in eastern and tropical Asia, Australia, and eastern USA. The leaves are trifoliate, and the flowers are small but are usually borne in long racemes.

CULTIVATION: Grow these in a sunny position in deep, well-drained, fertile soil. In cooler areas they need a warm wall for protection. In spring prune out dead growth and cut back hard to rejuvenate the plant. Propagate from seed or from half-hardened cuttings.

Lespedeza thunbergii

MIYAGINO-HAGI, THUNBERG BUSH CLOVER

※ ❄ ↔ 5–10 ft (1.5–3 m) ↑ 3–8 ft (0.9–2.4 m)

From Japan and China. An erect semi-evergreen or deciduous shrubby perennial. Long, wiry, widely spreading, interlacing branches; arching fountain-like habit. Bluish green compound leaves with 3 sharp-tipped leaflets, smooth above, finely hairy beneath. Dense drooping racemes of numerous pea-flowers with rose-purple corollas in late summer–autumn. 'Alba', white flowers; 'Albiflora', smaller leaflets, small white flowers with violet markings; 'Edo Shindori', pink and white flowers; 'Gibraltar', profuse lavender pink flowers. Zones 4–9.

LEUCANTHEMUM

This genus from Europe and northern Asia contains 33 species of annual and perennial daisies (family Asteraceae), most of which have flowerheads with white ray florets, usually around a central boss of golden disc florets. They form often large clumps of deep green, usually toothed, linear to spatula-shaped leaves. The flowers appear from spring to autumn, depending on the species. Garden forms include pompon-centered flowers and various colors.

CULTIVATION: Grow in a sunny position in moist well-drained soil. Feeding and watering will result in more luxuriant plants but not

Leonotis nepetifolia

necessarily more flowers. Tall types may need staking. Propagate the species from seed, cultivars and hybrids by division or from basal cuttings.

Leucanthemum × superbum
syns *Chrysanthemum maximum* of gardens, *C. superbum*
SHASTA DAISY

☼/☀ ❋ ↔ 40 in (100 cm) ↑ to 48 in (120 cm)
Garden hybrid. Many upright flower stems emerging from dense basal clump of dark green, toothed, spatula-shaped leaves, to 8 in (20 cm) long. Flowerheads solitary, to 4 in (10 cm) across, ray florets white, disc florets golden yellow. 'Aglaia' ★, white semi-double flowers; 'Becky', large, single, white flowers in spring–summer; 'Cobham Gold', creamy yellow double flowers; 'Esther Read', feathery semi-double flowers; 'Horace Read', feathery double flowers; 'Marconi', very large, double,

Leucanthemum × superbum

white flowers; 'Silberprinzesschen', single white flowers in spring–autumn; 'Snow Lady', single white flowers in spring–autumn; 'Snowcap', large, white, single flowers; 'T. E. Killin', yellow-centered, white, semi-double flowers; 'Wirral Supreme', anemone-centered white flowers. Zones 5–10.

Leucanthemum vulgare
syn. *Chrysanthemum leucanthemum*
OX-EYE DAISY

☼/☀ ❋ ↔ 24 in (60 cm) ↑ 40 in (100 cm)
From Europe and northern Asia. Perennial, forming basal clump of toothed leaves, to 4 in (10 cm) long. Flower stems sometimes branched, with small leaves, flowerheads 1–3 in (2.5–8 cm) across, ray florets white, disc florets yellow, in summer. Zones 3–9.

LEWISIA
BITTER ROOT

This is a genus of 19 species of exquisite, semi-succulent, evergreen and deciduous, alpine and subalpine perennials in the purslane (Portulacaceae) family. They are found in western North America from New Mexico to southern Canada and usually form basal rosettes of fleshy, linear, lance- or spatula-shaped leaves. Their starry many-petaled flowers may be solitary or clustered and are borne in shades of yellow, apricot, and pink at the ends of short wiry stems from mid-spring through to early summer.
CULTIVATION: Most have deep tap roots and prefer gritty free-draining soil; keep moist in the growing season but otherwise dry. Plant in full or half-sun and use gravel mulch around the crown to prevent rotting. Deciduous species generally only reproduce from seed, but evergreens can also be propagated from offsets.

Lewisia columbiana
☼/☀ ❋ ↔ 8 in (20 cm) ↑ 12 in (30 cm)
Found over much of North America west of the Rockies. Evergreen. Crowded, fleshy, narrow, basal leaves, 1–4 in (2.5–10 cm)

long. Many-flowered heads of pink-veined white to magenta flowers, to 1 in (25 mm) across, with up to 11 petals, in spring–summer. Zones 5–9.

Lewisia cotyledon
☼/☀ ❋ ↔ 8 in (20 cm) ↑ 6–12 in (15–30 cm)
From California and Oregon, USA. Evergreen. Loose rosette of spatula-shaped leaves, to over 4 in (10 cm) long, often blue-green and/or pink-tinted, edges often wavy, rarely toothed. Panicles of 7- to 10-petaled flowers, to 1¾ in (40 mm) across, in spring–summer. Flowers usually purple-pink. *L. c.* f. *alba*, white flowers. Sunset Group, shades of yellow, orange, pink, and red; 'White Splendour', dark green foliage, pure white flowers. Zones 5–9.

Lewisia 'Pinkie'
☼/☀ ❋ ↔ 8 in (20 cm) ↑ 6–8 in (15–20 cm)
Evergreen hybrid. Resembles a compact *L. cotyledon* with slightly narrower leaves. Many broad-petaled apricot pink flowers with dark pink centers. Zones 5–9.

Lewisia rediviva
BITTERROOT

☼/☀ ❋ ↔ 8 in (20 cm) ↑ 4 in (10 cm)
Found over much of subalpine and alpine western North America. Deciduous. Dense basal tuft of many narrow leaves, to 2 in (5 cm) long. Flowers solitary, to over 2 in (5 cm) across, with up to 6 petals in pink to purple shades or white. Zones 4–9.

Lewisia tweedyi
☼/☀ ❋ ↔ 8 in (20 cm) ↑ 8 in (20 cm)
From Washington State, USA, and British Columbia, Canada. Evergreen. Small clump of often purple-tinted, broad, lance-shaped leaves, to 3 in (8 cm) long. Up to 8 soft pink or yellow, 7- to 12-petaled flowers, to over 2 in (5 cm) across, in spring–summer. Zones 5–9.

LIATRIS
BLAZING STAR, GAYFEATHER, SNAKE ROOT

Native to eastern North America and growing from corms or modified flattened roots, the 35 species of perennials in this genus of the daisy (Asteraceae) family make a bold splash of color in summer; very easy to grow. They form clumps of simple linear to lance-shaped leaves, sometimes finely hairy, bearing 24–60 in (60–150 cm) tall stems, topped with long, quite un-daisy-like, bottlebrush spikes of filamentous purple-pink flowers.
CULTIVATION: While hardiness varies, most species are frost resistant. They can be grown in any sunny position in moist, humus-rich, well-drained soil. Place at back of borders to disguise the foliage clump and make use of flower stem's height. Propagate by division or from seed.

Liatris aspera
ROUGH BLAZING STAR

☼/◑ ❄ ↔ 12–20 in (30–50 cm) ↑ 40 in (100 cm)
Found across most of eastern North America. Leaves narrow, to 6 in (15 cm) long. Spikes of up to 20 purple flowerheads in mid-summer to autumn. Zones 5–10.

Liatris pycnostachya
BUTTON SNAKE ROOT

☼/◑ ❄ ↔ 10–18 in (25–45 cm) ↑ 60 in (150 cm)
Native to southeastern USA. Strongly upright habit. Leaves narrow, sometimes downy, to 4 in (10 cm) long. Densely crowded purple-red flowerheads, in spikes to 12 in (30 cm) long, in mid-summer–autumn. 'Alexander', dark green foliage, purple flowerheads. Zones 3–10.

Liatris spicata ★
BLAZING STAR, BUTTON SNAKE ROOT, GAYFEATHER

☼/◑ ❄ ↔ 10–18 in (25–45 cm) ↑ 60 in (150 cm)
Found across most of eastern USA. Upright habit. Leaves narrow, sometimes linear, to 8 in (20 cm) long. Dense spikes, to 24 in (60 cm) long, with purple-red flowerheads in mid-summer to autumn. 'Callilepsis Purple', 24 in (60 cm) high, dark purple flowerheads; 'Floristan', 32 in (80 cm) high, deep violet flowerheads; 'Floristan White', 32 in (80 cm) high, white flowerheads; 'Kobold' (syn. 'Goblin'), 20 in (50 cm) high, dense heads of purple-pink flowers. Zones 3–10.

LIBERTIA
The 9 species of perennial rhizomatous plants in this genus, a Southern Hemisphere member of the iris (Iridaceae) family, have a creeping or tufted growth habit and a prolonged flowering season. They occur in eastern Australia, New Zealand, New Guinea, and the Andes of South America. The strap-like leaves are produced in sparse to dense tufts. The flowers, usually white and recognizably iris-like in form, are borne in clusters at the top of straight stems. Often the leaves partially obscure the flowers.
CULTIVATION: Most species are quite tolerant of both drought and poor soils; however, they will respond visibly to softer conditions and light feeding. Some species may be used for roadside plantings. Propagate in spring by division or from seed.

Liatris pycnostachya

Ligularia przewalskii

Libertia formosa
SHOWY LIBERTIA, SNOWY MERMAID

☼ ❄ ↔ 24 in (60 cm) ↑ 18–36 in (45–90 cm)
Chilean species. Clumping perennial. Dark green leaves, narrow, strap-shaped, and leathery. Tall spikes of white or pale yellow flowers in late spring. Zones 9–10.

Libertia grandiflora
MIKOIKOI, NEW ZEALAND IRIS, TUKAUKI

☼ ❄ ↔ 24 in (60 cm) ↑ 30 in (75 cm)
From New Zealand. Clumping perennial. Leaves green to yellowy green, narrow, leathery. Tall spike of white flowers, in dense clusters, in spring, followed by attractive, yellow, pear-shaped seed capsules. Zones 8–11.

Libertia ixioides
MIKOIKOI, NEW ZEALAND IRIS, TUKAUKI

☼ ❄ ↔ 24 in (60 cm) ↑ 8–12 in (20–30 cm)
From New Zealand. Clumping perennial. Leaves green to orange-brown, narrow, leathery. Spike of white flowers in late spring. Zones 8–11.

Libertia peregrinans

☼/◑ ❄ ↔ 20 in (50 cm) ↑ 15–27 in (38–70 cm)
From New Zealand. Long-running rhizomes. Leaves obviously veined, turning orange-brown in cold weather. White flowers with yellow anthers in spring. Needs well-drained soil. Zones 8–10.

LIGULARIA
This temperate Eurasian genus of the daisy (Asteraceae) family has some 125 species of perennials. In spring these vigorous

plants soon develop into clumps of long-stalked, broad, basal leaves, usually kidney- to heart-shaped, with toothed edges. In summer and autumn flowering stems develop, ranging from broadly forking panicles of large yellow to orange daisies to tall spike-like racemes of numerous smaller heads. CULTIVATION: Most species are very hardy. Grow in full to half-sun, in deep, fertile, humus-rich soil kept moist through the year. Cut back when flowers and foliage fade. Propagate by division when dormant or from seed.

Ligularia dentata

☀/◐ ❄ ↔ 40–60 in (100–150 cm) ↕ 30–60 in (75–150 cm)
From China and Japan. Vigorous clump-forming perennial. Impressive foliage. Leaves rounded to kidney-shaped, deeply toothed, with downy undersides, often red-tinted, to 16 in (40 cm) wide. Strong upright flower stems branching broadly with many gold to orange flowerheads to 4 in (10 cm) across. 'Desdemona', purple-red leaves, orange flowers on stems to 48 in (120 cm). Zones 4–10.

Ligularia przewalskii

SHAVALSKI'S LIGULARIA
☀/◐ ❄ ↔ 40–48 in (100–120 cm) ↕ 7 ft (2 m)
Northern Chinese vigorous perennial. Leaves deeply palmately lobed and toothed, basal leaves to 12 in (30 cm) long and wide. Stems dark purple-red. Narrow spikes of many spidery golden yellow flowerheads. Zones 4–9.

Ligularia stenocephala

☀/◐ ❄ ↔ 32–40 in (80–100 cm) ↕ 60 in (150 cm)
Native to Japan, China, and Taiwan. Leaves heart-shaped to tri-angular, toothed, basal leaves to 12 in (30 cm) long and wide. Stems deep purple-red. Deep yellow flowerheads, to over 2 in (5 cm) across. Zones 5–10.

Ligularia Hybrid Cultivars

☀/◐ ❄ ↔ 32–60 in (80–150 cm)
↕ 3–7 ft (0.9–2 m)
Bred with both foliage and flowers in mind, hy-brid ligularias are bold architectural plants ideally suited to moist partly shaded corners, especially near ponds and streams. 'Gregynog Gold', coarsely toothed green leaves, and pyramidal spikes of orange flowers; 'The Rocket', dark black-green stems contrasting with numerous bright yellow flowerheads; 'Weihenstephan', large deep golden yellow flowerheads; 'Zepter', slightly shorter than the species but with more densely crowded golden yellow flowerheads. Zones 5–9.

LIMONIUM

SEA LAVENDER, STATICE
Genus of about 150 species of mainly summer-flowering annuals, perennials, and small shrubs in the leadwort (Plumbaginaceae) family, widely dis-tributed around the world, but with the main concentration in southern Europe and North Africa. Most are low-growing, forming mounds of basal leaf rosettes. The leaves vary in size and tend to be lance- or spatula-shaped. Flowers are minute but showy, borne in billowing sprays held well clear of the foliage on branching wiry stems, in white, cream, and mauve to purple shades. The flowers are still widely sold as "statice." CULTIVATION: Many species are somewhat frost tender, thriving in coastal conditions, with a preference for sheltered sunny locations and light, well-drained, yet moist soil. If the flowers are not cut for indoor use, they should be removed, as allowing the plants to set seed can shorten their life. Propagate from seed or root cuttings, or by division, depending on the plant type.

Limonium brassicifolium

☀/◐ ❄ ↔ 12 in (30 cm) ↕ 16 in (40 cm)
From Canary Islands. Perennial with a woody rhizome producing winged stems and 4–12 in (10–30 cm) long, broad, pointed oval leaves. Panicles of many single-flowered spikes with purple calyces and a white corolla. Zones 9–11.

Limonium perezii

☀/◐ ❄ ↔ 20 in (50 cm) ↕ 27 in (70 cm)
From Canary Islands. Broad oval leaves, to 6 in (15 cm) long. Flower stems downy. Large heads of flowers with deep purple calyces and creamy yellow to white corolla. Zones 9–11.

Limonium sinuatum

syn. *Statice sinuata*
☀/◐ ❄ ↔ 16 in (40 cm) ↕ 16 in (40 cm)
Native to Mediterranean region. Perennial, often short-lived and treated as annual. All parts downy. Leaves lance-shaped, 1–4 in (2.5–10 cm) long. Flower stems winged, with many short com-pact spikes of papery flowers in summer. White, lavender, or pink flowers; cultivars in many colors. Can be invasive. 'Art Shades', pastel tones, most colors; **California Series**, bright tones, most colors; 'Forever Gold', deep golden yellow flowers. Zones 9–11.

Limonium brassicifolium

Linum grandiflorum 'Rubrum'

LINUM

FLAX

This genus, which gives its name to the family Linaceae, comprises about 180 species of tender and hardy annuals, biennials, perennials, and subshrubs, with flax, *L. usitatissum*, the important fiber and oilseed plant included among them. Native to temperate or subtropical regions of the world though mainly from the Northern Hemisphere. They are delicate but easy-to-grow plants. The stems are erect and branching, and the gray-green leaves are simple and narrow. The cup-to funnel-shaped 5-petalled flowers are carried in branched clusters at the stem tips, lasting only one day. Colors vary with the variety but are mostly shades of blue or yellow, less commonly red, pink, or white. However, they are produced in great numbers throughout summer.

CULTIVATION: For the best flowering effect, grow in well-drained humus-rich soil in full sun. Provide shelter in cool climates. Annuals and perennials are easily raised from seed or from cuttings of named varieties. Plant out perennials in autumn or early spring; sow annual species in early autumn or spring. Thin seedlings as needed.

Linum 'Gemmell's Hybrid'

☼ ❄ ↔ 8 in (20 cm) ↑ 6 in (15 cm)

Short golden yellow form best grown at the front of a border or in the rock garden. Zones 6–9.

Linum grandiflorum

FLOWERING FLAX

☼ ❄ ↔ 12 in (30 cm) ↑ 15–18 in (38–45 cm)

From Algeria. Annual. Slender stems; narrow, pointed, pale green leaves. Single, clear rose to purple, saucer-shaped flowers, 1½ in (35 mm) across, in early–late summer. 'Bright Eyes', to 15 in (38 cm) tall, white flowers, 2 in (5 cm) across, with carmine eye; 'Rubrum' (scarlet flax), to 12 in (30 cm) tall, brilliant crimson flowers. Zones 7–10.

Linum narbonense

☼ ❄ ↔ 12–18 in (30–45 cm) ↑ 12–24 in (30–60 cm)

From southern Europe. Perennial. Leaves gray-green, narrow. Rich blue cup-shaped flowers, 1–1¼ in (25–30 mm) across, with white eye, in late spring–autumn. Usually dies back in winter but may be evergreen in mild climates. 'Heavenly Blue', more compact, with ultramarine flowers. Zones 5–9.

Linum perenne

PERENNIAL BLUE FLAX

☼ ❄ ↔ 12 in (30 cm) ↑ 12–18 in (30–45 cm)

From Europe. Vigorous but short-lived perennial. Many sky blue flowers, 1 in (25 mm) across, in early–late summer. Easy to raise from seed; self-seeds freely. Zones 4–9.

LINARIA

SPURRED SNAPDRAGON, TOADFLAX

From the foxglove (Scrophulariaceae) family, this genus encompasses about 150 species of annuals and perennials found in Europe (mainly around the Mediterranean) and temperate Asia. Toadflaxes are closely related to snapdragons, with similar but smaller flowers. They are easy to cultivate but stop flowering in hot weather. For best effect, plant in masses, as the individual plants are wispy.

CULTIVATION: Grow in full or half-sun in well-drained soil. Cut perennials down to ground level in autumn. Propagate annuals and perennials from seed; perennials also by division and from cuttings. Sow seed outdoors in late autumn or early spring (even when snow is still on ground) or indoors. Annuals also self-seed.

Linaria maroccana

ANNUAL TOADFLAX, BUNNY RABBITS, MOROCCO TOADFLAX

☼ ❄ ↔ 6–12 in (15–30 cm) ↑ 8–10 in (20–25 cm)

From Morocco; naturalized in northeastern USA. Annual. Leaves narrow, grass-like, alternate. Profuse tiny snapdragon-like flowers in white, yellow, pink, red, and dark blue to purple shades in early summer. 'Fairy Bouquet', flowers ranging from lavender, purple, and pink to crimson; 'Fantasy Blue', dwarf form, compact habit, will grow year-round in mild climates; 'Northern Lights', faintly violet-scented, jewel-like, bicolored flowers in pink, red, yellow, and purple; Soda Pop Series, magenta-rose, blue, or pink flowers. Zones 9–11.

Linaria purpurea

PURPLE TOADFLAX

☼ ❄ ↔ 6–12 in (15–30 cm) ↑ 20–36 in (50–90 cm)

From southern Europe. Narrow bushy perennial. Slender gray-green leaves. Bright blue-purple flowers with white stripes in mid-summer–early autumn. 'Canon Went', tall, with grayish foliage and soft pink flowers. Zones 5–10.

LIRIOPE

LILY TURF

This small genus in the family Ruscaceae has 5 or 6 species of evergreen or semi-evergreen frost-hardy perennials. From acid-soil woodland habitats in East Asia. Tough, mat-forming, trouble-free plants, which soon establish a dense fibrous root system and in some species develop nutrient-storing fleshy tubers. The grass-like leaves are arching, linear, and dense. Flowers are clustered and grape-like on blunt stems, usually showy for extended late summer period, followed by black, berry-like seeds. **CULTIVATION:** Grow in shade in mild climates; allow more sun in cold climates. Propagate by division or by fresh ripe seed sown in a sandy medium.

Liriope muscari 'Monroe White'

Liriope muscari

☼/☀ ❄ ↔ 18 in (45 cm) ↑ 12 in (30 cm)

Native to China, Taiwan, and Japan. Woodland plant; drought-tolerant, tough, sturdy, evergreen, spreading ground cover. Leaves narrow, glossy deep green. Dense, bead-like, steely deep lavender flowers, held on blunt spikes, in late autumn. '**Christmas Tree**', large form, resplendent flowers; '**John Burch**', large flowers on tall spikes, wide leaves with yellow-green central stripe; '**Majestic**', violet flowers; '**Monroe White**', numerous white flowers, requires full shade; '**Variegata**', leaves boldly edged in yellow. Zones 4–10.

Liriope spicata

☼/☀ ❄ ↔ 18 in (45 cm) ↑ 10 in (25 cm)

From China and Vietnam. Drought-tolerant evergreen ground cover. Leaves glossy, dark, dense. Pale lavender flowers in late summer. '**Silver Dragon**', compact, to about 8 in (20 cm) tall, narrow dark leaves silver striped, pale purple flowers. Zones 5–10.

LOBELIA

Lobelia is a large, enormously variable, and widespread genus of the bellflower (Campanulaceae) family, including over 350 species of annuals, perennials, and shrubs. Other than the annuals, with their massed summer display of blue, white, or pink flowers, cultivated lobelias are mainly perennials from the Americas, most of which form a basal clump of simple leaves, from which emerge upright flower stems bearing spikes of tubular 5-lobed flowers, the lower 3 lobes enlarged. **CULTIVATION:** Requirements vary but most *Lobelia* species prefer a sunny position with moist well-drained soil. Tall types may need staking. Propagate the annuals from seed sown in spring and the perennials by division or from basal cuttings.

Lobelia cardinalis

CARDINAL FLOWER

☼/☀ ❄ ↔ 12–16 in (30–40 cm) ↑ 36 in (90 cm)

North American short-lived perennial forming clump of upright stems with often red-tinted, narrow, pointed oval to lance-shaped leaves, to 4 in (10 cm) long. Long spikes of bright red flowers, to over 1 in (25 mm) wide, from summer to autumn. Zones 6–9.

Lobelia erinus

BEDDING LOBELIA, EDGING LOBELIA

☼/☀ ❄ ↔ 12–16 in (30–40 cm) ↑ 8 in (20 cm)

South African, small, long-flowering perennial usually treated as an annual. Dense mounding habit; fine stems; small, often purple-tinted, deep green leaves, roughly oval, toothed. Masses of small pale-centered flowers, blue, mauve, purple. Seedling strains differ mainly in size and growth habit. **Cascade Series**, for hanging baskets; '**Kathleen Mallard**', mounding, with deep blue double flowers; '**Mrs. Clibran**', mounding, with dark blue flowers; **Palace Series**, dwarf and heavy flowering, for borders and pots; '**Periwinkle Blue**', trailer, bright blue flowers; **Regatta Series**, trailer, mixed colors; **Royal Jewels** seed mix, flowers in blue, mauve, and purple-red shades. Zones 8–11.

Lobelia × gerardii

☼/☀ ❄ ↔ 20–24 in (50–60 cm) ↑ 60 in (150 cm)

Garden hybrid. Vigorous perennial forming a clump of upright stems with pointed oval to elliptical leaves, to 6 in (15 cm) long, mainly crowded at base. Large heads of white-marked pink or violet to purple flowers. '**Bee's Flame**', bronze foliage, red flowers; '**Cherry Ripe**', dark green leaves, red flowers; **Compliment Series**, seedling strain, blue or red flowers; '**Fan Scarlet**', green foliage, purple-red flowers; '**Queen Victoria**' ★, deep red foliage and stems, bright red flowers; '**Russian Princess**', green foliage, green flowers; '**Tania**', red-tinted foliage, deep magenta flowers; '**Vedrariensis**', red-tinted foliage, purple flowers. Zones 7–10.

Lobelia laxiflora

TORCH LOBELIA

☼/☀ ❄ ↔ 4 ft (1.2 m) ↑ 3 ft (0.9 m)

From southern Arizona, USA, through the Mexican highlands to Colombia, occurring in oak and pine forests. Variable species with shrubby habit. Leaves pointed, lance-shaped. Long-stalked tubular flowers, scarlet with yellow tips, in summer. Zones 8–11.

Lobelia × *gerardii* 'Tania'

Lobelia laxiflora

Lobelia tupa

flowers. Cultivars vary in size and color. **'Carpet of Snow'**, to 4 in (10 cm) tall, pure white flowers; **Easter Bonnet Series**, to 6 in (15 cm) tall, flowers white and pink to purple; **'Snow Crystals'**, to 8–10 in (20–25 cm) tall, large white flowers. Zones 7–10.

LOTUS

This genus in the pea-flower subfamily of the legume (Fabaceae) family has around 150 species of annuals, perennials, and deciduous and evergreen subshrubs. They are found almost worldwide in open grasslands and rocky places. The leaves are small and pinnate, often with only 4 or 5 leaflets and sometimes closely hairy, giving them a silvery appearance. The pea-flowers are white to yellow, pink, or red, and are borne singly or in clusters in the leaf axils. The most colorful are species from the Canary Islands and Madeira, with yellow or red flowers. The trailing types are suited to hanging baskets or pots.
CULTIVATION: Most prefer well-drained soil in full sun. Propagate from seed in spring or autumn, from cuttings in early summer.

Lobelia siphilitica
BLUE CARDINAL FLOWER
☼/◐ ❋ ↔ 16 in (40 cm) ↑ 24 in (60 cm)
From eastern USA. Bushy perennial with mainly basal foliage. Leaves pointed oval to lance-shaped, toothed, to 4 in (10 cm) long. Flower stems upright, with long spikes of deep blue flowers, to 1 in (25 mm) across, in summer–autumn. Zones 5–9.

Lobelia tupa
☼ ❋ ↔ 3 ft (0.9 m) ↑ 6 ft (1.8 m)
From Chile, growing in sandy hills near the sea. Attractive leaves lightly felted, grayish green. Terminal spikes of scarlet or brick-red flowers in summer–autumn. Zones 8–10.

LOBULARIA
ALYSSUM, BEDDING ALYSSUM
This genus of 5 species of annuals and perennials belongs to the cabbage (Brassicaceae) family and is from the northern temperate zones. They are small mounding plants with simple linear to lance-shaped leaves, sometimes with fine silvery hairs. Tiny, often sweet-scented flowers appear in the warmer months, in rounded heads. Garden forms are available in white and shades of primrose, apricot, mauve, and purple.
CULTIVATION: These plants are hardy, and easily grown in sun in light free-draining soil. Water to encourage flowering, but plants often remain more compact if kept dry. Propagate from seed, or the seed may be broadcast; often self-sows.

Lobularia maritima
BEDDING ALYSSUM
☼ ❋ ↔ 8–16 in (20–40 cm) ↑ 10 in (25 cm)
Widespread in northern temperate zones. Annual or short-lived perennial. Narrow dull green leaves, about 1 in (25 mm) long. Tiny flowers in massed rounded heads. Usually white to cream

Lotus berthelotii
CORAL GEM, PARROT'S BEAK, PELICAN'S BEAK
☼ ✛ ↔ 3–6 ft (0.9–1.8 m) ↑ 8 in (20 cm)
From the Canary Islands. Popular, trailing, evergreen plant. Leaves silvery gray, with needle-like leaflets. Yellow-orange to red flowers, 1½ in (35 mm) long, in spring–summer. Zones 10–11.

Lotus maculatus
syn. *Heinekenia maculata*
FIRE VINE
☼ ✛ ↔ 3–6 ft (0.9–1.8 m) ↑ 8 in (20 cm)
From the Canary Islands. Trailing perennial well suited to hanging baskets and pots. Mid-green needle-like leaflets.

Lotus maculatus 'Gold Flash'

Yellow-tipped red-orange flowers in spring–summer. '**Amazon Sunset**', long-flowering, with silvery leaves and deep red flowers; '**Gold Flash**', red-orange flowers; '**New Gold Flash**', improved form of 'Gold Flash', abundant red-orange flowers. Zones 10–11.

LUDWIGIA

syn. *Jussiaea*

This genus of about 75 herbaceous or woody, aquatic or marginal perennials belongs to the evening-primrose (Onagraceae) family and is widely distributed in bogs and marshes in warmer climates in both the Northern and Southern Hemispheres. The leaves are simple. The inconspicuous flowers may be solitary, arising from the leaf axils, or in clusters at the branch tips. They may be white or yellow, and have a long calyx tube with 4 or 5 sepals and 4 spreading petals (or sometimes no petals).
CULTIVATION: Grow near to, or in, shallow water in acid soil in a protected sunny position. Propagate from cuttings or by division.

Ludwigia peruviana

COMMON PRIMROSE WILLOW, EVENING PRIMROSE, PERUVIAN PRIMROSE WILLOW
☼ ❄ ↔ 20 in–8 ft (50 cm–2.4 m) ↕ 20 in–8 ft (50 cm–2.4 m)
Occurring from southeastern USA to South America. Woody shrubby perennial growing out from air-filled roots at water's edge to form floating mat, sometimes free-floating. Leaves finely hairy, oval, with impressed veins, deciduous in cooler climates. Solitary bright yellow flowers, clawed, with rounded petals, in late spring–autumn. Rusty red sepals remaining attached to brown seed capsule in star shape. Zones 7–10.

LUNARIA

This genus of 3 species of biennials and herbaceous perennials belongs to the cabbage (Brassicaceae) family. They are best raised in containers, as they can be somewhat weedy and invasive. They are primarily grown for their silvery flat seed pods, which are used in dried flower arrangements.
CULTIVATION: Grow these species in full sun or partial shade in light, fertile, moist, well-drained soil. Propagate the perennials from seed or by division in autumn or spring. Propagate biennials and annuals from seed in spring. These plants will readily self-seed.

Lunaria annua

HONESTY, MONEY PLANT, MONEYWORT, SILVER DOLLAR
☼/◑ ❄ ↔ 12 in (30 cm) ↕ 30 in (75 cm)
Fast-growing biennial from southern Europe. Has naturalized in parts of Europe and North America. Leaves bright green, alternate, heart-shaped, coarsely serrated. Rosy magenta, white, or violet-purple flowers, with 4 petals, in spring or early summer,

Lunaria rediviva

Ludwigia peruviana

followed by circular seed pods covered with silvery translucent membrane. *L. a.* var. *albiflora*, white flowers. *L. a.* '**Variegata**', variegated crimson flowers. Zones 8–10.

Lunaria rediviva

☼/◑ ❄ ↔ 24 in (60 cm)
↕ 36–42 in (90–105 cm)
Native to Europe. Hairy-stemmed perennial with somewhat smaller flowers and seed pods than the annual species. Pale mauve flowers, sweetly scented. Spring- to summer-flowering. Zones 8–10.

LUPINUS

LUPIN, LUPINE

There are about 200 species of annuals, perennials, and evergreen shrubs in this genus in the pea-flower subfamily of the legume (Fabaceae) family. They are native to North and South America, southern Europe, and northern Africa, usually found in dry habitats. Many have ornamental flowers, borne in showy terminal panicles or racemes. The leaves are palmate, with 5 to 15 leaflets, and the stems are often covered in fine soft down.
CULTIVATION: Although these generally tolerate poor dry conditions, they are best grown in full sun in moderately fertile well-drained soil. Propagate from seed or cuttings. The seedlings should be planted out when small, as these plants dislike root disturbance.

Lupinus chamissonis

☼ ❆ ↔ 4–10 ft (1.2–3 m) ↕ 2–7 ft (0.6–2 m)
From seashores of California, USA. Often mound-forming shrub. Leaves gray to blue-green from dense hairs. Blue flowers, on 4 in (10 cm) long spikes, from mid-spring to mid-summer. Tolerates drought and salt spray. Zones 9–10.

Lupinus polyphyllus

BLUE-POD LUPINE
☼ ❄ ↔ 20–40 in (50–100 cm)
↕ 24–60 in (60–150 cm)
From mountains of western North America, from British Columbia to California, growing in moist ground. Perennial with thick rootstock, chief ancestor of Russell lupins. Leaves large, basal, long-stalked, up to 17 leaflets, to 6 in (15 cm) long. Dense tapering spikes of very showy flowers, usually blue, often in shades of red, purple, or pink, in early–mid-summer. Zones 5–9.

Lupinus texensis

TEXAS BLUEBONNET
☼ ❄ ↔ 12 in (30 cm) ↕ 12–24 in (30–60 cm)
From Texas, USA. Drought-tolerant annual blooming in early–late spring with dark blue and white flowers. Must be planted in well-drained soil. Zones 7–10.

Lupinus, Hybrid Cultivar, 'Candy Floss'

Lupinus Hybrid Cultivars

☼ ❄ ↔2–5 ft (0.6–1.5 m) ↕2–4 ft (0.6–1.2 m)
Many of the later perennial hybrids are infor-
mally referred to as Russell lupins, and can be
invasive. **Band of Nobles Series**: rich colors of
blue, purple, intense reds ('The Page'); deep
pinks, creamy whites ('Noble Maiden'); and
many bicolors ('The Governor', blue and
white, 'The Chatelaine', soft pink and white).
'Bishop's Tipple', to 48 in (120 cm) tall,
mauve and lilac flowers with ivory flecks;
'Blue Moon', to 18 in (45 cm) tall, late-
blooming, tall narrow spikes of mauve-blue and white flowers;
'Candy Floss', to 24 in (60 cm) tall, delicate blush pink and
white flowers, becoming deep pink with age; **'Chandelier'**,
36–40 in (90–100 cm) tall, yellow flowers in early summer;
Gallery Series, compact plants, to 20 in (50 cm) tall, 10 to
12 spikes of red, blue, or pink sweet-pea-like flowers in late
spring or early summer; **'My Castle'**, 30–36 in (75–90 cm) tall,
bright brick-red blooms; **'Pagoda Prince'**, 36–48 in (90–120 cm)
tall, early-blooming, soft lilac to purple and white bicolor flowers;
'Red Arrow', to 36 in (90 cm) tall, pure red flowers flecked with
yellow, ageing to mulberry; **'Terracotta'**, 36–48 in (90–120 cm)
tall, early-blooming, large rusty-colored bells. Zones 3–9.

LYCHNIS

CAMPION, CATCHFLY
This genus of 20 species of biennials and perennials in the pink
(Caryophyllaceae) family is found in the northern temperate
zone. *Lychnis* species are quite variable, often forming large
clumps of foliage, sometimes with silver-gray leaves. While their
flowers are simple 5-petalled structures, they are brightly colored
and showy, occurring in heads usually held well clear of the foliage, maximizing the summer color effect.
CULTIVATION: They are mostly very hardy and easily grown in sun
or part-shade in moist well-drained soil. The silvery *L. coronaria*
prefers fairly dry conditions, but most others can be given routine

watering. Deadhead frequently to encourage
continuous flowering. Propagate from seed or
from basal cuttings or by division, depending
on the growth form.

Lychnis × *arkwrightii*

☼/◐ ❄ ↔16–24 in (40–60 cm)
↕12–30 in (30–75 cm)
Garden hybrids. Sometimes short-lived perennials. Bristly bright to dark green foliage.
Small heads of vivid flowers, held above foliage, in summer. **'Vesuvius'**, to 18 in (45 cm)
tall, dark green to purplish foliage, large,
striking, orange-red flowers. Zones 6–10.

Lychnis chalcedonica

MALTESE CROSS
☼/◐ ❄ ↔12–16 in (30–40 cm)
↕20 in (50 cm)
Upright, bristly, Eurasian perennial forming
clump of large, pointed, oval, basal leaves
with smaller leaves up the flower stems.
Heads of up to 50 small bright red flowers
in summer. Zones 4–10.

Lychnis × *arkwrightii* 'Vesuvius'

Lychnis coronaria

DUSTY MILLER, ROSE CAMPION
☼/◐ ❄ ↔20–40 in (50–100 cm)
↕16–32 in (40–80 cm)
From southeastern Europe. Spreading
mounding biennial or short-lived perennial.
Stems and foliage with dense silver-gray hairs. Leaves lance-
shaped, to about 3 in (8 cm) long, often smaller. Small heads
of flowers, usually in vivid shades of pink or purple-red. **'Alba'**,
white flowers; **'Atrosanguinea'**, very light foliage and deep magenta
flowers; **'Oculata'** ★, red-centered white flowers. Zones 4–10.

Lychnis flos-cuculi

RAGGED ROBIN
☼/◐ ❄ ↔16 in (40 cm) ↕30 in (75 cm)
Bristly Eurasian perennial. Basal leaves broad, lance- to spatula-
shaped; upper leaves almost linear. Open flowerheads, with few
pale purple flowers with fine petals divided in two. Zones 6–9.

Lychnis flos-jovis

☼/◐ ❄ ↔16 in (40 cm) ↕32 in (80 cm)
From Europe. Upright alpine perennial. Downy white stems and
foliage. Leaves lance- to spatula-shaped, broader at base. Small
heads of bright red flowers with petals divided in two, sometimes
almost completely, in summer. Zones 5–9.

Lychnis viscaria

GERMAN CATCHFLY, VISCARIA
☼/◐ ❄ ↔16 in (40 cm) ↕24 in (60 cm)
Found from Europe to Siberia. Upright perennial, with stems
and leaves bristly, and sticky leaf bases. The leaves are elliptical to

lance-shaped. The flower spikes are narrow, carrying small mauve to purple-red flowers, in summer. *L. v.* subsp. *atropurpurea*, deep purple flowers. *L. v.* 'Flore Pleno' (syn. 'Splendens Plena'), bright magenta double flowers; 'Splendens', pale to deep pink single flowers. Zones 4–10.

LYSICHITON
SKUNK CABBAGE

The 2 species in this genus in the arum (Araceae) family grow in bogs in northeast Asia and western North America. They are herbaceous rhizomatous perennials with large paddle-shaped leaves, preceded in spring by almost stemless arum-type flowers of yellow or white. Spikes of green-skinned fruit follow in summer. CULTIVATION: Plant in damp to wet humus-rich mud in sun or semi-shade in cool climates. They usually take several years to settle down and flower. Propagate from seed sown as soon as it is ripe. Division is possible, but given the habitat and the deeply buried rhizomes, this would be a very messy and difficult job.

Lysichiton americanus
YELLOW SKUNK CABBAGE

☼/◐ ❄ ↔ 4–5 ft (1.2–1.5 m)
↑ 3–4 ft (0.9–1.2 m)
From western North America. Flowers with bright yellow spathe, rising to 16 in (40 cm), in early spring, followed by tall, bright green, paddle-shaped leaves. Zones 6–10.

LYSIMACHIA
LOOSESTRIFE

This genus of about 150 species of perennials and subshrubs belonging to the primrose (Primulaceae) family is found over much of Europe and Asia, as well as in North America and South Africa. A few species are low-spreading plants, but most are clump-forming perennials with narrow lance-shaped leaves and upright spikes of small 5-petalled flowers, often in shades of yellow, rarely white or purple-pink. The flowers appear from early summer to autumn. CULTIVATION: Some species prefer the damp soil of pond edges or stream banks, others thrive in rockeries, but most are perfectly happy in full sun or half-sun in moist well-drained garden soil. Propagate by division or from basal cuttings or layers, depending on the growth type.

Lysimachia ciliata
☼ ❄ ↔ 20 in (50 cm) ↑ 40 in (100 cm)
From North America. Perennial with upright stems and whorls of lance-shaped leaves, to nearly 6 in (15 cm) long. The yellow flowers, solitary or paired, appear in the upper leaf axils, in summer. 'Purpurea', deep purple-red foliage. Zones 4–10.

Lysimachia clethroides
GOOSENECK LOOSESTRIFE

☼ ❄ ↔ 24 in (60 cm) ↑ 40 in (100 cm)
Native to China and Japan. Upright perennial with narrow, finely downy, lance-shaped leaves, to 5 in (12 cm) long. Produces

Lysimachia congestiflora
'Outback Sunset'

densely packed spikes of small white flowers, at the stem tips, during summer. The initially nodding flower spikes later become erect. Can become invasive. Zones 4–9.

Lysimachia congestiflora
☼ ❄ ↔ 8–16 in (20–40 cm) ↑ 6 in (15 cm)
From temperate East Asia. Perennial, forming densely foliaged mound of dark green, often red-tinted, pointed oval leaves, topped with clusters of golden yellow flowers in late spring. Prefers damp soil. 'Outback Sunset', yellow-green leaves with darker central zone. Zones 7–10.

Lysimachia ephemerum
☼ ❄ ↔ 16–24 in (40–60 cm) ↑ 40 in (100 cm)
From southwestern Europe. Upright perennial. Opposite pairs of narrow, lance-shaped, gray-green to blue-green leaves, to 6 in (15 cm) long. Terminal spikes of small white flowers, initially curved, later becoming erect. Summer-flowering. Zones 7–10.

Lysimachia nummularia
CREEPING JENNY, MONEYWORT

☼/◐ ❄ ↔ 24–40 in (60–100 cm)
↑ 2–4 in (5–10 cm)
Found in Europe, Turkey, and the Caucasus region. Low-spreading, sometimes mounding perennial. Leaves light-textured, wavy-edged, rounded, to 1 in (25 mm) wide. Bright yellow flowers, usually solitary, sometimes paired, in leaf axils, in summer. Can become invasive. 'Aurea', bright yellow-green to golden foliage. Zones 4–10.

Lysimachia punctata
☼ ❄ ↔ 16–24 in (40–60 cm) ↑ 40 in (100 cm)
Upright Eurasian perennial. Opposite pairs and/or whorls of downy, finely pointed, lance-shaped leaves, to 3 in (8 cm) long. Terminal heads or spikes of bright yellow flowers, to over ½ in (12 mm) across, in summer. 'Alexander', striking cream-edged foliage. Zones 5–10.

Lysichiton americanus

LYTHRUM

This genus of about 35 species is a member of the loosestrife (Lythraceae) family. It comprises mainly herbaceous perennials but includes some annuals and small herbs. Two of the hardy herbaceous perennials have been used to produce very adaptable varieties that grow in a wide range of conditions, thriving just about anywhere except in full shade. *(See note of caution for L. salicaria.)* The flowers are small, rather star-shaped, and carried in racemes. They are attractive cut and in borders.
CULTIVATION: Grow in ordinary garden soil in full or half-sun. Ideal conditions would be a damp or wet spot in part-shade, where some species can become invasive. Cut back in autumn. Propagate by dividing the roots in autumn or spring. Named varieties will not come true from seed.

Lythrum salicaria
PURPLE LOOSESTRIFE, STRIPED LOOSESTRIFE

☼/◐ ❄ ↔ 24 in (60 cm) ↕ 24–60 in (60–150 cm)

From temperate Eurasia, Africa, and Australia, but widely naturalized in North America. Invasive, declared illegal in some areas; both it and *L. virgatum* should be used with caution. Mid-green leaves. Spikes, 9–12 in (22–30 cm) long, of small red-purple flowers in early summer–early autumn. **'Blush'**, large-petalled blushed pale pink flowers; **'Feuerkerze'** (syn. 'Firecandle'), tall plant for back of border, intensely rosy red flowers; **'Robert'**, bright cerise pink flowers. Zones 3–10.

MACLEAYA
PLUME POPPY

This genus is a member of the poppy (Papaveraceae) family and includes 2 species of hardy herbaceous perennials, sometimes sold under the name *Bocconia*. These bold attractive plants can be invasive, forming dense thickets, and spread by means of underground suckers. They have scalloped, deeply lobed, heart-shaped, gray to olive green leaves, 6–8 in (15–20 cm) long. Tiny flowers are borne in large plume-like panicles, 12 in (30 cm) long.

Lythrum salicaria

CULTIVATION: Plant in autumn or early spring in a sheltered sunny position in deep loamy soil. Remove spent flowerheads and cut down stems in autumn. Soils with high fertility will encourage their invasive nature. Propagate from seed or by division of roots in autumn or early spring. Plants will self-seed.

Macleaya cordata
syn. *Bocconia cordata*
PLUME POPPY, TREE CELANDINE

☼ ❄ ↔ 3 ft (0.9 m) ↕ 8 ft (2.4 m)

Plume poppy from China and Japan. Lower stem has large deeply lobed leaves, gray-green above, gray-white beneath. Feathery plumes, to 36 in (90 cm) tall, of small, pearly white or pink flowers in summer. Zones 3–10.

Macleaya microcarpa
syn. *Bocconia microcarpa*

☼ ❄ ↔ 3 ft (0.9 m) ↕ 8 ft (2.4 m)

Plume poppy from central China. Leaves grayish green to olive with white undersides, downy. Flowers pink outside, bronze inside. Autumn-flowering. Can be very invasive. **'Coral Plume'**, pinker flowers; **'Kelway's Coral Plume'**, showy deep buff to coral flowers. Zones 3–10.

MAIANTHEMUM
syn. *Smilacina*
FALSE SOLOMON'S SEAL

This genus consists of about 35 species of herbaceous perennials in the family Ruscaceae, most from eastern Asia and North America but with a few in the highlands of Central America and one extending across northern Asia and into Europe. They have creeping underground rhizomes and erect or arching, unbranched stems, each bearing 2 to 15 ovate leaves, usually in 2 rows. Plants will grow into clumps or, in some species, into substantial colonies. Small white flowers are borne in spring and summer in terminal panicles or spikes, followed by small red berries.
CULTIVATION: All species grow best in moist humus-rich soils in full sun or partial shade under deciduous shrubs and trees. Plants should not be allowed to dry out when in leaf. Propagate by division while dormant, or by sowing seed as soon as it is ripe.

Maianthemum bifolium
FALSE LILY-OF-THE-VALLEY, MAY LILY

◐ ❄ ↔ 40–48 in (100–120 cm) ↕ 5–6 in (12–15 cm)

Spreading perennial found from western Europe to Japan. Upright unbranched stems bearing 2 heart-shaped leaves to 3 in (8 cm) long. Narrow spike of tiny flowers in spring. *M. b.* subsp. *kamtschaticum* (syn. *M. dilatatum*), stems to 14 in (35 cm) high, leaves to 8 in (20 cm) long. Zones 3–10.

Maianthemum canadense
syn. *Unifolium canadense*
TWO-LEAFED SOLOMON'S SEAL

◐ ❄ ↔ 36–40 in (90–100 cm) ↕ 7–8 in (18–20 cm)

Woodland plant, native to Canada and northern parts of USA. Good ground cover. Leaves oval, 1 to 3 per stem, to 4 in (10 cm)

long. Tiny, fragrant, white flowers, on spikes
2 in (5 cm) long, in spring. Zones 1–7.

Maianthemum racemosum
syn. *Smilacina racemosa*
FALSE SOLOMON'S SEAL, FALSE SPIKENARD
◗/◉ ❋ ↔ 2–4 ft (0.6–1.2 m)
↕ 2–3 ft (0.6–0.9 m)
Occurs right across USA and in parts of
northern Mexico. Arching cane-like stems,
each with up to 12 pointed oval leaves to 6 in
(15 cm) long. Panicles to 6 in (15 cm) long of
tiny creamy white flowers in summer. Red-
tinted green berries. Zones 4–10.

Maianthemum racemosum

MALCOLMIA
MAHON STOCK, MALCOLM STOCK, VIRGINIA STOCK
This genus of the cabbage (Brassicaceae) fam-
ily includes some 35 species of annuals and perennials, found
from southwest Europe to Afghanistan. They are mainly small
mounding plants, with variably shaped foliage that is often finely
hairy with toothed edges. The purplish red, often fragrant flowers
are 4-petalled, carried in open racemes, and appear from spring
to autumn, varying with the species.
CULTIVATION: Hardiness of these species varies, though most do
best in fairly mild climates. Plant in full sun with free-draining
soil that can be kept moist. Avoid over-watering or over-feeding,
which can result in very few flowers. Propagate common annuals
from seed; perennials from basal cuttings.

Malcolmia maritima
VIRGINIA STOCK
☀ ❋ ↔ 12 in (30 cm) ↕ 14 in (35 cm)
Native of Greece and Albania. Fast-growing
annual with upright branching stems. Leaves
hairy, 2 in (5 cm) long, elliptical, smooth-
edged or toothed. Racemes of fragrant pinkish
purple flowers, to 1 in (25 mm) wide, in
spring–summer. Zones 8–11.

MALVA
MALLOW, MUSK MALLOW
Like the hollyhock, to which it is related,
Malva is a member of the mallow (Malvaceae)
family. These easily cultivated plants are native
to Europe, North Africa, and Asia, but have

Malva moschata 'Alba'

naturalized in other areas. This genus contains at least 30 species
of annuals, biennials, and short-lived herbaceous perennials that
are similar to hollyhocks, but bushier and with smaller leaves.
The single flowers are 5-petalled, appearing in shades of white,
pink, blue, or purple.
CULTIVATION: Grow in herbaceous or annual borders. They do
best in a sunny position but will tolerate partial shade in well-
drained soil. Remove spent flowers to encourage a second flowering; cut down to the ground in autumn. Propagate from cuttings
or seed in spring. Plants will self-seed.

Malva alcea
☀ ❋ ↔ 24 in (60 cm) ↕ 40 in (100 cm)
Southern European herbaceous perennial, naturalized in USA.
Deeply lobed light green leaves with toothed edges. Mauve-pink
flowers, in mid-summer to mid-autumn. Zone 3–10.

Malva moschata
MUSK MALLOW
☀ ❋ ↔ 18 in (45 cm) ↕ 40 in (100 cm)
European perennial. Narrow, finely cut, mid-green leaves; musky
smell when brushed or crushed. Abundant, saucer-shaped, rose-
pink flowers, in summer. 'Alba', white flowers;
'Rosea', pink flowers. Zones 3–10.

Malva sylvestris
CHEESES, COMMON MALLOW, HIGH MALLOW
☀ ❋ ↔ 7–25 ft (2–8 m) ↕ 3 ft (0.9 m)
Biennial or perennial from Europe. Leaves
green, alternate, to 4 in (10 cm) long. Flowers
rose-purple with dark veins, in early summer–
early autumn. 'Primley Blue', bluish purple
flowers, dark blue veins. Zones 3–9.

MARANTA
PRAYER PLANT
This genus of the arrowroot (Marantaceae)
family includes around 32 species of evergreen tropical perennials from the forests of
Central and South America and the West Indies. The elliptical
leaves are spread flat by day and closed "in prayer" at night;
they are usually attractively blotched and veined. The tiny, white,
2-lipped flowers are insignificant. These plants can be grown as
attractive indoor foliage plants in cooler climates.
CULTIVATION: Grow these as house plants in a light, warm, humid
site or in a greenhouse out of direct sun. Potting mix should be
well-drained but never wet. In tropical climates they make good
ground covers under the shade of trees. Propagate by division or
from basal cuttings in spring with bottom heat.

Maranta leuconeura

PRAYER PLANT, RABBIT TRACKS, TEN COMMANDMENTS

☀ ⚘ ↔ 10–12 in (25–30 cm) ↕ 10–12 in (25–30 cm)

Perennial herb from Brazil. Almost prostrate, spreading rhizome. Leaves broad, dark green, oval, zoned gray or maroon, veined silver, red, or purple above, grayish green or maroon below, fold upward at night. Solitary spike of white or violet flowers, spotted purple, in spring–summer. *M. l.* var. *kerchoveana* (rabbit's foot), grayish green leaves, purplish brown to dark olive blotches on both sides of midrib. *M. l.* 'Erythroneura' (syn. 'Erythrophylla') (herringbone plant), velvety blackish green leaves, red veins, lime green central zone; 'Tricolor', large oval leaves, strong red veining, dark green blotches on each midrib. Zones 10–11.

Maranta leuconeura

MARRUBIUM

HOREHOUND

This is a genus of some 40 species of woolly gray-leafed perennials from Asia, the Mediterranean region, and North Africa. They are members of the mint (Lamiaceae) family, and as such usually feature rounded leaves that have quite a strong smell. They have square stems and 2-lipped pink to mauve flowers. Some species can become invasive.

CULTIVATION: These sun-loving perennials are drought-tolerant and enjoy a dry summer climate. Prune hard each winter to clean up the plant and encourage bushiness. Propagate by division or from spring-sown seed, which is inclined to germinate in an erratic fashion.

Marrubium incanum

syn. *Marrubium candidissimum*

☀ ❄ ↔ 24 in (60 cm) ↕ 20 in (50 cm)

Perennial from Italy and the Balkans. Densely woolly white shoots; gray-green, scalloped, rounded leaves. Dense clusters of pale mauve to nearly white flowers, in summer. Zones 6–10.

Marrubium incanum

Matthiola incana, Vintage Series, 'Vintage Lavender'

MATTHIOLA

GILLYFLOWER, STOCK

This genus, a member of the cabbage (Brassicaceae) family, contains 55 mainly temperate Eurasian species of annuals, perennials, and subshrubs. They usually have simple leaves, often gray-green and sometimes toothed. Their flowers, which are 4-petalled and often evening-scented, are borne on upright, often branching stems. There are many garden strains available in a wide range of flower forms and colors.

CULTIVATION: Plant in full sun with moist well-drained soil. A light dressing of lime is beneficial. Taller types need shelter from strong wind or can be supported by staking. Propagate mostly from seed, which can be sown in succession for continuous spring and summer flowering.

Matthiola incana

BROMPTON STOCK

☼/☀ ❄ ↔ 12 in (30 cm) ↕ 32 in (80 cm)

Woody-based biennial from southern and western Europe. Leaves elliptical, gray-green, downy, 2 in (5 cm) long. Upright spikes of scented purple, pink, or white flowers, in summer. Long seed pods. 'Annua' (ten weeks stock), matures and flowers in one season; Cinderella Series, single-stemmed, most colors; Lady Series, biennial, branching, dense spikes, most colors, many double flowers; Vintage Series, compact plants, branching, most colors, many doubles. Zones 8–11.

Matthiola longipetala

NIGHT-SCENTED STOCK

☼/☀ ❄ ↔ 10 in (25 cm) ↕ 20 in (50 cm)

Summer-flowering annual found from Greece and the Middle East to the Crimean region. Narrow leaves, to 3 in (8 cm) long, toothed or pinnately lobed. Creamy yellow or pink 4-petalled flowers, 1 in (25 mm) across, with evening fragrance, borne in summer. Horned seed pods. *M. l.* subsp. *bicornis*, usually double flowers. Zones 8–11.

MAZUS

The 30 species of ground-covering and mat-forming perennials in this genus belonging to the foxglove (Scrophulariaceae) family are found in Asia, Australia, and New Zealand. The foliage color varies from mid- to bright greens through to brown and bronze shades. The prostrate stems hug the ground and new roots form as the plant creeps along. Often found in damp sheltered areas, they creep through and over rocks. The narrow tubular flowers sit up on the mats of foliage in spring and summer. The flowers vary in color from purples and blues through to pale lavender, white, and yellow. Depending on the species, flowers may have a splash of lilac-mauve in the throat, or be marked with white and yellow. They are excellent ground cover plants.

CULTIVATION: These plants prefer full sun, good drainage, and open porous soils. Propagate from half-hardened stem cuttings in summer and autumn.

Mazus radicans

syn. *Mimulus radicans*

☼ ❄ ↔ 12 in (30 cm) ↑ 2 in (5 cm)

New Zealand perennial species. Round bronze-brown leaves, 1¼–2 in (3–5 cm) long, with very tight, nearly impenetrable, foliage mats. Flowers are white, lilac streaked, and 1½–2 in (3.5–5 cm) across, in spring–summer. Zones 7–9.

Mazus reptans

☼ ❄ ↔ 20 in (50 cm) ↑ 2 in (5 cm)

Himalayan species. Mid-green, almost glossy leaves cover its stems. Flowers purple-blue, ¾ in (18 mm) wide, with dark center fleck, in spring–summer. Zones 7–9.

MECONOPSIS

The 40 or more species in this genus are mainly native to the Himalayan region, with one notable exception. The genus belongs to the poppy (Papaveraceae) family, and includes annuals, biennials, and perennials, some of which die after flowering. The genus is known for its blue-flowered species, but the other more traditional poppies of yellow, pink, or red are often more easily grown. They form compact mounds of coarsely hairy lower leaves that may be round, pinnately lobed, or deeply toothed. The flowers, carried singly on short stems or in heads on taller stems, open in spring or summer.

CULTIVATION: Most species grow best in woodland conditions in a cool-temperate climate with reliable rainfall. Plant in a sheltered part-shaded position with moist, deep, humus-rich, well-drained soil. Water well in spring and early summer. Propagate from seed.

Meconopsis betonicifolia

BLUE POPPY

☼/◐ ❄ ↔ 8–20 in (20–50 cm) ↑ 3–6 ft (0.9 m–1.8 m)

Perennial, often short-lived, from Himalayan China. Stems and foliage bristly, golden brown hairs. Oblong, often shallowly serrated leaves, to 12 in (30 cm) long. Open heads of up to 6 bright blue flowers, to 2 in (5 cm) long, in late spring–early summer. *M. b.* var. *alba*, white flowers. Zones 7–9.

Meconopsis cambrica

WELSH POPPY

☼ ❄ ↔ 8–16 in (20–40 cm) ↑ 12–24 in (30–60 cm)

Perennial, native to western Europe. Small clumps of ferny mid-green leaves, to 8 in (20 cm) long. Flowers solitary, on hairy stems, bright yellow, to 2 in (5 cm) wide, in late spring–summer. Often self-sows freely. *M. c.* var. *aurantiaca*, orange flowers. Zones 6–10.

Meconopsis grandis

☼ ❄ ↔ 16–24 in (40–60 cm) ↑ 4 ft (1.2 m)

Himalayan perennial. Foliage and stems have rusty brown hairs. Lower leaves to 12 in (30 cm) long, elliptical, serrated to coarsely toothed. Long-stemmed flowers, in groups of 3 or more, deep blue to purple-blue, in late spring–early summer. Zones 5–9.

Mazus reptans

Meconopsis horridula

☼ ❄ ↔ 16 in (40 cm) ↑ 32 in (80 cm)

Often short-lived Himalayan perennial. Very bristly foliage and stems. Leaves elliptical, gray-green, to 10 in (25 cm) long. Long-stemmed flowers in upper leaf axils, solitary or paired, blue to light purple or white, in summer. Zones 6–9.

Meconopsis napaulensis

syn. *Meconopsis wallichii*

SATIN POPPY

☼/◐ ❄ ↔ 20–32 in (50–80 cm)
↑ 6–8 ft (1.8–2.4 m)

Vigorous upright perennial. Found from central Nepal to southwestern China. Stems and foliage covered with fine hairs. Leaves deeply lobed. Red or purple flowers, rarely blue or white, on drooping heads, in spring–summer. Zones 8–10.

Meconopsis × sheldonii

☼ ❄ ↔ 16–24 in (40–60 cm) ↑ 4 ft (1.2 m)

Colorful, easy-to-grow garden hybrid. Bristly oblong leaves, 6–10 in (15–25 cm) long. Leafy flower stems. Blue flowers, 1¼ in (30 mm) wide, in upper axils, in spring–summer. Zones 6–9.

MELAMPODIUM

The 37 annual or perennial herbs and subshrubs in this genus from the daisy (Asteraceae) family are native to the warmer parts of North America and Mexico. They have narrow to oval toothed or simple leaves, and carry heads of daisy-like flowers with white to yellow ray florets and yellow disc florets.

CULTIVATION: These plants are best suited to a sunny position in moist well-drained soil, although they will tolerate dry conditions. During winter reduce the amount of water given. They can be propagated from seed.

Meconopsis grandis

Melampodium paludosum 'Showstar'

Mentha pulegium

PENNYROYAL

☼/◐ ❄ ↔ 20 in (50 cm)
↕ 8–12 in (20–30 cm)

Carpeting, spreading, aromatic herb from southwest and central Europe, and the Mediterranean to Iran. Small, dark green, sometimes gray, leaves, flat on stems. Balls of tubular lilac flowers, on top of foliage, in summer–autumn. Oils deter houseflies. Zones 7–10.

Mentha requienii

syn. *Mentha corsica*

CORSICAN MINT

☼/◐ ❄ ↔ 27 in (70 cm) ↕ ¾ in (1.8 cm)

Carpeting herb naturally found in France and Italy. Tight mats of tiny leaves spread on creeping stems. Dark green foliage, pales in hot sun, very aromatic when rubbed. Tiny heads of lavender flowers, in summer. Zones 7–10.

Melampodium paludosum

BUTTER DAISY, GOLD MEDALLION FLOWER

☼ ✈ ↔ 36 in (90 cm) ↕ 24 in (60 cm)

Annual herb, from Mexico. Light green oblong leaves on purplish green stems. Solitary, yellow, daisy-like flowers, darker centers, in late spring–early autumn. May self-seed in suitable conditions. '**Showstar**', golden yellow daisy-like flowers. Zones 11–12.

MENTHA

A genus of 25 species of aromatic rhizomatous perennials in the mint (Lamiaceae) family from Europe, Africa, Asia, and Australia,. They naturalize in damp moist areas. Shallow-rooted plants, they spread easily. They have an upright branching habit and form dense bushy plants from a few inches to 5 ft (1.5 m) high. Tiny flowers are borne at the ends of the stems in clusters or spikes from ¼ in (6 mm) to 4 in (10 cm) long. Foliage is aromatic. Many are used in teas, as food flavoring, or for medicinal purposes; some are grown for their essential oils. Species can be evergreen or deciduous. CULTIVATION: Mints grow in any open, fertile, moist soil, in part-shade or full sun. Propagate by dividing the rhizomes throughout the year; roots will appear in a few weeks. Sow seed in spring.

Mentha × *gracilis*

☼ ❄ ↔ 36 in (90 cm) ↕ 12 in (30 cm)

Low-growing, ground-hugging perennial from temperate Eurasia. Crinkly, dark green, rounded leaves with minty, slightly ginger taste. Tubular lilac flowers, in summer–autumn. '**Variegata**' (variegated ginger mint), leaves with yellow streaks. Zones 7–9.

Mentha × *villosa*

BOWLES MINT

☼ ❄ ↔ 5 ft (1.5 m) ↕ 3 ft (0.9 m)

Spreading mound-forming mint. Delicate hairs on round bright green leaves. Large spikes of pink tubular flowers. Summer-flowering. Zones 5–8.

MENYANTHES

This genus of a single species of perennial aquatic or marginal herbs is native to the cooler regions of Europe, Asia, and North America and gives its name to the Menyanthaceae family. Grown for both its attractive foliage and fragrant flowers, it has smooth, dark green, compound leaves with elliptic to oval leaflets, with slightly serrated edges. These are carried on sheathed stalks arising from a thick, rooting, creeping, then rising rhizome. It carries erect racemes of 10 to 20 short-lived flowers. These heavily fringed and bearded blooms each feature 5 petals that are white, flushed with pink. CULTIVATION: This plant prefers an open, sunny position in shallow water. Keep tidy by removing fading flowerheads and foliage. Propagate from seed or by division of overcrowded clumps in spring.

Menyanthes trifoliata

Menyanthes trifoliata

BOG BEAN, BUCK BEAN, MARSH TREFOIL

☼ ❄ ↔ 8–12 in (20–30 cm) ↕ 10–16 in (25–40 cm)

Smooth, dark green, compound leaves; elliptic to oval leaflets, slightly serrated edges, on sheathed stalks. Erect racemes of short-lived, fringed, white flowers, flushed pink, in summer. Zones 3–9.

MERTENSIA

This genus, found in Europe, temperate Asia, and North America, is a member of the borage (Boraginaceae) family. It contains about 40 species of hardy herbaceous perennials, although only 4 or 5 are cultivated. Their leaves are usually lance-shaped and hairy. Most species are relatively small and produce terminal panicles of usually blue tubular or bell-shaped flowers in spring. Some species are used in wild or rock gardens. CULTIVATION: Plant these in full sun or half-sun in early spring. The plants prefer soil that is moist, well-drained, and rich in humus. Propagate from seed or by division after flowering.

Mertensia sibirica

SIBERIAN BLUEBELLS

☼ ❄ ↔ 12 in (30 cm)
↑ 12–18 in (30–45 cm)
Perennial from East Asia, northern China, and Siberia. Light green leaves on long stems. Deep blue-purple funnel-shaped flowers, in spring–early summer. Zones 3–7.

Mertensia simplicissima

syn. *Mertensia asiatica*

OYSTER PLANT

☼ ❄ ↔ 18 in (45 cm) ↑ 6 in (15 cm)
Perennial, native to Japan and Korea. Long trailing stems of fleshy silver-gray leaves. Sky blue flowers, in spring–early autumn. Needs well-drained soil. Zones 5–9.

Mertensia virginica

syn. *Mertensia pulmonaroides*

BLUEBELLS, COWSLIP, ROANOKE BELLS, VIRGINIA BLUEBELLS

☼ ❄ ↔ 12–24 in (30–60 cm)
↑ 12–24 in (30–60 cm)
Perennial from North America. Oval gray-green leaves, 8 in (20 cm) long. Very attractive blue-purple flowers, in nodding clusters, in spring. Foliage dies after blooming, so plant among other perennials. Zones 3–9.

MEUM

BALDMONEY, BEARWORT, SPIGNEL

This monotypic genus is a member of the carrot (Apiaceae) family. Its single species is a herbaceous perennial native to temperate Europe where it grows in grassland and rough rocky areas, usually on limestone. It forms a clump of finely divided, feathery, aromatic, rich green foliage. In summer small white to pinkish flowers are borne in the umbels that are typical of the carrot family. Both the roots and leaflets are edible, having a warm spicy taste. CULTIVATION: Grow these plants in a sunny position in well-drained but moisture-retentive fertile soil at the front of the border. Suitable for naturalizing in sunny wild gardens. Propagate from seed or by division.

Meum athamanticum

☼ ❄ ↔ 12–18 in (30–45 cm) ↑ 18–24 in (45–60 cm)
Perennial herb, native to Europe. Forms clumps of attractive, fresh green, feathery foliage. Umbels of small white flowers, sometimes flushed purple, in summer. Zones 6–9.

MIMULUS

MONKEY FLOWER, MUSK

While it is best known for its annuals and perennials, this mostly American genus in the foxglove (Scrophulariaceae) family has some 180 species and includes a few shrubs. *Mimulus* are vigorous plants with stems covered in fine hairs and sticky glands, which may also be present on the leaves. The flowers form in the leaf axils and are short tubes with widely flared throats. The annuals and perennials often have flowers with vividly contrasting color patterns; this is less common among the shrubs. CULTIVATION: In suitably mild climates, *Mimulus* species are easy to grow, provided they are given a position in full sun as well as a well-drained soil that remains moist throughout the summer months. They are quick growing, and may be inclined to become untidy unless they are routinely pinched back. They also tend to be short lived. Propagate from seed or half-hardened cuttings.

Mimulus cardinalis

Mimulus aurantiacus

BUSH MONKEY FLOWER

☼ ❄ ↔ 3 ft (0.9 m) ↑ 4 ft (1.2 m)
Upright plant found in western USA from southern Oregon to California. Narrow, bright to dark green leaves, serrated edges. Stems and foliage have sticky coating. Flowers funnel-shaped, yellow, gold, and orange, in spring–summer. Zones 8–10.

Mimulus cardinalis

SCARLET MONKEY FLOWER

☼/☼ ❄ ↔ 24–27 in (60–70 cm) ↑ 32–36 in (80–90 cm)
Vigorous clumping herbaceous perennial from southern North America. Roots down when a stem touches ground. Stems are sticky. Leaves to 5 in (12 cm) long. Scarlet tubular flowers, in leaf axils, in summer. Zones 6–10.

Mimulus luteus

MONKEY MUSK, YELLOW MONKEY FLOWER

☼ ❄ ↔ 24–32 in (60–80 cm) ↑ 12–16 in (30–40 cm)
Vigorous spreading perennial from Chile, naturalized in other moist habitats. Leaves to 1¼ in (30 mm) long. Yellow tubular flowers, to 2 in (5 cm) long, in leaf axils, in spring–autumn. 'Variegatus', variegated foliage, less vigorous. Zones 7–10.

Mimulus, Hybrid Cultivar, 'Puck'

Mimulus ringens
ALLEGHENY MONKEY FLOWER

☼ ❄ ↔ 4–5 ft (1.2–1.5 m) ↑ 3–4 ft (0.9–1.2 m)

Perennial herb from North America and Europe. Smooth, 4-cornered, narrowly winged stems. Narrow green leaves. Violet-blue tubular flowers, occasionally white or pink, thin throat, on erect stalks, in summer. Zones 3–9.

Mimulus Hybrid Cultivars

☼ ❄ ↔ 12–32 in (30–80 cm) ↑ 8–36 in (20–90 cm)

Mimulus hybrids are strong and vigorous with a wide range of striking colors to choose from. '**Highland Park**', varying shades from apricot to tomato red; '**Highland Pink**', strong red velvet colors with paler undersides; '**Malibu Red**', larger blooms in rich red; '**Puck**', clear yellow; '**Roter Kaiser**', larger trumpet-shaped blooms in rich red. Zones 3–9.

MINUARTIA
SANDWORT

This genus belonging to the pink (Caryophyllaceae) family contains about 100 annuals and perennials that are widely distributed through the temperate and arctic regions of the Northern Hemisphere. Many of the perennials have a mat-forming habit, and are often very compact. The plants have narrow leaves and clusters of 5-petalled open flowers; some of the neater ones are suited to rock gardens.
CULTIVATION: *Minuartia* species require a moist, rich, well-drained soil in an open sunny position. Propagate from seed in spring or cuttings in late summer.

Minuartia stellata
syns *Alsine parnassica, A. stellata*

☼ ❄ ↔ 18 in (45 cm) ↑ 2 in (50 mm)

Cushion-forming plant from eastern Mediterranean grasslands. Smooth, short, pointed leaves. White flowers, about 2½ in (6 cm) wide, elongated, 5 partially opening petals, in summer. Zones 4–9.

MIRABILIS

A genus of about 50 species of annuals and tuberous-rooted perennials in the four-o-clock (Nyctaginaceae) family, native to southern North America, Central America, and South America. The leaves are in opposite pairs and are simple and smooth-edged, modified into small bracts below the flower clusters. The flowers are short lived and fragrant, and are available in a wide range of bright colors.
CULTIVATION: Grow these plants in a sunny moist aspect in rich soil. In frost-prone areas, lift the tubers of perennials and store as you would dahlias. Propagate annual species from seed sown where it is to grow, or by division of tuberous perennial species.

Mirabilis jalapa
FOUR O'CLOCK FLOWER, MARVEL OF PERU, VIERUURTJIE

☼ ❄ ↔ 20–24 in (50–60 cm) ↑ 20–24 in (50–60 cm)

Widespread in tropical and subtropical regions of the Americas, so widely cultivated and naturalized that its exact origin is uncertain. Bushy herbaceous perennial. Tuberous roots and leaves to 4 in (10 cm) long. Short-lived, flared, trumpet-flowers, 2 in (5 cm) wide, mainly magenta, or yellow, red, or white, striped, in summer. Zones 8–11.

MITCHELLA
PARTRIDGE BERRY

There are 2 species of trailing, mat-forming, evergreen herbs in this genus belonging to the madder (Rubiaceae) family. One is native to North America and the other to Japan and Korea. They grow naturally in rather sandy soils on wooded hillsides. Dark green leaves are glossy and broadly oval. Small white or pinkish flowers are borne in pairs in summer. They are tubular with flaring lobes and velvety interiors. Although fairly inconspicuous they have a pleasant fragrance. The pea-sized scarlet berries have a noticeable dimple and are edible but have little flavor. They persist on the plant for long periods.
CULTIVATION: Grow these plants as ground cover in shady areas or in the rock garden in a rich soil, neutral to acid. Propagate from pieces of stem from which roots have emerged, or from seed.

Mitchella repens

☼ ❄ ↔ 24 in (60 cm) ↑ 3 in (8 cm)

Trailing prostrate perennial from North America. Roots along the stems. Small rounded leaves, whitish veins. Small pinkish white flowers, in summer. Scarlet berries. Zones 3–9.

MOLTKIA

This genus, belonging to the borage (Boraginaceae) family, is composed of 6 species of perennials, some of which become shrubby, especially in mild climates. Found from Italy through to Greece and into western Asia, they are small plants with hairy dark green foliage. Related to *Lithospermum*, they usually have a more upright, less spreading growth habit and considerably larger leaves than their relatives. In summer they bear cymes of small, tubular, 5-petalled flowers in shades of mauve, blue, and sometimes yellow.
CULTIVATION: Sun-loving plants, these are hardy to moderate frosts and reasonably drought tolerant once established. They thrive in well-drained gritty soil, of most soil types, to which some humus has been added to aid moisture retention, and are lime tolerant.

Light trimming after winter or after flowering will keep them tidy, though often they are not long lived. Propagate from seed, layers, or small cuttings.

Moltkia × intermedia

☼ ❋ ↔ 16–20 in (40–50 cm) ↑ 8–10 in (20–25 cm)
Spreading herbaceous perennial, native to Europe and Asia. Narrow bristly leaves, up to 6 in (15 cm) long. Indigo blue tubular flowers, up to ¾ in (18 mm) wide, in summer. Zones 5–8.

MONARDA
BEE BALM, BERGAMOT, HORSEMINT

This genus, a member of the mint (Lamiaceae) family, contains 16 species of annuals and perennials from North and Central America. They form large clumps, dying away completely in winter but recovering quickly in spring to form thickets of angled stems, densely clothed in lance-shaped leaves, often red-tinted and hairy, with serrated edges. In summer the top of each stem carries several whorls of tubular flowers backed by leafy bracts.
CULTIVATION: Very hardy, these plants are easily grown in any open sunny position with moist well-drained soil. Mildew is often a problem in late summer and good ventilation is important. Propagate by division when dormant, or from basal cuttings.

Monarda didyma ★
BEE BALM, OSWEGO TEA

☼/◗ ❋ ↔ 24–40 in (60–100 cm) ↑ 3–4 ft (0.9–1.2 m)
Perennial species from Canada and USA. Finely downy, often purple-red-tinted, serrated leaves, to 6 in (15 cm) long. Flowerheads 2 in (5 cm) wide, usually red shades. Summer-flowering. 'Cambridge Scarlet', heavy-flowering, bright light red; 'Mahogany', purple-red flowers, persistent red-brown bracts. Zones 4–9.

Monarda fistulosa ★

☼/◗ ❋ ↔ 24–40 in (60–100 cm)
↑ 3–4 ft (0.9–1.2 m)
Perennial found from Canada to Mexico. Very similar to *M. didyma*. Leaves seldom over 4 in (10 cm) long, may be smooth-edged. Flowers lavender to pink, in summer. Zones 4–9.

Monarda Hybrid Cultivars

☼/◗ ❋ ↔ 20–32 in (50–80 cm)
↑ 20–60 in (50–150 cm)
The 2 most commonly grown species, *M. didyma* and *M. fistulosa*, hybridize freely resulting in excellent garden varieties. 'Beauty of Cobham', 50 in (130 cm) high, lavender-pink flowers; 'Cambridge Scarlet' ★, large ruby red flowers; 'Croftway Pink' ★, 40 in (100 cm) tall, bright mid-pink flowers; 'Ruby Glow', 24 in (60 cm) tall, bright red flowers, red-tinted foliage; 'Scorpion', 40 in (100 cm) tall, purple-pink flowerheads, purple-red-tinted foliage; 'Vintage Wine', 27 in (70 cm) high, deep purple-red flowers. Zones 4–9.

Monarda fistulosa

Musa ornata

MUSA
BANANA

There are about 40 species in this genus of evergreen suckering perennials found from Asia to Australia. They belong to the banana (Musaceae) family. Leaves are large, paddle-shaped, and smooth-edged. The flowers appear on a spike that can be pendent or erect. The female or hermaphrodite flowers are near the base and the male flowers are near the tip. The fruit can be long, slim, and curved, or stubby, nearly round, sausage-shaped, or cylindrical. Although they are usually grown commercially for the fruit, some species are cultivated for their foliage or flowers.
CULTIVATION: *Musa* species are found in light woodland and forest margins and will do best in humus-rich fertile soil in full sun, with shelter from wind. In temperate areas where frosts occur, grow in a greenhouse in loam-based compost with added leafmold. Water and feed regularly during the growing months. Propagate by division of suckers, or by seed in spring.

Musa ornata
FLOWERING BANANA

☼ ✿ ↔ 6 ft (1.8 m) ↑ 6–10 ft (1.8–3 m)
Ornamental suckering perennial, native to Myanmar and Bangladesh. Waxy green leaves, 6 ft (1.8 m) long. Inflorescences of flowers, orange to yellow, light purple bracts, in summer. Yellow or pink fruit. Zones 11–12.

Musa velutina
VELVET BANANA

☼ ✿ ↔ 3 ft (0.9 m) ↑ 5 ft (1.5 m)
Rhizomatous plant from northeastern India. Dark green leaves, paler undersides, red midrib. Red bracts, white or yellowish flowers. Spring-flowering. Pink velvety fruit, will split when ripe. Zones 9–12.

MYOSOTIDIUM

The sole species in this genus in the borage (Boraginaceae) family is endemic to the wet, windswept Chatham Islands off the east coast of New Zealand. It has very large, leathery, glossy leaves on stalks like small rhubarb stalks. In spring and early summer, rounded heads of tiny, 5-petalled, bright blue to purple-blue flowers appear among the leaves.

CULTIVATION: This prefers cool-temperate conditions with no extremes of cold or heat. Plant in part- or full shade with moist, humus-rich, well-drained soil. Water and feed well for best results. Watch for aphids. Propagate from seed rather than by division, as established clumps are best left to naturalize.

Myosotidium hortensia

CHATHAM ISLANDS FORGET-ME-NOT

◑/◐ ❄ ↔ 24–40 in (60–100 cm)
↑ 12–16 in (30–40 cm)

Evergreen perennial. Forms clump of long-stemmed, deeply veined, dark green, heart- to kidney-shaped leaves to 12 in (30 cm) long. Upright flower stems, large heads crowded with white-centered blue flowers, in early summer. Zones 8–10.

MYOSOTIS

FORGET-ME-NOT

Around 100 species of annuals, biennials, and perennials belong to this genus of the borage (Boraginaceae) family. They are found in Europe, Asia, Africa, North and South America, Australia, and New Zealand. Most are small tufted plants with simple, usually lance-shaped leaves that are sometimes grayish and often finely hairy. Their 5-petalled flowers are tiny but quite showy and are usually borne in sprays on short branching stems. Most bloom in spring and early summer and are commonly white, cream, pink, or various shades of blue and mauve.

CULTIVATION: Easily grown in any position, sunny or shady, that remains moist during summer. Alpine species benefit from a gritty free-draining soil. Propagate perennials by careful division in late winter, otherwise raise from seed, which often self-sows.

Nelumbo nucifera

Myosotis alpestris

◐ ❄ ↔ 16 in (40 cm) ↑ 12 in (30 cm)

Long-flowering temperate Eurasian and North American perennial. Simple, bright green, pointed oval to lance-shaped leaves, to 3 in (8 cm) long. Small sprays of bright to dark blue tiny flowers, in spring. 'Alba', white flowers. Zones 3–9.

Myosotis sylvatica

BEDDING FORGET-ME-NOT

◐ ❄ ↔ 8–16 in (20–40 cm)
↑ 6–16 in (15–40 cm)

Biennial to short-lived perennial, often treated as an annual, from Europe and Asia. Bright green leaves, to 4 in (10 cm) long. Spikes of pale-centered, tiny flowers, blue or pink, in summer. 'Blue Ball', deep blue flowers; 'Music', large deep blue flowers; 'Royal Blue Improved', many deep blue flowers; 'Spring Symphony Blue', bright blue; Victoria Series, blue, pink, and white flowers. Zones 5–10.

Myosotis sylvatica

NELUMBO

This genus of 2 species of aquatic perennials belongs to the lotus (Nelumbonaceae) family. One species is native to eastern North America, and the other is found throughout Asia and in Australia. The round leaves are borne umbrella-like on long stalks, usually above the water. The showy fragrant flowers are also borne on long stalks, often over 36 in (90 cm) tall, in shades of pink, yellow, and white. They are followed by decorative seed heads. Stalks, rootstock, and seeds are all edible.

CULTIVATION: In warm subtropical climates, they can be grown in outdoor ponds. In cool-temperate climates, plant in shallow water or in tubs. Plant rhizomes in baskets or beds of heavy rich soil mix. Grow in calm water in full sun. Propagate by division of rhizomes or from seed.

Nelumbo lutea

syn. *Nelumbium luteum*

AMERICAN LOTUS, WATER CHINQUAPIN, YANQUAPIN

◔ ❄ ↔ 7 ft (2 m) ↑ 7 ft (2 m)

From eastern North America. Round bluish green leaves, to 24 in (60 cm) across. Pale yellow flowers, to 10 in (25 cm) wide, in summer. Flat-topped seed heads studded with small holes resemble showerheads. Zones 4–9.

Nelumbo nucifera

syn. *Nelumbium nelumbo*

SACRED LOTUS

◔ ⬥ ↔ 7 ft (2 m) ↑ 7 ft (2 m)

Found from Iran to Japan and in Australia. Bluish green wavy-edged leaves on prickly stems. Very fragrant pink or white flowers, to 12 in (30 cm) wide, in summer. 'Carolina Queen', large pink flowers, creamy at base; 'Momo Botan', smaller with dark pink to rosy red flowers; 'Mrs Perry D. Slocum', deep pink flowers, ageing to creamy yellow; 'Sharon', large double flowers, pink to red; 'Speciosum' with light pink flowers. Zones 9–12.

Nemesia caerulea

Nemesia, Hybrid Cultivar, 'Fragrant Cloud'

Nemophila menziesii 'Pennie Black'

NEMESIA

Confined to South Africa, this genus belonging to the foxglove (Scrophulariaceae) family includes around 65 species of annuals, perennials, and subshrubs. They form small mounds of toothed linear to lance-shaped foliage. Their flowers, borne in clusters on short stems, have a conspicuous lower lobe, often with a blotch of contrasting color. The annuals are popular short-lived bedding plants in a range of bright colors. The less colorful perennials are sometimes mildly scented and ideal for borders, rockeries, or pots.
CULTIVATION: Grow in a sunny position in light free-draining soil that is kept moist. Pinch back to keep compact. Sow annuals in succession for continuous bloom. Perennials will tolerate light frosts and grow from cuttings of non-flowering stems. Propagate from seed in late autumn or early spring.

Nemesia caerulea
↔ 16–24 in (40–60 cm) ↕ 16–24 in (40–60 cm)
Woody-based perennial from South Africa. Bright green, narrow, lance-shaped leaves, often finely toothed. Heads of small pink to light purple-blue flowers with yellow eye, in summer. Bluebird/ 'Hubbird', violet flowers with yellow eye. Zones 8–10.

Nemesia strumosa
↔ 8–16 in (20–40 cm) ↕ 6–20 in (15–50 cm)
Fast-growing mounding annual native to South Africa. Lower leaves to 3 in (8 cm) long, bright green, toothed, upper leaves much smaller. Small flowers in crowded heads, often in warm shades of yellow-orange and apricot, sometimes purple or white, in summer. 'Blue Gem', bright blue flowers; 'KLM', two-tone flowers, dark blue upper petals, white lower petals. Zones 9–11.

Nemesia Hybrid Cultivars
↔ 8–16 in (20–40 cm) ↕ 6–16 in (15–40 cm)
Many hybrids have been bred to produce early-flowering compact plants in a wide range of colors. 'Fleurie Blue', low spreader, bright blue flowers; 'Fragrant Cloud', fragrant pale pink and white flowers; 'Innocence', pure white flowers, each with a small yellow throat; Maritana Series, low-spreading, heavy-flowering plants, wide color range including bicolors; Sachet Series, compact, heavy-flowering, often fragrant plants in single colors, such as 'Blueberry Sachet', blue to purple, and 'Vanilla Sachet', white; 'Sundrops', compact rounded plants in warm tones. Zones 11–12.

NEMOPHILA

There are 11 species of annuals in this genus, a member of the waterleaf (Hydrophyllaceae) family. Native to western North America, they have small pinnate leaves on wiry stems, and form spreading mounds of ferny foliage that are smothered in small 5-petalled flowers, usually borne singly in the leaf axils, in late spring and summer. The plants are graceful and often intriguingly colored, with flowers in various shades and patterns of blue and white. They are most at home in full to half-sun.
CULTIVATION: These are superb plants for narrow borders, banks, hanging baskets, and window boxes. They require moist well-drained soil. Propagation is from seed, which is best sown in situ, as once it has germinated, the young plants resent disturbance.

Nemophila maculata
FIVE SPOT
↔ 12–20 in (30–50 cm) ↕ 8–12 in (20–30 cm)
Annual species from central California, USA. Initially upright, later spreading. Soft green pinnate leaves, up to 7 lobes. White flowers, purple blotch near petal tip, in summer. Zones 7–11.

Nemophila menziesii
↔ 12–20 in (30–50 cm) ↕ 4–6 in (10–15 cm)
Low spreading annual from California, USA. Ferny light green leaves, up to 11 lobes. Many white-centered mid-blue flowers, sometimes entirely white, in summer. N. m. subsp. atromaria, white flowers spotted with purple-black. N. m. 'Oculata', pale blue flowers with purple-black center; 'Pennie Black', very dark purple-black flowers, edged with white. Zones 7–11.

NEOMARICA

This genus of 15 species of tender rhizomatous perennials is a member of the iris (Iridaceae) family. They are native to tropical America and western Africa. The thick leaves are erect and sword-shaped, with strong veins or ribs, and are arranged in fans. Tall stems bear short-lived, flattened, iris-like flowers, in summer. The outer petals are larger and spreading; the inner 3 petals are upright and reflexed. Some species have fragrant flowers.
CULTIVATION: In suitably warm climates, grow outdoors in a sunny position in well-drained soil. In temperate areas, grow in the greenhouse in a fertile well-drained mix, in bright filtered light or full sun. Propagate by division or from seed.

Neomarica caerulea
syn. *Marica caerulea*

☼ ✣ ↔ 12 in (30 cm) ↑ 24–36 in (60–90 cm)

Rhizomatous perennial, native to Brazil. Leaves mid-green, sword-shaped, erect. Flowers on tall stems, 3–4 in (8–10 cm) wide, pale blue to lilac outer petals, deep blue inner petals, marked with yellow, white, and brown, in summer. Flowers rarely last more than one day but are quickly replaced. Zones 11–12.

NEOREGELIA

These variable members of the bromeliad (Bromeliaceae) family range from small tubular plants to large, flat, circular plants. Their leaves are generally strap-like, forming a rosette, and they can be green, silvery green, purplish, banded, spotted, striped in white, cream, or red, or marbled in a number of colors, or even tipped red. In some species the center leaves turn red or reddish blue, sometimes white. The flower stem is short, and the globular flowerhead, with up to 100 flowers, generally nestles in the center of the leaf rosette. This genus contains over 70 species, mainly from South America. One group from southeastern Brazil are common and easy to grow, especially in tropical to warm-temperate areas. This group provides almost all of the nearly 3,000 hybrids listed for this genus.

CULTIVATION: Grow *Neoregelia* indoors or in a conservatory or greenhouse in cool-temperate areas, or outdoors with protection from direct sunlight and extremes of rain in warmer areas. Water when the potting mix is dry. Try to keep the water in the leaf rosette clean. Do not add extra fertilizer. Propagate from offsets.

Neomarica caerulea

Neoregelia carolinae
☼ ✣ ↔ 24 in (60 cm) ↑ 12 in (30 cm)

From Rio de Janeiro, Brazil. About 20 green leaves, with a few small spines on edges. Flower stem short. Flowerhead globular, with up to 50 flowers opening over a long period. Center leaves turn red before flowering. Petals blue. *N. c.* f. *tricolor,* variegated form. Zones 11–12.

Neoregelia, Hybrid Cultivar, 'Empress'

Neoregelia concentrica
☼ ✣ ↔ 32 in (80 cm) ↑ 12 in (30 cm)

Brazilian species. Leaves strap-like, green with varying purple blotches and broken stripes, with large black teeth on edges, forming a spreading rosette. Center leaves turn purple just before flowering, lasting for many weeks. Flower stem short. Flowerhead globular, with up to 100 flowers, in summer. Petals bluish. Zones 11–12.

Neoregelia marmorata
☼ ✣ ↔ 40 in (100 cm) ↑ 20 in (50 cm)

Brazilian species. Leaves strap-like, green with many purplish spots and splashes, underside has reverse colors, medium-sized teeth on edges, forming an open funnel-shaped rosette. Flower stem short. Flowerhead globular, with up to 40 flowers, in summer. Petals white. Zones 11–12.

Neoregelia Hybrid Cultivars
☼ ✣ ↔ 4–40 in (10–100 cm) ↑ 6–20 in (15–50 cm)

Mostly from Australia, Brazil, and USA, these are all easy to grow in warm areas. '**Amazing Grace**', upright rosette in pale lime green, the whole plant blushes red in good light at flowering; '**Barbie Doll**', light green leaves, red tips; '**Beef Steak**', magnificent, symmetrically layered, wide-leafed rosette; '**Blushing Bride**', center turns bright red on flowering; '**Bobby Dazzler**', broad rich red leaves, heavy apple green spotting; '**Charm**', bright wine red leaves, tiny lime green spots—impostors grown from seed have large spotting; '**Chili Verde**', rich red in center at flowering; '**Chirripo**', glazed centrally in rich reddish purple; '**Debbie**', shy bloomer, inner leaves at first almost vertical; '**Empress**', strap-like green and pink leaves; '**Fireball**', shy flowering, petals blue; '**George's Prince**', pale lilac leaves; '**Gespacho**', wide red leaves with yellow-green markings; '**Green Apple**', leaves apple green; '**Lambert's Pride**', leaves with red to orange-red barring; '**Manoa Beauty**', leaves with unique speckling in yellow-green; '**Medallion**', inner leaves form dense crested rosette of brilliant red; '**Meyendorffii**', center turns red at flowering; '**Midnight**', deep burgundy central leaves, almost black; '**Ounce of Purple**', dull green leaves covered in tiny purple spots; '**Painted Desert**', symmetrical rosette of yellow-green leaves, developing more color in strong light; '**Passion**', chartreuse-green leaves with hot lilac-pink intense areas; '**Perfection**', yellow-cream central variegation; '**Red of Rio**', mahogany red with small random green markings; '**Rosella**', at flowering, green part of leaves turns red; '**Spots and Dots**', dark red spots, blotches, and wavy lines; '**Takemura Grande**', greenish plum-colored; '**Vulkan**', varying darker purple blotches and broken stripes. Zones 11–12.

NEPENTHES
MONKEY CUPS, TROPICAL PITCHER PLANT

A remarkable genus of carnivorous plants, *Nepenthes* are found through tropical Southeast Asia, with outlying species in Australia and Madagascar. They belong to their own pitcher-plant

Nepenthes alata

Nepenthes ampullaria

Nepenthes rajah

(Nepenthaceae) family. In all, there are over 70 species, divided into 2 main groups: highland species and lowland species. Tropical pitcher plants are climbers that reach up high into the jungle canopy. They have 2 types of pitchers: rounded lower ones, and upper pitchers that are longer and narrower. The flowers are small, with dozens carried along an upright stem. Attracted by bright colors and sweet nectar around the pitcher rim, the prey—usually insects, but sometimes small birds and even rats—once inside, slips down the waxy sides into the digestive liquid and drowns. CULTIVATION: Lowland species can be grown outside in tropical and subtropical regions. In the tropics, use an open soil like bark chips, while in subtropical and temperate areas, use a mix of equal parts peat and scoria. In cooler areas, they are best grown in a warm greenhouse or conservatory. Water overhead, never by tray. Most species prefer part-shade and high humidity. Fertilize with a light foliar feed once a month in spring and summer. Highland species prefer a cooler night temperature. Propagate from stem cuttings; plant in sphagnum moss. Mist regularly.

Nepenthes alata
WINGED NEPENTHES
☀/☀ ⚥ ↔ 20 in (50 cm) ↑ 15 ft (4.5 m)
Native to the Philippines, Malaysia, and Sumatra, in highlands and lowlands. Stem prostrate or climbing. Elongated green leaves, to 10 in (25 cm) long. Pitchers cylindrical, bulbous at base, green in shade, pinkish in full sun. Lower pitchers 4 in (10 cm) long, with 2 fringed wings; upper pitchers to 10 in (25 cm) long, with 2 wings. Also a spotted form. Zones 11–12.

Nepenthes ampullaria
☀/☀ ⚥ ↔ 20 in (50 cm) ↑ 20 ft (6 m)
From Borneo, Malaysia, New Guinea, Singapore, and Sumatra. Lowland climbing species, woody vine, leaves to 10 in (25 cm) long. Lower pitchers squat, about 3 in (8 cm) high, with 2 fringed wings, large spur behind lid. Upper pitchers rare. Zones 11–12.

Nepenthes burbidgeae
PAINTED PITCHER PLANT
☀ ⚥ ↔ 16 in (40 cm) ↑ 40 ft (12 m)
Beautiful climbing highland species native to Borneo. Lower pitchers ivory or cream with burgundy blotches, rim with burgundy stripes. Upper pitchers funnel-shaped, pale green with purple to burgundy blotches. Zones 11–12.

Nepenthes fusca
☀ ⚥ ↔ 14 in (35 cm) ↑ 35 ft (10 m)
From the highlands of Borneo. Tubular lower pitchers to 6 in (15 cm) long, with 2 fringed wings, usually purple with green blotches. Upper pitchers are similar size but funnel-shaped, green with purple blotches. Zones 11–12.

Nepenthes lowii
☀ ⚥ ↔ 26 in (65 cm) ↑ 25 ft (8 m)
Unusual highland species from Borneo. Lower pitchers cylindrical, with 2 prominent ribs. Upper pitchers hourglass-shaped, deep red inside, green to red outside. Lid is upright, the interior covered with bristly hairs. Zones 11–12.

Nepenthes maxima
☀ ❄ ↔ 30 in (75 cm) ↑ 10 ft (3 m)
Beautiful varied highland species found in Borneo, New Guinea, and Malaku and Sulawesi Islands, Indonesia. Three-angled climbing stem. Lower pitchers to 8 in (20 cm) high with 2 prominent wings. Upper pitchers usually tubular but can be slightly funnel-shaped. Color varies from yellow-green to white with burgundy blotches, to purple with white blotches. *N. m.* × *mixta*, 6–8 in (15–20 cm) pitchers, very easy to grow. Zones 8–12.

Nepenthes rajah
☀ ⚥ ↔ 40 in (100 cm) ↑ 7 ft (2 m)
Magnificent highland species from Borneo. *N. rajah* is the "king" of *Nepenthes*. Usually a scrambling vine rather than a climber. Lower pitchers are oval-shaped, to 14 in (35 cm) high, burgundy to purple, with large mouth and even larger lid. Upper pitchers are similar except they are funnel-shaped. Zones 11–12.

Nepenthes spathulata
☀ ⚥ ↔ 20 in (50 cm) ↑ 7 ft (2 m)
Beautiful highland species native to southern Sumatra. Lower pitchers are green, with large bright red rim and 2 lightly fringed wings. Upper pitchers are more slender and totally green. *N. s.* × *maxima*, pitchers spotted with red. Zones 11–12.

Nepenthes tentaculata

☀ ✂ ↔ 20 in (50 cm) ↑ 7 ft (2 m)

Small, scrambling, highland species from Borneo and Sulawesi. Lower pitchers are cream to green, burgundy blotches, narrowing toward mouth, with 2 heavily fringed wings. Upper pitchers burgundy to purple, with prominent ribs. Lid covered with thick bristles. Zones 11–12.

Nepenthes × ventrata

☀ ❀ ↔ 16 in (40 cm) ↑ 7 ft (2 m)

Naturally occurring hybrid; varies considerably in size and color. Pitchers usually cylindrical, bulging a little in lower third, totally green or almost bronze to red, with many variations in between. Robust easily grown plant. Zones 8–12.

Nepenthes ventricosa ★

☀ ❀ ↔ 16 in (40 cm) ↑ 7 ft (2 m)

Lovely highland species from the Philippines. Pitchers hourglass-shaped, without wings or ribs, yellow to green, often red in upper half, with red rim. *N. v. × mikei*, green pitchers spotted with red. Zones 8–12.

NEPETA

CATMINT, CATNIP

A member of the mint (Lamiaceae) family, this genus of around 250 mainly temperate Eurasian and North African aromatic perennials is represented in cultivation by just a few species, and one widely grown hybrid group. Commonly grown in herbaceous borders or for edging large beds, they are valued for the hazy effect created by their gray-green foliage and mauve-blue to purple flowerheads. They are mainly low-growing sprawling plants, with small toothed leaves. In summer, the foliage disappears under upright spikes of tiny flowers.
CULTIVATION: Grow in full sun with light free-draining soil. Pinch back in spring to encourage compact growth, and water well. Propagate from seed or cuttings of non-flowering stems.

Nepeta camphorata

☼/☀ ❀ ↔ 24 in (60 cm) ↑ 18 in (45 cm)

Very aromatic species from Greece. Somewhat sticky, toothed, pointed, oval leaves, to 1 in (25 mm) long. Foliage and stems camphor-scented when crushed. Heads of fairly widely spaced, purple-spotted, white flowers, in summer. Zones 8–10.

Nepeta clarkei

HIMALAYAN CATMINT

☼/☀ ❀ ↔ 24 in (60 cm) ↑ 24–36 in (60–90 cm)

Himalayan native. Leaves light green to silvery, broad-based, toothed, lance-shaped, in whorls at base, in opposite pairs on flower stems. Long upright spikes of purple-blue flowers, white lower lobes, in summer. Zones 6–10.

Nepeta × faassenii ★

☼/☀ ❀ ↔ 40 in (100 cm) ↑ 24 in (60 cm)

Often sprawling hybrid. Leaves toothed, lance-shaped to pointed oval. Spikes of lavender to purple-blue flowers, in summer. 'Walker's Low', mounding habit, lavender-blue flowers. Zones 3–10.

Nepeta grandiflora

☼/☀ ❀ ↔ 24 in (60 cm) ↑ 24 in (60 cm)

Bushy eastern European species. Leaves toothed, downy, broad-based, pointed oval. Spikes of lavender-blue flowers in summer. 'Bramdean', compact flowerheads; 'Dawn to Dusk', gray-green foliage, mauve flowers. Zones 3–10.

Nepeta sibirica

SIBERIAN CATMINT

☼/☀ ❀ ↔ 40 in (100 cm) ↑ 40 in (100 cm)

Quick-growing native of Siberia. Leaves sparsely hairy, toothed, dark green. Flowerheads crowded but individual whorls widely spaced, blue to soft purple, in spring–summer. Zones 3–9.

NICOTIANA

TOBACCO

Famous as the source of tobacco leaf, this genus, which is a member of the nightshade (Solanaceae) family, encompasses over 65 species, the bulk of which are annuals and perennials, most native to tropical and subtropical America, with a smaller number in Australia and the South Pacific. A few species are shrubby in habit, though they tend to be softwooded and short-lived. The leaves are usually very large and covered with fine hairs, sticky to the touch, and may exude a fragrance when crushed. The flowers are tubular or bell-shaped, usually white or in pastel shades of green, pale yellow, pink, or soft red, and if fragrant their scent is generally released at night. Some species, notably *N. alata,* are grown especially for their fragrant blooms
CULTIVATION: Most tobacco species are marginally frost tolerant. They grow best in warm humid climates with ample summer rainfall, in full sun or partial shade. The soil should be well drained and reasonably fertile. Cut back old flower stems to encourage reblooming. Propagate from seed sown in spring, though some will grow from cuttings. Some species may self sow.

Nicotiana alata

syn. *Nicotiana affinis*

FLOWERING TOBACCO, JASMINE TOBACCO

☼/☀ ❀ ↔ 12 in (30 cm) ↑ 24–36 in (60–90 cm)

Native to South America. Sticky-stemmed perennial often grown as an annual. Rosette-forming. Large oval leaves. Tall flower stems. Clusters of narrow, tubular, greenish white flowers with flaring starry ends, in summer. They are very fragrant and open at night. Zones 4–11.

Nepenthes × ventrata

Nicotiana langsdorffii

☀ ❄ ↔ 15 in (38 cm) ↕ 5 ft (1.5 m)

Native to Brazil. Upright tall annual with dark green, deeply veined, ovate leaves. Masses of twiggy flower spikes, lime green tubular flowers. Summer-flowering. Zones 8–11.

Nicotiana × sanderae

☀/◐ ❄ ↔ 10 in (25 cm)
↕ 15–24 in (38–60 cm)

Garden hybrid between *N. alata* and *N. forgetiana*. Bushy hairy-leafed annual. Slightly crinkled, wavy, dark green, ovate leaves. Fragrant, flaring, tubular flowers, red, purple, and white, open all day. **Domino Series**, compact, upward-facing flowers in antique shades such as salmon pink; '**Lime Green**', bright yellow-green flowers; **Nikki Series**, prolonged flowering, red, pink, yellow, and white flowers; **Saratoga Series**, uniform in size, flowers in mixed color range of reds, pinks, white, and lime. Zones 7–10.

Nicotiana sylvestris

☀/◐ ❄ ↔ 18–24 in (45–60 cm) ↕ 3–5 ft
(0.9–1.5 m)

Native to Argentina. Vigorous annual with very large sticky leaves. Tall stems bear terminal panicles of long, white, pendulous flowers, very fragrant, in summer. Zones 8–11.

Nicotiana × *sanderae*, Nikki Series

Nicotiana sylvestris

NIDULARIUM

From southern and eastern Brazil, this genus contains 45 species and belongs to the bromeliad (Bromeliaceae) family. Closely related to *Neoregelia*, these medium-sized plants prefer shadier conditions. They have small-toothed strap-like leaves, mainly green, often with darker green spots, and sometimes purplish on either side, forming an open rosette with some water-holding capacity. The flower stem varies from short to just emerging above the water level in the leaf tank. The flowerhead is globular, with flat flower clusters, and large, stiff, flattened bracts, mostly red but sometimes greenish. Each flowerhead contains many flowers, with petals that are white, red, or blue, but which never open wide. CULTIVATION: Grow indoors if in flower, or in a greenhouse or conservatory in cool-temperate areas, or outdoors with shade protection in warm-temperate, subtropical, and tropical areas. Water when potting mix is dry. Extra fertilizer is not necessary. Propagate from offsets.

Nidularium fulgens

☀ ⚘ ↔ 32 in (80 cm) ↕ 12 in (30 cm)

From Rio de Janeiro, Brazil. Leaves strap-like, green, with scattered dark green spots, teeth up to almost ¼ in (6 mm) long on edges, forming broad funnelform rosette. Flowerhead globular, with up to 10 flat flower clusters and large bright red to orange bract with strong teeth and spreading widely, in spring–summer. Petals blue with white edges. Zones 11–12.

Nidularium innocentii

☀ ⚘ ↔ 36 in (90 cm) ↕ 14 in (35 cm)

Native to southeast Brazil. Leaves green, or with purplish wine underneath, small teeth on edges forming a dense funnelform rosette. Flowerhead globular, with up to 9 flat flower clusters, and a large broad bract, green with a red tip to totally red, in spring–summer. Petals greenish. Several variegated forms available. Zones 11–12.

Nidularium Hybrid Cultivars

☀ ⚘ ↔ 20–40 in (50–100 cm)
↕ 12–20 in (30–50 cm)

Diverse color range and ease of care. Most prefer a subtropical garden. '**Madonna**', white bracts becoming bright red at flowering, petals white; '**Miranda**', variegated form of 'Madonna'; '**RaRu**', apple green rosette, whitish pink flowers; '**Ruby Lee**', leaves with longitudinal lines throughout on a background of green, or green and red, or totally red. Zones 10–12.

Nidularium fulgens

Nigella damascena 'Miss Jekyll'

Nierembergia caerulea 'Purple Robe'

Nolana paradoxa

NIEREMBERGIA
CUPFLOWER

There are about 23 species of annuals, perennials, and subshrubs in this genus, which is a member of the nightshade (Solanaceae) family. They are native to South America where they grow in moist sunny situations. They are slender-stemmed plants, creeping, spreading, or erect, with small narrow leaves. The showy flowers are open and upward-facing, in shades of blue, purple, or white, often with yellow throats. They are borne for long periods from summer to autumn.

CULTIVATION: Grow these in a sunny sheltered position in gritty moisture-retentive soil. In cold climates grow in pots or as annuals. Plants flower in the first year from seed. Propagate all species from seed, and perennials also by division or from cuttings.

Nierembergia caerulea
syn. *Nierembergia hippomanica*

☼ ❄ ↔ 8 in (20 cm) ↕ 8–15 in (20–38 cm)

From Argentina. Small, upright, densely branching perennial often grown as an annual. Narrow pointed leaves. Numerous lavender flowers with yellow throats, in summer. **'Purple Robe'**, darker purple flowers with yellow throats. Zones 9–11.

Nierembergia repens
syn. *Nierembergia rivularis*

☼ ❄ ↔ 18 in (45 cm) ↕ 2 in (5 cm)

Native to South America. Low spreading rhizomatous perennial with spoon-shaped leaves. Flaring white flowers, about 1 in (25 mm) wide, tinged with yellow or pink at base, in summer. May be invasive. Zones 9–11.

NIGELLA
FENNEL FLOWER, LOVE-IN-A-MIST, WILD FENNEL

This genus of about 15 species of annuals, from the Mediterranean region and western Asia, is a member of the buttercup (Ranunculaceae) family. All the species are easy to grow and feature finely divided green foliage with bushy growth. Flower colors are sky blue and mixes of white, blue, pink, purple, mauve, and rosy red. Nigellas bloom profusely and make good cut flowers. Their decorative seed pods and foliage are also used in dried floral arrangements.

CULTIVATION: Grow in full sun to half-sun in any well-drained soil and fertilize once a month with a relatively high phosphorus fertilizer. Deadhead to prolong flowering. Propagate from seed sown directly where it is to grow, since *Nigella* seedlings resent being transplanted. Plants will reseed.

Nigella damascena
LOVE-IN-A-MIST

☼ ❄ ↔ 10 in (25 cm) ↕ 20 in (50 cm)

European species. Bright green finely cut foliage, somewhat like fennel. Fluffy flowers, in blue, pink, or white. Make successive plantings for blooms all summer. **'Miss Jekyll'**, semi-double, sky blue flowers. Zones 8–10.

NOLANA
CHILEAN BELLFLOWER

This genus of around 18 perennials from South America belongs to the nightshade (Solanaceae) family. They are grown as annuals in the Northern Hemisphere. These are heat-tolerant sprawling plants, frequently found in maritime areas in their native habitat. Their leaves are spoon-shaped. The showy, tubular, blue or purple flowers have white throats and 5 lobes. The flowers open in the sun but stay closed on cloudy days. They are attractive edging plants and a good choice in a hanging basket.

CULTIVATION: Drought tolerant, these plants will grow in any sandy garden soil in full sun. Propagate from seed, sown directly where it is to grow, in spring.

Nolana humifusa
SNOWBIRD

☼ ✈ ↔ 12 in (30 cm) ↕ 4–6 in (10–15 cm)

Quite rare species from Peru. Leaves mid-green, oval. Long trailing stems with small, bell-shaped, pale blue flowers, in summer. Zones 11–12.

Nolana paradoxa

☼ ✈ ↔ 12 in (30 cm) ↕ 4–6 in (10–15 cm)

From Chile. Trailing plant, suitable for rock gardens or hanging baskets. Mid-green oval leaves, pointed. Large blue-purple flowers, pale yellow or white throats, in summer. **'Blue Bird'**, blue flowers, white throat. Zones 11–12.

NUPHAR

This genus belongs to the waterlily (Nymphaeaceae) family. It contains about 25 species of aquatic perennial herbs, native to temperate regions of the Northern Hemisphere, growing in still or slow-moving water. The large oval to round leaves may be floating, submerged, or held above the water. Floating and emergent leaves are leathery. The small flowers are held above the water and have prominent yellow sepals, with smaller yellow petals.
CULTIVATION: Plant rhizomes in baskets containing a rich soil mix. Baskets can be lowered gradually to acclimatize plants to the water depth. Grow in full sun in still water. They can be invasive where conditions suit. Propagate from seed or by division.

Nuphar lutea
YELLOW WATERLILY
☼/◑ ✳ ↔ 3–8 ft (0.9–2.4 m) ↕ 3–15 in (8–38 cm)
Widespread in northern temperate regions. Invasive plant with broadly oval or rounded, floating or emergent, leathery and shiny leaves. Produces small, globular, bright yellow flowers, in summer. Blooms emit a distinct odor. Zones 4–9.

NYMPHAEA

This genus of aquatic perennials, in the waterlily (Nymphaeaceae) family, is of varied distribution in ponds over most of the world. There are about 50 species, split into hardy and tropical groups. The leaves are broadly oval or round, with the base cleft in 2 lobes. Flowers with pointed or rounded petals cover the color spectrum. They may be on stalks above the foliage, or sit at water level. Some are fragrant or night-opening.
CULTIVATION: Hardy water lilies are suitable for permanent pond positions in temperate climates. Tropical plants need a summer water temperature of 65–70°F (18–21°C), and a winter temperature of 50°F (10°C). Plant rhizomes in baskets in a rich soil mix, the water depth varying with plant size. Grow in full sun in still water. Propagate by dividing rhizomes.

Nymphaea alba
EUROPEAN WHITE LILY
☼ ✳ ↔ 3–10 ft (0.9–3 m) ↕ 3–15 in (8–38 cm)
From temperate Eurasia and northern Africa. Round leaves, 12 in (30 cm) across, red then green. Floating white flowers, 8 in (20 cm) wide, open during day, in summer. Zones 5–9.

Nymphaea caerulea
syn. *Nymphaea capensis*
CAPE BLUE WATERLILY
☼ ✈ ↔ 3–12 ft (0.9–3.5 m)
↕ 3–15 in (8–38 cm)
From southern and eastern Africa. Round wavy-edged leaves, to 16 in (40 cm) wide. Fragrant blue flowers, held above foliage, open during day, in spring–summer. 'Colorata' (syn. *N. colorata*), smaller leaves with overlapping lobes, and smaller, mauve to blue flowers. Zones 10–12.

Nymphaea × daubenyana
☼ ✈ ↔ 3–6 ft (0.9–1.8 m) ↕ 3–15 in (8–38 cm)
Hybrid of garden origin. Small, fragrant, light blue flowers held well above the water. New plants arise within axils of leaves and stalks. Day-opening, in spring–summer. Zones 11–12.

Nymphaea lotus
EGYPTIAN WATERLILY, LOTUS, WHITE LILY
☼ ✈ ↔ 3–12 ft (0.9–3.5 m) ↕ 3–15 in (8–38 cm)
From Egypt and tropical southeastern Africa. Large, rounded, wavy-edged leaves to 20 in (50 cm) wide. Flowers, to 10 in (25 cm) wide, white, fragrant, usually night-opening, closing the following noon, in spring–summer. Zones 11–12.

Nymphaea mexicana
YELLOW WATERLILY
☼ ✈ ↔ 3–12 ft (0.9–3.5 m) ↕ 3–15 in (8–38 cm)
From southern USA and Mexico. Vigorous plant with round to oval leaves, green blotched with purplish brown. Lightly fragrant flowers, pale to bright yellow, in spring–summer. Zones 10–12.

Nymphaea odorata
FRAGRANT WATERLILY, POND LILY
☼ ✳ ↔ 3–8 ft (0.9–2.4 m) ↕ 3–15 in (8–38 cm)
From eastern USA. Round dull green leaves to 10 in (25 cm) wide. Fragrant white flowers open during day, in summer. Zones 3–10.

Nymphaea tetragona
syn. *Nymphaea pygmaea*
PYGMY WATERLILY
☼ ✳ ↔ 12–48 in (30–120 cm) ↕ 3–15 in (8–38 cm)
Found throughout Europe, Asia, and Japan. Small, oval, dark green leaves, dull red beneath. Slightly fragrant flowers, about 2 in (5 cm) wide, white with yellow stamens, in summer. 'Alba', small leaves, purple beneath, white flowers. Zones 3–9.

Nymphaea tetragona 'Alba'

Nymphaea Hybrid Cultivars

Nymphaea hybrids are divided into hardy and tropical hybrids, with the tropical hybrids further divided into day- and night-blooming hybrids.

HARDY HYBRIDS

☼ ❋ ↔ 3–8 ft (0.9–2.4 m) ↕ 3–15 in (8–38 cm)

Suitable for cooler climates. Day-blooming flowers, usually held close to water level, all colors except blue shades. Some "change-ables," altering their coloring dramatically as they age. '**Charlene Strawn**', scented yellow flowers held above water; '**Ellisiana**', scented deep pink to red flowers; '**Fire Crest**', scented clear pink flowers with red stamens; '**Gladstoneana**', large white flowers with gold stamens; '**Gonnère**', large pure white flowers; '**James Brydon**', large-cupped, bright red, scented flowers; '**Odorata Sulphurea Grandiflora**', mottled leaves and large, starry, bright yellow flowers; '**Pink Sensation**', rich pink flowers held above water; '**Pygmaea Helvola**', mottled leaves, bright yellow flowers, orange stamens; '**Texas Dawn**', large yellow flowers; '**William B. Shaw**', large creamy pink flowers; '**William Falconer**', blood red flowers with yellow stamens.

Marliacean hybrids, from mid-nineteenth century, still popular. '**Marliacea Albida**', white; '**Marliacea Carnea**', soft pink with yellow stamens; '**Marliacea Chromatella**', soft yellow. Zones 3–10.

TROPICAL DAY-BLOOMING HYBRIDS

☼ ❀ ↔ 3–12 ft (0.9–3.5 m) ↕ 3–15 in (8–38 cm)

These hybrids need a water temperature of 70°F (21°C). Some produce flowers to 15 in (38 cm) wide. All colors, including blue shades, are covered. Flowers are usually held above the foliage. '**Evelyn Randig**', hot pink flowers; '**General Pershing**', deep pink fragrant flowers, to 12 in (30 cm) across; '**Margaret Randig**', deep blue-purple scented flowers; '**Mrs George H. Pring**', scented, white, star-shaped flowers, to 10 in (25 cm) across; '**Pamela**', starry sky blue flowers; '**Panama Pacific**', deep plum flowers with yellow stamens; '**Pink Platter**', open soft pink flowers. Zones 11–12.

TROPICAL NIGHT-BLOOMING HYBRIDS

☼ ❀ ↔ 3–12 ft (0.9–3.5 m) ↕ 3–15 in (8–38 cm)

These need a water temperature of 70°F (21°C). Flowers open about dusk and close by the following noon. They are mostly in shades of red, pink, and white. '**Emily Grant Hutchings**', rich pinkish red cupped flowers, to 12 in (30 cm) wide; '**Mrs George C. Hitchcock**', large clear pink flowers with orange stamens; '**Red Flare**', starry, vivid red, scented flowers; '**Sir Galahad**', flowers of starry white with yellow stamens; '**Sturtevantii**', pearly pink scented flowers; '**Trudy Slocum**', large, flat, white flowers with yellow stamens. Zones 11–12.

NYMPHOIDES

This genus of about 20 species of aquatic perennial herbs belongs to the bogbean (Menyanthaceae) family. They are of cosmopolitan distribution. The floating leaves are oval to round with heart-shaped bases. Starry 5-petalled flowers of yellow or white are borne on stems above the water.

CULTIVATION: Most species are invasive and not suitable for small ponds. Grow in full sun, in still water, planting the rhizomes in a rich soil mix. Propagate from seed or by division.

Nymphoides crenata

WAVY MARSHWORT

☼ ☙ ↔ 6 ft (1.8 m) ↕ 2–5 ft (0.6–1.5 m)

From Australia, growing in water up to 5 ft (1.5 m) deep, can persist on drying mud. Leaves to 5 in (12 cm) wide with shallow wavy teeth. Flowers yellow, to 1¼ in (35 mm) across, with fringed petals, in many-flowered umbels, in spring–autumn. Zones 9–11.

Nymphoides peltata

YELLOW FLOATING HEART

☼ ❋ ↔ 3–8 ft (0.9–2.4 m) ↕ 12 in (30 cm)

Native to temperate Eurasia and naturalized in North America. Small, mottled, heart-shaped, floating leaves. Bright yellow, starry, fringed flowers, in summer. Zones 6–10.

OCHAGAVIA

The 4 members of this genus in the bromeliad (Bromeliaceae) family are native to Chile. They form clumps of dense non-water-retaining rosettes. The leaves are very numerous, narrow and stiff, with many teeth on the edges. The stemless globular flowerhead, with up to 50 flowers, is sunk in the middle of the leaf rosette and surrounded with bright red bracts. The flower petals are mainly in shades of red. The innermost leaves are sometimes reddish at the base. These plants require winter temperatures down to around 32°F (0°C) to promote flowering.

Nymphaea, Hybrid Cultivar, Hardy, 'Ellisiana'

Nymphaea, Hybrid Cultivar, Tropical Day-blooming, 'Margaret Randig'

Nymphaea, Hybrid Cultivar, Tropical Night-blooming, 'Trudy Slocum'

CULTIVATION: These are recommended for pot culture in a green-house or conservatory in cold-temperate areas, or for outdoor culture in cool- to warm-temperate areas. Water when potting mix is dry. Do not overfertilize. Propagation is mainly from offsets.

Ochagavia carnea

☼ ❄ ↔ 32 in (80 cm) ↑ 20 in (50 cm)

From Chile. Clumping plant of dense rosettes, to 20 in (50 cm) across. Leaves green, stiff, with strongly toothed edges. Flower-head bears up to 50 pink-petalled flowers, surrounded by large fluffy pink bracts, in winter. Zones 8–10.

OENOTHERA

EVENING PRIMROSE

This genus of more than 120 species of annuals, biennials, and perennials in the evening-primrose (Onagraceae) family is found in temperate zones of the Americas. Some have tap roots and tend to be upright, others have fibrous roots and a more sprawling habit. These plants' most attractive feature is their short-lived but pretty summer flowers, which are cup-shaped, 4-petalled, and mainly yellow, sometimes pink, in color. Many species open from evening or night, sometimes not lasting beyond the following morning. Elongated seed capsules follow.

CULTIVATION: Mostly very hardy, these tough adaptable plants prefer full sun and light, gritty, free-draining soil. Summer watering produces stronger growth, but they will tolerate drought. Fibrous-rooted species can be divided when dormant, otherwise propagate from seed or basal cuttings. May self-sow and naturalize.

Oenothera acaulis

☼ ❄ ↔ 16–24 in (40–60 cm) ↑ 6 in (15 cm)

Biennial or perennial from Chile. Spreading clump of often red-tinted stems. Irregularly lobed pinnate leaves. White flowers, ageing to pale pink, to 3 in (8 cm) wide, in summer. Zones 5–10.

Oenothera caespitosa

FRAGRANT EVENING PRIMROSE, WHITE EVENING PRIMROSE

☼ ❄ ↔ 24 in (60 cm) ↑ 4–10 in (10–25 cm)

Low, bushy, mounding perennial, native to western USA. Loose rosettes of variably sized leaves, narrow lance- to spatula-shaped, shallowly toothed, wavy edges. Fragrant white flowers ageing to pink, to 2½ in (6 cm) wide, open in evening, in summer. Zones 4–9.

Oenothera 'Lemon Sunset'

Oenothera 'Crown Imperial'

☼ ❄ ↔ 12 in (30 cm) ↑ 16–20 in (40–50 cm)

Hybrid. Forms clump of bright green, lance-shaped, basal leaves. Upright flower stems, fritillary-like heads of bright yellow flowers, to over 1¼ in (30 mm) wide, in summer. Zones 7–10.

Oenothera fruticosa

☼ ❄ ↔ 12–16 in (30–40 cm) ↑ 20–32 in (50–80 cm)

Sometimes short-lived biennial or perennial from eastern North America. Leaves to over 4 in (10 cm) long, lance-shaped, midrib

Ochagavia carnea

and stems usually red-tinted. Heads of golden yellow flowers, in summer. *O. f.* subsp. *glauca*, broad blue-green leaves, red-tinted when young. *O. f.* 'Fyrverkeri' (syns 'Feuerwerkeri', 'Fireworks'), foliage tinted purple-red, bright yellow flowers. Zones 4–9.

Oenothera 'Lemon Sunset'

☼ ❄ ↔ 16–32 in (40–80 cm) ↑ 40 in (100 cm)

Erect hybrid perennial of uncertain parentage. Forms mounding clump of small deep green leaves. Red stems. Fragrant flowers, to 4 in (10 cm) in diameter, light yellow, ageing to deep pink or red, in summer. Zones 5–9.

Oenothera macrocarpa

MISSOURI PRIMROSE, OZARK SUNDROPS

☼ ❄ ↔ 16–32 in (40–80 cm)

↑ 8–16 in (20–40 cm)

Spreading, sometimes mounding perennial from south-central USA. Stems initially erect then sprawling. Downy leaves, to 3 in (8 cm) long. Bright yellow flowers, to 4 in (10 cm) wide, in summer. Zones 5–9.

Oenothera speciosa

WHITE EVENING PRIMROSE

☼ ❄ ↔ 12–24 in (30–60 cm)

↑ 12–24 in (30–60 cm)

Perennial from southwestern USA and Mexico. Upright mounding habit. Rosettes of broad lance-shaped leaves, usually irregularly toothed, sometimes lobed. Flowers open white, ageing to deep pink, in summer–early autumn. 'Alba', white flowers; 'Rosea', pale pink flowers; 'Siskiyou', pale pink to mauve flowers. Zones 5–10.

Oenothera versicolor

☼ ❄ ↔ 16 in (40 cm) ↑ 24 in (60 cm)

Native range unclear, possibly of garden origin. Upright perennial; red-tinted stems; narrow elliptic leaves taper to fine point, toothed. Terminal heads of bright orange flowers ageing to red, in summer. Zones 6–10.

OMPHALODES
NAVELSEED, NAVELWORT

There are about 28 species of annuals, biennials, and perennials in this genus, which belongs to the borage (Boraginaceae) family. They are native to Europe, northern Africa, Asia, and Mexico, where they grow in habitats such as shady rocks and cliffs, damp woodland, or streamsides. The leaves vary from heart-shaped to lance-shaped and may be slightly hairy. The small blue or white flowers are borne in terminal clusters, in spring or early summer, and resemble forget-me-nots.
CULTIVATION: Most species prefer a cool, somewhat shaded situation in any moist but well-drained soil high in organic matter. Low-growing species are suitable for rockeries or make excellent ground covers, while taller plants can be grown in the border. Propagate all species from seed in spring. Perennials can also be propagated by division in autumn, but care should be taken as they resent root disturbance.

Omphalodes cappadocica
NAVELWORT

☀ ❅ ↔ 12–18 in (30–45 cm) ↑ 8 in (20 cm)
Native to Turkey. Perennial, forming low clumps of heart-shaped leaves. Small, blue, forget-me-not flowers, in early–mid-summer. 'Cherry Ingram', taller vigorous form, deeper blue flowers; 'Starry Eyes', darker blue central stripe on each pale petal, creating a starry effect. Zones 6–9.

Omphalodes linifolia
VENUS' NAVELWORT

☀ ❅ ↔ 6–10 in (15–25 cm)
↑ 12–18 in (30–45 cm)
From western Europe. Annual with narrow grayish green leaves. Sprays of slightly scented white flowers, borne profusely in summer. Unlike other members of the genus, should be grown in a sunny situation. Zones 6–9.

Omphalodes verna
BLUE-EYED MARY, CREEPING FORGET-ME-NOT

☀ ❅ ↔ 24 in (60 cm) ↑ 6 in (15 cm)
Native to Europe. Low-growing perennial, suitable for ground cover. Long, creeping, rooting stems; pointed oval to heart-shaped leaves. White-centered, blue, forget-me-not flowers, in spring. Zones 6–9.

Omphalodes cappadocica

ONOPORDUM

This genus of about 40 thistles in the daisy (Asteraceae) family is from the Mediterranean region and western and central Asia. They are gray-leafed plants, in some cases of impressive dimensions, with white cobwebbed foliage well armed with vicious spines. They are biennials and in their second year produce purple thistle-flowers on candelabra-like thorny and webbed stems, followed by the classic feathery seeds that are caught by the wind to be spread far and wide.
CULTIVATION: Grow in any sunny well-drained site. Propagation is from seed, best sown where it is to grow. Care must be taken in

Onopordum acaulon

choice of site as these plants can become invasive out of their native environment. On reaching seeding stage the plants will look shabby and should be removed.

Onopordum acanthium
COTTON THISTLE, SCOTCH THISTLE

☀ ❅ ↔ 6–7 ft (1.8–2 m) ↑ 8–10 ft (2.4–3 m)
Found from southern Europe to central Asia. Impressive biennial starting as rosette of large, spiny, woolly leaves; in second year sends up branched, prickly, gray stem topped by purple thistle-flowers surrounded by fierce spines, in summer. White-flowered form sometimes grown. Zones 6–10.

Onopordum acaulon
STEMLESS THISTLE

☀ ❅ ↔ 12–18 in (30–45 cm) ↑ 6 in (15 cm)
Annual from Spain and northwestern Africa. Considered a weed in many places. Low stemless rosette with white, woolly, spiny leaves. White or purple flowerheads open from yellow buds, sitting within center of rosette, in summer. Zones 7–10.

OPHIOPOGON
MONDO GRASS

This is a small genus of 4 species of evergreen perennials from Japan belonging to the family Ruscaceae. They form clumps of grassy leaves arising from underground rhizomes, and in summer bear small lily-like flowers of white to purple that are followed by blue-black berries. These grass-like plants are related to lilies, not grasses. They are cultivated for their attractive foliage and have become popular both as ground covers and for edging. Cultivars with dwarf, giant, and variously colored leaves are available.
CULTIVATION: Grow in full sun or part-shade in moist but well-drained soil. All species will withstand at least short periods of frost but in cooler areas they can be treated as bedding or container plants. Propagation is from seed sown in autumn or by division in spring.

Ophiopogon japonicus

☼/◑ ❄ ↔ 18 in (45 cm) ↕ 12 in (30 cm)

Native to Japan; popular species for ground cover. Very narrow, dark green, curving leaves form dense mats. White to pale lilac flowers, on short stems, in summer. '**Kyoto Dwarf**', tightly clumped, grows 2–4 in (5–10 cm) high; '**Nana**', slightly taller, to 5–6 in (12–15 cm) high. Zones 7–10.

Ophiopogon planiscapus

☼/◑ ❄ ↔ 18 in (45 cm)
↕ 12–18 in (30–45 cm)

From Japan. Similar to *O. japonicus*. Form most usually seen is the cultivar '**Nigrescens**' (syns 'Arabicus', 'Black Dragon', 'Ebony Knight'), commonly known as black mondo grass. Lower growing plant, purple-black foliage. Zones 6–10.

Ophiopogon planiscapus 'Nigrescens'

ORIGANUM

Found from the Mediterranean to east Asia and known mainly as a genus of perennials, including some of the best known culinary herbs, *Origanum* belongs to the mint (Lamiaceae) family. It has aromatic foliage on short stems. Flowers are borne in spikes with conspicuous bracts that enclose the flowers.
CULTIVATION: Grow in light well-drained soil in a sunny position. Hardiness varies, but most tolerate moderate frosts. Propagate from seed, small half-hardened cuttings, or by layering.

Origanum × hybridum

☼ ❄ ↔ 12 in (30 cm) ↕ 8 in (20 cm)

Hybrid between *O. dictamnus* and *O. sipyleum*. Downy, grayish green, oval leaves. Pink flowers, in drooping clusters of bracts, from late summer to autumn. '**Santa Cruz**', pink to purple flowers held above foliage. Zones 9–11.

Origanum Hybrid Cultivars

☼ ❄ ↔ 12–24 in (30–60 cm)
↕ 4–12 in (10–30 cm)

Some hybrids grown for globular flower-heads with shell-like pink to red bracts, others for attractive aromatic foliage. '**Barbara Tingey**', small, rounded, bluish leaves, flowers green at first, ageing to rosy pink; '**Betty Rollins**', crowded dark green leaves, small pink flowers, in summer; '**Kent Beauty**', small rounded leaves, small pink flowers enclosed within drooping, overlapping, pink and green bracts; '**Norton Gold**', aromatic bright golden foliage in spring, later becoming greenish gold, with pinkish purple flowers. Zones 6–9.

ORONTIUM

GOLDEN CLUB

This genus in the arum (Araceae) family contains only a single species of aquatic perennial. It is native to streams and shallow lakes and ponds of North America. The oblong leaves may be floating or upright. The narrow yellow spadix is borne on a long white stalk above a small green spathe, which withers and drops at flowering.
CULTIVATION: Grow these in large tubs or as a marginal plant in water 4–18 in (10–45 cm) deep. Grow in full sun in a fertile soil mix. Propagation is by division or from seed.

Orontium aquaticum

GOLDEN CLUB

☼ ❄ ↔ 18–24 in (45–60 cm) ↕ 12–18 in (30–45 cm)

Native to eastern USA. Aquatic perennial with leathery oblong leaves, to 12 in (30 cm) long, dark metallic green. Erect white flowering stems, to 24 in (60 cm) long, in summer. Zones 7–10.

Origanum, Hybrid Cultivar, 'Kent Beauty'

Origanum, Hybrid Cultivar, 'Betty Rollins'

ORTHOPHYTUM

Mainly from restricted locations in the dry areas of eastern Brazil, the 30 species in this genus belong to the bromeliad (Bromeliaceae) family. These clump-forming plants grow in the ground or on rocks, with or without elongating stems. The furry or smooth leaves, edged with strong teeth, form an open non-water-retaining rosette. Non-stemmed species have stalkless flowerheads that nestle in the center of the rosette, or long-stalked flowerheads. CULTIVATION: These plants are recommended for indoor culture in cool-temperate areas, or for outdoor culture with protection from continuous direct sunlight and extremes of rain in warm-temperate to tropical areas. Water when potting mix is dry. Do not over-fertilize. Propagation is usually by offsets.

Orthophytum navioides
☀ ❄ ↔ 40 in (100 cm) ↕ 4 in (10 cm)
From eastern Brazil. Dense flattened rosettes; leaves small-toothed, very narrow. Globular flowerhead, up to 10 white-petalled flowers. Most of plant turns red at flowering. Zones 9–10.

Orthophytum Hybrid Cultivars
☀ ❄ ↔ 4 in (10 cm) ↕ 10 in (25 cm)
These hybrids are bred for color and texture of foliage and inflorescence bracts. Cultivars include 'Blaze', 'Copper Penny', 'Iron Ore', and 'Star Lights'. Zones 9–10.

ORTHOSIPHON

Genus of about 40 species found in tropical regions of Africa, Asia, and Australasia, belonging to the mint (Lamiaceae) family. They are mainly softwooded shrubs with simple leaves in opposite pairs that may be smooth-edged or toothed. The elongated tubular flowers, with long prominent stamens, are borne in spiked whorls for long periods in spring and summer.
CULTIVATION: Frost tender, these plants prefer a protected sunny or shaded spot and a moist, moderately fertile, well-drained soil. Trim excess growth regularly, especially after flowering, to maintain density. Propagation is usually from seed or from cuttings.

Orthosiphon aristatus
CAT'S MOUSTACHE, CAT'S WHISKERS
☀ ✿ ↔ 36 in (90 cm) ↕ 36 in (90 cm)
Found from Southeast Asia to northern Australia, often growing near streams. Dark green ovate leaves, coarsely toothed edges. White or pale mauve flowers, in terminal racemes, in spring–summer. Zones 10–12.

OSTEOSPERMUM

Mainly from southern Africa, this genus in the daisy (Asteraceae) family comprises some 70 species of annuals, perennials, and sub-shrubs. They are valued for their carpeting of flowers during the warmer months, and year-round in mild areas. They are mainly low, mounding or spreading plants with simple, broadly toothed, elliptic to spatula-shaped leaves. The flowerheads are large, with showy ray florets, mainly in pinks and purples, or white. Disc florets are purple-blue, contrasting with the golden anthers.
CULTIVATION: Most tolerate only light frosts and do better in mild climates. They prefer a sunny position with light well-drained soil. Pinch back and deadhead to keep compact. Propagate annuals from seed and perennials from tip cuttings.

Osteospermum jucundum
syn. *Osteospermum barberae* of gardens
☀ ❄ ↔ 20–32 in (50–80 cm) ↕ 12–20 in (30–50 cm)
South African perennial. Narrow lance-shaped leaves, irregularly toothed. Flowerheads over 4 in (10 cm) wide, ray florets mauve-pink to purple, disc florets purple-black, in late spring–autumn.

Orthosiphon aristatus

O. j. subsp. *compactum*, high-altitude form, many small flowers; 'Purple Mountain' ★, purple-pink ray florets. *O. j.* 'Blackthorn Seedling', purple-pink ray florets. Zones 8–10.

Osteospermum Hybrid Cultivars
☀ ❄ ↔ 16–24 in (40–60 cm)
↕ 8–12 in (20–30 cm)
Osteospermum species hybridize freely, especially in cultivation. New forms are constantly being introduced. Most are low spreading. 'Buttermilk', warm buff-yellow petals, dark reverse; 'Hopleys', pink flowers; 'Pink Whirls' ★, pink ray florets, crimped, dark reverse; 'Pixie', soft pink flowers; 'Silver Sparkler', variegated leaves, white flowers; 'Stardust', deep pink flowers; 'Sunny Dark Gustaf', pink and white flowers; 'Weetwood', white flowers with blue eye; 'Whirligig', gray-green foliage, dusky gray-green flowers, crimped ray florets. Seedling strains include the Nasinga Series, various colors, some have crimped ray florets, and the Symphony Series, mainly bright warm colors. Zones 9–11.

OTACANTHUS

Native to Brazil, this genus of 4 species of soft-wooded evergreen shrubs is a member of the foxglove (Scrophulariaceae) family. These plants have simple smooth-edged leaves borne in opposite pairs and attractive spikes of snapdragon-like flowers.
CULTIVATION: These frost-tender plants require a humus-enriched well-drained soil in a warm sheltered position in full sun or partial shade. Pinch out tips in spring to promote bushy growth. Propagate from half-hardened cuttings.

Otacanthus caeruleus
☀/☀ ✿ ↔ 20 in (50 cm) ↕ 36 in (90 cm)
Upright plant; woody stems; bright green leaves, lance-shaped, rough-textured. Violet-blue tubular flowers, 2 flat lobes, about 1 in (25 mm) across, most of year. 'Little Boy Blue', attractive cultivar. Zones 10–12.

OXALIS

A huge genus occurring worldwide of about 500 species belonging to the wood-sorrel (Oxalidaceae) family. These mainly bulbous

plants also include evergreen ground-covering perennials, succulents, and shrubs. Many have clover-shaped leaves that close at night. Flower buds are rolled like an umbrella and open to bowl- or cup-shaped 5-petalled blooms, some species opening only in full sunlight. Some are troublesome weeds.
CULTIVATION: The bulbous winter-growers like almost frost-free sunny sites, dry in summer. Evergreen and woodland summer-growing species prefer shade and moist soil. Some of the succulent and shrubby forms, in all but frost-free climates, should be grown as green-house plants. Propagation is from seed, by division, or from cuttings of shrubby species.

Osteospermum, Hybrid Cultivar, 'Sunny Dark Gustaf'

Oxalis acetosella
CUCKOO BREAD, WOOD SORREL
☀/☀ ✽ ↔ 18–36 in (45–90 cm) ↑ 2–4 in (5–10 cm)
Creeping perennial ground cover from North America, Asia, and Europe. Clover-shaped leaves. White flowers, veined with purple, in summer. *O. a.* var. *subpurpurascens*, rose pink flowers with purple veins. Zones 3–10.

Oxalis oregana
RED WOOD SORREL
☀ ✽ ↔ 40 in (100 cm) ↑ 7–8 in (18–20 cm)
Creeping perennial. Native to the woods of western North America. Leaves with 3 mid-green leaflets. Flowers pink to lilac, sometimes white, to 1 in (25 mm) across, from spring to autumn. Zones 7–10.

PACHYSANDRA
SPURGE
Pachysandra belongs to the box (Buxaceae) family and contains 5 species of low-growing shrubby or creeping perennials native to North America and East Asia. Some are deciduous, some are semi-evergreen or evergreen, depending on the climate. They are

Oxalis oregana

used for ground cover in shady places and although slow to get started they are reliable once established. They spread by underground runners and have the advantage of being able to grow over tree roots. They have a compact growth and attractive tidy foliage, growing in whorls at the tip of the stem. The flowers are insignificant but scented and appear in spring.
CULTIVATION: Ideal conditions for these plants include a shady position, in moist slightly acidic soil, with organic matter incorporated. If too much light is admitted to their growing area, the foliage will turn yellow and the plants will not grow well. Propagation is by division or from cuttings taken in summer.

Pachysandra terminalis
JAPANESE PACHYSANDRA, JAPANESE SPURGE
☀ ✽ ↔ 18 in (45 cm) ↑ 8–12 in (20–30 cm)
Native to Japan. Shiny dark green leaves, slightly toothed edges. Small white flowers in spring. Withstands heavy shade and tree roots. 'Green Spike', popular cultivar; 'Variegata', green and gray-green leaves variegated with creamy white. Zones 5–10.

PAEONIA
PEONY
There are 30 or so species in this genus belonging to the peony (Paeoniaceae) family. While most of the species are herbaceous perennials native to temperate parts of the Northern Hemisphere, the genus also contains shrubs and subshrubs known as tree peonies, which have persistent woody stems, brilliantly colored flowers, and highly decorative foliage.
CULTIVATION: *Paeonia* species are best suited to deep fertile soils of basaltic origin, heavily fed annually with organic matter; soils should not be allowed to dry out in summer. Protection from strong winds and scorching sun is essential, and they require some protection from early spring frost. The only pruning that is necessary is the removal of spent flowerheads and dead or misplaced shoots. Propagation is from seed, which can be slow and difficult, or by division of herbaceous peonies, or by apical grafting of tree peonies, with the graft union being buried 3 in (8 cm) below soil level.

Paeonia cambessedesii
MAJORCAN PEONY

☼ ❄ ↔ 24 in (60 cm) ↕ 24 in (60 cm)

From the Balearic Islands. Leathery ovate leaves, purple-suffused veining, wavy edges; reddish stems. Single flowers, deep rose to magenta, darker veins, in spring. Zones 8–9.

Paeonia × *chamaeleon*

☼ ❄ ↔ 20 in (50 cm) ↕ 20 in (50 cm)

Naturally occurring hybrid between *P. mlokosewitschii* and *P. caucasica*, from mountains of Georgia. Oval bluish green leaflets. Flower color variable, from pink to creamy yellow, in late spring. Zones 6–9.

Paeonia lactiflora
syn. *Paeonia albiflora*
CHINESE PEONY

☼ ❄ ↔ 24 in (60 cm) ↕ 24 in (60 cm)

Perennial, native to steppes and scrub of Siberia, Tibet, and China. Erect stems; lobed, pointed leaves; good autumn color. Two or more scented white flowers per stem, to 4 in (10 cm) diameter, in early–mid-summer. Parent of thousands of cultivars and hybrids. Easy to grow in well-drained soil; tolerates winter temperatures to –22°F (–30°C). Cultivars mostly taller, to 40 in (100 cm) high, including: '**A La Mode**', scented white flowers, petals shiny, serrated, mid-spring; '**Angel Cheeks**', double pink flowers; '**Barrington Belle**', deep red outer petals, gold-edged pink or deep red, petal-like staminodes (narrow inner petals); '**Bowl of Beauty**', large, rose pink, rounded outer petals, mass of creamy staminodes; '**Carrara**', tall, white outer petals, mass of white staminodes; '**Cora Stubbs**', tall, pale lilac outer petals, cream and pale pink petaloids; '**Dawn Pink**', large, single, pink flowers, late spring; '**Duchesse de Nemours**', scented, double cream flowers flushed pale yellow toward center; '**Globe of Light**', petals almost white-edged, becoming bright pink toward center, free flowering, early summer; '**Haku-Gah**', white flowers; '**Heirloom**' ★, fully double pale pink flowers; '**Helen**', old cultivar, single pink flowers; '**Kelway's Supreme**', scented, single or semi-double, blush pink flowers, free flowering, late spring to mid-summer; '**Miss America**', beautiful, large, semi-double, scented, pure white flowers flushed creamy yellow at center,

spring; '**Moonstone**', large flowers, blush pink fading to white; '**Nellie Shaylor**', red flowers; '**Peppermint**', double flowers, opening blush pink, fading to white, cream flush at center, outer petals with crimson streak, early summer; '**Pillow Talk**', fully double, outer petals rose pink, pale yellow staminodes surround pink center, late spring; '**Pink Lemonade**', anemone- or double-flowered, pink and yellow petals; '**Pink Princess**' (syn. 'Pink Dawn'), rather crinkled petals, pale pink outer edge, fading to white at center; '**Reine Wilhelmine**', fully double, scented, rose pink flowers, fine carmine markings in center, very free flowering, early summer; '**Requiem**', spicy-scented, single blush cream flowers, free flowering, late spring; '**Sarah Bernhardt**', fully double, scented, large, rose pink flowers fading to blush on outer edges; '**Sorbet**', fully double, rose pink outer petals surrounding ring of finely fringed cream petals enclosing pink center; '**White Wings**', scented, purple-streaked buds opening to pure white single flowers, mid-summer. Zones 6–9.

Paeonia mascula
MALE PEONY

☼ ❄ ↔ 24 in (60 cm) ↕ 24–36 in (60–90 cm)

Variable species from forests of southern Europe. Large, spreading clumps; dark green ovate leaves, bluish green below. Single flowers, 5 in (12 cm) wide, usually deep rose red or pink, sometimes magenta or white, in mid- to late spring. Good autumn color. *P. m.* subsp. *arietina*, from Turkey and eastern Europe, leaves biternate, narrowly elliptic, light or dark green, bluish green below, red or pink single flowers; '**Mother of Pearl**', single, large, pale pink flowers; '**Northern Glory**', single, carmine flowers; '**Purple Emperor**', single magenta flowers; '**Rosy Gem**', rosy pink, single flowers. *P. m.* subsp. *russoi,* shorter, from Mediterranean islands and central Greece; mid-green oval leaflets, purple below, purplish stems; flowers single, deep pink, in mid-spring. Zones 8–9.

Paeonia mlokosewitschii ★
CAUCASIAN PEONY, MOLLY THE WITCH

☼ ❄ ↔ 40 in (100 cm) ↕ 40 in (100 cm)

One of the most famous peonies, from sunny hillsides and oak forests of the Caucasus. Oval leaves, blue-green above, lighter below, good autumn color. Bowl-shaped flowers, clear glowing yellow, in late spring. Zones 6–9.

Paeonia cambessedesii

Paeonia lactiflora 'Heirloom'

Paeonia officinalis 'Rosea Plena'

Paeonia officinalis
FEMALE PEONY

☀ ❄ ↔ 24 in (60 cm) ↕ 15–24 in (38–60 cm)
Native to Europe. Lower leaves dark green,
biternate, deeply cut into narrow segments.
Single flowers, 5 in (12 cm) across, magenta
to deep red. '**Rosea Plena**', double flowers,
bright pink; '**Rubra**', single, deep red flowers;
'**Rubra Plena**' (syn. 'Memorial Day'), double
flowers, deep red, very vigorous. Zones 8–9.

Paeonia peregrina
RED PEONY OF CONSTANTINOPLE

☀/◐ ❄ ↔ 20 in (50 cm) ↕ 20 in (50 cm)
From the Balkans and Turkey. Shiny, dark
green, biternate leaves, up to 18 segments,
turning yellow in autumn. Deep red, cup-
shaped, single flowers up to 5 in (12 cm)
across, in mid- to late spring. '**Fire King**',
shiny petals, scarlet; '**Otto Froebel**', red;
'**Sunbeam**', orange-red. Zones 8–9.

Paeonia, Hybrid Cultivar, 'Sanctus'

Paeonia tenuifolia
☀ ❄ ↔ 20–27 in (50–70 cm) ↕ 20–27 in (50–70 cm)
Herbaceous species, found from southeastern Europe to the
Caucasus. Finely dissected feathery leaves; single, blood red,
bowl-shaped flowers to 3 in (8 cm) across, yellow stamens, in
spring. '**Plena**', full double red selection. Zones 8–9.

Paeonia veitchii
☀ ❄ ↔ 20 in (50 cm) ↕ 24 in (60 cm)
From central China, found in subalpine meadows and scrub.
Bronze-green deeply divided leaves; good autumn color. Slightly
nodding, single flowers, deep rosy pink, 2 or more per stem, in
early summer. Ideal for rock gardens. Zones 8–9.

Paeonia Hybrid Cultivars
☀ ❄ ↔ 30–36 in (75–90 cm) ↕ 30–36 in (75–90 cm)
Breeding of herbaceous peonies has resulted in countless cultivars
including: '**America**', large, single, scented, scarlet flowers; '**Avant
Garde**', single flowers, pale pink petals with darker veins; '**Blaze**',
single red flowers, golden yellow centers; '**Buckeye Belle**', unusual
semi-double flowers, very dark red, crinkled petals; '**Burma Ruby**',
single red flowers; '**Claire de Lune**', large single flowers, palest yellow; '**Coral Charm**', large, semi-double, coral peach flowers;
'**Defender**', single blooms, rich crimson, lightly scented; '**Early
Windflower**', small, single, white flowers; '**Fairy Princess**', single
red flowers; '**Flame**', single, orange-tinted, bright red flowers;
'**Gauguin**', large, single, yellow flowers with red center; '**Hakuo-
jisi**' (syns 'King of White Lion', 'White Tailed Lion'), Japanese
tree peony, double white flowers flushed purple toward center;
'**Honor**', single deep pink flowers; '**Moonrise**', single flowers, pale
yellow, ageing to rich cream; '**Nymph**', single flowers, delicate
pink, yellow at center; '**Paula Fay**', semi-double, bright pink,
scented flowers, flushed white in center; '**Pink Hawaiian Coral**',
scented, semi-double, coral pink flowers, white stripe on outer

petals; '**Prairie Moon**', single to semi-double flowers, pale yellow;
'**Red Charm**', fully double, deep red, ruffled petals; '**Salmon
Surprise**', single salmon pink flowers; '**Sanctus**', single white
flowers; '**Scarlett O'Hara**', single bright red flowers; '**Vesuvian**',
deep, dark red flushed purple, almost black flowers; and '**Yellow
Dream**', large, scented, double flowers, rich yellow. Zones 6–9.

PAPAVER
POPPY

This widespread group of around 50 species of annuals and perennials gives its name to the poppy (Papaveraceae) family. Bristly
upright flower stems emerge from basal rosettes of usually finely
lobed, often hairy, leaves, each with one nodding bud, rarely 2
or 3. The flowers most often have 4 crape-like petals around a
central ovary topped with a prominent stigmatic disc.
CULTIVATION: Most poppies are very hardy and prefer a sunny position with light, moist, and well-drained soil. Propagate perennial
poppy cultivars by root cuttings, otherwise raise from seed.

Papaver alpinum
ALPINE POPPY

☀/◐ ❄ ↔ 8–16 in (20–40 cm) ↕ 10 in (25 cm)
Variable perennial from mountains of southern Europe, possibly
conglomerate of closely related species. Basal clump of finely divided, downy, gray-green to blue-green leaves. Orange, yellow, or
white flowers borne singly in summer. Zones 5–9.

Papaver atlanticum
☀/◐ ❄ ↔ 8–12 in (20–30 cm) ↕ 18 in (45 cm)
Moroccan perennial. Broad, hairy, lance-shaped leaves, coarsely
toothed or lobed. Flowers usually solitary, stems sometimes
forked, light orange to red, in summer. '**Flore Pleno**', orange
double flowers on stocky stems. Zones 6–10.

Papaver commutatum

Flower stems usually leafy on lower half. Solitary flowers, to 4 in (10 cm) wide, red, orange, or pink, often darker blotched. Cultivars include '**Black and White**', large white flowers with black center; '**Cedric Morris**' ★, very hairy leaves, dark-blotched soft pink flowers; the **Goliath Group**, sturdy plants, very large flowers in bright colors with dark centers, such as '**Beauty of Livermere**', deep red with small black blotches; '**Mrs Perry**', large salmon pink flowers with dark blotches; and '**Princess Victoria Louise**', ruffled apricot pink flowers with dark blotches. Zones 3–9.

Papaver rhoeas
CORN POPPY, FIELD POPPY, FLANDERS POPPY

☀/◐ ❄ ↔ 12–16 in (30–40 cm) ↕ 36–48 in (90–120 cm)

Vigorous hardy annual from Old World temperate zones. Pinnate leaves to 6 in (15 cm) long. Bristly flower stems, solitary bright red flowers to 3 in (8 cm) wide, sometimes with black basal blotch, in summer. Mixed color strains include '**Mother of Pearl**', in pastel shades, and **Shirley Mixed**, single or double flowers, range of colors. Zones 5–9.

Papaver commutatum

☀/◐ ❄ ↔ 16 in (40 cm) ↕ 16 in (40 cm)

Annual from western Asia. Leaves to 6 in (15 cm) long, sometimes shallowly lobed. Red flowers with black basal blotches, 2 in (5 cm) wide, in summer. '**Lady Bird**', slightly taller, bright red flowers liberally splashed with black. Zones 8–10.

Papaver × hybridum
ROUGH POPPY

☀/◐ ❄ ↔ 6–10 in (15–25 cm) ↕ 8–20 in (20–50 cm)

Naturally occurring hybrid. Eurasian annual. Finely divided pinnate leaves to 4 in (10 cm) long. Bright red flowers with purple blotch at base of petals. Zones 6–9.

Papaver nudicaule
syns *Papaver croceum, P. miyabeanum*
ARCTIC POPPY, ICELAND POPPY

☀/◐ ❄ ↔ 8–12 in (20–30 cm) ↕ 12–16 in (30–40 cm)

Perennial, native to subarctic regions. Pinnate leaves, often light blue-green, hairy. Solitary long-stemmed flowers to 3 in (8 cm) wide, in many colors, in spring–summer. *P. n.* **var.** *croceum*, orange to orange-red flowers. *P. n.* '**Pacino**', yellow flowers on stocky stems; mixed-color seedling strains include **Meadhome's Strain**, and **Artist Mixed**. Zones 2–10.

Papaver orientale
ORIENTAL POPPY

☀/◐ ❄ ↔ 12–20 in (30–50 cm) ↕ 24–40 in (60–100 cm)

Summer-flowering western Asian perennial. Forms sturdy clump of bristly, pinnate, often blue-green leaves to 10 in (25 cm) long.

Papaver somniferum
OPIUM POPPY

☀ ❄ ↔ 12–24 in (30–60 cm) ↕ 36–48 in (90–120 cm)

From southeastern Europe and western Asia. Vigorous annual. Leaves light blue-green, heavy textured, deeply cut with jagged teeth. Strong leafy flower stems. Flowers 4 in (10 cm) wide, white, mauve, or purple, sometimes with a dark basal blotch, in summer. *P. s.* var. *paeoniflorum*, deep blue-green leaves, maroon-black, double, peony-like flowers. *P. s.* '**Hen and Chickens**', lavender flowers; '**White Cloud**', tall, white, double flowers. Zones 7–10.

Paradisea liliastrum

PARADISEA
PARADISE LILY, ST BRUNO'S LILY

A genus of 2 species in the asphodel (Asphodelaceae) family, native to the woods and alpine pastures of Europe. Perennials with a short underground rhizome, strappy basal leaves, and stems of fragrant white trumpet flowers in summer. Excellent cut flowers. CULTIVATION: These species prefer moist but well-drained humus-rich soil in full sun or partial shade. Propagate from seed sown fresh or divide when dormant.

Paradisea liliastrum

☀/◐ ❄ ↔ 10–12 in (25–30 cm) ↕ 16–24 in (40–60 cm)

Clump-forming perennial. Narrow, gray-green, grass-like foliage to 10 in (25 cm) long. Upright spikes of slightly drooping, fragrant, white trumpets to 2½ in (6 cm) long, in summer. '**Major**' has larger trumpets. Zones 7–9.

PARAHEBE

Revised in recent years, this genus of some 30 species belonging to the foxglove (Scrophulariaceae) family grows largely in New Zealand with a few species in Australia and New Guinea. Low, spreading plants best regarded as subshrubs, sometimes developing a few woody branches with age. The leaves, on pliable wiry stems, are small, dark green, and elliptical, often with toothed edges. Racemes of small, rounded flowers, usually white, pink, or mauve with contrasting veining, appear in late spring and summer.

CULTIVATION: Parahebes are easily cultivated in moist well-drained soil and a reasonably sunny aspect. They tolerate moderate frosts but will not withstand drought without becoming sparsely foliaged and untidy. If necessary, trim back after flowering. Propagate from seed, layers (which often form naturally), or by small tip cuttings taken in summer–autumn.

Parahebe catarractae

Parahebe × bidwillii

☼ ❋ ↔ 6 in (15 cm) ↕ 4 in (10 cm)
Native to New Zealand. Mat-forming sub-shrub; cross between *P. decora* and *P. lyallii*. Tiny, round, leathery, dark green leaves. Small, saucer-shaped, white flowers stained crimson. Summer-flowering. Zones 6–11.

Parahebe catarractae

☼ ❋ ↔ 24 in (60 cm) ↕ 12 in (30 cm)
New Zealand native. Serrated lance-shaped leaves; purple-red-tinted stems. Flowers white, purple veining. Pale blue, pink, and mauve-flowered forms, such as '**Falling Skies**'. Zones 8–10.

Parahebe lyallii

☼ ❋ ↔ 18 in (45 cm) ↕ 8 in (20 cm)
Native to New Zealand. Dense mound of fine stems; leaves less than ½ in (12 mm) long, with toothed edges. White to pale pink flowers, held in sprays above the foliage, in summer. Zones 8–10.

PARIS

A genus of over 20 species of perennials in the honey-flower (Melanthiaceae) family, found in woodlands from Europe across to eastern Asia. Extremely slow-growing rhizomes produce erect stems, with a whorl of leaves at the top surrounding the flowers. The summer flowers have spidery or lance-shaped petals.

CULTIVATION: Grow in a cool aspect with moist not wet humus-rich soil. Propagate from seed, which can take 2 years or more to germinate, or by division of old clumps when dormant.

Paris polyphylla

Paris polyphylla

syn. *Daiswa polyphylla*
☼/◐ ❋ ↔ 8–12 in (20–30 cm) ↕ 36–40 in (90–100 cm)
Perennial, found from the Himalayas to Myanmar and Thailand. Upright stems; lance-shaped leaves to 7 in (18 cm) long. Flowers with narrow green sepals, thread-like yellow petals, purple ovary. *P. p.* var. *yunnanensis* f. *alba*, white filament-like petals. Zones 6–9.

Paris quadrifolia

HERB PARIS
☼/◐ ❋ ↔ 10–12 in (25–30 cm) ↕ 8–16 in (20–40 cm)
Perennial from Europe and East Asia. Upright stems; leaves to 6 in (15 cm) long. Flowers with 4 mid-green sepals and narrow white petals. Blue-black seed capsules. Zones 6–9.

PELARGONIUM

STORKSBILL
Most of the 250 species of annuals, perennials, and subshrubs in this genus of the geranium (Geraniaceae) family come from South Africa, a few from the rest of Africa, the Middle East, and Australia. The rounded or hand-shaped leaves have conspicuous lobes, fine hairs, and darker blotches. The simple 5-petalled flowers are often massed and/or brightly colored.

CULTIVATION: Tolerant of light frosts only, many pelargoniums are treated as annuals in areas with cold winters. Plant most species in a position in full sun in light well-drained soil. Propagate annuals and species from seed; perennials and shrubs from cuttings.

Pelargonium australe

☼ ✥ ↔ 20 in (50 cm) ↕ 12 in (30 cm)
Perennial from southeastern Australia including Tasmania. Rather straggling habit; downy, rounded, 5- to 7-lobed leaves to 4 in (10 cm) across. Clusters of 5 to 10 dark-veined pale pink or white flowers to slightly over ½ in (12 mm) wide, from spring to summer. Zones 9–10.

Pelargonium crispum

LEMON-SCENTED GERANIUM
☼ ✥ ↔ 36 in (90 cm) ↕ 30 in (75 cm)
South African aromatic shrub. Small, 3-lobed leaves, crinkled edges. Pink flowers, dark markings, ¾ in (18 mm) wide. Foliage has strong lemon scent when crushed. Cultivars with small fragrant leaves include '**Major**', larger leaves; '**Minor**', upright habit with tiny leaves; '**Peach Cream**', pink flowers, subtle peach scent; '**Variegatum**', cream-edged leaves. Zones 9–11.

Pelargonium graveolens

ROSE-SCENTED GERANIUM
☼ ✥ ↔ 26 in (65 cm) ↕ 48 in (120 cm)
South African summer-flowering species, possibly a hybrid. Erect stems; rounded, deeply divided leaves release strong scent of rosewater when crushed. Foliage and young stems covered with fine hairs. Clusters of small, purple-veined, pink flowers. '**Lady Plymouth**', compact growth, cream-edged strongly scented leaves, often used in floral decorations. Zones 9–11.

Pelargonium odoratissimum

APPLE GERANIUM

☼/◑ ⚬ ↔ 24 in (60 cm) ↑ 12 in (30 cm)

Low-spreading perennial from South Africa. Apple-scented leaves, rounded, pale green, and toothed, to around 1½ in (35 mm) wide. Branching flower stems with heads of up to 10, ½ in (12 mm) wide, red-marked, white flowers, in spring–summer. Zones 9–11.

Pelargonium quercifolium

ALMOND GERANIUM, OAK-LEAF GERANIUM

☼ ⚬ ↔ 24–32 in (60–80 cm) ↑ 3–5 ft (0.9–1.5 m)

South African native. Upright growth habit; hairy, aromatic, deeply lobed leaves, often with toothed edges, olive green, dark central zone. Small heads of ½ in (12 mm) wide purple-pink flowers in spring–summer. Zones 9–11.

Pelargonium rodneyanum

MAGENTA STORKSBILL

☼ ⚬ ↔ 12–20 in (30–50 cm) ↑ 8–12 in (20–30 cm)

Spreading, tuberous perennial. Native to Australia. Dark green, elongated, heart-shaped leaves to 4 in (10 cm) long, notched edges. Short wiry stems, heads of small bright pink flowers, in spring. Zones 9–11.

Pelargonium tomentosum

☼ ⚬ ↔ 40 in (100 cm) ↑ 20 in (50 cm)

South African perennial. Peppermint-scented, 3- to 5-lobed, velvety, rounded leaves, around 3 in (8 cm) wide. Erect stems; heads of white flowers, to over ½ in (12 mm) wide. Upper petals purple-marked. Spring- to summer-flowering. Zones 9–11.

Pelargonium Hybrid Cultivars

☼ ⚬ ↔ 8–40 in (20–100 cm) ↑ 6–60 in (15–150 cm)

Pelargonium species interbreed freely; there is a range of hybrid groups of mostly compact plants with large showy flowers.

Ivy-Leafed Hybrids: Derived mainly from *P. peltatum*. Large range of growth forms. Very hardy for outdoor planting; tolerant of humidity and damp soil. 'Barbe Bleu', deep purple double flowers ageing to deep red; 'Crocketta', light veined leaves, white flowers with red markings; 'Evka', white-edged leaves, bright red flowers; and 'Mutzel', gray-green and white variegated leaves, bright red flowers.

Angel Hybrids: Similar to Regal Hybrids, but usually only 12 in (30 cm) tall or less. They do not produce double flowers. 'Captain Starlight', upper petals purple-red, lower petals pink-flushed white; 'Oldbury Duet', white-edged bright green leaves, upper petals burgundy with mauve markings, lower petals shades of mauve; 'Quantock Marjorie', upper petals purple-red, lower petals very pale pink; 'Quantock Matty', upper petals deep purple, lower petals pink-flushed white; 'Quantock Rita', upper petals maroon, lower petals pink-flushed white; 'Quantock Star', upper and lower petals dark red with broad pale pink edge; 'Spanish Angel', upper petals purple-red edged with mauve, lower petals mauve with maroon blotch and veins; 'Suffolk Garnet', large red flowers; 'The Culm', royal purple upper petals with delicate mauve edging, lower petals lavender pink with deeper pink markings; 'Tip Top Duet', upper petals maroon, lower petals lavender.

Dwarf Hybrids: Resembling Zonal Hybrids in foliage and stature; differing from Angel Hybrids often with fully double blooms. 'Beryl Read', pink flowers, darker blotch; 'Brackenwood', salmon pink double flowers; 'Brenda', mid-pink flowers, red blotch; 'Brookside Flamenco', vivid pink double flowers; 'Hope Valley', golden yellow leaves, pink double flowers; 'Little Alice', deep green leaves, dark salmon pink flowers; 'Orion', orange-red double flowers; 'Redondo', large, red, double flowers.

Regal Hybrids: Also known as Martha Washington Hybrids. Around 20 in (50 cm) tall, though plant size ranges from dwarfs under 12 in (30 cm) tall through to shrubs of 4 ft (1.2 m) or more. Flowers large, reminiscent of evergreen azaleas; may be single or double; huge range of colors and patterns. 'Askham Fringed Aztec', frilly white flowers with red veining; 'Australian Mystery', cut-edged upper petals, magenta with lighter veining, lower petals white with magenta veining and blotch; 'Bert Pearce', large, frilly, pink flowers with red veining; 'Bosham', pink with dark purple-red upper blotch and magenta veining; 'Cherry Orchard', bright red with lighter center and dark red upper veining; 'Delhi', white flowers tinted dark pink at petal edge; 'Eileen Postle', bright mid-pink with purple-red upper blotch; 'Harbour Lights', bright pink with pink-edged, dark-blotched, light red upper petals; 'Joan Morf', white flushed mid-pink with red upper blotch; 'Kimono', lavender-pink with white throat, deep magenta veining; 'Lara Susan', single, pale pink-edged purple-red upper petals, near white lower petals with small purple-red blotch; 'Lavender Sensation', lavender-pink with purple-red upper blotch; 'Lord Bute',

Pelargonium, Hybrid Cultivar, Angel, 'Suffolk Garnet'

simple single flowers, dark maroon with narrow bright pink edge; '**Rembrandt**' ★, purple edged with mauve-pink; '**Rimfire**', black-red with red to pink edge; '**Rosmaroy**', bright pink, pale red upper blotch, lower spotting; '**Springfield Black**', dark purple-red, lighter center; '**Super Spoton-bonanza**', white flecked and sectored bright orange-red; '**Virginia Louise**', pale pink, blotched deeper pink.

Scented-leafed Hybrids: Grown mainly for aroma of foliage; flowers can be very showy. '**Camphor Rose**', minty camphor scent, small lavender flowers; '**Lara Ballerina**', sharp citrus scent, white to pale pink flowers flushed with purple-red; '**Lara Starshine**', mild citrus scent, many small, deep pinkish red flowers; '**Pink Champagne**', dwarf habit, green and gold foliage, bright pink double flowers.

Unique Hybrids: Woody-based perennials; most have *P. fulgidum* parentage. Aromatic foliage; large flowers. '**Bolero**', single, vivid pink flowers, darker center; '**Mystery**', red flowers with darker blotch; '**Scarlet Unique**', rich red flowers, velvety leaves; '**Shrubland Pet**' (syn. 'Shrubland Rose'), dwarf form, rose-red petals, deeper colored toward edges.

Zonal Hybrids: Mainly of *P. inquinans* × *P. zonale* parentage, many now classified as *P.* × *hortorum*. Low bushy habit; succulent stems; light green, kidney-shaped to rounded, shallowly lobed leaves with dark zonal markings. Heads of brightly colored flowers, held above foliage on upright stems in warmer months, year-round in frost-free areas. Many cultivars and seedling strains, including: '**Dolly Vardon**', tricolored leaves, red and green with creamy white edges, red single flowers; and '**Retah's Crystal**', variegated leaves, large soft pink flowers. Stellar forms have narrow, pointed petals and more sharply lobed leaves. These include: '**Annsbrook Gemini**', bright pink double flowers with red flecks; '**Bird Dancer**', very dark foliage, spidery, salmon pink, single flowers; '**Grandad Mac**', dark foliage, orange-pink double flowers; '**Laura Parmer**', dark foliage, mid-pink single flowers; '**Mrs Pat**', golden brown leaves, salmon pink single flowers; '**Pagoda**', pale pink double flowers; '**Red Cactus**', starry bright red flowers with long petals; '**Vancouver Centennial**', red leaves with light green edges, small, bright magenta, single flowers. Zones 9–11.

Pelargonium, Hybrid Cultivar, Regal, 'Delhi'

Pelargonium, Hybrid Cultivar, Regal, 'Rembrandt'

PELTANDRA

ARROW ARUM

The 3 aquatic, rhizomatous, perennial herbs in this genus of the arum (Araceae) family inhabit the bogs and marshes of eastern North America. They have simple arrowhead-shaped leaves on long sheathed stalks, and spikes of tiny unisexual flowers, carried on stalks as long or longer than the leaf stalks, and enclosed by wavy spathes with overlapping edges. The fruit is a berry.

CULTIVATION: Arrow arums thrive in full sun or half-sun in damp, acidic soil adjacent to water, or in water up to 12 in (30 cm) deep. Propagate by division in spring or from seed, which should be stratified prior to sowing.

Peltandra virginica

GREEN ARROW ARUM, TUCKAHOE

☼ ❋ ↔ 12–36 in (30–90 cm) ↕ 12–36 in (30–90 cm)

From eastern and southeastern USA. Large, glossy, dark green leaves, 12–36 in (30–90 cm) long, in spring, on long succulent stalks. Yellowish green spathe, up to 8 in (20 cm) long, edged with white or yellow; erect whitish green flower spike; green berries in late summer–autumn. Zones 5–9.

PENSTEMON

This genus of around 250 species of perennials and subshrubs in the foxglove (Scrophulariaceae) family is found from Alaska to Guatemala, with one straggler in cool-temperate Asia. Some are shrubby, some mat-forming, but most form clumps of simple linear to lance-shaped leaves in opposite pairs. Their flowers, borne mainly in summer on upright terminal spikes reminiscent of foxgloves *(Digitalis)*, are tubular to bell-shaped, with 2 upper lobes and 3 larger lower lobes.

CULTIVATION: Some species and garden forms are frost tender, and considerable work has recently been put into producing hardy hybrids. Plant in full or half-sun with moist well-drained soil. Propagate by division or from cuttings of non-flowering stems. The species may be raised from seed.

Penstemon barbatus

BEARDLIP, CORAL PENSTEMON

 ↔ 12–20 in (30–50 cm) ↕ 40 in (100 cm)

Perennial from Colorado, Arizona, and New Mexico, USA. Narrow lance-shaped leaves to 3 in (8 cm) long. Heads of pink to red flowers, extended upper lobes, in summer. '**Coccineus**', bright red flowers; '**Elfin Pink**', bright pink flowers; '**Rose Elf**', deep pink flowers; '**Schooley's Yellow**', bright yellow flowers. Zones 3–9.

Penstemon digitalis 'Husker Red'

Penstemon procerus var. tolmiei

Penstemon campanulatus

☼/◑ ⁛ ↔ 8–12 in (20–30 cm) ↑ 12–24 in (30–60 cm)
Perennial from mountains of Mexico and Guatemala. Narrow,
toothed, lance-shaped leaves, to 3 in (8 cm) long. Deep pink
to purple flowers, in late spring–early summer. Zones 9–10.

Penstemon davidsonii

☼/◑ ❄ ↔ 20–24 in (50–60 cm) ↑ 4 in (10 cm)
Low spreading perennial from western USA. Forms mat of fine
stems; ½ in (12 mm) long elliptical leaves. Short inflorescences
of bright pink flowers in summer. Zones 6–9.

Penstemon digitalis

FOXGLOVE BEARDTONGUE
☼/◑ ❄ ↔ 12–24 in (30–60 cm) ↑ 5 ft (1.5 m)
Perennial from central USA. Leaves glossy, purple-tinted, blue-
green, 4–6 in (10–15 cm) long. Purple-pink flushed white flowers
in summer. 'Husker Red', deep purple-red foliage. Zones 3–9.

Penstemon fruticosus

SHRUBBY PENSTEMON
☼/◑ ❄ ↔ 20 in (50 cm) ↑ 16 in (40 cm)
Perennial from western USA. Bushy clump of mostly erect stems;
lance-shaped leaves to 2 in (5 cm) long, sometimes toothed. Lavender to purple flowers in spring–summer. Zones 4–9.

Penstemon grandiflorus

LARGE BEARDTONGUE
☼/◑ ❄ ↔ 12–20 in (30–50 cm) ↑ 40 in (100 cm)
Perennial found in central USA from North Dakota to Texas.
Leathery, rounded, blue-green leaves, 1–4 in (2.5–10 cm) long.
lavender to pale blue flowers in summer. 'Prairie Snow', heavy-
blooming, white flowers. Zones 3–9.

Penstemon heterophyllus

FOOTHILLS PENSTEMON
☼/◑ ❄ ↔ 8–12 in (20–30 cm) ↑ 12–20 in (30–50 cm)
Shrubby Californian perennial. Narrow, dark green to blue-green
leaves to 2 in (5 cm) long. Fairly short heads of lavender-pink

to bright blue flowers, in summer. 'Blue Bedder' ★, compact,
bright blue flowers; 'Heavenly Blue', dark mauve-blue to blue
flowers. Zones 8–10.

Penstemon hirsutus

☼/◑ ❄ ↔ 8–12 in (20–30 cm) ↑ 16–32 in (40–80 cm)
Clump-forming perennial from eastern North America. Erect
stems; toothed lance-shaped leaves, 2–4 in (5–10 cm) long,
downy uppersurfaces. Slightly pendulous flowers, purple with
white-edged lobes, in late summer. 'Pygmaeus', 6 in (15 cm)
tall, purple flowers. Zones 3–9.

Penstemon isophyllus

☼/◑ ⁛ ↔ 40 in (100 cm) ↑ 27 in (70 cm)
Mexican perennial. Purple-tinted stems initially spreading, then
upright. Leaves leathery, lance-shaped, to 1½ in (35 mm) long,
with slightly rolled edges. Inflorescence to 12 in (30 cm) long;
5-lobed, white-haired, red flowers. Spring-flowering. Zones 9–11.

Penstemon pinifolius

☼/◑ ❄ ↔ 16–24 in (40–60 cm) ↑ 16 in (40 cm)
Perennial from Arizona and New Mexico, USA, and nearby parts
of Mexico. Very narrow filament-like leaves. Bright red flowers in
summer. 'Mersea Yellow', bright yellow flowers. Zones 8–10.

Penstemon procerus

SMALL-FLOWERED PENSTEMON
☼/◑ ❄ ↔ 12–16 in (30–40 cm) ↑ 6–16 in (15–40 cm)
Perennial from northwestern North America. Slender stems; broad,
dark green, lance-shaped leaves, 2 in (5 cm) long. White-centered
lavender-blue and purple-pink flowers in summer. P. p. var. tolmiei, 4 in (10 cm) tall, bright lavender-blue flowers. Zones 3–9.

Penstemon strictus

STIFF BEARDTONGUE
☼/◑ ❄ ↔ 12–16 in (30–40 cm) ↑ 32 in (80 cm)
Clumping perennial from mountains of southwestern USA.
Long-stemmed spatula-shaped basal leaves to over 3 in (8 cm)

Penstemon heterophyllus

long, upper leaves linear to lance-shaped. Narrow heads of large-lobed violet to purple-blue flowers in summer. Zones 3–9.

Penstemon superbus

☼/◑ ❄ ↔ 20–32 in (50–80 cm) ↑ 5–6 ft (1.5–1.8 m)

Vigorous, erect, Mexican perennial. Blue-green, leathery, pointed oval leaves to 6 in (15 cm) long, sometimes partly or entirely encircling stems. Bright red flowers in summer. Zones 9–11.

Penstemon Hybrid Cultivars

☼/◑ ❁ ↔ 8–16 in (20–40 cm) ↑ 24–48 in (60–120 cm)

Modern hybrids bred with large flowers, compact habit, bright colors, and frost tolerance. 'Alice Hindley', mauve flowers, white center; 'Andenken an Friedrich Hahn' (syn. 'Garnet'), flowers paler at first, becoming purple-red; 'Apple Blossom', pink-tipped, white flowers; 'Burgundy', deep purple-red flowers; 'Chester Scarlet' ★, bright red flowers, darker throat stripes; 'Countess of Dalkeith', deep purple flowers, white throat; 'Hewell Pink Bedder', gray-green foliage, reddish pink flowers; 'Hidcote Pink', gray-green foliage, deep pink flowers, darker throat markings; 'Maurice Gibbs', purple-red flowers, white throat; 'Myddleton Gem', vivid pinkish red flowers, white throat; 'Osprey', pink flowers, white throat; 'Peace', pink and white flowers; 'Pennington Gem', deep pink flowers, red-marked white throat; 'Raven', purple-red flowers, white throat; 'Rich Ruby', purple-red flowers, darker throat; 'Schoenholzeri' (syn. 'Firebird'), deep red flowers; 'Stapleford Gem', violet and light purple tones; 'White Bedder', white flowers, sometimes pink in bud, compact habit. Zones 6–10.

PENTAS

Mainly biennials and perennials, the 30 to 40-odd species in this genus of the madder (Rubiaceae) family from tropical parts of Arabia, Africa, and Madagascar also include a few shrubs. They have ovate to lance-shaped leaves and small flowers in showy terminal heads. Flowers occur in all shades of pink, white, purple, mauve, and red. Dry seed heads follow the flowers.

CULTIVATION: These tender plants will not tolerate frosts or prolonged cold conditions. Cultivated outdoors in the tropics and subtropics, they are treated as house or greenhouse plants elsewhere. They are not drought tolerant and need plenty of moisture while actively growing and flowering. Plant in a moist, fertile, humus-rich, well-drained soil. Keep stem tips pinched back to ensure a compact habit. Propagate from seed or half-hardened cuttings, which strike quickly.

Pentas lanceolata

STAR CLUSTER

☼ ✦ ↔ 3 ft (0.9 m) ↑ 6 ft (1.8 m)

Found from Yemen to tropical east Africa, smaller in cultivation. Dark green velvety leaves. Large heads of flowers, white through

shades of pink to magenta to lavender-blue, in summer. 'New Look Red' ★, scarlet flowers; 'New Look Rose', deep pink flowers. The Butterfly Series includes 'Butterfly Blush', 'Butterfly Cherry Red', and 'Butterfly Light Lavender'. Zones 10–12.

PEPEROMIA

Genus of around 1,000 evergreen herbs from the pepper (Piperaceae) family, mainly originating from South America, with 17 species from Africa, and valued for their ornamental foliage. They feature fleshy leaves, usually on long stalks, and dense, erect, slender spikes of minute bisexual flowers, normally whitish cream, which are mostly produced in late summer.

CULTIVATION: In warm climates *Peperomia* species can be grown as ground covers or as epiphytes on tree trunks. Otherwise, they can be grown in pots or hanging baskets in light, well-drained compost; a soil-less mixture is best for epiphytic species. Avoid over-watering; protect from slugs and snails. Propagation is by division or from stem, tip, or leaf cuttings.

Peperomia caperata

Peperomia argyreia

syn. *Peperomia sandersii*

WATERMELON BEGONIA, WATERMELON PEPPER

◑/☀ ❄ ↔ 6–9 in (15–22 cm) ↑ 6–12 in (15–30 cm)

Evergreen succulent perennial from northern South America to Brazil. Broadly heart-shaped, thick, wrinkled, dark green, concave leaves, pointed at tip, rounded at base, silvery gray above, with dark green stripes resembling watermelon rind, on erect red stalks. White flower spikes covered with tiny yellowish white flowers. 'Emerald Ripple', corrugated, deep green leaves, greenish white flower spikes on pinkish stalks; 'Little Fantasy', dwarf form; 'Silver Ripple', tight clusters of showy, deeply corrugated or ribbed heart-shaped leaves, with variable colors from green to red and even variegated, often highlighted with frosted ridges; 'Tricolor' (syn. 'Variegata'), small leaves with broad white borders. Zones 9–12.

Peperomia caperata

◑/☀ ❄ ↔ 6–10 in (15–25 cm) ↑ 6–10 in (15–25 cm)

Bushy perennial from Brazil. Heart-shaped, dark green, deeply veined leaves; pinkish stems. White flowers. Zones 10–12.

Peperomia clusiifolia

◑/☀ ❄ ↔ 6–10 in (15–25 cm) ↑ 6–10 in (15–25 cm)

Erect semi-succulent perennial, native to the West Indies and parts of northern South America. Oval to elliptical, glandular leaves, 3 in (8 cm) long, pointed or rounded tips, taper toward base; mid-green or tinged with purple, with edges flushed with maroon, and a reddish main vein, on dark red stalks. 'Variegata', light green leaves, variegated with cream toward the edges and red margins. Zones 9–11.

Peperomia griseoargentea
IVY-LEAF PEPPER, PLATINUM PEPPER, SILVER-LEAF PEPPER

☀ ✣ ↔ 6–8 in (15–20 cm) ↑ 6–8 in (15–20 cm)

Erect perennial herb from Brazil. Heart-shaped, leathery leaves, 1½ in (35 mm) long, pointed tips, rounded base, grayish green above, paler beneath, with deeply impressed veins, on pale green to pink stalks. Zones 9–11.

Peperomia obtusifolia
AMERICAN RUBBER PLANT, BABY RUBBER PLANT, PEPPER-FACE

☀ ✤ ↔ 6–8 in (15–20 cm) ↑ 6–8 in (15–20 cm)

Erect or sprawling perennial found from Mexico to northern South America and the West Indies. Stems to 6 in (15 cm) long. Alternate, thick, elliptical to oval leaves, to 4 in (10 cm) long, rounded tips, wedge-shaped at base, winged stalks. 'Golden Gate', yellow-blotched leaves; 'Variegata', more pointed variegated pale green leaves, marked with cream or yellow toward edges; 'White Cloud', bluish green leaves, yellow markings. Zones 10–12.

Peperomia orba
☀ ✣ ↔ 4–6 in (10–15 cm) ↑ 4–6 in (10–15 cm)

Bushy erect perennial. Leathery and hairy, oval or elliptical, dull green leaves, lighter central stripe, pointed tips, rounded at base. Spikes of tiny green flowers. Zones 9–11.

PERICALLIS
CINERARIA

This genus of 14 species of perennials and shrubs in the daisy (Asteraceae) family, are mostly Canary Island natives. With soft, bristly or hairy leaves, some of the species carry their flowers singly but cultivated plants produce large heads of daisies. Pink to purple is the predominant flower color in the wild, but the hybrids occur in a wide range of shades.

CULTIVATION: Cinerarias prefer temperate climates; in cool areas treat as summer annuals or winter-flowering indoor plants. They like shade in summer but require more light in winter. Plant in humus-rich, cool, moist, well-drained soil. Usually propagated by seed, but the shrubby types will grow from cuttings.

Pericallis × hybrida

Pericallis × *hybrida*
CINERARIA

✣/☀ ✣ ↔ 16–40 in (40–100 cm) ↑ 16–32 in (40–80 cm)

Perennial hybrids ranging from small mounding plants to taller, more open, shrubby forms. Compact types have downy, angular, heart-shaped leaves, toothed edges, sometimes purplish undersides; flowerheads clustered, often densely, in a wide range of colors, from early spring to summer. Zones 9–11.

Perilla frutescens var. crispa

PERILLA
A genus of 6 annual herbs in the mint (Lamiaceae) family, found naturally in Asia from India to Japan. They feature tight dense spikes of tiny flowers with a 5-toothed bell-shaped calyx, and a shorter 5-lobed corolla tube. Opposite pairs of leaves are often variegated or colored. Fruit consists of 4 joined nutlets.

CULTIVATION: Space plants about 12 in (30 cm) apart, in rich but well-drained soil and full sun to light shade. Sow seeds outdoors in warm soil; the seeds require light to sprout. Deadhead to prevent invasive self-sowing.

Perilla frutescens
BEEFSTEAK PLANT, CHINESE BASIL, WILD SESAME

✣/✣ ❊ ↔ 18–24 in (45–60 cm) ↑ 24–40 in (60–100 cm)

Erect, finely hairy, annual herb; resembles basil. Native to the Himalayas and eastern Asia. Leaves purple or green, sometimes speckled with purple, often wrinkled, broadly oval, heavily serrated, pointed, 1½–5 in (3.5–12 cm) long, cinnamon-like scent. Spikes of small, white, pink, or reddish flowers, corolla to 4 mm across, in late summer to autumn. *P. f.* var. *crispa* (syn. *P. f.* var. *nankinensis*), with extra-crinkled bronze or dark purplish brown leaves. Zones 8–11.

PEROVSKIA
A genus of 7 deciduous subshrubs or perennials in the mint (Lamiaceae) family, and native to central Asia and the Himalayas. They are grown for their grayish foliage and large sprays of small blue flowers produced in late summer and autumn.

CULTIVATION: Plant in a sunny well-drained position. Prune heavily each winter. Propagate from softwood or half-hardened cuttings.

Perovskia atriplicifolia

RUSSIAN SAGE

☼ ❄ ↔ 18–36 in (45–90 cm) ↑ 30–60 in (75–150 cm)

Deciduous perennial from Iran, Afghanistan, and western Pakistan. Upright stems; grayish green leaves, 2–2½ in (5–6 cm) long, coarsely toothed to lobed, pungent when crushed. Narrow spikes of tiny, tubular, blue to lavender flowers in late summer–autumn. Zones 5–9.

PERSICARIA

KNOTWEED

A large and somewhat confused genus of between 50 and 80 species in the knotweed (Polygonaceae) family, found around the world. Many are alternatively listed in the genera *Bistorta, Polygonum, Tovara, Antenoron,* or *Aconogonon*. Most cultivated species are creeping perennials or occasionally subshrubs, grown for their attractive foliage or for their upright or drooping spikes of small flowers, which are usually pink turning to red as they age. Some can be quite weedy.

CULTIVATION: Most knotweeds like a moist to very moist soil, in full sun to partial shade. Propagate by division or from softwood cuttings in spring.

Persicaria affinis

syns *Bistorta affinis, Polygonum affine*

☼ ❄ ↔ 20–24 in (50–60 cm) ↑ 8–10 in (20–25 cm)

Evergreen creeping perennial from the Himalayas. Upright stems; leaves to 6 in (15 cm) long. Upright spikes of tiny pink flowers in late summer. '**Darjeeling Red**', larger leaves, flowers pink then red; '**Superba**', tiny pink flowers turn red then brown. Zones 3–10.

Persicaria amplexicaulis

syns *Bistorta amplexicaulis, Polygonum amplexicaule*

KNOTWEED, MOUNTAIN FLEECE

☼ ❄ ↔ 3–4 ft (0.9–1.2 m) ↑ 3–4 ft (0.9–1.2 m)

Upright perennial, native to the Himalayas. Large, dense, bushy, slowly spreading clumps. Stem-clasping, dark green, sword-shaped to oval, pointed leaves, 3–10 in (8–25 cm) long, heart-shaped at base, downy underneath, on long stalks. Dense, bottlebrush-like, erect flower spikes, 3–6 in (8–15 cm) long; tiny rose red to purple or white flowers from early summer to early autumn. '**Firetail**', low-growing, bright crimson flowers. Zones 4–9.

Persicaria bistorta

syn. *Polygonum bistorta*

BISTORT, EASTER LEDGES, SNAKEWEED

☼ ❄ ↔ 6–30 in (15–75 cm) ↑ 6–30 in (15–75 cm)

Perennial from northern Europe and northern and western Asia. Wavy, triangular, oval, or oblong leaves, 4–8 in (10–20 cm) long, rounded tips, flattened bases, winged stalks. Dense cylindrical spikes of white or rose pink flowers in summer. '**Superba**' ★ (syn. '**Superbum**'), dense spikes of soft pinkish red flowers. Zones 3–9.

Persicaria capitata

syn. *Polygonum capitatum*

KNOTWEED

☼ ❄ ↔ 6–12 in (15–30 cm) ↑ 3–6 in (8–15 cm)

Spreading perennial from the Himalayas. Silvery grayish green heart-shaped or oval leaves, 1–2 in (25–50 mm) long, with purplish maroon bands. Dense trailing heads of pink to red flowers from summer–autumn. Can become invasive in warmer regions. '**Magic Carpet**', creeping form, to 4 in (10 cm) high. Zones 5–10.

Persicaria orientalis

syn. *Polygonum orientale*

KISS-ME-OVER-THE-GARDEN-GATE, ORIENTAL PERSICARY, PRINCE'S FEATHER

☼ ❄ ↔ 15–18 in (38–45 cm) ↑ 36–60 in (90–150 cm)

Annual, native to eastern and southeastern Asia and northern Australia, naturalized in North America. Oval leaves, 4–8 in (10–20 cm) long, bronze-green, soft fine hairs, branching stems. Drooping many-branched spikes of bead-like, pink, rose-purple, or white flowers, in late summer–early autumn. Zones 8–10.

Persicaria virginiana

syn. *Polygonum virginianum*

☼/◐ ❄ ↔ 32–60 in (80–150 cm) ↑ 24–48 in (60–120 cm)

Large perennial found from the Himalayas to Japan, and in northeastern USA. Pointed oval leaves, up to 6 in (15 cm) long, downy to bristly, dark markings. Tiny, pink-tinted, greenish white flowers, in late summer. '**Painter's Palette**', variegated leaves, cream with yellow, green, and red-brown patches. Zones 5–9.

PETUNIA

This tropical South American genus in the nightshade (Solanaceae) family includes some 35 species of annuals, perennials, and shrubs. Most are low spreading plants with soft, downy, rounded leaves and large funnel-shaped flowers with 5 fused lobes.

CULTIVATION: Plant in full sun in moist, humus-rich, well-drained soil. Flowers are vulnerable to water spray and wet weather, although modern types are sturdier. Most are raised from seed; the more reliably perennial forms all grow well from cuttings.

Persicaria bistorta

Petunia × hybrida, Surfinia Series, Surfinia Blue Vein/'Sunsolos'

Petunia axillaris

LARGE WHITE PETUNIA

☼/◐ �$ ↔ 16–24 in (40–60 cm) ↕ 12–20 in (30–50 cm)

Annual from Argentina, Uruguay, and southern Brazil. Sticky, short-haired, thin leaves, rounded tips. Conical white or creamy yellow flowers, night-scented, in summer. Zones 10–12.

Petunia × hybrida

☼/◐ ◊ ↔ 8–40 in (20–100 cm) ↕ 4–16 in (10–40 cm)

Garden hybrids, generally low, spreading, short-lived perennials treated as annuals. 'Colorwave', a distinct cultivar propagated vegetatively. Forms are sometimes grouped in classes such as Grandiflora (large flowers), Milliflora (small flowers, compact habit), and Multiflora (many flowers, spreading habit). Popular forms include: **Carpet Series,** mounding bushes in many colors; **Celebrity Series,** compact, heavy-flowering, several color mixes; **Daddy Series,** shades of pink and purple, large flowers, veins in contrasting colors; **Fantasy Series,** very compact, many small flowers, good container plant; **Giant Victorious Series,** all-double flowers, huge color range including bicolors and picotées; **Marco Polo Series,** double-flowered, mainly pinks, mauves, and purples; **Mirage Series,** large single flowers, often light colors, striking contrasting dark veins; **Super-cascade Series,** compact but with trailing habit, wide color range; **Surfinia Series,** mainly purples, pinks, and blues; **Wave Series,** mounding bushes, large flowers. Zones 9–10.

Petunia integrifolia

☼/◐ ❀ ↔ 16–24 in (40–60 cm) ↕ 12–20 in (30–50 cm)

Annual or short-lived perennial from Argentina. Sticky, downy, elliptical leaves. Long-tubed violet flowers, purple-pink interior, to nearly 2 in (5 cm) wide, in summer. Zones 8–10.

PHACELIA

SCORPION WEED

This genus of about 150 glandular, hairy, annual, biennial, or perennial herbs belongs to the waterleaf (Hydrophyllaceae) family, and originates from North and South America. The plants have alternate leaves, divided or smooth-edged, and they bear dense terminal heads of white to purple flowers, which have a narrow 5-lobed calyx and an open to spreading bell-shaped corolla with lobed petals. The capsular fruits contain one to many brownish seeds with a pitted or furrowed appearance. The bristly hairs of this plant may cause severe dermatitis, and some species can become invasive and weedy. CULTIVATION: Sow seed for both annuals and biennials in spring where plants are to grow, in full sun in fertile well-drained soil. Perennial species can be propagated by division.

Phacelia campanularia

syn. *Phacelia minor* var. *campanularia*

CALIFORNIA BLUEBELL, DESERT BLUEBELL, WILD CANTERBURY BELL

☼ ❀ ↔ 6–24 in (15–60 cm) ↕ 6–24 in (15–60 cm)

Annual herb from southern California, USA. Erect stems; elliptical to oval, hairy, toothed leaves. Dark blue bell-shaped flowers in early spring. Oval fruits, 40 to 80 pitted seeds. Zones 7–10.

Phacelia tanacetifolia

FIDDLENECK

☼ ❀ ↔ 4–24 in (10–60 cm) ↕ 6–60 in (15–150 cm)

Moderately fast-growing annual from California, USA, to Mexico. Covered with bristly hairs; erect, sparsely branched stem; compound, oval to oblong, toothed or lobed leaves. Blue, lilac, or mauve flowers in spring. Fruits have 1 or 2 wrinkled pitted seeds. Zones 7–10.

Phacelia tanacetifolia

PHLOMIS

This genus of about 100 low-growing shrubs, subshrubs, and herbs in the mint (Lamiaceae) family is found through Europe and Asia, from the Mediterranean regions to China. Most have felted leaves and tubular flowers in whorls along the stems. The yellow, cream, pink, mauve, or purple flowers have 2 lips at the tips. CULTIVATION: Most are quite frost hardy, and best planted in exposed sunny positions. Drought tolerant, they generally resent receiving too much water in summer. Propagate from seed or tip cuttings from non-flowering shoots.

Phlomis cashmeriana

☼ ❀ ↔ 36 in (90 cm) ↕ 36 in (90 cm)

Native to Kashmir and the western Himalayas. Very woolly stems; narrow oval leaves, downy, white undersides. Pale lilac flowers, in crowded whorls, in summer. Zones 8–11.

Phlomis 'Edward Bowles'

☼ ❋ ↔ 36 in (90 cm) ↕ 36 in (90 cm)

Robust hybrid of uncertain parentage. Pointed oval, bright green, felted leaves, up to 6 in (15 cm) in length, wrinkled surfaces. Whorls of sulfur yellow flowers. Summer-flowering. Zones 7–11.

Phlomis purpurea

☼ ❋ ↔ 24 in (60 cm) ↕ 24 in (60 cm)

From Spain and Portugal. Woolly-stemmed; narrow, wrinkled, leathery, grayish green leaves, very hairy undersides. Whorls of downy purple to pink flowers in summer. Zones 8–11.

Phlomis russeliana

☼ ❋ ↔ 24 in (60 cm) ↕ 36 in (90 cm)

Native to just a small area of western Syria; common in cultivation. Long-stemmed heart-shaped leaves, fine hairs, especially on undersides. Spikes of pale yellow hooded flowers in summer. Does not thrive in prolonged wet conditions. Zones 7–9.

Phlomis russeliana

Phlomis tuberosa

☼ ❋ ↔ 36 in (90 cm) ↕ 36 in (90 cm)

Tuberous-rooted deciduous perennial found from central Europe to central Asia. Lightly hairy, pointed oval leaves to 10 in (25 cm) long. Whorls of purple to pink flowers, more crowded near stem ends, in summer. Zones 6–10.

PHLOX

This North American genus of 67 annuals and perennials belongs in the phlox (Polemoniaceae) family. All types have similar terminal heads of small bell-shaped flowers with long widely flaring tubes, but growth habits differ markedly. Annual species tend to be small mounding bushes; the ground-hugging rock phlox has tiny leaves; trailing forms have long stems; and border phlox species are upright and bushy, often with plenty of foliage.
CULTIVATION: All *Phlox* species prefer well-drained soil that can be kept moist; annual and rock phlox need full sun; border and trailing forms will take part shade. Border phlox need good ventilation to prevent late-season mildew. Propagate by seed, by division, or from cuttings.

Phlox adsurgens

WOODLAND PHLOX

☼/◑ ❋ ↔ 12–20 in (30–50 cm) ↕ 4–6 in (10–15 cm)

Spreading perennial from western USA. Stem tips sometimes partly erect; oval leaves, ½–1 in (12–25 mm) long. Open flower-heads of pink to purple blooms in late spring–summer. Zones 6–10.

Phlox bifida

SAND PHLOX

☼/◑ ❋ ↔ 12–16 in (30–40 cm) ↕ 4–8 in (10–20 cm)

Tufted perennial from central USA. Sparse hairy leaves, elliptical to near-linear. Honey-scented, starry, white to lavender flowers, with notched petals, in spring–summer. Zones 6–10.

Phlox divaricata

BLUE PHLOX, WILD SWEET WILLIAM

☼/◑ ❋ ↔ 24–40 in (60–100 cm) ↕ 12–18 in (30–45 cm)

Spreading low-clump-forming perennial from central North America. Wiry stems; pointed oval to narrow lance-shaped leaves. Small heads of lavender-pink, mauve, or white flowers in spring. *P. d.* subsp. *laphamii* is best known for cultivar 'Chattahoochee' ★, 6 in (15 cm) tall, lavender flowers with red eye. Zones 4–9.

Phlox douglasii

☼/◑ ❋ ↔ 12–20 in (30–50 cm) ↕ 2–6 in (5–15 cm)

Perennial from northwestern USA. Usually mat-forming, sometimes stem tips ascend slightly. Fine downy stems; very narrow hair-fringed leaves. Flowers in showy, tightly clustered heads, mainly in deep pink, red, mauve, and purple, in spring–early summer. 'Boothman's Variety', dark-centered lavender flowers; 'Crackerjack', compact habit, magenta flowers; 'Kelly's Eye', pale pink flowers, purple-red center; 'Red Admiral', mounding to 4 in (10 cm) high, crimson flowers; 'Rosea', silvery pink flowers. Zones 5–10.

Phlox drummondii

☼/◑ ❋ ↔ 8–16 in (20–40 cm) ↕ 6–16 in (15–40 cm)

Annual from Texas, USA; now widely established as a wild-flower. Upright, sometimes sprawling stems; pointed oval to narrow lance-shaped leaves. Showy heads of small flowers, often with notched petals, bright lavender to purple-red. Summer-flowering. Mixed color seedling strains include **Beauty Series**, many colors, including yellow; **Brilliancy Series**, wide color range; **Buttons and Bows Series**. mainly bright colors, often with contrasting eye; **Phlox of Sheep Series**, primrose-centered, pastel shades including yellow, orange-red, and apricot; **Tapestry Series**, wide range of pastel shades with contrasting eye color, fragrant. Zones 6–10.

Phlox divaricata subsp. *laphamii* 'Chattahoochee'

Phlox maculata
MEADOW PHLOX, WILD SWEET WILLIAM

☼/◐ ✳ ↔ 16 in (40 cm) ↕ 27 in (70 cm)

Erect rhizome-rooted perennial from eastern USA. Thick, lustrous, dark green leaves, usually pointed oval, sometimes linear. Densely packed heads of pink, violet, or white flowers, often with purplish centers, in summer. 'Alpha', fragrant lavender pink flowers; 'Omega', fragrant white flowers, deep violet centers. Zones 5–10.

Phlox paniculata
BORDER PHLOX, SUMMER PHLOX

☼/◐ ✳ ↔ 16–40 in (40–100 cm) ↕ 24–48 in (60–120 cm)

Eastern USA perennial. Upright stems; pointed oval to lance-shaped leaves, often toothed, sometimes downy. Large rounded flowerheads, usually pink, lavender, and purple, in summer. Cultivars include 'Brigadier', apricot pink; 'Europa', white, scarlet eye, honey-scented; 'Eva Cullum', dark pink, deep pink center; 'Eventide', mauve-blue; 'Fujiyama' ★, white; 'Le Mahdi', purple-blue; 'Mother of Pearl', pale silvery pink; 'Prospero', lavender to light purple; 'Starfire', deep red; 'Tenor', scarlet; 'White Admiral', pure white; 'Windsor', white, suffused lavender blue. Zones 4–10.

Phlox subulata
MOSS PHLOX, MOUNTAIN PHLOX

☼/◐ ✳ ↔ 12–20 in (30–50 cm) ↕ 2–4 in (5–10 cm)

Prostrate mat-forming perennial from eastern USA. Small, narrow, pointed leaves. Few blooms per head, but densely clustered; usually pink to lavender or white, often with notched petals, in spring–early summer. Cultivars include 'Bonita', bright pink; 'Emerald Blue', mid-blue; 'Emerald Pink', vivid pink; 'Late Red', purple-red; 'McDaniel's Cushion', bright pink; 'Scarlet Flame', deep purple-red. Zones 3–9.

PHORMIUM
FLAX LILY, NEW ZEALAND FLAX

Phormium is a genus of only 2 species of large evergreen perennials in the daylily (Hemerocallidaceae) family, and is restricted to New Zealand and Norfolk Island. The leaves are long and fibrous, and in summer the plants produce large candelabras of upright curved flowers, dripping nectar that is highly attractive to birds. Glossy decorative seed pods follow.
CULTIVATION: Give these plants a sunny spot in moisture-retentive soil; in frosty climates, cover them in winter. Propagate from seed, or by division of the colored leaf or dwarf clones in early spring.

Phlox paniculata

Phormium cookianum
syn. *Phormium colensoi*
NEW ZEALAND MOUNTAIN FLAX

☼ ✳ ↔ 7–8 ft (2–2.4 m) ↕ 4–8 ft (1.2–2.4 m)

Arching leaves to 5 ft (1.5 m) long. Yellow-green flowers, thick petals. Glossy brown seed pods, curled and pendulous. *P. c.* subsp. *hookeri* 'Cream Delight', narrow creamy yellow bands toward edges of leaves, broader bands further in; 'Tricolor', leaves with irregular bands of creamy yellow and fine red edges. Zones 8–11.

Phormium Hybrid Cultivars

☼ ✳ ↔ 1–6 ft (0.3–1.8 m) ↕ 1–6 ft (0.3–1.8 m)

In the wild and in cultivation, the 2 *Phormium* species hybridize readily. Large number of cultivars available, in dwarf to tall sizes, with weeping or erect foliage, and range of colors and variegations. Cream and green striped cultivars include: 'Duet', to 3 ft (0.9 m); 'Tricolor', to 4 ft (1.2 m); and 'Yellow Wave', to 3 ft (0.9 m). Variegated cultivars in tones of pink, red, and bronze include: 'Rainbow Maiden' (syn. 'Maori Maiden') and 'Sundowner', both erect forms, and 'Evening Glow' and 'Pink Panther', both weeping forms. Cultivars with dark purple to black foliage include: 'Bronze Baby' and 'Tom Thumb', dwarf forms, and 'Black Prince' and 'Dark Delight', taller weeping forms. Zones 8–11.

PHYSALIS
GROUND CHERRY, HUSK TOMATO

This genus in the nightshade (Solanaceae) family consists of about 80 erect, bushy, or sprawling annual and rhizomatous perennial herbs. It is widely distributed, especially in the Americas, but also in temperate Eurasia and Australia. Alternate simple or divided leaves, sometimes roughly opposite and often in groups of 2 or 3, grow from erect or straggling stems, sometimes woody at the base. Nodding, mostly solitary flowers, on short stalks or none, grow from the leaf axils, with widely bell-shaped to open, blue, yellowish, or white corollas. The bell-shaped calyx features 5 lobes and enlarges into a papery husk enclosing the spherical, 2-celled, greenish, yellowish, orange, or purple fruits, which contain many seeds. The husks split open as fruits ripen in late summer to autumn. Unripe berries may be toxic to humans and livestock, although those of some species are edible.
CULTIVATION: Sow seed in autumn or early spring and plant out seedlings of annual species in a warm, sunny, exposed or part-shaded position, in fertile well-drained soil. Perennials can be propagated by division of rhizomes or from tip cuttings in spring.

Physalis alkekengi
ALKEKENGI, BLADDER CHERRY, CHINESE LANTERN, WINTER CHERRY

☼ ✳ ↔ 12–24 in (30–60 cm) ↕ 12–24 in (30–60 cm)

Perennial from central and southern Europe, and from western Asia to Japan. Long, creeping, underground rhizomes. Erect, leafy, finely glandular, hairy stems. Mid-green triangular to oval leaves, to 5 in (12 cm) long. Inconspicuous drooping flowers, calyx expands to 2 in (5 cm) enclosing the fruit, yellow to cream corolla, red to scarlet berries, in late summer. 'Gigantea' (syn. 'Monstrosa'), larger growing, larger fruits. Zones 4–9.

PHYSOSTEGIA

FALSE DRAGON HEAD, OBEDIENT PLANT

A member of the mint (Lamiaceae) family, this North American genus has just 2 species of upright perennials, one widely cultivated. They normally form a clump of unbranched stems, with simple, dark green, toothed, narrow, elliptical to lance-shaped leaves. In summer to autumn flowerheads of many 5-lobed tubular to bell-shaped blooms, mainly pink and purple, develop at most stem tips.
CULTIVATION: These plants are hardy, and are easily grown in full or half-sun in moist well-drained soil. They spread by rhizomes that can become invasive, but provided the clumps are broken up occasionally this causes few problems. Propagate by division.

Physostegia virginiana

OBEDIENT PLANT

☼/◐ ❄ ↔ 12–20 in (30–50 cm)
↑ 32–48 in (80–120 cm)

Phormium cookianum, in the wild, New Zealand

Summer- to autumn-flowering perennial from eastern USA. Upright stems; narrow, toothed, lance-shaped leaves. Narrow conical flower spikes to 8 in (20 cm) long, downy, tubular, purple-pink flowers. Cultivars include '**Alba**', '**Rose Queen**', '**Rosea**', '**Summer Snow**', '**Variegata**', and '**Vivid**'. Zones 5–10.

PHYTOLACCA

From temperate, warm-temperate, and subtropical regions throughout the world, this genus in the pokeweed (Phytolaccaceae) family comprises 35 species of perennials, subshrubs, and deciduous or evergreen shrubs and trees, usually upright in form, with simple, often large leaves that can develop vivid colors in autumn. Their petal-less flowers are followed by conspicuous berries that in many species are poisonous.
CULTIVATION: Apart from variable frost hardiness and an intolerance of drought, most species are easily grown in moist, moderately fertile, well-drained soil in a position in sun or part-shade. Prune at any time, but winter is often best as it will not affect the flower and fruit production or the autumn color. Propagate from seed, from rooted basal shoots, or from cuttings taken during the growing season.

Phytolacca americana

POKE, POKEBERRY, POKEWEED

☼ ❄ ↔ 3 ft (0.9 m) ↑ 12 ft (3.5 m)

Phytolacca americana

Perennial from North and Central America. Can be herbaceous in severe winters. Young stems purple-red; leaves take on purple-red and pink tones in autumn. Racemes of tiny cream to pink flowers in summer–autumn. Clusters of berries follow, turning red and purple-black as they ripen. Zones 4–10.

PILEA

This genus of about 600 creeping, sprawling, or erect annual or perennial herbs, sometimes with a woody base, is a member of the nettle (Urticaceae) family, and is native to tropical regions worldwide except for Australia. The leaves are usually opposite, often unequal, smooth-edged or serrated, covered with calcium deposits that give the appearance of opalescent spots. Minute whitish green flowers that become pinkish brown are produced on solitary flowerheads or loose panicles. The fruits are achenes.
CULTIVATION: These plants require abundant moisture during active growth, in any moist well-drained soil, out of direct sunlight and drafts. Pinch out terminal buds to encourage compact bushy growth. Propagate perennial species from stem cuttings or by division in spring or summer, and annual species from seed in spring or autumn.

Pilea involucrata

FRIENDSHIP PLANT, PANAMICA

◐ ♣ ↔ 6–12 in (15–30 cm) ↑ 4–18 in (10–45 cm)
Evergreen, bushy, hairy, trailing to erect herb. From tropical regions of Central and South America. Branches 8–12 in (20–30 cm) long; hairy, oval, toothed leaves, to 2½ in (6 cm) long, marked with bronze, red, or silver. Tiny pink or red flowers in summer. Cultivars include '**Moon Valley**', and '**Norfolk**'. Zones 10–12.

Pilea peperomioides

◐ ♣ ↔ 6–20 in (15–50 cm) ↑ 6–20 in (15–50 cm)
Erect herb from the West Indies. Smooth elongated stems; succulent, elliptical to nearly circular, pale green, prominently veined leaves, to 3½ in (9 cm) long, on stalks to 2½ in (6 cm) long. Insignificant flowers in summer. Zones 10–12.

Pinguicula emarginata × P. vulgaris

Pinguicula moranensis

Pistia stratiotes

PINGUICULA

BUTTERWORTS, PINGS

A varied genus of more than 75 carnivorous plants belonging to the bladderwort (Lentibulariaceae) family, found in a variety of damp tropical and temperate habitats in North America, Asia, and Europe. In South America they favor drier conditions, sometimes as epiphytes. Most are perennials, with fibrous roots, very pale to bright green leaves forming a rosette, and beautiful flowers held singly on leafless stems. Some species form a tight winter resting-bud (hibernacula). Tiny glandular hairs covering the leaves produce a greasy mucilage.
CULTIVATION: Tropical species prefer an equal mix of sand, peat, and perlite, and filtered sun; keep moist in spring and summer, and just damp in winter, when succulent non-carnivorous leaves form. Feed each week in spring and summer with a weak foliar fertilizer. In temperate areas, grow in a warm greenhouse or on a sunny windowsill. Propagate from leaf cuttings of winter leaves. Temperate species prefer an equal mix of peat and sand or vermiculite, and filtered light. If grown in pots, water by tray in spring and summer; keep plants with hibernacula fairly dry in winter. Propagate from leaf cuttings. Re-pot in winter.

Pinguicula emarginata

☼/◐ ❋ ↔ 4 in (10 cm) ↕ 1½ in (35 mm)
From Mexico, found in damp sandy soil. Oval leaves, 2 in (5 cm) long. White to violet flowers, with violet to purple veins. *P. e.* × *P. vulgaris*, purple or violet flowers spotted with white. Zones 8–11.

Pinguicula moranensis ★

syn. *Pinguicula caudata*
◐ ❋ ↔ 10 in (25 cm) ↕ 2 in (5 cm)
From Mexico. Oval leaves, to 5 in (12 cm) long, slightly curved edges, sometimes tinged pink. Lavender or pink flowers, sometimes pink and white or all white. Zones 8–11.

Pinguicula vulgaris ★

COMMON BUTTERWORT
☼/◐ ❋ ↔ 5 in (12 cm) ↕ 6 in (15 cm)
From rocky mountainous areas of Europe and North America, in open grass or bogs. Leaves yellow to green, curved inward at edge. Single violet-like flowers on 6 in (15 cm) tall stems. Zones 2–7.

PISTIA

SHELL FLOWER, WATER LETTUCE

This genus, with just 1 aquatic evergreen herb, belongs to the arum (Araceae) family. Found on Lake Victoria, on Africa's Nile River, it is now widely distributed through the tropics. It has spreading feathery roots and floating rosettes of broadly wedge-shaped, ribbed, bluish green leaves in lettuce-like arrangements.
CULTIVATION: Water lettuce is best grown in aquariums and ponds in warmer climates, in a protected sunny position, out of direct sunlight in the middle of the day. Propagation is by division of plantlets in summer.

Pistia stratiotes

☼ ⁂ ↔ 4–6 in (10–15 cm) ↕ 4–6 in (10–15 cm)
Aquatic herb. Rosettes of oval to hairy, round, bright green leaves, to 8 in (20 cm) long; fine, water-repellent hairs. Small flowers without petals, enclosed by a leaf-like spathe. Zones 9–11.

PITCAIRNIA

There are more than 350 species in this genus, one of the more primitive genera in the bromeliad (Bromeliaceae) family, found throughout more humid areas in the American tropics, with a single species native to Guinea, in West Africa. The few species in cultivation are very popular. Species vary greatly in size, most growing in the ground but sometimes on rocks, rarely on trees. Leaves are generally narrow and grass-like, sometimes wider, the edges sometimes toothed, forming an open erect rosette. Some species have both grass-like and short, very prickly leaves. Conspicuous red, sometimes yellow, white, or violet flowerheads are held on long slender stems above leaves. The fruit is a dry capsule.
CULTIVATION: Recommended for greenhouse or conservatory cultivation in cool temperate areas, and outdoors with protection from direct continuous sunlight in warmer areas. Water when potting mix is almost dry. Extra feeding is not necessary. Propagation is by seed or offsets.

Pitcairnia atrorubens

◐ ⁂ ↔ 8 in (20 cm) ↕ 32 in (80 cm)
Found from Mexico to Colombia. Erect, open, rosettes; strap-like leaves, few small teeth. Flower stem erect; cylindrical flowerhead, erect bright red bracts spiraling to top, whitish petals. Zones 10–12.

Pitcairnia heterophylla

☀ ✿ ↔ 20 in (50 cm) ↕ 20 in (50 cm)

From Mexico to Venezuela and Peru. Large bulb; forms clumps; leaves very thin, brown, very spiny. Short flower stem or second set of leaves emerges from center of leaf rosette. Leaves narrow, smooth-edged, to 27 in (70 cm) long. Globular flowerhead, up to 10 flowers, reddish, petals of red, orange, or white. Zones 10–12.

PLATYCODON

BALLOON FLOWER, CHINESE BELLFLOWER

The sole species in this genus in the bellflower (Campanulaceae) family is a vigorous herbaceous perennial found in Japan and nearby parts of China. It forms a clump of bold, lance-shaped leaves with toothed edges. The flowers open from enlarged, balloon-like buds and are cup- to bell-shaped, white, pink, or blue, with 5 broad lobes.
CULTIVATION: Suitable for a distinctly seasonal temperate climate. Plant in sun or part-shade in moist, humus-rich, well-drained soil. May be raised from seed; cultivars by division.

Platycodon grandiflorus

Platycodon grandiflorus

BALLOON FLOWER, CHINESE BELLFLOWER

☼/☀ ✿ ↔ 24 in (60 cm) ↕ 27 in (70 cm)

Broad lance-shaped, toothed leaves; sturdy, usually upright, sometimes sprawling stems. Bell-shaped blue, purple, white, or pink flowers open from inflated buds in summer. 'Apoyama', low growing, large deep lavender flowers; 'Fuji Blue' ★, erect habit, flowers large, blue; 'Fuji White', white flowers; 'Perlmutterschale' (syn. 'Mother of Pearl'), large pale pink flowers; 'Sentimental Blue', dwarf habit, large mauve-blue flowers. Zones 4–9.

PLECTRANTHUS

Over 200 species of annuals, perennials, and shrubs make up this large genus of herbaceous, semi-succulent or succulent plants in the mint (Lamiaceae) family. They come from Africa, Asia, Australia, and the Pacific Islands. Most are grown for their attractive evergreen foliage and ease of growing, either in the garden, in pots, or as hanging basket specimens in greenhouses where necessary. Although individual tubular flowers are usually insignificant, the massed flower display provided by the spikes is impressive.
CULTIVATION: Many of these undemanding plants can be grown as ground covers in lightly shaded areas in warmer climates or as easy-care specimens for pot or basket. Others of shrub-like proportions can be grown in a warm sheltered position. Any fertile soil or potting mix will suit; provide ample water during growing season. They are quite rapid growers; the succulent stems are easily pruned and can be used for propagating.

Plectranthus ciliatus

☀ ❧ ↔ 4 in (10 cm) ↕ 2–4 in (5–10 cm)

Straggling evergreen herb or shrub. Native to eastern South Africa; spreads by runners. Hairy trailing stems; opposite pairs of shining hairy leaves, to 5 in (12 cm) long, purple beneath, dotted with glands. Tiny flowers, white corolla tube, 2-lobed upper lip, purple dots in lower lip, in winter–autumn. Dark brown nutlets follow the flowers. Zones 9–11.

Plectranthus ecklonii

☀ ❧ ↔ 3 ft (0.9 m) ↕ 5 ft (1.5 m)

Bushy South African plant. Mid-green tapering leaves, prominent veining. Upright clusters of pale lilac flowers in autumn. Zones 9–11.

Plectranthus forsteri

☀ ❧ ↔ 10 ft (3 m) ↕ 3–8 ft (0.9–2.4 m)

Sprawling herb from eastern Australia and nearby Pacific Islands. Oval, serrated, hairy leaves. Pale to mid-blue or mauve flowers. 'Marginatus' (syn. 'Variegatus'), white flowers, leaves variegated with cream. Zones 8–10.

Plectranthus neochilus

FLY BUSH, LOBSTER FLOWER, SKUNK LEAF

☼/☀ ❧ ↔ 24 in (60 cm) ↕ 18 in (45 cm)

Sprawling succulent perennial from southern Africa. Mat-forming branches; succulent fragrant leaves, prominent veins, strong garlic-like smell when crushed. Flowerheads distinctly 4-sided, to 4 in (10 cm) long. Blue 2-lipped flowers emerge from large overlapping bracts throughout most of summer. Zones 8–11.

Plectranthus oertendahlii

☀ ✿ ↔ 36 in (90 cm) ↕ 8–12 in (20–30 cm)

Semi-succulent, freely branching, perennial herb. Native to South Africa. Oval to nearly round, purple, hairy, scalloped leaves, to 1½ in (35 mm) long, white veins above, reddish green beneath. White or pale mauve flowers, irregularly during the year. Zones 10–11.

Plectranthus ciliatus

Plectranthus verticillatus

SWEDISH IVY

☼ ◑ ↔ 40 in (100 cm) ↑ 12 in (30 cm)

Succulent, sprawling, perennial herb from Southeast Asia, Swaziland, and Mozambique. Smooth or slightly hairy stems, to over 40 in (100 cm) long; leaves oval to rounded, toothed, to 1½ in (35 mm) long; single or pairs of cymes; 1 to 3 white to pale mauve flowers, speckled with purple, without stalks. Zones 9–11.

PODOPHYLLUM

MAY APPLE

This genus of 7 perennial herbs from the barberry (Berberidaceae) family, found from eastern North America to eastern Asia and the Himalayas, grows from stout rhizomes. Large, palm-shaped, lobed leaves, on long stalks, and groups of single or several, overlapping, ruff- or parasol-like flowers with 6 to 9 petals, rise on erect stems, to 16 in (40 cm) tall. Large, fleshy, egg-shaped berries follow the flowers. CULTIVATION: Most may apples prefer a shady position, often in wet or marshy ground. Propagate by division or from seed.

Podophyllum peltatum

AMERICAN MANDRAKE, DEVIL'S APPLE, HOG-APPLE, INDIAN APPLE, MAY APPLE

☼ ❋ ↔ 24 in (60 cm) ↑ 24 in (60 cm)

From woodlands of eastern USA south to Texas. Single, round, simple, forked stem; 2 leaves, to 12 in (30 cm) across, with 3 to 9 lobes, finely hairy beneath. Flowering stem with 2 to 3 leaves or leafless; solitary, nodding, fragrant flowers, white or rose pink petals, with toothed points, in spring. Fruit is single berry, greenish yellow, occasionally red, flesh pulpy; ripens in late summer, only part of plant not poisonous. Zones 4–6.

POLEMONIUM

JACOB'S LADDER, SKY PILOT

A genus of 25 erect or spreading or rhizomatous annual or sometimes short-lived perennial herbs from the phlox (Polemoniaceae) family, native from temperate to Arctic regions of the Americas, Europe, and Asia. Plants have pinnate leaves with simple or divided leaflets, with or without stalks. Heads of 5-lobed, tubular,

Polemonium reptans

bell- or funnel-shaped flowers, in blue, purplish, white, or yellow, grow from the leaf axils or at the ends of sprawling or erect stems. Fruit contain 3 to 10 brown or black seeds per compartment. CULTIVATION: These plants grow well in sun or part-shade in rich, well-drained, moist, loamy soil. Propagate by division in autumn or early spring, or from seed sown in autumn or winter.

Polemonium caeruleum

CHARITY, GREEK VALERIAN, JACOB'S LADDER

☼ ❋ ↔ 12–20 in (30–50 cm) ↑ 12–36 in (30–90 cm)

Hairy and glandular perennial, from northern and central Europe and northern Asia. Leaves to 16 in (40 cm) long, 11 to 27 sword-shaped to oblong leaflets, growing from a central base. Blue flowers,

Polemonium caeruleum, Brise d'Anjou/'Blanjou'

occasionally white, widely bell-shaped corollas, oval lobes, in late spring–summer. *P. c.* subsp. *caeruleum*, many blue flowers, stamens protruding beyond corolla. *P. c.* Brise d'Anjou/ 'Blanjou' ★, variegated form. Zones 2–4.

Polemonium pulcherrimum

SHOWY POLEMONIUM, WESTERN SKY PILOT

☼/◑ ❋ ↔ 20–24 in (50–60 cm) ↑ 20–24 in (50–60 cm)

Erect, clumping, deciduous perennial. From moist to dry, often rocky slopes in northwestern North America. Slender branching rhizomes; sprawling or erect stems, 4 to 10, soft hairs; leaves grow from central base, 9 to 37 bright green, oval leaflets, fine hairs. Dense glandular clusters of flowers, bell-shaped, blue, violet, or white corolla, 2 leaf-like bracts, yellow inside, on stalks to 1 in (25 mm) long, in late spring–summer. Zones 4–7.

Polemonium reptans

ABSCESS ROOT, CREEPING JACOB'S LADDER, GREEK VALERIAN

☼ ❋ ↔ 12–27 in (30–70 cm) ↑ 8–27 in (20–70 cm)

Erect or spreading perennial, native to eastern USA. Fleshy roots; many erect, smooth, hollow, branching, herbaceous stems, sometimes tinged red, growing from small crown. Leaves 8 in (20 cm) long; 7 to 19 elliptical to oval, dull green leaflets, silvery green beneath. Drooping flowers; densely glandular, bell-shaped calyx; lilac to light blue, funnel-shaped corolla, in spring–early summer. 'Blue Pearl', to 10 in (25 cm) high, blue flowers. Zones 4–7.

POLYGALA

Covering over 500 species of almost every growth form, except tall trees, this genus, a member of the milkwort (Polygalaceae) family, is very widespread. The foliage ranges from small and linear to large and oval but is usually simple with smooth edges. The flowers have a pea-flower-like structure with distinct wings and a keel, which usually has a feathery tuft unique to polygalas. The flowers, carried in clusters or racemes, come in a range of colors, with purple and pink dominant, and are followed by small seed pods. CULTIVATION: Most prefer a light well-drained soil in sun or part-shade. European and American alpine species are ideal subjects for pots or troughs. Shrubby species can be trimmed or pruned to shape in spring. Propagate from seed, layers, or cuttings.

Polygala chamaebuxus
✸ ✽ ↔ 15 in (38 cm) ↕ 2–6 in (5–15 cm)

Tiny spreading shrublet from mountains of central Europe. Long, elliptical, leathery, glossy leaves. White-winged, yellow-keeled, pea-flowers. *P. c.* var. *grandiflora*, purple-winged flowers. Zones 6–9.

POLYGONATUM
SOLOMON'S SEAL

There are approximately 50 species in this genus, which is a member of the family Ruscaceae. They are found in the temperate zones of the Northern Hemisphere. Spreading by slow-growing underground rhizomes, most of these easy-to-grow herbaceous perennials are fully hardy. The taller species have graceful arching stems, attractive leaves, and carry the delicate flowers in small pendulous clusters from the upper leaf axils. Small blue-black berries often follow the flowers.
CULTIVATION: Plant in a shady or partly shady position in a rich, moist, peaty soil. Cut the stems down to soil level in late autumn. Mulch annually with leaf mold. Propagate from seed or divide the rhizomes in spring or autumn.

Polygonatum odoratum
syn. *Polygonatum officinale*
ANGULAR SOLOMON'S SEAL
✸ ✽ ↔ 24 in (60 cm) ↕ 36 in (90 cm)

From Europe, northern Iran, Siberia, and Japan. Grows in woods, in limestone. Flowers mid-spring to early summer. 'Flore Pleno' ★, double flowers; 'Variegatum', white leaf edges and tips. Zones 3–9.

PONTEDERIA

A genus of 5 perennial aquatic or marginal herbs, members of the pickerel-weed (Pontederiaceae) family, from the east of North and South America and the Caribbean. Erect or prostrate stems grow from a branching, often submerged rhizome, with smooth-edged, sword-shaped, dark green leaves on long stalks. Spikes of small tubular flowers are produced, usually blue with 3 lobes, the largest lobe spotted with yellow.
CULTIVATION: Plant these perennials in full sun in ponds and bog gardens, in water 8–12 in (20–30 cm) deep. Propagate in spring by division or from seed.

Pontederia cordata
PICKEREL RUSH, PICKEREL WEED, WAMPEE
✸ ✽ ↔ 27 in (70 cm) ↕ 48 in (120 cm)

Deciduous marginal water plant found mostly in eastern North America and the Caribbean. Dense cylindrical spikes, 1–6 in (2.5–15 cm) long; blue to white flowers, to ¾ in (18 mm) wide; erect stalks, to 14 in (35 cm) tall, in late summer. Zones 2–5.

PORTEA

There are 8 species, all from the eastern states of Brazil, in this genus belonging to the bromeliad (Bromeliaceae) family. They are medium to large plants, with green strap-like leaves, toothed on the edges, forming an open rosette. The flowerhead is branched, sometimes reaching 5 ft (1.5 m) tall, each flower borne on a slender stem. The petals are generally blue-violet but sometimes red.

Pontederia cordata

CULTIVATION: These plants are recommended for greenhouse cultivation in cool temperate areas, or outdoors with protection from direct continuous sunlight and extremes of rain in warm temperate, subtropical, and tropical areas. Water when potting mix is dry. Extra feeding is not necessary. Propagation is mainly from offsets.

Portea petropolitana
✸ ✛ ↔ 3 ft (0.9 m) ↕ 7 ft (2 m)

From central eastern Brazil. Open rosette of long, toothed-edged, strap-like, green leaves. Flower stem to 32 in (80 cm) tall, many-branched, pyramidal flowerheads to 4 ft (1.2 m) high, each branch with open cluster of red-stemmed violet flowers, long red bract below each branch. Zones 10–12.

PORTULACA
PURSLANE

This genus of some 40 species occurring in the warmer parts of the world is a member of the purslane (Portulacaceae) family. They are mostly succulent herbs, usually with tuberous roots. The leaves are flat or cylindrical, opposite or spirally arranged, usually with hairs in their axils, though these are absent in the Australian species (subgenus *Portulacella*). Flowers are solitary or in heads, surrounded by a whorl of bracts formed by the upper leaves, the Australian species with distinct stalks. There are 2 sepals and usually 5 pink, purple, or yellow petals, which open in direct sun and close in shade. There are 8 to many stamens. The fruit is a small conical capsule, opening when the top falls off to release the many small seeds. The various species are often very difficult to distinguish. Some are grown as ornamentals, some for eating.
CULTIVATION: *Portulaca* species are easily grown from seed in well-drained soils in sunny but sheltered positions.

Portulaca grandiflora, Sundial Series, 'Sundial Fuchsia'

Portulaca grandiflora

syn. *Portulaca pilosa* subsp. *grandiflora*

ELEVEN-O'CLOCK, GARDEN PORTULACA, MOSS ROSE, ROSE MOSS, SUN PLANT

☀ ❄ ↔ 6–12 in (15–30 cm) ↕ 6–12 in (15–30 cm)

Slow-growing annual. Native to Brazil, Argentina, and Uruguay. Partially prostrate or climbing stem, to 12 in (30 cm) long, reddish twigs; alternate, thick, fleshy, lance-shaped, cylindrical, pale green leaves. Single or double flowers of rose, red, purple, lavender, yellow, or white, often striped, open only in sunlight. '**Sundance**', semi-double flowers remain open most of the day. Other popular cultivars include: '**Double Mix**', '**Margarita Rosita**', the **Sundial Series**, and '**Tutti Frutti Mix**'. Zones 8–10.

POTAMOGETON

PONDWEED

A genus of about 90 aquatic perennials from the pondweed (Potamogetonaceae) family, widely distributed, mostly in temperate regions of the Northern Hemisphere. They have submerged or floating, simple, elliptical, flat, green, leathery, alternate leaves growing from cylindrical or flattened upright stems, rooting at the lower nodes and usually growing from a bottom-rooting, simple or branched rhizome. Fleshy cylindrical spikes of inconspicuous flowers grow on stalks above or below the water. Plants also produce small, bulb-like, winter buds and stalkless, egg-shaped, floating fruit. CULTIVATION: They suit aquariums and pond cultivation, in full sun. Propagate from stem cuttings in spring and summer, by division, or by planting out bulb-like winter buds.

Potamogeton perfoliatus

CLASPING LEAF PONDWEED, PERFOLIATE PONDWEED, REDHEAD GRASS

☀ ❄ ↔ 15 ft (4.5 m) ↕ 2 in (5 cm)

Freshwater pondweed. Native to eastern North America, temperate Eurasia, and eastern Australia. Branching, densely crowded stem. Stalkless, deep green, glossy, oval to heart-shaped, submerged leaves, up to 4 in (10 cm) long, heart-shaped base. Spikes of small green flowers in summer. Zones 3–10.

POTENTILLA

This is a large genus of some 500 species in the rose (Rosaceae) family from the Northern Hemisphere. While most are herbaceous perennials, the shrubby species are very hardy, thriving in most soils, in sun and in partial shade. The flowers are like small single roses, and are produced over a long period, from spring throughout summer and, in some species, well into autumn. CULTIVATION: These plants prefer a fertile well-drained soil. Cultivars with orange, red, or pink flowers tend to fade in very strong sunshine and should be given a position where they receive some shade in the hottest part of the day. Propagation is usually from seed in autumn or cuttings in summer.

Potentilla alba

WHITE CINQUEFOIL

☀ ❄ ↔ 10 in (25 cm) ↕ 10 in (25 cm)

Low-growing, spreading, mat-forming, perennial herb from central, southern, and eastern Europe. Lower leaves dark green, palm-shaped, 5 oblong leaflets, to 2½ in (6 cm) long, toothed tips; stem leaves smaller, simple or divided into leaflets, silvery silky at first. Sprays of 5 white single flowers in spring–summer. Zones 3–9.

Potentilla atrosanguinea

syns *Potentilla argyrophylla* var. *atrosanguinea*, *P. leucochroa*

RED CINQUEFOIL

☀ ❄ ↔ 36 in (90 cm) ↕ 36 in (90 cm)

Clump-forming perennial herb from grassland and thickets of the Himalayas and western China. Branching stems; few branches. Semi-evergreen leaves, 3 elliptical to oval, toothed, silky leaflets, up to 3 in (8 cm) long, white hairs beneath, on long stems. Clusters of deep red to reddish purple, orange, or yellow flowers, usually with dark eyes, in late summer–early autumn. Zones 3–9.

Potentilla aurea

syns *Potentilla chrysocraspeda*, *P. halleri*, *P. ternata*

☀ ❄ ↔ 12 in (30 cm) ↕ 12 in (30 cm)

Rounded, mat-forming, perennial herb with woody base. Native to grassland and thickets of the European Alps and the Pyrenees. Hand-shaped leaves grow from a central base; 5 oblong leaflets, silver hairs along the edges and veins, toothed at tips; smaller leaves on stems. Loose clusters of few golden yellow flowers, with deeper orange centers. Spring- to summer-flowering. Zones 3–9.

Potentilla nepalensis 'Miss Willmott'

Potentilla megalantha

syn. *Potentilla fragiformis*

☀ ❄ ↔ 8–12 in (20–30 cm)

↕ 8–12 in (20–30 cm)

Clump-forming, softly hairy, tufted perennial herb. Native to Japan and the Siberian and North American tundra.

Soft, palm-shaped, thick basal leaves to 3 in (8 cm) wide, 3 broad oval leaflets, scalloped edges; leaves finely hairy underneath. Solitary, rich bright yellow, 5-petalled, saucer-shaped flowers. Summer- to autumn-flowering. Zones 5–9.

Potentilla nitida 'Rubra'

Potentilla nepalensis

CINQUEFOIL

☼ ❈ ↔ 12–24 in (30–60 cm) ↕ 12–24 in (30–60 cm)
Clump-forming perennial herb. Found in thickets and grassland of the western Himalayas. Slender, erect, leafy, branching, purple stems. Palmate strawberry-like leaves, 1¼–3 in (3–8 cm) long, on tall stalks, 5 oval coarsely toothed leaflets, grow from a central base. Pink, purplish red, or crimson 5-petalled flowers in summer. 'Miss Willmott' ★ (syn. 'Willmottiae'), dwarf form, salmon pink flowers, darker pink center and veining. Zones 5–8.

Potentilla neumanniana

syns *Potentilla crantzii, P. tabernaemontani, P. verna*
SPRING CINQUEFOIL

☼ ❈ ↔ 6–12 in (15–30 cm) ↕ 3–4 in (8–10 cm)
From temperate northern, western, and central Europe. Prostrate, mat-forming, evergreen, perennial herb. Sprawling woody stem, spreads by runners. Spicily scented, strawberry-like, shiny, hand-shaped, deep green leaves, usually 5 leaflets, occasionally 3, up to 1½ in (35 mm) long, with toothed tips. Up to 12 buttery yellow 5-petalled flowers in spring. 'Nana' (syn. *P. verna* 'Nana'), vivid green leaves, gold flowers. Zones 5–8.

Potentilla nitida

☼ ❈ ↔ 5–16 in (12–40 cm) ↕ 2–4 in (5–10 cm)
From rocky areas of European Alps. Dense, tufted, downy, carpet-forming, perennial herb. Compound leaves; 3 silvery, silky leaflets, oval to nearly sword-shaped, to ½ in (12 mm) long, with 3-toothed tips. White or deep pink flowers in summer. 'Rubra', pink to rose-pink flowers. Zones 3–8.

Potentilla × tonguei

☼ ❈ ↔ 12–20 in (30–50 cm) ↕ 6–10 in (15–25 cm)
Perennial herb of garden origin. Sprawling, non-rooting stems; compound leaves, 3 to 5 narrowly oval, coarsely toothed leaflets. Apricot corolla and carmine red eye, in summer. Zones 3–5.

PRIMULA

COWSLIP, POLYANTHUS, PRIMROSE

This widespread, mainly Northern Hemisphere, perennial genus gives its name to the family Primulaceae. Most primulas form basal rosettes of heavily veined leaves from which emerge the flower stems, sometimes with just a single bloom, but often with a large terminal head or several well-shaped whorls of flowers. CULTIVATION: The majority of *Primula* species prefer dappled shade in woodland gardens and moist, humus-rich, well-drained soil. So-called bog primroses like damper conditions and often naturalize along streams. Propagate from seed or by dividing thriving clumps when dormant.

Primula alpicola

☼/◕ ❈ ↔ 10–16 in (25–40 cm) ↕ 16–36 in (40–90 cm)
Native to the Himalayas. Prefers wet peaty soil. Toothed elliptical leaves. Flowers white, yellow, mauve, purple, on stems with powdery white coating, in late spring–early summer. Zones 6–9.

Primula auricula

☼/◕ ❈ ↔ 6–16 in (15–40 cm) ↕ 4–8 in (10–20 cm)
From mountains of southern Europe. Clump-forming; foliage and stems with dusty coating. Leaves fleshy, light green, rounded to broad lance-shaped, usually toothed; heads of few to many flat, ½–1 in (12–25 mm) wide spring flowers on 6 in (15 cm) stems, in the wild mostly yellow or purple-red with yellow center, some with white band. Cultivars include 'Alicia', dark purple-red, edges lighter; 'Beatrice', purple, mauve border, cream center; 'Butterwick', red-brown, golden yellow center; 'C. W. Needham', dark purple-blue, yellow-green center; 'Dales Red', red, heavy powdery white coating and white band, yellow center; 'Hawkwood', red, white edge and band, yellow center; 'Jeannie Telford', purple-red, mauve edge, cream center; 'Lavender Lady', light purple, white center; 'Lucy Locket', buff yellow, cream center; 'Rowena', maroon, lavender edges, yellow center, white band; 'Sirius', coffee-colored, purplish red markings, yellow center; 'Spring Meadows', cream, yellow-green center, light green edges; and 'Trouble', pinkish beige double flowers. Zones 3–9.

Primula alpicola

Primula beesiana

☼/◕ ❈ ↔ 20 in (50 cm) ↕ 32 in (80 cm)
Native to Himalayan area of western China. Narrow, toothed leaves lengthen as seed heads ripen. Candelabra-style flowerheads with up to 8 whorls; flowers deep pink, yellow-centered, in summer. Zones 5–9.

Primula bulleyana

☼/◕ ❈ ↔ 12–27 in (30–70 cm) ↕ 24 in (60 cm)
Native to southwestern China. Basal rosette; leaves toothed and tapering to narrow base. Candelabra-style flowerheads with up to 7 whorls of golden yellow to orange flowers in late spring–early summer. Zones 6–9.

Primula denticulata

Primula juliae

Primula, Pruhonicensis Hybrid, 'Iris Mainwaring'

Primula capitata

☽/☀ ❄ ↔ 12–18 in (30–45 cm) ↑ 10–15 in (25–38 cm)

From the Himalayas. Stems and undersides of foliage powdery white; leaves coarsely toothed. Sturdy erect flower stems, somewhat flattened heads of many small, violet to purple flowers, in late spring–early summer. Zones 5–9.

Primula denticulata

DRUMSTICK PRIMULA

☽/☀ ❄ ↔ 10–18 in (25–45 cm) ↑ 8–12 in (20–30 cm)

Found from mountains of Afghanistan to Myanmar. Flower stems and undersides of toothed leaves are downy white. Overwinters as conical bud; rounded heads of mauve to purple-red, rarely white, flowers in spring, with or before new leaves. Zones 5–9.

Primula elatior

OXLIP

☽/☀ ❄ ↔ 6–16 in (15–40 cm) ↑ 6–12 in (15–30 cm)

Eurasian perennial. Forms clump of long-stemmed, toothed, rounded to elliptical leaves, undersides sometimes downy. Rather wiry flower stems; heads of pale yellow flowers, in spring–early summer. Zones 5–9.

Primula farinosa

☽/☀ ❄ ↔ 12 in (30 cm) ↑ 8 in (20 cm)

Found from Scotland to northwestern Pacific. Bright green leaves, spatula-shaped, wavy edges can be toothed or smooth. Short flower stems; heads of usually a few, sometimes many, bright pink, starry flowers, notched petals. Spring-flowering. Zones 4–9.

Primula florindae

☽/☀ ❄ ↔ 8–16 in (20–40 cm) ↑ 36 in (90 cm)

Native to Tibet. Long-stemmed, broad pointed oval, toothed leaves. Tall sturdy flower stems; heads of up to 40 scented yellow flowers in late spring–early summer. **Keillour Group** (hybrids with *P. × waltonii*), flowers in oranges, reds, and yellow tones. Zones 6–9.

Primula japonica

☽/☀ ❄ ↔ 12–24 in (30–60 cm) ↑ 18 in (45 cm)

Native to Japan. Clump-forming; broad, coarsely toothed, spatula-shaped leaves to 10 in (25 cm) long. Stems bear up to 6 whorls

of white, pink, magenta to red flowers, to ¾ in (18 mm) wide, in late spring–early summer. '**Postford White**', white flowers, pink eye; '**Valley Red**', bright pinkish red flowers. Zones 5–9.

Primula juliae

☽/☀ ❄ ↔ 6–10 in (15–25 cm) ↑ 2 in (5 cm)

Native to the Caucasus. Rounded, toothed leaves, red-tinted leaf stems. Flowers among foliage, solitary, mauve to purple-red, conspicuous yellow eye, in spring. Flowers can appear before foliage. Zones 5–9.

Primula × kewensis

☽/☀ ❄ ↔ 12–18 in (30–45 cm) ↑ 12 in (30 cm)

Hybrid, probably between *P. floribunda* and *P. verticillata*. Faintly powdery, toothed, spatula-shaped leaves. Closely spaced whorls of fragrant yellow flowers in spring. Zones 9–10.

Primula malacoides

☽/☀ ❄ ↔ 16 in (40 cm) ↑ 12 in (30 cm)

From China. Winter-flowering, usually short lived; treated as annual. Long-stemmed, downy, rounded leaves, lobed and coarsely toothed. Numerous flower stems; heads of up to 20 lavender flowers. Cultivars in pink, lavender, purple, and white. Zones 8–10.

Primula obconica

GERMAN PRIMROSE, POISON PRIMROSE

☽/☀ ❄ ↔ 8–16 in (20–40 cm) ↑ 8 in (20 cm)

Perennial from southern China. Broad elliptical leaves; fine downy hairs, frequently causing contact dermatitis. Open heads of up to 15 lavender to purple flowers, notched petals, in winter. Mixed-color seed strains include '**Libre Mixed**', large flowers in apricots, pinks, mauves, purples, and white. Zones 9–10.

Primula, Pruhonicensis Hybrids

POLYANTHUS

☽/☀ ❄ ↔ 6–16 in (15–40 cm) ↑ 4–12 in (10–30 cm)

Complex group of garden and natural hybrids, ranging from very small, long-lived, rock-garden types, such as '**Wanda**' (purple-red flowers) to large showy hybrid polyanthus (usually mixed color seedling selections, such as the **Crescendo**, **Kaleidoscope**, **Pacific Giants**, and **Rainbow Series**), which are often treated as annuals.

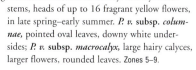

Also single-flowered hybrids; rosebud-double-flowered types ("double primroses"); hose-in-hose, appearing to have two blooms sleeved one within the other, and "gold-" or "silver-laced" forms with light-edged brownish black flowers. Popular single-flowered forms include: **'Dorothy'**, pale yellow flowers; **'Guinevere'** (syn. 'Garryard Guinevere'), bronze-green leaves, white flowers, red stems and sepals; **'Iris Mainwaring'**, mauve-blue suffused with pink; **'Old Port'**, deep purple-red; **'Schneekissen'**, dark green foliage, pure white flowers; and **'Velvet Moon'**, very dark foliage, deep velvet red flowers. Double primroses include: **'April Rose'**, deep red flowers; **Bon Accord Series**, series of doubles mainly named by color, such as **'Bon Accord Purple'**; **'Ken Dearman'**, apricot-pink suffused with yellow, deep pink buds; and **'Sunshine Susie'**, bright yellow to gold flowers. Zones 7–9.

Primula × *pubescens*

☼◐/☀ ❋ ↔ 10 in (25 cm) ↑ 6 in (15 cm)
Hybrid between *P. auricula* and *P. hirsuta*. Leaves often powdery, toothed, usually quite rounded, to 4 in (10 cm) long. Small flowerheads, short stems, most shades, except darker blue. **'Boothman's Variety'** (syn. 'Carmen'), deep crimson, white center; **'Harlow Car'**, cream; **'Wharfedale Buttercup'**, sulfur yellow. Zones 5–9.

Primula pulverulenta

☼◐/☀ ❋ ↔ 20 in (50 cm) ↑ 36 in (90 cm)
Native to China. Coarsely toothed leaves to 12 in (30 cm) long. Tall flower stems, candelabra-like; several whorls of purple-red flowers, dark red centers, in late spring–summer. **Bartley hybrids**, typically dark-centered pink-red flowers. Zones 6–9.

Primula rosea

☼◐/☀ ❋ ↔ 6–15 in (15–38 cm) ↑ 4–6 in (10–15 cm)
From northwest Himalayas. Toothed leaves develop slowly, often flushed bronze when young. Glowing deep pink flowers appear before foliage, or before it is fully expanded. Heads of up to 12 flowers, notched petal tips, in spring. **'Grandiflora'**, large flowers on tall stems. Zones 6–9.

Primula sieboldii

☼◐/☀ ❋ ↔ 12–24 in (30–60 cm) ↑ 12 in (30 cm)
Native to Japan and nearby parts of temperate mainland Asia. Leaves very coarsely toothed, indented heart-shaped base. White, pink, or purple flowers, in small heads, in late spring–summer. **'Blush Pink'** ★, bright pink flowers, hint of apricot; **'Cloth of Mist'**, pale lavender flowers; **'Mikado'**, dark purple-pink flowers. Zones 5–9.

Primula sikkimensis

☼◐/☀ ❋ ↔ 10–24 in (25–60 cm)
↑ 12–36 in (30–90 cm)
Native to Nepal and the Chinese western Himalayas. Dark green, serrated to toothed leaves.

Primula rosea

Heads of partly pendulous flowers, white to yellow and funnel-shaped, sturdy erect stems, in late spring–early summer. Zones 6–9.

Primula veris

COWSLIP
☼◐/☀ ❋ ↔ 16 in (40 cm) ↑ 12 in (30 cm)
Eurasian species. Leaves smooth-edged to coarsely toothed, 2–8 in (5–20 cm) long, undersides sometimes downy. Downy flower stems, heads of up to 16 fragrant yellow flowers, in late spring–early summer. *P. v.* subsp. *columnae,* pointed oval leaves, downy white undersides; *P. v.* subsp. *macrocalyx,* large hairy calyces, larger flowers, rounded leaves. Zones 5–9.

Primula vulgaris

ENGLISH PRIMROSE, PRIMROSE
☼◐/☀ ❋ ↔ 6–16 in (15–40 cm)
↑ 4–6 in (10–15 cm)
European species. Leaves toothed, sometimes coarsely, undersides often faintly downy. Fragrant pale yellow flowers emerge at ground level on thin stems in spring. Extensively hybridized. *P. v.* subsp. *sibthorpii,* very compact, light mauve-pink flowers. *P. v.* **'Blaue Auslese'** (syn. 'Blue Selection'), lavender blue flowers; **'Quaker's Bonnet'**, lavender pink flowers. Zones 6–9.

PRUNELLA

syn. *Brunella*
HEAL ALL, SELF-HEAL
These 7 semi-evergreen, spreading, sprawling perennial herbs in the mint (Lamiaceae) family are from temperate Eurasia, North Africa, and North America. Leaves are opposite with generally smooth-edged blades, on stalks from the base of the plant or from the stems. Bluish violet or purplish red, tubular to bell-shaped flowers, with an erect, hooded, 2-lipped corolla with 3 lobes, are surrounded by leaf-like bracts. Fruit is an egg-shaped nutlet.
CULTIVATION: They grow well in sun or shade in dry to moist well-drained soil. Propagate from seed or by division in spring.

Primula sieboldii 'Mikado'

Prunella grandiflora 'Loveliness'

Prunella grandiflora
BIGFLOWER, LARGE SELF-HEAL, SELF-HEAL

☼ ❋ ↔ 12–24 in (30–60 cm) ↕ 12–24 in (30–60 cm)

European mat-forming herb. Woody branching stems; tiny, oval to sword-shaped leaves, scalloped edges. Off-white, pale blue, or purple flowers, deep violet lips, in summer. '**Loveliness**' ★, pale lilac flowers; '**Pink Loveliness**', pink flowers. Zones 4–9.

Prunella laciniata
☼ ❋ ↔ 9–12 in (22–30 cm) ↕ 9–12 in (22–30 cm)

From southwestern and central Europe. Lobed or divided leaves, to 3 in (8 cm) long, densely covered with fine hairs. Spikes of yellowish white flowers, sometimes rose pink or purple, in spring–summer. Zones 6–9.

PSYLLIOSTACHYS
A genus of around 10 species of annuals in the leadwort (Plumbaginaceae) family, ranging in the wild from the eastern Mediterranean and Black Sea region to central Asia. Often treated in the past as species of the larger genus *Limonium* (statice). The leaves are mostly in a basal rosette and may be deeply lobed. Flowers are tiny, usually pink, in small clusters that are densely crowded onto branched cylindrical spikes.

CULTIVATION: *Psylliostachys* species are readily grown in full sun in any reasonably fertile soil. Water freely in warmer months, do not over-fertilize. Sow seed in spring, covering seed trays as germination requires darkness and even then may be erratic.

Psylliostachys suworowii
syns *Limonium suworowii*, *Statice suworowii*

☼ ❋ ↔ 12–16 in (20–40 cm)
↕ 12–36 in (30–90 cm)

Erect branching annual. Native to central Asia and Iran. Glossy green leaves, 6 in (15 cm) or more long, wavy-edged to deeply lobed. Flowers pale pink to deep rose pink, in summer–early autumn. Zones 7–10.

PULMONARIA
LUNGWORT

This genus of 14 temperate Eurasian perennials of the borage (Boraginaceae) family overcomes its rather unappealing name by being indispensable for woodland, perennial border, and rock-garden cultivation. Their simple, long-stemmed, lance-shaped leaves are sometimes white spotted and can grow to a considerable size. The first flowers, while welcome, are sparse but, as spring warms further, the plants carry larger heads of small 5-petalled blooms. Flowers are usually blue, though white and pink forms are common.

CULTIVATION: Lungworts are very hardy and need a temperate climate with distinct seasons. They can be grown in full sun, but are best cultivated in moist, humus-rich, well-drained soil, in a partly shaded position. Propagate by division, or from basal cuttings or seed.

Pulmonaria angustifolia
BLUE COWSLIP, BLUE LUNGWORT

◑/☼ ❋ ↔ 16–40 in (40–100 cm) ↕ 8–16 in (20–40 cm)

Native to Europe. Spreading mat of unspotted, pointed oval leaves to 12 in (30 cm) long. Heads of bright blue flowers in spring. Often blooms before foliage is fully expanded. *P. a.* **subsp.** *azurea*, intense gentian blue flowers, no purple tones. Zones 3–9.

Pulmonaria mollis
◑/☼ ❋ ↔ 40 in (100 cm) ↕ 16 in (40 cm)

European species. Leaves downy, usually unspotted, to 20 in (50 cm) long. Flowers violet to purple-blue; in early spring–summer. Several pink- or white-flowered cultivars. Zones 6–9.

Pulmonaria rubra
◑/☼ ❋ ↔ 20–40 in (50–100 cm) ↕ 12–18 in (30–45 cm)

Native to Europe. Leaves often spotted white or silver-gray. Small heads of light red flowers, sometimes mauve tinted; flower stems tend to be erect. Spring- to early summer-flowering. '**Bowles' Red**', white-spotted leaves, red-pink flowers; and '**David Ward**', creamy white-edged leaves, red-pink flowers. Zones 6–9.

Pulmonaria saccharata

Pulmonaria saccharata
JERUSALEM SAGE

◑/☼ ❋ ↔ 16–32 in (40–80 cm)
↕ 12–16 in (30–40 cm)

Native to northern Italy, flowers after foliage is well developed. Spring leaves are small, lance-shaped, spotted, summer leaves larger. Flowers white, or shades of mauve to purple or purple-red. **Argentea Group**, silver-mottled leaves, mauve-blue flowers; '**Dora Bielefeld**', white- or lighter green-spotted leaves, mauve-pink flowers; '**Janet Fisk**', silver-spotted and marbled leaves, purple flowers opening from red buds; '**Leopard**', white-spotted leaves, purplish pink flowers; and '**Mrs Moon**', white-spotted leaves, red-tinted mauve flowers. Zones 3–9.

Pulmonaria vallarsae

☀/◐ ❋ ↔ 20–40 in (50–100 cm)
↑ 12–18 in (30–45 cm)

Northern Italian species. Forms clump of finely hairy, often white-spotted or variegated leaves. First flowers appear with new growth, red-tinted buds open to purple flowers, in early spring–early summer. Zones 6–9.

Pulmonaria Hybrid Cultivars

☀/◐ ❋ ↔ 16–40 in (40–100 cm)
↑ 8–16 in (20–40 cm)

Lungworts hybridize freely, in the wild and in cultivation; many widely grown hybrids. Modern forms tend to have showy variegated foliage and short flower stems. 'Benediction', silver-flecked leaves, mauve-blue flowers; 'Beth's Pink', broad spotted leaves, mauve-pink flowers; 'Blue Pearl', small rounded leaves, light blue flowers; 'High Contrast', silver-gray leaves, with irregular green edges, flowers deep pink ageing to purple-blue; 'Lewis Palmer', white-spotted leaves, purple-blue flowers; 'Margery Fish' ★, silver-mottled foliage, pink flowers ageing to blue; 'Purple Haze', white-spotted leaves, purple flowers; 'Roy Davidson', long silver-spotted leaves, light blue flowers; 'Silver Mist', leaves spotted silvery white, red-pink flowers; 'Silver Streamers', large silver-gray leaves with ruffled edges, pink flowers darkening with age; 'Sissinghurst White', large white-spotted leaves, white flowers, produced early in season; 'Smoky Blue', dark green white-spotted leaves, purplish blue flowers; and 'Trevi Fountain', silver-spotted leaves, open sprays of deep blue flowers. Zones 6–9.

PULSATILLA

PASQUE FLOWER

These beautiful Eurasian and North American relatives of the anemones race into growth in early spring. They are members of the buttercup (Ranunculaceae) family. They form clumps of ferny leaves, which are silvery in most species from a dense covering of fine hairs. Long-stemmed, very graceful, cup- or bell-shaped flowers in a wide color range. Carried singly, the blooms have 5 to 8 petals and a prominent boss of golden stamens. CULTIVATION: Pasque flowers need a seasonal temperate climate. They grow well in woodland conditions but are at their best in rock gardens with sun or part-shade, in gritty, humus-rich, well-drained yet moist soil. Propagate by division when dormant, or raise from seed.

Pulsatilla albana

☀/◐ ❋ ↔ 8 in (20 cm) ↑ 8 in (20 cm)

From alpine meadows of the Caucasus and northeastern Turkey. Finely cut pinnate foliage. Hairy stems and buds; nodding, bell-shaped, yellow flowers, in late spring–early summer. Zones 5–9.

Pulmonaria, Hybrid Cultivar, 'Silver Mist'

Pulsatilla halleri

☀/◐ ❋ ↔ 12 in (30 cm) ↑ 10 in (25 cm)

From mountains of central and southeastern Europe. Densely covered with silky silvery hairs. Blooms often well advanced before finely divided feathery foliage appears. Flowers erect, usually upward-facing, violet to lavender blue. Zones 5–9.

Pulsatilla patens

EASTERN PASQUE FLOWER

☀/◐ ❋ ↔ 8–12 in (20–30 cm) ↑ 6–10 in (15–25 cm)

Found from northern Europe to Siberia and Alaska, USA. Leaves lightly hairy, heavy textured, less finely divided than most silvery species. Flowers quite late in season, purple shades, sometimes with yellow tint, rarely white, stems silky. Zones 4–9.

Pulsatilla pratensis

☀/◐ ❋ ↔ 16 in (40 cm) ↑ 12 in (30 cm)

Found throughout most of Europe. Entire plant covered with dense, silky, silvery hairs. Foliage very finely divided. Pendent, narrow bell-shaped flowers, to 1½ in (40 mm) wide, mauve to deep purple. Spring-flowering. *P. p.* subsp. *bohemica,* small flowers, very dark purple. Zones 5–9.

Pulsatilla vulgaris

Pulsatilla vulgaris

syn. *Anemone pulsatilla*
PASQUE FLOWER

☀/◐ ❋ ↔ 8–16 in (20–40 cm) ↑ 8–15 in (20–38 cm)

From Britain through Europe to Ukraine. Covered in fine, silky, silvery hairs. Very finely divided feathery foliage. Mauve to purple flowers usually upward-facing, open bell-shaped, in spring. 'Alba', white flowers; 'Papageno' (syn. *P. v.* subsp. *grandis* 'Papageno'), mixed color strain; 'Rubra', red flowers. Zones 5–9.

Puya berteroniana

Puya venusta

PUYA

More than 200 species, mainly from the South American Andes,
make up this ground-dwelling genus in the bromeliad (Bromeliaceae) family, most of which prefer colder conditions than other
bromeliads. Many are large plants forming trunks, and are not
often seen in private gardens; they are popular in botanic gardens
in subtropical areas. One species reaches a height of 35 ft (10 m)
in flower; the smallest species reaches only 3 in (8 cm) high. They
form rosettes of narrow-triangular leaves, usually with large spines
along the edges. Flowerheads may be cylindrical or pyramidal
and branched, and the flowers are generally large and showy.
CULTIVATION: Recommended for greenhouse, conservatory, or outdoor cultivation in cool temperate areas; some species will adapt
to warmer areas if kept on the dry side. Water when potting mix
is dry. Extra feeding may speed up their slow-growing habit.
Propagation is by seed or from offsets of most species.

Puya berteroniana
☀ ❄ ↔ 7 ft (2 m) ↑ 15 ft (4.5 m)
From central Chile. Forms trunk with age. Leaves green, narrow-
triangular, strongly toothed edges; form dense rosette. Flower
stem stout, to 10 ft (3 m) high. Flowerhead to 40 in (100 cm)
long and 20 in (50 cm) wide, up to 100 side branches, each with
about 15 large blue-green flowers. Upper part of branches without flowers. Zones 7–9.

Puya chilensis
☀ ❄ ↔ 7 ft (2 m) ↑ 15 ft (4.5 m)
From central Chile. Forms trunk with age. Leaves green, narrow-
triangular, strongly toothed edges; form dense rosette. Stout erect
flower stem to 12 ft (3.5 m) tall. Flowerhead over 40 in (100 cm)
long, up to 100 side branches, each with up to 12 large yellow
flowers. Upper part of branches without flowers. Zones 7–9.

Puya venusta
☀ ❄ ↔ 20 in (50 cm) ↑ 40 in (100 cm)
From coastal Chile. Clump-forming, branching plant. Leaves
gray-green, narrow-triangular, toothed-edged; form dense rosette.

Flower stem stout, bright red. Flowerheads reddish, like pine
cones, at end of some branches, flowers deep violet. Zones 8–9.

QUESNELIA

The 16 species in this genus in the bromeliad (Bromeliaceae)
family are indigenous to southeastern Brazil and fall into two
main groups: one containing plants that form large clumps and
have a flowerhead in the form of an elongated cone with start-
lingly bright, red, erect bracts; the other made up of plants that
are not clump-forming and mostly having an open flowerhead
reminiscent of *Billbergia* but with the petals uniform rather than
opening at an angle. The leaves are green and strap-like, with
some teeth on the edges, forming an open rosette. Petals may be
red, blue, or yellow.
CULTIVATION: Recommended for indoor culture in the greenhouse
or conservatory in cool-temperate areas, or outdoors with protection from direct continuous sunlight and extremes of rain in
warmer areas. Water when soil is dry. Extra feeding is generally
not necessary. Propagation is mainly by offsets.

Quesnelia liboniana
☀ ❅ ↔ 4 in (10 cm) ↑ 32 in (80 cm)
From Brazil's Rio de Janeiro area. Forms offsets on small rhizomes; leaves few, strap-like, few teeth on edges, forming a tube
that soon flares out. Slender flower stem; short cylindrical flowerhead, with about 8 well-separated red flowers emerging at all
angles. Petals are blue. Zones 9–12.

Quesnelia marmorata
☀ ❅ ↔ 4 in (10 cm) ↑ 24 in (60 cm)
From central eastern Brazil. Few stiff, strap-like leaves, dark green
or brown irregular cross-bands and toothed edges, forming tight
tube that flares at top. Flowerhead just emerging from leaf tube,
pyramidal, spreading branches on all sides becoming smaller toward top. Large red bracts below branches tend to droop. Flowers
mainly violet, petals blue. Zones 10–12.

RAMONDA

The 3 species in this small genus in the African violet (Gesneriaceae) family are evergreen, rosette-forming, alpine plants, found
from the mountains of northeastern Spain to the Balkans. The
flowers, held well above the rich green heavily veined leaves in
late spring and early summer, are 4- or 5-petalled, somewhat flat-
faced, and come in white to pink and lavender to violet-blue.
CULTIVATION: These plants are for cool to cold climates only, and
due to their dislike of winter wet they are usually grown in a cool
greenhouse or on their sides in a drystone wall. Propagation is
quite difficult from seed. They are usually propagated by division
or, better still, from leaf cuttings taken in late summer.

Ramonda myconi
syn. *Ramonda pyrenaica*
☀ ❅ ↔ 7–8 in (18–20 cm) ↑ 4–5 in (10–12 cm)
Rosette-forming perennial. Native to northeastern Spain. Ovate,
hairy, crinkled, rich green leaves. Violet-blue 5-petalled flowers, to
1 in (25 mm) across, yellow anthers, in clusters held above leaves, in

late spring–early summer. '**Rosea**', pink-flowered form; a white form is also grown. Zones 6–9.

RAOULIA
SCABWEED

Found in screes or open rocky places from sea level to alpine areas throughout New Zealand, the 20 to 30 species of tiny-leafed, cushion- or mat-forming, evergreen perennials or subshrubs that make up this genus are members of the daisy (Asteraceae) family. The leaves are green or silvery in appearance, caused by minute silky hairs. The flowers are tiny, disc-like, and pale white, cream, or yellow. Many botanists now regard *Raoulia* as an unnatural group and propose that some of the species should go into a distinct genus, *Psychrophyton*.

CULTIVATION: Grow *Raoulia* species in full sun in moist well-drained soil. They will do well in pots, troughs, or rock gardens. Propagate from seed or from sections of the mat (rooted stems).

Raoulia australis
syn. *Raoulia lutescens*
COMMON MAT DAISY, GOLDEN SCABWEED
☼ ❄ ↔ 12 in (30 cm) ↕ ½ in (12 mm)
From New Zealand's South Island. Mat-forming perennial; layers itself as it creeps. Tiny leaves, gray or silver. Yellow flowers, 5 mm wide, in summer. Zones 7–9.

Raoulia eximia
TUTAHUNA, VEGETABLE SHEEP
☼ ❄ ↔ 20 in (50 cm) ↕ 12 in (30 cm)
From New Zealand's South Island. Dense cushion-like perennial, eventually forming large mounds. Tiny flowers, yellowish white. Summer-flowering. These plants resemble sheep sitting down, giving rise to one of the common names. Zones 7–9.

RATIBIDA
CONEFLOWER

This genus in the daisy (Asteraceae) family contains 5 biennial or perennial species that are found throughout North America, from Ontario, Canada, through to New York, Minnesota, South Dakota, Nebraska, south to Georgia and Texas, USA, and into northern Mexico. These plants are stiff and erect, with deeply cut leaves that are covered with rigid hairs. The flowerheads are similar to those of *Rudbeckia* species but have fewer ray florets and a round or cylindrical central disc, unlike the flat disc of the *Rudbeckia* flower-heads. The crushed seed heads have an aromatic anise scent.

Ramonda myconi 'Rosea'

CULTIVATION: Ideal for casual settings, in native flower gardens, or cottage gardens. Plant in full sun in a very well-drained soil. Propagation is from seed, which will self-sow.

Ratibida columnifera
MEXICAN HAT, PRAIRIE CONEFLOWER
☼ ❄ ↔ 18 in (45 cm) ↕ 24 in (60 cm)
Perennial, from North America and Mexico. Hairy gray-green leaves. Flowers bright yellow or brown-purple, in drooping rays; cylindrical or columnar brown floral disc. Summer- to autumn-flowering. Zones 4–9.

Ratibida pinnata
GRAY-HEAD CONEFLOWER, PRAIRIE CONEFLOWER, YELLOW CONEFLOWER
☼ ❄ ↔ 12–18 in (30–45 cm) ↕ 48 in (120 cm)
Perennial from eastern North America. Leaves lance-shaped, blue-green, toothed. Yellow ray flowers, rounded brown disc, from mid-summer to early autumn. Zones 3–8.

Ratibida columnifera, in the wild, Mexico

REHMANNIA
CHINESE FOXGLOVE

This genus of up to 9 species of herbaceous perennials in the fox-glove (Scrophulariaceae) family is native to the woods and hills of China. The foliage is heavily serrated and hairy to sticky. The blooms, produced over a long period, are usually a magenta-pink with patterns of brown and yellow in the throat.
CULTIVATION: Grow these perennials in moisture-retentive but not wet, humus-rich soil in a spot that receives lots of light but not the very hottest sun. Propagate from seed, or from stem cuttings early in the growth cycle, or more usually by division.

Rehmannia elata
syn. *Rehmannia angulata* of gardens
CHINESE FOXGLOVE

☀ ❄ ↔ 20–32 in (50–80 cm) ↕ 40–60 in (100–150 cm)
Vigorous suckering perennial from China. Lobed hairy leaves, to 10 in (25 cm) long, in basal foliage. Slightly drooping trumpet flowers, to 4 in (10 cm) long, heavily spotted in throat, in late spring–summer. Zones 8–10.

REINECKEA

This genus, a member of the family Ruscaceae, contains 1 species of grassy-leafed, rhizomatous, evergreen perennial, and is native to China and Japan. Its prostrate stems form clumps of narrow glossy foliage. Flowering stems, to 6 in (15 cm) in height, bear small fragrant flowers in varying shades of pink.
CULTIVATION: This perennial will do well in half-sun in a rich, moisture-retentive, but well-drained soil. Where summers are cool, flowering may be limited. Propagate from seed or by division.

Reineckea carnea
☀ ❄ ↔ 6–12 in (15–30 cm) ↕ 8 in (20 cm)
Native to China and Japan. Clump-forming perennial. Narrow arching leaves. Pink buds open to near-white flowers, spreading starry petals, in late spring. Small scarlet berries. Zones 7–10.

RESEDA
MIGNONETTE

This genus of some 50 to 60 species of annuals and perennials gives its name to the mignonette (Resedaceae) family. Although mainly from the Mediterranean area, some species come from India, Asia, and East Africa. They have small leaves that can be smooth-edged or lobed to toothed, and bear tiny flowers in up-right spikes that are rarely showy, usually green or white, and in some species sweetly fragrant. All are good bee-attractant plants.
CULTIVATION: These plants will all grow well in a sunny site in fertile, well-drained, and preferably alkaline soil. Propagate from seed planted in position and thin out as seedlings get larger.

Reseda lutea
YELLOW MIGNONETTE

☀ ❄ ↔ 20–27 in (50–70 cm) ↕ 20–27 in (50–70 cm)
From the Mediterranean to Iran. Annual herb; deep roots; many erect, very fast-growing stems; leaves with simple blades or 1 to 3 deep lobes, with or without stalks. Flowers with 4 to 8 white-edged sepals, 4 to 8 yellow petals, each with 2 to 3 lobes, in summer. Erect 3-part capsule contains smooth seed. Zones 7–9.

Reseda luteola
☀ ❄ ↔ 8–12 in (20–30 cm) ↕ 36–48 in (90–120 cm)
From Europe and central Asia. Upright annual or short-lived perennial. Leaves smooth-edged, to 1 in (25 mm) long. Sometimes branched, upright, 24 in (60 cm) tall flower spikes; tiny, yellow-green, unscented flowers, in summer. Zones 6–10.

Reseda odorata
BASTARD ROCKET, MIGNONETTE, SWEET RESEDA

☀ ❄ ↔ 7–8 in (18–20 cm) ↕ 12–24 in (30–60 cm)
Annual from the Mediterranean region. Smooth-edged leaves, occasionally 3-lobed. Loose clusters of highly scented, tiny, greenish white flowers, soft orange stamens, in early summer. Zones 6–10.

RHEUM
RHUBARB

This genus of 50 robust perennials, native to a wide area of temperate Asia, includes several ornamental foliage plants as well as the popular edible rhubarb, and belongs to the knotweed (Polygonaceae) family. The large leaves, which are often wavy-edged or palmately lobed, are borne on stout stalks and form basal clumps. The small greenish white or red tinged flowers are wind-pollinated and borne in large panicles on strong upright stems.

Rehmannia elata

Reineckea carnea

Reseda lutea

Rhodanthe chlorocephala

CULTIVATION: Ornamental *Rheum* species make excellent feature plants. They do best when grown in sun or part-shade in a rich, deep, moisture-retentive but well-drained soil. Edible rhubarb should be planted at a 30–36 in (75–90 cm) spacing in a deeply cultivated soil with plenty of compost added. Plants require plenty of moisture but should be well-drained. Propagate from seed or by division; cultivars are propagated by division of the crown.

Rheum australe
syn. *Rheum emodi*
HIMALAYAN RHUBARB, RED-VEINED PIE PLANT
☼/◖ ❋ ↔ 5 ft (1.5 m) ↑ 5 ft (1.5 m)
From the Himalayas. Leaves rounded or broadly oblong, prominently veined, wavy edges. Stout red-tinged flowering stalks; dense clusters of small white to red flowers in summer. Zones 6–9.

Rheum palmatum
☼/◖ ❋ ↔ 5 ft (1.5 m) ↑ 5–8 ft (1.5–2.4 m)
Native to northwestern China. Deeply lobed and toothed leaves, to 40 in (100 cm) wide, purplish red when young. Fluffy panicles of small pink flowers, on tall stems, in summer. *R. p.* var. *tanguticum*, more robust, very deeply lobed leaves. *R. p.* 'Atrosanguineum', cerise flowers, leaves open vivid red; and 'Bowles' Crimson', leaves crimson beneath. Zones 6–9.

RHODANTHE
STRAWFLOWER
This genus in the daisy (Asteraceae) family, one of several in the complex *Helichrysum* group, was extensively revised in the early 1990s and is now considered to be exclusively Australian. The 40 species in the genus are annuals, perennials, and small shrubs with simple, narrow, light green to silver-gray leaves. They are rather sprawling plants, grown for their long-lasting flowers, which are made colorful by dry papery bracts enclosing the yellowish flowerheads. Some species have long-stemmed flowerheads that last well when cut. Some are ephemeral plants native to desert regions, remaining in the ground as seeds for many years ready to burst into a carpet of bloom with the arrival of rain.
CULTIVATION: Hardiness varies but most are surprisingly tough and are ideal for dry banks or rockeries. Plant in full sun with light, gritty, very free-draining soil. These plants will tolerate poor soil. Propagate from seed or cuttings. Some will self-layer.

Rhodanthe chlorocephala
syn. *Helipterum roseum*
☼ ◿ ↔ 8–12 in (20–30 cm) ↑ 12–24 in (30–60 cm)
Annual from southwestern Australia; usually erect or rounded. Narrow gray-green leaves, around 1 in (25 mm) long. Flowerheads 1–2 in (25–50 mm) wide, white to pink papery bracts around a conspicuous soft yellow disc, from late spring to early summer; winter-flowering in mild areas. *R. c.* subsp. *rosea*, flowerheads with bright pink ray florets; *R. c.* subsp. *splendida*, white flowerheads with many ray florets. Zones 9–11.

Rhodanthe manglesii
syn. *Helipterum manglesii*
SWAN RIVER EVERLASTING
☼ ❋ ↔ 6–12 in (15–30 cm) ↑ 12–18 in (30–45 cm)
Western Australian annual. Erect stems; pointed oval to narrow heart-shaped, gray-green to blue-green leaves, to 2 in (5 cm) long. Many white to pink flowerheads, 1¼ in (30 mm) wide, in spring or after rain. 'Sutton's Rose', attractive cultivar. Zones 8–11.

RHODANTHEMUM
A mainly alpine Eurasian and North African genus of some 15 to 20 species that was established with the revision of *Chrysanthemum* in the 1960s to 1990s, and belongs to the daisy (Asteraceae) family. These shrubby perennials have ferny, usually silver-gray foliage, sometimes in whorls or loose rosettes, and develop into dense mounds. In spring and early summer they are covered in wiry-stemmed flowerheads with white ray florets, often pink-tinted, around a yellow disc. In mild areas flowers occur less heavily throughout the year.
CULTIVATION: Although generally frost tolerant, few *Rhodanthemum* species will withstand prolonged cold damp winter conditions. They are best grown in an alpine house or dry winter climate. Plant in full sun or half-sun in gritty free-draining soil with a little added humus. Water in summer and feed very lightly. Propagation is from seed or from small basal cuttings of non-flowering shoots.

Rodgersia podophylla

Rhodanthemum gayanum

syns *Chrysanthemum gayanum, C. mawii, Pyrethropsis gayana*
☼ ❀ ↔ 24–40 in (60–100 cm) ↕ 8–12 in (20–30 cm)
Low-growing perennial subshrub. Native to Morocco and Algeria. Forms dense spreading cushion; lacy, finely divided, dark
green, glossy foliage. Abundant, bright pink, daisy-like flowers,
yellow to burgundy centers, from winter to spring. Zones 8–10.

Rhodanthemum hosmariense

syns *Chrysanthemum hosmariense,*
Pyrethropsis hosmariensis
MOROCCAN DAISY
☼ ❀ ↔ 12–16 in (30–40 cm)
↕ 4–8 in (10–20 cm)
Spreading, drought-resistant, bushy perennial
herb. Native to Morocco's Atlas Mountains.
Forms compact cushion; finely cut silvery
gray leaves. Scaly decorative floral buttons
in winter open to white daisy-like flowers
with yellow centers, from spring to autumn,
scattered blooms throughout year. Zones 8–10.

Rodgersia pinnata 'Rosea'

RODGERSIA

The 6 large perennial species of this genus are members of the
saxifrage (Saxifragaceae) family. Found naturally among the woodlands and streamsides of temperate Asia, these plants have a preference for damp conditions. They have large pinnate leaves with
toothed edges and are grown primarily as foliage plants. Their
astilbe-like plumes of tiny flowers are also attractive, although
they are quite short lived. The foliage develops quickly in spring,
and the flowers, which are white, cream, or pink in color, open
at about the time the leaves reach their maximum size.
CULTIVATION: Plant *Rodgersia* species in a position in part-shade
or full shade in cool, moist, humus-rich soil. Although these
plants prefer constant moisture, they are not happy in stagnant
boggy conditions and often do better when planted alongside
moving water rather than ponds. Propagation is from seed or
by division when dormant.

Rodgersia aesculifolia

☼ ❀ ↔ 3–7 ft (0.9–2 m) ↕ 5–7 ft (1.5–2 m)
From China. Large palmate leaves, to over 16 in (40 cm) long,
reminiscent of horse chestnut *(Aesculus)* foliage. White flowers,
in dense panicles, to 24 in (60 cm) long, in summer. Zones 5–9.

Rodgersia pinnata

☼ ❀ ↔ 3–7 ft (0.9–2 m) ↕ 32–48 in (80–120 cm)
Native to southwestern China. Leaves partly pinnate, with 5 to
9 dark green, deeply veined leaflets, to 8 in (20 cm) long. Deep
pink to red, rarely white, flowers, in long-stemmed panicles held
well clear of foliage, in summer. 'Rosea', deep pink flowers;
'Superba' ★, bronze- to purple-tinted foliage, large panicles of
pink flowers. Zones 6–9.

Rodgersia podophylla

☼ ❀ ↔ 3–7 ft (0.9–2 m) ↕ 32–48 in (80–120 cm)
Native to Japan and Korea. Broad palmate leaves, usually 5-lobed,
to over 12 in (30 cm) long and wide, with lobes at tips. Foliage
reddens in autumn, sometimes brilliantly. White flowers, in
heads to 12 in (30 cm) long, in summer. Zones 6–9.

Rodgersia sambucifolia

☼ ❀ ↔ 24–48 in (60–120 cm) ↕ 24–36 in (60–90 cm)
Perennial from China. Pinnate leaves, to over 12 in (30 cm)
in length; up to 11 deeply veined, finely hairy, dark green leaflets. Flat-topped, often rather open panicles
of white to light pink flowers. Summer-
flowering. Zones 6–9.

ROMNEYA

This is a genus of only 2 species in the
poppy (Papaveraceae) family, native to western North America and Mexico, both with
glaucous stems and deeply cut leaves. The
flowers are large, 6-petalled, white and
poppy-like, with a central mass of golden
yellow stamens. *Romneya* species are sometimes difficult to establish but once settled
they spread quickly by underground stems,
so should be allowed plenty of space.
CULTIVATION: These attractive plants thrive in a warm sunny
position and are quite frost hardy. They prefer a fertile and well-
drained soil and resent being transplanted. Propagation is from
seed or from cuttings.

Romneya coulteri

CALIFORNIA TREE POPPY
☼ ❀ ↔ 7 ft (2 m) ↕ 8 ft (2.4 m)
Small to medium-sized shrubby perennial from southern
California, USA. Persistent stems; leaves silvery gray, finely
cut. Flowers solitary, buds smooth, slightly conical, opening to
large white flowers, crumpled crape-like petals, in late summer
to mid-autumn. Cultivars include 'Butterfly', smaller flowers,
pure white ruffled petals; 'White Cloud', large white flowers,
silvery gray leaves. Zones 7–10.

RUDBECKIA

BLACK-EYED SUSAN, CONEFLOWER

This North American genus contains 15 species of perennials in the daisy (Asteraceae) family. They are popular in gardens for their great hardiness, ease of cultivation, and late-season flower display. Most are fairly bulky plants, over 4 ft (1.2 m) tall, and carry masses of large golden yellow daisies, usually with dark brown to black disc florets. Available in dwarf, double-flowered, and variously colored forms, they bloom from late summer until cut back by frost.

CULTIVATION: Plant in a sunny open position in moist well-drained soil. Deadhead to encourage continued blooming. Mildew can occur but usually only late in the season. Propagate by division, from basal cuttings or seed.

Romneya coulteri

Rudbeckia fulgida

BLACK-EYED SUSAN, ORANGE CONEFLOWER

☼/◐ ❈ ↔ 24–48 in (60–120 cm) ↑ 40 in (100 cm)

Perennial from southeastern USA. Lance-shaped leaves, to over 4 in (10 cm) long, often bristly. Flowerheads to almost 3 in (8 cm) wide, ray florets yellow to orange, disc florets dark purple-brown, in summer–autumn. Several natural varieties, including: *R. f.* **var.** *deamii*, 24 in (60 cm) tall, hairy pointed oval leaves; *R. f.* **var.** *speciosa*, 36 in (90 cm) tall, hairy elongated lance-shaped leaves; and *R. f.* **var.** *sullivantii*, 36 in (90 cm) tall, pointed oval leaves often downy, flowerheads to 4 in (10 cm) wide; 'Goldsturm', to 24 in (60 cm) tall, slightly larger flower-heads. Zones 4–9.

Rudbeckia 'Herbstsonne'

syn. *Rudbeckia* 'Autumn Sun'

☼ ❈ ↔ 3 ft (0.9 m) ↑ 6 ft (1.8 m)

Vigorous *R. nitida* hybrid; perennial with strongly erect habit. Flowerheads to well over 4 in (10 cm) wide, yellow ray florets, tall yellow-green cone. Summer- to autumn-flowering. Zones 3–10.

Rudbeckia hirta

BLACK-EYED SUSAN

☼/◐ ❈ ↔ 32–48 in (80–120 cm)
↑ 5–7 ft (1.5–2 m)

Biennial or short-lived perennial, native to central USA. Dwarf forms often treated as annuals. Narrow, 4 in (10 cm) long, lance-shaped leaves, toothed. Flowerheads to nearly 4 in (10 cm) wide, ray florets yellow, disc florets purple-brown, in summer–autumn. Cultivars and seedling strains include 'Becky Mix', 10 in (25 cm) tall, mixed color dwarf seedling strain with yellow-, orange-, and red-flowered forms; 'Irish Eyes' ★, olive green disc florets; 'Marmalade', 18 in (45 cm) tall,

golden orange ray florets; 'Rustic Dwarfs', 24 in (60 cm) tall, flowers in warm shades of gold, orange, terracotta, and red-brown; 'Toto', 10 in (25 cm) tall, golden yellow ray florets, large deep purple-brown disc florets. Zones 4–9.

Rudbeckia laciniata

CUT-LEAF CONEFLOWER

☼/◐ ❈ ↔ 3–7 ft (0.9–2 m) ↑ 7–10 ft (2–3 m)

Vigorous North American perennial. Leaves deeply lobed to pinnate, bluish-green, often with hairy undersides. Flowerheads over 5 in (12 cm) wide, ray floret yellow, disc florets yellow-green, in late summer–autumn. 'Gold-quelle' (syn. 'Gold Drop'), 30 in (75 cm) tall, large, yellow, fully double flowerheads; 'Hortensia' (syn. 'Golden Glow'), 6 ft (1.8 m) tall, yellow double flowerheads. Zones 3–9.

Rudbeckia nitida

SHINY CONEFLOWER

☼/◐ ❈ ↔ 32–48 in (80–120 cm) ↑ 5–7 ft (1.5–2 m)

Perennial, native to North America. Leaves to 6 in (15 cm) long, deeply lobed, almost to midrib. Flowerheads to 4 in (10 cm) wide, ray florets yellow, disc florets yellow-green, in late summer–autumn. Zones 3–9.

Rudbeckia occidentalis

☼/◐ ❈ ↔ 32–48 in (80–120 cm) ↑ 5–7 ft (1.5–2 m)

Perennial, native to western USA. Pointed oval leaves, to over 4 in (10 cm) long, sometimes toothed. Flowerheads to over 3 in (8 cm) wide, yellow ray florets, central cone brown-black, to over 2 in (5 cm) high. Summer-flowering. 'Green Wizard', no ray florets but elongated bright green sepals around a large near-black disc. Zones 7–10.

Rudbeckia hirta

RUELLIA

Mostly from tropical and subtropical regions, with a few species in temperate North America, this is a genus containing some 150 species of evergreen perennials and soft-stemmed shrubs, belonging to the acanthus (Acanthaceae) family. They are grown for their showy funnelform flowers, usually red, pink, or mauve, that may occur singly, or in dense terminal panicles or axillary clusters. The attractive, smooth-edged, oblong to lance-shaped leaves have prominent veins.
CULTIVATION: Although some species from temperate America are quite frost hardy, most need a warm climate and a fertile, moist, well-drained soil in partial shade. In cooler areas they are grown indoors or in a greenhouse. Water potted specimens adequately during the growing season and keep just moist during winter. Trim excess growth regularly and especially after flowering to maintain density of foliage. Propagation is from seed or softwood cuttings in spring.

Ruellia brittoniana
COMMON RUELLIA
↔ 18–24 in (45–60 cm) ↑ 24–36 in (60–90 cm)
Upright evergreen perennial shrub from Mexico and southwestern USA. Purple fleshy stems; lower branches drooping over with age and taking root. Narrow, sword-shaped, serrated, dark green leaves, prominent purple veins. Funnel-shaped, purple or blue, petunia-like flowers, 2 in (5 cm) long, in leaf axils, from mid-spring until first autumn frosts. Dies back in winter and self-seeds aggressively. 'Alba' (syn. 'Clean White Katie'), low-growing form, up to 8 in (20 cm) high, white flowers throughout summer; 'Chi Chi', 24–36 in (60–90 cm) tall, pale pink flowers throughout summer; 'Katie' (dwarf blue bells), low-growing form, 6–8 in (15–20 cm) high, purple flowers all summer; 'Texas Blue', up to 10 in (25 cm) tall, purple summer flowers. Zones 8–11.

Ruellia makoyana
MONKEY PLANT, TRAILING VELVET PLANT
↔ 15–18 in (38–45 cm) ↑ 6–12 in (15–30 cm)
Perennial from Brazil. Spreading habit; trailing branching stems. Variegated leaves, 2–3 in (5–8 cm) long, velvet-textured, veined

Ruscus aculeatus

white above and purple beneath. Brilliant reddish purple trumpet-shaped flowers, to 2 in (5 cm) wide, growing from leaf axils, all year round, mostly autumn–spring. Zones 10–12.

RUMEX
DOCK, SORREL

This genus, comprising some 200 species of annuals, biennials, and often tap-rooted perennials, belongs to the knotweed (Polygonaceae) family. Its members are distributed worldwide, and are found in most countries with temperate climates. The leaves are usually basal and the typically small flowers are produced in terminal racemes or spikes. The seeds are enclosed in a papery membrane that allows them to float. Although some species are ornamental and some are edible, this genus also includes some dreadfully weedy species that have hitchhiked around the world with human travelers.
CULTIVATION: Most *Rumex* species do best in a deep, fertile, and moist to even damp soil in full sun. Propagation is usually from seed, which will often self-sow; root cuttings are another option.

Rumex sanguineus
BLOODY DOCK, RED-VEINED DOCK
↔ 12–36 in (30–90 cm) ↑ 20–40 in (50–100 cm)
Clumping species. Native to Europe, southwestern Asia, and northern Africa. Dark stems; lance-shaped bright green leaves, to 6 in (15 cm) long, beetroot red veins. Panicles of tiny green flowers, from early to mid-summer. Brown seeds. Zones 6–10.

Rumex vesicarius
syn. *Acetosa vesicaria*
ROSY DOCK
↔ 6–8 in (15–20 cm) ↑ 8–10 in (20–25 cm)
Annual from northern Africa and southwest Asia. Fleshy leaves, spearhead-shaped, to ¾ in (18 mm) long. Tiny flowers, deep pink, in panicles, in late spring. Conspicuous fruits, rose pink, bladder-like. A weed in arid southern Australia. Zones 6–10.

RUSCUS

This genus, containing about 6 species of evergreen subshrubs from the Mediterranean region, belongs to the family Ruscaceae. The plants form clumps, spreading slowly by underground rhizomes. Their leaves are more correctly called "cladodes," which are flattened stems that function as a leaf. The real leaf is a small protuberance on the surface of the cladode, from whence emerge the tiny greenish or white starry flowers. These are followed by red pea-sized fruits if both male and female plants are present. Some forms appear to be hermaphrodite.
CULTIVATION: These hardy plants perform well in dry shade. Grow in well-drained soil in a position in full sun to half-sun. Propagate from seed or by division.

Ruscus aculeatus
BUTCHER'S BROOM
↔ 40 in (100 cm) ↑ 30–40 in (75–100 cm)
From southern Europe and the Mediterranean region. Clump-forming; spreads by rhizomes. Small, oval-shaped, leathery, dark

green cladodes, ¾–1¼ in (18–30 mm) long, prickly tips. Bright red berries in summer–winter. Zones 6–10.

Ruscus hypoglossum
☼/◗ ❄ ↔ 40 in (100 cm)
↕ 18–26 in (45–65 cm)
Native to southern Europe and elsewhere in the Mediterranean region. Clumping subshrub; spreads by rhizomes. Oval mid-green cladodes, to 4 in (10 cm) long. Arching stems; green flowers; red fruit. Flowers and fruit borne on a cladode under a tongue-like leaf. Zones 7–11.

SAGINA
PEARLWORT

This Northern Hemisphere genus contains approximately 20 species of annual and perennial, ground-

Sagina subulata

covering, mat-forming plants, which are found growing on rocky outcrops in the wild. Members of the pink (Caryophyllaceae) family, a great number of the species in this genus are garden weeds, and can prove extremely difficult to eradicate because of their highly developed reproductive system. Their fine linear leaves are arranged in pairs, and they quickly form dense mats of growth that cover both soil and rocky areas. Tiny white 4- or 5- petalled flowers are typically borne in spring and summer. CULTIVATION: Pearlworts do not like prolonged periods of hot dry weather; they prefer low temperatures and cool free-draining soils, with full sun or part-shade. Some of the golden forms of pearlwort will die if temperatures exceed 86°F (30°C). These plants can be propagated very easily, either from seed in spring or by division at any time of year.

Sagina subulata
GOLDEN PEARLWORT
☼/◗ ❄ ↔ 12 in (30 cm) ↕ 1 in (25 mm)
Mat-forming perennial. Native to central Europe. Soft foliage; forms dense ground-covering mounds; leaves bright green, tiny. Solitary white flowers in summer. 'Aurea', lime green to canary yellow foliage. Zones 4–7.

SAGITTARIA
ARROWHEAD

This genus of some 30 mostly perennial species is distributed throughout the world, but is particularly well represented in the Americas. It belongs to the family Alismataceae. Sagittaria species are aquatic plants, usually with flowers of a single sex on the same plant. Some have rhizomes or runners; many have tubers, which are sometimes edible. The leaves are smooth-edged, and are borne below, on, or above the water. The flower-heads are erect, floating, or submerged, in racemes or panicles,

rarely umbel-like. The 3-petalled flowers are white, sometimes with a pink spot. Fruits are compressed achenes, with a con-spicuous dorsal wing and sometimes lateral wings. CULTIVATION: Sagittaria species are grown as marshy garden or pond-edge plants. They can also be grown in deep fast-flowing water and will tolerate light shade. Weighted tubers thrown into water to 24 in (60 cm) deep will grow well. Propagation is by division in spring.

Sagittaria graminea
☼ ❄ ↔ 12 in (30 cm) ↕ 20 in (50 cm)
Cormous aquatic perennial. Native to eastern USA. Narrow, strap-like, submerged leaves, emergent leaves being wider and pointed. Upright flowering stems; whorls of white 3-petalled male flowers above small, green, petal-less female flowers. Summer-flowering. S. g. var. platyphylla, flowers with longer beaks. Zones 6–12.

SAINTPAULIA
AFRICAN VIOLET

This genus of 20 perennials from tropical East Africa is a mem-ber of the African violet (Gesneriaceae) family. Only a few species are cultivated, with the majority of those grown being hybrids or cultivars. They are soft-stemmed rosette-forming plants, generally low-growing, with finely hairy, rounded leaves that have toothed edges and long stalks. The velvety 5-petalled flowers are produced in clusters at the center of the rosettes throughout the year. CULTIVATION: Rarely grown outdoors, even in the tropics, African violets are popular pot plants that prefer constant temperatures, moderate to high humidity, and fertile, moist, humus-rich soil. They need bright but not sunny conditions. Propagate from leaf-stalk cuttings. The seed is very fine, and is cultured rather like orchid seed.

Saintpaulia, Hybrid Cultivar, 'Patty'

Saintpaulia ionantha

AFRICAN VIOLET, USAMBARA VIOLET

☀ ✝ ↔8–16 in (20–40 cm) ↑4–10 in (10–25 cm)

Perennial, native to Tanzania. Rounded to heart-shaped, downy, wavy-edged or softly toothed leaves. Sprays of flowers held above the foliage, 8 to 10 blooms per head. Flowers pale lavender to purple or white, with violet throat. Zones 11–12.

Saintpaulia shumensis

☀ ✝ ↔6–10 in (15–25 cm)

↑2–6 in (5–15 cm)

Perennial, native to Tanzania. Slightly glossy, rounded, hairy, serrated to toothed leaves, undersides often red-tinted. Heads of up to 5 flowers, to over 2 in (5 cm) wide, white to pale mauve, sometimes with darker markings. Zones 11–12.

Saintpaulia Hybrid Cultivars

☀ ✝ ↔4–12 in (10–30 cm)

↑2–8 in (5–20 cm)

All the plants in this group are commonly known as hybrids, but most of the widely grown and popular African violets are in fact cultivars of *S. ionantha* (although some are true hybrids between *S. ionantha* and other species, such as *S. shumensis*). Compact, lavishly foliaged, long-flowering plants; attractive flowers range in color from mainly pink to purple, but may also come in white, in near-red shades, and in yellow. Hybrids and cultivars include 'Akira', lush dark foliage, deep crimson flowers; 'Chantiana', dwarf form, bright pink double flowers; 'Chimera Monique', dwarf form, white flowers, dark purple edges; 'Concord', deep maroon flowers, white edges; 'Diana', very dark foliage, deep red velvety flowers; 'Dorothy', pink flowers, fine white edges; 'Emi', very profuse pale mauve flowers, light edges; 'Hisako', deep purple-blue flowers, fine white edges; 'Irish Flirt', white flowers suffused with green, double; 'Jolita', dwarf form, lavender double flowers; 'Melodie Kimi', purple upper petal, white lower petals with broad purple edges; 'Milky Way Trail', pure white flowers; 'Optimara Colorado', bright purplish red flowers; 'Patty', purple-red and white

flowers; 'Rococo Pink', semi-double, dusky dark pink flowers; 'Shades of Autumn', cream variegated foliage, ruffled pink and mauve flowers, semi-double; 'Zoja', purple-blue flowers, white edges, semi-double. Zones 11–12.

SALPIGLOSSIS

This genus containing 2 species of annuals or short-lived perennials is a member of the nightshade (Solanaceae) family. Natives of the southern and central Andes, they are small upright plants with alternate, simple linear to elliptical, dark green leaves with finely toothed edges. The stems and foliage are rather sticky to the touch. The petunia-like flowers are funnel-shaped and 5-lobed; they are borne singly in the leaf axils near the stem tips, and are strikingly colored and patterned, often velvety-textured. Seedling strains in a range of sizes and colors are widely available.

CULTIVATION: Treated as annuals, *Salpiglossis* species are best grown in an area with cool moist summer conditions. Plant in a sunny position with fertile, moist, well-drained soil, and water well. They make excellent cut flowers and are useful for border planting. Taller plants may need staking. In mild almost frost-free regions these species can be overwintered. They are usually propagated by seed sown in situ.

Salpiglossis sinuata, Festival Strain

Salpiglossis sinuata

PAINTED TONGUE

☼/◑ ❄ ↔8–12 in (20–30 cm)

↑16–24 in (40–60 cm)

Annual, biennial, or short-lived perennial, usually treated as an annual. Native of Chile. Narrow, dark green, sticky leaves to 4 in (10 cm) long, often toothed, sometimes lobed. Heads of funnel-shaped flowers, to 2 in (5 cm) wide, yellow to reddish purple, darker veins and markings, in summer–autumn. Mixed color seedling strains include **Bolero Hybrids**, 12 in (30 cm) tall, wide color range; **Casino Mixed**, 12 in (30 cm) tall, wide color range with contrasting veining; **Emperor Royal Series**, 24 in (60 cm) tall, large petunia-like flowers, conspicuously veined; and **Festival Strain**, dark red-maroon flowers. Zones 8–11.

SALVIA

SAGE

The largest genus in the mint (Lamiaceae) family, *Salvia* contains annuals, perennials, and softwooded evergreen shrubs. They grow in habitats ranging from coastal to alpine; over half the 900 or so species are native to the Americas. The leaves are opposite and carried on squared hairy stems, and are aromatic when crushed. The flowers are tubular, with the petals split into 2 straight or flaring lips. Colors may be shades of blue to purple and pink to red, as well as white and some yellows.

CULTIVATION: Shrubby sages grow in a range of soils, but dislike heavy wet soil. Most do best in full sun; all require a well-drained situation. Prune in spring to remove straggly, bare, and frost-damaged stems. Propagate shrubby species from softwood cuttings in the growing season. Seed of all species can be sown in spring.

Salvia argentea
SILVER SAGE

☼ ❄ ↔ 24–36 in (60–90 cm)
↕ 24–36 in (60–90 cm)
Perennial, native to southern Europe. Large, woolly, silvery-looking leaves form flat rosette up to 36 in (90 cm) wide on young plants. Tall candelabra-like stems; white flowers produced in second year. Pinch out developing flower stem to promote foliage growth. Zones 8–11.

Salvia blepharophylla
EYELASH-LEAFED SAGE

☼ ⚘ ↔ 20–27 in (50–70 cm)
↕ 8–12 in (20–30 cm)
Native to Mexico. Mat-forming perennial, spreads by runners. Glossy green oval leaves, edged with tiny hairs; tubular flowers, orange-red, in early summer–late autumn. Zones 9–11.

Salvia chiapensis
CHIAPAS SAGE

☼/☀ ⚘ ↔ 16–24 in (40–60 cm) ↕ 16–24 in (40–60 cm)
Perennial, native to Mexico. Glossy olive green leaves to 3 in (8 cm) in length. Cerise-pink flowers, velvety green calyces. Long-flowering in mild climates. Zones 9–11.

Salvia coccinea
syn. *Salvia coccinea* var. *pseudococcinea*
TEXAS SAGE, TROPICAL SAGE

☼ ⚘ ↔ 20–32 in (50–80 cm) ↕ 40 in (100 cm)
Annual or short-lived shrub from tropical South America; in mild climates may be perennial, elsewhere treated as annual. Mostly triangular, hairy leaves, scalloped edges. Flowers usually scarlet, may be red, pink, or white. '**Lady in Red**', red flowers. Zones 9–12.

Salvia coccinea

Salvia discolor
ANDEAN SILVER SAGE

☼/☀ ⚘ ↔ 32–40 in (80–100 cm) ↕ 32–40 in (80–100 cm)
Perennial from Peru. White, wiry, sprawling stems; leaves green above, silver below. Dark purple to navy blue flowers, green calyces and silver bracts, in late summer–early autumn. Zones 9–11.

Salvia dorisiana
FRUIT-SCENTED SAGE, PEACH SAGE

☼ ⚘ ↔ 36 in (90 cm) ↕ 36–48 in (90–120 cm)
From Honduras; hairy heavily branched plant; long velvety leaves. Spikes of bright pink loosely tubular flowers, 2 in (5 cm) long, in winter. Flowers and leaves scented; flowers attract hummingbirds. Zones 10–12.

Salvia elegans
PINEAPPLE SAGE

☼ ❄ ↔ 3 ft (0.9 m) ↕ 6 ft (1.8 m)
From high mountain regions of Central Mexico and Guatemala. Perennial or sub-shrub; shorter growth habit in cold areas. Light green leaves, soft and downy, finely serrated edges. Crushed leaves have distinctive pineapple aroma. Small, narrow, scarlet-red flowers in well-spaced whorls, from spring to autumn. Flowers attract hummingbirds. '**Scarlet Pineapple**' (syn. *S. rutilans*), stronger pineapple scent than the species, larger flowers. Zones 8–11.

Salvia farinacea
MEALY SAGE

☼ ⚘ ↔ 24 in (60 cm) ↕ 36–48 in (90–120 cm)
Popular perennial, often treated as an annual, from Texas and New Mexico, USA. Leaves oval, green, glossy. Flowers at ends of stems in shades of blue, purple, or white; dusted with flour-like substance. Cultivars include '**Strata**', shorter habit, blue flowers, mealy white stem and calyces; '**Victoria**', blue flowers, blue stems and calyces; '**Victoria Blue**', shorter habit, flowers deeper blue, larger. Zones 9–11.

Salvia dorisiana

Salvia elegans

Salvia farinacea (purple flowers)

Salvia fulgens
CARDINAL SAGE

☼ ✂ ↔ 30 in (75 cm) ↕ 48 in (120 cm)

Perennial subshrub. Native of Mexico. Woody-stemmed and shrubby in mild climates. Ovate to poplar-shaped leaves, cleft at base, toothed edges, downy undersides. Spikes of 2 to 6 bright red flowers, densely coated with soft hairs, in summer. Zones 9–10.

Salvia gesneriiflora
☼ ✂ ↔ 10 in (25 cm) ↕ 26 in (65 cm)

Perennial shrub or subshrub occurring from Mexico to Colombia. Dense mound of hairy, somewhat wrinkled, ovate leaves with toothed edges. Flower spikes to 8 in (20 cm) long; orange-red flowers, 2 in (5 cm) long, resembling those of *Columnea* species, in summer–autumn. 'Tequila', large shrub, scarlet flowers, black calyx. Zones 9–11.

Salvia greggii
AUTUMN SAGE

☼ ✂ ↔ 12–36 in (30–90 cm)
↕ 12–36 in (30–90 cm)

Variable species from Texas, USA, and Mexico. Hybridizes freely with related *S. microphylla*. Small leathery leaves, usually smooth. Flowers usually red or shades of pink, purple, and white, in summer–late autumn. Cultivars named for flower color include 'Alba', 'Iced Lemon', 'Peach', and 'Raspberry Royale'. Zones 9–11.

Salvia guaranitica ★
syns *Salvia ambigens, S. concolor*
ANISE-SCENTED SAGE

☼ ❄ ↔ 16–27 in (40–70 cm) ↕ 4–5 ft (1.2–1.5 m)

South American perennial, suckering lightly to form large clumps. Flowers on 10 in (25 cm) long spike, true blue with green calyces, in early summer–autumn. 'Black and Blue', shorter cultivar, less

Salvia involucrata

spreading, blue flowers, almost black calyces; 'Blue Enigma', shorter cultivar, earlier flowering, deep blue flowers, green calyces; 'Costa Rica Blue', tall cultivar, violet-blue flowers, yellow-green calyces. Zones 8–11.

Salvia indica
☼ ✂ ↔ 24 in (60 cm) ↕ 24–36 in (60–90 cm)

Perennial, native to the Middle East. Hairy gray leaves, edges scalloped; forms mound of basal foliage. Tall spikes of purple flowers, white markings on bottom lip. Spring-flowering. May die down during warmer months. Zones 9–11.

Salvia involucrata
ROSELEAF SAGE

☼/◐ ✂ ↔ 5 ft (1.5 m) ↕ 5 ft (1.5 m)

Perennial from Mexico. Some wood at base. Purplish green leaves. Beetroot red flowers and calyces. Summer- to autumn-flowering. 'Bethellii', more compact, sometimes suckering, large heart-shaped leaves, flowers sugar pink. Zones 9–11.

Salvia leucantha
MEXICAN BUSH SAGE, VELVET SAGE

☼ ✂ ↔ 36 in (90 cm) ↕ 36 in (90 cm)

Native to Mexico and tropical America. Woolly stems; soft, narrow, wrinkled leaves, dull green, thickly felted beneath. White or purple flowers; purple velvety calyces, in late summer. 'Midnight' (syn. 'Purple Velvet'), purple flowers. Zones 9–11.

Salvia microphylla
LITTLE-LEAFED SAGE

☼ ❄ ↔ 3 ft (0.9 m) ↕ 4 ft (1.2 m)

Variable species, widespread in its native southern USA and Mexico. Slightly hairy serrated-edged leaves; blackcurrant-like aroma when crushed. Flower color variable, shades of pink, red, and deep purple, in summer–autumn. *S. m.* var. *microphylla*, crimson flowers, heavily blooming; 'La Foux', shrubby, glossy green oval leaves, flowers hot pink to red with purple stems and calyces. *S. m.* 'Coral', deep salmon pink flowers; 'Huntington Red', bright scarlet flowers; 'Kew Red', deep red flowers; 'La Trinidad Pink', bright pink to magenta flowers; 'Newby Hall', vivid deep scarlet flowers; 'Pink Blush', magenta-pink flowers; 'San Carlos Festival', continual display of crimson flowers. Zones 8–11.

Salvia nemorosa
BALKAN CLARY, STEPPE SAGE

☼ ❄ ↔ 12–24 in (30–60 cm)
↕ 24–36 in (60–90 cm)

Perennial found from Europe to central Asia. Simple, oval to oblong, wrinkled, green

Salvia leucantha

Salvia patens

Salvia roemeriana

Salvia × sylvestris 'Mainacht'

leaves. Racemes of mauve to purple flowers, sometimes white to pink, in summer–autumn. **'Lubecca'** (syn. *S. × superba* 'Lubecca'), dwarf cultivar, gray-green leaves, tall spikes of mauve flowers with rich burgundy bracts, in spring; **'Ostfriesland'** (syn. 'East Friesland'), vivid violet-blue flowers, slightly taller than 'Lubecca', in late spring. Zones 5–10.

Salvia patens
GENTIAN SAGE

↔ 12–24 in (30–60 cm) ↕ 12–24 in (30–60 cm)
Perennial from Mexico. Dies back to tubers in winter. Oval green leaves to 8 in (20 cm) long. Spikes of gentian blue flowers, in pairs, 12 in (30 cm) long, green calyces, in summer–autumn. **'Cambridge Blue'**, sky blue flowers. Zones 9–11.

Salvia pratensis
MEADOW CLARY, MEADOW SAGE

↔ 12 in (30 cm) ↕ 36 in (90 cm)
Perennial of meadows across Europe. Basal clump of rich green wrinkled leaves with irregular edges. Violet flowers (also blue, pink, and white forms), brown calyces, green bracts, in spring. **Haematodes Group** (syn. *S. haematodes*), large erect sprays of pale lilac-blue flowers, reddish brown stems, in summer; **'Indigo'**, superb indigo blue flowers in early summer. Zones 4–10.

Salvia przewalskii

↔ 12–24 in (30–60 cm)
↕ 12–24 in (30–60 cm)
Chinese species; forms basal clump of yellow-green foliage. Some leaves grow to 12 in (30 cm) long. Much-branched stems; flowers purplish red, reddish brown calyces, in summer. Zones 8–11.

Salvia roemeriana
CEDAR SAGE

↔ 12 in (30 cm) ↕ 12 in (30 cm)
Small perennial. Native to Arizona and Texas, USA, and Mexico. Rounded geranium-like leaves. Bright red flowers on 8 in (20 cm) long stalks, in summer. Zones 8–11.

Salvia spathacea
CRIMSON SAGE, HUMMINGBIRD SAGE, PITCHER SAGE

↔ 12–36 in (30–90 cm) ↕ 12–36 in (30–90 cm)
From California, USA. Suckering perennial; forms large mats. Large spear-shaped leaves. Tall stems; crimson-pink flowers, prominent reddish black calyces and bracts, in early spring–summer. **'Powerline Pink'**, taller stems, pink flowers. Zones 8–11.

Salvia splendens
SCARLET SAGE

↔ 8–32 in (20–80 cm) ↕ 8–48 in (20–120 cm)
Native of Brazil. Variable perennial, often treated as an annual. Upright growth habit; many-branched. Oval bright green to dark green leaves, serrated edges. Spikes of flowers, usually red, from summer to autumn; many cultivars in other colors. Popular cultivars include **'Blaze of Fire'**, brillian orange-red flowers; **'Empire Purple'**, deep reddish purple flowers; **'Red Arrows'**, bright red flowers; **'Red Riches'** (syn. 'Ryco'), early-blooming, vivid scarlet flowers, dark green leaves; **'Scarlet King'**, traditional bedding variety, big dense spikes of scarlet flowers, dark green foliage; **Sizzler Series**, compact foliage, early-flowering, long-lasting, flowers burgundy, lavender, pink, red, salmon, white, and bicolored; **'Vanguard'**, compact, early flowering, dark leaves, red flowers; **'Vista Salmon'**, compact, well-branched, dark green leaves, well-packed spikes of salmon flowers, pink inner petals. Zones 9–11.

Salvia spathacea

Salvia × sylvestris

↔ 20–40 in (50–100 cm)
↕ 20–40 in (50–100 cm)
Very hardy and widespread European perennial. Small narrow leaves; scalloped edges. Flowers usually purple. Summer-flowering. **'Blauhügel'** (syns 'Blue Hills', 'Blue Mount'), deep blue flower spikes on low plants to 15 in (38 cm) high; **'Mainacht'** (syn. 'May Night'), midnight violet flowers, in early spring; **'Tänzerin'**, erect, deep violet flower spikes to 32 in (80 cm) long. Zones 5–10.

Salvia uliginosa

BOG SAGE

☼ ⬡ ↔ 3 ft (0.9 m) ↑ 3–6 ft (0.9–1.8 m)

From Brazil, Uruguay, and Argentina. Clump-forming perennial; spreads by underground runners. Yellowish green lance-shaped leaves on erect stems. Whorls of small sky blue and white flowers in late summer–autumn. Needs moist soil. Zones 9–11.

Salvia verticillata

LILAC SAGE

☼ ✿ ↔ 32 in (80 cm) ↑ 40 in (100 cm)

Perennial, widespread throughout Europe and western Asia, naturalized in North America. Leafy clump of hairy, pale green leaves. Branched inflorescences; whorls of lavender-violet flowers, green calyces, in summer. 'Alba', white flowers, lime green calyces; 'Purple Rain', dusky purple flowers, violet calyces. Zones 6–10.

Salvia Hybrid Cultivars

☼◐ ✿/⬡ ↔ 16–48 in (40–120 cm) ↑ 20–60 in (50–150 cm)

Hybrids have been developed from a wide range of species—some are known crosses, others chance seedlings—and are a diverse group. Grown mainly for their flowers, but many cultivars also have attractive or unusual foliage. Many are probably perennial, but are often treated as annuals, especially in cold climates. 'Costa Rica Blue', vibrant green heart-shaped leaves, bright blue flowers; 'Hot Lips', white, red, and red/white flowers on same plant; 'Indigo Spires' ★, deep violet flowers, double white bee-line, lower lip, dark purple calyces; 'Maraschino', sprawling plant, long-flowering, cherry red flowers; 'Phyllis's Fancy', long-flowering, white flowers, bluish tinge, calyces purple; 'Plum', flowers bright magenta, calyces deep reddish purple; 'Purple Majesty', flowers and calyces rich dark purple, growing in spikes 10 in (25 cm) long. Zones 6–10.

SANGUINARIA

BLOODROOT, RED PUCCOON

This genus, belonging to the poppy (Papaveraceae) family, consists of a single species that is found only in eastern North America. The plant is a hairless perennial that grows in woodlands. It has a branching rhizome, usually with a single palmately

Salvia uliginosa

Salvia, Hybrid Cultivar, 'Plum'

incised leaf. The small, white, starry flowers appear early, unfurling to reveal their rounded scalloped shape. The fruit capsules open from the middle to both the base and the apex. The many seeds have a juicy aril that is attractive to ants, which then help to disperse the seeds. This plant is an ephemeral and will die down by mid-summer—so mark its location. It will eventually spread to make a good woodland ground cover.

CULTIVATION: Grow this plant in half-sun or shade in rich moist soil, and keep well watered. It prefers a damp shaded area, where it can be left to spread. Sow seed when ripe, or divide rhizomes when the plant is dormant.

Sanguinaria canadensis

◑/◐ ✿ ↔ 4 in (10 cm) ↑ 8 in (20 cm)

Native to eastern North America. Perennial woodland plant. Branching rhizome; large leaves, up to 12 in (30 cm) wide, green-gray, deep indentations. Starry white or pinkish flowers, 1 per stalk. Spring-flowering. Many-seeded fruit capsules follow flowers. Ephemeral, dies back in mid- to late summer. 'Flore Pleno' and 'Multiplex' (syn. 'Plena'), showy double white flowers. Zones 2–8.

SANGUISORBA

syn. *Poterium*

BURNET

Genus comprising about 10 species of shrubs and rhizomatous perennials found in temperate parts of Eurasia, North America, and the Canary Islands, is a member of the rose (Rosaceae) family. Spirally arranged leaves. Flowers are small, either unisexual or hermaphroditic, green, white, or pink, stalkless, and arranged in dense heads. The calyx tube has 4 petal-like lobes, and there are no petals. Fruits are leathery achenes.

CULTIVATION: Grow in moist rich soils that do not dry out in summer. Propagate by division, or from seed.

Sanguisorba canadensis

CANADIAN BURNET, GREAT BURNET

☼ ✿ ↔ 24–36 in (60–90 cm) ↑ 48–60 in (120–150 cm)

Clump-forming perennial found from Newfoundland, Canada, through Michigan, and south to Georgia, USA. Bright green

Salvia verticillata 'Purple Rain'

compound leaves, small regular indentations on edges. White bottlebrush-like flowers, in late summer. Zones 4–8.

SANVITALIA

This genus of 7 species extends from southwestern USA through Central America to northwestern South America, and belongs to the daisy (Asteraceae) family. They are small ornamental shrubs or low-growing perennials or annuals. The leaves are opposite, with sheathing bases, and may be smooth-edged or lobed. The flowers resemble daisies. Outer florets have orange to yellow to white rays; disc florets are usually a deep purple.
CULTIVATION: Garden species are usually annuals, and are best suited to an open sunny position in well-drained good soil. Propagate from seed sown in situ in spring or autumn.

Saponaria ocymoides

Sanvitalia procumbens
CREEPING ZINNIA
☀ ❋ ↔ 12 in (30 cm) ↕ 6–8 in (15–20 cm)
Native to southwestern USA and Mexico. Low spreading annual; forms mats of hairy, mid-green, ovate leaves. Heads of many bright yellow to orange daisies, purple-black centers, in summer. 'Aztec Gold', bright yellow daisies, green centers; 'Gold Braid', double golden daisies; 'Mandarin Orange', bright orange flowers, black centers. Zones 6–11.

SAPONARIA
SOAPWORT
This genus, belonging to the pink (Caryophyllaceae) family, contains some 20 species of temperate Eurasian annuals and perennials that contain saponin, a glycoside that forms a soapy colloidal solution when mixed with water, and the extract is sometimes used in detergents and foaming agents. They are mainly low-growing, ranging from tufted mounds to fairly wide-spreading ground covers. They have blue-green linear to spatulate leaves, sometimes toothed, and in summer they are smothered in heads of small, starry, 5-petalled, pink flowers.
CULTIVATION: *Saponaria* species are mainly very hardy and easily grown, and do best spilling over banks or in perennial borders or rockeries. They prefer gritty, moist, free-draining, humus-rich soil, however, they will tolerate slightly alkaline soil. Propagate from cuttings or seed, or by layering.

Saponaria officinalis

Saponaria ocymoides
ROCK SOAPWORT
☀ ❋ ↔ 12–20 in (30–50 cm) ↕ 6–12 in (15–30 cm)
Found from Spain to the Balkans. Mound-forming, alpine perennial; small, downy, lance-shaped leaves. Clusters of tiny deep pink flowers, sometimes red or white, in summer. 'Rubra Compacta' ★, dense mounding habit, deep crimson flowers. Zones 3–10.

Saponaria officinalis
BOUNCING BET, SOAPWORT
☀ ❋ ↔ 20–40 in (50–100 cm) ↕ 12–24 in (30–60 cm)
Perennial found over much of Europe. Billowing mound of wiry stems, green to gray-green; pointed oval leaves to ½ in (12 mm) long. Heads of 5 or more small flowers, pale to bright pink, sometimes red or white, in late summer–autumn. Cultivars include 'Rosea Plena' and 'Rubra Plena'. Zones 4–10.

Saponaria × olivana
☀ ❋ ↔ 8 in (20 cm) ↕ 2 in (5 cm)
Dwarf cushion-forming hybrid. Dense mound; tiny green to gray-green leaves. Abundant pink flowers in late spring. Zones 3–10.

SARRACENIA
AMERICAN PITCHER PLANT, TRUMPET PITCHER
The 8 species in this genus are carnivorous pitcher plants in the family Sarraceniaceae. They hybridize easily, both in the wild and in cultivation. They are found in swamps, wetlands, and pine forest edges, mainly in southeastern USA. They are perennial, growing from a rhizome, and the leaves or pitchers form a basal rosette. Most have long tubular pitchers. The nodding scented flowers grow singly on tall leafless stalks. Inside, downward-pointing hairs prevent their prey—usually small insects—from escaping out of a well of digestive liquid.
CULTIVATION: Grow in full sun in peat moss or a mix of peat and sand. Water by tray, keeping level constant. Suits warmish temperate climate, with cold winters for dormancy. Most will withstand light frosts. Propagate by division during winter dormancy. Divide and repot potted plants every 2 to 3 years.

Sarracenia × *exornata*

Sarracenia alata ★
FLYCATCHER, PALE PITCHER PLANT
☼ ❋ ↔ 12 in (30 cm) ↑ 27 in (70 cm)
Pitcher plant from Texas, Louisiana, Mississippi, and Alabama, USA. Light green pitchers to 26 in (65 cm) high, sometimes red veined, red pitcher lid. Yellow to white flowers, 2 in (5 cm) wide, on long stalks, in spring. *S. a.* × *S. flava* '**Maxima**', vigorous, pitchers to 24 in (60 cm), flowers yellow to green. Zones 7–9.

Sarracenia × *catesbaei*
☼ ❋ ↔ 12 in (30 cm) ↑ 18 in (45 cm)
Hybrid of *S. purpurea* × *S. flava*. Tall pitchers, large frilled lid, red veined to fully red. Flowers in late spring–summer. Zones 7–9.

Sarracenia × *exornata*
☼ ❋ ↔ 12 in (30 cm) ↑ 14 in (35 cm)
Naturally occurring hybrid of *S. purpurea* × *S. alata*. Pitchers red veined to totally burgundy, frilled lid. Zones 7–9.

Sarracenia flava ★
YELLOW TRUMPET
☼ ❋ ↔ 12 in (30 cm) ↑ 30 in (75 cm)
Varied pitcher plant found along the Atlantic coastal plain of USA. Tall pitchers, widening toward the mouth, large green lid. Yellow to greenish yellow flowers in spring. '**Red Veined**', red veined, red around throat. Zones 7–9.

Sarracenia '**Juthatip Soper**'
☼ ❋ ↔ 12 in (30 cm) ↑ 18 in (45 cm)
Stunning award-winning cultivar of *S. mitchelliana* crossed with very pink form of *S. leucophylla*. Rich reddish purple pitchers. Zones 7–9.

Sarracenia leucophylla
WHITE TRUMPET
☼ ❋ ↔ 12 in (30 cm) ↑ 24 in (60 cm)
Pitcher plant found along Atlantic coastal plain of USA. Showy species, beautiful pitchers, green at base, top white, red veined.

Deep burgundy flowers, fragrant, in spring. *S. l.* × *S. oreophila*, robust, narrow, bright green pitchers, crimson veining. Zones 7–9.

Sarracenia minor
HOODED PITCHER PLANT
☼ ❋ ↔ 12 in (30 cm) ↑ 24 in (60 cm)
Found on floating sphagnum islands in North and South Carolina, Georgia, and Florida, USA. Pale green to red pitchers, hood curls over pitcher mouth. Upper pitcher covered with fenestrations. Yellow flowers in spring. Zones 7–9.

Sarracenia × *mitchelliana*
☼ ❋ ↔ 12 in (30 cm) ↑ 18 in (45 cm)
Hybrid of *S. purpurea* and *S. leucophylla*. Curved pitchers, hood usually ruffled, lower parts green, red and white around top and hood. Zones 7–9.

Sarracenia × *moorei*
☼ ❋ ↔ 12 in (30 cm) ↑ 40 in (100 cm)
Cross between *S. flava* and *S. leucophylla*. Very tall pitchers, 40 in (100 cm) or more. '**Brook's Hybrid**', red around throat, pink to red flowers. Zones 7–9.

Sarracenia oreophila
BUGLE GRASS, FROG BONNETS, GREEN PITCHER PLANT
☼ ❋ ↔ 12 in (30 cm) ↑ 24 in (60 cm)
Rare pitcher plant from Alabama, Georgia, and North and South Carolina, USA. Green pitchers, red veined to almost totally red, wide mouth, heart-shaped lid. Pale yellow fragrant flowers. Endangered species since 1979. Zones 7–9.

Sarracenia psittacina
LOBSTER POT, PARROT PITCHER PLANT
☼ ❋ ↔ 20 in (50 cm) ↑ 10 in (25 cm)
Unusual species, native to southeastern coastal plain of USA. Pitchers grow upward, then fall back horizontally, forming a rosette with pitcher openings facing center of plant. Pitchers

Sarracenia 'Juthatip Soper'

Sarracenia × *moorei* 'Brook's Hybrid'

green to red, puffed up hood. Red flowers. Prefers very wet soil; can survive flooding, during which it preys on small swimming creatures. Zones 7–9.

Sarracenia purpurea ★
HUNTSMAN'S CAP, NORTHERN PITCHER PLANT, SIDESADDLE PLANT

※ ❄ ↔ 24 in (60 cm) ↑ 12 in (30 cm)

Found east of Canadian Rockies and southward along coastal USA to Gulf of Mexico. Green to purple bulging pitchers 12 in (30 cm) high, prominent rib, hood ruffled or unruffled. Green, pink, or burgundy flowers. *S. p.* subsp. *venosa*, fat green to red pitchers. *S. p.* f. *heterophylla*, narrow, green, wide mouth pitchers. Zones 2–9.

Sarracenia × readii
※ ❄ ↔ 12 in (30 cm) ↑ 24 in (60 cm)

Naturally occurring cross between *S. leucophylla* and *S. rubra*. Bright green slender pitchers, ruffled lids white and veined with red. Zones 7–9.

Sarracenia × stevensii
※ ❄ ↔ 12 in (30 cm) ↑ 24 in (60 cm)

Origins of this Dutch hybrid are disputed; believed to be a cross between *S. rubra* and *S. leucophylla*. Green pitchers, heavily veined with red. Zones 7–9.

SAXIFRAGA

This genus in the saxifrage (Saxifragaceae) family is very extensive, comprising a wide range of perennial, annual, or biennial ground-hugging plants, many of which are alpines. They are found throughout much of the temperate and subarctic zones of the Northern Hemisphere, with outposts in places such as Ethiopia, Mexico, and the Arctic. There are some 480 known species, as well as numerous garden hybrids. The 3 main sections that are of garden interest are the "mossies," the "silvers," and the Kabschia and Engleria subsections. These plants are not only diverse in themselves but come from a variety of habitats, such as exposed mountains and moist woodlands.
CULTIVATION: Being shallow-rooted plants, *Saxifraga* species require free-draining relatively fertile soil and a position in either sun or part-shade. Propagate by division at any time, or from seed in autumn.

Saxifraga andersonii
※ ❄ ↔ 12 in (30 cm) ↑ 4 in (10 cm)

Cushion-forming perennial. Native to Nepal and Tibet. Loose rosettes

of gray-green leaves. Tall flower stalks, to 4 in (10 cm) high; clear white or pink flowers. Spring-flowering. Zones 6–8.

Saxifraga callosa
syn. *Saxifraga lingulata*

※ ❄ ↔ 8 in (20 cm) ↑ 10 in (25 cm)

Evergreen perennial from western and eastern Spain, the southwestern alpine areas of Europe, Sardinia, Sicily, and southern Italy. Rosettes of broad, round, silver-gray foliage growing in dense clumps. White flowers, star-shaped, ½ in (12 mm) wide, in early summer. Grows on limestone formations. Zones 7–9.

Saxifraga cochlearis
SNAIL SAXIFRAGE

※ ❄ ↔ 6 in (15 cm) ↑ 8 in (20 cm)

Very tight, dense, mat-forming cushion plant from the maritime Alps of France. Rosettes of mid-green spoon-shaped leaves. Tall hairy stems, 4 in (10 cm) high; clusters of red-spotted white flowers in summer. 'Probynii', pure white flowers. Zones 7–8.

Saxifraga oppositifolia

Saxifraga oppositifolia
PURPLE MOUNTAIN SAXIFRAGE

※/❂ ❄ ↔ 8 in (20 cm) ↑ 1 in (2.5 cm)

Very small, clumping and dense mat-forming perennial herb from arctic-latitude mountains of Europe, western Asia, and North America. Rosettes of stiff, elliptical, dark green leaves. Single, almost stemless, dark red to purple to pale pink flowers in summer. Zones 1–7.

Saxifraga callosa

Saxifraga, Hybrid Cultivar, 'Purple Robe'

Saxifraga paniculata

syn. *Saxifraga aizoon*

☼ ❄ ↔ 10 in (25 cm) ↕ 6 in (15 cm)

Mat-forming perennial from Canada, Norway, Greenland, and Iceland. Rosettes of narrow gray-green leaves, 2½ in (6 cm) long, lime-encrusted edges. Creamy white to pink flowers, in early summer. Zones 1–6.

Saxifraga spathularis

ST PATRICK'S CABBAGE

☼/◑ ❄ ↔ 6–8 in (15–20 cm) ↕ 8–12 in (20–30 cm)

Summer-flowering species. Native to Ireland, Spain, and Portugal. Forms clumped rosettes; rounded, 1–2 in (25–50 mm) long, leathery, bright green leaves, coarsely toothed edges. Wiry stems; sprays of tiny pinkish purple flowers. Zones 5–9.

Saxifraga stolonifera

syn. *Saxifraga sarmentosa*

MOTHER OF THOUSANDS, STRAWBERRY BEGONIA

☼/◑ ❄ ↔ 12 in (30 cm) ↕ 16 in (40 cm)

Perennial from East Asia. Rounded, kidney-shaped, mid- to dark green, serrated leaves form dense mounds of foliage. Tall loose stems, 16 in (40 cm) long; white flowers, spotted with red or yellow, in summer. 'Eco Butterfly', golden yellow leaves, green centers; 'Harvest Moon', moon-shaped golden green to reddish leaves; 'Tricolor', leaves edged in tones of red, white, and/or pink. Zones 5–10.

Saxifraga umbrosa

☼ ❄ ↔ 12 in (30 cm) ↕ 12 in (30 cm)

From the Pyrenees. Clump-forming perennial; stiff rosettes of green leaves. Flowers on 10 in (25 cm) long stems, rose pink, irregular red blotches, in late spring–early summer. Zones 1–5.

Saxifraga × *urbium*

syn. *Saxifraga umbrosa* 'London Pride'

LONDON PRIDE

☼ ❄ ↔ 18–36 in (45–90 cm) ↕ 12 in (30 cm)

Of garden origin; quick-growing ground-covering perennial. Large rosettes of spoon-shaped, leathery, dark green leaves. Arching stems; small pale pink flowers in summer. 'Aureovariegata', variegated leaves, gray-green and gold. Zones 6–7.

Saxifraga Hybrid Cultivars

☼/◑ ❄/❄ ↔ 6–18 in (15–45 cm) ↕ 3–12 in (8–30 cm)

Saxifraga species hybridize freely in the wild, and many garden plants are of indeterminate parentage. Suited to rock and alpine gardens. Cultivars include 'James Bremner', 6 in (15 cm) tall, creamy white flowers; 'Purple Robe', dense foliage cushion, many tall sprays of purple-pink flowers; 'Southside Seedling' dark green spoon-shaped leaves in rosettes, arching panicles of white saucer-like flowers; 'Tumbling Waters' (syn. *S. longifolia* 'Tumbling Waters'), dark green rosettes, arching racemes of star-shaped white flowers; 'Whitehill', gray-green foliage with crusty white edges, white flowers on stems to 12 in (30 cm) tall. Zones 6–9.

SCABIOSA

SCABIOUS

Belonging to the teasel (Dipsacaceae) family, the genus comprises around 80 species of annuals and perennials found throughout Europe, parts of Africa, and Japan. Most species form a spreading basal clump of light green to gray-green, rounded to lance-shaped leaves with deeply incised notches or lobes. A few species have an erect or branching habit. The flowers are individually tiny, but occur in rounded to flattened composite heads on stems held clear of the foliage. White and pale yellow to soft pink or powder blue and mauve are the usual colors.

CULTIVATION: *Scabiosa* species are hardy and easily grown in any sunny position in fertile, moist, free-draining, slightly alkaline soil. Propagate annuals from seed and perennials from seed and basal cuttings, or by division.

Scabiosa atropurpurea 'Chile Black'

Scabiosa atropurpurea

EGYPTIAN ROSE, MOURNFUL WIDOW, SWEET SCABIOUS

☼/◑ ❄ ↔ 16–30 in (40–75 cm) ↕ 16–36 in (40–90 cm)

Annual, biennial, or short-lived perennial herb from southern Europe. Basal cluster of light green to gray-green, lobed or toothed leaves, to 6 in (15 cm) long, upper leaves shorter and more deeply lobed, almost pinnate. Flowerheads crimson to deep purple-black, fragrant, to 2 in (5 cm) wide, in summer–early autumn. 'Blue Cockade', 36 in (90 cm) tall, rounded, deep blue, double flowerheads; '**Chile Black**', 24 in (60 cm) tall, deep black-red flowers with minute flecks of lavender; '**Peter Ray**', 24 in (60 cm) tall, large purple-black flowerheads; '**Salmon Queen**', 36 in (90 cm) tall, deep salmon pink to light red double flowers. Zones 8–10.

Scabiosa caucasica
☼/◐ ❄ ↔16–18 in (40–45 cm) ↕20–36 in (50–90 cm)
Perennial, native to the Caucasus region. Gray-green to blue-green leaves, basal foliage lance-shaped, large, smooth-edged; upper leaves lobed almost to midrib. Powder blue flowers bloom in heads to 3 in (8 cm) wide. Summer- to autumn-flowering. Cultivars include '**Alba**', white flowers; '**Bressingham White**', white flowers; '**Clive Greaves**' ★, pale lavender blue flowers; '**Fama**', bright blue flowers; '**Floral Queen**', tall, vigorous, flowers light blue; '**Miss Willmott**', tall, flowers cream; '**Nachtfalter**', dark purple flowers; '**Pink Lace**', bright pink flowers. Zones 4–10.

Scabiosa columbaria
☼/◐ ❄ ↔16 in (40 cm) ↕24 in (60 cm)
Biennial or short-lived perennial from temperate Eurasia and North Africa. Stems and foliage gray-green, woolly; basal leaves smooth-edged to deeply lobed, upper leaves pinnate, often further divided. Lavender to purple-blue flowerheads to 1¾ in (40 mm) wide, in summer. *S. c.* **var.** *ochroleuca*, 36 in (90 cm) tall, primrose flowerheads. *S.c.* '**Butterfly Blue**', 28 in (70 cm) tall, lavender blue; '**Pink Mist**', 24 in (60 cm) tall, light pink. Zones 6–10.

Scabiosa lucida
☼ ❄ ↔12–20 in (30–50 cm) ↕12 in (30 cm)
Low spreading perennial from central Europe. Deeply divided, hairy, dark green to silvery leaves. Lavender-pink to purple-red flowerheads to 1¾ in (40 mm) wide. Summer- to autumn-flowering. '**Rosea**'. pale pink flowers. Zones 5–10.

SCAEVOLA
This genus from the family Goodeniaceae contains nearly 100 plants from Australia and islands in the Indian and Pacific Oceans, and includes shrubs, subshrubs, and perennials. Many have a ground-hugging habit, and provide reliable ground cover in temperate areas. The leaves of most species are small, somewhat succulent, often hairy, and usually carried on short, often brittle stems. The foliage is covered in fan-shaped flowers in varying shades of blue, sometimes white, over a long period from mid-winter onward.
CULTIVATION: Full sun and freely draining soil are the main requirements. Many species are resistant to salt spray, making them ideal plants for coastal sites, but they do need a frost-free position. Propagate from cuttings taken in the warmer months.

Scaevola aemula
☼ ◑ ↔20 in (50 cm) ↕6 in (15 cm)
Perennial from southern and eastern Australia. Variable, usually prostrate habit; oblong, wedge-shaped, toothed leaves. Pale mauve-blue fan-shaped flowers, 1¼ in (30 mm) wide, along stems. Spring- to summer-flowering. Cultivars include '**Blue Fan**', '**Blue Wonder**', and '**New Wonder**', more vigorous and upright growth habit; '**Mauve Clusters**' ★, mauve-pink flowers; '**Purple Fanfare**', large flowers produced throughout most of year. Zones 9–11.

Scaevola aemula

SCHAUERIA
This genus, a member of the acanthus (Acanthaceae) family, contains 8 species of evergreen shrubs and subshrubs, native to Brazil. They are grown for their spikes of narrow tubular flowers; the bristly calyces give a brush-like appearance.
CULTIVATION: In tropical climates, plant *Schaueria* species outdoors in a rich moist soil. In cool climates they are suitable for the conservatory or greenhouse, but will require shading during the hottest part of the day. Propagate by softwood cuttings.

Schaueria flavicoma
☼ ✦ ↔24 in (60 cm) ↕36 in (90 cm)
Erect perennial subshrub from Brazil. Glossy green leaves, prominent pale veins and midribs. Dense spikes of narrow, soft yellow, tubular flowers; downy to bristly yellow-green calyces. Zones 10–12.

Schaueria flavicoma

SCHIZANTHUS

POOR MAN'S ORCHID

This Chilean genus of 12 species of annuals and biennials belongs to the nightshade (Solanaceae) family, although the relationship is not an obvious one. The species are small upright plants around 12 in (30 cm) tall, with soft, green, ferny foliage, often covered with fine hairs. Flowers are borne in branching panicles that are held above the foliage. They are beautifully marked and shaped, with a prominent lower lip, hence the common name. Modern strains are available in a wide range of colors and sizes.
CULTIVATION: These plants are easily grown as annuals where summer temperatures are warm and consistent. Elsewhere they are best treated as greenhouse plants, as they are intolerant of cold. Grow in a bright position in fertile, moist, well-drained soil. Raise from seed, with several sowings to ensure continued flowering.

Schizanthus pinnatus

☼/◐ ⬧ ↔ 8–16 in (20–40 cm)
↕ 8–20 in (20–50 cm)
Annual; bushy habit; lance-shaped, usually lobed, light green leaves. Tightly clustered heads of flat flowers, lobes almost evenly sized, in summer–autumn. White-throated deep pink flowers, yellow and black central markings. Garden forms in many colors. Zones 9–11.

Schizanthus × wisetonensis

Schizanthus × wisetonensis

☼/◐ ⬧ ↔ 12 in (30 cm) ↕ 12–20 in (30–50 cm)
Garden hybrid annual; S. pinnatus × S. grahamii parentage. Several cultivars resembling S. pinnatus in foliage and habit. Flowers in various colors. Zones 9–11.

SCLERANTHUS

This genus, a member of the pink (Caryophyllaceae) family, contains up to 10 species that occur naturally in Europe, Asia, Africa, South America, Australia, New Guinea, and New Zealand. Perennials or annuals, they have a densely tufted ground-covering habit. The small, linear, usually green leaves are joined at the base of the stems. The pale creamy green flowers are small, often less than ¼ in (6 mm) wide, and are hard to see on some species. The plants are shallow-rooted, and generally all species creep along the ground, forming dense cushions.

Scleranthus biflorus

CULTIVATION: These plants like sun or shade, but not long periods of dry or heavy wet weather. Propagate from stem cuttings in autumn or from fresh seed.

Scleranthus biflorus

☼ ✳ ↔ 12 in (30 cm) ↕ 2–4 in (5–10 cm)
From New Zealand; dense, perennial, mat-forming plant. Tiny, needle-like, bright green, sometimes lime green, foliage. Conspicuous pale creamy green flowers, in summer. Zones 5–9.

SCROPHULARIA

FIGWORT

The members of this genus of some 200 species in the foxglove (Scrophulariaceae) family are mainly perennials. Often marsh-dwellers, they come mostly from temperate parts of the Northern Hemisphere, although some species are found as far south as Central America. The stems are 4-angled; their leaves may be compound or simple, and alternate or opposite. The flowers are usually small, like tiny, fat, inflated foxgloves (Digitalis) with a lower lip, in bronze, copper, or dull red. Some species are garden weeds.
CULTIVATION: Most species grow well in moist humus-rich soil in dappled shade; some are aquatic. Propagation is by seed sown in situ, or from basal cuttings taken in spring.

Scrophularia auriculata

syn. Scrophularia aquatica
WATER BETONY, WATER FIGWORT
◐ ✳ ↔ 36–48 in (90–120 cm) ↕ 36–48 in (90–120 cm)
Vigorous marginal aquatic species from western Europe. Opposite leaves, to 10 in (25 cm) long, slightly toothed. Open sprays of tiny, rounded, reddish brown flowers, drooping lip, yellowish green interior, in summer. 'Variegata', leaves with bold white edges. Zones 5–10.

SCUTELLARIA

HELMET FLOWER, SKULLCAP

This genus of about 300 species of annuals and perennials is a member of the mint (Lamiaceae) family. They are found mostly in temperate Northern Hemisphere regions, where they grow in scrub, open woodland, and grassland. The roots are often rhizomatous, and the plants are erect or sprawling, ranging from 6 in (15 cm) to 4 ft (1.2 m) high. The leaves are opposite and simple, sometimes pinnate or toothed. The 2-lipped tubular flowers emerge from hooded calyces, which give the genus its common names. The blue, white, or yellow flowers appear in summer singly, in pairs, or on the ends of spikes. A number of species are grown ornamentally, and some are used in herbal medicine for their anti-spasmodic properties.
CULTIVATION: Plant taller species in borders and smaller species at the edges of borders or in rock gardens. Grow in full sun in any reasonable soil. Water well in dry summers. Propagate from seed or by division.

Scutellaria alpina

☼ ❋ ↔ 18 in (45 cm) ↕ 6–10 in (15–25 cm)

Found in mountains from southern Europe to Siberia. Sprawling perennial; often roots at nodes; mats of small oval leaves. Small flowers in crowded racemes, purple to pale pink, often with yellow on lower lip, in late spring–early summer. *S. a.* subsp. *supina*, soft lemon flowers. *S. a.* 'Arcobaleno', bluish purple to white, rose, and pale yellow flowers, contrasting colors on lower lip. Zones 5–9.

Scutellaria incana

DOWNY SKULLCAP

☼ ❋ ↔ 24 in (60 cm) ↕ 24–48 in (60–120 cm)

Bushy perennial from eastern North America. Oval leaves, to 3 in (8 cm) long, grayish green, with minute hairs. Dense panicles of velvety purplish blue flowers in summer–autumn. Zones 4–9.

Scutellaria indica

☼ ❋ ↔ 12 in (30 cm) ↕ 6 in (15 cm)

Low-growing mat-forming perennial; native to Japan, Korea, and China. Small, rounded, grayish green leaves, toothed edges. Pale purplish blue flowers in summer. *S. i.* var. *parvifolia* ★, dark green leaves, relatively large lavender-blue flowers. Zones 5–9.

Scutellaria orientalis

☼ ❋ ↔ 6–10 in (15–25 cm) ↕ 12–18 in (30–45 cm)

Low mounding subshrub; native to southeastern Europe. Small oval leaves, dark green above, woolly gray beneath. Dense racemes of lemon yellow flowers, sometimes tinged or spotted with red. Summer-flowering. Zones 7–10.

SEDUM

STONECROP

This very diverse group of succulent species in the stonecrop (Crassulaceae) family has many hybrids. Of Northern Hemisphere origins, with over 300 species they vary enormously in foliage and form. Some are shrubby, with flattened, oval, gray-green leaves; others are trailing, with succulent jellybean-like leaves; and some form very compact mats. Most species produce small heads of tiny, bright yellow, 5-petalled flowers in summer and autumn. The autumn-flowering types have been reclassified, mainly to the genera *Hylotelephium* and *Rhodiola*. Their name is derived from the Latin *sedo* (to sit), referring to their low spreading habit. Some species are used medicinally and as salad vegetables.
CULTIVATION: Plant in full sun in gritty well-drained soil. Most appreciate water at flowering time, but are otherwise drought tolerant. Propagate by division, from cuttings, or from seed, depending on the growth type.

Sedum spectabile ★

syn. *Hylotelephium spectabile*

ICE PLANT

☼ ❋ ↔ 16–32 in (40–80 cm) ↕ 27 in (70 cm)

Perennial from Korea and nearby parts of China. Erect thickened stems; fleshy, toothed,

Scutellaria orientalis

elliptical leaves, 2–4 in (5–10 cm) long. Large 3-branched heads of small pink to red flowers in late summer–autumn. 'Brilliant' ★, pink flowers; 'Iceberg', white flowers, sometimes tinted with pink; 'Indian Chief', deep pink to purple-red flowers. Zones 6–10.

Sedum telephium

syn. *Hylotelephium telephium*

LIVE-FOREVER, ORPINE

☼ ❋ ↔ 24–32 in (60–80 cm) ↕ 24 in (60 cm)

Found from eastern Europe to Japan. Perennial; erect thickened stems; fleshy, toothed, pointed oval leaves, to 3 in (8 cm) long. Heads of many purple-red flowers in late summer. *S. t.* subsp. *maximum* 'Atropurpureum', deep purple-red foliage, red flowers. *S. t.* 'Matrona', stems tinted red, very pale pink flowers. Zones 6–10.

Sedum Hybrid Cultivars

☼ ❋ ↔ 12–24 in (30–60 cm) ↕ 12–24 in (30–60 cm)

Several popular interspecies garden hybrids are placed in the subgenus *Hylotelephium*; these are mainly autumn-flowering, though foliage is also attractive. 'Herbstfreude' (syn. 'Autumn Joy') (*S. telephium* × *S. spectabile*), blue-green foliage, salmon pink flowers ageing to bronze; 'Ruby Glow' (*S. cauticolum* × *S. telephium*), purple-green foliage, often pink-edged, deep red flowers; 'Vera Jameson' ('Ruby Glow' × *S. telephium* subsp. *maximum* 'Atropurpureum'), purple foliage, light pink flowers. Zones 6–10.

Sedum, Hybrid Cultivar, 'Ruby Glow'

Semiaquilegia ecalcarata

Senecio cineraria 'Silver Dust'

Serissa japonica 'Flore Pleno'

SEMIAQUILEGIA

This genus, belonging to the buttercup (Ranunculaceae) family, contains 7 species of low perennial plants closely related to *Aquilegia*. Native to Asia, they grow in high mountain grassland and scrub in damp conditions. The lacy foliage resembles maidenhair fern *(Adiantum)*, with leaves comprising 3 leaflets. The nodding flowers are in shades of pink, red, and purple, often plump with many petals, but lacking the spurs typical of *Aquilegia* species. CULTIVATION: Suitable for the rock garden, these plants should be grown in full sun to half-sun. They require a moist but well-drained soil. Propagate from seed or by division.

Semiaquilegia ecalcarata
☼/◗ ❄ ↔ 8–10 in (20–25 cm) ↕ 12 in (30 cm)
Perennial species, native to western China. Clumps of deeply divided ferny foliage, often with purplish tinge. Nodding cup-like flowers, pink to purple, in loose panicles, in summer. Zones 6–9.

SENECIO

There are 1,250 species in this cosmopolitan genus of trees, shrubs, annuals, biennials, lianes, perennials, and some succulent species in the daisy (Asteraceae) family; this is one of the largest genera of flowering plants. The leaves are lobed or smooth-edged, and the daisy-like flowers are usually arranged in clusters, with or without florets. The flowers are usually yellow, but can be purple, white, red, or blue. Many species are toxic to livestock. CULTIVATION: With such a large genus, the cultivation requirements are diverse; therefore general guidelines only can be given. These species grow in either moderately fertile well-drained soil in full sun, or in moderately fertile soil that retains moisture; a few will grow in bogs. Plants that are grown in pots in colder climates need fertile well-drained soil with added grit and leaf mold. They should be fed and watered moderately during the growing season. Propagation is from seed or cuttings.

Senecio cineraria
syn. *Cineraria maritima*
DUSTY MILLER, SEA RAGWORT
☼ ❄ ↔ 16 in (40 cm) ↕ 20 in (50 cm)
From southern Europe; naturalized in southern England. Mounding subshrub; leaves deeply dissected and lobed, intensely silver-white.

Small heads of yellow daisies in summer. 'Cirrus', grayish blue rounded-lobed leaves; 'Silver Dust' ★, broad, deeply cut, pewter leaves; 'Silver Lace', rounded leaves deeply lobed but less dissected; 'White Diamond', finely dissected white leaves, compact habit. Zones 7–10.

Senecio vira-vira
syn. *Senecio leucostachys*
DUSTY MILLER
☼ ❄ ↔ 12–24 in (30–60 cm) ↕ 16–24 in (40–60 cm)
Shrubby perennial; native to Argentina. Covered in dense white hairs. Lacy effect of finely divided, soft, silvery gray leaves. Small, creamy, button-like flowers in summer. Zones 8–11.

SERISSA

The sole species in this genus from the madder (Rubiaceae) family is a small, densely branched, evergreen shrub from warm-temperate Southeast Asia. It is a neat little bush with tiny leaves that emit an unpleasant smell when crushed. It produces small white flowers followed by berries, but it is often grown as a foliage plant; there are several variegated cultivars. CULTIVATION: Somewhat frost tender, *Serissa* likes a warm, moist, humid climate and a rich soil with plenty of humus. For cooler climates, it makes an excellent greenhouse or conservatory plant. Propagate from cuttings or from self-layered pieces.

Serissa japonica
syn. *Serissa foetida*
☼ ◖ ↔ 18 in (45 cm) ↕ 18 in (45 cm)
Attractive plant; popular bonsai subject. White flowers in spring–autumn. 'Flore Pleno', very compact bush with double flowers; 'Mount Fuji', very compact, leaves edged and striped with white; 'Variegata Pink', pink flowers, white-edged leaves. Zones 9–11.

SHORTIA

syn. *Schizocodon*
This genus in the family Diapensiaceae comprises 6 dainty, rhizomatous, clumping, evergreen perennials. Five are native to East Asia, the other to the woodlands of southeastern USA. The leaves are heart-shaped, rounded, or elliptical, toothed and leathery, and are usually glossy dark green, often turning red in winter. In early

spring they bear bell-, trumpet-, or funnel-shaped, white to deep pink flowers with toothed or fringed petals.

CULTIVATION: All appreciate humus-rich, acidic, moist but well-drained soil and part- to full shade. They are a challenge to grow in dry regions, even with adequate water; regions with cool damp summers are preferred. Sow seed when ripe in autumn, or propagate by basal cuttings in early summer or runners in mid-summer.

Shortia galacifolia

OCONEE BELLS

☼ ❄ ↔ 10 in (25 cm) ↕ 6 in (15 cm)

Perennial species; native of southeastern USA. Large clump of roundish glossy green leaves, scalloped edges, bronze-red in winter. Nodding, rose-flushed white, bell-shaped flowers, toothed edges. Spring-flowering. Zones 6–9.

Shortia soldanelloides

FRINGE BELLS, FRINGED GALAX

☼ ❄ ↔ 10 in (25 cm) ↕ 6 in (15 cm)

Evergreen perennial from Japan. Round coarsely toothed leaves. Pinkish rose flowers, deeply fringed, whitish edges, in spring. *S. s.* var. *ilicifolia,* smaller, with smaller sparsely and coarsely toothed leaves, white or occasionally pink flowers. Zones 6–9.

SIDALCEA

FALSE MALLOW

This genus, containing about 22 annual and perennial species, is a member of the mallow (Malvaceae) family. Native to western parts of North America, these plants can be found growing on lime-free sandy grasslands along stream beds, and in damp mountain meadows. Resembling a small hollyhock *(Alcea rosea),* to which they are related, they have glossy, round, palmately lobed basal leaves and stiffly upright flower spikes that bear stalkless or short-stemmed, white, pink, or purple, open, cup-shaped flowers at the ends. These are popular plants for perennial borders, and many improved varieties are bred for their color and length of flowering. CULTIVATION: *Sidalcea* species require a humus-rich free-draining soil in a sunny position. They will flower freely throughout summer if spent flower spikes are removed. Propagation is by division or from seed.

Sidalcea candida

☼ ❄ ↔ 20 in (50 cm) ↕ 24–36 in (60–90 cm)

From Utah, New Mexico, Wyoming, and Colorado, USA. Roundish, 7-lobed, glossy leaves on long stalks. White flowers with bluish anthers, on branching stems, in early summer. Parent, with *S. malviflora,* of many modern cultivars. Zones 5–9.

Sidalcea malviflora

CHECKERBLOOM

☼/☼ ❄ ↔ 16–30 in (40–75 cm) ↕ 24–40 in (60–100 cm)

Clump-forming perennial found from Oregon, USA, to Baja California, Mexico. Erect stems; 7- to 9-lobed leaves, 1–2 in (25–50 mm) long, shallow-toothed. Racemes of many pink to lavender flowers, 1–2 in (25–50 mm) wide, from spring to autumn. Zones 6–10.

Sidalcea Hybrid Cultivars

☼/☼ ❄ ↔ 16–24 in (40–60 cm) ↕ 24–32 in (60–80 cm)

Compact heavy-blooming plants, flowers usually held well above foliage. 'Elsie Heugh', dainty shell pink flowers; 'Little Princess', miniature, compact, soft pink flowers; 'Rose Queen' ★, deep rose pink flowers; 'Sussex Beauty', large pale pink flowers; 'Monarch', taller cultivar, pink flowers. Zones 6–10.

SILENE

CAMPION, CATCHFLY, CUSHION PINK

This large and varied genus in the pink (Caryophyllaceae) family contains about 500 annuals and perennials widely distributed throughout the Northern Hemisphere and southern Africa. The flowers are 5-petalled, generally white or shades of pink, and may be solitary or borne in one-sided spikes. The leaves and stems of many species are downy and sticky to the touch. CULTIVATION: Good drainage is essential for cultivation of these plants, as is a light loamy soil in a sunny position. Propagation is from seed or cuttings, or by division.

Silene acaulis

CUSHION PINK, MOSS CAMPION

☼ ❄ ↔ 4 in (10 cm) ↕ 2 in (5 cm)

Perennial from Eurasia and North America extending into higher mountain regions further south. Low, dense, tufted cushion; bright green linear leaves. Solitary deep pink to purple flowers sit just above foliage. Numerous cultivars. Zones 2–8.

Silene alpestris

syns *Heliosperma alpestre, Silene quadrifida*

☼/☼ ❄ ↔ 12 in (30 cm) ↕ 6–12 in (15–30 cm)

Found from the southern European Alps to Caucasus region. Low loose cushion of linear-lanceolate leaves. Starry flowers, white, rarely pink, with cleft or fringed petals, in summer. Zones 5–9.

Sidalcea, Hybrid Cultivar, 'Elsie Heugh'

Silene dioica

RED CAMPION

☀/☽ ❄ ↔ 12 in (30 cm) ↕ 24 in (60 cm)

From woods, rocky hillsides, and cliffs of Europe. Perennial; rosettes of downy leaves. Tall, stiff, branching stems; bright pink flowers, rarely white, in summer. Zones 6–10.

Silene fimbriata

☀/☽ ❄ ↔ 24 in (60 cm) ↕ 40 in (100 cm)

Perennial, native to damp woodlands of the Caucasus region. Rosettes of dark green, hairy, oval leaves. Open panicles of fringed white flowers, swollen globular calyces. Early summer-flowering. Zones 5–8.

Silene laciniata

FRINGED INDIAN PINK, MEXICAN CAMPION

☀ ❄ ↔ 8 in (20 cm) ↕ 36 in (90 cm)

From California and New Mexico, USA, and Mexico. Narrow oval leaves. Upright stems; large, starry, crimson flowers. Zones 7–10.

Silene schafta

☀ ❄ ↔ 8 in (20 cm) ↕ 4 in (10 cm)

Perennial from Caucasus region. Upright stems; small, bright green, linear leaves form loose mat. Star-shaped, rosy magenta flowers, cleft petals, in late summer–autumn. Zones 5–9.

Silene uniflora

syn. *Silene vulgaris* subsp. *maritima*

BLADDER CAMPION, SEA CAMPION

☀ ❄ ↔ 4 in (10 cm) ↕ 4–8 in (10–20 cm)

Perennial, native to coasts of western Europe and North Africa. gray-tinged oval to spathulate leaves. Upright flower stems; profuse, solitary, white blooms, pronounced inflated calyx like a small bladder. Summer-flowering. '**Robin Whitebreast**' (syn. 'Flore Pleno'), gray leaves, abundant double white flowers. Zones 5–9.

Silphium perfoliatum

SILPHIUM

This genus of 23 species of coarse-leafed perennials native to central and eastern North America is in the daisy (Asteraceae) family. The simple to deeply divided leaves are opposite to whorled, the basal ones forming a rosette, those on the inflorescence stalks spirally arranged. The daisy-like flowerheads are large and have numerous outer rayed white or yellow florets growing in 2 or 3 rows, with small yellow disc florets.

CULTIVATION: Mostly suited to the wild garden, *Silphium* species grow in a position in full sun or very light shade in any soil that is not too nitrogen-rich. Seed is the best method of propagation, because the deep root system of larger species makes them difficult to propagate vegetatively.

Silphium laciniatum

COMPASS PLANT

☀/☽ ❄ ↔ 3–4 ft (0.9–1.2 m)

↕ 5–10 ft (1.5–3 m)

From central USA. Strongly erect, hairy, fern-like leaves, 4–16 in (10–40 cm) long, aligned north–south. Clusters of bright yellow flowerheads in summer. Zones 4–9.

Silphium perfoliatum

CUP PLANT

☀/☽ ❄ ↔ 3 ft (0.9 m) ↕ 5 ft (1.5 m)

From damp woodlands and prairies of eastern North America. Forms large clump of rough, irregularly toothed, ovate leaves, upper leaves stem-clasping. Stiffly upright stems branching toward top; single yellow daisy flowers. Zones 5–10.

Silphium terebinthinaceum

PRAIRIE DOCK

☀/☽ ❄ ↔ 3–6 ft (0.9–1.8 m) ↕ 7–10 ft (2–3 m)

From southern Canada to southeastern USA. Dense clump of large, long-stemmed basal leaves, to over 12 in (30 cm) long, heart-shaped at base, toothed or lobed near tip. Erect red-brown flower stems; sprays of 1–2 in (25–50 mm) wide golden flowerheads with many ray florets, in summer. Zones 4–9.

SILYBUM

This genus, belonging to the daisy (Asteraceae) family, contains just 2 species of annual or biennial plants grown for their ornamental foliage. They are native to the Mediterranean region and eastern Africa, where they grow in sunny free-draining areas. They are robust upright plants forming basal rosettes from which the stout flowering stems arise. The long leaves are lobed or pinnate with extremely spiny edges. They have prominent white veins or variegations. The purple thistle flowers are borne on tall stems in spring or summer.

CULTIVATION: Ideal candidates for border planting, grow *Silybum* species in full sun and in free-draining soil. To prolong the display of attractive foliage, the flowering stem can be removed. When allowed to flower, seed will self-sow freely. Young plants need protection from slugs and snails.

Silene fimbriata

Silybum marianum

Sinningia cardinalis

Sinningia speciosa, Lawn Hybrid

Silybum marianum

BLESSED THISTLE, OUR LADY'S MILK THISTLE

☀ ❄ ↔ 2 ft (0.6 m) ↕ 4 ft (1.2 m)

Biennial, native to Europe; naturalized in the Americas. Basal rosette of long, deeply lobed, dark green leaves, with prominent white veins and spiny edges. Purplish thistle flowers. Spring- to summer-flowering. Zones 6–10.

SINNINGIA

GLOXINIA

This genus, a member of the African violet (Gesneriaceae) family, is made up of about 40 species of tuberous perennials and small shrubs found from Mexico to Argentina. The commonly cultivated species are perennials with large lance- to heart-shaped leaves made velvety by a dense covering of fine hairs. The well-known florist's gloxinia (*S. speciosa*) has large, upward-facing, bell-shaped flowers; other species have tubular flowers, which are sometimes scented.
CULTIVATION: These plants prefer warm humid conditions with a bright but not sunny exposure and moist, well-drained, humus-rich soil. They are widely grown as indoor or greenhouse plants in pots, and are also raised outdoors as a summer annual, or year-round in warm areas. The flower trumpets collapse if filled with water. Propagate by lifting and dividing plants after the foliage has died back, or by seed or leaf-stalk cuttings. Tubers may be stored dry.

Sinningia canescens

☀/◐ ⚘ ↔ 10 in (25 cm) ↕ 10 in (25 cm)

Perennial, native to Brazil. Heavy thickened tubers; upright stems; heart-shaped, velvety, deep green leaves, finely toothed. Small heads of up to 5 long-stemmed, tubular, bright orange flowers. Zones 11–12.

Sinningia cardinalis

☀/◐ ⚘ ↔ 12 in (30 cm) ↕ 8–12 in (20–30 cm)

Tuberous perennial from Brazil. Paired, long-stemmed, rounded to heart-shaped, velvety deep green, finely toothed leaves. Red tubular flowers, overarching upper lip, in heads of many blooms, not all open at same time. '**Innocent**', low-growing cultivar, tubular white flowers. Zones 11–12.

Sinningia × pumila

☀/◐ ⚘ ↔ 6–12 in (15–30 cm) ↕ 4–6 in (10–15 cm)

Low mounding garden hybrid between *S. pusilla* and *S. eumorpha*. Short-stemmed, rounded, velvety leaves. Slightly flared, mauve, tubular flowers, to 1¼ in (30 mm) long. Zones 11–12.

Sinningia speciosa

FLORIST'S GLOXINIA, GLOXINIA

☀/◐ ⚘ ↔ 12–20 in (30–50 cm) ↕ 8–12 in (20–30 cm)

Brazilian species, popular house plant. Lush, deep green, velvety, soft-toothed, rounded to heart-shaped leaves. Upright flower stems; large bell-shaped flowers, mauve to purple with light center and contrasting spots. Cultivars have larger flowers and wider color range, including '**Boonwood Yellow Bird**', yellow flowers; '**Buell's Queen Bee**', white flowers, 2 conspicuous pink blotches; and '**Kiss of Fire**', many small bright red flowers. Seedling strains such as **Lawn Hybrids** ★ available as individual colors or mixed. Zones 10–12.

SISYRINCHIUM

This genus contains about 90 species of annuals and perennials, and is a member of the iris (Iridaceae) family. These plants are native to North and South America, but have also been known to naturalize in other temperate countries. They produce clumps of stiff, upright, linear or sword-shaped leaves, which arch out into a fan shape. During spring and summer, clusters of trumpet-shaped flowers appear on spikes that hold the flowers just above the top of the foliage.
CULTIVATION: While frost tolerance varies with the species, these are otherwise undemanding plants that will do well when grown in poor to moderately fertile, well-drained soil. Though they will tolerate some shade, they do best in a position in full sun. Both species and cultivars propagate readily from seed and the rhizomatous clumps divide easily in autumn and spring.

Sisyrinchium 'Biscutella'

☀ ❄ ↔ 6 in (15 cm) ↕ 12 in (30 cm)

Clumping evergreen perennial; mid-green linear leaves. Upright flower stems; spikes of pale yellow flowers, dark brown to purple veining, to 1 in (25 mm) across; short-lived. Summer-flowering. Zones 7–9.

Sisyrinchium 'Californian Skies'

Sisyrinchium 'Californian Skies'

☀ ❄ ↔ 8 in (20 cm) ↑ 12 in (30 cm)

Hybrid with dark green lance-shaped foliage. Sturdy flower stems; mid-blue flowers in summer–late autumn. Zones 8–9.

Sisyrinchium californicum

syns *Sisyrinchium boreale, S. brachypus*

GOLDEN EYE GRASS

☀ ❄ ↔ 6 in (15 cm) ↑ 24 in (60 cm)

Found from California, USA, to British Columbia, Canada. Semi-evergreen perennial; often short-lived. Linear to sword-shaped gray-green leaves, 4–6 in (10–15 cm) long. Sturdy stems; star-shaped yellow flowers, 1 in (25 mm) wide, in summer. Zones 8–10.

Sisyrinchium graminoides

syns *Sisyrinchium angustifolium, S. bermudiana*

BLUE-EYED GRASS

☀ ✿ ↔ 8 in (20 cm) ↑ 20 in (50 cm)

Tight clump-forming perennial from North America. Rush-like dark green foliage year round. Star-shaped flowers, dark blue with distinctive yellow center dot, in summer–autumn. Zones 5–10.

Sisyrinchium striatum

syn. *Phaiophleps nigricans*

☀ ❄ ↔ 14 in (35 cm) ↑ 32 in (80 cm)

From Chile and Argentina. Clump-forming upright perennial; gray-green linear foliage. Sturdy spikes of pale yellow star-shaped flowers push up on stems through foliage, in summer. '**Aunt May**', creamy yellow variegated foliage. Zones 8–10.

SMITHIANTHA

This genus of 4 species of rhizomatous perennials belongs to the African-violet (Gesneriaceae) family, and grows in high-rainfall mountain areas of tropical Mexico. They are compact plants with one to several short fleshy stems and broadly heart-shaped leaves with a coating of velvety hairs. Borne in erect racemes, the long-stalked flowers are trumpet-shaped with upward-turned mouths, spotted on the inside. Many attractive hybrid cultivars exist.

CULTIVATION: Grown as indoor plants except in the humid tropics and subtropics, these plants prefer high light levels but not direct sun and should not be allowed to dry out except during their winter dormancy period, when they should be kept dry. Resume watering in late spring. Propagate by division of rhizomes in spring.

Smithiantha zebrina

☀ ⚘ ↔ 10–18 in (25–45 cm) ↑ 18–24 in (45–60 cm)

Known in Europe since 1840 and cultivated around the world, now rare in the wild in Mexico. Leaves 6 in (15 cm) long, irregularly banded along veins with brownish purple. Racemes of few flowers in summer, stalks erect, but flowers pointing down, orange to red on outside, inside yellow with red spots. Zones 10–12.

SOLANUM

syns *Cyphomandra, Lycianthes*

Distinguished by potato (*S. tuberosum*) in its many forms, this genus in the nightshade (Solanaceae) family includes some 1,400 species of annuals, perennials, vines, shrubs, and trees with a cosmopolitan distribution, most from tropical America. The trees and shrubs may be deciduous or evergreen, and many are armed with thorns. While variable, their flowers are all remarkably similar, being simple, small, 5-petalled structures carried singly or in clusters with a central cone of yellow stamens. Fleshy berries follow the flowers. The berries are usually somewhat poisonous and, because of their conspicuous color, may be attractive to children.

CULTIVATION: Hardiness varies: although a few species are really frost tolerant, most are tender. They are generally easily grown in any well-aerated well-drained soil; some have become serious weeds in various parts of the world. Most species prefer sun or part-shade. Propagate from seed or cuttings, or in a few cases by division.

Solanum quitoense

NARANJILLA

☀ ⚘ ↔ 7 ft (2 m) ↑ 7 ft (2 m)

Shrubby perennial, native to South America; straggly growth habit; densely covered with fine hairs. Stems and leaves light green, purple toned; leaves angularly lobed. Clusters of white flowers. Tomato-like edible orange fruit. Zones 10–12.

SOLDANELLA

This genus, belonging to the primrose (Primulaceae) family, contains 10 species of tiny alpine perennials native to the European Alps, the Carpathians, and the Balkans. They grow naturally in short damp turf and rocky places in the mountains. Plants form basal rosettes of leathery round or kidney-shaped leaves. The flowering stems often penetrate the snow cover in early spring. They bear heads of 1 to 6 hanging flowers in shades of blue to violet and white. The small funnel-shaped or bell-shaped flowers have fringed petals and are very dainty in appearance.

CULTIVATION: Grow in well-drained rich soil that in most cases should be neutral to slightly acid. Plant in an open cool position with protection from the hot midday sun. Protect from winter wet and also from slugs at flowering time. Alternatively, grow in a cool greenhouse in a gritty soil mix in bright filtered light with good ventilation. Propagation is from seed or by division.

Soldanella alpina

ALPINE SNOWBELL

☼ ❄ ↔ 8 in (20 cm) ↑ 3–6 in (8–15 cm)

From the Pyrenees and Alps, Europe. Leathery, kidney-shaped to round, dark green leaves. Violet flowers, crimson markings inside, 2 to 4, on 6 in (15 cm) stems, in spring–early summer. Zones 5–9.

Soldanella carpatica

☼ ❄ ↔ 8 in (20 cm) ↑ 3–6 in (8–15 cm)

From the Carpathian Mountains, Europe. Broad dark green leaves, to 2 in (5 cm) wide. Flowers small, fringed, violet, 2 to 5 blooms on 6 in (15 cm) stems, in spring. Zones 5–9.

Soldanella alpina

Soldanella villosa

☼ ❄ ↔ 8–12 in (20–30 cm) ↑ 6–12 in (15–30 cm)

Perennial from the Pyrenees, Europe. Round or kidney-shaped leaves to 2½ in (6 cm) wide, pale green beneath. Hairy flowering stalks, to 12 in (30 cm) high; 3 to 4 violet fringed flowers per stalk in early spring. Zones 5–9.

SOLEIROLIA

BABY'S TEARS, MIND-YOUR-OWN-BUSINESS

The sole species in this genus is an evergreen mat-forming perennial native to the islands of the western Mediterranean, notably Corsica, and widely naturalized in warm countries. It is a member of the nettle (Urticaceae) family. The branches are fine and root at the nodes. The tiny leaves are almost circular and spirally arranged but appear alternate. The white flowers are pink-tinged, minute, solitary, 4-petalled, and held in the leaf axils. CULTIVATION: Makes a neat ground cover in greenhouses, and in terraria, for temperate regions. Its invasive habit makes it less welcome in warmer climates. Plant in humus-rich well-drained soil; it is intolerant of scorching midday sun. Propagate by division.

Soleirolia soleirolii

syn. *Helxine soleirolii*

ANGEL'S TEARS, BABY'S TEARS, MIND-YOUR-OWN-BUSINESS

☼/◐ ✲ ↔ 2–4 ft (0.6–1.2 m) ↑ 2–4 in (5–10 cm)

Mat-forming perennial. Tightly packed, small, rounded, bright green leaves. Tiny, 4-petalled, solitary flowers, white tinged with pink, in summer. 'Aurea', yellowish green leaves. Zones 9–12.

SOLENOSTEMON

This genus, belonging to the mint (Lamiaceae) family, contains 60 species of shrubby plants native to tropical Africa and Asia. They may be erect, prostrate, or sprawling and are sometimes downy or succulent. Some of the species were previously included in the closely related genera *Plectranthus* and *Coleus*. Species of *Solenostemon* are grown for their colorful foliage that is often strikingly blotched or variegated, the leaves being pointed oval with toothed or scalloped edges. The

flowers have little importance for their appearance, and are the typical tubular 2-lipped flowers of the mint family.

CULTIVATION: In cool temperate climates, grow species in the conservatory, as house plants, or outdoors as annual bedding plants. In frost-free areas the plants can remain outdoors. Grow in any reasonable soil or potting mix in direct sunlight. Pinch back the growing tips regularly to maintain the plant's bushy shape and to prevent flowering. Propagate from seed or cuttings.

Solenostemon scutellarioides

syns *Coleus blumei, C. scutellarioides, Plectranthus scutellarioides*

COLEUS, PAINTED NETTLE

☼/◐ ✲ ↔ 12–24 in (30–60 cm) ↑ 12–24 in (30–60 cm)

From southeastern Asia. Shrubby plant; square, semi-succulent, lightly downy stems. Pointed oval, scallop-edged leaves, extremely variable, with green, red, purple, white, and yellow combinations. Insignificant flowers. 'Cantigny Royale', reddish purple leaves; 'Crinkly Bottom', deep blue-purple leaves, bright green edges; 'Display', burnt orange leaves, bright green edges; **Dragon Series**, large leaves, serrated-edged, scarlet to purple and black, gold edging; 'Frogfoot Purple', magenta leaves with deep purple edges; 'Jupiter', beet red crinkly leaves, edged pale green; 'Kiwi Fern', deeply serrated crimson leaves, edged lemon; 'Lemon Dash', brilliant green leaves, yellow center; 'Pineapple Beauty', deep maroon splashed, golden green leaves; **Rainbow Series**, variegated in greens, creams, and purples, irregularly marked leaves of yellow, red, copper, purple, and green, including 'Rainbow Fringed Mix', cut frilly edged leaves; 'Solar Eclipse', serrated edges; 'Walter Turner', red to dark red leaves, bright green edges; 'White Pheasant', serrated-edged rich green leaves, pale lemon center; 'Winsley Tapestry', serrated bright green leaves, beet red center; 'Winsome', vivid green leaves, red to black centers. Zones 10–12.

Solenostemon scutellarioides, Dragon Series, 'Black Dragon'

SOLIDAGO

GOLDENROD

Although a few species are found in other temperate regions, this genus of around 100 species of perennials is primarily North American, and belongs to the daisy (Asteraceae) family. They form clumps of upright, sometimes branching stems, the upper half of which develops panicles of tiny golden yellow flowers. The leaves may be linear, lance-shaped, or pointed oval, and usually have toothed edges. Often, by the time flowering starts in late summer, many of the lower leaves have withered somewhat. CULTIVATION: Very hardy plants, easily grown in full sun or half-sun in any position, in reasonably fertile, moist, and well-drained soil. They will grow in poor soil and withstand drought but will not flower well or reach maximum size in such conditions. Propagate from seed, basal cuttings, or by division. May self-sow.

Solidago bicolor

SILVERROD

☼/◐ ❄ ↔ 24 in (60 cm) ↑ 40 in (100 cm)

Perennial, native to eastern and central North America. Broad lance-shaped leaves, smooth-edged or toothed, to 8 in (20 cm) long. White to pale yellow flowerheads, in upright spikes, sometimes widely spaced, in late summer–autumn. Zones 4–9.

Solidago californica

CALIFORNIA GOLDENROD

☼/◐ ❄ ↔ 24–32 in (60–80 cm) ↑ 40–48 in (100–120 cm)

From southwestern USA east to New Mexico and south to Mexico. Narrow, pointed oval leaves, to more than 4 in (10 cm) long. Deep yellow flowerheads, in slightly overarching spikes, in autumn. Zones 8–10.

Solidago canadensis

☼/◐ ❄ ↔ 40 in (100 cm) ↑ 60 in (150 cm)

Erect species widespread throughout North America. Narrow lance-shaped leaves, to 4 in (10 cm) long, serrated edges. Short

Solidago canadensis

panicles of golden yellow flowers in late summer–autumn. *S. c.* subsp. *elongata*, minutely bristly stems and leaves. Zones 3–9.

Solidago rugosa

ROUGH-STEMMED GOLDENROD

☼/◐ ❄ ↔ 40 in (100 cm) ↑ 60 in (150 cm)

From eastern North America. Densely foliaged basal clump; broad lance-shaped leaves to over 5 in (12 cm) long, bristly, toothed. Small bright yellow flowerheads in late summer. 'Fireworks', heavy flowering, starburst-like array of panicles. Zones 3–9.

Solidago virgaurea

☼/◐ ❄ ↔ 24 in (60 cm) ↑ 40 in (100 cm)

Herbaceous perennial, native to Europe. Downy, finely toothed, broad lance-shaped leaves, to 4 in (10 cm) long near plant base, becoming smaller higher up. Elongated branching sprays of yellow flowers. Summer- to autumn-flowering. Zones 5–9.

Solidago Hybrid Cultivars

☼/◐ ❄ ↔ 12–48 in (30–120 cm) ↑ 24–60 in (60–150 cm)

Goldenrods, especially the hardier species from northern North America, interbreed freely, often producing vigorous heavy-flowering hybrids that generally make better garden plants. Examples include: 'Cloth of Gold', 24 in (60 cm) high, flowers deep yellow; 'Golden Wings', 60 in (150 cm) tall, toothed lance-shaped leaves, feathery panicles of bright yellow flowers; 'Goldenmosa' ★, 40 in (100 cm) tall, with strongly erect cane-like stems and small, overarched, bright yellow plumes; and 'Summershine', panicles of golden yellow flowers. Zones 4–9.

Solidago californica

× SOLIDASTER

This is a hybrid genus, arising in cultivation, of a single clump-forming perennial. It is most probably a cross between *Solidago canadensis* and *Aster ptarmicoides*, both members of the daisy (Asteraceae) family, and was found in 1910 in a nursery in Lyons, France. It bears tiny daisy flowers from late summer through to autumn. This plant is an ideal candidate for border plantings, and the blooms make good cut flowers for fresh or dried floral arrangements.

CULTIVATION: This attractive plant will grow well in a sunny well-drained border with moist but not wet soils. It will do best in a non-humid Mediterranean climate: it is fully frost hardy. Propagation is by dividing dormant plants in winter or from basal cuttings taken in spring.

× *Solidaster luteus*
syn. × *Solidaster hybridus*
☼ ❄ ↔ 12–15 in (30–38 cm)
↕ 32–36 in (80–90 cm)
Erect clump-forming perennial; leaves to 6 in (15 cm) long. Sprays of tiny daisy flowers, soft yellow, darker disc florets, from late summer to autumn. 'Lemore', profuse flowers, paler yellow. Zones 6–10.

SPATHIPHYLLUM
PEACE LILY

This genus of 36 species of evergreen perennials originates mainly in the American tropics, and is a member of the arum (Araceae) family. Peace lilies are large clump-forming plants with strong rhizomes, from which emerge lush, dark green, long-stemmed leaves that taper to a fine point and have a prominent midrib and veining. The tiny flowers, which are usually cream, are borne on an upright spike backed and partially enclosed by a large leafy spathe, which is often pure white but may be cream or pale green. In recent years, peace lilies have gained a reputation for their ability to remove vaporized solvents from the atmosphere. This characteristic, along with their ability to flower with fairly low light levels, has resulted in peace lilies being widely used as pot plants in shopping malls and offices.

CULTIVATION: *Spathiphyllum* species will perform best in a warm humid environment with fertile, deep, moist, humus-rich, well-drained soil. Water and feed well. Propagate by division.

Spathiphyllum cannifolium
☼ ❄ ↔ 40 in (100 cm) ↕ 40 in (100 cm)
Evergreen perennial, native to tropical South America and Trinidad. Long-stemmed leaves, lighter colored, less heavily veined than most species, on long stalk. Spathe usually folded back, white inside, green-tinted exterior. White to pale gray-green spadix. Zones 11–12.

Spathiphyllum wallisii
☼ ❄ ↔ 20–40 in (50–100 cm) ↕ 24–48 in (60–120 cm)
From Panama and Costa Rica. Dark green, heavily veined, lustrous, lance-shaped leaves, to 14 in (35 cm) long. Spathes white, ageing to green. White spadix, fragrant flowers. 'Clevelandii', large spathes, drooping leaves, deeply veined, glossy, to 16 in (40 cm) long, flowers indoors. Zones 11–12.

Spathiphyllum Hybrid Cultivars
☼ ❄ ↔ 12–60 in (30–150 cm) ↕ 12–72 in (30–180 cm)
A number of hybrid peace lilies have been raised, ranging from the fairly compact, heavy-flowering 'Tasson', to the largest hybrid cultivar in general cultivation, 'Sensation', which reaches over 6 ft (1.8 m) in height. Zones 11–12.

Spathiphyllum wallisii

SPHAERALCEA
syn. *Iliamna*
FALSE MALLOW, GLOBE MALLOW

This genus consists of 60 species belonging to the mallow (Malvaceae) family. Deciduous or evergreen perennials, subshrubs, and shrubs, they are native to the dry, even volcanic, mountain slopes of the warmer areas of North America, South America, and South Africa. The leaves are arranged in spirals, come in a variety of shapes, and are usually downy and toothed. The saucer-shaped flowers are red, pale purple, pink, white, orange, or yellow, and are produced singly or in clusters or inflorescences.

CULTIVATION: Grow outdoors in full sun in well-drained moderately fertile soil and provide protection from winter moisture. If grown in pots, provide added grit to loam-based compost and feed and water moderately. Propagate by sowing seed in spring and dividing perennials at the same time. In areas with heavy winter rain, they are best protected in a cool greenhouse as excess wet, rather than cold, often kills the hardier species.

Sphaeralcea coccinea
syn. *Malvastrum coccineum*
GLOBE MALLOW, PRAIRIE MALLOW, RED FALSE MALLOW
☼ ❄ ↔ 6–12 in (15–30 cm) ↕ 6–18 in (15–45 cm)
Found from southern Canada to Arizona, USA. Well-branched perennial; white or gray felted stems. Pinnately parted leaves, rough-textured, grayish green. Short racemes of orange to red flowers in summer. Zones 4–9.

Sphaeralcea munroana
☼ ❄ ↔ 12–27 in (30–70 cm) ↕ 8–36 in (20–90 cm)
Short-lived perennial; native to western North America. Felted gray stems; small, deeply toothed, 5-lobed, hairy leaves. Apricot-pink to red or orange saucer-shaped flowers in summer. Zones 4–9.

STACHYS

BETONY, HEDGE NETTLE, WOUNDWORT

There are about 300 species in this genus in the mint (Lamiaceae) family, and they range from stoloniferous and rhizomatous perennials through to a few evergreen shrubs. In the wild these plants can be found in a range of situations, from dry mountain areas through to scrub areas, wastelands, meadows, and streamsides, particularly in northern temperate zones. The hairy, soft to touch, lance-shaped, sometimes round leaves vary in color from pale silvery grays to greens. Flowers are tubular, sometimes hooded, and vary from red, pink, and purple through to white and yellow. The foliage is often aromatic, lending itself to many uses in the ornamental garden.

CULTIVATION: *Stachys* species require well-drained open soil in full sun. They do not cope well in shade or humid areas. Propagate from seed in spring and autumn or from softwood cuttings when material is available.

Stachys byzantina

syns *Stachys lanata*, *S. olympica*

LAMBS' EARS, WOOLLY BETONY

☼ ❅ ↔ 24 in (60 cm) ↕ 18 in (45 cm)

Ground-hugging perennial found from the Caucasus region to Iran. Oblong to elliptical gray-green leaves with silvery white down. Upright stems of pink to purple flowers in late spring–early summer. **'Cotton Boll'** ★ (syn. 'Sheila McQueen'), longer leaves, modified cottonball-like flowers. Zones 4–8.

Stachys citrina

☼ ❅ ↔ 12 in (30 cm) ↕ 8 in (20 cm)

Spreading, low-growing, woody perennial. Native to Turkey. Ovate, minutely serrated, delicately downy, soft green leaves. Spikes of yellow flowers in summer. Zones 5–7.

Stachys coccinea

SCARLET HEDGE NETTLE

☼ ❅ ↔ 18 in (45 cm) ↕ 24 in (60 cm)

Mounding perennial species found from Arizona and Texas, USA, to Mexico. Ovate to lance-shaped, slightly downy, crinkly, mid-green leaves. Upright stems of scarlet-pink flowers from mid-spring to late autumn. Zones 7–9.

Stachys byzantina

Stachys coccinea

Stachys macrantha

syns *Stachys grandiflora*, *S. spicata*

BIG BETONY

☼ ❅ ↔ 12–18 in (30–45 cm) ↕ 18–24 in (45–60 cm)

Upright hairy perennial from northeastern Turkey and northwestern Iran. Rosettes of wide, ovate, crinkly, veined, dark green leaves, to 3 in (8 cm) long. Spikes of hooded dark cerise-purple flowers, 1¼ in (3 cm) wide, on erect stems, in summer. **'Superba'**, bright cerise-purple flowers. Zones 5–7.

Stachys officinalis

syn. *Stachys betonica*

BISHOP'S WORT, WOOD BETONY

☼ ❅ ↔ 18–36 in (45–90 cm) ↕ 12–36 in (30–90 cm)

Perennial from Europe. Upright, almost completely hairless, oblong, wrinkled, mid-green leaves, to 5 in (12 cm) long. Erect stems of oblong flower spikes; purple, reddish pink, or white flowers in early summer–early autumn. **'Alba'**, white flowers; **'Rosea Superba'**, rose pink flowers. Zones 5–8.

STELLARIA

CHICKWEED, STITCHWORT

This large genus of plants belongs to the pink (Caryophyllaceae) family. About 120 species are distributed worldwide; they are annuals and perennials with brittle stems and generally tiny white flowers. Some species, such as *S. media*, commonly known as chickweed, are weeds.

CULTIVATION: *Stellaria* species with some ornamental value are only suitable in wild gardens, as fillers under large shrubs, or as light airy plants among bolder woodland perennials. Grow these plants in humus-rich soil in half-sun and propagate by division or from seed.

Stellaria holostea

GREATER STITCHWORT

☼ ❅ ↔ 3–7 ft (0.9–2 m) ↕ 20–24 in (50–60 cm)

Suckering perennial from Europe, North Africa, and western Asia. Narrow leaves to 3 in (8 cm) long. Open airy sprays of dainty white flowers in spring–early summer. Zones 5–10.

Stellaria holostea

STOKESIA

STOKES ASTER

The sole species in this genus in the daisy (Asteraceae) family has been extensively developed in cultivation. This late summer- to autumn-flowering perennial from southeastern USA is an upright plant with 6–8 in (15–20 cm) long lance-shaped leaves and large cornflower-like heads of white, yellow, or mauve to deep purple-blue flowers.

CULTIVATION: Plant in full sun or half-sun in light free-draining soil. Water and feed well. Watch for mildew in late summer. Propagate by division near end of dormant period or from seed.

Stokesia laevis

STOKES ASTER

☼/◐ ❄ ↔ 8–16 in (20–40 cm)
↑ 10–30 in (25–75 cm)

Found from South Carolina to Louisiana and northern Florida, USA. Narrow, deep green, lance-shaped leaves, smooth-edged, sometimes spiny-toothed at base. Flowerheads to 4 in (10 cm) wide, solitary or in small clusters, usually mauve to purple. 'Blue Danube' ★, 16 in (40 cm) tall, deep blue with white center; 'Bluestone', 10 in (25 cm) tall, bright blue; 'Mary Gregory', pale yellow with darker center; 'Purple Parasols', 20 in (50 cm) tall, deep violet-blue; 'Silver Moon', 18 in (45 cm) tall, pure white; 'Wyoming', 20 in (50 cm) tall, very dark blue flowers. Zones 6–10.

Stokesia laevis 'Purple Parasols'

STRELITZIA

Originating in South Africa, the 4 or 5 species in this genus are large evergreen perennials in the strelitzia (Strelitziaceae) family. Usually treated as shrubs or trees, they are clump-forming and have very long oblong to lance-shaped leaves that are borne on stout stalks. A large bud or spathe, borne at the end of the stem, is usually held clear of the foliage; from it opens a succession of flowers, each with a long projecting corolla and wing-like sepals, often in a striking range of contrasting colors.

CULTIVATION: They prefer full sun or partial shade, and are tender to all but the lightest frosts. Plant in moist well-drained soil; most species will tolerate brief periods of drought once established and prefer to be kept on the dry side in winter. Roots are very strong, so take care when siting. Propagate from seed, by removing suckers, or by division.

Strelitzia juncea

syns *Strelitzia* × *kewensis* var. *juncea*,
S. reginae var. *juncea*

☼ ⧓ ↔ 3–5 ft (0.9–1.5 m) ↑ 5 ft (1.5 m)

Native to South Africa's Cape region; ever-green perennial. Thick, rush-like, grayish green leaves lack blades, tapering to point. Orange flowers emerge from beaked bract, like those of *S. reginae*. Zones 10–12.

Strelitzia reginae

BIRD OF PARADISE

☼ ⧓ ↔ 3 ft (0.9 m) ↑ 6 ft (1.8 m)

Leaves 12–30 in (30–75 cm) long; stems to 6 ft (1.8 m) tall. Deep purple-blue corolla, orange calyces, in winter–spring. Cultivars include 'Kirstenbosch Gold' and 'Mandela's Gold' ★. Zones 10–12.

STREPTOCARPUS

CAPE PRIMROSE

Although widespread in the African and Asian tropics and sub-tropics, most of the cultivated plants in this genus of around 130 species of annuals and perennials are natives of southern Africa, and belong to the African violet (Gesneriaceae) family. Despite the di-versity of form among species in the genus, they share some features. The leaves are vel-vety and heavily veined. The flowers are long-tubed, primrose-like, usually with 5 petals; they occur in heads on short upright stems.

CULTIVATION: Cold tolerance varies, though none withstand more than the lightest frost. Plant in a bright but not sunny, warm, draft-free position, in fertile, moist, humus-rich, well-drained soil. Propagate by division, from leaf-stalk cuttings or from seed.

Streptocarpus candidus

◐/☼ ⧓ ↔ 10–16 in (25–40 cm) ↑ 12 in (30 cm)

From South Africa. Vertical rhizome; rosettes of deep green, heavily veined, irregularly toothed leaves. Heads of up to 25 pale mauve to white flowers, usually fragrant, in summer. Zones 10–11.

Streptocarpus caulescens

◐/☼ ⧓ ↔ 12–20 in (30–50 cm) ↑ 12–20 in (30–50 cm)

From Tanzania and Kenya; erect to sprawling perennial. Woody-based stems; broad, pointed oval leaves. Airy sprays of up to 12 white-centered purple flowers, in autumn–winter. Zones 11–12.

Strelitzia reginae

Streptocarpus, Hybrid Cultivar, 'Party Doll'

Streptocarpus cyaneus

◐/☀ ✛ ↔ 12–20 in (30–50 cm)
↑ 6–8 in (15–20 cm)
From South Africa. Rosettes of toothed leaves
up to 16 in (40 cm) long. Dark-veined light
pink to violet flowers, usually paired, on stems
to 6 in (15 cm) long, in spring–summer. *S. c.*
subsp. *polackii*, mauve-pink flowers, leaves
and stalks red-tinted. Zones 10–11.

Streptocarpus glandulosissimus

◐/☀ ✛ ↔ 12–20 in (30–50 cm)
↑ 12–20 in (30–50 cm)
Kenyan species; upright to sprawling habit.
Downy pointed oval leaves to over 4 in
(10 cm) long, often smaller. Airy sprays of
violet flowers, most of year. Zones 11–12.

Streptocarpus kirkii

◐/☀ ✛ ↔ 8–12 in (20–30 cm) ↑ 12–16 in (30–40 cm)
Native to Kenya and Tanzania. Erect stems become woody and
trailing as they mature. Opposite pairs of sparsely hairy, pointed
oval, serrated or smooth-edged leaves. Airy sprays of up to 10
small violet-pink flowers, deep purple spots in throat. Winter-
flowering. Zones 11–12.

Streptocarpus saxorum

syn. *Streptocarpella saxorum*
◐/☀ ✛ ↔ 8–16 in (20–40 cm) ↑ 4–6 in (10–15 cm)
Compact, long-flowering species, native to Kenya and Tanzania.
Low spreading clump of velvety pointed oval leaves to 1¼ in
(30 mm) long. Relatively large, solitary or paired, white to pale
mauve flowers, small upper lobes. Blooms throughout most of
year. Zones 10–12.

Streptocarpus wendlandii

◐/☀ ✛ ↔ 30 in (75 cm) ↑ 12 in (30 cm)
South African native. Single, very large, heart-
shaped, finely toothed, deep green leaf, to
30 in (75 cm) long, covered with fine hairs,
red underside. Small, white to mauve, purple-
marked flowers, in summer. Zones 10–12.

Streptocarpus Hybrid Cultivars

◐/☀ ✛ ↔ 12–20 in (30–50 cm)
↑ 12–20 in (30–50 cm)
Wide-ranging group of fancy-flowered, compact, rosette-forming hybrids developed by
interbreeding mainly South African species.
Flower most heavily from spring into summer, sometimes blooming sporadically year-
round. Cultivated as house plants. 'Albatross',
white flowers, yellow throat; 'Amanda', blue,
dark-veined, white throat; 'Bethan', mauve,
yellow throat; 'Blue Heaven', pale lavender,
semi-double, white throat; 'Blushing Bride',
white flushed pink, semi-double, long-tubed;
'Bristol's Very Best', magenta, double; 'Carys',
mauve-blue, purple-blue throat and veining;
'Chorus Line', white with mauve-blue veining, double; 'Concord Blue', continual pale
violet-blue mid-pink, purple-red center;
'Falling Stars', pale lavender, white throat;
'Flexii White', white, dark purple veins;
'Happy Snappy', red, yellowish throat;
'Heidi', mauve-blue; 'Jennifer', dark blue,
white throat; 'Kim', purple, white throat;
'Lisa', pink, white throat; 'Lynette', soft
deep burgundy; 'Megan', deep purple, yellow throat; 'Melanie', mauve-blue, purple-
pink veining; 'Midnight Flame', intense
bright red; 'Nymph', bright purple, yellow
throat; 'Party Doll', purple-edged, pale lavender, yellow throat; 'Passion Pink', deep
pink with dark lines; 'Pink Souffle', frilly
pink double; 'Rosebud', deep pink, double; 'Rosemary', light
pink, double; 'Ruby' ★, pure deep crimson; 'Sian', bright blue,
white and yellow throat; 'Sophie', purple-red, dark throat;
'Tina', pale pink, dark pink center and veining. Zones 10–11.

Streptocarpus wendlandii

STROBILANTHES

This genus of more than 250 species of evergreen or deciduous
perennials and soft-stemmed shrubs is native to tropical Asia
and Madagascar, and belongs to the acanthus (Acanthaceae)
family. A few species are grown both indoors and out for their
attractive tubular or funnel-shaped flowers, in varying shades of
blue and purple. *Strobilanthes* species have colorful purplish foliage; the opposite paired leaves are frequently of unequal size.
CULTIVATION: Frost tender, these plants require a warm climate
and prefer a position in full sun or part-shade in well-drained
humus-enriched soil. They can be pruned lightly to shape, or

clipped to form a hedge. The new growth has the most attractive coloring. Propagation is from seed, cuttings, or by division.

Strobilanthes anisophyllus

GOLDFUSSIA

☀ ♣ ↔ 5 ft (1.5 m) ↕ 5 ft (1.5 m)

Shrubby plant, native to Assam in northern India. Narrow silvery purple leaves in unequal-sized pairs. Tubular flowers, lavender-blue, 1 in (25 mm) long, at ends of branches, in late summer–autumn. Zones 10–11.

Strobilanthes dyerianus

syn. *Perilepta dyeriana*

☀ ♣ ↔ 36 in (90 cm) ↕ 36 in (90 cm)

Originally a native of Myanmar. Evergreen species grown mostly as an indoor plant for its attractive foliage. Lance-shaped irides-cent purple leaves, to 6 in (15 cm) long, toothed edges. Short spikes of funnel-shaped pale blue flowers, held above leaves, in spring–summer. Zones 10–12.

Strobilanthes gossypinus

☀ ♣ ↔ 20–30 in (50–75 cm) ↕ 3–5 ft (0.9–1.5 m)

Shrubby species native to southern India and Sri Lanka. Green leaves, 2–4 in (5–10 cm) long, lance-shaped, tapering to fine point, densely coated with cream hairs. Small heads of soft blue to lavender flowers clustered at stem tip and in upper leaf axils, in summer. Zones 10–12.

STROMANTHE

This genus of 15 species of leafy perennials growing 3–10 ft (0.9–3 m) high belongs to the arrowroot (Marantaceae) family. In their native Central and South America they grow on the forest floor, where they are rampant and often weedy. Their appearance is similar to related plants such as *Ctenanthe* and *Maranta* with long oblong orna-mental leaves, which emerge from sheathed stems. The leaves are often marked or veined with white or lighter or darker shades of green. Although they are grown as house plants for their foliage, the flowers often have showy colorful bracts, which add interest to their ornamental appeal. CULTIVATION: In suitably warm climates grow these plants in a shady and sheltered position. In tem-perate climates they are widely cultivated as in-door plants. Grow in bright filtered light in a rich soil mix. During active growth, water moderately and apply liquid fertilizer fortnightly. Propagation is by division or from cuttings.

Stromanthe sanguinea

☀/◐ ♣ ↔ 2–3 ft (0.6–0.9 m) ↕ 3–5 ft (0.9–1.5 m)

Handsome foliage plant, native to Brazil. Large, thick, glossy, oblong leaves, emerge from pinkish red sheaths, dark green above, purple beneath. White flowers, showy red floral bracts. 'Stripestar', leaves with distinctive white stripes. Zones 10–12.

Strobilanthes gossypinus

STYLIDIUM

TRIGGERPLANT

This genus, belonging to the self-named triggerplant (Stylidi-aceae) family, contains around 110 species of perennials. Most are native to Australia, where they often grow in sandy coastal areas. The foliage is usually grass-like, sometimes with short leaves on narrow stems. The dainty flowers, in white, pink, or yellow, are borne on upright spikes in summer. Stamens and stigma are fused in a column; when an insect alights on the flower, they react like a trigger, hitting the insect's back and thereby transferring pollen. It is this unusual trigger mecha-nism, which is only activated on warm sunny days, that gives the genus its common name. CULTIVATION: In very warm dry areas, plant *Stylidium* species in well-drained sandy soil, but these plants are better suited to pot culture. In cool temperate climates they can be grown in the greenhouse in full light in a sandy potting mix. They should be watered moderate-ly when in growth, but plants should be kept almost dry in winter. Propagate from seed or cuttings or by division.

Stylidium graminifolium

TRIGGERPLANT

☀ ❅ ↔ 10 in (25 cm) ↕ 10–20 in (25–50 cm)

Native to eastern and southern Australia; found from coastal to mountain regions. Variable per-ennial; stiff grass-like leaves. Spikes of pale pink to magenta flowers, on hairy stems, in summer. Zones 9–11.

Stylidium lineare

☀ ❅ ↔ 4 in (10 cm) ↕ 6–12 in (15–30 cm)

Native to New South Wales, Australia. Small plant forming rosettes of short, narrow, grass-like leaves. Upright central stems; spikes of dainty pink flowers. Summer- to autumn-flowering. Zones 9–11.

Stylidium lineare

Sutera cordata

STYLOPHORUM

This genus in the poppy (Papaveraceae) family contains 3 species of hairy perennials, and is native to eastern North America and eastern Asia, where they grow in woodlands. They form basal rosettes of long divided, irregularly lobed and toothed leaves. The stem leaves are much smaller and usually stalkless. Clear yellow or orange, 4-petalled, saucer-shaped flowers are borne in small clusters in spring. The blooms are followed by narrow cylindrical seed pods that are covered in fine silvery hairs.
CULTIVATION: *Stylophorum* species are woodland plants suitable for shady positions in the garden. Unlike most plants in the poppy family, which resent disturbance, these plants can be readily transplanted, and will perform best in any reasonably fertile moist but well-drained soil. Propagate from seed or by division.

Stylophorum diphyllum

Stylophorum diphyllum
CELANDINE POPPY, WOOD POPPY
☀ ❋ ↔ 12 in (30 cm) ↑ 18 in (45 cm)
Downy perennial, native to eastern USA. Deeply and irregularly lobed leaves, scalloped or toothed edges. Simple, yellow, saucer-shaped, 4-petalled flowers, to 2 in (5 cm) wide, on delicate stems, in spring. Zones 5–9.

Stylophorum lasiocarpum
CHINESE CELANDINE POPPY
☀ ❋ ↔ 12 in (30 cm) ↑ 12 in (30 cm)
Perennial from central and eastern China. Long irregularly lobed and toothed leaves, rather like those of the dandelion (*Taraxacum* species). Clear yellow, 4-petalled, saucer-shaped flowers, in clusters, 4–5 in (10–12cm) wide, in spring. Zones 5–9.

SUTERA

This genus of about 130 perennials and annuals from the foxglove (Scrophulariaceae) family originates from South Africa. They have become well known in recent years as hanging basket plants. Small, rounded, toothed, green leaves sit on thin stems that hug the ground. Starry white, mauve, lilac, pink, or blue flowers sit face-up on the foliage. These plants can produce flowers for up to 10 months of the year.
CULTIVATION: *Sutera* species are adaptable to sun and shade and require free-draining fertile soil. During warmer months they need extra water to keep blooming. Propagate from stem cuttings in autumn or by sowing seed in spring.

Sutera cordata
syn. *Bacopa cordata*
☼ ❅ ↔ 20 in (50 cm) ↑ 3 in (8 cm)
Low-growing, ground covering, South African perennial, pale green leaves all year. Pure white flowers, delicate yellow eye, almost year round in warm climates. '**Blue Showers**', lilac to pale blue flowers; '**Lavender Showers**', pale lavender star-shaped flowers; '**Snowflake**', tiny white flowers in leaf axils; '**Snowstorm**' ★, large white flowers, more compact growth habit. Zones 9–10.

Sutera grandiflora
PURPLE MORNING GLORY PLANT
☼ ❅ ↔ 24 in (60 cm) ↑ 40 in (100 cm)
Bushy perennial, native to South Africa. Small, elliptical, green leaves. Lavender-blue flowers with white throat. Summer- to autumn-flowering. Zones 9–11.

SWAINSONA

Around 50 species of perennials and subshrubs from the pea-flower subfamily of the legume (Fabaceae) family, all but one of the species in this genus are Australian natives. They are leguminous plants and have small racemes of ridged pea-flowers, often red or pink, but also occur in mauve- or white-flowered forms. The foliage is pinnate, usually with many small leaflets, often gray-green and covered in fine downy hairs. The flowering season varies—some species bloom in winter, others in spring to summer, and those from very arid areas burst into bloom after rain.
CULTIVATION: Although some *Swainsona* species will tolerate very light frosts, most perform best in a mild frost-free climate in a position in full sun. They vary in their soil requirements; those species from hot arid areas prefer to be dry over winter, while those from cooler zones require constant moisture. Good drainage is also most important. Propagation is from seed, which needs to be soaked before sowing, or from half-hardened summer cuttings.

Swainsona formosa

syn. *Clianthus formosus*

GLORY PEA, STURT'S DESERT PEA

☼ ❄ ↔ 3–7 ft (0.9–2 m) ↕ 3–4 ft (0.9–1.2 m)

Sprawling subshrub. Silky, grayish green, pinnate leaves. Showy pea-flowers to 3 in (8 cm) long, in clusters of 5 to 6; brilliant red, black spot, from winter–summer. Zones 9–11.

Swainsona galegifolia

☼ ❄ ↔ 6 ft (1.8 m) ↕ 2 ft (0.6 m)

Upright or trailing perennial or softwooded shrub from eastern Australia. Gray- to dark green pinnate leaves, 25 tiny leaflets edged with fine hairs. Pink, mauve, purple, white, or reddish purple pea-flowers, in spring–summer. Zones 9–11.

SYMPHYANDRA

RING BELLFLOWER

This genus of some 12 rather short-lived perennial species, occurs from the eastern Mediterranean region to central Asia, and belongs to the bellflower (Campanulaceae) family. They differ from *Campanula* merely in the anthers being united to form a collar around the style. The basal leaves are often heart-shaped and toothed, with long stalks. The flowers are held in racemes or panicles. The calyx has 5 long lobes; the corolla is bell-shaped with 5 lobes. There are 5 stamens with free filaments and united anthers. The fruit is a capsule.

CULTIVATION: These plants suit the herbaceous border or rock garden in temperate areas. They grow best in good well-drained soils. Some die after flowering, though setting seed freely. They can be propagated by careful division of the fleshy rootstocks or from seed sown in autumn.

Symphyandra hofmannii

☼/❂ ❄ ↔ 6–12 in (15–30 cm) ↕ 12–24 in (30–60 cm)

From Bosnia and Herzegovina. Can be monocarpic in cultivation. Rosette-forming; leaves oval to lance-shaped. Pendulous cream or pale yellow bell-flowers, in racemes, in summer. Zones 4–9.

SYMPHYTUM

COMFREY, KNITBONE

This genus contains 35 species of hardy perennials belonging to the borage (Boraginaceae) family. Of temperate Eurasian origin, they favor damp woodlands, streamsides, and wasteland. Plants are characterized by vigorous growth and prolific flowering. A basal rosette of coarse tapering leaves emerges from a fleshy tap root. Clusters of small bell-shaped flowers, red-tipped in bud, reddish to blue in bloom, are arranged in 1-sided coils at the tips of branching stems. Hummingbirds are attracted to the flowers. Comfrey has a long history of use in herbal medicine. If taken internally in quantity, comfrey could be carcinogenic.

CULTIVATION: *Symphytum* species favor damp soil and will grow in full sun or partial shade. They are adaptable to dry conditions where their growth is restrained. They can be grown in full sun

Swainsona formosa

in cold climates if the soil is heavy and moisture-retentive. Control and propagate these plants by chopping out extra growth; they should be cut back after blooming.

Symphytum asperum

PRICKLY COMFREY

☼ ❄ ↔ 5–7 ft (1.5–2 m) ↕ 4–5 ft (1.2–1.5 m)

From Europe, the Caucasus region, and Iran. Oval bristly leaves to 10 in (25 cm) long. Small tubular flowers, initially pink, ageing to blue or lilac, in summer. Zones 5–10.

Symphytum caucasicum

☼ ❄ ↔ 24–32 in (60–80 cm) ↕ 24–32 in (60–80 cm)

Native to the Caucasus region. Basal leaves mid-green, 10 in (25 cm) long. Flared trumpets of rich blue flowers, to ½ in (12 mm) long, in summer. 'Eminence', smaller than the species, leaves gray tinged, blue flowers in early summer. Zones 5–10.

Symphytum 'Goldsmith' ★

syns *Symphytum ibericum* 'Jubilee', *S. i.* 'Variegatum'

☼/❂ ❄ ↔ 12–20 in (30–50 cm) ↕ 10–12 in (25–30 cm)

Spreading bristly perennial. Leaves to 10 in (25 cm) long, irregularly and broadly edged with yellow. Drooping blue and white flowers, to ¾ in (18 mm) long, open from pink buds, in late spring–early summer. Zones 5–10.

Symphytum grandiflorum

☼ ❄ ↔ 20–24 in (50–60 cm) ↕ 15–16 in (38–40 cm)

Native to Europe and the Caucasus region. Deciduous species; rosette-forming; bristly leaves, to 10 in (25 cm) long. Clusters of trumpet-shaped flowers open to pale yellow from red-tipped buds, at the end of branching stems, in late spring–early summer. Zones 5–10.

Symphytum 'Goldsmith'

Symphytum 'Hidcote Blue'

☼ ❋ ↔ 18–20 in (45–50 cm) ↑ 18–20 in (45–50 cm)
Leaves to 10 in (25 cm) long. Red buds, pale blue trumpets,
to ¾ in (18 mm) long, in late spring–early summer. Zones 5–10.

Symphytum ibericum

syn. *Symphytum grandiflorum* of gardens
☼/◑ ❋ ↔ 12 in (30 cm) ↑ 16 in (40 cm)
Creeping rhizomatous perennial, native to Turkey and eastern
Europe. Hairy oval leaves. Clusters of pendulous tubular cream
flowers in spring–summer. Can be invasive. Zones 5–10.

SYNTHYRIS

KITTENTAILS

This genus, belonging to the foxglove (Scrophulariaceae) family,
contains 14 species of perennials from northern and western
North America where they are found growing in woodland and
alpine areas. Closely related to *Veronica*, they are low-growing,
rhizomatous, tufted plants. The leathery leaves, which are heart-
shaped, kidney-shaped, or deeply cut, become smaller and bract-
like on the flowering stems. The flowers are blue or violet-blue
with a short tube and 4 erect or spreading lobes.
CULTIVATION: The woodland species will tolerate quite poor soils
such as those occurring under deciduous trees, but will do best
in a fertile well-drained soil with added organic matter in light
shade. Alpine species will perform best in a sunny open site with
protection from the hottest summer sun. Propagation is from
seed or by division.

Tacca integrifolia

Synthyris missurica

☼/● ❋ ↔ 12 in (30 cm) ↑ 16–24 in (40–60 cm)
Tufted perennial native to northern and western North America.
Dark green, leathery, heart-shaped to kidney-shaped, toothed
leaves. Bright bluish purple tubular flowers, in loose spikes, in
spring–summer. 'Alba', white flowers. Zones 3–9.

Synthyris reniformis

SNOW QUEEN, SPRING QUEEN
☼/● ❋ ↔ 4 in (10 cm) ↑ 2–6 in (5–15 cm)
From moist shady forests of Washington and Oregon, USA.
Round to heart-shaped leaves, shallowly lobed, paler beneath.
Short racemes of bluish purple flowers in early spring. Zones 6–9.

TACCA

This genus, comprising 10 species native to the African and Asian
tropics with 9 from the Malay Archipelago alone, is now a member of the yam (Dioscoreaceae) family, though it was formerly
placed in Taccaceae. The plants are herbaceous perennials that
arise from tubers. The long-stalked leaves have blades that are
smooth and elliptical, or deeply dissected. The hermaphrodite
flowers are regular, in cymes surrounded by a whorl of bracts
and are pollinated by flies. The 6 tepals are petal-like, greenish
to brown-purple. The fruit is a berry or more rarely a capsule
with 10 to many seeds. These plants are found in semi-evergreen
monsoon forests and are useful foliage plants in tropical gardens.
They are used as flowering pot plants for indoor decoration in
more temperate countries.
CULTIVATION: In the tropics these perennials are grown in shaded
sites with humus-rich soils; in temperate regions they need a
humid greenhouse. To maintain vigor, such plants should be
re-rooted and repotted every 2 years. They are propagated by
division or from cuttings from old tubers. Seeds sown on the
soil surface will yield flowering plants in 3 years.

Tacca integrifolia

BAT FLOWER, BAT PLANT, WHITE BAT FLOWER
☼ ⚘ ↔ 24 in (60 cm) ↑ 24–48 in (60–120 cm)
Perennial from eastern India, southern China, and Indonesia.
Vertical rhizome; large, broad, oblong or sword-shaped leaves.
Long-stalked heads of nodding bat-like flowers, green to dark
purplish black bracts (white in one popular form), green to dark
purple bracteoles, in spring–summer. Zones 10–12.

TAGETES

MARIGOLD

All but one of the 50 or so species of this genus in the daisy
(Asteraceae) family comes from the American tropics and subtropics. They are mainly upright annuals or perennials with dark
green, sometimes aromatic, pinnate leaves with toothed edges.
The flowers are usually yellow or orange, and often daisy-like.
CULTIVATION: Marigolds prefer a warm sunny position in light
well-drained soil. Water well and feed if the foliage begins to
yellow. Deadhead frequently to ensure continuous blooming
is maintained. Propagate from seed, which is usually started
indoors in early spring.

Tagetes, Hybrid Cultivar, Safari Series, 'Safari Red'

Tagetes, Hybrid Cultivar, Atlantis Series, 'Atlantis Primrose'

Tagetes, Hybrid Cultivar, 'Jolly Jester'

Tagetes lucida

MEXICAN MINT, SPANISH TARRAGON, SWEET MACE

☼/◐ ⊰ ↔ 16–32 in (40–80 cm) ↕ 16–40 in (40–100 cm)

Perennial from Mexico and Guatemala. Woody-based, branching a little way up stem. Lance-shaped leaves, toothed, pleasantly aromatic. Small bright golden yellow flowerheads in late summer. Can be used as tarragon substitute. Zones 9–11.

Tagetes patula

FRENCH MARIGOLD

☼ ✾ ↔ 6–12 in (15–30 cm) ↕ 8–20 in (20–50 cm)

Compact bushy annual from Mexico and Guatemala. Pinnate leaves, narrow, toothed, lance-shaped segments. Flowers solitary or in small clusters, usually yellow to orange, in early summer–autumn. Garden forms available in many colors. Zones 11–12.

Tagetes tenuifolia

SIGNET MARIGOLD, STRIPED MARIGOLD

☼ ✾ ↔ 12–24 in (30–60 cm) ↕ 12–32 in (30–80 cm)

Annual, found naturally from Mexico to Colombia. Sometimes narrowly upright, usually bushy, with fine branches. Pinnate, many-toothed leaves, narrow lance-shaped segments. Abundant bright yellow flowerheads, short ray florets, in early summer–autumn. 'Starfire', seedling mix in various shades of yellow, orange, and red. Zones 11–12.

Tagetes Hybrid Cultivars

☼ ✾ ↔ 6–12 in (15–30 cm) ↕ 8–12 in (20–30 cm)

Mainly derived from *T. patula*. Border marigolds make ideal summer bedding plants. Usually marketed as seedling series, in mixed or single colors; mostly double flowers with few visible ray florets, chiefly in yellow, orange, and red. **Antigua Series**, flowerheads up to 3 in (8 cm) wide; **Atlantis Series,** pompon-like flowerheads up to 4 in (10 cm) wide; **Bonanza Series**, crested flowerheads up to 2 in (5 cm) wide; **Boy Series**, crested flowerheads up to 1½ in (35 mm) wide; **Crush Series**, flowerheads to 4 in (10 cm) wide; **Disco Series,** many single flowers up to 2 in (5 cm) wide; **Gate Series,** double flowerheads up to 3 in (8 cm) wide; **Girl Series,** dwarf, double flowerheads; **Inca Series,** flowerheads up to 5 in (12 cm) wide; '**Jolly Jester**', red petals with yellow striping; **Little Hero Series,** double flowerheads up to 2 in (5 cm) wide;

'**Naughty Marietta**' ★, single yellow flowers, red mid-band; **Safari Series,** double flowers to 3 in (8 cm) wide; **Zenith Series,** heavy foliage, double flowers to 3 in (8 cm) wide. Zones 11–12.

TALINUM

This genus of over 40 species of succulent shrubs or herbs from Africa and the Americas, belongs to the purslane (Portulacaceae) family. They usually have deciduous leaves and branches arising from a perennial tuber or caudex. Leaves are alternate, often irregularly spaced, flat to cylindrical, more or less succulent and often soft and limp. Flowerheads are often solitary and usually held at the stem tips. The flowers open once, often for only a few hours, some setting seed without opening. The seed pod is a 3-chambered, spherical to oval capsule. Some are regarded as weeds. **CULTIVATION:** These plants are extremely easy to grow in any well-drained soil. Most mature plants will readily set seed. Underground roots may be raised for display. Propagate from seed.

Talinum paniculatum

JEWELS OF OPAR

☼/◐ ⊰ ↔ 16–20 in (40–50 cm) ↕ 40 in (100 cm)

Found from southern USA to central Argentina, naturalized in tropics and subtropics. Leaves elliptical to oblong. Small flowers, 5-petalled, pink, yellow, or white, in spring–summer. Seed pods yellow. Often a weed. Zones 9–10.

Tagetes tenuifolia 'Starfire'

Tanacetum corymbosum subsp. *clusii*

Tanacetum camphoratum

TANACETUM

This genus of about 70 annuals and perennials belonging to the daisy (Asteraceae) family originates in northern temperate regions. Foliage is diverse, often strongly aromatic, sometimes silvery, and can be fringed, ferny, scalloped, or toothed. Flowers are daisy-like or rayless buttons, mainly yellow, white, and red, produced in a mass on vigorous plants of mounding, upright, or shrubby habit. CULTIVATION: These plants require poor to moderately fertile well-drained soil, full sun, and dry growing conditions. There are forms that are suitable for a variety of situations, from rock gardens and borders to natural-izing. Cut back plants after blooming to encourage new growth and to prevent pro-lific self-seeding of some types. Propagate by division or from seed in spring.

Tanacetum balsamita

syns *Balsamita major, Chrysanthemum balsamita*

ALECOST, COSTMARY

☼ ❄ ↔ 18 in (45 cm)

↕ 36 in (90 cm)

Hardy mat-forming perennial found growing naturally from central Asia to Europe. Silvery gray leaves, scalloped, slightly hairy, aromatic. Small, white, button-like flowers with yellow eye, in late summer–autumn. Zones 6–10.

Tanacetum camphoratum

DUNE DAISY

☼ ❄ ↔ 20 in (50 cm)

↕ 27 in (70 cm)

Rare perennial from temperate zones of North America. Bright green serrated foliage all year round. Bright yellow button-like flowers, 1 in (25 mm) wide. Summer- to autumn-flowering. In some areas, can die back over winter months. Zones 8–10.

Tanacetum coccineum

syns *Chrysanthemum coccineum, Pyrethrum coccineum*

PAINTED DAISY, PYRETHRUM

☼ ❄ ↔ 18 in (45 cm)   ↕ 18–30 in (45–75 cm)

Compact low-growing perennial found from southwest Asia and the Caucasus. Fern-like, elliptical to oblong, silver-gray, aromatic foliage. White, pink, or red daisy flowers, yellow eye, in early summer–late autumn. Oils of leaves used to deter pests. Cultivars include 'Brenda', bright cerise-pink flowers with yellow eye; 'Eileen May Robinson', larger pale pink flowers with soft yellow eye; 'James Kelway' ★, vibrant crimson-pink flowers. Zones 5–9.

Tanacetum corymbosum

☼ ❄ ↔ 18 in (45 cm)   ↕ 36 in (90 cm)

Woody perennial, native to southern and central Europe. Clump-forming plant; leaves mid-green, elliptical to oblong, aromatic. Clusters of white daisy-like flowers, from early summer to late autumn. *T. c.* subsp. *clusii*, white daisy-like flowers, drooping petals. Zones 6–9.

Tanacetum coccineum

Tanacetum niveum

SILVER TANSY

☼ ❄ ↔ 24 in (60 cm)   ↕ 36 in (90 cm)

Superb species, native to southern and central Europe. Mound-forming; striking silver-gray, deeply cut, fragrant leaves. Hundreds of *Chrysanthemum*-like flowers, white with yellow centers, in late spring–summer. Zones 6–9.

TAPEINOCHILUS

This genus is a member of the ginger (Zingiberaceae) family and contains about 15 species of perennial herbs that are found in Southeast Asia, Indonesia, New Guinea, and Australia. Like the related *Costus*, they are plants of the forest floor and have spirally arranged leaves. As is typical of the ginger family, the flowers are of less significance than the colorful showy bracts that surround them, which are usually red. The flowerheads may be on leafy shoots or a separate flowering stem.

CULTIVATION: In tropical areas, *Tapeinochilus* species can be grown in a shady border in rich, moist but well-drained soil. In cool-temperate climates, grow these plants in the greenhouse in a rich soil-based mix, providing high humidity, plenty of water, and fortnightly feeding in summer. They should be watered sparingly in winter and humidity should be reduced. Propagation is from seed or bulbils or by division.

Tapeinochilus ananassae

☀ ✿ ↔ 2–3 ft (0.6–0.9 m) ↑ 5–7 ft (1.5–2 m)
Rhizomatous perennial found from Malaysia to Australia. Cane-like stems; spirally arranged, bright green, oblong leaves. Yellow flowers held within a cone-like structure of densely packed overlapping red bracts, in summer. Zones 11–12.

TELEKIA

This genus, comprising a single species found from central Europe eastward to the Caucasus region, is a member of the daisy (Asteraceae) family. The plant is a coarse perennial herb. Leaves are large and heart-shaped, deeply toothed, and hairy, with long stalks. The large flowerheads have ray florets and form loose terminal corymbs. The receptacle has scales, which persist after flowering. The whorl of bracts is cup-shaped and the bracts are heart-shaped and herbaceous. Ray florets are female, each with a very long, narrow, yellow petal. The dry fruits are linear and flattened.

CULTIVATION: This plant grows wild by streamsides and in wet woodlands up to the subalpine zone. It is easily grown in open or lightly shaded moist places in a garden but can readily become invasive. Propagate by division or from seed.

Telekia speciosa
syn. *Buphthalmum speciosum*
OXEYE DAISY, TELEKIA SUNFLOWER
☀ ✿ ↔ 4–6 ft (1.2–1.8 m) ↑ 4–6 ft (1.2–1.8 m)
Strongly scented perennial. Coarsely serrated leaves, finely hairy underneath. Clusters of 2 to 8 flowerheads, up to 35 tiny yellow ray florets, in summer. Zones 3–9.

TELLIMA

This genus in the saxifrage (Saxifragaceae) family contains just a single species of perennial herb. Native to western North

America, it is found in cool moist woodland and rocky areas. The hairy, heart-shaped or round, lobed or toothed leaves form spreading clumps. In summer, tall wiry stems bear spikes of small creamy flowers, tinged with green and red. The blooms deepen in color as they age.

CULTIVATION: Fringecups are ideal plants for cool woodland gardens, shady borders, and rockeries. They prefer moist humus-rich soil. Propagate by division in autumn or from seed sown in spring.

Tellima grandiflora
FRINGECUPS
☀ ✿ ↔ 24 in (60 cm) ↑ 24 in (60 cm)
Perennial herb. Almost round, lobed, hairy, basal leaves, 2–4 in (5–10 cm) wide. Creamy flowers with deeply fringed petals, in summer. **Rubra Group** (syn. 'Purpurea'), rounder leaves, scallop-edged, tinted bronze, green, flowers fringed with pink. Zones 6–9.

Tapeinochilus ananassae

TEUCRIUM
GERMANDER

This genus of about 100 species of herbs, shrubs, and subshrubs is a member of the mint (Lamiaceae) family. They are found growing in warm-temperate regions, but are particularly concentrated around the Mediterranean region. The shrubs are attractive and often colorful flowering plants. All have characteristic squarish stems with opposite leaves that are usually downy or hairy, oval to lance-shaped, and have notched or slightly toothed edges. The summer flowers are borne in whorls on loose stems and are cream, purple, or pink.

CULTIVATION: These reliable plants are mostly frost hardy, and will perform best in a sunny position with well-drained soil. While they will tolerate the dry heat of the inland, they prefer coastal conditions. Lightly prune the ends of the branchlets to remove spent inflorescences and stimulate lateral growth immediately after the summer-flowering period. Propagation is best from firm tip cuttings taken in summer.

Tellima grandiflora

Teucrium chamaedrys
GROUND OAK, WALL GERMANDER

✻ ❄ ↔ 24–36 in (60–90 cm) ↑ 12–24 in (30–60 cm)
Woody-based perennial, native to central and southern Europe;
naturalized further north. Small oval leaves, toothed edges, shiny
green above, downy below. Whorls of pink to purple flowers,
on terminal spikes, in summer. Zones 5–10.

Teucrium cossonii
syns *Teucrium gussonei, T. majorcum*

✻ ❄ ↔ 24 in (60 cm) ↑ 8 in (20 cm)
Low-growing shrubby perennial from the
Mediterranean island of Majorca, Spain.
Small, narrow, gray leaves. Whorls of lav-
ender flowers, on short leafy spikes, almost
year-round in warm climates. Zones 8–11.

Teucrium hircanicum

✻ ❄ ↔ 24 in (60 cm) ↑ 24 in (60 cm)
Woody-based perennial, native to western
Asia and the Caucasus region. Soft, green,
downy leaves, somewhat wrinkled on upper-
surface. Terminal spikes of closely packed whorls of small purple
to reddish purple flowers from summer to autumn. Zones 6–9.

Teucrium cossonii

Teucrium polium
GOLDEN GERMANDER

✻ ❄ ↔ 6–12 in (15–30 cm) ↑ 4–16 in (10–40 cm)
Low mound-forming subshrub from the Mediterranean and
western Asia. Woody-based, with downy stems; small gray leaves,
wrinkled surface. Small heads of white, yellow, pink, or purple
velvety flowers in summer. Zones 7–10.

Teucrium scorodonia
MOUNTAIN SAGE, WOOD GERMANDER, WOOD SAGE

✻/☀ ❄ ↔ 18 in (45 cm) ↑ 24 in (60 cm)
From southern and western Europe. Downy rhizomatous perennial. Wrinkled, toothed, grayish green leaves. Small yellowish
green flowers, in terminal spikes, in summer–autumn. 'Crispum
Marginatum', crimped, frilly-edged, green leaves. Zones 6–10.

Thalictrum aquilegiifolium

THALIA
ALLIGATOR FLAG

This genus of 12 aquatic perennial herbs belongs to the arrowroot
(Marantaceae) family, and is native to the tropical and subtropical
Americas and tropical Africa. Growing from thick rhizomes, the
overlapping blue-green leaves have large sword-shaped to oval
blades that fold upward at night, and long stalks with sheaths at
the base. Two ranks of tubular, often waxy
flowers are produced in curving tassel-like
branches on long-stalked panicles that extend beyond the leaves.
CULTIVATION: These plants grow in water
12–18 in (30–45 cm) deep, or in moist to
wet loamy soil in an open sunny position.
Propagate by division in spring.

Thalia dealbata
POWDERY ALLIGATOR FLAG, WATER CANNA

✻ ☙ ↔ 20–30 in (50–75 cm)
↑ 3–6 ft (0.9–1.8 m)
Native to southeastern North America. Erect
perennial; unbranching stems. Large, tex-
tured, grayish green leaves; fine red edges, powdery white underneath. Branching heads of 6-petalled, violet, waxy flowers, from
late summer to early autumn. Zones 9–11.

THALICTRUM
MEADOW RUE

This genus of around 130 species of tuberous or rhizome-rooted
perennials, belonging to the buttercup (Ranunculaceae) family, is
found mainly in the northern temperate zone, with a few species
straying south of the equator into the tropics. They are upright
plants with lacy, pinnate, blue-green leaves that are reminiscent
of *Aquilegia* or *Adiantum* (maidenhair fern) foliage. Tall elegant
flower stems extend well above the foliage and from late spring
to autumn, depending on the species, produce inflorescences of
small fluffy flowers, which are mainly pink or mauve, but can
be white and yellow.
CULTIVATION: *Thalictrum* species are useful plants in woodland
gardens, borders, or rock gardens. The ferny foliage is an effective
backdrop in floral arrangements. Usually very
hardy, these plants are easily grown in temperate climates in full sun or half-sun in fertile, humus-rich, well-drained soil. Propagate
these perennials by division, as the cultivated
plants are mainly selected forms.

Thalictrum aquilegiifolium
FEATHERED COLUMBINE, FRENCH MEADOW RUE

✻/☀ ❄ ↔ 20–40 in (50–100 cm)
↑ 60 in (150 cm)
Multi-stemmed perennial found from Europe
to Japan. Blue-green fern-like foliage, leaves
to 12 in (30 cm) wide. Panicles of greenish
white through pink to purple flowers, inconspicuous sepals, in early summer. Zones 6–9.

Thalictrum delavayi

☼/◑ ❄ ↔ 16–24 in (40–60 cm)
↕ 4–5 ft (1.2–1.5 m)
Perennial, native to the Himalayas. Dark-stemmed; blue-green foliage. Erect showy heads of large, long-lasting, purple-pink, rarely white flowers, sepals similarly colored, yellow stamens. Summer-flowering. '**Hewitt's Double**' ★, double flowers, slightly shorter than the species. Zones 7–9.

Thalictrum dioicum

EARLY MEADOW RUE

◑/☼ ❄ ↔ 12–16 in (30–40 cm)
↕ 12–30 in (30–75 cm)
Found from Ontario, Canada, to Tennessee, USA. Aquilegia-like blue-green foliage; tiny leaflets, deeply scalloped edges. Flowers with pendulous pink filaments below conspicuous pale green, sometimes purple-tinted sepals, in summer. Zones 4–9.

Thalictrum rochebruneanum

Thalictrum flavum

FALSE RHUBARB, YELLOW MEADOW RUE

☼/◑ ❄ ↔ 16–20 in (40–50 cm)
↕ 40 in (100 cm)
Perennial, native to in southwestern Europe and North Africa. Finely divided, blue-green, aquilegia-like, pinnate foliage. Small heads of fluffy cream to yellow flowers, inconspicuous sepals. Flowers held above foliage on tall stems. Summer-flowering. *T. f.* subsp. *glaucum*, intensely blue-green foliage. Zones 6–10.

Thalictrum kiusianum

☼ ❄ ↔ 12–20 in (30–50 cm)
↕ 6–12 in (15–30 cm)
Small species, native to Japan. Dense clump of short-stemmed, small, doubly trifoliate, blue-green leaves, 3- to 5-lobed segments. Abundant small flowerheads, held above foliage, white to purple-pink blooms, inconspicuous sepals. Summer-flowering. Zones 8–10.

Thalictrum minus

☼/◑ ❄ ↔ 20–32 in (50–80 cm) ↕ 3–5 ft (0.9–1.5 m)
Erect perennial, found throughout Europe and Asia. Finely divided, blue-green, pinnate leaves. Panicles of yellow, sometimes purple-tinted flowers, inconspicuous sepals, in summer. Zones 6–9.

Thalictrum rochebruneanum

☼/◑ ❄ ↔ 16–20 in (40–50 cm) ↕ 40 in (100 cm)
Japanese perennial. Finely divided foliage, smooth-edged or lobed leaflets, to over 1 in (25 mm) long. Airy sprays of small pendulous flowers, many yellow filaments, showy purple-pink sepals, in summer. '**Lavender Mist**', large heads of tiny, bell-shaped, violet flowers. Zones 8–10.

Thalictrum delavayi

THERMOPSIS

FALSE LUPIN

This genus, which is a member of the pea-flower subfamily of the legume (Fabaceae) family, contains 23 species of rhizome-rooted perennial herbs. They are native to North America, Siberia, and parts of Asia, and are found growing in habitats such as riverbanks and open woods. The attractive 3-part leaves are often silvery. Their nectar-rich yellow or purple flowers are typical of the pea-flower family. The blooms are borne in spring or summer in dense or loose terminal racemes, often resembling lupins (*Lupinus*), a fact that is recognized in the common name applied to a number of the species.

CULTIVATION: *Thermopsis* species make ideal subjects for border planting and are suitable for naturalizing in larger areas. They are fully frost hardy plants, and will do well if planted in a position in full sun in any reasonably fertile soil that is moist but well drained. Some of the species can spread rapidly by their rhizomes. Propagate from seed or by division, which must be undertaken carefully as these deep-rooted plants resent disturbance.

Thermopsis rhombifolia

FALSE LUPIN, GOLDEN BANNER

☼ ❄ ↔ 24 in (60 cm) ↕ 36 in (90 cm)
Found from the Rocky Mountains to New Mexico, USA. Leaflets broadly oval, undersides coated with silvery hairs. Yellow, softly hairy flowers, densely or loosely packed in racemes to 12 in (30 cm) long. Spring- to summer-flowering. Upright downy seed pods. Zones 4–9.

Thermopsis villosa

syn. *Thermopsis caroliniana*

CAROLINA LUPIN

☼ ❄ ↔ 2 ft (0.6 m) ↕ 3–5 ft (0.9–1.5 m)

Stout perennial, native to southeastern USA. Bluish green leaves, downy undersides. Yellow flowers in terminal, downy, lupin-like racemes, in spring–summer. Silky-hairy seed pods. Zones 6–9.

THYMUS

THYME

Well known as the source of one of the most widely used culinary herbs, this genus in the mint (Lamiaceae) family is composed of around 350 species of mainly evergreen aromatic perennials and subshrubs, many of which become quite shrubby. The distribution range of the genus extends to most parts of Europe, temperate Asia, and northwest Africa, but the highest concentration is found around the Mediterranean and in the Middle East. Small wiry-stemmed plants, they have tiny, often downy leaves and heads of equally small, mauve, pink, or sometimes white flowers that are very attractive to bees. Late spring to mid-summer is the main flowering season.
CULTIVATION: Frost hardiness varies with the species, though most *Thymus* species will withstand moderate frosts. Thyme grows best in light, rather gritty soil that has been enriched with humus for moisture retention. Plant in full sun and trim lightly after flowering to keep the plants compact and well-foliaged. When growing thyme indoors, place plant in a well-lit position. Propagate from seed, by removing naturally formed layers, or by taking half-hardened cuttings.

Thymus Coccineus Group

Thymus polytrichus subsp. *britannicus*

Thymus caespititius

☼ ❄ ↔ 15 in (38 cm) ↕ 2 in (5 cm)

Dwarf mat-forming shrub, found in Portugal and nearby parts of Spain, also Madeira and the Azores. Narrow, tiny, paddle-shaped leaves, edged with fine hairs. Flowers deep pink, lavender, or white, in late spring. Zones 7–10.

Thymus × *citriodorus*

LEMON-SCENTED THYME, LEMON THYME

☼ ❄ ↔ 24 in (60 cm) ↕ 6–12 in (15–30 cm)

Erect subshrub; of garden origin; *T. pulegioides* × *T. vulgaris* hybrid. Branching stems; glossy dark green leaves. Dense lavender-pink flowerheads in summer. Strong lemon scent. 'Aureus', upright spreading plant, gold-splashed leaves; 'Bertram Anderson' (golden lemon thyme), gray-green leaves suffused with gold, new growth tinged red; 'Lime', low, creeping, lime green foliage, white flowers; 'Silver Queen', silver-green to cream marbled foliage. Zones 5–10.

Thymus Coccineus Group

☼ ❄ ↔ 14 in (35 cm) ↕ 3–4 in (8–10 cm)

Mat-forming creeper, garden origin, possibly forms of *T. serpyllum*. Tiny dark green leaves. Magenta flowers, in terminal clusters, in summer. 'Coccineus Minor', dwarf form, tiny leaves, pink flowers. Zones 4–9.

Thymus herba-barona

CARAWAY THYME

☼ ❄ ↔ 24 in (60 cm) ↕ 4 in (10 cm)

Wide-spreading species from Corsica and Sardinia. Carpet of glossy dark green leaves, spicy scent. Loose clusters of pink-mauve flowers in mid-summer. Zones 7–9.

Thymus mastichina

☼ ❄ ↔ 16 in (40 cm)
↕ 6–12 in (15–30 cm)

Native of Spain and Portugal. Upright perennial; hairy shoots and leaves. Elliptical green leaves, aromatic. Clusters of white flowers. Summer-flowering. Zones 7–10.

Thymus polytrichus

☼ ❄ ↔ 24 in (60 cm) ↕ 2 in (5 cm)

Perennial, native to southern Europe. Tight mat-forming species; dark green oval leaves. Pale to deep purple flowers, splashed with white, in summer. *T. p.* subsp. *britannicus*, slightly downy foliage, dark pink flowers; 'Minor', dwarf habit, tiny pink and white flowers; 'Thomas's White' (syn. *T. praecox* subsp. *arcticus* 'Albus'), compact, crisp clear white flowers. Zones 5–9.

Thymus pseudolanuginosus

syn. *Thymus lanuginosus*

WOOLLY MOTHER-OF-THYME, WOOLLY THYME

☼ ❋ ↔ 24 in (60 cm) ↑ 1–3 in (2.5–8 cm)

Of unknown origin. Forms low-spreading mat of woolly leaves. Scentless pink flowers in early summer. Sparse flowering. Must have sharp drainage. Plant between rocks. Zones 5–9.

TIARELLA

This genus in the saxifrage (Saxifragaceae) family is made up of 5 perennials—4 from North America and 1 found from the Himalayas to Japan. They spread by rhizomes or an underground network of thin fleshy stems, forming clumps of lobed heart-shaped leaves with long stalks. The flower stems carry airy open racemes of tiny white and/or pink to red, 5-petalled flowers, in late spring and summer. Foliage and flower stems are covered in fine hairs. *Tiarella* has been crossed with *Heuchera* to produce the intergeneric hybrid × *Heucherella*.

CULTIVATION: *Tiarella* species are very hardy, especially the American species. They are easily grown in woodlands or perennial borders; spreading but seldom invasive. Plant in a position in half-sun or full shade in humus-rich, moist, well-drained soil. Propagation is by division in late winter to early spring or from seed.

Tiarella cordifolia

FOAMFLOWER

☼/☀ ❋ ↔ 16–20 in (40–50 cm) ↑ 12 in (30 cm)

Perennial, occurring naturally in eastern North America; spreads by underground stems. Stems and leaves finely hairy; leaves lobed, toothed, heart-shaped, up to 4 in (10 cm) in length, on long stalks.

Tiarella, Hybrid Cultivar, 'Tiger Stripe'

Airy sprays of tiny, often pink-tinted flowers, 5-petalled, on fine stems, in early summer. '**Major**', salmon pink flowers that darken with age. Zones 3–9.

Tiarella polyphylla

☼/☀ ❋ ↔ 16–20 in (40–50 cm) ↑ 12–18 in (30–45 cm)

Found from the Himalayas to Japan. Toothed, 5-lobed, heart-shaped leaves, to nearly 3 in (8 cm) long and wide. Sturdy purple-red-tinted flower stems; branching sprays of small, pink-tinted, cream flowers, from late spring to early summer. '**Rosea**', deep pink flowers. Zones 7–9.

Tiarella wherryi

☼/☀ ❋ ↔ 16–20 in (40–50 cm) ↑ 8–12 in (20–30 cm)

Perennial from North America, closely allied to *T. cordifolia*. Leaves usually have 5 pronounced lobes, reddening in autumn.

Racemes of narrow, cream, 5-petalled flowers open from base upward from pink to maroon buds. Summer-flowering. '**Bronze Beauty**', red-brown leaves, pink flowers; '**Oakleaf**' ★, leaves with dark center and more pronounced lobes, flowers strongly pink-tinted. Zones 5–9.

Tiarella Hybrid Cultivars

☼/☀ ❋ ↔ 16–20 in (40–50 cm) ↑ 12–18 in (30–45 cm)

North American species interbreed freely and intermediate forms are common. Range of attractive garden forms available. Cultivars include '**Crow Feather**', foliage with dark central feather marking intensifying in winter, cream to pink flowers on spikes; '**Dark Star**', bright green leaves with dark center, pink-tinted white flowers; '**Elizabeth Oliver**', deep maroon-veined foliage, maroon-tinted flowers; '**Spring Symphony**', long-lobed dark-centered leaves, pale pink flowers from dark buds; and '**Tiger Stripe**', dark-veined bronze foliage, reddening in autumn, pink-tinted cream flowers. Zones 6–9.

TILLANDSIA

AIR PLANT

This large genus of over 500 mostly epiphytic species in the bromeliad (Bromeliaceae) family has a distribution range that extends from southern USA to southern Argentina. Plants vary in size from minute to 15 ft (4.5 m) tall in flower. Some species have leaves that are covered with moisture-absorbing gray-white hairs, while others have green strap-like leaves. The flowerheads are typically globular or pyramidal, with side-branches and prominent bracts that are showy and colorful. Flowers are mostly tubular, sometimes scented, and are bluish, pink, white, or yellow. The seed has a feathery parachute.

CULTIVATION: Gray-leafed forms are usually grown attached to a substrate. Mist-spray weekly in cooler months, as often as daily (in the early morning) in warmer periods. They like some air movement. Green-leafed forms are generally grown in pots. Grow them indoors in light and airy situations, in a greenhouse or conservatory in cool-temperate areas, outdoors with protection from direct sunlight and extremes of rain in warm areas. Propagation is mainly by offsets.

Tillandsia aeranthos

☀ ⚘ ↔ 6 in (15 cm) ↑ 6 in (15 cm)

Clump-forming species, found from northeastern Argentina to southern Brazil. Narrow triangular leaves form elongated rosette. Flower stem red, a little taller than leaf rosette. Flowerhead egg-shaped, mainly red, large dark blue petals. Summer-flowering. Zones 11–12.

Tillandsia butzii

Tillandsia crocata

Tillandsia cyanea

Tillandsia bergeri
☀ ✛ ↔6 in (15 cm) ↑6 in (15 cm)

From southeastern Argentina. Clump-forming; narrow triangular leaves, gray-green, form elongated rosette. Flower stem a little taller than leaf rosette, pale red. Egg-shaped flowerhead, mainly pale red; large, wavy, pale blue petals, in summer. Zones 11–12.

Tillandsia butzii
☀ ✛ ↔4 in (10 cm) ↑12 in (30 cm)

Found from southern Mexico to Panama. Tall, clump-forming; base of leaves forms dense globular bulb, gray-green with darker spots and broken lines, upper parts almost tubular, contorted, spreading. Flower stem red, slender. Flowerhead with few sword-shaped spikes, petals blue-violet, rolled into tight tube. Summer-flowering. Zones 11–12.

Tillandsia crocata
☀ ✛ ↔6 in (15 cm) ↑8 in (20 cm)

Tiny clump-forming species, found from Bolivia to southern Brazil. Leaves narrow, almost cylindrical, furry gray, in opposite rows on single plane. Short flowerhead, furry, gray, sword-shaped; on slender stem; wide-spreading petals bright yellow. Summer-flowering. Zones 11–12.

Tillandsia cyanea
☀ ✛ ↔10 in (25 cm) ↑10 in (25 cm)

Small plant from Ecuador. Closely linked with *Tillandsia lindenii,* often hybridizing. Leaves narrow triangular, green, often with red lines underneath, forming an open rosette. Flowerhead sword-shaped, fragrant, petals deep violet, sometimes white eye in center, in summer. Zones 11–12.

Tillandsia dyeriana
☀ ✛ ↔6 in (15 cm) ↑6 in (15 cm)

From Ecuador. Leaves strap-like, green and purple spotted, forming funnel-shaped rosette. Flower stem slender, soon hanging. Sword-shaped flowerhead, single or cluster of several branches, bright reddish orange, petals white, spreading wide, just emerging from bracts, in summer. Zones 11–12.

Tillandsia fasciculata
☀ ✛ ↔20 in (50 cm) ↑40 in (100 cm)

Large varied species, native to Mexico, Central America, and the West Indies. Narrow triangular leaves, gray-green, rigid; form open rosette. Simple sword-shaped spike or cluster of up to 10 spikes, wholly red or yellow, or yellow and red, petals purple, rolled into tube. Summer-flowering. Eight varieties are recognized. Zones 11–12.

Tillandsia fuchsii
☀ ✛ ↔4 in (10 cm) ↑8 in (20 cm)

Small species, found naturally in Mexico. Leaves almost tubular, very thin, and grayish, bottom part forms tight bulb, upper part spreading, forming globular rosette. Dark wine red flower stem. Cylindrical flowerhead, wine red, petals violet, rolled into tight tube, in summer. Zones 11–12.

Tillandsia imperialis
☀ ✛ ↔16 in (40 cm) ↑20 in (50 cm)

Large species from Mexico. Green, narrow triangular leaves, form spreading rosette. Cone-shaped flowerhead, many red overlapping bracts, tip bending outward and sometimes green; emerging petals violet, rolled tightly into a tube; in summer. Zones 11–12.

Tillandsia ionantha

Tillandsia ionantha
BLUSHING BRIDE

☀ ✛ ↔3 in (8 cm) ↑2 in (5 cm)

Variable clump-forming species native to Mexico and Central America. Narrow triangular leaves, gray-green, erect, tips bent outward, almost forming a ball. Hidden flowerhead, globular, with up to 5 flowers, petals violet, forming a tight tube. Summer-flowering. Center leaves turn bright red at flowering. 'Druid', albino form. Zones 11–12.

Tillandsia leiboldiana
☀ ✛ ↔10 in (25 cm) ↑24 in (60 cm)

Tall evergreen perennial, native to Mexico and Central America. Funnel-shaped rosette; strap-like green leaves. Erect to curved flower stem. Bright red, narrow pyramidal flowerhead, up to 12 side branches, large red bract below each, petals violet, rolled into tight tube. Summer-flowering. Variegated form also occurs. Zones 11–12.

Tillandsia lindenii

☀ ⚹ ↔ 16 in (40 cm) ↕ 27 in (70 cm)

Tall species, native to Ecuador and northern Peru. Open rosette; narrow triangular green leaves, striped red underneath. Tall flower stem; sword-shaped flowerhead, petals opening wide, deep blue, white eye in center, fragrant. Summer-flowering. Zones 11–12.

Tillandsia magnusiana

☀ ⚹ ↔ 6 in (15 cm) ↕ 6 in (15 cm)

Tiny species, found from southern Mexico to El Salvador. Globular rosette; leaves very thin, almost tubular, gray-green, furred. Flowerhead almost globular, violet petals rolled into tight tubes emerging above leaves, in summer. Zones 11–12.

Tillandsia recurvata

BALL MOSS

◑ ⚹ ↔ 2½–8 in (6–20 cm) ↕ 4 in (10 cm)

Minute clump-forming species, found from southern USA to Argentina. Stemmed leaves almost tubular, gray-green, furred, in opposite rows on single plane. Flowerhead with 1 or 2 flowers; petals pale violet or white, in summer. Zones 11–12.

Tillandsia streptophylla

☀ ⚹ ↔ 8 in (20 cm) ↕ 18 in (45 cm)

Tall species, found from southern Mexico to Honduras. Leaves narrow triangular, gray-green, bottom part forms erect bulb, top part bends downward, contorted, spiralling. Flowerhead pyramidal, up to 10 narrow sword-shaped side branches, gray-green; center axis and large bracts below branches bright red, petals purple, rolled into a tube. Summer-flowering. Zones 11–12.

Tillandsia stricta

☀ ⚹ ↔ 6 in (15 cm) ↕ 8 in (20 cm)

Widespread species, especially in eastern South America. Epiphytic; open rosette, sometimes with leaves pointing in the same direction; leaves narrow triangular, green-gray, covered with hairs. Flower stem curving downward. Flowerhead egg-shaped, many overlapping red bracts, petals blue, in summer. Zones 11–12.

Tillandsia tectorum

☀ ⚹ ↔ 12 in (30 cm) ↕ 20 in (50 cm)

Larger species, native to Ecuador and northern Peru. Open rosette; sometimes stemmed leaves, narrow triangular, gray with long gray wool. Flowerhead with up to 5 sword-shaped spikes, reddish gray, petals blue with white band, in summer. Dislikes wet conditions. Zones 11–12.

Tillandsia streptophylla

Tillandsia tenuifolia

☀ ⚹ ↔ 6 in (15 cm) ↕ 6 in (15 cm)

Tiny epiphytic species, native to eastern South America. Stems can reach up to 10 in (25 cm) in length. Leaves sometimes stemmed, narrow triangular, gray-green, usually forming open rosette, but sometimes pointing in one direction. Egg-shaped flowerhead, red overlapping bracts, petals white or blue. Summer-flowering. Zones 11–12.

Tillandsia usneoides

OLD MAN'S BEARD, SPANISH MOSS

☀ ⚹ ↔ 4 in (10 cm)

↕ 24 in (50 cm)

Tall narrow species; perennial herb; found from southern USA to Argentina. Forms large clumps; leaves clothed in woolly hairs, gray, opposite and on same plane, forming long strands that twist and twine. Single flowerhead, green petals, fragrant. Summer-flowering. Zones 11–12.

Tillandsia leiboldiana

Tillandsia Hybrid Cultivars

☀ ✂ ↔4–24 in (10–60 cm) ↕4–36 in (10–90 cm)

Cultivars are extremely varied in size, however, all produce showy and colorful flowers. Popular cultivars include '**Anita**', which has links with *Tillandsia cyanea* and *T. lindenii*, striking lavender instead of more usual light pink, with large, cinnamon-scented flowers; '**Creation**', hybrid between *T. platyrhachis* and *T. cyanea*, flowerhead erect, many spreading branches, sword-shaped spikes in pink to dark rose, spreading violet-blue flowers; '**Curly Slim**', leaves narrow triangular, gray-green, flowerhead pyramidal, gray-green with pinkish tinge, central axis dull red, petals purple; '**Curra**', numerous inner leaves turn red at flowering, conical flowerhead, many overlapping bright red bracts, emergent violet petals; '**Eric Knobloch**', gray-green leaves, forming a bulbose base, flowers pointing upward, petals violet; at time of flowering, upper half of plant blushes yellow-orange, orange-scarlet, then deep rosy red; and '**Wildfire**', flower stem appears to be an extension of plant, with up to 25 green bracts taking the place of leaves; brilliant red sword-shaped spike emerges from each bract, petals purplish. Zones 11–12.

TITHONIA

MEXICAN SUNFLOWER

This genus is made up of 10 species of annuals, perennials, and shrubs that are native to Mexico and Central America. It is a member of the daisy (Asteraceae) family. Quite shrubby species, they are robust plants, sometimes with hairy stems, and have alternate leaves that are often lobed. They bear large daisy flowers in shades of yellow and orangey scarlet.

CULTIVATION: These plants are useful for providing a bright spot in the garden in late summer and autumn. Grow in a well-drained, moderately fertile soil in full sun. Propagation is from seed or from cuttings.

Tithonia rotundifolia
syn. *Tithonia speciosa*
MEXICAN SUNFLOWER

☀ ✂ ↔2 ft (0.6 m) ↕3–6 ft (0.9–1.8 m)

Annual, native to Mexico and Central America; rapidly forming, large, many-branched plant. Velvety-hairy leaves, to 12 in (30 cm) long. Orange ray flowers, tufted yellow centers, from summer to autumn, or first frost. Cultivars include '**Aztec Sun**', 4 ft (1.2 m) tall, golden flowers; '**Fiesta del Sol**', earlier-blooming dwarf; '**Goldfinger**', bushy selection, deep orange flowers; and '**Torch**', orange-red flowers. Zones 9–10.

Tithonia rotundifolia 'Torch'

TOLMIEA

Native to the coastal mountains of western North America, from northern California and north to Alaska, USA, this genus in the saxifrage (Saxifragaceae) family contains a single mat-forming herbaceous perennial. It has shallowly lobed pale green leaves that are sometimes evergreen. Young plants are borne on the leaves where the leaf stalk and leaf blade meet.

CULTIVATION: This plant prefers neutral to acidic, cool, moist, humus-rich soil in partial to deep shade. Sun can scorch the leaves, particularly the variegated form. It is sometimes grown as a house plant, requiring cool temperatures and filtered light. Propagation is by division in spring, or from seed in autumn. Plantlets may also be removed from leaves in mid- to late summer and potted up.

Tolmiea menziesii
PICKABACK PLANT, PIGGYBACK PLANT, THOUSAND MOTHERS

☀ ❄ ↔3–6 ft (0.9–1.8 m) ↕18–24 in (45–60 cm)

Shade-loving perennial from the west coast of North America. Shallowly lobed leaves, slightly hairy, mid-green. Small, inconspicuous, reddish brown flowers, borne on top of 12–24 in (30–60 cm) stems, from late spring to summer. '**Taff's Gold**' (syns 'Maculata', 'Variegata'), leaves splashed with gold in spring; foliage fades somewhat in summer. Zones 6–9.

TORENIA

WISHBONE FLOWER

This is a genus of up to 50 species of low-growing, spreading, bushy annual and perennial plants from tropical parts of Africa and Asia. They are members of the foxglove (Scrophulariaceae) family. These plants are noted for their ability to bloom well in both shady and sunny conditions. The toothed oval leaves, up to 4 in (10 cm) long, cover the pale creamy green stems. The flowers are pale violet with dark blue-purple lower lips and a yellow throat blotch. A pair of stamens unites at the anthers in a shape resembling the wishbone of a chicken, hence the common name. The flowers generally appear from late spring and finish once the first frosts start.

CULTIVATION: These plants make excellent edging plants for beds, borders, and shade or woodland gardens, as well as for containers or window boxes. They need a warm spot in order to flourish and will not cope with frost, cold persistent winds, or cold wind-chill factors. They are best grown in consistently moist, organically rich, well-drained soils in part-shade to full sun. Propagate from seed in spring, or once the last of the frosts has finished.

Torenia fournieri
BLUEWINGS, WISHBONE FLOWER

☀/☀ ✂ ↔10 in (25 cm) ↕12 in (30 cm)

Small bushy species, native to tropical Asia. Pale green lightly serrated leaves, 2 in (5 cm) long, form mounds on stems. Trumpet-shaped, pale purple flowers. Summer- to autumn-flowering. Ideal hanging basket plant. '**Blue Panda**', compact

Torenia fournieri 'Blue Panda'

habit, lilac-blue flowers; **Clown Series**, mix containing several colors, some with a contrasting rim to each flower. Zones 11–12.

Torenia Hybrid Cultivars

☀/◐ ≯ ↔ 10 in (25 cm) ↕ 12–15 in (30–38 cm)

Cultivars expand the range of flower colors to include shades of burgundy, pink, rose, lavender, as well as white. '**Duchess Deepblue**', deep purplish blue flowers with orange spotting; '**Duchess White and Blue**' ★, white flowers with very deep blue blotches; '**Duchess White and Pink**', white flowers with deep magenta markings. Zones 11–12.

TOWNSENDIA

This genus of about 21 annual or perennial herbs is a member of the daisy (Asteraceae) family, and is native to western North America. It features soft gray-green spatula-shaped leaves that are covered in very fine hairs. The flowers are very daisy-like with wide discs surrounded by pointed ribbed petals in grayish pink, pinkish white, and mauve. The disc florets are yellow.
CULTIVATION: These plants prefer a position in full sun with deep well-drained soil. Propagate from cuttings in spring or from seed when ripe.

Townsendia formosa

☀ ❋ ↔ 10–12 in (25–30 cm)
↕ 12–16 in (30–40 cm)

Tufting rhizomatous perennial from dry stony grasslands of southwestern USA. Spatula-shaped leaves, midribs and edges finely hairy. Purple or white ray florets and yellow disc florets, in summer. Zones 8–10.

Townsendia parryi

PARRY'S TOWNSENDIA

☀ ❋ ↔ 10–15 in (25–38 cm) ↕ 10–15 in (25–38 cm)

Biennial or short-lived hairy perennial from northwestern North America. Spatula-shaped leaves. Large solitary flowerheads, ray florets bluish purple or violet, disc florets yellow, in early summer. Prefers subalpine to alpine habitats. Zones 5–8.

TRACHELIUM

A small genus of 7 species of perennial herbs belonging to the bellflower (Campanulaceae) family. They are native to Mediterranean regions, and are usually found growing in rocky crevices. They range from tiny cushion-forming species to more robust, erect, woody-based plants. Their simple leaves are alternately arranged. The flowers, in shades of purple and white, usually appear in clusters in summer. They are tubular with prominently protruding styles. *T. caeruleum,* which is suitable for border planting, is most commonly seen, flowering from seed in its first year or grown as an annual.
CULTIVATION: Grow *Trachelium* species in a sunny position in reasonably fertile, well-drained soil. The smaller species, requiring perfectly drained alkaline soil, are better suited to the rock garden, pots, or alpine house. Provide protection from the hottest sun and from winter wet. Propagate from seed or cuttings.

Trachelium caeruleum ★

☀ ❄ ↔ 18 in (45 cm) ↕ 24–36 in (60–90 cm)

Upright perennial from the Mediterranean region. Serrated-edged, pointed, oval leaves. Rounded clusters of tiny, starry, pleasantly perfumed, purple flowers, in summer. Very long protruding styles give flowerheads a soft fluffy appearance. Zones 9–11.

Townsendia parryi, in the wild, Colorado, USA

Trachystemon orientalis

Tradescantia, Andersoniana Group, 'Bilberry Ice'

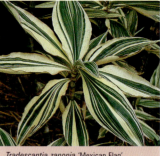

Tradescantia zanonia 'Mexican Flag'

TRACHYSTEMON

RUSSIAN BORAGE

This small genus of only 2 species of herbaceous perennials is a member of the borage (Boraginaceae) family and is native to eastern Europe. They have large bristly leaves, very similar to those of comfrey *(Symphytum),* and bright blue starry flowers in very early spring as the leaves come up. Only *T. orientalis* is in general cultivation.
CULTIVATION: These exceptionally hardy plants do best in light to heavy shade in moist humus-rich soil where they will make large weed-smothering clumps. Propagate by division when dormant. Plants will self-seed.

Trachystemon orientalis
syn. *Borago orientalis*
RUSSIAN BORAGE
☀ ❄ ↔ 3–7 ft (0.9–2 m) ↕ 2–3 ft (0.6–0.9 m)
Coarse herbaceous perennial from Europe. Paddle-shaped, bristly, green leaves, to 12 in (30 cm) long. Open sprays of bright blue starry flowers, white at center, to ¾ in (18 mm) across, in late winter–early spring. Zones 5–10.

TRADESCANTIA

SPIDER LILY, SPIDERWORT

This genus is made up of around 70 species of annuals and perennials from the Americas, and is a member of the spiderwort (Commelinaceae) family. It includes a few species that, while attractive as garden plants, have become serious pests in some areas. Tuberous or fibrous-rooted and often evergreen, they have rather succulent stems and fleshy, pointed elliptical, lance-shaped, or narrow leaves. The clusters of small 3-petalled flowers, subtended by bracts, appear throughout the warmer months. They are sometimes very bright magenta, though white, soft pink, and blue to mauve predominate. Variegated and colored foliage forms are common.
CULTIVATION: Most of these plants are tolerant of light to moderate frosts. Some prefer a sunny aspect and are drought tolerant, but most prefer part-shade and

Tradescantia virginiana

moist well-drained soil. Propagation is by division, or from self-struck layers, tip cuttings, or seed, depending on the growth form.

Tradescantia Andersoniana Group
☀ ❄ ↔ 12–48 in (30–120 cm) ↕ 8–20 in (20–50 cm)
Often wrongly called *T. × andersoniana.* Hybrids of several species, mostly derived from *T. virginiana.* Mainly clumping hybrids with narrow foliage and flowering habits of *T. virginiana.* Hybrids include '**Bilberry Ice**', blue-green foliage, pale silver-mauve flowers; '**Blue and Gold**' (syn. 'Sweet Kate'), long, narrow, bright yellow leaves, vivid blue flowers; '**Concord Grape**', blue-green foliage, deep magenta flowers; '**Innocence**', bright green foliage, white flowers; '**Isis**', green foliage, bright blue flowers; '**J. C. Weguelin**', green foliage, striking sky blue flowers; '**Little Doll**', very compact, bright green foliage, soft mauve-blue flowers; '**Osprey**', green foliage, flowers white to palest mauve with mauve-blue center; '**Purple Dome**', green foliage, deep purple flowers; and '**Zwanenburg Blue**', green foliage, blue to violet flowers. Zones 7–10.

Tradescantia fluminensis
syn. *Tradescantia albiflora*
WANDERING JEW
☀/☀ ⊰ ↔ 24–60 in (60–150 cm) ↕ 12–20 in (30–50 cm)
Somewhat invasive perennial from South America; naturalized in southern USA. Thick succulent stems, closely spaced. Broadly lance-shaped fleshy leaves, lighter central area, to over 3 in (8 cm) long; large white flowers. Cultivated forms occur in wide range of foliage colors and patterns. Zones 9–11.

Tradescantia spathacea
syn. *Rhoeo discolor*
BOAT LILY, CRADLE LILY, MOSES-IN-HIS-CRADLE
☀/☀ ⊰ ↔ 12–16 in (30–40 cm)
↕ 15 in (38 cm)
From southern Mexico, Guatemala, and Belize. Short-stemmed clumping perennial; erect leaves, to 14 in (35 cm) long, broadly spear-shaped, dark green above, purple-red below. Small white flowers in boat-shaped bract near leaf base, all year. '**Vittata**' ★ (syn. 'Variegata'), cream-and-pink striped foliage. Zones 10–12.

Tradescantia virginiana

☀️ ❄️ ↔ 20–48 in (50–120 cm) ↕ 12–20 in (30–50 cm)

Mounding spreading perennial, native to eastern USA. Narrow, rather grass-like leaves. Small heads of white, pink, mauve-blue, or purple flowers, similarly colored bracts, in summer. Widely hybridized to produce a range of garden forms. Zones 7–10.

Tradescantia zanonia

syn. *Campelia zanonia*

☀️/❄️ ☀️ ↔ 5 ft (1.5 m) ↕ 24–40 in (60–100 cm)

Erect to spreading perennial from Central and South America. Leaves simple lance-shaped, silvery beneath. Inflorescence to 8 in (20 cm) long, tiny magenta-tinted white flowers, large purple-tinted green bracts, in summer–winter. 'Mexican Flag', leaves with broad cream stripes. Zones 10–12.

TRICHOSTEMA

This genus of 16 species of aromatic annuals and small shrubs is a member of the mint (Lamiaceae) family and is found throughout most parts of North America. They have simple lance-shaped leaves that have a woolly underside. They produce blue, or occasionally pink or white, tubular flowers, which resemble those

Trichostema lanatum

of the related *Salvia* genus, during most of spring and summer. CULTIVATION: The shrubby species should be grown in a well-drained soil of medium fertility. In cool climates they are best overwintered in the greenhouse. Propagate from seed sown in spring, or from half-hardened cuttings in autumn.

Trichostema lanatum

BLUE CURLS, WOOLLY BLUE CURLS

☀️ ❄️ ↔ 2 ft (0.6 m) ↕ 2–5 ft (0.6–1.5 m)

Shrubby species from California, USA. Dark green lance-shaped leaves, woolly beneath, rolled edges. Woolly, tubular, purple-blue flowers on 15 in (38 cm) spikes, in spring–summer. Zones 8–10.

TRICYRTIS

TOAD LILY

A genus of 16 graceful, rhizomatous, woodland perennials belonging to the lily-of-the-valley (Convallariaceae) family, and found growing in moist woodlands and on mountains and cliffs from the eastern Himalayas to the Philippines, and in Japan and Taiwan. Their oblong to lance-shaped, pointed, often glossy and sometimes spotted leaves clasp upright on arching stems. The star-, bell-, or funnel-shaped flowers are terminal or in upper leaf axils and can be pure white, golden yellow, lavender, or purple, usually spotted, with a somewhat waxen or iridescent quality. They usually bloom in late summer and autumn. CULTIVATION: These perennials need moist, well-drained, humus-rich soil, and a position in part-shade to full sun. In warmer areas, they will do best in part-shade to full shade. Some species may be propagated from seed in autumn. All may be divided in spring when dormant.

Tricyrtis formosana

syn. *Tricyrtis stolonifera*

FORMOSA TOAD LILY

☀️ ❄️ ↔ 18 in (45 cm) ↕ 36 in (90 cm)

Erect species, native to Taiwan. Spreads by runners. Green leaves mottled deeper green. Brown or maroon buds open to white or pale lilac, purple-spotted flowers tinged yellow, in mid-summer to autumn. Zones 5–9.

Tricyrtis hirta

HAIRY TOAD LILY

☀️ ❄️ ↔ 24 in (60 cm) ↕ 36 in (90 cm)

From Japan. Arching stems; slightly hairy, soft green foliage. White flowers speckled with dark purple, along stems in leaf axils, in early to mid-autumn. Cultivars include 'Myzaki' and 'Myazaki Gold'. Zones 4–9.

Tricyrtis macrantha

☀️ ❄️ ↔ 24 in (60 cm) ↕ 30 in (75 cm)

Upright plant from Japan. Arching stems; glossy green, ovate-oblong, bamboo-like leaves. Brownish slightly fuzzy stems; pendulous bell-shaped flowers, lemon yellow with chocolate spots inside, in early autumn. Zones 7–9.

Tricyrtis macropoda

syn. *Tricyrtis dilatata*

☀️ ❄️ ↔ 24 in (60 cm) ↕ 30 in (75 cm)

Handsome species, native to China. Rhizomatous perennial; oblong-ovate leaves on erect stems. Branched inflorescence of lavender flowers, spotted with darker purple, in mid- to late summer. Zones 5–9.

Tricyrtis hirta

Trifolium pannonicum

Trifolium rubens

☼/◐ ❄ ↔ 18–24 in (45–60 cm)
↑ 12–24 in (30–60 cm)
Bushy perennial, native to southern Europe.
Silver-haired, deep green, trifoliate leaves,
elliptical leaflets. Large conical heads of
crimson flowers. Summer-flowering.
Zones 7–10.

Trifolium uniflorum ★
ONE-FLOWERED CLOVER

☼/◐ ❄ ↔ 8–16 in (20–40 cm)
↑ 2–4 in (5–10 cm)
Trailing rhizome-rooted perennial found
from Sicily to the eastern Mediterranean.
Trifoliate leaves, leaflets rounded, often
downy undersides. White flowers, sometimes
flushed with pink, solitary or in heads of up
to 3, in spring–summer. Zones 7–10.

TRIFOLIUM
CLOVER

A vitally important component of the world's pastures, at the
same time clover is far less welcome in lawns. A member of the
pea-flower subfamily of the legume (Fabaceae) family, it is found
naturally throughout the temperate and subtropical zones except
Australasia and consists of around 230 species of annuals, biennials, and perennials. Typically trifoliate and bright green, the
leaves may have up to 9 leaflets, sometimes darkly marked. The
individual flowers, which are carried in rounded heads, are very
much like pea-flowers.
CULTIVATION: Generally hardy and easily grown, clover is rarely
deliberately cultivated in gardens. Plant in full sun or half-sun in
moist well-drained soil. Propagate by division but usually self-sows.

Trifolium pannonicum
HUNGARIAN CLOVER

☼/◐ ❄ ↔ 8 in (20 cm) ↑ 8 in (20 cm)
Perennial from eastern Europe; upright bushy
habit. Fine silky hairs on stems and leaves.
Red-tinted stems; narrow elliptical leaflets.
Inflorescence erect, to 4 in (10 cm) long; soft
creamy yellow flowers, in summer. Zones 5–9.

Trifolium repens
WHITE CLOVER

☼/◐ ❄ ↔ 8–16 in (20–40 cm) ↑ 2 in (5 cm)
Low-growing widely naturalized perennial
from Europe. Creeping rhizomes; leaves usu-
ally trifoliate, leaflets rounded, finely serrated, deep green with
darker chevron markings. Tiny flowers, fragrant, white or soft
pink. Summer-flowering. Cultivars include '**Atropurpureum**',
red-bronze leaves, variable green edge; '**Green Ice**', 2-tone gray-
green foliage; '**Purpurascens**', vigorous, leaflets with central
purple-red zone; and '**Purpurascens Quadrifolium**', purplish
brown leaves with 4 leaflets. Zones 4–10.

TRILLIUM
WAKE ROBIN, WOOD LILY

This group of 30 rhizome-rooted, spring-flowering, woodland
perennials from North America and temperate Asia is the type
genus for the wake-robin (Trilliaceae) family. Ranging from the
tiny *T. rivale*, to 2 in (5 cm) high, to species 24 in (60 cm) tall
in flower, the genus is remarkably consistent in form. The leaflets are bright green, often mottled and usually broadly oval,
tapering to a point. At the center of the 3-leafed cluster is a
simple 3-petalled flower that may be white, cream, pink, or
deep maroon-red. The common name comes from their early
flowering habit—the plant that wakes the robin in spring.
CULTIVATION: Plant in part-shade or full shade in a cool, moist,
humus-rich, well-drained soil. All species die back completely in
autumn but race into growth in early spring.
Propagate by division or from seed.

Trillium chloropetalum

Trillium chloropetalum

◐/☼ ❄ ↔ 20 in (50 cm) ↑ 20 in (50 cm)
Perennial from California, USA. Thick
stems; rounded, often maroon-mottled leaves
developing rapidly from early spring to form
full ruff behind flowers. Fragrant, white to
greenish white, soft yellow, or maroon flowers
with slightly reflexed petals, in early spring.
T. c. var. *giganteum*, robust, usually dark
red-flowered form, with maroon-mottled
foliage. Zones 6–9.

Trillium cuneatum
SWEET BETSY, TOAD SHADE

◐/☼ ❄ ↔ 16 in (40 cm) ↑ 24 in (60 cm)
Variegated species from southeastern USA. Mottled gray-green
and olive foliage, said to resemble pattern of a toad's skin. Leaves
pointed oval, not quite making a full circle. Flowers burgundy to
yellowish green, musk-scented, in early spring. Zones 6–9.

Trillium erectum ★

BETHROOT, BIRTHROOT

☼/◐ ❋ ↔ 20 in (50 cm) ↑ 20 in (50 cm)

From eastern North America. Large, light textured, bright green leaves, sometimes making complete ruff. Flowers at or slightly above foliage level, dark velvety red, rarely white, narrow petals, unpleasantly scented, in early spring. Zones 4–9.

Trillium grandiflorum

GRAND TRILLIUM, SHOWY TRILLIUM

☼/◐ ❋ ↔ 20 in (50 cm) ↑ 18 in (45 cm)

Late-flowering species from eastern North America. Rounded to pointed oval leaves, sometimes overlapping to form full circle. Flowers open white, age to pink, in early summer. *T. g.* f. *roseum* (syn. 'Roseum'), flowers pink, age to deep dusky shade. Zones 5–9.

Trillium luteum

WOOD TRILLIUM, YELLOW WAKE ROBIN

☼/◐ ❋ ↔ 18 in (45 cm) ↑ 18 in (45 cm)

Native to southeastern USA. Broad pointed oval, mottled leaves, not overlapping. Yellow to yellow-green, very fragrant flowers, erect petals to over 3 in (8 cm) long, in early spring. Zones 5–9.

Trillium ovatum

WAKE ROBIN, WESTERN TRILLIUM

☼/◐ ❋ ↔ 20 in (50 cm) ↑ 20 in (50 cm)

Erect species, native to Oregon, USA. Conspicuously veined, deep green, pointed oval to rhomboidal leaves. Flowers held above foliage; white ageing to pink, musk-scented, in early spring. Zones 5–9.

Trillium sessile

TOAD SHADE

☼/◐ ❋ ↔ 12–16 in (30–40 cm) ↑ 12 in (30 cm)

Native to northeastern USA. Elliptical to rounded leaves with dark mottling, often slightly drooping, leaves encircle flower but seldom overlap. Flowers musk-scented, petals deep purple-red, sepals green tinted purple-red, in early spring. Zones 4–9.

TROLLIUS

GLOBE FLOWER

There are around 31 species of perennial herbs in this genus, which belongs to the buttercup (Ranunculaceae) family. They are found in almost all northern temperate regions from the Himalayas to Turkey, China, Europe, and North America. The roots are thick and fibrous and the plants form basal tufts or rosettes of palmately lobed and divided leaves with toothed edges. The flowers, often cupped, are up to 3 in (8 cm) wide, with spirally arranged sepals and petals of white, yellow, or orange, sometimes tinged with red or lilac. They grow

Trollius chinensis 'Golden Queen'

in damp sunny meadows and on stream banks, often in heavy soils. CULTIVATION: These plants will grow best in full sun or part-shade in permanently moist soil or in boggy areas beside water. Propagate from seed or by division.

Trillium cuneatum

Trollius chinensis

syn. *Trollius ledebourii*

☼/◐ ❋ ↔ 18 in (45 cm) ↑ 36 in (90 cm)

Clumping species, found growing naturally in northern China. Deeply lobed, finely toothed leaves. Tall stems; bowl-shaped flowers, golden yellow, prominent stamens, in summer. '**Golden Queen**' ★, deep orange-yellow flowers. Zones 5–9.

Trollius × cultorum

☼/◐ ❋ ↔ 18 in (45 cm) ↑ 24–36 cm (60–90 cm)

Garden hybrids; finely divided foliage; lemon to orange flowers, in summer. '**Cheddar**', pale lemon to almost white flowers; '**Feuertroll**', rich orangey yellow flowers. Zones 5–9.

TROPAEOLUM

CANARY BIRD VINE, FLAME CREEPER, NASTURTIUM

The type genus for the nasturtium (Tropaeolaceae) family, this group of over 80 species of sometimes tuberous annuals and perennials is found from southern Mexico to the southern tip of South America. Many climb using their twining leaf stalks. Though variable, the leaves are often shield-shaped and tinted blue-green. All have long-spurred 5-petalled flowers in a wide range of mainly warm shades.

CULTIVATION: Hardiness varies considerably in these species. Plant in full sun or half-sun in moist well-drained soil. May need trimming back occasionally. Propagate by division, from basal cuttings or seed.

Tropaeolum ciliatum

☼/◐ ❋ ↔ 20 ft (6 m) ↑ 20 ft (6 m)

Vigorous, climbing, herbaceous perennial, native to Chile. Leaves mid-green, 5 to 7 lobes. Bright golden yellow trumpet-shaped flowers, deep red center and veining. Summer-flowering. Capable of spreading over a large area in one season. Zones 8–10.

Utricularia inflata

Tropaeolum peregrinum

CANARY CREEPER

☼/☀ ❄ ↔ 8 ft (2.4 m) ↕ 8 ft (2.4 m)

Quick-growing perennial climber from Peru and Ecuador, often treated as an annual in gardens. Light green, 5-lobed leaves. Clusters of long-stemmed, 1 in (25 mm) wide, sulfur yellow to gold flowers, cut-edged petals. Summer- to autumn-flowering. Zones 9–11.

UTRICULARIA

BLADDERWORT

This genus in the bladderwort (Lentibulariaceae) family has around 200 species of small carnivorous plants. Highly adaptable, these plants grow in areas of perennial or seasonal wetness in a wide range of environments. Having no real root system, they form rhizomes or stolons with green leaves of varying size and shape and/or tiny stalked bladders, spreading rapidly in the growing season. Traps found on the stems or runners have tiny trigger hairs that "vacuum" insects into the bladder. Most have attractive 2-lipped flowers on slender scapes from spring to early summer. CULTIVATION: Growing conditions can be divided into 4 main groups. All can be grown in a peat/sand mix (4:1). Grow terrestrial species in part-shade in permanently wet peat soil occasionally flooded with shallow water. Allow seasonal species to dry out, then put in a shallow tray of water in the growing season. Tropical/epiphytic species prefer warm, wet, humid conditions in part-shade. Grow aquatic species in full sun in a small tank of water with a peat base, taking care to prevent algae from forming. Propagate by division in the growing season or from seed.

Utricularia alpina

ALPINE BLADDERWORT

☀ ❄ ↔ 6 in (15 cm) ↕ 12 in (30 cm)

Perennial tropical epiphyte or ground species from highland rainforests of Central and South America and the West Indies. Oval leaves, 6 in (15 cm) long, arise from tuberous root stock. Up to 4 white and yellow flowers, to 2 in (5 cm) wide. Zones 9–11.

Utricularia bisquamata

syn. *Utricularia capensis*

☀ ❄ ↔ 3 in (8 cm) ↕ 2 in (5 cm)

Terrestrial species from South Africa. Profuse small flowers on scapes to 1 in (25 mm) long, in a color combination of violet, orange, white, and yellow. Spreads by seed. Zones 9–11.

Utricularia calycifida

☀ ❄ ↔ 4 in (10 cm) ↕ 6 in (15 cm)

Tropical species, native to Guyana, Venezuela, and Surinam. Teardrop-shaped leaves with purple streaks, sometimes tinged red. Several purple flowers with yellow center, on scapes to 6 in (15 cm) tall. Zones 10–11.

Utricularia bisquamata

Utricularia reniformis

Utricularia uniflora

Utricularia dichotoma ★

FAIRY APRONS

☀ ❄ ↔ 8 in (20 cm) ↑ 6–18 in (15–45 cm)

Tropical and temperate terrestrial species from New Zealand and temperate Australia. Leaves to 1 in (25 mm) long. Pale pink to purple flowers, white to yellow centers, 1 to 2 pairs per scape. Zones 9–11.

Utricularia inflata

syn. *Utricularia ceratophylla*

FLOATING BLADDERWORT

☀ ❄ ↔ 12 in (30 cm) ↑ 12 in (30 cm)

North American tropical and subtropical perennial aquatic. Leaves to 7 in (18 cm) long. Star-shaped whorl of 5 to 7 hollow tubes make it float. To 17 yellow flowers per scape. Zones 9–11.

Utricularia menziesii

REDCOAT

☀ ❄ ↔ 2 in (5 cm) ↑ 3 in (8 cm)

From southwestern Western Australia. Leaves to 2 in (5 cm) long. Single orange to burgundy flower, yellow center. Forms a tuber during hot dry summer months. Zones 9–11.

Utricularia praelonga

☀ ❄ ↔ 12 in (30 cm) ↑ 18 in (45 cm)

Tropical and subtropical Brazilian species. Forms 2 types of leaves: long, thin; circular, flat on ground. Large yellow flowers on long stems. Zones 10–11.

Utricularia reniformis ★

☀ ❄ ↔ 18 in (45 cm) ↑ 18 in (45 cm)

Tropical terrestrial species from Venezuela and Guyana. Thick fleshy rhizomes bearing traps. Large kidney-shaped leaves. Tall spikes of long-lasting, large, pinkish violet flowers. Zones 10–11.

Utricularia uniflora

☀ ❄ ↔ 3 in (8 cm) ↑ 8 in (20 cm)

Perennial terrestrial found in the wet sandy soil of streams and on waterfall rockfaces of the Australian east coast. Small egg-shaped leaves; 1 to 2 mauve flowers on each slim stalk. Zones 9–11.

UVULARIA

BELLWORT, MERRYBELLS

This genus contains 5 species of easy-to-grow herbaceous perennials in the lily-of-the-valley (Convallariaceae) family. From eastern North America, they are found in moist, well-drained, deciduous woodlands. Stems are erect or arching; the lance-shaped leaves are a bright green. Leaves are perfoliate (wrapping around the stem at the base) on all species except *U. sessilifolia*. Yellow bell-shaped flowers dangle from the stem and have long, slender, pointed, slightly twisted

Utricularia praelonga

petals. Blooms last for 2 to 3 weeks in early spring to mid-summer, depending on species, but foliage remains visible all summer. CULTIVATION: Grow these plants in shade in deep, moist, slightly acid soil. Propagate by dividing clumps in spring or autumn, from ripened seed in late summer, or by transplanting underground stems, which spread easily.

Uvularia grandiflora

BIG MERRYBELLS, GREAT MERRYBELLS

☀ ❄ ↔ 12–24 in (30–60 cm)

↑ 12–24 in (30–60 cm)

Found from Quebec to Ontario, Canada, south to Minnesota, Georgia, Tennessee, and Kansas, USA. Light green foliage, arching stems. Bright yellow flowers, from mid-spring to early summer. Fruit a small triangular capsule. *U. g.* var. *pallida*, pale sulfur yellow flowers. Zones 3–9.

Uvularia perfoliata

PERFOLIATE BELLWORT, STRAW BELL, WOOD MERRYBELLS

☀ ❄ ↔ 12–18 in (30–45 cm) ↑ 16 in (40 cm)

From Quebec to Ontario, Canada, south to Mississippi and Florida, USA. Flowers pale yellow from mid-spring to early summer. Zones 3–9.

VALERIANA

VALERIAN

This is a widely distributed (excluding Australasia) genus of vigorous annuals, hardy perennials, and small shrubs in the family Valerianaceae that favor moist habitats in woodlands, meadows, and mountainous regions. They are creeping or tap-rooted, and leaves vary from simple to lobed, pointed or deeply divided, sometimes arranged along the stems like the rungs of a ladder, disappearing near the top of the plant. Small flowers are produced, often in clusters, in pink, lavender-pink, white or yellow shades. CULTIVATION: Grow in moist soil and full sun or part-shade. Propagate from seed in autumn or early spring, or from cuttings.

Uvularia grandiflora

Valeriana montana

☀ ❄ ↔ 10 in (25 cm) ↕ 10 in (25 cm)
From the Alps and the Caucasus region. Clumps of oval to round leaves. Small rounded clusters of lilac, pink, or white flowers in early summer. Zones 4–9.

Valeriana phu

☀ ❄ ↔ 18 in (45 cm) ↕ 36 in (90 cm)
Native to Europe and the Caucasus. Tall perennial; basal leaves mostly undivided. Tiny white flowers, in clusters, in summer. 'Aurea' leaves yellow when young. Zones 3–9.

VANCOUVERIA

This genus is made up of 3 species of herbaceous creeping perennials that are native to the woodlands of northwestern North America. Like *Epimedium,* they are members of the barberry (Berberidaceae) family and are useful ground covers in shady areas, but they

Valeriana montana

will not do well in dry soil. Their leathery divided leaves grow on wiry stems from crowns arising from branched underground rhizomes. The small and pendulous flowers are held on tall stems above the foliage.
CULTIVATION: Grow *Vancouveria* species in partial shade in cool, moist, organic, acid soil. Additions of leaf mold or humus will ensure success. They will not perform well in areas with hot dry summers. Given ideal conditions they will spread quickly. Propagate by dividing the rhizomes in spring or autumn.

Vancouveria chrysantha

☀ ❄ ↔ 12 in (30 cm) ↕ 12 in (30 cm)
Creeping evergreen perennial from Oregon, USA. Stiff green leaves, bronze-tinged. Small golden yellow flowers in early summer. Zones 7–9.

Vancouveria hexandra ★

AMERICAN BARRENWORT
☀/☀ ❄ ↔ 12 in (30 cm) ↕ 12 in (30 cm)
Creeping perennial, found from Washington to California, USA. Deciduous; pale green foliage, similar to maidenhair fern (*Adiantum*). Drooping white flowers from late spring to early summer. Zones 7–9.

VERATRUM

FALSE HELLEBORE
This genus of rhizomatous herbaceous perennials, belonging to the bunchflower (Melanthiaceae) family, includes 20 species distributed throughout temperate Europe, North Africa, Asia, and North America that are usually found in damp meadows and open woodlands. Typically grown for their foliage, these plants feature alternate, pleated, prominently veined, mid- to dark green leaves, which form mounds. The numerous tiny flowers, typically bell-shaped, occur in white, green, brownish, or purple-black, and are held in terminal panicles. All parts of the plants are extremely toxic.

CULTIVATION: Generally frost tolerant, these plants prefer a position in full sun or light shade in rich moisture-retentive soil. A few species will tolerate dry summer conditions. Propagate from root cuttings in spring or by division or from seed in autumn. It may take a decade for them to flower from seed.

Veratrum album

WHITE FALSE HELLEBORE
☀ ❄ ↔ 24 in (60 cm) ↕ 24 in (60 cm)
Rhizomatous herb, native to Europe, North Africa, and northern Asia. Large, oblong or elliptic, pleated leaves. Dense racemes of green and white flowers. Summer-flowering. Zones 5–9.

Veratrum nigrum

BLACK HELLEBORE
☀ ❄ ↔ 24 in (60 cm) ↕ 24–48 in (60–120 cm)
Found from southern Europe to Siberia and Asia. Pleated, broadly elliptic to linear or lance-shaped leaves. Numerous purple-black flowers in dense racemes. Summer-flowering. Zones 6–9.

VERBASCUM

MOTH MULLEIN, MULLEIN
This genus of some 300 species of annuals, biennials, perennials, and subshrubs in the foxglove (Scrophulariaceae) family includes cultivated plants and many that have become weeds outside their natural temperate Eurasian and North African range. The commonly cultivated species usually form basal rosettes of large elliptic leaves, which are often heavily veined and sometimes felted. Tall upright flower spikes emerge from the rosettes, carrying massed, small, 5-petalled flowers, usually in white, yellow, or pink to lavender shades.
CULTIVATION: Hardiness varies with the species, but the majority of *Verbascum* species and cultivars prefer a sunny position with light, gritty, free-draining soil. They can tolerate summer drought but need moisture until after flowering. Propagate by division or from seed, depending on the growth form.

Verbascum acaule

☀/☀ ❄ ↔ 4 in (10 cm) ↕ 4 in (10 cm)
Tiny species, native to the Peloponnesian region of Greece. Tight rosette of dark green, toothed, elliptic leaves. Glowing yellow 5-petalled flowers throughout warmer months. Ideal for alpine troughs. Zones 7–10.

Verbascum blattaria

MOTH MULLEIN
☀/☀ ❄ ↔ 12–20 in (30–50 cm) ↕ 5–6 ft (1.5–1.8 m)
Widely naturalized temperate Eurasian biennial. Basal rosettes of downy, toothed, lance-shaped, green leaves, up to 10 in (25 cm) long. Strong, erect, leafy flower stems; many ¾ in (18 mm) wide, white, sometimes pale yellow or pink flowers. Cultivated forms may have considerably larger flowers. Zones 6–10.

Verbascum bombyciferum

☼/☀ ❄ ↔ 24–40 in (60–100 cm) ↑6–8 ft (1.8–2.4 m)
Western Asian biennial. Forms large rosettes of broadly oval, wavy-edged, white-felted leaves, to 20 in (50 cm) long. Flower stems to over 6 ft (1.8 m) tall, leafy at base but leafless from point where flowers commence. Stems and buds woolly, sometimes branching, flowers deep yellow, to over 1¼ in (30 mm) wide, in summer. 'Polarsommer' (syn. 'Arctic Summer'), yellow flowered cultivar, named for especially heavy silver felting on leaves. Zones 6–10.

Verbascum chaixii

NETTLE-LEAFED MOTH MULLEIN
☼/☀ ❄ ↔ 12–24 in (30–60 cm) ↑36–48 in (90–120 cm)
Perennial, occurring from central Europe to Spain and east to Russia. Forms clump of rosettes of deeply veined, toothed, gray-green to dark green, downy leaves, to 12 in (30 cm) long. Narrow erect flower stems; flowers less than 1 in (25 mm) wide, bright yellow with purple-red stamens, in summer. 'Album' ★, to 33 in (85 cm) tall, white flowers, mauve stamens. Zones 5–9.

Verbascum dumulosum

☼/☀ ❄ ↔ 12–16 in (30–40 cm) ↑8 in (20 cm)
Turkish perennial. Dense clump of velvety, toothed, soft green, basal leaves to 2 in (5 cm) long. Many 10- to 35-flowered heads of bright yellow blooms in summer. Zones 8–10.

Verbascum olympicum

☼/☀ ❄ ↔ 20–40 in (50–100 cm) ↑5–6 ft (1.5–1.8 m)
Turkish summer-flowering biennial or short-lived perennial. Forms dense basal clump of smooth-edged, lance-shaped, white, woolly leaves, around 12 in (30 cm) long, sometimes more than 24 in (60 cm) long. Branching leafy-based stems; dozens of 1 in (25 mm) wide, bright yellow flowers. Zones 6–10.

Verbascum phoeniceum

PURPLE MULLEIN
☼/☀ ❄ ↔ 12–16 in (30–40 cm) ↑8–16 in (20–40 cm)
Southern Eurasian biennial or short-lived perennial. Usually one large rosette of sparsely hairy, dark green, wavy-edged or finely toothed, pointed oval leaves, to 6 in (15 cm) long. Simple or few-branched stems with mauve to purple, rarely white, pink, or yellow flowers, around 1 in (25 mm) wide, in summer. Zones 6–10.

Verbascum thapsus

AARON'S ROD
☼/☀ ❄ ↔ 20–32 in (50–80 cm) ↑6–7 ft (1.8–2 m)
Extremely vigorous, widely naturalized, summer-flowering, temperate Eurasian biennial. Forms large rosettes of woolly white to gray leaves, up to 20 in (50 cm) long. Strong erect flower stem, usually leafy at base, many ½–1¼ in (12–30 mm) wide, deep yellow flowers. Zones 3–9.

Verbascum Hybrid Cultivars

☼/☀ ❄ ↔ 12–20 in (30–50 cm) ↑12–60 in (30–150 cm)
Moth mulleins hybridize freely, and British breeders in particular have produced a range of hybrids that combine lush velvety foliage with beautifully shaded flowers. Some of the best include members of the **Cotswold Group** such as 'Cotswold Beauty', to 48 in (120 cm) tall, with buff to apricot-pink flowers, purple-pink anthers; 'Gainsborough', to 48 in (120 cm) tall, bright yellow flowers, gray felted foliage; 'Mont Blanc', to 36 in (90 cm) high, pure white flowers, gray felted foliage; and 'Pink Domino', to 48 in (120 cm) tall, bright pink with a dark center. Other excellent cultivars include 'Helen Johnson', 24–32 in (60–80 cm) tall, variable dusky apricot-pink shades, gray-felted foliage; 'Jackie', to 24 in (60 cm) high, dusky pink with deep magenta center; 'Letitia', to 12 in (30 cm) tall, shrubby habit, many bright yellow flowers. Zones 6–10.

Verbascum chaixii 'Album'

Verbascum dumulosum

Verbascum olympicum

Verbascum, Hybrid Cultivar, 'Cotswold Beauty'

VERBENA

VERVAIN

This member of the self-named vervain (Verbenaceae) family contains 250 species of annuals, perennials, and subshrubs native to tropical and subtropical America. Plants are sprawling to erect; leaves are opposite and variously divided. Terminal flowerheads range from narrow and overlapping to broader, rounder clusters. Individual flowers are tubular with flaring, sometimes notched, lobes and blooms come in shades of purple, pink, red, and white. Some botanists, particularly in North America, recognize the genus *Glandularia* as distinct from *Verbena*. As such, *Glandularia* includes most lower-growing verbenas with more colorful flowers in short broad heads, in contrast to the erect slender spikes of flowers that characterize *Verbena* in the narrower sense.
CULTIVATION: Grow these plants in the border in full sun in moderately fertile, moist but well-drained soil. A number of cultivars are suitable for hanging baskets. Propagate annuals from seed and perennials from seed, cuttings, or by division.

Verbena bonariensis

PURPLE TOP, SOUTH AMERICAN VERVAIN, TALL VERBENA

☀ ❄ ↔ 24 in (60 cm) ↕ 3–5 ft (0.9–1.5 m)
South American perennial; also grown as annual. Erect, square, rough stems. Sparsely foliaged; lance-shaped serrated leaves. Tiny purple flowers in flat-topped clusters. Self-sows. Zones 7–10.

Verbena canadensis

syn. *Glandularia canadensis*

CREEPING VERVAIN, ROSE VERVAIN

☀ ❄ ↔ 16 in (40 cm) ↕ 8 in (20 cm)
From North America. Semi-prostrate perennial, rooting at nodes. Leaves toothed, deeply divided. Small showy heads of fragrant rosy pink to purple flowers, in spring–autumn. Zones 4–9.

Verbena rigida

syn. *Verbena venosa*

VEINED VERBENA

☀ ❄ ↔ 12 in (30 cm) ↕ 24–36 in (60–90 cm)
Creeping perennial, native to South America. Stiff upright stems; stalkless oblong leaves, rough, irregularly toothed. Vivid purple to magenta flowers, in clusters, in summer. 'Polaris', silver-blue flowers. Zones 8–10.

Verbena tenera

syn. *Glandularia tenera*

☀ ❄ ↔ 12–20 in (30–50 cm) ↕ 12–20 in (30–50 cm)
Shrubby, clumping perennial, found from Brazil to Argentina. Sprawling stems rooting at nodes; small, finely hairy, divided leaves. Elongated spikes of purplish or rose violet flowers. *V. t.* var. *maonetti*, reddish violet flowers edged with white; *V. t.* var. *pulchella*, spikes of rose-violet flowers. *V. t.* 'Kleopatra', crimson-pink flowers. Zones 9–11.

Verbena tenuisecta

syns *Glandularia tenuisecta*, *Verbena pulchella gracilior*

MOSS VERBENA

☀ ❄ ↔ 12–20 in (30–50 cm) ↕ 12–20 in (30–50 cm)
Annual or perennial from South America. Prostrate, sprawling, aromatic stems, square in cross-section. Leaves with 3 narrow, toothed leaflets. Spikes of broad-lobed lilac, mauve, purple, blue, or white flowers. Zones 9–11.

Verbena Hybrid Cultivars

syn. *Glandularia* Hybrid Cultivars

☀ ❄ ↔ 24–40 in (60–100 cm) ↕ 12–24 in (30–60 cm)
Fragrant perennials flowering from summer to autumn. 'Homestead Purple', vigorous, trailing dark green foliage, purple flowers; 'Imagination', violet-blue flowers; 'Peaches and Cream', peach and cream flowers; 'Quartz Burgundy', dwarf form, deep wine red flowers with tiny white eyes; 'Quartz Scarlet', vigorous, scarlet flowers; 'Silver Ann', vigorous, pale and deep pink flowers; 'Sissinghurst', mat-forming, magenta pink flowers, can be invasive; Tapien Series, low-growing, long-blooming, heat-resistant forms, in blue, violet-blue, lavender, and pink; Temari Series, low-growing, trailing, long-flowering, dense mats of ferny foliage, large flowerheads in pink, burgundy, blue, and scarlet. Zones 7–10.

VERONICA

BIRDSEYE, SPEEDWELL

This genus in the foxglove (Scrophulariaceae) family, containing 250 species of annuals and perennials, is widespread in northern temperate zones. Most are creeping mat-forming plants that sometimes strike root as they spread. The leaves tend to be small, oval to lance-shaped, often shallowly toothed, and rarely pinnately lobed. A few of the species have solitary flowers, but more often

Verbena bonariensis

Verbena tenera 'Kleopatra'

Verbena, Hybrid Cultivar, 'Homestead Purple'

many-flowered upright spikes develop in spring and summer. The color range is mainly white and pink to purple-blue shades, including some striking deep blue flowers.

CULTIVATION: Speedwells are mostly very hardy and easily grown in full sun to half-sun, with moist well-drained soil. Some are superb rock garden plants, others are suited to borders. Propagate from cuttings or seed, or by self-rooted layers or division.

Veronica alpina

☼/◐ ❄ ↔ 8–16 in (20–40 cm) ↕ 2–6 in (5–15 cm)

Creeping Arctic and temperate Eurasian perennial. Forms clump of wiry stems; pointed oval leaves, 1 in (25 mm) long, faintly toothed, sparsely hairy. Short erect spikes, few light-centered, purple flowers, ¼ in (6 mm) wide, in spring–summer. 'Alba', white-flowered form, but the name *Veronica alpina* 'Alba' is sometimes used in the nursery trade to refer to *Veronicastrum virginicum* 'Album', which is a completely different plant. Zones 2–9.

Veronica austriaca

☼/◐ ❄ ↔ 10–24 in (25–60 cm) ↕ 6–16 in (15–40 cm)

Spreading European perennial. Wiry stems; sparsely hairy, narrow lance-shaped, ½ in (12 mm) long leaves. Upright spikes of many bright purple-blue flowers, in late spring–summer. *V. a.* subsp. *teucrium*, broader, more deeply toothed leaves, parent of best garden forms, such as '**Crater Lake Blue**' ★, 10 in (25 cm) tall, intense blue flowers; and '**Shirley Blue**', 10 in (25 cm) tall, bright mid-blue flowers. Zones 6–10.

Veronica beccabunga

BROOKLIME

☼/◐ ❄ ↔ 8–20 in (20–50 cm)
↕ 4–6 in (10–15 cm)

Eurasian perennial. Fleshy, often red-tinted stems, upturned at tips. Oval leaves, 1¾ in (40 mm) long, usually finely toothed, Tiny lilac to purple flowers, in small clusters at stem tips and nearby axils, in summer. Zones 5–9.

Veronica chamaedrys

ANGELS' EYES, BIRD'S EYE, GERMANDER SPEEDWELL

☼/◐ ❄ ↔ 12–20 in (30–50 cm)
↕ 6–10 in (15–25 cm)

Temperate Eurasian perennial, widely naturalized in North America. Forms small mounding clump of bright green, sparsely hairy, and toothed, ½–1¾ in (12–40 mm) long, oval leaves. Flowers tiny, bright blue, white center, in sprays of up to 30 blooms, in late spring–summer. Zones 3–9.

Veronica cinerea

☼/◐ ❄ ↔ 6–10 in (15–25 cm) ↕ 2–4 in (5–10 cm)

Summer-flowering perennial from the Middle East and western Asia. Forms dense cushion; ½ in (12 mm) long, sometimes toothed leaves, covered with silver-gray hairs. Foliage color contrasts well with short spikes of light-centered deep blue to purple-blue flowers. Zones 5–9.

Veronica chamaedrys

Veronica longifolia

Veronica gentianoides

☼/◐ ❄ ↔ 12–24 in (30–60 cm) ↕ 12–24 in (30–60 cm)

Spreading perennial from the Caucasus region and western Asia. Forms dense clump; upright stems, narrow, toothed, pointed oval leaves, to nearly 3 in (8 cm) long, at base of clump. Erect spikes, to 12 in (30 cm) long; abundant flowers, usually pale blue, sometimes white, in late spring–summer. Cultivars include '**Tissington White**', white flowers; and '**Variegata**', attractive cream-variegated foliage, pale blue flowers. Zones 4–9.

Veronica longifolia

☼/◐ ❄ ↔ 16–30 in (40–75 cm)
↕ 20–48 in (50–120 cm)

Found over much of continental Europe, widely naturalized in northeastern North America. Erect perennial; whorls of narrow, lance-shaped leaves, toothed, sometimes sparsely hairy. Basal leaves to over 4 in (10 cm) long, upper leaves much smaller. Terminal flower spikes to 10 in (25 cm) long, numerous tiny blue to lavender flowers. Summer- to autumn-flowering. Cultivars include '**Alba**', to 36 in (90 cm) tall, flowers pure white; '**Blauriesin**' (syn. 'Blue Giantess'), reaches up to 32 in (80 cm) tall, bright blue flowers; '**Lilac Fantasy**', compact, flowers lilac; '**Pink Damask**', to 36 in (90 cm) tall, soft pastel pink flowers; '**Rose Tone**', to around 36 in (90 cm) high, rose pink flowers; and '**Schneeriesin**', to 36 in (90 cm) tall, profuse white flowers. Zones 4–9.

Veronica pectinata

☼/◐ ❄ ↔ 12–16 in (30–40 cm) ↕ 2–8 in (5–20 cm)

Evergreen southern Eurasian subshrub. Forms mat of hairy, deeply toothed or cut leaves, each around 1 in (25 mm) long. Racemes, up to 8 in (20 cm) long, form in leaf axils; numerous light-centered deep blue flowers, from late spring. Zones 3–9.

Veronica petraea

☼/◐ ❄ ↔ 8–12 in (20–30 cm) ↑ 4–6 in (10–15 cm)
Caucasian perennial. Forms small tuft; wiry, often purple-tinted stems; downy, sometimes toothed leaves, to ¾ in (18 mm) long. Stem tips usually erect; heads of up to 20 tiny flowers, blue or pink, at tips and in nearby leaf axils, in summer–autumn. 'Madame Mercier', lilac-blue flowers. Zones 6–9.

Veronica prostrata

☼/◐ ❄ ↔ 8–16 in (20–40 cm) ↑ 2–4 in (5–10 cm)
European perennial. Forms small mat; wiry stems; toothed, narrow pointed oval leaves, to 1 in (25 mm) long. Spikes of many small pale to deep blue flowers in late spring–summer. 'Heavenly Blue', bright blue flowers; 'Spode Blue', deepest blue flowers; 'Trehane', golden leaves and violet-blue flowers. Zones 5–9.

Veronica spicata

☼/◐ ❄ ↔ 12–32 in (30–80 cm) ↑ 12–24 in (30–60 cm)
European perennial. Forms clump; erect stems; narrow lance-shaped, 1–3 in (25–80 mm) long leaves, downy, finely toothed. Terminal spikes of many ¼ in (6 mm) wide deep blue flowers in summer. *V. s.* subsp. *incana,* velvety silver-gray to white flowers, sometimes classified as distinct species, with cultivars including 'Rotfuchs' (syn. 'Red Fox'), 'Silbersee', and 'Wendy'. *V. s.* 'Barcarolle', bright pink flowers; 'Heidekind', purple-red flowers; 'Icicle', white flowers; 'Rosea', deep pink flowers; 'Sunny Border Blue', dark violet-blue flowers over long season. Zones 3–9.

Veronica wormskjoldii

AMERICAN ALPINE SPEEDWELL
☼/◐ ❄ ↔ 8–20 in (20–50 cm) ↑ 4–12 in (10–30 cm)
Clump-forming perennial from North America and southern tip of Greenland. Spreads by rhizomes; erect sparsely hairy stems; pointed elliptic leaves to 2 in (5 cm) long sometimes toothed. Terminal heads of few tiny violet-blue blooms in summer. Zones 4–9.

VERONICASTRUM

Belonging to the foxglove (Scrophulariaceae) family, this genus of 2 upright perennials is from northeastern Asia and northeastern

Veronica petraea 'Madame Mercier'

Veronica spicata 'Heidekind'

North America. The plants have whorls of simple leaves and a terminal raceme of spikes of flowers. Blooms feature a calyx with 4 to 5 lobes, and a saucer-shaped corolla with 2 stamens.
CULTIVATION: These perennials like moist, humus-rich soil and will grow in full sun or half-sun. Propagate from seed or by division.

Veronicastrum virginicum

syns *Leptandra virginica, Veronica virginica*
BLACKROOT, BOWMAN'S ROOT, CULVER'S ROOT
☼ ❄ ↔ 1–3 ft (0.3–0.9 m) ↑ 2–6 ft (0.6–1.8 m)
From northeastern America. Whorls of 4 to 7 simple, sword-shaped, serrated leaves. Slender spikes, to 12 in (30 cm) tall, tiny pale blue or white flowers in summer. *V. v.* var. *sibiricum,* narrow spikes of lilac flowers. *V. v.* 'Album', white flowers; 'Pointed Finger', lilac flowers; 'Roseum', soft pink flowers. Zones 3–6.

VICTORIA

GIANT WATER LILY
The 2 species of aquatic perennials in this genus, members of the waterlily (Nymphaeaceae) family, are native to tropical South America, where they are found growing in slow-moving or still water. These giant plants are grown for their large flat leaves, reputed to be able to bear the weight of a small child, and for their beautiful perfumed flowers. Arising from stout rhizomes, they produce floating round leaves, which can reach up to 7 ft (2 m) wide, with upturned rims. Opening at night, the many-petalled flowers are white at first, deepening to pink on the second day, and purple on the third day before dying.
CULTIVATION: Ideal for large warm pools in tropical greenhouses, these plants are usually grown as annuals because of their rapid growth rate. Grow in full sun. Propagate from seed and gradually increase pot size and water depth as plants grow.

Victoria amazonica

syn. *Victoria regia*
AMAZON WATER LILY, ROYAL WATER LILY
☼ ⚘ ↔ 15–20 ft (4.5–6 m) ↑ 10–12 in (25–30 cm)
From the Amazon region. Leaves to 7 ft (2 m) wide, upturned rim to about 6 in (15 cm) high. Leaf underside is reddish purple and spiny. Perfumed flowers in summer and autumn. Zones 10–12.

Veronicastrum virginicum var. *sibiricum*

Victoria 'Longwood Hybrid'

↔12–40 ft (3.5–12 m)
↑10–12 in (25–30 cm)
Vigorous hybrid of *V. amazonica* and *V. cruziana* raised at Longwood Gardens, Philadelphia, USA. Large leaves, to 8 ft (2.4 m) wide. Flowers open earlier in evening. Zones 10–12.

VIGUIERA

Native to North and South America, this genus, containing about 150 annual or perennial herbs and shrubs, is a member of the daisy (Asteraceae) family. They feature several stems that grow from a central base, and simple, alternate or opposite leaves. The solitary flowerheads, about 2 in (5 cm) across, are borne on long stalks, usually with yellow daisy-like flowers.
CULTIVATION: *Viguiera* species prefer a position in full sun, and will perform well in most well-drained soils. Propagate from seed.

Victoria amazonica

Viguiera multiflora

↔30–40 in (75–100 cm) ↑30–40 in (75–100 cm)
Resinous perennial herb, native to southern, central, and western USA, and south to Mexico. Smooth-edged or sparsely toothed leaves, narrowly oval to sword-shaped. Yellow daisy-like flowers in summer. Zones 10–12.

VINCA
PERIWINKLE

This genus of 7 species of evergreen groundcovering perennials found in woodland areas of Europe, North Africa, and central Asia, belongs to the dogbane (Apocynaceae) family. These plants are distinctive for their opposite, simple, lance-shaped leaves that cover the slender, often cream or pale green, ground-hugging stems. The foliage varies in color from pale to dark green and many variations occur with attractive variegations. The star-shaped flowers are produced from spring through to late autumn, and vary in color from dark purple to blue and white.
CULTIVATION: These plants prefer a light free-draining soil with a reasonable level of organic matter, in sun or shade. The plant sends out long trailing and rooting shoots, which make new plants. They will spread indefinitely and can become invasive if neglected. Propagation is easy any time of year by separating the new offshoots or by layering new shoots.

Vinca minor

Vinca difformis

↔5–10 ft (1.5–3 m) ↑12 in (30 cm)
Low-growing evergreen perennial, native to North Africa, and southern and western Europe. Narrowly lance-shaped, glossy, dark green leaves, up to 3 in (8 cm) long. Flowers 5-petalled, soft blue, fading to white as the season develops. Early spring-flowering. Zones 8–9.

Vinca major
BLUE BUTTONS, GREATER PERIWINKLE

↔5–10 ft (1.5–3 m) ↑18 in (45 cm)
Mounding plant from western parts of Mediterranean. Arching stems; dark green leaves, 3½ in (9 cm) long. Rich violet-blue flowers from early spring to late autumn. 'Variegata' (syn. 'Elegantissima'), creamy white-streaked green leaves. Zones 7–11.

Vinca minor
CREEPING MYRTLE

↔5–10 ft (1.5–3 m) ↑8 in (20 cm)
From Europe, southern Russia, and northern Caucasus. Mat-forming; dark green leaves, to 2 in (5 cm) long. Violet-blue star-shaped flowers from early spring to mid-autumn. 'Alba', white flowers; 'Argenteovariegata' (syn. 'Variegata'), variegated leaves pale lavender flowers; 'Atropurpurea', dark plum flowers; 'Azurea Flore Pleno', pale blue, frilly, double flowers; 'Bowles' Variety', pale lavender-blue flowers; 'Gertrude Jekyll', white flowers; 'Illumination', variegated leaves, mainly yellow, some green marking; 'Multiplex', double, red wine colored flowers; 'Ralph Shugert', deep green leaves, white variegations. Zones 4–9.

VIOLA
HEARTSEASE, PANSY, VIOLET

The type genus for the family Violaceae, *Viola* includes some 500 species of annuals, perennials, and subshrubs, found in all the world's temperate zones from the mountains of New Zealand to the subarctic. Most species are small clump-forming plants with lobed, elliptic, kidney- or heart-shaped leaves. All have 5-petalled flowers, with the lower petal often carrying dark markings. White, yellow, and purple predominate but flowers occur in every color, at least among the garden forms.
CULTIVATION: Pansies are mostly very hardy and easily grown in sun or shade. Woodland species prefer a humus-rich soil, while the rock-garden types like something grittier, but most do well in any moist well-drained soil. Propagation is from seed or basal cuttings or by division, depending on the growth form.

Viola cornuta 'Magnifico'

Viola cornuta 'Pat Kavanagh'

Viola jooi

Viola adunca

HOOKED-SPUR VIOLET, PURPLE VIOLET, WESTERN DOG VIOLET

☼◐/☀ ❋ ↔ 12–16 in (30–40 cm) ↕ 2–4 in (5–10 cm)

Spreading perennial from northern USA. Heart-shaped to rounded leaves, up to 1¾ in (40 mm) long. Spurred lavender to violet flowers in spring, deepen in color with age. Zones 4–9.

Viola blanda

SWEET WHITE VIOLET, WILLDENOW VIOLET, WOODLAND WHITE VIOLET

☼◐/☀ ❋ ↔ 12–20 in (30–50 cm) ↕ 3–6 in (8–15 cm)

Stemless North American perennial. Shallowly toothed, sparsely downy, deep green, heart-shaped leaves, to over 2 in (5 cm) long. White flowers, dark central veining, in spring. Zones 2–9.

Viola canina

HEATH DOG VIOLET, HEATH VIOLET

☀ ❋ ↔ 12–20 in (30–50 cm) ↕ 4–12 in (10–30 cm)

Perennial found over much of northern temperate Eurasia. Deep green, shallowly toothed, pointed oval to heart-shaped leaves, to 1 in (25 mm) long. Erect stems; mauve, purple, or white flowers, pale yellow spur, in summer. Zones 6–9.

Viola cornuta

BEDDING PANSY, HORNED VIOLET

☼◐/☼ ❋ ↔ 8–14 in (20–35 cm) ↕ 6–12 in (15–30 cm)

Rhizome-rooted perennial from the Pyrenees and northern Spain; initially prostrate then more mounding. Oval, 1 in (25 mm) long, shallowly toothed leaves. Spurred, broad-petalled, violet flowers, darker veining, yellow center, in late spring–summer. **Alba Group**, white-flowered forms, **'Belmont Blue'** (syn. 'Boughton Blue'), lilac flowers; **'Jewel White'**, compact habit, white flowers; **'Magnifico'**, white flowers, mauve-edged; **'Pat Kavanagh'**, pale lemon yellow flowers; **'Victoria's Blush'**, mid-pink flowers, narrow petals. Mixed color seedling strains include **Penny Series** and **Princess Series**. **Sorbet Series** includes **'Sorbet Black Delight'**, almost black flowers; and **'Sorbet Coconut'**, pure white flowers. Zones 7–10.

Viola cucullata

syn. *Viola obliqua*

MARSH BLUE VIOLET

☼◐/☼ ❋ ↔ 8–16 in (20–40 cm) ↕ 4–6 in (10–15 cm)

Perennial from North America. Low spreading habit; broad, pointed oval to kidney-shaped leaves, to more than 3 in (8 cm) wide, shallowly toothed. Short-spurred, 5-petalled, white flowers, washed with mauve to purple, in spring–early summer. Zones 4–9.

Viola hederacea

AUSTRALIAN VIOLET, TRAILING VIOLET

☀ ❋ ↔ 6–12 in (15–30 cm) ↕ 2–3 in (5–8 cm)

Small creeping perennial native to southeastern Australia. Broad, oval to kidney-shaped, sometimes shallowly toothed leaves, to over 1¼ in (30 mm) wide. Dark-centered pale lavender or white flowers throughout warmer months. Zones 8–10.

Viola jooi

☼◐/☼ ❋ ↔ 8–14 in (20–35 cm) ↕ 2–4 in (5–10 cm)

Perennial from southeastern Europe. Stemless habit; spreads by runners. Shallowly toothed heart-shaped leaves, to 3 in (8 cm) long. Short-spurred, dark-streaked, mauve flowers, in spring–summer. Zones 5–10.

Viola odorata

SWEET VIOLET

☼◐/☀ ❋ ↔ 12–24 in (30–60 cm) ↕ 4–6 in (10–15 cm)

Southern and western European perennial. Spreads by runners; heart-shaped dark green leaves, to over 2 in (5 cm) long. Highly fragrant, spurred, lavender, purple, yellow, or white flowers, in spring–early summer. Can be weedy. Numerous cultivars available, with single or double flowers in range of colors. **'Purple Robe'** ★, low spreading habit, masses of deep purple flowers. Zones 7–10.

Viola pedata

BIRD'S FOOT VIOLET, PANSY VIOLET

☀ ❋ ↔ 8–16 in (20–40 cm) ↕ 4–6 in (10–15 cm)

Stemless eastern North American perennial. Spreads by runners; foliage differs from most violets: palmate, with up to 5 narrow lobes. Spurred flowers, faintly downy petals, lavender with darker upper petals and veining, in spring. Zones 4–9.

Viola riviniana

DOG VIOLET, WOOD VIOLET

☼◐/☀ ❋ ↔ 8–24 in (20–60 cm) ↕ 4–6 in (10–15 cm)

European and North African perennial. Broad, pointed oval to rounded, toothed, often purple-tinted leaves, about 2 in (5 cm) long. Short-spurred lavender-blue flowers in spring–early summer. **'Purpurea'**, purplish-tinted foliage. Zones 5–9.

Viola septentrionalis

NORTHERN BLUE VIOLET

☼/◐ ✿ ↔ 6–16 in (15–40 cm) ↑ 4–6 in (10–15 cm)

North American perennial; spreads by rhizomes. Pointed oval to rounded heart-shaped leaves, to 2 in (5 cm) long, edged with fine hairs. Downy dark-veined flowers, lavender, less commonly white or purple, in spring–early summer. Zones 4–9.

Viola sororia

☼/◐ ✿ ↔ 6–16 in (15–40 cm) ↑ 2–6 in (5–15 cm)

Eastern North American perennial. Leaves broad, rounded, light-textured, toothed, downy, up to 4 in (10 cm) long. Light-centered violet flowers, less commonly white with purple veining, in spring–early summer. 'Freckles', white flowers heavily purple-spotted; 'Priceana', flowers white, deep blue center. Zones 4–9.

Viola tricolor

HEARTSEASE, JOHNNY JUMP-UP, LOVE-IN-IDLENESS

☼/◐/● ↔ 6–16 in (15–40 cm) ↑ 4–14 in (10–35 cm)

Annual, biennial, or perennial from temperate Eurasia; usually treated as an annual; often self-sows and naturalizes. Pointed oval to lance-like, shallowly lobed or toothed leaves. Small bicolored or multi-colored pansy flowers, often with face-like pattern, in spring–early summer. Many cultivars and seedling strains, such as 'Bowles' Black' (syn. 'E. A. Bowles'), intense velvety black flowers with small yellow center; 'Czar Bleu', pink to purple; and Tinkerbelle Series, small flowers in various pure shades and combinations. Zones 4–10.

Viola sororia 'Freckles'

Viola Hybrid Cultivars

PANSY, VIOLA

☼/◐/● ✿ ↔ 8–16 in (20–40 cm) ↑ 6–12 in (15–30 cm)

Annual or short-lived perennial garden hybrids developed from *V. cornuta*, *V. tricolor*, *V. corsica*, and other mainly European species. Mostly neat, slowly spreading clumps of fleshy, dark green, shallowly lobed, ½–2 in (12–50 mm) long, pointed oval to lance-shaped leaves. Flowers variably sized from small to giant styles nearly 3 in (8 cm) wide. Virtually all colors and many beautiful combinations and patterns. **Baby Face Series**, bicolored to multi-colored flowers with central "face" markings; **Banner Series**, vigorous plants with massed display of mainly bright clear colors; **Crystal Bowl Series**, large flowers, bright pure colors; **Delta Series**, large flowers, wide color range in pure and bicolor; **Dynamite Series**, large flowers, pure colors and several multi-tone forms; **Fama Series**, semi-trailing habit, abundant mid-sized flowers, usually selfs but some pastel blends; **Imperial Series**, similar colors to 'Antique Shades' but larger flowers, such as 'Imperial Antique Shades', large heat-tolerant flowers in delicate pale creams, mauves, peachy apricots, blues, rosy pinks;

Joker Series, boldly patterned mid-sized flowers usually combining blue and another color; **Panola Series**, narrow leaves and abundant small flowers with dark faces; **Penny Series**, including 'Penny Primrose', creamy white upper petals, pale yellow lower petals, and 'Penny Violet Flare', deep violet petals; **Turbo Series**, hardy plants, bright colors; **Ultima Series**, fast-growing, large flowers, wide color range, including selfs, blotched and pastel types in lavender, scarlet, yellow, bronze-apricot, pale salmon orange, including Ultima Supreme, compact form bred to withstand very cold temperatures, with mid-sized early-flowering blooms; **Universal Series**, tolerant of hot and cold weather, 18 prolific bloomers, masses of early-flowering blooms with 13 clear colors, including blue, white, burgundy, orange, purple and yellow, or the typical pansy face; **Velour Series**, medium to large, velvet-textured flowers in intense shades, often with dark markings. Other cultivars include 'Antique Shades', mid-sized, dusky pink and apricot pastel tones; 'Black Moon', rich black petals; and 'Elaine Quin', deep velvety rosy mauve with cream stripes, giving a marbled effect.

Viola Group, more compact pansies, usually fragrant, flowers often patterned. 'Baby Lucia', clear blue blooms, 6 in (15 cm) high mounding plant, heavy bloomer, cold tolerant; 'Etain', cream-yellow petals edged with lavender, refreshing scent; 'Fiona', sweet scent, creamy white flowers, suffused with lavender-blue; 'Irish Molly' ★, gold-bronze yellow petals, dark maroon eye; 'Jackanapes', lower sections bright yellow, upper chocolate brown; 'Maggie Mott', a silvery mauve with creamy center and golden eye; 'Martin', violet flowers with a creamy center; 'Masterpiece', large ruffled flowers, purple-blue with bronze; 'Molly Sanderson', long-lasting, nearly black, velvety flowers with purple veins and golden eye, green heart-shaped leaves; 'Nellie Britton', originally called 'Haslemere', rosy pink; 'Vita', small dainty flowers, with delicate lavender-pink petals and a creamy eye.

Violetta Group, similar to Viola Group but smaller, more compact fragrant flowers. 'Dawn', pale cream flowers deepening to gold; 'Little David' ivory flowers; 'Melinda', white with mauve-blue edges and gold centers; 'Zoe', flowers soft lilac-purple and yellow. Zones 7–10.

Viola, Hybrid Cultivar, Viola Group, 'Irish Molly'

VRIESEA

From Mexico, Central and South America, and the West Indies, this genus of over 250 species and 650 listed hybrids in the bromeliad (Bromeliaceae) family is closely related to *Tillandsia*. They mainly have green leaves, only a few have gray-green leaves, and they have 2 small appendages at the base of each petal. The spineless leaves form a dense rosette capable of storing water. The flowerhead is usually colorful, and some can reach 7 ft (2 m) high. CULTIVATION: Grow indoors or in the greenhouse in cool-temperate areas, or outdoors with protection from prolonged sunlight and heavy rain in warm-temperate, subtropical, and tropical areas. Water when potting mix is dry. A foliar feed high in potash and low in nitrogen (other than in the form of urea) will increase flower size. Propagate from offsets.

Vriesea carinata

☀ ✣ ↔ 12 in (30 cm) ↕ 14 in (35 cm)

From Rio de Janeiro, Brazil. Leaves strap-like, green, forming a funnel-shaped rosette. Flower stem erect, longer than the rosette. Flowerhead sword-shaped, made up of mainly red bracts with green edges. Petals tubular, yellow, green tipped. Zones 11–12.

Vriesea erythrodactylon

☀ ✣ ↔ 16 in (40 cm) ↕ 16 in (40 cm)

From Brazil. Leaves strap-like, green, forming funnel-shaped rosette. Erect flower stem, shorter than rosette. Broadly sword-shaped flowerhead, center portion solid and green, outer edges deeply notched and red, with yellow tubular petals. Zones 11–12.

Vriesea fenestralis

☀ ✣ ↔ 27 in (70 cm) ↕ 40 in (100 cm)

From Brazil. Broad rosette; strap-like green leaves, dark green, narrow, longitudinal lines and irregular, broken, thick crossbands. Sturdy flower stem, longer than rosette. Sword-shaped flowerhead, green bracts with red spots. Petals greenish white. Zones 11–12.

Vriesea fosteriana

☀ ✣ ↔ 40 in (100 cm) ↕ 60 in (150 cm)

From Brazil. Spreading rosette; leaves strap-like, rigid, green or purplish, wavy broken crossbands in dark green, purple, or white. Flower stem erect, longer than rosette. Flowerhead sword-shaped, yellowish bracts with red spots. Petals creamish purple. Zones 11–12.

Vriesea malzinei

☀ ✣ ↔ 16 in (40 cm) ↕ 32 in (80 cm)

Native to Mexico. Funnel-shaped rosette; leaves strap-like, green above, red below. Flower stem erect, longer than rosette.

Cylindrical red flowerhead; pale green or yellow overlapping bracts; long, white, tubular petals with flared tips. Zones 11–12.

Vriesea saundersii

☀ ✣ ↔ 16 in (40 cm) ↕ 24 in (60 cm)

Native to Brazil. Broad funnel-shaped rosette; leaves strap-like, leathery, dull green or gray-green above; undersides with small brown or purplish speckles. Erect flower stem, taller than rosette. Pyramidal flowerhead, 3 to 4 side-branches, bracts mainly yellow; bright yellow tubular petals. Zones 11–12.

Vriesea splendens

FLAMING SWORD

☀ ✣ ↔ 20 in (50 cm) ↕ 40 in (100 cm)

From Venezuela and the Caribbean Islands. Broad funnel-shaped rosette; strap-like green leaves, often with broad dark irregular crossbands. Erect flower stem, about equal in length to rosette. Long, sword-shaped, bright red flowerhead, yellow tubular petals. Zones 10–12.

Vriesea Hybrid Cultivars

☀ ✣ ↔ 8–20 in (20–50 cm) ↕ 16–36 in (40–90 cm)

Hybrids feature larger flower spike and strongly patterned foliage. '**Bananas**', upright rosette, reddish flower stem, flowerhead sword-shaped at top, with up to 8 sword-shaped side-branches, mostly bright yellow but sometimes with reddish edges; '**Carlsbad**', leaves pointed, green with red mottling, flushed red near base, flower stem red; '**Charlotte**', broad sword-shaped flowerhead, with up to 7 side-branches, all red toward base, bright yellow above; '**Christiane**', flowerhead bright red, yellow tubular petals; '**Eva**', open rosette of strap-like leaves, green tinged maroon; '**Grafton Sunset**', mainly golden orange flowerhead suffused with red, petals yellow; '**Gunther**', flowerhead bright red; '**Komet**', overlapping, mainly red, yellow-tipped bracts, pale yellow petals; '**Likely Lad**', flowerhead pyramidal, red side-branches, each with up to 5 flowers and large red bract below each branch; '**Little Chief**', flowerhead glossy orange tinted red; '**Mariae**', petals tubular, yellow with green tips; '**Poelmanii**', sword-shaped flowerhead, up to 7 bright red branches, yellow petals; '**Purple Cockatoo**', flowerheads purple, deep serrations around edge resembling a cockatoo's crest; '**Red Chestnut**', yellowish bracts with small reddish spots, creamish purple petals; '**Splendide**', sword-shaped flowerhead, up to 4 bright red side-branches, pinkish yellow tubular petals. Zones 11–12.

Vriesea, Hybrid Cultivar, 'Mariae'

WACHENDORFIA

This genus of some 25 species of mostly deciduous strappy-leafed perennials from South Africa is a member of the bloodroot

(Haemodoraceae) family. The deciduous species have bright red tubers, and both deciduous and the sole evergreen species have orange-red roots. The leaves are usually bright green and heavily pleated, with each leaf sheathing the next one in a flat fan arrangement. The yellow star-shaped flowers are produced in tall narrow spikes or, in the case of smaller species, in open clusters. Regarded as weeds in southern Australia.

CULTIVATION: In more or less frost-free climates, grow in a sunny moist position; in other areas, protect from frost by growing these plants in large pots which can be overwintered in a greenhouse. Raise from fresh seed or by division in late winter.

Wachendorfia thyrsiflora (at front), South Africa

Wachendorfia thyrsiflora

◐ ⚘ ↔ 2–4 ft (0.6–1.2 m)
↕ 4–7 ft (1.2–2 m)

Only evergreen species. Strongly pleated, rich green leaves to 40 in (100 cm) long. Star-shaped rich yellow flowers, to 1¼ in (30 mm) wide, on tall upright spikes, in early summer. Zones 10–11.

WALDSTEINIA

This genus of 6 species of creeping fleshy-stemmed perennials belongs to the rose (Rosaceae) family. They are native to northern temperate regions, where they are found in woodland areas. Plants form low mats of lobed and toothed leaves that are similar to those of the related strawberry and cinquefoil *(Potentilla)*. The leaves sometimes take on bronze tones in winter. The saucer-shaped, 5-petalled, yellow flowers are carried for long periods in spring and early summer.

CULTIVATION: *Waldsteinia* species are suited to the rock garden, the front of a border, or a woodland edge, and make useful ground covers. Grow in partial shade in moist but well-drained soils. Where soils remain moist in summer, they can be grown in full sun. Propagate by division of rooted runners or from seed.

Waldsteinia fragarioides

BARREN STRAWBERRY

◐/◑ ❄ ↔ 12–20 in (30–50 cm) ↕ 2 in (5 cm)
Mat-forming species, native to eastern USA. Trifoliate bronze-green leaves with toothed, pointed oval leaflets to nearly 3 in (8 cm) long. Clusters of up to 8 yellow flowers, ¾ in (18 mm) wide, in spring. Zones 3–9.

Waldsteinia ternata

Waldsteinia ternata ★

◐ ❄ ↔ 24 in (60 cm) ↕ 6 in (15 cm)
Found from Europe to China and Japan. Dark green, 3-lobed, toothed, somewhat hairy leaves. Flowers borne in groups of 3 to 7 in spring–summer. Can become invasive. Zones 3–9.

WITTROCKIA

This small genus of 6 species, related to *Canistrum,* is a member of the bromeliad (Bromeliaceae) family. They are medium to large plants from southeastern Brazil, with strap-like toothed leaves forming a broad cup-shaped rosette. The flowerhead bears many flowers, usually with bright red bracts around the bottom edge.

CULTIVATION: In cool-temperate areas. grow in a greenhouse or conservatory. In warm-temperate, subtropical, and tropical areas, grow outdoors with protection from prolonged sunlight and heavy rain. Propagate from offsets.

Wittrockia superba

☀ ✦ ↔ 55 in (140 cm) ↕ 16 in (40 cm)
Large plant from Rio de Janeiro, Brazil. Strap-like large-toothed leaves, dark green with bright red tip, forming broad cup-shaped rosette. Flower stem very short. Flowerhead globular, with many flowers, surrounded by bright red bracts. Petals white. Zones 10–12.

XANTHORRHOEA

Now classified in their own family—Xanthorrhoeaceae—there are around 30 species of grass trees found across Australia. They are slow-growing long-lived woody perennials with long narrow leaves that emerge in tufts from the extremities of the branches; there are also species that have substantial subterranean stems. The white or cream flowers are clustered on long-stalked spikes, and are usually produced in spring or as a reaction to fire. Leathery capsular fruits are clustered along the spikes.

CULTIVATION: The young plants may take 20 years to develop stems and more than 100 years to flower. Plant in an open sunny spot with well-drained soil. Propagation is from seed sown in spring or autumn in a coarse free-draining mix.

Xanthorrhoea quadrangulata, in the wild, South Australia

Xanthorrhoea australis
SOUTHERN GRASS TREE

☀ ⬡ ↔ 3 ft (0.9 m) ↕ 3 ft (0.9 m)

From southeastern Australia. May develop short trunk. Dense rosette; narrow arching leaves, finely hairy. Spring flowers, white or cream, fragrant, on long "spears," after many years. Zones 9–11.

Xanthorrhoea glauca
NARROW-LEAFED GRASS TREE

☀ ❀ ↔ 3 ft (0.9 m) ↕ 20 ft (6 ft)

From Great Dividing Range country of New South Wales and southeastern Queensland, Australia. Branched blackish trunks; Leaves bluish green. Flower spike to 7 ft (2 m) tall. Zones 8–11.

Xanthorrhoea johnsonii
QUEENSLAND GRASS TREE

☀ ⬡ ↔ 3 ft (0.9 m) ↕ 7 ft (2 m)

Fire-blackened trunk; bright green grass-like leaves. Huge cylindrical spikes, hundreds of nectar-rich cream flowers. Zones 9–10.

Xanthorrhoea quadrangulata
SQUARE-LEAF GRASS TREE

☀ ⬡ ↔ 4–7 ft (1.2–2 m) ↕ 7–10 ft (2–3 m)

From southern Australia. Trunk to 10 ft (3 m) tall; very narrow, tough, dark green leaves, quadrangular in section, to 24–36 in (60–90 cm) long. Narrow whitish flower spikes, 3–4 ft (0.9–1.2 m) tall, in autumn. Drought tolerant. Zones 9–11.

XANTHOSOMA
TANNIA, YAUTIA

This genus of around 50 species of tuberous-rooted perennials from tropical America belongs to the arum (Araceae) family. The leaves are variable, often long and arrowhead-shaped but sometimes pointed, oval, or divided into large segments. The flowerheads are usually short-stemmed, with a bulbous base and a green, white, or creamy yellow spathe that partly encloses a short spadix.
CULTIVATION: These plants demand warm humid conditions with moist humus-rich soil. They will not tolerate frosts or prolonged

cold. Outside the tropics they are mainly cultivated as house or greenhouse plants. Propagate from seed or by division of clumps.

Xanthosoma undipes

☀ ⬡ ↔ 7–10 ft (2–3 m) ↕ 7–10 ft (2–3 m)

Found from Mexico to Peru; widely cultivated in the Caribbean. Stem to 7 ft (2 m) long. Broadly heart-shaped leaves, 20 in–7 ft (0.5–2 m) long, on stalks to 40 in (100 cm) long. Egg-shaped spathe tube, to 3 in (8 cm) long, yellowish green inside, limb to 10 in (25 cm) long. Zones 10–11.

XERANTHEMUM

This genus of 6 upright annual herbs in the daisy (Asteraceae) family is found from the Mediterranean region to southwestern Asia. They have alternate smooth leaves and solitary, terminal, disc-like flowerheads resembling daisy flowers, in white, mauve, rose, or lilac shades, with papery petal-like bracts.
CULTIVATION: These plants prefer an open sunny position in most well-drained fertile soils. Propagation is from seed.

Xeranthemum annuum
COMMON IMMORTELLE

☀ ✳ ↔ 10–36 in (25–90 cm) ↕ 10–36 in (25–90 cm)

Found from southeastern Europe to the Caucasus and Iran, naturalized elsewhere. Upright branching stems; alternate, smooth, narrow, oblong leaves, with fine white hairs, denser underneath. Flowerheads have spreading, oblong, bright pink or white inner bracts and many florets, in summer–autumn. Zones 6–10.

XEROCHRYSUM
ALPINE EVERLASTING, ORANGE EVERLASTING

A small genus of 6 Australian species in the daisy (Asteraceae) family, formerly classified in the genus *Bracteantha*. They feature dry papery bracts, which are golden yellow in many species.
CULTIVATION: These attractive daisies will do best in a position in full sun, in light well-drained soil. Propagate from seed.

Xerochrysum bracteatum
syns *Bracteantha bracteatum*, *Helichrysum bracteatum*
GOLDEN EVERLASTING, STRAWFLOWER

☀ ✳ ↔ 16 in (40 cm) ↕ 36 in (90 cm)

Australian annual or short-lived perennial. Narrow, pointed lance-shaped, often sticky, leaves to over 4 in (10 cm) long. Flowerheads to nearly 3 in (8 cm) wide, deep golden yellow. 'Bright Bikini' strain in all shades except blue and mauve; 'Coco', pale yellow flowers; 'Dargan Hill Monarch' (syn. *Bracteantha bracteata* 'Dargan Hill Monarch'), buttery yellow flowers; 'Golden Beauty', all-over deep golden yellow; 'Pink Sunrise', orange and cream flowerheads opening from pink buds; 'Princess of Wales', compact habit, golden yellow flowerheads. Zones 8–10.

ZALUZIANSKYA

A genus of about 35 species of sticky-leafed annuals, perennials, and subshrubs from southern and eastern Africa belonging to the foxglove (Scrophulariaceae) family. Their leaves are smooth or toothed and the flowers have 5 spreading notched petals at

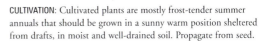

the end of a long tube. The outside color of the flowers is quite different from the inside, and the majority are night scented.
CULTIVATION: These plants like full sun and a well-drained soil in almost frost-free climates. Where frost is usual, they can be grown in a cool greenhouse. Keep almost dry in winter. Take tip cuttings in the summer or sow seed in spring with bottom heat.

Zaluzianskya ovata
☼ ⚘ ↔ 20–24 in (50–60 cm) ↑ 8–10 in (20–25 cm)
Brittle-stemmed evergreen perennial, native to South Africa. Toothed leaves to 1¾ in (40 mm) long. Flowers white inside, rich crimson on petal backs, in summer–autumn. Zones 10–11.

ZINGIBER
GINGER
This genus, containing about 60 herbaceous and evergreen rhizomatous, clumping, perennial herbs from Asia and northern Australia, gives its name to the ginger (Zingiberaceae) family. The leaves are usually narrow, and are arranged in 2 ranks on upright stems. The inflorescences, which are often intensely colored and cone-like with overlapping waxy-looking bracts, arise from the base of the plant in summer.
CULTIVATION: Most species are frost tender, although some prove surprisingly hardy in temperate gardens. The majority prefer nutrient-rich, well-drained, moist soil and full sun to part shade in warm humid conditions. Propagate by division in early spring.

Zingiber spectabile
BEEHIVE GINGER
☼ ⚘ ↔ 3 ft (0.9 m) ↑ 5–7 ft (1.5–2 m)
From Malaysia. Deep green leaves; paler, downy beneath. Long inflorescences, yellow bracts turning scarlet. Small creamy flowers, 2-lobed purple lip with yellow spots, in late summer. Zones 9–12.

Zingiber zerumbet
syn. *Zingiber amaricans*
AWAPUHI, PINE-CONE GINGER, SHAMPOO GINGER
☼ ❄ ↔ 3 ft (0.9 m) ↑ 6–8 ft (1.8–2.4 m)
Upright species from India. Arching stems; shiny dark green leaves. Large cone-shaped inflorescences, pale green turning bright red. Flowers white with pale yellow lip in late summer. 'Variegatum' (syns *Z. darceyi, Z.* 'Darceyi'), smaller, more frost tender, leaves striped with cream. Zones 8–12.

ZINNIA
This genus of around 20 species of annuals, perennials, and small shrubs in the daisy (Asteraceae) family is found from south-central USA to Argentina, with its center in Mexico. Zinnias have soft light green leaves that range from linear to broadly spatula-shaped. The flowers of the wild species are typically daisy-like with conspicuous ray and disc florets. Modern seed strains are mainly doubles with the disc florets largely hidden or absent. The color range is very wide, though mostly warm tones.

Zinnia elegans, Ruffles Series, 'Cherry Ruffles'

CULTIVATION: Cultivated plants are mostly frost-tender summer annuals that should be grown in a sunny warm position sheltered from drafts, in moist and well-drained soil. Propagate from seed.

Zinnia angustifolia
☼ ⚘ ↔ 12–20 in (30–50 cm) ↑ 8–16 in (20–40 cm)
Annual from southeastern USA and Mexico. Needle-like to narrow lance-shaped leaves. Bright orange ray florets, orange disc florets. 'Classic', white ray florets; 'Coral Beauty', orange-pink; 'Crystal White', white ray florets; 'Golden Eye', white ray florets, creamy yellow at center; 'Star White', white ray florets, orange disc. Zones 9–11.

Zinnia elegans
syn. *Zinnia violacea*
☼ ⚘ ↔ 8–18 in (20–45 cm)
↑ 8–40 in (20–100 cm)
Popular garden flowers; some newer varieties are disease resistant. Cultivars include 'Aztek', white flowers; 'Canary Yellow', bright yellow flowers; Dreamland Series, double flowers, many colors; 'Envy', light green fully double flowers; 'Giant Purity', fully double white flowers; 'Halo', red flowers; Mammoth Exhibition Series, double flowers, large color range; Oklahoma Series, semi-double and fully double flowers, wide color range; 'Polar Bear', white double flowers; Profusion Series, single flowers, red, orange, or white; 'Pulcino', semi-double and fully double flowers, wide color range; Ruffles Series, double flowers in most colors; Splendor Series, fully double flowers, red, pink, orange, or yellow; Sun Series, double flowers, in a variety of bright warm colors. Zones 9–11.

Zinnia haageana
syn. *Zinnia angustifolia* of gardens
☼/◐ ⚘ ↔ 12–24 in (30–60 cm) ↑ 24 in (60 cm)
From Mexico. Narrow lance-shaped leaves. Golden to red-brown ray florets, orange disc. Fully double-flowered forms include 'Old Mexico' and 'Stargold'. Zones 9–11.

Zingiber spectabile

Index to Plant Names

Italicized page numbers refer to a photograph on the page, while plain page numbers indicate a reference in either the text or the tables.

Acknowledgments

Proofreading Puddingburn Publishing Services

Photographers David Banks, Chris Bell, Rob Blakers, Lorraine Blyth, Greg Bourke, Ken Brass, Geoff Bryant, Derek Butcher, Claver Carroll, Leigh Clapp, Mike Comb, David Austin Roses, Grant Dixon, Heather Donovan, e-garden Ltd, Bruce Elder, Katie Fallows, Derek Fells, Stuart Owen Fox, Richard Francis, Robert Gibson, William Grant, Denise Greig, Barry Griffith, Barry Grossman, Gil Hanly, Ivy Hansen, Dennis Harding, Jerry Harpur, Jack Hobbs, Neil Holmes, Paul Huntley, Richard I'Anson, Jason Ingram, Steve Johnson, David Keith Jones, Ionas Kaltenbach, Willie Kempen, Colin Kerr, Robert M. Knight, Carol Knoll, Albert Kuhnigk, Stan Lamond, Mike Langford, Gary Lewis, Geoff Longford, Stirling Macoboy, John McCann, David McGonigal, Richard McKenna, Ron Moon, Eberhard Morell, Barry Myers-Rice, Steve Newall, Connall Oosterbrock, Ron Parsons, Luke Pellatt, Larry Pitt, Craig Potton, Janet Price, Geof Prigge, Nick Rains, Christo Reid, Howard Rice, Jamie Robertson, Tony Rodd, Rolf Ulrich Roesler, Luke Saffigna, Don Skirrow, Raoul Slater, Michael Snedic, Peter Solness, Ken Stepnell, Warren Steptoe, Angus Stewart, Oliver Strewe, J. Peter Thoeming, David Titmuss, Wayne Turville, Georg Uebelhart, Ben-Erik van Wyk, Sharyn Vanderhorst, Kim Westerskov, Murray White, Vic Widman, Brent Wilson, Geoff Woods, Gary Yong Gee, Grant Young, James Young

Produced by Global Book Publishing Pty Ltd

Level 8, 15 Orion Road, Lane Cove, NSW 2066, Australia   Ph: (612) 9425 5800   Fax: (612) 9425 5804   Email: rightsmanager@globalpub.com.au